CQ's State Fact Finder
1996

CQ's State Fact Finder 1996

Rankings Across America

Harold A. Hovey

Congressional Quarterly Inc.
Washington, D.C.

Copyright © 1996 Congressional Quarterly
1414 22nd Street, N.W., Washington, D.C. 20037

Printed in the United States of America.

The first edition of this title contained the following
Library of Congress Cataloging-in-Publication data:

CQ's state fact finder: rankings across America

    1. United States—Statistics. 2. State governments—
United States—Statistics. I. Title.
HA214.V36 1993
317.3—dc20   93-8929

ISBN 1-56802-216-6 (cloth)
ISBN 1-56802-213-1 (paper)
ISSN 1079-7149

Contents

Detailed Contents of Subject Rankings

Government

Federal Impacts

Taxes

Revenues and Finances

Education

Health

Crime and Law Enforcement

Transportation

Welfare/Families/Social Services

Introduction

CQ's State Fact Finder 1996 is the second edition of an important new information source and analytical tool for any person interested in developments in America's fifty states and the District of Columbia. This book is a valuable reference source for anyone looking to uncover trends in the states, whether a policy expert seeking detailed data or an individual wishing to learn more about today's social, political, and economic currents.

This book was first published by Congressional Quarterly in 1993 as part of CQ's fifty-year tradition of providing comprehensive, reliable, and focused information about national public policy issues in America. This effort has broadened in recent years to include developments and trends in the states through books such as *State Fact Finder* and the creation of *Governing*, a magazine covering all aspects of state government. Favorable response to the first edition of this book prompted CQ to update and expand the work with the expectation of putting it on the road to annual publication. To accomplish these goals, CQ joined with State Policy Research, an Ohio firm that is known to state government experts everywhere as one of the most reliable and knowledgeable organizations dealing with state-level information. State Policy Research publishes the periodicals *State Policy Reports* and *State Budget & Tax News* and for a decade has been publishing *States in Profile*, which has now merged into *State Fact Finder*.

What's New in This Edition

The editors at State Policy Research have used their extensive experience in state issues to refine and focus the tables that constitute the core of this volume. To make the book more user-friendly, they have included tables that focus on information people commonly want to know about states. In addition, they have added tables that present data from sources that are not widely published and therefore are not available to much of the public. The editors have provided a "value-added" element to raw data in some tables by relating different sets of information and establishing measurements. This has allowed the editors, for example, to establish in Table B-28 an Index

of State Economic Momentum, and in Table D-11 a Governor's Performance Rating.

A second important new component of *State Fact Finder* is the essay that begins the volume—Finding What Information Users Want to Know—in which the editors guide the reader through the use of the information. This section helps readers understand the scope of information available to them.

A third new feature is a carefully documented source notes section that lists the origins of the statistics in each table and guides the reader to sources where more information on the same topic can be obtained.

Information Development

Any data book is by definition a work in progress. What is useful one year may be less helpful the next, as new information needs arise. For these and many other reasons, the editors welcome reaction from readers, suggestions for additional information or changes in presentation, and, of course, any corrections or clarifications that come to the readers' attention. These should be sent to Harold Hovey or Kendra Baker (who was responsible for table preparation) at State Policy Research, 182 West Royal Forest Blvd., Columbus, Ohio 43214. They can be reached by phone at 614-262-9229 or by fax at 614-447-2077.

Organization of the Volume

State Fact Finder is organized in five sections, which are described on the next page. Readers can find specific information by using the index at the end, referring to the summary table of contents for a section and then leafing through the tables dealing with that subject, or looking at the detailed table of contents. The tables of contents take readers to tables identified by section letter and table number. For example, A-1 is the first table in the Population section. Source notes, which appear in a separate section, are keyed to these table titles. State rankings pages appear alphabetically by state. All other sections use conventional page numbering.

Finding Information Users Want to Know

Readers differ in their preferences on many things—from what they value in a place to live to the amount of state government spending they consider appropriate. They will not agree on such subjects as where they should move or which state is governed best.

In this section, rather than impose personal values as though they were facts by ranking some states as the "best place" to live or do business, the editors have provided guideposts on how to use the tables so that readers can obtain the information they need. Utilizing a question-and-answer format, this section leads readers to groups of tables that can be consulted together to deal with the broad questions, such as which state might have the best schools or the best business opportunities.

The section is divided into three parts, each based on particular types of decisions people use state statistics to make. The first covers personal and family decisions, such as job opportunities. The second focuses on business decisions, such as where to locate a new plant. The third provides information about the government to assist people in their roles as voters and in influencing public policy.

Subject Rankings

This section forms the heart of the book. It is organized in twelve subject areas that are challenging policy makers throughout the country: population, economies, geography, government, federal impacts, taxes, revenues and finances, education, health, crime, transportation, and welfare. States are listed alphabetically in each table. The information also is presented in rankings that allow a reader to see how each state compares with the others. The rankings are from highest to lowest, unless otherwise noted.

Source Notes

This section is designed to be used in tandem with the subject rankings to understand the specific usefulness of, and any caveats about, the data. The sources for all the statistics in the book are documented so that the calculations can be replicated or expanded upon by those who need more detail than space allows here. These source notes allow the reader to locate other information sources that may be useful.

State Rankings

The state rankings section provides the reader with a composite view of each state. In this section, the editors bring together the rankings for each state of most of the data included in the volume. This compilation gives readers a quick summary of their states' positions in each subject area.

Index

The index guides the reader to topics presented in the various sections of the book.

Introduction to the Data

Rankings: There is nothing magical about rankings, though *State Fact Finder* generally follows the convention of most statisticians by ranking from highest to lowest. Most rankings can be interpreted similarly by reversing them. For example, a table showing tax burdens from highest to lowest can be reversed to show tax burdens from lowest to highest by ranking the fiftieth state first, the forty-ninth state second, and so on.

Data Accuracy: The statistics in this volume vary greatly in their accuracy. Some, such as the land area of states or the number of state legislators, can be measured precisely. Other data, such as birth rates or finances of local governments, are estimates. The source notes generally explain how the data were developed or direct readers to the statistical providers, who usually have available detailed technical papers on their methods.

In preparing this report, the editors worked with data as presented by the statistical source. In presenting the data in tables, figures were rounded to a manageable number of digits (such as by expressing financial data as $24.5 million rather than $24,515,078). As a result, the rankings that are based on detailed data will show one state ranked above another even though they are apparently tied in the data published in the table.

Junk Data: Many special interest groups have strong opinions about appropriate policies for governments, and they translate these opinions into rankings of which states are "best" for the subject of their interest, such as protecting the environment, providing mental health, or keeping a favorable climate for business. Sometimes the resulting statistics themselves are unreliable. Sometimes they combine individually reliable statistics into measures that simply reflect the policy preferences of those who rank the composite results. Such reports are generally not included in *State Fact Finder,* but the editors are familiar with them and are willing to help *State Fact Finder* readers deal with them.

Time Periods: The tables all deal with the specific time periods indicated in the headings. These are normally calendar years. In the case of fiscal data, the time period is fiscal years that end in the year shown.

District of Columbia: The District of Columbia has a unique status in any statistical compilation. It is not a state in the sense that it has no voting representatives in Congress and is counted as a city, not a state, in all Census Bureau statistics on government finances. However, the Census Bureau does include its residents within the total population of the United States. Federal agencies and private statistics-gathering organizations differ in how they treat the District, Puerto Rico, the Virgin Islands, and other entities in their statistics.

State Fact Finder presents information for the District of Columbia in each table but does not include it in the state rankings. Some other rankings (including the previous edition of *State Fact Finder*) do include the District, but State Policy Research has consistently avoided including the District for two reasons. First, users of rankings find this inclusion cumbersome to explain, often having to resort to particular explanations of rankings (such as a state being ranked fifth, fourth among states and also behind the District of Columbia). Second, the District is economically and demographically a central city with fiscal and other attributes of most central cities—high taxes, high crime rates, large percentages of population in poverty and receiving government benefits, and so forth. When ranked along with states, the District often ranks first or last in the tables, distorting other rankings. For example, if the District of Columbia were to be included in the crime rate rankings, it would have the highest rate. Most people would interpret the statement that Florida is the state with the second highest crime rate as meaning some other state had a higher rate, when in fact it was surpassed only by the District of Columbia. *State Fact Finder* lists Florida as having the highest crime rate, meaning no state has a higher rate.

Finding What Information Users Want to Know

Most people look at state statistics to answer specific questions related to a decision they need to make but often discover that the statistics they seek do not appear in the reference books they consult. Alternatively, they find some comparisons that seem to be relevant but wonder if they are.

This edition of *State Fact Finder* introduces a new feature—one not found in other compilations of data about states. Besides finding tables, readers can consult this section to find a list of frequently asked questions. Under each question they will find information about which statistics in this book should be helpful in trying to find answers, as well as road maps to other statistics that might be useful. Readers sometimes will be informed that the statistics they seek are not available anywhere and why.

This section is divided into three parts, each based on particular types of decisions people use state statistics to make. The first covers personal and family decisions, such as finding the states with the best job opportunities, the best health care, and even the best chances for finding a spouse. The second covers business decisions, such as where to locate a new business or where to find the most productive workers. This section is also useful for investors. The third contains information about government to assist people in their roles as voters and in influencing public policy.

About Personal Decisions on Where to Live or Visit

1 Where is the best place to find a job?

As a general rule, people find it easier to get a job, higher pay, better opportunities for advancement, and better opportunities for building professional practices if they locate in rapidly expanding economies. If they go to places in economic decline they will find few job opportunities and stiff competition to get the positions that do exist.

To find states with rapidly expanding economies, look at measures of recent economic growth, particularly the

Index of State Economic Momentum (B-28), population growth (A-3), job growth (B-29, B-30), and projections of future population growth (A-4). The Index (B-28) is especially useful because it summarizes the three elements of economic growth important to job-seekers: population growth, income growth, and increases in the number of jobs.

Growth rates are particularly important if you seek jobs that are inherently related to growth, such as jobs in the construction industry. Because the need for construction relates to *changes* in the need for homes and buildings, there are massive differences between fast- and slow-growing states. For example, in 1995 there were 60 new homes being built for every 1,000 residents of Nevada but only 4 for every 1,000 residents of New York (B-20).

When a state is classified as rapidly growing, this does not necessarily mean that all local areas in the state are growing. For example, the fast growth in Nevada is concentrated in the Las Vegas area. Growth in the Pacific Northwest is occurring along the Pacific Coast between Seattle and Portland, but there are few job opportunities in the eastern parts of Oregon and Washington. To find which areas are growing and in what types of industries and jobs, you can consult local sources, such as state economic development departments, local chambers of commerce, or even friends familiar with the area. For nationwide statistics on growth in metropolitan areas, you can get information on recent job growth from the Bureau of Labor Statistics. Somewhat less current statistics on income and other economic factors are available from the Department of Commerce, including detailed books on major counties called *County Business Patterns*.

2 Where will tax burdens be least for me and my family?

The tables in the Taxes section are good guides to average tax burdens. Table F-1 shows what share of personal income goes to state and local taxes in each state. Tables F-6, F-9, and F-13 do this for each of the major taxes: property, sales, and personal income. The range among states is very large. For example, New York governments take 15.8 percent of income in state and local taxes, while governments in Tennessee take only 9.1 percent.

The taxes you actually pay will depend on your circumstances, such as how much property you plan to own in relation to your income. You can see the major differences on Tables F-16 and F-23. For example, Florida and Texas have tax systems that wealthy retirees will like—no income, inheritance, or estate taxes. Young couples without much income will pay heavy sales taxes and find that renters do not share in special property tax breaks for homeowners. For them, states like Oregon, which has no sales tax but steep income taxes, might be a better deal.

The state and local taxes you pay will be a combination of state government taxes, which are uniform throughout entire states, and local taxes. These vary greatly from place to place within a state. There are about 50,000 local governments in the United States with the power to set tax rates and 50 states, so figure about 1,000 different local governments in each state.

Depending on where you decide to live, you may find you are paying property taxes that are the sum of individual taxes levied by a county; a municipality or township; a school district; perhaps a second school district, such as a community college or vocational district; and hosts of special districts, such as road districts, transit districts, mosquito control districts, and levee districts—to mention just a few of the possibilities. Local governments in many states also levy sales taxes and a few states have significant local income taxes, such as the steep income taxes of New York City and Philadelphia. All these taxes are reflected in the state averages.

Because of these differences, what you pay will depend on where you live even though state government taxes are uniform throughout each state. To find local areas with low taxes within a state, look for places that have large business sources of tax revenues combined with small numbers of people to serve. In most metropolitan areas, there are suburbs with concentrations of office buildings, shopping centers, and businesses that have much lower property taxes than surrounding areas. Realtors in metropolitan regions will be able to identify them. For property taxes, check the county government where you want to locate. The county officials who collect property taxes will have rate information for each local area.

Most state tax departments, with offices in state capitols and major cities, publish free booklets describing all their state taxes and tax rates.

3   Which state has the best public schools

To compare how well students do, consider the first five tables in the Education section. Use Tables H-1 and H-2 for overall comparisons, H-3 for students not going to college right away, and H-4 and H-5 for the college preparation programs. You can also use the tables to compare states on measures of what they spend per student (H-15), what they pay teachers (H-16), class sizes (H-9), and more.

Except in Hawaii, all schools are local. Expect to find immense variations within areas in every state; these are as important as the variations from state to state. All state education departments, located in state capitols, keep statistics for each school district on spending and number of teachers and pupils. Some states issue "report cards" comparing district performance measures, such as how students do on standardized tests. You can use these or research locally such indicators as percentage of graduates that go on to college, percentages winning National Merit Scholarships and other awards, and local reputations for good schools.

How well students do depends heavily on how much help and motivation they get at home, not just on what happens at school. Much of the difference among states is caused by differences in the students, not in the schools. This is true for districts within a state as well.

One key is getting a child into the right school, not just the right school district. Some of the best specialized programs, and some of the worst schools, are found in central cities.

If you want to send children to private schools, do not expect much help from government. Many states are considering "voucher" plans that would help with tuition, but such plans are only available now in Ohio and Wisconsin, where they mostly serve poor, inner-city children. Iowa and Minnesota provide limited income tax breaks if you pay private school tuition.

4   Which state is best for children?

Throughout *State Fact Finder* you will find many tables comparing states on aspects of life important to children, including health, education, crime, and economic opportunity. If you crave even more comparisons, detailed ones are available from the Children's Defense Fund (Washington, D.C.) and from the Annie E. Casey Foundation (One Lafayette Place, Greenwich, CT 06830, 203-661-2773) in their annual *Kids Count Data Booklet*.

Children grow up in small worlds, such as school buildings and neighborhoods, so do not expect to rely totally on facts about states, metropolitan areas, or even individual cities and counties for information important to your child's life. Where your child is within one of these areas is often much more important than which area the child is in. State differences are important in such fields as the quality of education and the possibilities for getting a job.

5   Which is the best state for retirement?

Most people retire within twenty miles of where they lived when they stopped working. For them, finding the right place is more a matter of finding the right house or apartment in the right community rather than finding the right state. If you are thinking about retirement in another state, *State Fact Finder* can be helpful but you will need to go beyond it to make an informed decision.

Do not start with statistics comparing places, unless your overriding concern is minimizing the taxes you will pay. Start with your own preferences. Decide first on how far you are willing to be from your family and old friends and on key climate issues, such as whether you want to avoid ice and snow and whether you will like places that do not have changing seasons of the year. Most people will be able to narrow their choices considerably this way before they look at statistics. If you are willing to take the time to look systematically at what is important to you about a place, take a "preference inventory" such as the one found in *Retirement Places Rated* by David Savageneau. It will force you to consider whether being able to get a part-time job, see and hear a symphony orchestra, follow a professional sports team, and other items are important to you.

In the tables in *State Fact Finder*, you will see systematic differences among the states in such characteristics as income and education levels of residents, living costs, crime, and taxes.

There are many books designed to help with retirement decisions. A library or good bookstore should be able to recommend some reference book choices. Some describe places to live and provide information on investments, Medicare, and estate planning. *The Only Retirement Guide You'll Ever Need* by Kathryn and Ross Petras (1991) is an example. Some deal only with places to retire, often with different emphases, such as health (*The 50 Healthiest Places to Live and Retire in the United States* by Normal D. Ford, 1991) or specialized retirement areas (*Retirement Places Rated*, which covers Kauai, Hawaii, and Hilton Head, South Carolina, but not New York City or any place in Ohio or Illinois).

The American Association of Retired Persons is a good source for a variety of publications on retirement, including specialized guides on state taxes. One topic of particular interest to retirees is what percentage of income from Social Security is taxed by each state.

6 Which state universities are best?

State Fact Finder contains some important statistics that are relevant to selecting among state university systems. Look for them in Tables H-19 to H-24. State statistics alone cannot pick a university to attend because state systems include everything from community colleges to medical schools. California even has systems within systems. They vary from the University of California, with campuses at Berkeley and elsewhere, which contains some of the finest institutions in the country; to California State University, which enjoys less of a national reputation but has some outstanding specialized programs; to community colleges with diverse and varying strengths and weaknesses. Students attend schools, not states. Consult guides and ratings on individual schools that contain information on the numbers of students, types of curriculum, costs, and attempted assessments of the quality of students and faculty.

7 Which state has the best cultural attractions and recreation?

Recreational opportunities cannot be adequately measured by statistics. Attempts to do so often are misleading.

For example, you will find by far the best ratio of park land to people in Alaska, but much of the state is covered by glaciers that are not fit for hiking or camping. Some fine experiences—the "big sky" of Montana, the bustle of the streets of New York, and the beauty of fall foliage in New England—are not specific places and do not count attendance.

There are fairly good statistics about how many people participate in various sports in each state. Tables C-5 and C-6 are examples. See the notes to these tables for how to obtain specific information on other sports. Most sports have specialized equipment stores, magazines, and guidebooks that are superior to state statistics for making personal recreational choices. For example, just because there are more golfers and courses per capita in one state than another does not mean you will not find more than enough courses and players to make foursomes in the lower ranked states.

Cultural opportunities are listed in the many guidebooks and specialized magazines published in nearly every possible field of interest. Government spending on the arts, shown in Table C-8, is not a useful indicator of the extent or quality of arts in that state. States spend, on average, less than $1 per year per capita funding the arts—amounts that are dwarfed by sales revenues, admissions, and donations.

8 Where is the best place to invest in property?

Nearly everyone interested in owning real estate has heard the old saw about the three keys to real estate investment: location, location, and location. This applies to states and metropolitan areas among states. For example, statistics in Table B-21 from Freddie Mac (which buys mortgages from banks that issue them) show that in the three years from 1991 to 1994, the average house in Utah appreciated by 40 percent while the average house in California lost 11 percent of its value. Of course, how much your investment will lose or appreciate depends on the property you buy, whether you pay the right price, and local market conditions.

It is hard to pick a winner in a field of losers and hard to pick a loser in a field of winners. You want to pick the right state (and metropolitan area in that state) for your investment.

Real estate prices depend on supply and demand. Supply does not go down much in poor markets—who would tear down a house or office building just because values were dropping? Supply responds to increased demand in good markets, but prices rise because new construction usually costs more than established buildings, prices of lots and construction labor tend to rise, and the most desirable locations generally already have buildings on them.

The best strategy for real estate investment is to pick an area with an expanding economy, where lots of new jobs are being created. Look at the answer to Question 1 (where to find a job) for tips on using *State Fact Finder* to identify those places.

9 Can picking the right states help pick winners in stocks and bonds?

Few economists or investment professionals would suggest picking which company's stocks to buy based on the states in which their headquarters or plants are found. The important questions are how good are the products and how well are they marketed. Some successful companies operate from unlikely places. For example, computer-maker Gateway is based in farm country in South Dakota and apparel seller L. L. Bean is based in rural Maine.

For making things, being in a fast-growing economy is bad news, not good news. In fast-growing economies, it is harder to get and keep good workers, their pay is often higher, and transportation facilities are often congested. Only look for strong state and regional economies when looking for regionally oriented companies that sell products, such as new homes and fast food, directly to consumers.

Most people who buy tax-exempt bonds do so through mutual funds or rely heavily on bond-rating agencies, such as Standard & Poor's and Moody's. Those professional investors rely heavily on the kinds of economic, population, and government statistics used in *State Fact Finder* and analyses of recent fiscal developments presented in publications like State Policy Research's *State Budget & Tax News* and *State Policy Reports*. People who buy individual bonds or buy mutual funds of tax-exempt bonds issued from a single state, like those that invest solely in the bonds of New York or California, can use these same statistics.

10 Which state government will interfere least with my freedom?

People occasionally say they would like to live where government interferes less with their daily lives.. Government intrusiveness cannot easily be compared because governments often restrict the freedom of some citizens to enhance that of others. The ultimate example is capital punishment, which is the most intrusive concept imaginable for the person being punished but is used in the name of increasing freedom from fear and crime for everyone else. State policies are not necessarily consistent on intrusiveness issues. For example, the states that are most likely to allow you to own weapons without restriction are least likely to let you grow marijuana on your own property for personal consumption.

Some elements of government intrusiveness can be measured. One is taxes, measured by the many comparisons in the Taxes section (F). *State Policy Reports* designed an experimental comparison of tax intrusiveness (Vol. 12, Issue 24, December 1994), giving extra weight to property taxes and counting only taxes paid by households, not businesses. With a national average set at 100, it showed variation from 142 in most intrusive New York to 32 in least intrusive Alaska.

Another way to look at intrusiveness is the ratio of state and local government employees to population (D-13). If you find local governments closer to citizens and less intrusive than state governments, look at measures of differences in state and local roles as indicated by public employees (D-15) and revenue raising (D-16).

11 Where are taxes likely to go up/down in the future?

Tax rates are set by state legislatures and local bodies (school boards, city councils, county commissions, etc.). Predicting where taxes will be raised or lowered would appear to be a matter of forecasting the views of those who now serve or will subsequently be elected to these bodies. The economic and population statistics in *State Fact Finder* provide some excellent clues to future tax rates, as does common sense thinking about why some states have higher taxes than others.

Right now, the states with the lowest taxes on people who live there are the states that get lots of their money from other sources—tourists, oil and gas, and gaming casinos, for example. States amply endowed with these—such as Alaska, Nevada, Texas, and Wyoming—have been able to keep taxes low while still offering extensive government services. Some states have been able to keep taxes on their residents relatively low because they have been able to draw new residents who pay substantial taxes but do not have children in public schools, which is the biggest single cause of state and local spending. Fast-growing states of the Southwest and Florida have been the best examples.

These same states will be under the strongest pressures to raise tax levels in the future. As more people come to them, the amount that their unique resources contribute to revenues *per resident* drops. Furthermore, as time passes, their populations become more like the national averages. For example, the childless young people who flocked to Florida in large numbers to work at tourist attractions and to provide health care and other services to retirees are having children in large numbers. Florida has to pay for putting nearly 100,000 additional students in its classrooms every year. California and Texas face similar pressures.

12 Which states have the least/most pollution?

State Fact Finder presents summary statistics on air and water pollution and hazardous waste (C-10 to C-14). More important, the notes to the tables provide leads to where to get more details on local areas. State averages are misleading for people seeking to decide where to live or visit. For example, western cities, like Denver and Salt Lake City, have some of the worst air pollution problems in the nation, but away from urban areas the air in these states is about as pure as you will find. An average for California that lumps downtown Los Angeles with the forests of northern California and the state's deserts will not give an accurate picture of any of these places.

13 Where do I find the best health care?

Because much more money is spent in gathering them, state-by-state statistics on health and health care (section I) are quite comprehensive compared with statistics in other fields. The statistics cover (1) health of average people in a state's population, (2) apparent availability of care, (3) cost of care, and (4) government programs, which are generally oriented to poor people. These statistics suggest strong concentrations of health professionals in northeastern states.

People worried about whether they can find adequate health care for themselves and their family need not be guided by these statistics. Most people are limited to amounts their insurance will pay. Because insurers will not pay for long-distance travel and hotel bills except in rare cases, the doctors capable of performing all types of operations have been locating in the areas across the country where paying patients are found. One result is the development of top-flight facilities across the country, such as the University of Iowa hospital, which serves as a specialized facility for patients throughout that state, and the medical complex around Birmingham, Alabama. There is no reason for anyone to avoid an entire state because of concerns about health care, unless they have a very specialized medical problem. The main limits on health care are primarily those that people accept by their decisions on where to locate within a state. People who seek near-wilderness isolation by buying ranchettes in Colorado or locating on small islands off the Atlantic Ocean must accept the consequences of their isolation on the availability of health care.

14   Where will I be safest from crime?

State statistics, and even city statistics, on crime are not much help in looking for a safe place to live. In every state, crime is most prevalent in the low-income areas of central cities. Violent crimes are most prevalent in these areas after dark. Reported crime statistics much overstate crime risks for people who do not spend evenings in low-income central city areas. A high crime rate for an entire state says more about the percentage of a state's population living in these areas than about safety in that state's suburban, small town, and rural areas as compared with similar areas in other states.

City and state crime rates are also misleading when used to consider which places are safe to visit on business or recreational trips. All statistics, like crime rates and per capita amounts, that relate a category to population use night-time population—the number of people whose regular beds are in a city or state. States such as Florida, Hawaii, and Nevada have many visitors for vacations and conventions. Cities have day-time commuters and business and vacation travelers. Crime rates in cities and these states are much lower for people at risk than when expressed in relation to the number of people who regularly sleep there.

15   Where is the best place to look for a mate?

People looking for an opposite sex partner can reasonably expect better opportunities in locations where they are outnumbered by persons of the opposite sex (A-13).

However, aggregate statistics can be misleading for people under fifty-five looking for a partner about their own age. Because women live longer than men, the states with predominately older populations (A-6) also tend to have high ratios of women to men. Careful research by several women on the Federal Reserve Bank of Boston's research staff found the worst sex ratios (from the standpoint of women seeking men) were found in older northeastern cities and the states with a high percentage of jobs in health care, government, and financial services, which are disproportionately filled by women. The best ratios, again from the perspective of women seeking men, were in booming western states where economic growth draws large numbers of young men to occupations such as mining and construction.

16   Where can I find the lowest living costs?

State Fact Finder includes the best information in use on comparative living costs (B-8), but the data must be used with care. For reasons appearing in the table notes, these measures are not likely to be accurate for what they try to measure—average living costs—and more accurate data are not likely to be available. Also, there are substantial variations within states. All costs, except state and local taxes, are about the same in midsize cities and rural areas throughout the nation. The major differences are taxes (see section F) and costs related to economic growth (see section B). In booming communities and states, housing prices soar, wage rates tend to be higher, and ample and growing sales discourage everyone from doctors to corner store owners from engaging in price wars. In depressed communities and slow-growth states (for example, West Virginia and older industrial communities such as Syracuse, Cleveland, and St. Louis), the reverse factors are reducing housing costs, wages, and prices.

Different people buy different things so the costs they experience will differ from averages, often by wide margins. Business travelers experience enormous price differences in what they buy—downtown hotel rooms, rental cars, and meals at restaurants catering to expense-account travelers. Highly paid executives with downtown jobs will find large differentials, particularly if they hope to live within fifteen minutes commuting time of their work. The largest differentials are associated with the size of metropolitan areas, not with states. New York, Chicago, and Los Angeles are expensive places for these people, but Rochester, Joliet, and Fresno are not.

Most people will not see such large differences in living costs. Much of what they buy—cars, furniture, alcoholic beverages and soft drinks, packaged foods, motion pictures and videotapes, books, sports equipment, clothing, and more—is produced long distances away. The prices generally reflect only minor differences in shipping costs among states, except Alaska and Hawaii where prices are higher. A large part of the housing costs will depend upon mortgage rates, which are nearly uniform nationwide. Most will select homes far enough away from congested central cities so that older home prices cannot get too far out of line with what it costs to build new houses, which is about the same nationwide.

About Business Decisions on Where to Locate and Expand

1 Where is the best place to locate a business?

State Fact Finder provides useful statistics for some kinds of business but not all. Businesses that depend on local customers—from doctors' offices to fast-food franchises—will usually do better in rapidly growing areas. To use *State Fact Finder* to identify these areas, see Question 1 in the previous section. Some local businesses have specialized markets, appealing primarily to clearly defined groups, such as children or the retired. To identify where such populations are large and growing, study the tables in the sections on population and the economy.

Sophisticated investors in consumer-oriented businesses, like franchises, often do extensive market research before committing their money. The same is true for companies deciding how and where to market consumer products, from cars to shampoo. The serious researchers are generally looking at geographic detail not found in sources like *State Fact Finder*—zip codes and even streets and Census tracts, rather than states or metropolitan areas. They rely on their own publications, most notably *American Demographics* and *Sales and Marketing Management.* Many private companies specialize in providing such information and in the computer software to use it. They advertise in these publications.

Some businesses, such as manufacturing companies, can separate where they produce products from where their consumers are located. Their business often limits their location choices. Mining and oil production companies need to be on top of their raw materials. Manufacturing needs an ample supply of labor and may have special transportation requirements, such as access to a rail line or deep-water port.

Among locations that satisfy manufacturers' needs, the factors that help determine what is the best location mostly relate to costs—labor costs, state and local taxes, electricity prices, and transportation costs. Every firm, indeed every plant, is different in where it gets supplies, where its customers are located, how much and what kind of energy it uses, and the relative use of labor and machinery. This means the best place to locate depends on the match between the needs of a particular firm and the attractions of a potential plant site.

State Fact Finder contains much useful information to compare business locations. The Population (A) and Economics (B) sections provide information about potential markets for selling products and hiring workers. The Government (D) section offers information about how states are governed. The Taxes (F) and Revenues (G) sections cover factors associated with each state's tax burdens. Elements of government-provided services that are important to business are discussed in the Education (H) and Transportation (K) sections.

In establishing a business oriented to local economic growth, the important question is what growth *will be,* not what growth *was.* Most statistics show what it was. As the warning about mutual funds goes, "past performance is no guarantee of future results." So, too, for state economic growth.

Future growth will depend on many factors, such as changes in oil prices, federal spending (particularly defense), and how well particular firms and industries (and thus the places where they are located) do in the marketplace. To make predictions on future growth, you can review trend statistics (A-2, B-29, and E-2) or look at the composite Index of State Economic Momentum (B-28). Forecasts can be purchased from firms specializing in forecasting or obtained free from the Department of Commerce (14th St. and Constitution Ave. N.W., Washington, D.C. 20230).

2 Which state has the most productive workers?

In their industrial development ads in business magazines, some states try to convince firms to locate within their borders because their workers are more productive. Productivity in this context is an elusive concept. Many experts are not even sure that national figures about changes in worker productivity are right, much less state-by-state numbers on the same subject.

Employers' ideas of a productive worker may vary from situation to situation. For example, software design and advertising place a premium on creativity and originality, so employees that work irregular hours still may be considered highly productive. An assembly line, however, will not work unless all the workers show up at the same time. Having lots of formal schooling may make engineers productive, but experience may be better for those who repair plumbing or who fish for a living.

State Fact Finder has many statistics on factors employers may consider to be signs of productivity, particularly in the Education (H) and Health (I) sections. *State Fact Finder* also includes the statistics usually used to compare productivity in states (B-6), but such data are misleading for the reasons explained in the notes to the table.

3 Which states have the lowest labor costs?

Most comparisons among states regarding labor costs are based on average annual pay (B-5), as well as annual averages in retailing (B-10) and manufacturing (B-9). However, they will not necessarily be correct for hiring new workers in a particular occupation in a particular location within a state. The wages that must be paid to get competent workers in such a situation will depend upon the supply of labor and the demand for it in that local labor market. Firms looking for low-wage workers should do just the opposite of workers looking for high-paying firms, as discussed in Question 1 of the Personal Decisions section.

The really important statistic is how much work an employer gets from a worker in relation to a dollar paid. That statistic is elusive because productivity per worker is hard to accurately calculate (see Question 2, above). For a sophisticated attempt to calculate this unit labor cost in relation to productivity, see the research presented by Regional Financial Associates (West Chester, Pa.), including *The High Costs of High Costs* (1995).

4 Where will my business pay the least taxes?

State taxes on business are a complex web of interlocking provisions made even more complex because many local governments have separate taxes on business. These combinations have different impacts on different types of business, depending on such factors as how profitable they are; how capital-intensive they are; whether they qualify for state and local economic development incentives; and whether they are organized as proprietorships, partnerships, S (small business) corporations, or C (regular) corporations. There is no substitute for learning the tax rules for the states and localities where you might operate and applying them to the expected characteristics (payroll, profits, etc.) of the business you plan to start or move. These calculations are so complicated that a major consulting industry has developed to make them.

State Fact Finder provides some good indicators of the possible results of these calculations. Start with the overall levels of taxes (F-1 to F-3). If these are high, you will pay them somewhere—if not in taxes on your firm, then in taxes on your salary, your house, and what your firm pays for utility services. Next, look at the burdens of the specific taxes important to your operations. If you will have high investments in property (plant and equipment), see Tables F-6 to F-8. If you are concerned about payroll taxes, see Tables F-13 to F-16. If you are concerned about taxes on your sales, see Tables F-9 to F-12

If yours is a local service business, such as a bakery or retail store, you do not have to worry much about state taxes on your business. Unless you are near a border with another state, your competitors will be paying the same taxes as you. This may not be true with local taxes, so you have to check them specifically. If yours is a small business, you may not be as worried about some taxes, particularly corporate income and franchise taxes, as large firms. You may be more concerned with certain taxes on individuals, such as income and estate taxes, as shown in Tables F-16 and F-23.

If yours is a nationally oriented business, such as manufacturing, you may be in for some pleasant and unpleasant surprises about taxes on your business. Some states with high overall tax levels, such as New York, are very competitive in taxes on manufacturing. Some states with low taxes on households, particularly those with no taxes on personal incomes, have relatively high taxes on firms. For multistate firms, opening a plant in one state affects corporate income taxes in all the states because of the way corporate income is apportioned among states for tax purposes. For samples of calculations of corporate taxes of different industries in many states, see studies that the accounting firm of KPMG Peat Marwick has prepared for states studying their "tax competitiveness." Recent studies have been made for Kentucky, New York, and North Carolina.

5 Which states provide the best incentives to locate in them?

The amounts and types of assistance available from state and local governments in tax breaks, grants, and loans for locating in their jurisdiction depend upon the kind of business. If your business inherently serves local customers—an auto dealership, restaurant, retail store, or repair business, for example—expect no significant help from these governments. Your new business is not going to increase the wealth or income of the area you serve but rather just move it from those already there and competing for the same business you want. You may get some technical assistance and even loans, but mostly from state and local agencies administering federal small business money. If you pick the right state and right local government within that state, you may get some tax breaks because local communities compete for tax base with other local communities.

If your business will draw money from out-of-state, your business (large or small) will likely be offered major incentives from just about any state. There are so many incentives and the number is growing so fast that a directory of them published by the Urban Institute in 1991 was obsolete the day it was released. Do not try to find national directories of these. Even if you do you will miss the deals that states might be willing to tailor to fit your business. Nearly every community of any size and all states employ "developers"—economic development professionals whose mission is to draw employers to their community or state by providing information and administering incentives. These people are eager to provide you with details about sites, taxes, worker availability, and state and local incentives. Look for state agencies with *development* in their titles and find local agencies through county or city governments or chambers of commerce.

6 Which states have the lowest utility rates?

Statistics comparing state averages of electric rates for various consumers appear in Tables B-33 and B-34. They are indicative of rate differentials for other fuels as well. In general, the farther you locate from the sources of inexpensive energy (the gas fields of the Southwest and hydroelectric sites), the more expensive energy will be. Taxes make a big difference in what you pay for energy. So do state policies that determine how the total bill is divided between household, commercial, and industrial uses, as Table B-34 dramatically illustrates. There are price variations within states among users of differing quantities and among types of industrial service (such as cheaper rates for those who will close their plants on high-use days). Many concessions are made to firms newly locating in an area or who demonstrate they can obtain service from a competitor utility. There is no substitute for checking the prices the local utilities charge.

7 Which states regulate business the least?

There is no statistical way to compare state and local regulation of business across the board because there are so many different ways government regulation touches business operations. There is also great variation in policies among states and local areas. Many of the regulatory differences are not systematic. For example, some southern states have less stringent regulation of workplace conditions while imposing more stringent regulation on how corporations are governed.

8 Where is the transportation system best?

The interstate transportation systems—road, rail, air, and even barge lines—form an interconnected network that reaches every state in some way. Once your products or raw materials reach this network, service is close to uniform until they leave it. For businesses with large shipping requirements, the key aspect is how easily you can connect with the national networks used by your particular business. This varies with geography, not state lines, and is critically dependent on exactly where your site is located relative to rail and other transportation access points. As every driver knows, the quality and capacity of roads depends on exactly which roads you use.

However, there are systematic differences among states. These appear most dramatically in measures of maintenance and construction, the condition of bridges (K-3), and highway pavement (K-2).

9 Which states have pro-business attitudes?

Like the rest of us, business owners and managers have differing needs and differing views of appropriate public policies. For example, a company engaged in a low-technology, labor-intensive activity such as poultry processing is not much concerned with the education of its workers but is highly concerned with pollution control costs, state labor regulations, and taxes. A company engaged in high-tech competition for improved designs of computer chips or software is not as affected by such state regulation or even taxes; it is highly sensitive to how well educated employees are and whether governments offer strong university systems and cultural and recreational opportunities. Thus, a state with relatively high taxes that is accustomed to paying for top-flight schools and state universities will appear anti-business to some business leaders and pro-business to others.

The phrase *business climate* was widely used in the 1980s in discussions of state policies for economic development, regulation, labor laws, and taxes. The statistics were developed by the Grant Thornton accounting firm, based on opinions of which characteristics were important to those manufacturing firms that participated in state manufacturing associations. The state rankings much favored southeastern states with low taxes, low wages, and little business regulation. The influence of these ratings on state policies encouraged the development of countersta-

tistics, particularly the annual *Development Report Card for the States*, published by the Corporation for Economic Development, whose sponsors include many unions. As the name implies, the *Report Card* gives letter grades, not aggregate rankings, to reflect the complexity and controversy associated with deciding which state policies are pro-business and which are successful in causing state economic development. The state grades are nearly a flip-flop from the business climate rankings. In this evaluation, southeastern states tend to have the lowest grades.

The availability of these more sophisticated measures discouraged use of the old business climate rankings, which are no longer published. The term *business climate* has been appropriated by the publishers of the business-oriented quarterly *Site Selection*. Its ranking procedure, associated with the number of new jobs primarily in manufacturing, inherently favors large states over less populous ones. Using the test of which states are drawing the most new work, see Table B-30, which shows growth in manufacturing jobs. Using the test of where firms locate their headquarters, see Tables B-16 and B-17.

10 Which states are the best places to sell business-to-business?

Many companies do not sell to consumers; they sell goods and services to other businesses. Finding firms that might want to buy office supplies, parts, maintenance services, and other business-to-business offerings is different from finding individual consumers (which is discussed in Question 1). The statistics needed for finding business customers are too specialized for this book but exist in abundance from government sources. The Bureau of Labor Statistics in the Department of Labor keeps up-to-date statistics on the number of jobs in each state, with breakdowns by major industry. The Commerce Department keeps detailed data and publishes them on a county level in *County Business Patterns*. The Commerce Department also does major surveys of industries, such as the Census of Manufacturing and the Census of Retail Trade.

State governments have even more detailed information, though some do a better job than others in keeping it current and making it available in usable form. The state agencies that administer Unemployment Compensation (UC)—typically called the Department of Labor or Employment Services Administration—know details on every private firm because they collect UC payroll taxes from them every quarter. Corporations, from mom-and-pop stores to General Motors, are chartered by states and often need some kind of permit to operate in states where they are not chartered. Secretaries of state are the keepers of these records. Many state economic development departments have detailed statistics on businesses operating in the state, and some publish directories.

About Government and Public Policy

1 Which state is the best managed?

No one has ever found a way to use statistics to determine which states, or for that matter which private companies, are best managed. Bottom-line results—good schools, low taxes, and high and growing business profits—count, but some companies and states face greater challenges than others in achieving them because of circumstances beyond the control of their managers. There are awards for well-managed companies and governments, but these are like civic awards. Who gets them depends on who is on the selection committees, the criteria those particular people think are important, and their personal knowledge of the award candidates.

Somewhat more objective measures of state financial management are available. Bond rating agencies, such as Standard & Poor's, assess credit risks (G-15) much like a bank would determine how much to loan a family seeking a mortgage. Like personal credit ratings, these concern only the likelihood that loans will be repaid, not whether the borrower is competent, efficient, or doing the right things.

States can also be compared in financial management practices, such as whether they conform to generally accepted accounting principles and whether they use performance-oriented budgeting. Most experts believe these practices improve the quality of state decisions. These comparisons can be found in Table G-20. For a more detailed discussion of these and comparisons of such state practices as balanced budget requirements, governors' item-veto powers, and use of stabilization or "rainy day" funds, see *State Policy Reports* (vol. 13, issue 5, March 1995).

2   Which state has the fairest tax system?

Fairness in taxes depends entirely on one's perspective about who should bear what share of tax burdens—a specific example of the old maxim, "Where you stand depends on where you sit." The data needed to form opinions are found in Tables F-6 through F-22 in the Taxes section. Included are tables on progressivity of taxes; relative reliance on sales, income, and other tax bases; and tax burdens on high- and low-income households.

A large group of experts and state officials—including governors, legislators, and tax commissioners—have jointly published a study about the elements of good tax systems. *Financing State Government in the 1990s* is available from the National Conference of State Legislatures in Denver or the National Governors' Association in Washington, D.C. The study advocates keeping rates of all taxes as low as possible, given the money to be raised, by avoiding lots of special exemptions and balancing reliance on property, income, and sales tax. Look for balance in percentage of three-tax revenue in Tables F-8, F-11, and F-15.

3   Which states keep the share of taxes paid by business low?

Economists argue that all taxes must reduce some person's income in order to make it available for government. They do not believe that legal abstractions, such as corporations and partnerships, bear the burden of any taxes. Instead, the tax burdens find their way into prices paid by customers, lower wages paid to workers, lower prices paid to suppliers, and lower profits credited to stockholders.

Many people do not agree with this. Public opinion polls usually show that voters would rather see taxes on corporations than taxes they *know* they pay, such as sales and personal income taxes. While many business leaders do not agree with the economists' outlook, others believe it but want to protect everyone involved—stockholders, suppliers, workers, and customers—by avoiding taxes on their business. As a result there is a lot of interest in comparing how states distribute tax burdens between businesses and people.

Good data to make such comparisons will never exist because the people who might gather the information, the tax collectors, do not care about it. Most collect the same property tax on houses and stores whether they are owned by occupants, individual landlords, or a corporate landlord. When someone buys a yellow pad of paper and pays sales tax no one asks if they are buying it for grocery lists or for a business project. The family farm is both a business and a home, but most states do not divide the value between the two or make the tax lower or higher if the family is organized as a sole proprietorship, partnership, or corporation.

Consequently, comparisons of states on the share of taxes paid by businesses inherently involve guesswork and arbitrary distinctions, such as calling all severance taxes business taxes and all farm taxes people taxes. The most recent comparison was published in 1993 in *Business Tax Competitiveness*, a report for a special commission studying business tax policy for Massachusetts. It found business paid the lowest share of state and local taxes in Iowa (19.3 percent) and the highest in Alaska (78.8 percent). These data deliberately are not included in *State Fact Finder*.

4   Which state has the highest taxes?

The three standard measures of tax burdens are found in the first three tables of the Taxes section (F-1, F-2, and F-3). None of them are as good as the other tables in this section for considering what taxes are likely to be on an individual household or business. For those answers, see the answers to Question 2 in the Personal Decisions section and Question 4 in the Business Decisions section.

5   Which state has the best education policies?

People disagree about the best policies in education and other public policy fields. To answer questions like these, there are sporadic publications of evaluations of aggregate policies that rank states, but these simply reflect the policy preferences of the interest group issuing them. The scores and rankings are useful to those who share their biases, misleading to those who do not. *State Fact Finder* provides statistics on education (section H) and lets you decide which ones are most important to you.

6 Which states help the poor the most?

There is much disagreement about what is truly helpful to the poor. For example, some people believe providing welfare cash helps, but others argue that this hurts in the long run because it discourages working and hinders the opportunity to rise out of poverty. *State Fact Finder* has many tables on programs for the poor, including food stamps (L-3), welfare (L-2, L-9, L-15, and L-16), Medicaid (I-12, I-13, I-16, I-17, and I-18), and school aid for the disadvantaged (H-12), as well as on tax policies affecting low income households (L-11). If you want to look further into this question, consult the Center for Budget and Policy Priorities (in Washington, D.C.). This group has analyzed which states are most generous to the poor in their spending and how regressive state and local tax policies are—that is, whether they take away in taxes a larger percentage of the purchasing power of the poor than of the rich.

7 Which states have the best roads?

Comparing state policies on a topic such as education does not work well because different people have different ideas about what constitutes good or bad policy. However, for some services, such as providing well-maintained roads, people generally agree on what is good and bad. Even when people can agree on desirable results (for example, how children should perform on standard reading tests), it is difficult to judge states on these outcomes because so much of the result is determined by factors governments do not control. Because state and local governments maintain their own roads, few extraneous factors are involved.

Highways provide a good example of how services can be compared (see Tables K-2 and K-3). Truckers run their own surveys, which can be found in the special interest magazine *Overdrive*.

8 Overall, which states use tax dollars in the most cost-effective manner?

For conceptual reasons, this question cannot be answered. Conceptual problems arise because people do not agree on what governments should do and how they should do it. For example, most people would agree that administrative costs for welfare should be kept at a minimum so all available money can be devoted to real work. Most people would agree that it is bad for society if large numbers of people are allowed to cheat their governments and most would also agree that welfare recipients should be encouraged to find jobs. These beliefs produce contradictory results when applied to available data, such as costs per case of administering welfare (L-17) and collecting child support (L-13). These costs are lowest if a state does little counseling and does not spend much money checking for fraud. Another example of a conceptual problem is the size of elementary school classes (H-9); some people think really small classes are ideal for all schools, while others believe small classes result in unnecessary spending.

Conceptual problems are not unique to governments. How can a company effectively measure whether its public relations or shareholder relations departments are cost-effective?

Even if conceptual problems could be solved, there are enormous difficulties in collecting the relevant data. For many functions, we do not have good measures of effectiveness. Do you know an effective police officer when you meet one, or an effective state university professor, or an effective state legislator? If you do, can you think how you would apply your effectiveness tests to every police officer, state university professor, or legislator in the nation? Often good measures of costs are not available either, at least not ones that are related closely to particular services or outputs of government. This problem is not unique to government. What percentage of the cost of a steer goes with the beef and what percentage with the leather?

Most attempts to measure the cost-effectiveness of government are experimental, usually confined to activities that can be measured fairly easily, such as gathering refuse, maintaining highways, and collecting bills. For more information, see the many useful books by Harry Hatry, published by the Urban Institute in Washington, D.C.

9 Which states have the best government institutions?

Beauty is clearly in the eye of the beholder when it comes to deciding how governments ought to be organized, their policies established, and their leaders selected. Some people have strong preferences on these matters, which are from time to time reflected in comparisons oriented to showing the states with the "best" practices.

For the past thirty years, experts have advocated and states have moved to organizing the executive branches of state government in ways that strengthen the power of governors. These moves include (1) strengthening the veto power, including "line item" vetoes; (2) reducing the number of executive officials (comptrollers, education superintendents, and insurance commissioners, etc.) selected by elections rather than appointed; (3) increasing the governor's role in preparing and administering budgets; and (4) extending governor's terms by converting two-year terms to four-year terms and allowing governors to run for reelection. Information on these developments and classifications of which states have which practices appear in the Government section (D).

For decades state legislatures were criticized as citadels of corrupt power removed from popular control and unresponsive to the needs of citizens. One major change came with a Supreme Court decision on reapportionment, requiring "one man (or woman), one vote." Now the Senate is the only governing body in the nation where voting power is not proportional to population. The National Conference of State Legislatures and some business groups and foundations have sponsored research on "modern" legislatures emphasizing (1) longer annual sessions, (2) more staff, and (3) higher legislative pay and expenses. Two measures of the results appear in Tables D-5, D-8, and D-9.

These ideas have come under considerable criticism recently. Some people saw more staffing and full-time legislators making the field a career as a move toward professionalizing the legislature; others saw this as a recipe for making bureaucrats out of legislators, creating "full-time politicians," and pulling legislators out of touch with the people they represent. One result has been a move to limit the number of terms legislators can serve (D-8), in effect encouraging turnover (D-7).

Surveys show that large numbers of Americans think corruption is common among elected officials at the state and federal level. There is no statistical way to compare ethics, but laws on conflict of interest and disclosure of personal financial information can be compared. The National Conference of State Legislatures does this, with the organization Common Cause providing a kind of watchdog role.

There is no prevailing doctrine on whether "bigger is better" for business and government. Sometimes the fashion is consolidation—forming conglomerates for business and merging regional governments to reduce the roughly 80,000 different state and local governments. Sometimes the emphasis is decentralization and local control, with spin-offs for business and special districts (for example, downtown revitalization areas, police service districts) and decentralized control of neighborhood schools within large school systems. One way to look at differing state policy is to compare the ratio of governments to people (D-4). Another approach is to examine the percentage of local government spending that local officials do not have to finance with their own taxes (D-16).

State Fact Finder provides in Table D-11 assessments of performance of governors, as seen by "experts" and voters.

10 Overall, which states have the best policies?

For some people, picking the best policy is simple: the best state is the one with the lowest taxes, or the one that spends the most on schools or taking care of the poor, or is active in some other area of interest to the person making the judgment. For most people, this question is too general to be answered meaningfully because opinions differ so markedly on "best." Even for a particular

person, one state may combine "good" policies on one subject with "bad" policies on another.

One thing is clear: State officials have to play the hands they are dealt, balancing the needs of their population and the tax base available for revenue to meet those needs. Needs appear in the form of children to be educated (H-10), poor people potentially eligible for services (A-11), and more. Tax bases are apparent from economic differences, as shown in the Economies section (B). State differences are summarized in Table G-21 for spending needs and Table F-3 for tax bases.

By comparing these statistics, some conclusions are pretty obvious. For example, compared with most states, it is easy for Connecticut officials to look good, as the state has both low taxes and high spending in relation to what they do, such as spending per school pupil. The state has a rich tax base and a comparatively small percentage of people needing service. Mississippi faces the exact opposite situation.

10 All things considered, which state is run the best?

Readers are advised not to pay attention to magazine rankings purporting to show which state governments are best, or which states are governed the best by the combination of state and local officials responsible for their policies. You can get a pretty good idea that there is something slippery about these just by comparing results. According to *Worth* magazine (November 1994), Wyoming is best and Alaska is second. Compare this with *Financial World,* which ranks Wyoming forty-third and puts Alaska next to last.

The rankings for cities and metropolitan areas are no better than those for states. For a good discussion of the pitfalls involved in such rankings, see "Why Nice Cities Finish Last" in *Governing* magazine (September 1995).

If you must rank states on something, pick some areas where they compete for the same prize, such as jobs (B-29); where residents are judged by the same test (H-3); or where the same objective criteria are being applied, such as tax levels (F-1).

There is widespread agreement on what constitutes a valuable football player or an outstanding actress. This is not true for governments. Many people think those that govern best govern least, but others are looking for good schools, good roads, and quick responses from police and fire departments.

Subject Rankings

Population

A-1 Population and Percent Distribution, 1994

State	Population 1994 (000)	% of nat'l total 1994 %	Rank by number (#) and percent (%)
Alabama	4,219	1.6	22
Alaska	606	0.2	48
Arizona	4,075	1.6	23
Arkansas	2,453	0.9	33
California	31,431	12.1	1
Colorado	3,656	1.4	26
Connecticut	3,275	1.3	27
Delaware	706	0.3	46
Florida	13,953	5.4	4
Georgia	7,055	2.7	11
Hawaii	1,179	0.5	40
Idaho	1,133	0.4	42
Illinois	11,752	4.5	6
Indiana	5,752	2.2	14
Iowa	2,829	1.1	30
Kansas	2,554	1.0	32
Kentucky	3,827	1.5	24
Louisiana	4,315	1.7	21
Maine	1,240	0.5	39
Maryland	5,006	1.9	19
Massachusetts	6,041	2.3	13
Michigan	9,496	3.6	8
Minnesota	4,567	1.8	20
Mississippi	2,669	1.0	31
Missouri	5,278	2.0	16
Montana	856	0.3	44
Nebraska	1,623	0.6	37
Nevada	1,457	0.6	38
New Hampshire	1,137	0.4	41
New Jersey	7,904	3.0	9
New Mexico	1,654	0.6	36
New York	18,169	7.0	3
North Carolina	7,070	2.7	10
North Dakota	638	0.2	47
Ohio	11,102	4.3	7
Oklahoma	3,258	1.3	28
Oregon	3,086	1.2	29
Pennsylvania	12,052	4.6	5
Rhode Island	997	0.4	43
South Carolina	3,664	1.4	25
South Dakota	721	0.3	45
Tennessee	5,175	2.0	17
Texas	18,378	7.1	2
Utah	1,908	0.7	34
Vermont	580	0.2	49
Virginia	6,552	2.5	12
Washington	5,343	2.1	15
West Virginia	1,822	0.7	35
Wisconsin	5,082	2.0	18
Wyoming	476	0.2	50
50 States	259,771	99.8	
DC	570	0.2	
United States	260,341	100.0	

Rank in order

By # & %

1. California
2. Texas
3. New York
4. Florida
5. Pennsylvania
6. Illinois
7. Ohio
8. Michigan
9. New Jersey
10. North Carolina
11. Georgia
12. Virginia
13. Massachusetts
14. Indiana
15. Washington
16. Missouri
17. Tennessee
18. Wisconsin
19. Maryland
20. Minnesota
21. Louisiana
22. Alabama
23. Arizona
24. Kentucky
25. South Carolina
26. Colorado
27. Connecticut
28. Oklahoma
29. Oregon
30. Iowa
31. Mississippi
32. Kansas
33. Arkansas
34. Utah
35. West Virginia
36. New Mexico
37. Nebraska
38. Nevada
39. Maine
40. Hawaii
41. New Hampshire
42. Idaho
43. Rhode Island
44. Montana
45. South Dakota
46. Delaware
47. North Dakota
48. Alaska
49. Vermont
50. Wyoming

A-2 Percent Change in Population 1993-94

State	Population 1993 (000)	% change in population 1993-1994 %	Rank by % change		Rank in order By %
Alabama	4,181	0.9	26		1. Nevada
Alaska	598	1.3	15		2. Arizona
Arizona	3,945	3.3	2		3. Idaho
Arkansas	2,426	1.1	21		4. Colorado
California	31,217	0.7	35		5. Utah
Colorado	3,564	2.6	4		6. New Mexico
Connecticut	3,278	-0.1	49		7. Georgia
Delaware	698	1.1	19		8. Texas
Florida	13,726	1.7	12		9. Montana
Georgia	6,902	2.2	7		10. North Carolina
Hawaii	1,166	1.1	20		11. Oregon
Idaho	1,100	3.0	3		12. Florida
Illinois	11,686	0.6	39		13. Washington
Indiana	5,706	0.8	29		14. Tennessee
Iowa	2,821	0.3	43		15. Alaska
Kansas	2,535	0.7	32		16. Wyoming
Kentucky	3,794	0.9	27		17. Virginia
Louisiana	4,290	0.6	37		18. New Hampshire
Maine	1,240	0.0	48		19. Delaware
Maryland	4,958	1.0	23		20. Hawaii
Massachusetts	6,018	0.4	40		21. Arkansas
Michigan	9,460	0.4	41		22. Mississippi
Minnesota	4,524	1.0	24		23. Maryland
Mississippi	2,640	1.1	22		24. Minnesota
Missouri	5,235	0.8	28		25. South Carolina
Montana	841	1.8	9		26. Alabama
Nebraska	1,613	0.6	36		27. Kentucky
Nevada	1,382	5.4	1		28. Missouri
New Hampshire	1,124	1.2	18		29. Indiana
New Jersey	7,859	0.6	38		30. Oklahoma
New Mexico	1,616	2.4	6		31. Wisconsin
New York	18,153	0.1	47		32. Kansas
North Carolina	6,952	1.7	10		33. South Dakota
North Dakota	637	0.2	46		34. Vermont
Ohio	11,061	0.4	42		35. California
Oklahoma	3,233	0.8	30		36. Nebraska
Oregon	3,035	1.7	11		37. Louisiana
Pennsylvania	12,030	0.2	45		38. New Jersey
Rhode Island	1,000	-0.3	50		39. Illinois
South Carolina	3,630	0.9	25		40. Massachusetts
South Dakota	716	0.7	33		41. Michigan
Tennessee	5,094	1.6	14		42. Ohio
Texas	18,022	2.0	8		43. Iowa
Utah	1,860	2.6	5		44. West Virginia
Vermont	576	0.7	34		45. Pennsylvania
Virginia	6,473	1.2	17		46. North Dakota
Washington	5,259	1.6	13		47. New York
West Virginia	1,818	0.2	44		48. Maine
Wisconsin	5,044	0.8	31		49. Connecticut
Wyoming	470	1.3	16		50. Rhode Island
50 States	257,206	1.0			
DC	579	-1.6			
United States	257,783	1.0			

State	Population 1980 (000)	% change in population 1980-94 %	rank by % change	Rank in order By %
Alabama	3,894	8.3	26	1. Nevada
Alaska	402	50.7	2	2. Alaska
Arizona	2,718	49.9	3	3. Arizona
Arkansas	2,286	7.3	32	4. Florida
California	23,668	32.8	5	5. California
Colorado	2,890	26.5	11	6. Utah
Connecticut	3,108	5.4	34	7. Washington
Delaware	594	18.9	17	8. Texas
Florida	9,746	43.2	4	9. Georgia
Georgia	5,463	29.1	9	10. New Mexico
Hawaii	965	22.2	14	11. Colorado
Idaho	944	20.0	16	12. New Hampshire
Illinois	11,427	2.8	42	13. Virginia
Indiana	5,490	4.8	37	14. Hawaii
Iowa	2,914	-2.9	49	15. North Carolina
Kansas	2,364	8.0	27	16. Idaho
Kentucky	3,661	4.5	38	17. Delaware
Louisiana	4,206	2.6	44	18. Maryland
Maine	1,125	10.2	24	19. South Carolina
Maryland	4,217	18.7	18	20. Oregon
Massachusetts	5,737	5.3	35	21. Vermont
Michigan	9,262	2.5	45	22. Tennessee
Minnesota	4,076	12.0	23	23. Minnesota
Mississippi	2,521	5.9	33	24. Maine
Missouri	4,917	7.3	30	25. Montana
Montana	787	8.8	25	26. Alabama
Nebraska	1,570	3.4	41	27. Kansas
Nevada	800	82.1	1	28. Wisconsin
New Hampshire	921	23.5	12	29. Oklahoma
New Jersey	7,365	7.3	31	30. Missouri
New Mexico	1,303	26.9	10	31. New Jersey
New York	17,558	3.5	40	32. Arkansas
North Carolina	5,882	20.2	15	33. Mississippi
North Dakota	653	-2.3	48	34. Connecticut
Ohio	10,798	2.8	43	35. Massachusetts
Oklahoma	3,025	7.7	29	36. Rhode Island
Oregon	2,633	17.2	20	37. Indiana
Pennsylvania	11,864	1.6	46	38. Kentucky
Rhode Island	947	5.3	36	39. South Dakota
South Carolina	3,122	17.4	19	40. New York
South Dakota	691	4.3	39	41. Nebraska
Tennessee	4,591	12.7	22	42. Illinois
Texas	14,229	29.2	8	43. Ohio
Utah	1,461	30.6	6	44. Louisiana
Vermont	511	13.5	21	45. Michigan
Virginia	5,347	22.5	13	46. Pennsylvania
Washington	4,132	29.3	7	47. Wyoming
West Virginia	1,950	-6.6	50	48. North Dakota
Wisconsin	4,706	8.0	28	49. Iowa
Wyoming	470	1.3	47	50. West Virginia
50 States	222,017	17.0		
DC	638	-10.7		
United States	226,546	14.9		

State	Projected Population 2005 (000)	% change in population 1993-2005 %	Rank by % change	Rank in order By %
Alabama	4,516	0.6	38	1. Nevada
Alaska	694	1.3	7	2. Utah
Arizona	4,881	1.8	3	3. Arizona
Arkansas	2,655	0.8	25	4. Florida
California	36,657	1.3	7	5. Colorado
Colorado	4,273	1.5	5	6. Washington
Connecticut	3,564	0.7	31	7. Alaska
Delaware	793	1.1	17	8. California
Florida	16,900	1.7	4	9. Georgia
Georgia	8,033	1.3	7	10. Hawaii
Hawaii	1,354	1.3	7	11. New Mexico
Idaho	1,277	1.2	12	12. Idaho
Illinois	12,677	0.7	31	13. Montana
Indiana	6,133	0.6	38	14. North Carolina
Iowa	2,949	0.4	45	15. Oregon
Kansas	2,772	0.7	31	16. Texas
Kentucky	4,086	0.6	38	17. Delaware
Louisiana	4,611	0.6	38	18. New Hampshire
Maine	1,352	0.7	31	19. South Carolina
Maryland	5,598	1.0	20	20. Maryland
Massachusetts	6,523	0.7	31	21. Tennessee
Michigan	9,927	0.4	45	22. Vermont
Minnesota	4,998	0.8	25	23. Virginia
Mississippi	2,819	0.5	43	24. South Dakota
Missouri	5,728	0.8	25	25. Arkansas
Montana	968	1.2	12	26. Minnesota
Nebraska	1,747	0.7	31	27. Missouri
Nevada	1,839	2.4	1	28. New Jersey
New Hampshire	1,276	1.1	17	29. Wisconsin
New Jersey	8,638	0.8	25	30. Wyoming
New Mexico	1,895	1.3	7	31. Connecticut
New York	18,654	0.2	50	32. Illinois
North Carolina	8,006	1.2	12	33. Kansas
North Dakota	661	0.3	48	34. Maine
Ohio	11,677	0.5	43	35. Massachusetts
Oklahoma	3,517	0.7	31	36. Nebraska
Oregon	3,493	1.2	12	37. Oklahoma
Pennsylvania	12,682	0.4	45	38. Alabama
Rhode Island	1,070	0.6	38	39. Indiana
South Carolina	4,116	1.1	17	40. Kentucky
South Dakota	794	0.9	24	41. Louisiana
Tennessee	5,771	1.0	20	42. Rhode Island
Texas	20,734	1.2	12	43. Mississippi
Utah	2,336	1.9	2	44. Ohio
Vermont	647	1.0	20	45. Iowa
Virginia	7,284	1.0	20	46. Michigan
Washington	6,237	1.4	6	47. Pennsylvania
West Virginia	1,884	0.3	48	48. North Dakota
Wisconsin	5,518	0.8	25	49. West Virginia
Wyoming	520	0.8	25	50. New York
50 States	287,734	n/a		
DC	554	-0.4		
United States	288,286	0.9		

State	Estimated 2000 Population (000)	Rank
Alabama	4,383	23
Alaska	657	47
Arizona	4,526	21
Arkansas	2,567	33
California	34,470	1
Colorado	3,996	24
Connecticut	3,434	27
Delaware	757	46
Florida	15,642	4
Georgia	7,602	11
Hawaii	1,281	40
Idaho	1,216	42
Illinois	12,260	6
Indiana	5,962	14
Iowa	2,893	30
Kansas	2,684	32
Kentucky	3,967	25
Louisiana	4,478	22
Maine	1,302	39
Maryland	5,347	18
Massachusetts	6,301	13
Michigan	9,741	8
Minnesota	4,816	20
Mississippi	2,750	31
Missouri	5,531	16
Montana	920	44
Nebraska	1,696	37
Nevada	1,664	38
New Hampshire	1,218	41
New Jersey	8,334	9
New Mexico	1,788	36
New York	18,472	3
North Carolina	7,610	10
North Dakota	651	48
Ohio	11,432	7
Oklahoma	3,406	28
Oregon	3,314	29
Pennsylvania	12,413	5
Rhode Island	1,037	43
South Carolina	3,919	26
South Dakota	763	45
Tennessee	5,521	17
Texas	19,724	2
Utah	2,147	34
Vermont	619	49
Virginia	6,953	12
Washington	5,833	15
West Virginia	1,858	35
Wisconsin	5,327	19
Wyoming	501	50
50 States	275,683	
DC	559	
United States	276,241	

Rank in order

By population

1. California
2. Texas
3. New York
4. Florida
5. Pennsylvania
6. Illinois
7. Ohio
8. Michigan
9. New Jersey
10. North Carolina
11. Georgia
12. Virginia
13. Massachusetts
14. Indiana
15. Washington
16. Missouri
17. Tennessee
18. Maryland
19. Wisconsin
20. Minnesota
21. Arizona
22. Louisiana
23. Alabama
24. Colorado
25. Kentucky
26. South Carolina
27. Connecticut
28. Oklahoma
29. Oregon
30. Iowa
31. Mississippi
32. Kansas
33. Arkansas
34. Utah
35. West Virginia
36. New Mexico
37. Nebraska
38. Nevada
39. Maine
40. Hawaii
41. New Hampshire
42. Idaho
43. Rhode Island
44. Montana
45. South Dakota
46. Delaware
47. Alaska
48. North Dakota
49. Vermont
50. Wyoming

A-6 Percentage of Population Over 65 Years Old, 1994			Rank in order

State	Percent over 65 Years Old 1994 %	Rank	By %
Alabama	13.1	23	1. Florida
Alaska	4.6	50	2. Pennsylvania
Arizona	13.4	20	3. Rhode Island
Arkansas	14.8	6	4. Iowa
California	10.6	45	5. West Virginia
Colorado	10.0	48	6. Arkansas
Connecticut	14.2	9	7. North Dakota
Delaware	12.6	27	8. South Dakota
Florida	18.4	1	9. Connecticut
Georgia	10.1	47	10. Nebraska
Hawaii	12.0	34	11. Missouri
Idaho	11.7	37	12. Massachusetts
Illinois	12.6	28	13. Maine
Indiana	12.8	24	14. Kansas
Iowa	15.4	4	15. Oregon
Kansas	13.9	14	16. New Jersey
Kentucky	12.8	25	17. Oklahoma
Louisiana	11.4	39	18. Wisconsin
Maine	14.0	13	19. Ohio
Maryland	11.2	41	20. Arizona
Massachusetts	14.1	12	21. Montana
Michigan	12.4	32	22. New York
Minnesota	12.5	29	23. Alabama
Mississippi	12.4	31	24. Indiana
Missouri	14.1	11	25. Kentucky
Montana	13.3	21	26. Tennessee
Nebraska	14.2	10	27. Delaware
Nevada	11.3	40	28. Illinois
New Hampshire	12.0	35	29. Minnesota
New Jersey	13.6	16	30. North Carolina
New Mexico	10.9	44	31. Mississippi
New York	13.2	22	32. Michigan
North Carolina	12.5	30	33. Vermont
North Dakota	14.7	7	34. Hawaii
Ohio	13.4	19	35. New Hampshire
Oklahoma	13.6	17	36. South Carolina
Oregon	13.7	15	37. Idaho
Pennsylvania	15.9	2	38. Washington
Rhode Island	15.5	3	39. Louisiana
South Carolina	11.9	36	40. Nevada
South Dakota	14.6	8	41. Maryland
Tennessee	12.7	26	42. Wyoming
Texas	10.2	46	43. Virginia
Utah	8.8	49	44. New Mexico
Vermont	12.1	33	45. California
Virginia	11.1	43	46. Texas
Washington	11.6	38	47. Georgia
West Virginia	15.4	5	48. Colorado
Wisconsin	13.4	18	49. Utah
Wyoming	11.1	42	50. Alaska
50 States	12.7		
DC	13.5		
United States	12.7		

State	Percent 17 and Under %	Rank
Alabama	25.6	33
Alaska	31.7	2
Arizona	28.0	10
Arkansas	26.1	25
California	27.6	12
Colorado	26.5	20
Connecticut	24.1	46
Delaware	24.8	41
Florida	23.4	50
Georgia	26.8	18
Hawaii	25.8	28
Idaho	29.9	4
Illinois	26.2	23
Indiana	25.6	32
Iowa	25.8	29
Kansas	27.0	15
Kentucky	25.3	35
Louisiana	28.6	8
Maine	24.7	42
Maryland	25.2	36
Massachusetts	23.6	48
Michigan	26.6	19
Minnesota	27.2	14
Mississippi	28.3	9
Missouri	26.1	24
Montana	27.8	11
Nebraska	27.2	13
Nevada	25.8	27
New Hampshire	25.7	31
New Jersey	24.4	44
New Mexico	30.1	3
New York	24.8	40
North Carolina	24.8	39
North Dakota	27.0	17
Ohio	25.7	30
Oklahoma	27.0	16
Oregon	25.4	34
Pennsylvania	24.0	47
Rhode Island	24.1	45
South Carolina	26.0	26
South Dakota	28.8	5
Tennessee	25.1	38
Texas	28.8	6
Utah	35.2	1
Vermont	25.2	37
Virginia	24.5	43
Washington	26.4	22
West Virginia	23.5	49
Wisconsin	26.5	21
Wyoming	28.8	7
50 States	26.1	
DC	20.9	
United States	26.1	

Rank in order

By %

1. Utah
2. Alaska
3. New Mexico
4. Idaho
5. South Dakota
6. Texas
7. Wyoming
8. Louisiana
9. Mississippi
10. Arizona
11. Montana
12. California
13. Nebraska
14. Minnesota
15. Kansas
16. Oklahoma
17. North Dakota
18. Georgia
19. Michigan
20. Colorado
21. Wisconsin
22. Washington
23. Illinois
24. Missouri
25. Arkansas
26. South Carolina
27. Nevada
28. Hawaii
29. Iowa
30. Ohio
31. New Hampshire
32. Indiana
33. Alabama
34. Oregon
35. Kentucky
36. Maryland
37. Vermont
38. Tennessee
39. North Carolina
40. New York
41. Delaware
42. Maine
43. Virginia
44. New Jersey
45. Rhode Island
46. Connecticut
47. Pennsylvania
48. Massachusetts
49. West Virginia
50. Florida

State	Median Age 1994	Rank
Alabama	34	20
Alaska	31	49
Arizona	33	41
Arkansas	35	12
California	32	47
Colorado	34	32
Connecticut	36	6
Delaware	34	26
Florida	37	1
Georgia	33	42
Hawaii	34	27
Idaho	33	43
Illinois	34	34
Indiana	34	21
Iowa	35	8
Kansas	34	33
Kentucky	35	18
Louisiana	32	44
Maine	36	5
Maryland	34	28
Massachusetts	35	13
Michigan	34	35
Minnesota	34	36
Mississippi	32	45
Missouri	35	14
Montana	35	9
Nebraska	34	22
Nevada	34	29
New Hampshire	34	19
New Jersey	36	7
New Mexico	32	46
New York	35	17
North Carolina	34	30
North Dakota	34	31
Ohio	35	15
Oklahoma	34	23
Oregon	36	4
Pennsylvania	36	3
Rhode Island	35	10
South Carolina	34	40
South Dakota	34	39
Tennessee	35	16
Texas	32	48
Utah	27	50
Vermont	35	11
Virginia	34	37
Washington	34	24
West Virginia	37	2
Wisconsin	34	25
Wyoming	34	38
50 States	34	
DC	35	
United States	34	

Rank in order

By #

1. Florida
2. West Virginia
3. Pennsylvania
4. Oregon
5. Maine
6. Connecticut
7. New Jersey
8. Iowa
9. Montana
10. Rhode Island
11. Vermont
12. Arkansas
13. Massachusetts
14. Missouri
15. Ohio
16. Tennessee
17. New York
18. Kentucky
19. New Hampshire
20. Alabama
21. Indiana
22. Nebraska
23. Oklahoma
24. Washington
25. Wisconsin
26. Delaware
27. Hawaii
28. Maryland
29. Nevada
30. North Carolina
31. North Dakota
32. Colorado
33. Kansas
34. Illinois
35. Michigan
36. Minnesota
37. Virginia
38. Wyoming
39. South Dakota
40. South Carolina
41. Arizona
42. Georgia
43. Idaho
44. Louisiana
45. Mississippi
46. New Mexico
47. California
48. Texas
49. Alaska
50. Utah

A-9 African-American Population and Percent of State Population, 1992

State	African-American Population	% of total population %	Rank by %	Rank in order By %
Alabama	1,049,082	25.4	5	1. Mississippi
Alaska	23,154	3.9	30	2. Louisiana
Arizona	111,391	2.9	36	3. South Carolina
Arkansas	379,740	15.9	11	4. Georgia
California	2,176,452	7.0	25	5. Alabama
Colorado	136,425	3.9	31	6. Maryland
Connecticut	266,045	8.1	21	7. North Carolina
Delaware	118,644	17.2	9	8. Virginia
Florida	1,814,747	13.5	15	9. Delaware
Georgia	1,842,375	27.2	4	10. Tennessee
Hawaii	26,778	2.3	38	11. Arkansas
Idaho	3,439	0.3	49	12. Illinois
Illinois	1,718,873	14.8	12	13. New York
Indiana	444,374	7.9	22	14. Michigan
Iowa	50,334	1.8	40	15. Florida
Kansas	145,813	5.8	27	16. New Jersey
Kentucky	266,650	7.1	24	17. Texas
Louisiana	1,327,269	31.0	2	18. Ohio
Maine	4,958	0.4	47	19. Missouri
Maryland	1,243,311	25.3	6	20. Pennsylvania
Massachusetts	289,141	4.8	29	21. Connecticut
Michigan	1,322,468	14.0	14	22. Indiana
Minnesota	104,787	2.3	37	23. Oklahoma
Mississippi	933,993	35.7	1	24. Kentucky
Missouri	560,907	10.8	19	25. California
Montana	2,217	0.3	50	26. Nevada
Nebraska	58,445	3.7	32	27. Kansas
Nevada	86,910	6.5	26	28. Wisconsin
New Hampshire	5,847	0.5	45	29. Massachusetts
New Jersey	1,012,105	12.9	16	30. Alaska
New Mexico	29,260	1.8	39	31. Colorado
New York	2,604,916	14.4	13	32. Nebraska
North Carolina	1,503,277	22.0	7	33. Rhode Island
North Dakota	3,553	0.6	44	34. West Virginia
Ohio	1,194,482	10.8	18	35. Washington
Oklahoma	240,675	7.5	23	36. Arizona
Oregon	47,999	1.6	41	37. Minnesota
Pennsylvania	1,101,393	9.2	20	38. Hawaii
Rhode Island	36,336	3.6	33	39. New Mexico
South Carolina	1,075,144	29.8	3	40. Iowa
South Dakota	3,544	0.5	46	41. Oregon
Tennessee	804,300	16.0	10	42. Wyoming
Texas	2,056,912	11.6	17	43. Utah
Utah	11,726	0.6	43	44. North Dakota
Vermont	1,947	0.3	48	45. New Hampshire
Virginia	1,213,280	19.0	8	46. South Dakota
Washington	156,654	3.0	35	47. Maine
West Virginia	56,121	3.1	34	48. Vermont
Wisconsin	256,892	5.1	28	49. Idaho
Wyoming	3,373	0.7	42	50. Montana
50 States	29,928,458	11.7		
DC	377,852	64.6		
United States	30,306,310	11.9		

A-10 Hispanic Population and Percent of State Population, 1992

State	Hispanic Population	% of state population %	Rank by %	By %
Alabama	26,768	0.6	46	1. New Mexico
Alaska	19,711	3.4	21	2. California
Arizona	750,850	19.6	4	3. Texas
Arkansas	22,434	0.9	41	4. Arizona
California	8,352,665	27.0	2	5. Colorado
Colorado	456,709	13.2	5	6. New York
Connecticut	227,663	6.9	12	7. Florida
Delaware	17,628	2.6	26	8. Nevada
Florida	1,732,850	12.9	7	9. New Jersey
Georgia	123,904	1.8	32	10. Illinois
Hawaii	90,064	7.8	11	11. Hawaii
Idaho	59,187	5.6	14	12. Connecticut
Illinois	975,161	8.4	10	13. Wyoming
Indiana	106,396	1.9	31	14. Idaho
Iowa	37,489	1.3	36	15. Massachusetts
Kansas	100,601	4.0	20	16. Utah
Kentucky	23,175	0.6	48	17. Rhode Island
Louisiana	98,230	2.3	27	18. Washington
Maine	7,121	0.6	49	19. Oregon
Maryland	143,105	2.9	23	20. Kansas
Massachusetts	314,028	5.2	15	21. Alaska
Michigan	215,361	2.3	28	22. Oklahoma
Minnesota	62,316	1.4	34	23. Maryland
Mississippi	17,402	0.7	45	24. Virginia
Missouri	66,277	1.3	37	25. Nebraska
Montana	13,372	1.6	33	26. Delaware
Nebraska	42,346	2.6	25	27. Louisiana
Nevada	149,148	11.2	8	28. Michigan
New Hampshire	11,575	1.0	39	29. Pennsylvania
New Jersey	807,038	10.3	9	30. Wisconsin
New Mexico	614,346	38.8	1	31. Indiana
New York	2,361,878	13.0	6	32. Georgia
North Carolina	84,386	1.2	38	33. Montana
North Dakota	5,036	0.8	42	34. Minnesota
Ohio	149,286	1.4	35	35. Ohio
Oklahoma	93,941	2.9	22	36. Iowa
Oregon	126,788	4.3	19	37. Missouri
Pennsylvania	253,600	2.1	29	38. North Carolina
Rhode Island	51,110	5.1	17	39. New Hampshire
South Carolina	34,685	1.0	40	40. South Carolina
South Dakota	5,625	0.8	43	41. Arkansas
Tennessee	37,595	0.7	44	42. North Dakota
Texas	4,688,696	26.5	3	43. South Dakota
Utah	93,542	5.2	16	44. Tennessee
Vermont	3,668	0.6	47	45. Mississippi
Virginia	178,476	2.8	24	46. Alabama
Washington	241,933	4.7	18	47. Vermont
West Virginia	9,082	0.5	50	48. Kentucky
Wisconsin	101,649	2.0	30	49. Maine
Wyoming	27,019	5.8	13	50. West Virginia
50 States	24,232,915	9.5		
DC	34,899	6.0		
United States	24,267,814	9.5		

Rank in order

A-11 Population in Poverty, 1994

State	Total Population in Poverty (000)	% of population in poverty %	Rank by %
Alabama	704	16.4	10
Alaska	61	10.2	38
Arizona	673	15.9	11
Arkansas	369	15.3	13
California	5,658	17.9	7
Colorado	335	9.0	43
Connecticut	344	10.8	32
Delaware	57	8.3	47
Florida	2,128	14.9	14
Georgia	1,012	14.0	21
Hawaii	97	8.7	46
Idaho	137	12.0	26
Illinois	1,464	12.4	25
Indiana	816	13.7	23
Iowa	302	10.7	33
Kansas	375	14.9	15
Kentucky	710	18.5	6
Louisiana	1,117	25.7	1
Maine	113	9.4	40
Maryland	541	10.7	34
Massachusetts	585	9.7	39
Michigan	1,347	14.1	19
Minnesota	523	11.7	28
Mississippi	515	19.9	3
Missouri	797	15.6	12
Montana	97	11.5	30
Nebraska	146	8.8	45
Nevada	168	11.1	31
New Hampshire	87	7.7	49
New Jersey	730	9.2	42
New Mexico	356	21.1	2
New York	3,097	17.0	8
North Carolina	980	14.2	18
North Dakota	65	10.4	36
Ohio	1,571	14.1	20
Oklahoma	540	16.7	9
Oregon	373	11.8	27
Pennsylvania	1,496	12.5	24
Rhode Island	99	10.3	37
South Carolina	501	13.8	22
South Dakota	107	14.5	17
Tennessee	779	14.6	16
Texas	3,603	19.1	4
Utah	154	8.0	48
Vermont	45	7.6	50
Virginia	710	10.7	35
Washington	614	11.7	29
West Virginia	336	18.6	5
Wisconsin	453	9.0	44
Wyoming	45	9.3	41
50 States	37,932	13.1	
DC	129	21.2	
United States	38,059	14.5	

Rank in order

By %

1. Louisiana
2. New Mexico
3. Mississippi
4. Texas
5. West Virginia
6. Kentucky
7. California
8. New York
9. Oklahoma
10. Alabama
11. Arizona
12. Missouri
13. Arkansas
14. Florida
15. Kansas
16. Tennessee
17. South Dakota
18. North Carolina
19. Michigan
20. Ohio
21. Georgia
22. South Carolina
23. Indiana
24. Pennsylvania
25. Illinois
26. Idaho
27. Oregon
28. Minnesota
29. Washington
30. Montana
31. Nevada
32. Connecticut
33. Iowa
34. Maryland
35. Virginia
36. North Dakota
37. Rhode Island
38. Alaska
39. Massachusetts
40. Maine
41. Wyoming
42. New Jersey
43. Colorado
44. Wisconsin
45. Nebraska
46. Hawaii
47. Delaware
48. Utah
49. New Hampshire
50. Vermont

State	# of children 5-17 in poverty (000)	% in poverty %	Rank by %	Rank in order By %
Alabama	157	19.5	15	1. Louisiana
Alaska	15	11.7	43	2. New Mexico
Arizona	189	23.4	9	3. Mississippi
Arkansas	87	20.4	13	4. Texas
California	1,550	25.3	6	5. Kentucky
Colorado	69	9.9	46	6. California
Connecticut	100	18.6	20	7. Missouri
Delaware	10	9.8	48	8. New York
Florida	563	22.1	10	9. Arizona
Georgia	267	18.5	21	10. Florida
Hawaii	21	12.0	42	11. West Virginia
Idaho	39	15.5	28	12. Oklahoma
Illinois	405	18.0	24	13. Arkansas
Indiana	164	13.7	31	14. Tennessee
Iowa	74	13.5	34	15. Alabama
Kansas	97	19.5	16	16. Kansas
Kentucky	200	26.6	5	17. Ohio
Louisiana	337	36.8	1	18. Pennsylvania
Maine	20	9.6	49	19. South Carolina
Maryland	143	17.2	26	20. Connecticut
Massachusetts	121	12.2	39	21. Georgia
Michigan	326	17.9	25	22. North Carolina
Minnesota	115	13.7	32	23. South Dakota
Mississippi	138	28.2	3	24. Illinois
Missouri	204	23.6	7	25. Michigan
Montana	20	12.3	38	26. Maryland
Nebraska	43	12.5	37	27. Nevada
Nevada	45	16.2	27	28. Idaho
New Hampshire	23	12.2	40	29. New Jersey
New Jersey	211	14.6	29	30. Washington
New Mexico	111	29.2	2	31. Indiana
New York	769	23.5	8	32. Minnesota
North Carolina	206	18.4	22	33. Oregon
North Dakota	15	11.6	44	34. Iowa
Ohio	448	19.5	17	35. Rhode Island
Oklahoma	140	21.5	12	36. Virginia
Oregon	81	13.7	33	37. Nebraska
Pennsylvania	400	19.0	18	38. Montana
Rhode Island	24	13.3	35	39. Massachusetts
South Carolina	121	18.7	19	40. New Hampshire
South Dakota	32	18.2	23	41. Wisconsin
Tennessee	206	20.1	14	42. Hawaii
Texas	1,084	26.8	4	43. Alaska
Utah	46	9.9	47	44. North Dakota
Vermont	7	7.0	50	45. Wyoming
Virginia	157	12.6	36	46. Colorado
Washington	146	14.6	30	47. Utah
West Virginia	66	22.0	11	48. Delaware
Wisconsin	120	12.1	41	49. Maine
Wyoming	12	10.7	45	50. Vermont
50 States	9,944	17.3		
DC	29	30.0		
United States	9,974	20.1		

A-13 Female Population, 1994

State	Female population (000)	As % of population %	Rank by %	Rank in order By %
Alabama	2,195	52.0	2	1. Mississippi
Alaska	287	47.3	50	2. Alabama
Arizona	2,061	50.6	39	3. Pennsylvania
Arkansas	1,270	51.8	10	4. Rhode Island
California	15,710	50.0	46	5. New York
Colorado	1,844	50.4	40	6. Louisiana
Connecticut	1,688	51.5	16	7. Massachusetts
Delaware	363	51.4	23	8. West Virginia
Florida	7,195	51.6	15	9. Tennessee
Georgia	3,626	51.4	22	10. Arkansas
Hawaii	582	49.3	48	11. Ohio
Idaho	568	50.1	45	12. Missouri
Illinois	6,035	51.4	25	13. South Carolina
Indiana	2,959	51.4	20	14. New Jersey
Iowa	1,454	51.4	21	15. Florida
Kansas	1,298	50.8	33	16. Connecticut
Kentucky	1,972	51.5	17	17. Kentucky
Louisiana	2,239	51.9	6	18. North Carolina
Maine	636	51.3	26	19. Maryland
Maryland	2,575	51.4	19	20. Indiana
Massachusetts	3,134	51.9	7	21. Iowa
Michigan	4,879	51.4	24	22. Georgia
Minnesota	2,321	50.8	34	23. Delaware
Mississippi	1,390	52.1	1	24. Michigan
Missouri	2,729	51.7	12	25. Illinois
Montana	431	50.3	42	26. Maine
Nebraska	830	51.2	28	27. Oklahoma
Nevada	715	49.1	49	28. Nebraska
New Hampshire	579	50.9	31	29. Virginia
New Jersey	4,080	51.6	14	30. Wisconsin
New Mexico	839	50.7	36	31. New Hampshire
New York	9,435	51.9	5	32. Vermont
North Carolina	3,640	51.5	18	33. Kansas
North Dakota	320	50.2	44	34. Minnesota
Ohio	5,743	51.7	11	35. South Dakota
Oklahoma	1,669	51.2	27	36. New Mexico
Oregon	1,565	50.7	37	37. Oregon
Pennsylvania	6,265	52.0	3	38. Texas
Rhode Island	518	51.9	4	39. Arizona
South Carolina	1,894	51.7	13	40. Colorado
South Dakota	366	50.8	35	41. Washington
Tennessee	2,681	51.8	9	42. Montana
Texas	9,318	50.7	38	43. Utah
Utah	959	50.3	43	44. North Dakota
Vermont	295	50.9	32	45. Idaho
Virginia	3,344	51.0	29	46. California
Washington	2,691	50.4	41	47. Wyoming
West Virginia	945	51.9	8	48. Hawaii
Wisconsin	2,590	51.0	30	49. Nevada
Wyoming	237	49.7	47	50. Alaska
50 States	132,960	51.2		
DC	304	53.4		
United States	133,265	51.2		

State	Births Per 1,000 Population	Rank
Alabama	14.5	25
Alaska	18.2	3
Arizona	16.7	7
Arkansas	13.9	39
California	18.5	2
Colorado	14.8	19
Connecticut	14.0	35
Delaware	14.2	31
Florida	13.8	40
Georgia	15.6	13
Hawaii	17.0	5
Idaho	15.0	17
Illinois	16.2	8
Indiana	14.4	26
Iowa	13.1	45
Kansas	14.5	24
Kentucky	13.6	41
Louisiana	16.0	9
Maine	12.1	48
Maryland	15.4	14
Massachusetts	13.9	38
Michigan	14.6	23
Minnesota	14.0	37
Mississippi	15.7	12
Missouri	14.2	29
Montana	12.9	46
Nebraska	14.2	30
Nevada	15.8	10
New Hampshire	14.1	34
New Jersey	14.7	21
New Mexico	16.9	6
New York	15.7	11
North Carolina	14.3	27
North Dakota	14.1	32
Ohio	14.2	28
Oklahoma	14.7	20
Oregon	13.3	43
Pennsylvania	13.2	44
Rhode Island	14.0	36
South Carolina	15.3	15
South Dakota	15.3	16
Tennessee	14.1	33
Texas	17.3	4
Utah	19.4	1
Vermont	12.1	50
Virginia	14.7	22
Washington	14.8	18
West Virginia	12.1	49
Wisconsin	13.6	42
Wyoming	12.6	47
50 States	n/a	
DC	19.3	
United States	15.3	

Rank in order

By rate

1. Utah
2. California
3. Alaska
4. Texas
5. Hawaii
6. New Mexico
7. Arizona
8. Illinois
9. Louisiana
10. Nevada
11. New York
12. Mississippi
13. Georgia
14. Maryland
15. South Carolina
16. South Dakota
17. Idaho
18. Washington
19. Colorado
20. Oklahoma
21. New Jersey
22. Virginia
23. Michigan
24. Kansas
25. Alabama
26. Indiana
27. North Carolina
28. Ohio
29. Missouri
30. Nebraska
31. Delaware
32. North Dakota
33. Tennessee
34. New Hampshire
35. Connecticut
36. Rhode Island
37. Minnesota
38. Massachusetts
39. Arkansas
40. Florida
41. Kentucky
42. Wisconsin
43. Oregon
44. Pennsylvania
45. Iowa
46. Montana
47. Wyoming
48. Maine
49. West Virginia
50. Vermont

State	Deaths Per 1,000 Population	Rank		Rank in order By rate
Alabama	10.0	12		1. South Dakota
Alaska	3.3	50		2. West Virginia
Arizona	8.3	33		3. Arkansas
Arkansas	11.0	3		4. North Dakota
California	7.1	43		5. Pennsylvania
Colorado	6.6	47		6. Florida
Connecticut	8.9	28		7. Missouri
Delaware	9.9	13		8. Iowa
Florida	10.6	6		9. Oklahoma
Georgia	7.5	41		10. Mississippi
Hawaii	5.9	48		11. Rhode Island
Idaho	7.1	45		12. Alabama
Illinois	9.2	24		13. Delaware
Indiana	9.2	23		14. Maine
Iowa	10.3	8		15. Kentucky
Kansas	9.4	18		16. New York
Kentucky	9.7	15		17. Massachusetts
Louisiana	9.3	20		18. Kansas
Maine	9.7	14		19. Ohio
Maryland	8.2	35		20. Louisiana
Massachusetts	9.4	17		21. Nebraska
Michigan	8.8	30		22. New Jersey
Minnesota	8.1	38		23. Indiana
Mississippi	10.1	10		24. Illinois
Missouri	10.4	7		25. Tennessee
Montana	8.2	37		26. Oregon
Nebraska	9.2	21		27. North Carolina
Nevada	8.2	34		28. Connecticut
New Hampshire	7.9	39		29. Wisconsin
New Jersey	9.2	22		30. Michigan
New Mexico	6.7	46		31. Vermont
New York	9.5	16		32. Wyoming
North Carolina	8.9	27		33. Arizona
North Dakota	11.0	4		34. Nevada
Ohio	9.4	19		35. Maryland
Oklahoma	10.1	9		36. South Carolina
Oregon	9.1	26		37. Montana
Pennsylvania	10.6	5		38. Minnesota
Rhode Island	10.0	11		39. New Hampshire
South Carolina	8.2	36		40. Washington
South Dakota	15.3	1		41. Georgia
Tennessee	9.1	25		42. Virginia
Texas	7.1	44		43. California
Utah	5.8	49		44. Texas
Vermont	8.6	31		45. Idaho
Virginia	7.3	42		46. New Mexico
Washington	7.7	40		47. Colorado
West Virginia	12.1	2		48. Hawaii
Wisconsin	8.9	29		49. Utah
Wyoming	8.4	32		50. Alaska
50 States	n/a			
DC	10.5			
United States	8.8			

State	Persons per square mile	Rank
Alabama	83	25
Alaska	1	50
Arizona	36	37
Arkansas	47	35
California	202	12
Colorado	35	38
Connecticut	676	4
Delaware	361	7
Florida	258	10
Georgia	122	20
Hawaii	184	13
Idaho	14	43
Illinois	211	11
Indiana	160	16
Iowa	51	33
Kansas	31	40
Kentucky	96	23
Louisiana	99	22
Maine	40	36
Maryland	512	5
Massachusetts	771	3
Michigan	167	14
Minnesota	57	31
Mississippi	57	32
Missouri	77	27
Montana	6	48
Nebraska	21	42
Nevada	13	45
New Hampshire	127	18
New Jersey	1,065	1
New Mexico	14	44
New York	385	6
North Carolina	145	17
North Dakota	9	47
Ohio	271	8
Oklahoma	47	34
Oregon	32	39
Pennsylvania	269	9
Rhode Island	954	2
South Carolina	122	21
South Dakota	9	46
Tennessee	126	19
Texas	70	29
Utah	23	41
Vermont	63	30
Virginia	165	15
Washington	80	26
West Virginia	76	28
Wisconsin	94	24
Wyoming	5	49
50 States	73	
DC	9,283	
United States	74	

Rank in order

By density

1. New Jersey
2. Rhode Island
3. Massachusetts
4. Connecticut
5. Maryland
6. New York
7. Delaware
8. Ohio
9. Pennsylvania
10. Florida
11. Illinois
12. California
13. Hawaii
14. Michigan
15. Virginia
16. Indiana
17. North Carolina
18. New Hampshire
19. Tennessee
20. Georgia
21. South Carolina
22. Louisiana
23. Kentucky
24. Wisconsin
25. Alabama
26. Washington
27. Missouri
28. West Virginia
29. Texas
30. Vermont
31. Minnesota
32. Mississippi
33. Iowa
34. Oklahoma
35. Arkansas
36. Maine
37. Arizona
38. Colorado
39. Oregon
40. Kansas
41. Utah
42. Nebraska
43. Idaho
44. New Mexico
45. Nevada
46. South Dakota
47. North Dakota
48. Montana
49. Wyoming
50. Alaska

A-17 Illegal Immigrant Population, 1994

State	Illegal immigrant Population (000)	% of population %	Rank by #	By #
Alabama	6	0.1	43	1. California
Alaska	3	0.4	23	2. New York
Arizona	59	1.4	7	3. Florida
Arkansas	4	0.1	41	4. Texas
California	1,553	4.9	1	5. New Jersey
Colorado	26	0.7	18	6. Illinois
Connecticut	30	0.9	14	7. Arizona
Delaware	3	0.4	24	8. Nevada
Florida	314	2.3	3	9. Hawaii
Georgia	33	0.5	21	10. Massachusetts
Hawaii	15	1.2	9	11. New Mexico
Idaho	7	0.6	19	12. Rhode Island
Illinois	191	1.6	6	13. Maryland
Indiana	10	0.2	38	14. Connecticut
Iowa	5	0.2	36	15. Washington
Kansas	9	0.4	25	16. Oregon
Kentucky	4	0.1	46	17. Virginia
Louisiana	12	0.3	32	18. Colorado
Maine	3	0.2	34	19. Idaho
Maryland	46	0.9	13	20. Utah
Massachusetts	74	1.2	10	21. Georgia
Michigan	32	0.3	26	22. Oklahoma
Minnesota	13	0.3	31	23. Alaska
Mississippi	3	0.1	44	24. Delaware
Missouri	8	0.2	40	25. Kansas
Montana	1	0.1	49	26. Michigan
Nebraska	5	0.3	27	27. Nebraska
Nevada	18	1.2	8	28. New Hampshire
New Hampshire	4	0.3	28	29. North Carolina
New Jersey	133	1.7	5	30. Pennsylvania
New Mexico	20	1.2	11	31. Minnesota
New York	501	2.8	2	32. Louisiana
North Carolina	20	0.3	29	33. Wisconsin
North Dakota	1	0.1	48	34. Maine
Ohio	22	0.2	35	35. Ohio
Oklahoma	15	0.5	22	36. Iowa
Oregon	24	0.8	16	37. Vermont
Pennsylvania	33	0.3	30	38. Indiana
Rhode Island	12	1.2	12	39. South Carolina
South Carolina	6	0.2	39	40. Missouri
South Dakota	0	0.0	50	41. Arkansas
Tennessee	7	0.1	42	42. Tennessee
Texas	364	2.0	4	43. Alabama
Utah	11	0.6	20	44. Mississippi
Vermont	1	0.2	37	45. Wyoming
Virginia	50	0.8	17	46. Kentucky
Washington	46	0.9	15	47. West Virginia
West Virginia	2	0.1	47	48. North Dakota
Wisconsin	13	0.2	33	49. Montana
Wyoming	1	0.1	45	50. South Dakota
50 States	n/a	n/a		
DC	17	3.0		
United States	3,750	1.4		

Economies

State	Personal income $ (millions)	Rank
Alabama	75,621	25
Alaska	14,184	46
Arizona	78,050	23
Arkansas	41,248	33
California	702,568	1
Colorado	81,595	22
Connecticut	95,127	21
Delaware	16,256	44
Florida	302,093	4
Georgia	142,501	12
Hawaii	28,335	38
Idaho	20,855	43
Illinois	277,424	5
Indiana	116,547	16
Iowa	57,083	30
Kansas	53,028	31
Kentucky	67,936	26
Louisiana	76,009	24
Maine	24,162	41
Maryland	124,391	14
Massachusetts	154,705	10
Michigan	210,559	9
Minnesota	101,654	19
Mississippi	42,152	32
Missouri	108,519	17
Montana	15,258	45
Nebraska	33,795	35
Nevada	34,702	34
New Hampshire	26,920	40
New Jersey	219,268	8
New Mexico	28,152	39
New York	467,511	2
North Carolina	138,401	13
North Dakota	11,880	48
Ohio	231,843	7
Oklahoma	57,349	29
Oregon	63,167	28
Pennsylvania	267,501	6
Rhode Island	21,877	42
South Carolina	64,898	27
South Dakota	14,156	47
Tennessee	100,637	20
Texas	362,398	3
Utah	32,763	36
Vermont	11,663	49
Virginia	147,415	11
Washington	120,444	15
West Virginia	31,146	37
Wisconsin	106,142	18
Wyoming	9,699	50
50 States	5,631,587	
DC	17,421	
United States	5,649,010	

Rank in order

By $

1. California
2. New York
3. Texas
4. Florida
5. Illinois
6. Pennsylvania
7. Ohio
8. New Jersey
9. Michigan
10. Massachusetts
11. Virginia
12. Georgia
13. North Carolina
14. Maryland
15. Washington
16. Indiana
17. Missouri
18. Wisconsin
19. Minnesota
20. Tennessee
21. Connecticut
22. Colorado
23. Arizona
24. Louisiana
25. Alabama
26. Kentucky
27. South Carolina
28. Oregon
29. Oklahoma
30. Iowa
31. Kansas
32. Mississippi
33. Arkansas
34. Nevada
35. Nebraska
36. Utah
37. West Virginia
38. Hawaii
39. New Mexico
40. New Hampshire
41. Maine
42. Rhode Island
43. Idaho
44. Delaware
45. Montana
46. Alaska
47. South Dakota
48. North Dakota
49. Vermont
50. Wyoming

State	GSP 92 (millions of 1987 dollars)	Rank
Alabama	65,975	24
Alaska	22,969	40
Arizona	62,299	26
Arkansas	37,342	32
California	652,328	1
Colorado	69,016	23
Connecticut	82,460	21
Delaware	18,422	43
Florida	222,553	5
Georgia	128,612	12
Hawaii	27,185	38
Idaho	17,674	45
Illinois	246,809	4
Indiana	103,313	15
Iowa	50,456	30
Kansas	47,090	31
Kentucky	63,689	25
Louisiana	79,942	22
Maine	20,122	42
Maryland	95,376	16
Massachusetts	135,079	10
Michigan	171,653	9
Minnesota	92,925	18
Mississippi	37,221	33
Missouri	93,597	17
Montana	12,956	46
Nebraska	31,589	34
Nevada	31,378	35
New Hampshire	21,569	41
New Jersey	184,080	8
New Mexico	27,348	37
New York	413,136	2
North Carolina	130,482	11
North Dakota	11,089	49
Ohio	203,155	7
Oklahoma	50,694	29
Oregon	52,480	28
Pennsylvania	222,088	6
Rhode Island	17,760	44
South Carolina	58,943	27
South Dakota	12,673	47
Tennessee	91,299	20
Texas	349,988	3
Utah	29,968	36
Vermont	10,002	50
Virginia	125,145	13
Washington	105,827	14
West Virginia	26,849	39
Wisconsin	92,808	19
Wyoming	12,025	48
50 States	4,606,784	
DC	32,004	
United States	5,001,445	

Rank in order

By $

1. California
2. New York
3. Texas
4. Illinois
5. Florida
6. Pennsylvania
7. Ohio
8. New Jersey
9. Michigan
10. Massachusetts
11. North Carolina
12. Georgia
13. Virginia
14. Washington
15. Indiana
16. Maryland
17. Missouri
18. Minnesota
19. Wisconsin
20. Tennessee
21. Connecticut
22. Louisiana
23. Colorado
24. Alabama
25. Kentucky
26. Arizona
27. South Carolina
28. Oregon
29. Oklahoma
30. Iowa
31. Kansas
32. Arkansas
33. Mississippi
34. Nebraska
35. Nevada
36. Utah
37. New Mexico
38. Hawaii
39. West Virginia
40. Alaska
41. New Hampshire
42. Maine
43. Delaware
44. Rhode Island
45. Idaho
46. Montana
47. South Dakota
48. Wyoming
49. North Dakota
50. Vermont

State	Per capita personal income $	Rank
Alabama	17,925	40
Alaska	23,395	10
Arizona	19,153	37
Arkansas	16,817	49
California	22,353	14
Colorado	22,320	15
Connecticut	29,044	1
Delaware	23,015	11
Florida	21,651	20
Georgia	20,198	29
Hawaii	24,042	6
Idaho	18,406	39
Illinois	23,607	9
Indiana	20,262	28
Iowa	20,176	30
Kansas	20,762	24
Kentucky	17,753	42
Louisiana	17,615	44
Maine	19,482	35
Maryland	24,847	5
Massachusetts	25,609	4
Michigan	22,173	18
Minnesota	22,257	16
Mississippi	15,793	50
Missouri	20,562	25
Montana	17,824	41
Nebraska	20,824	23
Nevada	23,817	7
New Hampshire	23,680	8
New Jersey	27,742	2
New Mexico	17,025	48
New York	25,731	3
North Carolina	19,576	34
North Dakota	18,621	38
Ohio	20,883	22
Oklahoma	17,602	45
Oregon	20,468	26
Pennsylvania	22,195	17
Rhode Island	21,948	19
South Carolina	17,712	43
South Dakota	19,630	33
Tennessee	19,446	36
Texas	19,719	32
Utah	17,172	46
Vermont	20,101	31
Virginia	22,501	13
Washington	22,542	12
West Virginia	17,094	47
Wisconsin	20,887	21
Wyoming	20,378	27
50 States	20,887	
	30,555	
	21,699	

Rank in order

By $

1. Connecticut
2. New Jersey
3. New York
4. Massachusetts
5. Maryland
6. Hawaii
7. Nevada
8. New Hampshire
9. Illinois
10. Alaska
11. Delaware
12. Washington
13. Virginia
14. California
15. Colorado
16. Minnesota
17. Pennsylvania
18. Michigan
19. Rhode Island
20. Florida
21. Wisconsin
22. Ohio
23. Nebraska
24. Kansas
25. Missouri
26. Oregon
27. Wyoming
28. Indiana
29. Georgia
30. Iowa
31. Vermont
32. Texas
33. South Dakota
34. North Carolina
35. Maine
36. Tennessee
37. Arizona
38. North Dakota
39. Idaho
40. Alabama
41. Montana
42. Kentucky
43. South Carolina
44. Louisiana
45. Oklahoma
46. Utah
47. West Virginia
48. New Mexico
49. Arkansas
50. Mississippi

State	wages & salaries $ (millions)	as % of personal income %	Rank by %
Alabama	43,191	57.1	22
Alaska	9,186	64.8	1
Arizona	44,057	56.4	25
Arkansas	22,549	54.7	32
California	395,707	56.3	26
Colorado	49,004	60.1	9
Connecticut	53,872	56.6	24
Delaware	10,359	63.7	2
Florida	149,010	49.3	48
Georgia	87,323	61.3	5
Hawaii	16,793	59.3	12
Idaho	10,955	52.5	41
Illinois	164,156	59.2	13
Indiana	68,886	59.1	14
Iowa	30,149	52.8	39
Kansas	28,530	53.8	35
Kentucky	38,090	56.1	28
Louisiana	41,715	54.9	31
Maine	12,446	51.5	45
Maryland	64,934	52.2	43
Massachusetts	92,922	60.1	8
Michigan	125,016	59.4	11
Minnesota	62,737	61.7	4
Mississippi	22,761	54.0	34
Missouri	62,798	57.9	21
Montana	7,412	48.6	49
Nebraska	18,388	54.4	33
Nevada	20,867	60.1	7
New Hampshire	13,602	50.5	46
New Jersey	121,483	55.4	30
New Mexico	15,959	56.7	23
New York	271,025	58.0	20
North Carolina	83,910	60.6	6
North Dakota	6,195	52.1	44
Ohio	136,246	58.8	16
Oklahoma	30,111	52.5	42
Oregon	35,292	55.9	29
Pennsylvania	143,728	53.7	37
Rhode Island	11,571	52.9	38
South Carolina	38,228	58.9	15
South Dakota	6,641	46.9	50
Tennessee	60,152	59.8	10
Texas	211,210	58.3	18
Utah	20,501	62.6	3
Vermont	6,272	53.8	36
Virginia	86,061	58.4	17
Washington	67,687	56.2	27
West Virginia	15,638	50.2	47
Wisconsin	61,801	58.2	19
Wyoming	5,104	52.6	40
50 States	3,202,230	56.9	
DC	28,783	165.2	
United States	3,231,012	57.2	

Rank in order

By %

1. Alaska
2. Delaware
3. Utah
4. Minnesota
5. Georgia
6. North Carolina
7. Nevada
8. Massachusetts
9. Colorado
10. Tennessee
11. Michigan
12. Hawaii
13. Illinois
14. Indiana
15. South Carolina
16. Ohio
17. Virginia
18. Texas
19. Wisconsin
20. New York
21. Missouri
22. Alabama
23. New Mexico
24. Connecticut
25. Arizona
26. California
27. Washington
28. Kentucky
29. Oregon
30. New Jersey
31. Louisiana
32. Arkansas
33. Nebraska
34. Mississippi
35. Kansas
36. Vermont
37. Pennsylvania
38. Rhode Island
39. Iowa
40. Wyoming
41. Idaho
42. Oklahoma
43. Maryland
44. North Dakota
45. Maine
46. New Hampshire
47. West Virginia
48. Florida
49. Montana
50. South Dakota

State	Average annual pay $	Rank	By $
Alabama	23,616	30	1. Connecticut
Alaska	32,657	4	2. New Jersey
Arizona	24,276	27	3. New York
Arkansas	20,898	46	4. Alaska
California	29,878	6	5. Massachusetts
Colorado	26,164	15	6. California
Connecticut	33,811	1	7. Michigan
Delaware	27,950	10	8. Illinois
Florida	23,925	29	9. Maryland
Georgia	25,306	22	10. Delaware
Hawaii	26,746	12	11. Pennsylvania
Idaho	21,938	44	12. Hawaii
Illinois	29,105	8	13. Minnesota
Indiana	24,908	23	14. Washington
Iowa	22,187	42	15. Colorado
Kansas	22,900	35	16. Ohio
Kentucky	22,747	37	17. Virginia
Louisiana	23,176	32	18. Texas
Maine	22,389	39	19. Nevada
Maryland	28,421	9	20. New Hampshire
Massachusetts	31,024	5	21. Rhode Island
Michigan	29,541	7	22. Georgia
Minnesota	26,425	13	23. Indiana
Mississippi	20,382	47	24. Oregon
Missouri	24,625	25	25. Missouri
Montana	20,219	48	26. Wisconsin
Nebraska	21,500	45	27. Arizona
Nevada	25,700	19	28. Tennessee
New Hampshire	25,555	20	29. Florida
New Jersey	33,439	2	30. Alabama
New Mexico	22,351	40	31. North Carolina
New York	33,438	3	32. Louisiana
North Carolina	23,449	31	33. Vermont
North Dakota	19,893	49	34. West Virginia
Ohio	26,133	16	35. Kansas
Oklahoma	22,292	41	36. Utah
Oregon	24,780	24	37. Kentucky
Pennsylvania	26,950	11	38. South Carolina
Rhode Island	25,454	21	39. Maine
South Carolina	22,477	38	40. New Mexico
South Dakota	19,255	50	41. Oklahoma
Tennessee	24,106	28	42. Iowa
Texas	25,959	18	43. Wyoming
Utah	22,811	36	44. Idaho
Vermont	22,964	33	45. Nebraska
Virginia	26,031	17	46. Arkansas
Washington	26,362	14	47. Mississippi
West Virginia	22,959	34	48. Montana
Wisconsin	24,324	26	49. North Dakota
Wyoming	22,054	43	50. South Dakota
50 States	25,109		
DC	40,919		
United States	26,939		

State	Earnings October-94 $	Rank
Alabama	10.78	39
Alaska	11.95	26
Arizona	10.92	38
Arkansas	9.71	48
California	12.52	14
Colorado	12.43	17
Connecticut	13.56	6
Delaware	13.88	4
Florida	9.92	47
Georgia	10.41	41
Hawaii	12.12	24
Idaho	11.76	30
Illinois	12.36	20
Indiana	13.78	5
Iowa	12.37	19
Kansas	12.27	22
Kentucky	12.07	25
Louisiana	13.00	9
Maine	12.15	23
Maryland	13.07	8
Massachusetts	12.67	10
Michigan	16.20	1
Minnesota	12.53	13
Mississippi	9.39	49
Missouri	11.79	29
Montana	12.50	16
Nebraska	11.13	37
Nevada	11.87	27
New Hampshire	11.83	28
New Jersey	13.27	7
New Mexico	10.12	45
New York	12.29	21
North Carolina	10.24	44
North Dakota	10.32	43
Ohio	14.32	3
Oklahoma	11.39	33
Oregon	12.51	15
Pennsylvania	12.54	12
Rhode Island	10.55	40
South Carolina	10.08	46
South Dakota	9.28	50
Tennessee	10.40	42
Texas	11.18	36
Utah	11.38	34
Vermont	11.50	32
Virginia	11.31	35
Washington	14.37	2
West Virginia	12.63	11
Wisconsin	12.43	18
Wyoming	11.58	31
50 States	11.89	
DC	13.42	
United States	12.10	

Rank in order

By $

1. Michigan
2. Washington
3. Ohio
4. Delaware
5. Indiana
6. Connecticut
7. New Jersey
8. Maryland
9. Louisiana
10. Massachusetts
11. West Virginia
12. Pennsylvania
13. Minnesota
14. California
15. Oregon
16. Montana
17. Colorado
18. Wisconsin
19. Iowa
20. Illinois
21. New York
22. Kansas
23. Maine
24. Hawaii
25. Kentucky
26. Alaska
27. Nevada
28. New Hampshire
29. Missouri
30. Idaho
31. Wyoming
32. Vermont
33. Oklahoma
34. Utah
35. Virginia
36. Texas
37. Nebraska
38. Arizona
39. Alabama
40. Rhode Island
41. Georgia
42. Tennessee
43. North Dakota
44. North Carolina
45. New Mexico
46. South Carolina
47. Florida
48. Arkansas
49. Mississippi
50. South Dakota

State	Value Added $ (millions)	Rank	By $
Alabama	21,056	24	1. California
Alaska	1,291	47	2. New York
Arizona	11,551	33	3. Ohio
Arkansas	12,826	31	4. Texas
California	144,908	1	5. Illinois
Colorado	13,704	28	6. Pennsylvania
Connecticut	23,832	20	7. Michigan
Delaware	4,231	40	8. North Carolina
Florida	29,055	17	9. New Jersey
Georgia	36,576	11	10. Indiana
Hawaii	1,383	46	11. Georgia
Idaho	3,895	42	12. Wisconsin
Illinois	70,104	5	13. Massachusetts
Indiana	43,805	10	14. Virginia
Iowa	19,062	25	15. Tennessee
Kansas	14,573	27	16. Missouri
Kentucky	23,714	21	17. Florida
Louisiana	22,126	23	18. Minnesota
Maine	5,428	38	19. Washington
Maryland	15,242	26	20. Connecticut
Massachusetts	34,472	13	21. Kentucky
Michigan	63,351	7	22. South Carolina
Minnesota	25,042	18	23. Louisiana
Mississippi	12,880	30	24. Alabama
Missouri	31,803	16	25. Iowa
Montana	1.093	49	26. Maryland
Nebraska	7,537	34	27. Kansas
Nevada	1,463	45	28. Colorado
New Hampshire	5,647	37	29. Oregon
New Jersey	44,332	9	30. Mississippi
New Mexico	3,931	41	31. Arkansas
New York	81,625	2	32. Oklahoma
North Carolina	59,915	8	33. Arizona
North Dakota	1,152	48	34. Nebraska
Ohio	78,876	3	35. Utah
Oklahoma	11,959	32	36. West Virginia
Oregon	13,344	29	37. New Hampshire
Pennsylvania	64,942	6	38. Maine
Rhode Island	5,140	39	39. Rhode Island
South Carolina	22,491	22	40. Delaware
South Dakota	1,691	44	41. New Mexico
Tennessee	32,499	15	42. Idaho
Texas	77,570	4	43. Vermont
Utah	6,689	35	44. South Dakota
Vermont	3,163	43	45. Nevada
Virginia	33,245	14	46. Hawaii
Washington	24,852	19	47. Alaska
West Virginia	6,009	36	48. North Dakota
Wisconsin	36,328	12	49. Montana
Wyoming	925	50	50. Wyoming
50 States	1,312,328		
DC	1,505		
United States	1,313,829		

State	Cost of Living Index	Rank
Alabama	92	40
Alaska	114	3
Arizona	100	17
Arkansas	90	49
California	103	13
Colorado	98	19
Connecticut	113	6
Delaware	104	11
Florida	94	30
Georgia	91	46
Hawaii	130	1
Idaho	94	29
Illinois	100	18
Indiana	96	25
Iowa	93	34
Kansas	93	38
Kentucky	91	48
Louisiana	93	39
Maine	104	10
Maryland	98	20
Massachusetts	114	4
Michigan	94	31
Minnesota	94	32
Mississippi	89	50
Missouri	93	37
Montana	95	28
Nebraska	94	33
Nevada	100	15
New Hampshire	107	8
New Jersey	115	2
New Mexico	97	23
New York	114	5
North Carolina	92	43
North Dakota	93	36
Ohio	98	21
Oklahoma	92	41
Oregon	97	22
Pennsylvania	105	9
Rhode Island	112	7
South Carolina	91	45
South Dakota	92	44
Tennessee	93	35
Texas	92	42
Utah	100	16
Vermont	103	12
Virginia	96	24
Washington	101	14
West Virginia	91	47
Wisconsin	95	27
Wyoming	95	26
50 States	n/a	
DC	106	
United States	100	

Rank in order

By Index

1. Hawaii
2. New Jersey
3. Alaska
4. Massachusetts
5. New York
6. Connecticut
7. Rhode Island
8. New Hampshire
9. Pennsylvania
10. Maine
11. Delaware
12. Vermont
13. California
14. Washington
15. Nevada
16. Utah
17. Arizona
18. Illinois
19. Colorado
20. Maryland
21. Ohio
22. Oregon
23. New Mexico
24. Virginia
25. Indiana
26. Wyoming
27. Wisconsin
28. Montana
29. Idaho
30. Florida
31. Michigan
32. Minnesota
33. Nebraska
34. Iowa
35. Tennessee
36. North Dakota
37. Missouri
38. Kansas
39. Louisiana
40. Alabama
41. Oklahoma
42. Texas
43. North Carolina
44. South Dakota
45. South Carolina
46. Georgia
47. West Virginia
48. Kentucky
49. Arkansas
50. Mississippi

State	Average annual pay in manufacturing $	Rank
Alabama	26,577	44
Alaska	29,346	30
Arizona	34,372	13
Arkansas	23,191	48
California	37,107	7
Colorado	33,762	15
Connecticut	42,541	3
Delaware	44,279	1
Florida	30,095	27
Georgia	27,611	40
Hawaii	28,670	34
Idaho	30,361	25
Illinois	35,984	9
Indiana	33,937	14
Iowa	29,991	28
Kansas	30,100	26
Kentucky	29,114	32
Louisiana	32,716	19
Maine	28,425	35
Maryland	35,434	11
Massachusetts	38,674	5
Michigan	43,725	2
Minnesota	34,390	12
Mississippi	22,602	49
Missouri	31,577	20
Montana	25,651	46
Nebraska	26,862	42
Nevada	29,314	31
New Hampshire	33,491	16
New Jersey	40,667	4
New Mexico	27,257	41
New York	38,148	6
North Carolina	26,641	43
North Dakota	24,447	47
Ohio	36,448	8
Oklahoma	28,419	36
Oregon	31,544	21
Pennsylvania	33,371	17
Rhode Island	28,673	33
South Carolina	27,880	38
South Dakota	22,536	50
Tennessee	28,071	37
Texas	33,045	18
Utah	27,671	39
Vermont	30,747	24
Virginia	29,394	29
Washington	35,971	10
West Virginia	31,339	22
Wisconsin	31,325	23
Wyoming	26,157	45
50 States	31,393	
DC	47,389	
United States	33,526	

Rank in order

By $

1. Delaware
2. Michigan
3. Connecticut
4. New Jersey
5. Massachusetts
6. New York
7. California
8. Ohio
9. Illinois
10. Washington
11. Maryland
12. Minnesota
13. Arizona
14. Indiana
15. Colorado
16. New Hampshire
17. Pennsylvania
18. Texas
19. Louisiana
20. Missouri
21. Oregon
22. West Virginia
23. Wisconsin
24. Vermont
25. Idaho
26. Kansas
27. Florida
28. Iowa
29. Virginia
30. Alaska
31. Nevada
32. Kentucky
33. Rhode Island
34. Hawaii
35. Maine
36. Oklahoma
37. Tennessee
38. South Carolina
39. Utah
40. Georgia
41. New Mexico
42. Nebraska
43. North Carolina
44. Alabama
45. Wyoming
46. Montana
47. North Dakota
48. Arkansas
49. Mississippi
50. South Dakota

B-10 Average Annual Pay In Retailing, 1994

State	Average annual pay in retailing $	Rank	Rank in order By $
Alabama	12,969	33	1. New Jersey
Alaska	17,556	2	2. Alaska
Arizona	14,671	15	3. Connecticut
Arkansas	13,163	31	4. California
California	16,545	4	5. Nevada
Colorado	14,498	16	6. Hawaii
Connecticut	17,216	3	7. New York
Delaware	13,901	20	8. Maryland
Florida	14,694	14	9. Massachusetts
Georgia	13,861	22	10. Washington
Hawaii	16,429	6	11. Oregon
Idaho	12,928	35	12. New Hampshire
Illinois	14,726	13	13. Illinois
Indiana	12,532	38	14. Florida
Iowa	11,806	46	15. Arizona
Kansas	12,699	37	16. Colorado
Kentucky	12,350	41	17. Texas
Louisiana	12,530	39	18. Rhode Island
Maine	13,489	26	19. Virginia
Maryland	15,690	8	20. Delaware
Massachusetts	15,625	9	21. Tennessee
Michigan	13,648	24	22. Georgia
Minnesota	13,537	25	23. Pennsylvania
Mississippi	12,054	43	24. Michigan
Missouri	13,441	27	25. Minnesota
Montana	12,019	44	26. Maine
Nebraska	11,665	48	27. Missouri
Nevada	16,459	5	28. North Carolina
New Hampshire	14,747	12	29. Vermont
New Jersey	17,696	1	30. Ohio
New Mexico	12,980	32	31. Arkansas
New York	16,196	7	32. New Mexico
North Carolina	13,440	28	33. Alabama
North Dakota	11,219	50	34. Utah
Ohio	13,288	30	35. Idaho
Oklahoma	12,393	40	36. South Carolina
Oregon	14,793	11	37. Kansas
Pennsylvania	13,782	23	38. Indiana
Rhode Island	14,221	18	39. Louisiana
South Carolina	12,894	36	40. Oklahoma
South Dakota	11,286	49	41. Kentucky
Tennessee	13,887	21	42. Wisconsin
Texas	14,351	17	43. Mississippi
Utah	12,969	34	44. Montana
Vermont	13,440	29	45. West Virginia
Virginia	14,069	19	46. Iowa
Washington	15,170	10	47. Wyoming
West Virginia	11,886	45	48. Nebraska
Wisconsin	12,227	42	49. South Dakota
Wyoming	11,781	47	50. North Dakota
50 States	13,828		
DC	15,765		
United States	14,385		

B-11 Labor Force, 1995

State	Labor force (000)	labor force as % of pop %	Rank by %
Alabama	2,048	48.5	44
Alaska	300	49.5	39
Arizona	2,132	52.3	22
Arkansas	1,217	49.6	38
California	15,474	49.2	40
Colorado	2,071	56.6	1
Connecticut	1,732	52.9	18
Delaware	383	54.2	11
Florida	6,930	49.7	36
Georgia	3,655	51.8	27
Hawaii	587	49.8	35
Idaho	601	53.0	16
Illinois	6,076	51.7	28
Indiana	3,134	54.5	9
Iowa	1,531	54.1	12
Kansas	1,351	52.9	17
Kentucky	1,875	49.0	41
Louisiana	1,969	45.6	48
Maine	641	51.7	29
Maryland	2,733	54.6	7
Massachusetts	3,154	52.2	24
Michigan	4,715	49.6	37
Minnesota	2,575	56.4	3
Mississippi	1,254	47.0	47
Missouri	2,816	53.4	14
Montana	438	51.1	32
Nebraska	884	54.5	10
Nevada	821	56.3	4
New Hampshire	642	56.5	2
New Jersey	4,108	52.0	26
New Mexico	750	45.3	49
New York	8,602	47.3	46
North Carolina	3,648	51.6	30
North Dakota	328	51.4	31
Ohio	5,550	50.0	34
Oklahoma	1,563	48.0	45
Oregon	1,682	54.5	8
Pennsylvania	5,868	48.7	43
Rhode Island	487	48.9	42
South Carolina	1,848	50.4	33
South Dakota	379	52.6	20
Tennessee	2,695	52.1	25
Texas	9,607	52.3	23
Utah	998	52.3	21
Vermont	319	55.1	6
Virginia	3,526	53.8	13
Washington	2,814	52.7	19
West Virginia	793	43.5	50
Wisconsin	2,840	55.9	5
Wyoming	253	53.2	15
50 States	132,396	51.0	
DC	285	50.0	
United States	132,681	51.0	

Rank in order

By %

1. Colorado
2. New Hampshire
3. Minnesota
4. Nevada
5. Wisconsin
6. Vermont
7. Maryland
8. Oregon
9. Indiana
10. Nebraska
11. Delaware
12. Iowa
13. Virginia
14. Missouri
15. Wyoming
16. Idaho
17. Kansas
18. Connecticut
19. Washington
20. South Dakota
21. Utah
22. Arizona
23. Texas
24. Massachusetts
25. Tennessee
26. New Jersey
27. Georgia
28. Illinois
29. Maine
30. North Carolina
31. North Dakota
32. Montana
33. South Carolina
34. Ohio
35. Hawaii
36. Florida
37. Michigan
38. Arkansas
39. Alaska
40. California
41. Kentucky
42. Rhode Island
43. Pennsylvania
44. Alabama
45. Oklahoma
46. New York
47. Mississippi
48. Louisiana
49. New Mexico
50. West Virginia

CQ State Fact Finder

B-12 Unemployed And Unemployment Rate, 1995

State	unemployed (000)	unemployment rate %	Rank by %	By %
Alabama	129	6.3	7	1. West Virginia
Alaska	21	6.9	5	2. California
Arizona	113	5.3	17	3. Rhode Island
Arkansas	57	4.7	34	4. Louisiana
California	1,216	7.9	2	5. Alaska
Colorado	83	4.0	40	6. New Jersey
Connecticut	92	5.3	18	7. Alabama
Delaware	15	4.0	41	8. Maine
Florida	357	5.2	21	9. New York
Georgia	188	5.1	26	10. Washington
Hawaii	31	5.2	22	11. Texas
Idaho	32	5.3	19	12. New Mexico
Illinois	308	5.1	27	13. Nevada
Indiana	151	4.8	32	14. Massachusetts
Iowa	47	3.1	47	15. Mississippi
Kansas	64	4.7	35	16. Pennsylvania
Kentucky	96	5.1	28	17. Arizona
Louisiana	139	7.1	4	18. Connecticut
Maine	40	6.2	8	19. Idaho
Maryland	140	5.1	29	20. Montana
Massachusetts	180	5.7	14	21. Florida
Michigan	242	5.1	30	22. Hawaii
Minnesota	95	3.7	44	23. Missouri
Mississippi	72	5.7	15	24. South Carolina
Missouri	145	5.2	23	25. Tennessee
Montana	23	5.3	20	26. Georgia
Nebraska	22	2.5	50	27. Illinois
Nevada	48	5.8	13	28. Kentucky
New Hampshire	25	3.9	43	29. Maryland
New Jersey	280	6.8	6	30. Michigan
New Mexico	47	5.9	12	31. Ohio
New York	533	6.2	9	32. Indiana
North Carolina	147	4.0	42	33. Oklahoma
North Dakota	10	3.0	48	34. Arkansas
Ohio	270	4.9	31	35. Kansas
Oklahoma	75	4.8	33	36. Oregon
Oregon	78	4.6	36	37. Wyoming
Pennsylvania	316	5.4	16	38. Virginia
Rhode Island	35	7.2	3	39. Vermont
South Carolina	95	5.2	24	40. Colorado
South Dakota	10	2.7	49	41. Delaware
Tennessee	140	5.2	25	42. North Carolina
Texas	578	6.0	11	43. New Hampshire
Utah	33	3.3	45	44. Minnesota
Vermont	13	4.2	39	45. Utah
Virginia	157	4.5	38	46. Wisconsin
Washington	174	6.2	10	47. Iowa
West Virginia	66	8.3	1	48. North Dakota
Wisconsin	94	3.3	46	49. South Dakota
Wyoming	12	4.6	37	50. Nebraska
50 States	7,336	n/a		
DC	26	9.0		
United States	7,362	(unweighted) 5.7		

CQ State Fact Finder

B-13 Employment and Employment Rate, 1995

State	employed (000)	Employment Rate %	Rank by %	By %
Alabama	1,767	86.3	36	1. Nevada
Alaska	262	87.4	30	2. Delaware
Arizona	1,763	82.7	45	3. North Carolina
Arkansas	1,073	88.2	27	4. Massachusetts
California	12,270	79.3	48	5. Georgia
Colorado	1,800	86.9	33	6. Ohio
Connecticut	1,542	89.1	21	7. Tennessee
Delaware	363	94.8	2	8. Minnesota
Florida	5,998	86.5	34	9. North Dakota
Georgia	3,402	93.1	5	10. New Mexico
Hawaii	530	90.3	17	11. Nebraska
Idaho	474	78.9	50	12. Utah
Illinois	5,539	91.2	14	13. New York
Indiana	2,745	87.6	29	14. Illinois
Iowa	1,355	88.5	24	15. Louisiana
Kansas	1,200	88.8	23	16. South Dakota
Kentucky	1,633	87.1	32	17. Hawaii
Louisiana	1,790	90.9	15	18. Missouri
Maine	541	84.4	39	19. Michigan
Maryland	2,162	79.1	49	20. Wisconsin
Massachusetts	2,962	93.9	4	21. Connecticut
Michigan	4,252	90.2	19	22. Pennsylvania
Minnesota	2,371	92.1	8	23. Kansas
Mississippi	1,050	83.7	42	24. Iowa
Missouri	2,540	90.2	18	25. South Carolina
Montana	350	80.1	47	26. Rhode Island
Nebraska	810	91.7	11	27. Arkansas
Nevada	782	95.3	1	28. New Jersey
New Hampshire	530	82.6	46	29. Indiana
New Jersey	3,608	87.8	28	30. Alaska
New Mexico	688	91.7	10	31. Virginia
New York	7,870	91.5	13	32. Kentucky
North Carolina	3,452	94.6	3	33. Colorado
North Dakota	302	92.1	9	34. Florida
Ohio	5,160	93.0	6	35. West Virginia
Oklahoma	1,307	83.6	43	36. Alabama
Oregon	1,425	84.7	38	37. Wyoming
Pennsylvania	5,211	88.8	22	38. Oregon
Rhode Island	430	88.2	26	39. Maine
South Carolina	1,634	88.5	25	40. Washington
South Dakota	343	90.5	16	41. Texas
Tennessee	2,487	92.3	7	42. Mississippi
Texas	8,042	83.7	41	43. Oklahoma
Utah	914	91.6	12	44. Vermont
Vermont	266	83.2	44	45. Arizona
Virginia	3,080	87.3	31	46. New Hampshire
Washington	2,365	84.0	40	47. Montana
West Virginia	685	86.4	35	48. California
Wisconsin	2,543	89.5	20	49. Maryland
Wyoming	218	86.1	37	50. Idaho
50 States	5,631,587	n/a		
DC	639	224.1		
United States	5,632,226	(unweighted) 90.7		

State	government employment (000)	Rank		Rank in order By #
Alabama	341	22		1. California
Alaska	73	44		2. Texas
Arizona	301	25		3. New York
Arkansas	176	33		4. Florida
California	2,099	1		5. Illinois
Colorado	306	23		6. Ohio
Connecticut	216	32		7. Pennsylvania
Delaware	50	49		8. Michigan
Florida	914	4		9. Virginia
Georgia	573	11		10. North Carolina
Hawaii	110	38		11. Georgia
Idaho	94	40		12. New Jersey
Illinois	791	5		13. Washington
Indiana	374	17		14. Maryland
Iowa	225	30		15. Missouri
Kansas	239	28		16. Massachusetts
Kentucky	285	26		17. Indiana
Louisiana	350	21		18. Tennessee
Maine	91	41		19. Minnesota
Maryland	421	14		20. Wisconsin
Massachusetts	392	16		21. Louisiana
Michigan	642	8		22. Alabama
Minnesota	365	19		23. Colorado
Mississippi	225	31		24. South Carolina
Missouri	393	15		25. Arizona
Montana	75	43		26. Kentucky
Nebraska	147	36		27. Oklahoma
Nevada	98	39		28. Kansas
New Hampshire	80	42		29. Oregon
New Jersey	569	12		30. Iowa
New Mexico	165	34		31. Mississippi
New York	1,393	3		32. Connecticut
North Carolina	577	10		33. Arkansas
North Dakota	66	46		34. New Mexico
Ohio	743	6		35. Utah
Oklahoma	270	27		36. Nebraska
Oregon	238	29		37. West Virginia
Pennsylvania	707	7		38. Hawaii
Rhode Island	62	47		39. Nevada
South Carolina	304	24		40. Idaho
South Dakota	68	45		41. Maine
Tennessee	368	18		42. New Hampshire
Texas	1,457	2		43. Montana
Utah	163	35		44. Alaska
Vermont	44	50		45. South Dakota
Virginia	594	9		46. North Dakota
Washington	444	13		47. Rhode Island
West Virginia	134	37		48. Wyoming
Wisconsin	365	20		49. Delaware
Wyoming	58	48		50. Vermont
50 States	19,230			
DC	251			
United States	19,481			

State	Manufacturing employment July-95 (000)	Rank	Rank in order By #
Alabama	381	19	1. California
Alaska	17	48	2. Ohio
Arizona	201	28	3. Texas
Arkansas	259	24	4. Michigan
California	1,763	1	5. Illinois
Colorado	194	29	6. New York
Connecticut	279	23	7. Pennsylvania
Delaware	63	41	8. North Carolina
Florida	485	14	9. Indiana
Georgia	585	11	10. Wisconsin
Hawaii	17	49	11. Georgia
Idaho	72	40	12. Tennessee
Illinois	957	5	13. New Jersey
Indiana	677	9	14. Florida
Iowa	250	26	15. Massachusetts
Kansas	193	30	16. Minnesota
Kentucky	308	22	17. Missouri
Louisiana	192	31	18. Virginia
Maine	92	37	19. Alabama
Maryland	177	32	20. South Carolina
Massachusetts	452	15	21. Washington
Michigan	971	4	22. Kentucky
Minnesota	425	16	23. Connecticut
Mississippi	253	25	24. Arkansas
Missouri	423	17	25. Mississippi
Montana	24	46	26. Iowa
Nebraska	113	35	27. Oregon
Nevada	36	45	28. Arizona
New Hampshire	101	36	29. Colorado
New Jersey	498	13	30. Kansas
New Mexico	47	42	31. Louisiana
New York	948	6	32. Maryland
North Carolina	862	8	33. Oklahoma
North Dakota	22	47	34. Utah
Ohio	1,093	2	35. Nebraska
Oklahoma	173	33	36. New Hampshire
Oregon	227	27	37. Maine
Pennsylvania	941	7	38. West Virginia
Rhode Island	81	39	39. Rhode Island
South Carolina	371	20	40. Idaho
South Dakota	46	43	41. Delaware
Tennessee	531	12	42. New Mexico
Texas	1,028	3	43. South Dakota
Utah	124	34	44. Vermont
Vermont	45	44	45. Nevada
Virginia	402	18	46. Montana
Washington	335	21	47. North Dakota
West Virginia	83	38	48. Alaska
Wisconsin	595	10	49. Hawaii
Wyoming	10	50	50. Wyoming
50 States	18,419		
DC	13		
United States	18,432		

B-16 Fortune 500 Companies, 1995

State	# of Fortune 500 companies	Fortune 500 companies per million population	Rank by #
Alabama	1	0.2	37
Alaska	0	0.0	n/a
Arizona	3	0.7	27
Arkansas	5	2.0	22
California	51	1.6	2
Colorado	4	1.1	26
Connecticut	23	7.0	8
Delaware	3	4.2	28
Florida	12	0.9	14
Georgia	15	2.1	12
Hawaii	0	0.0	n/a
Idaho	3	2.6	29
Illinois	40	3.4	3
Indiana	6	1.0	18
Iowa	2	0.7	32
Kansas	2	0.8	33
Kentucky	3	0.8	30
Louisiana	1	0.2	38
Maine	2	1.6	34
Maryland	6	1.2	19
Massachusetts	17	2.8	9
Michigan	16	1.7	10
Minnesota	16	3.5	11
Mississippi	1	0.4	39
Missouri	12	2.3	15
Montana	0	0.0	n/a
Nebraska	5	3.1	23
Nevada	0	0.0	n/a
New Hampshire	1	0.9	40
New Jersey	24	3.0	7
New Mexico	0	0.0	n/a
New York	65	3.6	1
North Carolina	7	1.0	16
North Dakota	0	0.0	n/a
Ohio	30	2.7	6
Oklahoma	5	1.5	24
Oregon	6	1.9	20
Pennsylvania	33	2.7	5
Rhode Island	3	3.0	31
South Carolina	2	0.5	35
South Dakota	1	1.4	41
Tennessee	6	1.2	21
Texas	36	2.0	4
Utah	2	1.0	36
Vermont	0	0.0	n/a
Virginia	13	2.0	13
Washington	7	1.3	17
West Virginia	0	0.0	n/a
Wisconsin	5	1.0	25
Wyoming	0	0.0	n/a
50 States	**495**	**1.9**	
DC	5	8.8	
United States	**500**	**1.9**	

Rank in order

By #

1. New York
2. California
3. Illinois
4. Texas
5. Pennsylvania
6. Ohio
7. New Jersey
8. Connecticut
9. Massachusetts
10. Michigan
11. Minnesota
12. Georgia
13. Virginia
14. Florida
15. Missouri
16. North Carolina
17. Washington
18. Indiana
19. Maryland
20. Oregon
21. Tennessee
22. Arkansas
23. Nebraska
24. Oklahoma
25. Wisconsin
26. Colorado
27. Arizona
28. Delaware
29. Idaho
30. Kentucky
31. Rhode Island
32. Iowa
33. Kansas
34. Maine
35. South Carolina
36. Utah
37. Alabama
38. Louisiana
39. Mississippi
40. New Hampshire
41. South Dakota

B-17 Business Week 1000 Companies, 1995

State	Business Week 1,000 companies #	Business Week companies per million population	Rank by #
Alabama	16	3.8	18
Alaska	0	0.0	n/a
Arizona	8	2.0	26
Arkansas	8	3.3	26
California	117	3.7	1
Colorado	10	2.7	23
Connecticut	44	13.4	7
Delaware	8	11.3	26
Florida	24	1.7	13
Georgia	29	4.1	12
Hawaii	4	3.4	38
Idaho	5	4.4	34
Illinois	76	6.5	3
Indiana	14	2.4	21
Iowa	9	3.2	24
Kansas	5	2.0	34
Kentucky	7	1.8	30
Louisiana	9	2.1	24
Maine	2	1.6	42
Maryland	14	2.8	21
Massachusetts	36	6.0	9
Michigan	31	3.3	10
Minnesota	30	6.6	11
Mississippi	2	0.7	42
Missouri	22	4.2	15
Montana	1	1.2	44
Nebraska	5	3.1	34
Nevada	7	4.8	30
New Hampshire	4	3.5	38
New Jersey	37	4.7	8
New Mexico	3	1.8	41
New York	103	5.7	2
North Carolina	17	2.4	16
North Dakota	0	0.0	n/a
Ohio	59	5.3	5
Oklahoma	7	2.1	30
Oregon	8	2.6	26
Pennsylvania	58	4.8	6
Rhode Island	5	5.0	34
South Carolina	7	1.9	30
South Dakota	1	1.4	44
Tennessee	16	3.1	18
Texas	69	3.8	4
Utah	4	2.1	38
Vermont	0	0.0	n/a
Virginia	24	3.7	13
Washington	15	2.8	20
West Virginia	0	0.0	n/a
Wisconsin	17	3.3	16
Wyoming	0	0.0	n/a
50 States	997	3.8	
DC	7	12.3	
United States	1,000	3.8	

Rank in order

By #

1. California
2. New York
3. Illinois
4. Texas
5. Ohio
6. Pennsylvania
7. Connecticut
8. New Jersey
9. Massachusetts
10. Michigan
11. Minnesota
12. Georgia
13. Florida
14. Virginia
15. Missouri
16. North Carolina
17. Wisconsin
18. Alabama
19. Tennessee
20. Washington
21. Indiana
22. Maryland
23. Colorado
24. Iowa
25. Louisiana
26. Arizona
27. Arkansas
28. Delaware
29. Oregon
30. Kentucky
31. Nevada
32. Oklahoma
33. South Carolina
34. Idaho
35. Kansas
36. Nebraska
37. Rhode Island
38. Hawaii
39. New Hampshire
40. Utah
41. New Mexico
42. Maine
43. Mississippi
44. Montana
45. South Dakota

B-18 Tourism Spending, 1993

State	Tourism spending 1993 ($million)	Share of US total %	Rank by $
Alabama	3,682	1.1	28
Alaska	1,085	0.3	45
Arizona	5,525	1.7	19
Arkansas	2,745	0.8	32
California	42,480	13.1	1
Colorado	6,122	1.9	17
Connecticut	3,458	1.1	30
Delaware	836	0.3	47
Florida	28,629	8.9	2
Georgia	9,186	2.8	9
Hawaii	5,866	1.8	18
Idaho	1,462	0.5	40
Illinois	13,804	4.3	5
Indiana	4,220	1.3	26
Iowa	2,746	0.8	31
Kansas	2,457	0.8	36
Kentucky	3,567	1.1	29
Louisiana	4,848	1.5	22
Maine	1,483	0.5	39
Maryland	4,922	1.5	21
Massachusetts	7,452	2.3	14
Michigan	7,498	2.3	13
Minnesota	4,492	1.4	24
Mississippi	2,236	0.7	37
Missouri	6,215	1.9	16
Montana	1,434	0.4	41
Nebraska	1,751	0.5	38
Nevada	12,539	3.9	6
New Hampshire	1,408	0.4	42
New Jersey	11,134	3.4	7
New Mexico	2,695	0.8	35
New York	19,950	6.2	4
North Carolina	7,884	2.4	12
North Dakota	828	0.3	49
Ohio	8,546	2.6	11
Oklahoma	2,698	0.8	34
Oregon	3,795	1.2	27
Pennsylvania	10,060	3.2	8
Rhode Island	708	0.2	50
South Carolina	4,831	1.5	23
South Dakota	834	0.3	48
Tennessee	6,779	2.1	15
Texas	20,215	6.3	3
Utah	2,712	0.8	33
Vermont	1,030	0.3	46
Virginia	9,076	2.8	10
Washington	5,318	1.6	20
West Virginia	1,371	0.4	43
Wisconsin	4,453	1.4	25
Wyoming	1,142	0.4	44
50 States	320,203	98.9	
DC	3,169	1.0	
United States	323,272	100.0	

By $

1. California
2. Florida
3. Texas
4. New York
5. Illinois
6. Nevada
7. New Jersey
8. Pennsylvania
9. Georgia
10. Virginia
11. Ohio
12. North Carolina
13. Michigan
14. Massachusetts
15. Tennessee
16. Missouri
17. Colorado
18. Hawaii
19. Arizona
20. Washington
21. Maryland
22. Louisiana
23. South Carolina
24. Minnesota
25. Wisconsin
26. Indiana
27. Oregon
28. Alabama
29. Kentucky
30. Connecticut
31. Iowa
32. Arkansas
33. Utah
34. Oklahoma
35. New Mexico
36. Kansas
37. Mississippi
38. Nebraska
39. Maine
40. Idaho
41. Montana
42. New Hampshire
43. West Virginia
44. Wyoming
45. Alaska
46. Vermont
47. Delaware
48. South Dakota
49. North Dakota
50. Rhode Island

State	Export related jobs (000)	Rank
Alabama	57	22
Alaska	7	43
Arizona	36	25
Arkansas	32	27
California	402	1
Colorado	32	28
Connecticut	62	19
Delaware	12	41
Florida	85	14
Georgia	81	15
Hawaii	3	48
Idaho	13	40
Illinois	182	5
Indiana	106	11
Iowa	33	26
Kansas	29	32
Kentucky	45	23
Louisiana	30	31
Maine	18	36
Maryland	31	29
Massachusetts	111	9
Michigan	175	6
Minnesota	69	17
Mississippi	31	30
Missouri	62	20
Montana	3	47
Nebraska	14	39
Nevada	4	46
New Hampshire	18	34
New Jersey	102	12
New Mexico	6	44
New York	190	4
North Carolina	122	8
North Dakota	2	49
Ohio	210	3
Oklahoma	27	33
Oregon	44	24
Pennsylvania	170	7
Rhode Island	17	37
South Carolina	63	18
South Dakota	5	45
Tennessee	78	16
Texas	221	2
Utah	18	35
Vermont	8	42
Virginia	57	21
Washington	110	10
West Virginia	16	38
Wisconsin	92	13
Wyoming	1	50
50 States	3341	
DC	1	
United States	3363	

Rank in order

By #

1. California
2. Texas
3. Ohio
4. New York
5. Illinois
6. Michigan
7. Pennsylvania
8. North Carolina
9. Massachusetts
10. Washington
11. Indiana
12. New Jersey
13. Wisconsin
14. Florida
15. Georgia
16. Tennessee
17. Minnesota
18. South Carolina
19. Connecticut
20. Missouri
21. Virginia
22. Alabama
23. Kentucky
24. Oregon
25. Arizona
26. Iowa
27. Arkansas
28. Colorado
29. Maryland
30. Mississippi
31. Louisiana
32. Kansas
33. Oklahoma
34. New Hampshire
35. Utah
36. Maine
37. Rhode Island
38. West Virginia
39. Nebraska
40. Idaho
41. Delaware
42. Vermont
43. Alaska
44. New Mexico
45. South Dakota
46. Nevada
47. Montana
48. Hawaii
49. North Dakota
50. Wyoming

B-20 Housing Permits, 1994

State	housing permits (000)	permits per 10,000 pop	Rank by # of total permits	By total #
Alabama	19.1	45.4	25	1. Florida
Alaska	2.1	34.0	49	2. Texas
Arizona	51.8	127.2	6	3. California
Arkansas	12.4	50.4	33	4. Georgia
California	97.0	30.9	3	5. North Carolina
Colorado	37.2	101.8	13	6. Arizona
Connecticut	9.5	28.9	37	7. Illinois
Delaware	5.0	70.4	40	8. Ohio
Florida	128.6	92.2	1	9. Virginia
Georgia	64.9	91.9	4	10. Michigan
Hawaii	7.3	62.2	39	11. Washington
Idaho	12.6	111.6	31	12. Pennsylvania
Illinois	49.3	41.9	7	13. Colorado
Indiana	34.4	59.9	15	14. Wisconsin
Iowa	12.5	44.1	32	15. Indiana
Kansas	13.0	50.8	30	16. Tennessee
Kentucky	18.6	48.5	27	17. New York
Louisiana	14.8	34.3	29	18. Nevada
Maine	4.6	36.9	42	19. Maryland
Maryland	29.0	57.9	19	20. Missouri
Massachusetts	18.1	30.0	28	21. Minnesota
Michigan	46.5	48.9	10	22. New Jersey
Minnesota	25.6	56.1	21	23. South Carolina
Mississippi	10.9	41.0	35	24. Oregon
Missouri	26.4	50.0	20	25. Alabama
Montana	3.0	35.4	46	26. Utah
Nebraska	7.9	48.6	38	27. Kentucky
Nevada	31.1	213.2	18	28. Massachusetts
New Hampshire	4.7	41.1	41	29. Louisiana
New Jersey	25.4	32.1	22	30. Kansas
New Mexico	11.6	69.8	34	31. Idaho
New York	31.1	17.1	17	32. Iowa
North Carolina	62.9	88.9	5	33. Arkansas
North Dakota	3.4	53.0	45	34. New Mexico
Ohio	47.2	42.5	8	35. Mississippi
Oklahoma	9.5	29.2	36	36. Oklahoma
Oregon	24.1	78.0	24	37. Connecticut
Pennsylvania	40.2	33.4	12	38. Nebraska
Rhode Island	2.5	25.5	47	39. Hawaii
South Carolina	24.6	67.1	23	40. Delaware
South Dakota	4.6	63.2	43	41. New Hampshire
Tennessee	31.9	61.6	16	42. Maine
Texas	102.6	55.8	2	43. South Dakota
Utah	18.6	97.4	26	44. West Virginia
Vermont	2.4	41.0	48	45. North Dakota
Virginia	46.8	71.5	9	46. Montana
Washington	44.0	82.4	11	47. Rhode Island
West Virginia	3.9	21.2	44	48. Vermont
Wisconsin	34.6	68.1	14	49. Alaska
Wyoming	2.0	42.4	50	50. Wyoming
50 States	1,371.5	52.8		
DC	0.2	3.7		
United States	1,371.6	52.7		

State	Change in Price %	Rank by %
Alabama	12	20
Alaska	n/a	n/a
Arizona	16	9
Arkansas	n/a	n/a
California	-11	35
Colorado	30	2
Connecticut	-6	33
Delaware	n/a	n/a
Florida	10	23
Georgia	8	26
Hawaii	n/a	n/a
Idaho	n/a	n/a
Illinois	14	14
Indiana	15	10
Iowa	18	6
Kansas	15	10
Kentucky	15	10
Louisiana	18	6
Maine	n/a	n/a
Maryland	0	32
Massachusetts	1	30
Michigan	13	17
Minnesota	14	14
Mississippi	n/a	n/a
Missouri	12	20
Montana	n/a	n/a
Nebraska	18	6
Nevada	9	24
New Hampshire	-7	34
New Jersey	2	29
New Mexico	28	3
New York	1	30
North Carolina	13	17
North Dakota	n/a	n/a
Ohio	15	10
Oklahoma	n/a	n/a
Oregon	28	3
Pennsylvania	6	27
Rhode Island	n/a	n/a
South Carolina	12	20
South Dakota	n/a	n/a
Tennessee	14	14
Texas	9	24
Utah	40	1
Vermont	n/a	n/a
Virginia	5	28
Washington	13	17
West Virginia	n/a	n/a
Wisconsin	22	5
Wyoming	n/a	n/a
50 States	n/a	
DC	8	
United States	n/a	

B-21 Change In Price of Existing Homes, 1991-1994

Rank in order

By %

1. Utah
2. Colorado
3. Oregon
4. New Mexico
5. Wisconsin
6. Nebraska
7. Louisiana
8. Iowa
9. Arizona
10. Ohio
11. Kentucky
12. Kansas
13. Indiana
14. Tennessee
15. Minnesota
16. Illinois
17. Washington
18. North Carolina
19. Michigan
20. South Carolina
21. Missouri
22. Alabama
23. Florida
24. Texas
25. Nevada
26. Georgia
27. Pennsylvania
28. Virginia
29. New Jersey
30. New York
31. Massachusetts
32. Maryland
33. Connecticut
34. New Hampshire
35. California

State	Net farm income (000)	Net farm income per capita $	rank by total amount
Alabama	1,122,756	266	16
Alaska	9,042	15	50
Arizona	481,649	118	30
Arkansas	1,418,880	578	10
California	5,077,147	162	1
Colorado	607,691	166	27
Connecticut	166,546	51	39
Delaware	126,788	180	41
Florida	2,250,864	161	6
Georgia	2,054,525	291	7
Hawaii	26,555	23	49
Idaho	665,135	587	23
Illinois	1,919,400	163	8
Indiana	857,124	149	20
Iowa	2,793,286	987	4
Kansas	1,678,097	657	9
Kentucky	1,209,151	316	13
Louisiana	520,189	121	29
Maine	97,749	79	44
Maryland	276,341	55	35
Massachusetts	139,938	23	40
Michigan	192,531	20	38
Minnesota	1,407,142	308	11
Mississippi	669,631	251	22
Missouri	964,479	183	17
Montana	453,882	530	32
Nebraska	2,264,221	1,395	5
Nevada	67,076	46	46
New Hampshire	45,769	40	47
New Jersey	248,933	31	36
New Mexico	377,503	228	33
New York	336,603	19	34
North Carolina	2,873,411	406	3
North Dakota	858,772	1,346	19
Ohio	1,169,684	105	14
Oklahoma	1,132,880	348	15
Oregon	523,483	170	28
Pennsylvania	673,328	56	21
Rhode Island	41,718	42	48
South Carolina	461,403	126	31
South Dakota	1,353,708	1,878	12
Tennessee	647,236	125	24
Texas	3,743,668	204	2
Utah	240,994	126	37
Vermont	114,300	197	43
Virginia	608,375	93	26
Washington	922,434	173	18
West Virginia	90,082	49	45
Wisconsin	626,223	123	25
Wyoming	121,731	256	42
50 States	46,730,053	180	
DC	n/a	n/a	
United States	46,730,053	179	

B-22 Net Farm income, 1994

Rank in order

By total #

1. California
2. Texas
3. North Carolina
4. Iowa
5. Nebraska
6. Florida
7. Georgia
8. Illinois
9. Kansas
10. Arkansas
11. Minnesota
12. South Dakota
13. Kentucky
14. Ohio
15. Oklahoma
16. Alabama
17. Missouri
18. Washington
19. North Dakota
20. Indiana
21. Pennsylvania
22. Mississippi
23. Idaho
24. Tennessee
25. Wisconsin
26. Virginia
27. Colorado
28. Oregon
29. Louisiana
30. Arizona
31. South Carolina
32. Montana
33. New Mexico
34. New York
35. Maryland
36. New Jersey
37. Utah
38. Michigan
39. Connecticut
40. Massachusetts
41. Delaware
42. Wyoming
43. Vermont
44. Maine
45. West Virginia
46. Nevada
47. New Hampshire
48. Rhode Island
49. Hawaii
50. Alaska

State	total assets (millions)	per capita assets $	Rank by total assets	By total assets
Alabama	53,683	12,724	24	1. New York
Alaska	5,539	9,140	50	2. California
Arizona	43,240	10,611	27	3. Illinois
Arkansas	30,377	12,384	34	4. Texas
California	604,687	19,239	2	5. Pennsylvania
Colorado	37,669	10,303	31	6. Florida
Connecticut	74,655	22,795	20	7. Ohio
Delaware	92,942	131,646	14	8. Massachusetts
Florida	195,259	13,994	6	9. Michigan
Georgia	106,178	15,050	12	10. New Jersey
Hawaii	28,243	23,955	35	11. North Carolina
Idaho	12,742	11,246	46	12. Georgia
Illinois	269,677	22,947	3	13. Maryland
Indiana	79,133	13,757	19	14. Delaware
Iowa	45,101	15,942	26	15. Virginia
Kansas	38,295	14,994	30	16. Missouri
Kentucky	55,024	14,378	23	17. Wisconsin
Louisiana	46,692	10,821	25	18. Washington
Maine	16,126	13,005	44	19. Indiana
Maryland	103,799	20,735	13	20. Connecticut
Massachusetts	159,717	26,439	8	21. Minnesota
Michigan	146,999	15,480	9	22. Tennessee
Minnesota	68,368	14,970	21	23. Kentucky
Mississippi	27,899	10,453	36	24. Alabama
Missouri	89,295	16,918	16	25. Louisiana
Montana	9,496	11,093	47	26. Iowa
Nebraska	32,360	19,938	33	27. Arizona
Nevada	26,732	18,347	37	28. South Carolina
New Hampshire	18,612	16,369	41	29. Oklahoma
New Jersey	128,431	16,249	10	30. Kansas
New Mexico	15,435	9,332	45	31. Colorado
New York	992,269	54,613	1	32. Oregon
North Carolina	127,268	18,001	11	33. Nebraska
North Dakota	16,859	26,425	43	34. Arkansas
Ohio	184,627	16,630	7	35. Hawaii
Oklahoma	38,461	11,805	29	36. Mississippi
Oregon	35,561	11,523	32	37. Nevada
Pennsylvania	223,214	18,521	5	38. South Dakota
Rhode Island	21,890	21,956	39	39. Rhode Island
South Carolina	39,207	10,701	28	40. West Virginia
South Dakota	25,108	34,824	38	41. New Hampshire
Tennessee	67,883	13,117	22	42. Utah
Texas	244,485	13,303	4	43. North Dakota
Utah	18,070	9,471	42	44. Maine
Vermont	8,219	14,171	48	45. New Mexico
Virginia	89,297	13,629	15	46. Idaho
Washington	79,225	14,828	18	47. Montana
West Virginia	21,637	11,875	40	48. Vermont
Wisconsin	79,554	15,654	17	49. Wyoming
Wyoming	6,966	14,634	49	50. Alaska
50 States	4,982,205	19,179		
DC	9,173	16,093		
United States	5,019,308	19,280		

State	Bankruptcy Petitions	Petitions per 1000 residents	Rank by per 1000 residents	Rank in order By per 1000
Alabama	23,684	5.61	3	1. Tennessee
Alaska	869	1.43	48	2. Georgia
Arizona	18,149	4.45	6	3. Alabama
Arkansas	6,652	2.71	28	4. Nevada
California	146,421	4.66	5	5. California
Colorado	12,993	3.55	12	6. Arizona
Connecticut	8,681	2.65	29	7. Oregon
Delaware	1,220	1.73	46	8. Oklahoma
Florida	42,347	3.03	21	9. Indiana
Georgia	40,836	5.79	2	10. Mississippi
Hawaii	1,566	1.33	50	11. Virginia
Idaho	3,317	2.93	24	12. Colorado
Illinois	36,408	3.10	15	13. Utah
Indiana	21,878	3.80	9	14. Washington
Iowa	5,380	1.90	41	15. Illinois
Kansas	7,845	3.07	18	16. Maryland
Kentucky	11,756	3.07	17	17. Kentucky
Louisiana	12,358	2.86	25	18. Kansas
Maine	1,783	1.44	47	19. Ohio
Maryland	15,405	3.08	16	20. Rhode Island
Massachusetts	14,581	2.41	32	21. Florida
Michigan	22,465	2.37	33	22. Minnesota
Minnesota	13,827	3.03	22	23. New Jersey
Mississippi	9,863	3.70	10	24. Idaho
Missouri	14,576	2.76	27	25. Louisiana
Montana	1,891	2.21	36	26. New Hampshire
Nebraska	3,527	2.17	37	27. Missouri
Nevada	7,448	5.11	4	28. Arkansas
New Hampshire	3,177	2.79	26	29. Connecticut
New Jersey	23,597	2.99	23	30. New York
New Mexico	3,500	2.12	39	31. Wyoming
New York	47,573	2.62	30	32. Massachusetts
North Carolina	13,266	1.88	42	33. Michigan
North Dakota	1,145	1.79	43	34. West Virginia
Ohio	34,075	3.07	19	35. Texas
Oklahoma	12,897	3.96	8	36. Montana
Oregon	12,708	4.12	7	37. Nebraska
Pennsylvania	26,130	2.17	38	38. Pennsylvania
Rhode Island	3,047	3.06	20	39. New Mexico
South Carolina	6,400	1.75	44	40. Wisconsin
South Dakota	1,246	1.73	45	41. Iowa
Tennessee	35,394	6.84	1	42. North Carolina
Texas	41,372	2.25	35	43. North Dakota
Utah	6,595	3.46	13	44. South Carolina
Vermont	796	1.37	49	45. South Dakota
Virginia	23,858	3.64	11	46. Delaware
Washington	17,422	3.26	14	47. Maine
West Virginia	4,236	2.32	34	48. Alaska
Wisconsin	10,438	2.05	40	49. Vermont
Wyoming	1,170	2.46	31	50. Hawaii
50 States	845,775	3.23		
DC	1,365	2.39		
United States	837,797	3.22		

State	patents issued	patents per 100,000 population	Rank by per 100,000
Alabama	339	8.0	47
Alaska	61	10.1	43
Arizona	1,027	25.2	18
Arkansas	155	6.3	49
California	10,472	33.3	8
Colorado	1,140	31.2	9
Connecticut	1,842	56.2	2
Delaware	513	72.7	1
Florida	2,241	16.1	29
Georgia	925	13.1	35
Hawaii	116	9.8	44
Idaho	350	30.9	10
Illinois	3,266	27.8	13
Indiana	1,137	19.8	24
Iowa	463	16.4	27
Kansas	319	12.5	36
Kentucky	343	9.0	45
Louisiana	475	11.0	38
Maine	149	12.0	37
Maryland	1,137	22.7	21
Massachusetts	2,669	44.2	3
Michigan	3,295	34.7	7
Minnesota	1,914	41.9	5
Mississippi	166	6.2	50
Missouri	730	13.8	33
Montana	94	11.0	39
Nebraska	173	10.7	42
Nevada	221	15.2	30
New Hampshire	452	39.8	6
New Jersey	3,328	42.1	4
New Mexico	270	16.3	28
New York	5,522	30.4	11
North Carolina	1,181	16.7	26
North Dakota	69	10.8	40
Ohio	3,078	27.7	14
Oklahoma	624	19.2	25
Oregon	772	25.0	19
Pennsylvania	3,085	25.6	17
Rhode Island	275	27.6	15
South Carolina	529	14.4	32
South Dakota	47	6.5	48
Tennessee	684	13.2	34
Texas	4,089	22.2	22
Utah	473	24.8	20
Vermont	173	29.8	12
Virginia	959	14.6	31
Washington	1,117	20.9	23
West Virginia	147	8.1	46
Wisconsin	1,381	27.2	16
Wyoming	51	10.7	41
50 States	64,038	24.7	
DC	44	7.7	
United States	64,119	24.6	

Rank in order

By per 100,000

1. Delaware
2. Connecticut
3. Massachusetts
4. New Jersey
5. Minnesota
6. New Hampshire
7. Michigan
8. California
9. Colorado
10. Idaho
11. New York
12. Vermont
13. Illinois
14. Ohio
15. Rhode Island
16. Wisconsin
17. Pennsylvania
18. Arizona
19. Oregon
20. Utah
21. Maryland
22. Texas
23. Washington
24. Indiana
25. Oklahoma
26. North Carolina
27. Iowa
28. New Mexico
29. Florida
30. Nevada
31. Virginia
32. South Carolina
33. Missouri
34. Tennessee
35. Georgia
36. Kansas
37. Maine
38. Louisiana
39. Montana
40. North Dakota
41. Wyoming
42. Nebraska
43. Alaska
44. Hawaii
45. Kentucky
46. West Virginia
47. Alabama
48. South Dakota
49. Arkansas
50. Mississippi

B-25 Patents Issued, 1994

State	WC Maximum Weekly Benefit $	Rank	Rank in order By $
Alabama	427	28	1. Iowa
Alaska	700	4	2. Illinois
Arizona	323	44	3. New Hampshire
Arkansas	270	49	4. Alaska
California	406	34	5. Connecticut
Colorado	443	24	6. Vermont
Connecticut	660	5	7. Massachusetts
Delaware	346	42	8. Washington
Florida	453	23	9. Maryland
Georgia	275	48	10. Minnesota
Hawaii	491	14	11. Pennsylvania
Idaho	361	39	12. Michigan
Illinois	735	2	13. Ohio
Indiana	428	27	14. Hawaii
Iowa	817	1	15. Oregon
Kansas	319	46	16. Wisconsin
Kentucky	416	33	17. North Carolina
Louisiana	323	45	18. Missouri
Maine	441	25	19. Rhode Island
Maryland	525	9	20. Texas
Massachusetts	586	7	21. New Jersey
Michigan	499	12	22. Virginia
Minnesota	517	10	23. Florida
Mississippi	253	50	24. Colorado
Missouri	476	18	25. Maine
Montana	373	37	26. Nevada
Nebraska	350	40	27. Indiana
Nevada	432	26	28. Alabama
New Hampshire	714	3	29. West Virginia
New Jersey	469	21	30. South Carolina
New Mexico	343	43	31. Wyoming
New York	400	35	32. Utah
North Carolina	478	17	33. Kentucky
North Dakota	366	38	34. California
Ohio	493	13	35. New York
Oklahoma	307	47	36. Tennessee
Oregon	489	15	37. Montana
Pennsylvania	509	11	38. North Dakota
Rhode Island	474	19	39. Idaho
South Carolina	422	30	40. Nebraska
South Dakota	349	41	41. South Dakota
Tennessee	383	36	42. Delaware
Texas	472	20	43. New Mexico
Utah	417	32	44. Arizona
Vermont	648	6	45. Louisiana
Virginia	466	22	46. Kansas
Washington	546	8	47. Oklahoma
West Virginia	423	29	48. Georgia
Wisconsin	479	16	49. Arkansas
Wyoming	421	31	50. Mississippi
50 States	454		
DC	702		
United States	459		

B-27 Average Weekly Unemployment Compensation Benefit, 1994

State	Average Weekly UC Benefit $	Rank	By $
Alabama	131	48	1. Hawaii
Alaska	170	25	2. New Jersey
Arizona	148	42	3. Massachusetts
Arkansas	161	32	4. Connecticut
California	154	38	5. Rhode Island
Colorado	195	12	6. Minnesota
Connecticut	222	4	7. Michigan
Delaware	183	20	8. Pennsylvania
Florida	169	27	9. Washington
Georgia	153	40	10. New York
Hawaii	266	1	11. Illinois
Idaho	167	29	12. Colorado
Illinois	199	11	13. Kansas
Indiana	158	36	14. Ohio
Iowa	183	19	15. Wisconsin
Kansas	192	13	16. Utah
Kentucky	159	35	17. Texas
Louisiana	118	50	18. Nevada
Maine	161	33	19. Iowa
Maryland	180	21	20. Delaware
Massachusetts	237	3	21. Maryland
Michigan	213	7	22. Oregon
Minnesota	217	6	23. North Carolina
Mississippi	129	49	24. Wyoming
Missouri	150	41	25. Alaska
Montana	156	37	26. Virginia
Nebraska	140	46	27. Florida
Nevada	185	18	28. Oklahoma
New Hampshire	146	43	29. Idaho
New Jersey	246	2	30. West Virginia
New Mexico	140	45	31. Vermont
New York	203	10	32. Arkansas
North Carolina	175	23	33. Maine
North Dakota	160	34	34. North Dakota
Ohio	191	14	35. Kentucky
Oklahoma	168	28	36. Indiana
Oregon	179	22	37. Montana
Pennsylvania	212	8	38. California
Rhode Island	220	5	39. South Carolina
South Carolina	154	39	40. Georgia
South Dakota	138	47	41. Missouri
Tennessee	142	44	42. Arizona
Texas	185	17	43. New Hampshire
Utah	187	16	44. Tennessee
Vermont	164	31	45. New Mexico
Virginia	169	26	46. Nebraska
Washington	206	9	47. South Dakota
West Virginia	167	30	48. Alabama
Wisconsin	188	15	49. Mississippi
Wyoming	173	24	50. Louisiana
50 States	n/a		
DC	220		
United States	182		

B-28 Index of State Economic Momentum, 1995

State	Index of State Economic Momentum, 1995	Rank
Alabama	-0.30	30
Alaska	-0.94	41
Arizona	2.47	2
Arkansas	0.61	12
California	-0.12	26
Colorado	1.03	8
Connecticut	-1.96	50
Delaware	-0.56	34
Florida	1.37	7
Georgia	1.64	4
Hawaii	-1.68	49
Idaho	1.00	10
Illinois	-0.80	40
Indiana	-0.57	35
Iowa	-0.26	27
Kansas	-0.09	23
Kentucky	-0.11	25
Louisiana	0.25	17
Maine	-0.59	37
Maryland	-1.00	43
Massachusetts	-0.47	32
Michigan	0.12	20
Minnesota	0.22	18
Mississippi	-1.12	44
Missouri	0.26	16
Montana	-0.28	29
Nebraska	0.44	15
Nevada	4.03	1
New Hampshire	-0.04	22
New Jersey	-0.59	36
New Mexico	1.61	5
New York	-1.39	47
North Carolina	0.56	14
North Dakota	-1.17	45
Ohio	-0.36	31
Oklahoma	-0.65	38
Oregon	1.43	6
Pennsylvania	-1.20	46
Rhode Island	-1.50	48
South Carolina	-0.28	28
South Dakota	-0.73	39
Tennessee	0.90	11
Texas	1.00	9
Utah	2.34	3
Vermont	-1.00	42
Virginia	0.07	21
Washington	0.59	13
West Virginia	-0.55	33
Wisconsin	0.22	19
Wyoming	-0.11	24
50 States	n/a	
DC	n/a	
United States	0.00	

Rank in order

By Index

1. Nevada
2. Arizona
3. Utah
4. Georgia
5. New Mexico
6. Oregon
7. Florida
8. Colorado
9. Texas
10. Idaho
11. Tennessee
12. Arkansas
13. Washington
14. North Carolina
15. Nebraska
16. Missouri
17. Louisiana
18. Minnesota
19. Wisconsin
20. Michigan
21. Virginia
22. New Hampshire
23. Kansas
24. Wyoming
25. Kentucky
26. California
27. Iowa
28. South Carolina
29. Montana
30. Alabama
31. Ohio
32. Massachusetts
33. West Virginia
34. Delaware
35. Indiana
36. New Jersey
37. Maine
38. Oklahoma
39. South Dakota
40. Illinois
41. Alaska
42. Vermont
43. Maryland
44. Mississippi
45. North Dakota
46. Pennsylvania
47. New York
48. Rhode Island
49. Hawaii
50. Connecticut

B-29 Employment Change, 1994-1995			Rank in order	
	Percentage change in employment June 94-95	Rank by % change		By %
State	%			
Alabama	9.2	38		1. Nevada
Alaska	7.7	42		2. Utah
Arizona	48.7	3		3. Arizona
Arkansas	35.4	8		4. New Mexico
California	9.4	36		5. Louisiana
Colorado	21.5	25		6. Oregon
Connecticut	0.7	47		7. Georgia
Delaware	4.7	44		8. Arkansas
Florida	34.9	9		9. Florida
Georgia	42.0	7		10. Texas
Hawaii	-7.8	49		11. South Dakota
Idaho	24.3	18		12. Missouri
Illinois	8.0	41		13. Washington
Indiana	14.4	33		14. Montana
Iowa	20.5	28		15. Kansas
Kansas	25.4	15		16. Tennessee
Kentucky	20.5	27		17. Wisconsin
Louisiana	44.3	5		18. Idaho
Maine	22.5	22		19. Michigan
Maryland	4.5	45		20. Virginia
Massachusetts	17.2	31		21. Oklahoma
Michigan	23.5	19		22. Maine
Minnesota	21.9	23		23. Minnesota
Mississippi	-11.4	50		24. North Dakota
Missouri	27.3	12		25. Colorado
Montana	25.4	14		26. West Virginia
Nebraska	17.8	30		27. Kentucky
Nevada	55.4	1		28. Iowa
New Hampshire	8.3	40		29. North Carolina
New Jersey	12.4	34		30. Nebraska
New Mexico	47.9	4		31. Massachusetts
New York	5.6	43		32. Ohio
North Carolina	17.9	29		33. Indiana
North Dakota	21.9	24		34. New Jersey
Ohio	16.5	32		35. South Carolina
Oklahoma	22.8	21		36. California
Oregon	42.6	6		37. Wyoming
Pennsylvania	1.4	46		38. Alabama
Rhode Island	-6.8	48		39. Vermont
South Carolina	10.2	35		40. New Hampshire
South Dakota	29.5	11		41. Illinois
Tennessee	25.0	16		42. Alaska
Texas	34.8	10		43. New York
Utah	55.0	2		44. Delaware
Vermont	8.3	39		45. Maryland
Virginia	23.3	20		46. Pennsylvania
Washington	27.0	13		47. Connecticut
West Virginia	21.4	26		48. Rhode Island
Wisconsin	24.5	17		49. Hawaii
Wyoming	9.2	37		50. Mississippi
50 States	19.4			
DC	-30.5			
United States	n/a			

State	% change in manufacturing employment, Aug. 94-95 %	Rank
Alabama	-1.41	43
Alaska	0.42	29
Arizona	3.79	4
Arkansas	1.71	17
California	-0.16	35
Colorado	1.14	23
Connecticut	-2.09	45
Delaware	-2.65	46
Florida	0.39	30
Georgia	0.79	26
Hawaii	-5.03	50
Idaho	2.17	10
Illinois	0.76	27
Indiana	1.84	15
Iowa	1.62	19
Kansas	2.98	5
Kentucky	1.04	24
Louisiana	1.27	22
Maine	0.21	31
Maryland	-0.84	40
Massachusetts	-0.07	33
Michigan	1.29	21
Minnesota	2.04	11
Mississippi	-3.78	49
Missouri	1.65	18
Montana	2.97	6
Nebraska	2.28	9
Nevada	4.62	3
New Hampshire	-0.79	39
New Jersey	-3.23	48
New Mexico	2.56	7
New York	-0.50	36
North Carolina	-0.59	37
North Dakota	0.46	28
Ohio	0.90	25
Oklahoma	1.93	13
Oregon	2.43	8
Pennsylvania	-0.67	38
Rhode Island	-2.86	47
South Carolina	-1.23	42
South Dakota	4.94	2
Tennessee	-1.61	44
Texas	1.31	20
Utah	7.46	1
Vermont	1.81	16
Virginia	-0.15	34
Washington	-1.19	41
West Virginia	1.95	12
Wisconsin	1.91	14
Wyoming	0.00	32
50 States	0.35	
DC		
United States		

B-30 Manufacturing Employment Change, 1994-1995

Rank in order

By %

1. Utah
2. South Dakota
3. Nevada
4. Arizona
5. Kansas
6. Montana
7. New Mexico
8. Oregon
9. Nebraska
10. Idaho
11. Minnesota
12. West Virginia
13. Oklahoma
14. Wisconsin
15. Indiana
16. Vermont
17. Arkansas
18. Missouri
19. Iowa
20. Texas
21. Michigan
22. Louisiana
23. Colorado
24. Kentucky
25. Ohio
26. Georgia
27. Illinois
28. North Dakota
29. Alaska
30. Florida
31. Maine
32. Wyoming
33. Massachusetts
34. Virginia
35. California
36. New York
37. North Carolina
38. Pennsylvania
39. New Hampshire
40. Maryland
41. Washington
42. South Carolina
43. Alabama
44. Tennessee
45. Connecticut
46. Delaware
47. Rhode Island
48. New Jersey
49. Mississippi
50. Hawaii

State	% of homes owner occupied %	Rank
Alabama	70.5	6
Alaska	56.1	46
Arizona	64.2	38
Arkansas	69.6	13
California	55.6	47
Colorado	62.3	42
Connecticut	65.6	33
Delaware	70.3	8
Florida	67.2	27
Georgia	64.9	36
Hawaii	53.9	49
Idaho	70.1	10
Illinois	64.2	39
Indiana	70.2	9
Iowa	70.0	11
Kansas	67.9	22
Kentucky	69.6	14
Louisiana	65.9	32
Maine	70.5	7
Maryland	65.0	35
Massachusetts	59.3	45
Michigan	71.0	4
Minnesota	71.8	2
Mississippi	71.5	3
Missouri	68.8	16
Montana	67.3	26
Nebraska	66.5	29
Nevada	54.8	48
New Hampshire	68.2	17
New Jersey	64.9	37
New Mexico	67.4	25
New York	52.2	50
North Carolina	68.0	20
North Dakota	65.6	34
Ohio	67.5	24
Oklahoma	68.1	18
Oregon	63.1	40
Pennsylvania	70.7	5
Rhode Island	59.5	44
South Carolina	69.9	12
South Dakota	66.1	31
Tennessee	68.0	21
Texas	60.9	43
Utah	68.1	19
Vermont	69.0	15
Virginia	66.3	30
Washington	62.6	41
West Virginia	74.1	1
Wisconsin	66.7	28
Wyoming	67.8	23
50 States	n/a	
DC	38.9	
United States	64.2	

Rank in order

By %

1. West Virginia
2. Minnesota
3. Mississippi
4. Michigan
5. Pennsylvania
6. Alabama
7. Maine
8. Delaware
9. Indiana
10. Idaho
11. Iowa
12. South Carolina
13. Arkansas
14. Kentucky
15. Vermont
16. Missouri
17. New Hampshire
18. Oklahoma
19. Utah
20. North Carolina
21. Tennessee
22. Kansas
23. Wyoming
24. Ohio
25. New Mexico
26. Montana
27. Florida
28. Wisconsin
29. Nebraska
30. Virginia
31. South Dakota
32. Louisiana
33. Connecticut
34. North Dakota
35. Maryland
36. Georgia
37. New Jersey
38. Arizona
39. Illinois
40. Oregon
41. Washington
42. Colorado
43. Texas
44. Rhode Island
45. Massachusetts
46. Alaska
47. California
48. Nevada
49. Hawaii
50. New York

B-32 Gambling, 1994				Rank in order
State	Gambling losses (millions)	$ per capita spent on gambling $	Rank by total losses	By losses
Alabama	87	21	36	1. Nevada
Alaska	46	76	43	2. New Jersey
Arizona	225	55	29	3. California
Arkansas	53	22	41	4. Illinois
California	2,423	77	3	5. New York
Colorado	556	152	16	6. Florida
Connecticut	379	116	22	7. Texas
Delaware	84	119	37	8. Mississippi
Florida	1,558	112	6	9. Louisiana
Georgia	591	84	15	10. Ohio
Hawaii	n/a	0	n/a	11. Massachusetts
Idaho	43	38	44	12. Pennsylvania
Illinois	2,102	179	4	13. Michigan
Indiana	335	58	25	14. Maryland
Iowa	245	87	27	15. Georgia
Kansas	137	54	32	16. Colorado
Kentucky	389	102	21	17. Washington
Louisiana	1,393	323	9	18. Virginia
Maine	92	74	35	19. Oregon
Maryland	718	143	14	20. South Carolina
Massachusetts	1,110	184	11	21. Kentucky
Michigan	840	88	13	22. Connecticut
Minnesota	375	82	23	23. Minnesota
Mississippi	1,499	562	8	24. Missouri
Missouri	336	64	24	25. Indiana
Montana	238	278	28	26. Wisconsin
Nebraska	79	48	38	27. Iowa
Nevada	7,071	4,853	1	28. Montana
New Hampshire	135	119	33	29. Arizona
New Jersey	4,430	560	2	30. South Dakota
New Mexico	47	28	42	31. West Virginia
New York	1,976	109	5	32. Kansas
North Carolina	8	1	46	33. New Hampshire
North Dakota	66	104	39	34. Rhode Island
Ohio	1,167	105	10	35. Maine
Oklahoma	57	18	40	36. Alabama
Oregon	453	147	19	37. Delaware
Pennsylvania	1,012	84	12	38. Nebraska
Rhode Island	128	128	34	39. North Dakota
South Carolina	409	112	20	40. Oklahoma
South Dakota	197	274	30	41. Arkansas
Tennessee	n/a	n/a	n/a	42. New Mexico
Texas	1,511	82	7	43. Alaska
Utah	n/a	n/a	n/a	44. Idaho
Vermont	30	52	45	45. Vermont
Virginia	478	73	18	46. North Carolina
Washington	497	93	17	47. Wyoming
West Virginia	143	78	31	
Wisconsin	335	66	26	
Wyoming	8	16	47	
50 States	35,748	139		
DC	104	183		
United States	36,195	139		

B-33 Average Annual Electricity Use Per Residential Customer, 1993

State	Avg. Annual Kwh use per customer residential	Rank
Alabama	13,442	7
Alaska	8,290	35
Arizona	10,967	23
Arkansas	11,370	18
California	6,112	49
Colorado	7,354	41
Connecticut	8,061	36
Delaware	10,215	27
Florida	12,412	13
Georgia	12,220	14
Hawaii	7,274	42
Idaho	14,244	2
Illinois	7,790	38
Indiana	10,990	22
Iowa	9,681	29
Kansas	9,280	31
Kentucky	12,529	12
Louisiana	13,955	3
Maine	6,373	46
Maryland	11,887	15
Massachusetts	6,662	45
Michigan	7,119	43
Minnesota	8,528	33
Mississippi	13,091	9
Missouri	11,082	21
Montana	10,662	24
Nebraska	10,647	25
Nevada	11,270	19
New Hampshire	6,915	44
New Jersey	7,467	40
New Mexico	5,332	50
New York	6,228	47
North Carolina	12,749	11
North Dakota	11,643	16
Ohio	9,715	28
Oklahoma	11,507	17
Oregon	13,527	6
Pennsylvania	8,717	32
Rhode Island	6,127	48
South Carolina	13,877	4
South Dakota	10,519	26
Tennessee	15,500	1
Texas	12,818	10
Utah	7,848	37
Vermont	7,525	39
Virginia	13,287	8
Washington	13,714	5
West Virginia	11,243	20
Wisconsin	8,351	34
Wyoming	9,408	30
50 States	10,150	
DC	8,452	
United States	9,874	

Rank in order

By kwh

1. Tennessee
2. Idaho
3. Louisiana
4. South Carolina
5. Washington
6. Oregon
7. Alabama
8. Virginia
9. Mississippi
10. Texas
11. North Carolina
12. Kentucky
13. Florida
14. Georgia
15. Maryland
16. North Dakota
17. Oklahoma
18. Arkansas
19. Nevada
20. West Virginia
21. Missouri
22. Indiana
23. Arizona
24. Montana
25. Nebraska
26. South Dakota
27. Delaware
28. Ohio
29. Iowa
30. Wyoming
31. Kansas
32. Pennsylvania
33. Minnesota
34. Wisconsin
35. Alaska
36. Connecticut
37. Utah
38. Illinois
39. Vermont
40. New Jersey
41. Colorado
42. Hawaii
43. Michigan
44. New Hampshire
45. Massachusetts
46. Maine
47. New York
48. Rhode Island
49. California
50. New Mexico

State	Average revenue cents per kwh industrial	Average revenue cents per kwh residential	residential as percent of industrial %	Rank by residential as percent of industrial %	Rank in order By %
Alabama	4.4	6.8	157	31	1. New York
Alaska	6.7	10.6	158	29	2. Ohio
Arizona	5.8	9.7	168	18	3. Delaware
Arkansas	5.0	8.2	165	20	4. Illinois
California	7.3	11.5	157	30	5. Montana
Colorado	4.5	7.3	164	23	6. Washington
Connecticut	8.3	11.4	137	42	7. Texas
Delaware	4.7	8.9	189	3	8. New Mexico
Florida	5.4	8.0	149	37	9. Virginia
Georgia	4.9	8.0	164	22	10. South Carolina
Hawaii	8.9	12.3	138	41	11. Iowa
Idaho	2.8	5.0	179	12	12. Idaho
Illinois	4.7	8.9	188	4	13. Wisconsin
Indiana	4.1	6.6	159	25	14. Utah
Iowa	3.9	7.1	181	11	15. Louisiana
Kansas	4.9	7.1	145	38	16. Oklahoma
Kentucky	4.3	5.7	134	44	17. Wyoming
Louisiana	4.5	7.8	174	15	18. Arizona
Maine	7.1	11.7	165	19	19. Maine
Maryland	5.5	8.2	151	34	20. Arkansas
Massachusetts	8.8	11.1	127	49	21. Minnesota
Michigan	5.7	8.2	143	39	22. Georgia
Minnesota	4.4	7.2	165	21	23. Colorado
Mississippi	4.7	7.2	154	33	24. North Carolina
Missouri	4.9	7.2	149	36	25. Indiana
Montana	3.1	5.8	187	5	26. Pennsylvania
Nebraska	4.0	6.4	159	27	27. Nebraska
Nevada	5.1	6.5	129	47	28. West Virginia
New Hampshire	9.0	11.9	132	45	29. Alaska
New Jersey	8.1	11.4	141	40	30. California
New Mexico	5.0	9.1	183	8	31. Alabama
New York	6.7	13.2	198	1	32. South Dakota
North Carolina	5.1	8.1	160	24	33. Mississippi
North Dakota	4.8	6.4	135	43	34. Maryland
Ohio	4.3	8.4	197	2	35. Oregon
Oklahoma	4.2	7.2	172	16	36. Missouri
Oregon	3.4	5.0	150	35	37. Florida
Pennsylvania	6.1	9.7	159	26	38. Kansas
Rhode Island	9.0	11.4	127	48	39. Michigan
South Carolina	4.1	7.3	181	10	40. New Jersey
South Dakota	4.6	7.1	156	32	41. Hawaii
Tennessee	4.7	5.9	125	50	42. Connecticut
Texas	4.3	8.0	184	7	43. North Dakota
Utah	3.9	6.9	175	14	44. Kentucky
Vermont	7.4	9.7	131	46	45. New Hampshire
Virginia	4.3	7.8	181	9	46. Vermont
Washington	2.5	4.7	185	6	47. Nevada
West Virginia	4.0	6.3	158	28	48. Rhode Island
Wisconsin	4.0	7.0	177	13	49. Massachusetts
Wyoming	3.5	5.9	169	17	50. Tennessee
50 States	5.2	8.2	157		
DC	5.9	7.2	121		
United States	4.9	8.3	169		

State	# of new companies per 1,000 employees	Rank	Rank in order By #
Alabama	5.8	37	1. Washington
Alaska	10.5	5	2. Idaho
Arizona	6.8	23	3. Colorado
Arkansas	6.2	33	4. Oregon
California	9.5	11	5. Alaska
Colorado	10.9	3	6. Montana
Connecticut	6.2	32	7. Georgia
Delaware	7.6	19	8. Wyoming
Florida	9.7	10	9. New Hampshire
Georgia	10.3	7	10. Florida
Hawaii	5.9	35	11. California
Idaho	11.2	2	12. New Mexico
Illinois	5.5	39	13. Nevada
Indiana	5.2	44	14. Utah
Iowa	4.6	47	15. Vermont
Kansas	6.6	29	16. Rhode Island
Kentucky	4.9	45	17. Nebraska
Louisiana	5.6	38	18. Maine
Maine	7.6	18	19. Delaware
Maryland	6.5	30	20. New Jersey
Massachusetts	5.4	42	21. Texas
Michigan	4.9	46	22. New York
Minnesota	5.5	41	23. Arizona
Mississippi	6.7	24	24. Mississippi
Missouri	5.8	36	25. Virginia
Montana	10.4	6	26. South Dakota
Nebraska	7.9	17	27. North Carolina
Nevada	8.9	13	28. Oklahoma
New Hampshire	9.8	9	29. Kansas
New Jersey	7.1	20	30. Maryland
New Mexico	9.2	12	31. Tennessee
New York	6.9	22	32. Connecticut
North Carolina	6.6	27	33. Arkansas
North Dakota	5.3	43	34. West Virginia
Ohio	3.8	50	35. Hawaii
Oklahoma	6.6	28	36. Missouri
Oregon	10.7	4	37. Alabama
Pennsylvania	4.4	49	38. Louisiana
Rhode Island	7.9	16	39. Illinois
South Carolina	5.5	40	40. South Carolina
South Dakota	6.7	26	41. Minnesota
Tennessee	6.3	31	42. Massachusetts
Texas	6.9	21	43. North Dakota
Utah	8.9	14	44. Indiana
Vermont	8.0	15	45. Kentucky
Virginia	6.7	25	46. Michigan
Washington	13.0	1	47. Iowa
West Virginia	6.1	34	48. Wisconsin
Wisconsin	4.6	48	49. Pennsylvania
Wyoming	10.1	8	50. Ohio
50 States	363.0		
DC	n/a		
United States	362.9		

Geography/Environment/Recreation

State	Land area square mile	Rank	Rank in order By sq. mile
Alabama	50,750	28	1. Alaska
Alaska	570,373	1	2. Texas
Arizona	113,642	6	3. California
Arkansas	52,075	27	4. Montana
California	155,973	3	5. New Mexico
Colorado	103,728	8	6. Arizona
Connecticut	4,845	48	7. Nevada
Delaware	1,954	49	8. Colorado
Florida	53,997	26	9. Wyoming
Georgia	57,919	21	10. Oregon
Hawaii	6,423	47	11. Utah
Idaho	82,751	12	12. Idaho
Illinois	55,593	24	13. Kansas
Indiana	35,870	38	14. Minnesota
Iowa	55,875	23	15. Nebraska
Kansas	81,823	13	16. South Dakota
Kentucky	39,732	36	17. North Dakota
Louisiana	43,566	33	18. Missouri
Maine	30,864	39	19. Oklahoma
Maryland	9,775	42	20. Washington
Massachusetts	7,838	45	21. Georgia
Michigan	56,809	22	22. Michigan
Minnesota	79,616	14	23. Iowa
Mississippi	46,914	31	24. Illinois
Missouri	68,898	18	25. Wisconsin
Montana	145,556	4	26. Florida
Nebraska	76,877	15	27. Arkansas
Nevada	109,805	7	28. Alabama
New Hampshire	8,969	44	29. North Carolina
New Jersey	7,419	46	30. New York
New Mexico	121,364	5	31. Mississippi
New York	47,224	30	32. Pennsylvania
North Carolina	48,718	29	33. Louisiana
North Dakota	68,994	17	34. Tennessee
Ohio	40,953	35	35. Ohio
Oklahoma	68,678	19	36. Kentucky
Oregon	96,002	10	37. Virginia
Pennsylvania	44,820	32	38. Indiana
Rhode Island	1,045	50	39. Maine
South Carolina	30,111	40	40. South Carolina
South Dakota	75,896	16	41. West Virginia
Tennessee	41,219	34	42. Maryland
Texas	261,914	2	43. Vermont
Utah	82,768	11	44. New Hampshire
Vermont	9,249	43	45. Massachusetts
Virginia	39,598	37	46. New Jersey
Washington	66,581	20	47. Hawaii
West Virginia	24,087	41	48. Connecticut
Wisconsin	54,314	25	49. Delaware
Wyoming	97,104	9	50. Rhode Island
50 States	3,536,868		
DC	61		
United States	3,536,338		

| C-2 Land Owned By Federal Government, 1991 | | | | Rank in order |
State	Total acres of federally owned land (000)	% of land federally owned %	Rank by total acres	By total acres
Alabama	1,075	3.3	27	1. Alaska
Alaska	248,021	67.9	1	2. Nevada
Arizona	34,308	47.2	4	3. California
Arkansas	2,762	8.2	18	4. Arizona
California	44,707	44.6	3	5. Utah
Colorado	24,154	36.3	11	6. Idaho
Connecticut	6	0.2	49	7. Oregon
Delaware	27	2.2	48	8. Wyoming
Florida	3,114	9.0	16	9. Montana
Georgia	1,488	4.0	24	10. New Mexico
Hawaii	634	15.5	36	11. Colorado
Idaho	32,614	61.6	6	12. Washington
Illinois	961	2.7	30	13. Minnesota
Indiana	401	1.7	39	14. Michigan
Iowa	336	0.9	42	15. Wisconsin
Kansas	422	0.8	38	16. Florida
Kentucky	1,080	4.2	26	17. South Dakota
Louisiana	745	2.6	31	18. Arkansas
Maine	155	0.8	45	19. Texas
Maryland	187	3.0	44	20. Missouri
Massachusetts	66	1.3	47	21. North Carolina
Michigan	4,589	12.6	14	22. North Dakota
Minnesota	5,367	10.5	13	23. Virginia
Mississippi	1,306	4.3	25	24. Georgia
Missouri	2,096	4.7	20	25. Mississippi
Montana	26,142	28.0	9	26. Kentucky
Nebraska	710	1.4	34	27. Alabama
Nevada	58,265	82.9	2	28. West Virginia
New Hampshire	734	12.7	32	29. Tennessee
New Jersey	149	3.1	46	30. Illinois
New Mexico	25,203	32.4	10	31. Louisiana
New York	209	0.7	43	32. New Hampshire
North Carolina	1,970	6.3	21	33. South Carolina
North Dakota	1,879	4.2	22	34. Nebraska
Ohio	342	1.3	41	35. Oklahoma
Oklahoma	705	1.6	35	36. Hawaii
Oregon	32,291	52.4	7	37. Pennsylvania
Pennsylvania	608	2.1	37	38. Kansas
Rhode Island	2	0.3	50	39. Indiana
South Carolina	722	3.7	33	40. Vermont
South Dakota	2,806	5.7	17	41. Ohio
Tennessee	994	3.7	29	42. Iowa
Texas	2,245	1.3	19	43. New York
Utah	33,661	63.9	5	44. Maryland
Vermont	358	6.0	40	45. Maine
Virginia	1,597	6.3	23	46. New Jersey
Washington	12,080	28.3	12	47. Massachusetts
West Virginia	1,028	6.7	28	48. Delaware
Wisconsin	3,537	10.1	15	49. Connecticut
Wyoming	30,477	48.9	8	50. Rhode Island
50 States	649,335	n/a		
DC	10	26.1		
United States	649,346	28.6		

State	State park acreage (000)	acreage per 1000 population	Rank by total acreage	Rank in order By total acreage
Alabama	50	11.9	39	1. Alaska
Alaska	3,240	5,417.9	1	2. California
Arizona	45	11.5	41	3. Texas
Arkansas	48	19.7	40	4. Florida
California	1,330	42.6	2	5. Illinois
Colorado	342	96.0	6	6. Colorado
Connecticut	174	53.1	18	7. Kansas
Delaware	14	20.3	49	8. New Jersey
Florida	428	31.2	4	9. Massachusetts
Georgia	57	8.3	36	10. Michigan
Hawaii	25	21.1	46	11. Pennsylvania
Idaho	42	38.0	44	12. New York
Illinois	391	33.5	5	13. Washington
Indiana	54	9.5	37	14. Maryland
Iowa	54	19.0	38	15. Minnesota
Kansas	324	127.9	7	16. Ohio
Kentucky	43	11.2	43	17. West Virginia
Louisiana	39	9.0	45	18. Connecticut
Maine	75	60.5	31	19. Nevada
Maryland	242	48.8	14	20. Nebraska
Massachusetts	292	48.6	9	21. North Carolina
Michigan	288	30.5	10	22. Tennessee
Minnesota	234	51.8	15	23. Wisconsin
Mississippi	22	8.3	47	24. Missouri
Missouri	126	24.1	24	25. New Mexico
Montana	44	52.0	42	26. Wyoming
Nebraska	142	88.0	20	27. Utah
Nevada	146	105.6	19	28. South Dakota
New Hampshire	75	66.3	32	29. Oregon
New Jersey	305	38.8	8	30. South Carolina
New Mexico	121	75.1	25	31. Maine
New York	260	14.3	12	32. New Hampshire
North Carolina	135	19.5	21	33. Oklahoma
North Dakota	19	30.4	48	34. Virginia
Ohio	209	18.9	16	35. Vermont
Oklahoma	72	22.3	33	36. Georgia
Oregon	91	30.1	29	37. Indiana
Pennsylvania	276	22.9	11	38. Iowa
Rhode Island	9	8.7	50	39. Alabama
South Carolina	80	22.1	30	40. Arkansas
South Dakota	93	129.5	28	41. Arizona
Tennessee	133	26.1	22	42. Montana
Texas	499	27.7	3	43. Kentucky
Utah	97	52.2	27	44. Idaho
Vermont	64	111.2	35	45. Louisiana
Virginia	67	10.4	34	46. Hawaii
Washington	247	46.9	13	47. Mississippi
West Virginia	199	109.3	17	48. North Dakota
Wisconsin	127	25.2	23	49. Delaware
Wyoming	120	255.0	26	50. Rhode Island
50 States	11,610	45.1		
DC	0	0.0		
United States	11,610	45.0		

State	state park total visitors (000)	visitors per capita	rank by total visitors	Rank in order By total #
Alabama	6,198	1.5	34	1. California
Alaska	6,590	11.0	32	2. New York
Arizona	1,858	0.5	46	3. Ohio
Arkansas	7,257	3.0	30	4. Washington
California	66,674	2.1	1	5. Oregon
Colorado	10,137	2.8	22	6. Illinois
Connecticut	7,314	2.2	29	7. Pennsylvania
Delaware	3,151	4.5	41	8. Tennessee
Florida	11,416	0.8	20	9. Kentucky
Georgia	15,637	2.3	14	10. Texas
Hawaii	15,178	13.0	15	11. Michigan
Idaho	2,701	2.5	42	12. Missouri
Illinois	35,851	3.1	6	13. Oklahoma
Indiana	10,381	1.8	21	14. Georgia
Iowa	9,794	3.5	23	15. Hawaii
Kansas	3,930	1.6	37	16. Massachusetts
Kentucky	28,396	7.5	9	17. North Carolina
Louisiana	1,221	0.3	47	18. New Jersey
Maine	1,942	1.6	45	19. Wisconsin
Maryland	9,666	1.9	24	20. Florida
Massachusetts	15,139	2.5	16	21. Indiana
Michigan	21,228	2.2	11	22. Colorado
Minnesota	7,492	1.7	28	23. Iowa
Mississippi	3,913	1.5	38	24. Maryland
Missouri	16,216	3.1	12	25. Nebraska
Montana	4,153	4.9	36	26. South Carolina
Nebraska	8,858	5.5	25	27. West Virginia
Nevada	2,600	1.9	43	28. Minnesota
New Hampshire	1,158	1.0	48	29. Connecticut
New Jersey	11,643	1.5	18	30. Arkansas
New Mexico	4,174	2.6	35	31. Utah
New York	62,376	3.4	2	32. Alaska
North Carolina	11,830	1.7	17	33. South Dakota
North Dakota	1,043	1.6	49	34. Alabama
Ohio	56,908	5.1	3	35. New Mexico
Oklahoma	16,049	5.0	13	36. Montana
Oregon	40,236	13.3	5	37. Kansas
Pennsylvania	35,641	3.0	7	38. Mississippi
Rhode Island	3,515	3.5	40	39. Virginia
South Carolina	8,189	2.3	26	40. Rhode Island
South Dakota	6,200	8.7	33	41. Delaware
Tennessee	28,701	5.6	8	42. Idaho
Texas	25,368	1.4	10	43. Nevada
Utah	6,607	3.6	31	44. Wyoming
Vermont	765	1.3	50	45. Maine
Virginia	3,779	0.6	39	46. Arizona
Washington	45,114	8.6	4	47. Louisiana
West Virginia	7,822	4.3	27	48. New Hampshire
Wisconsin	11,481	2.3	19	49. North Dakota
Wyoming	2,010	4.3	44	50. Vermont
50 States	725,500	2.8		
DC	0	0.0		
United States	725,500	2.8		

C-5 Exercisers at Clubs, 1994

State	Exercisers at clubs (000)	% of population %	Rank by %	By %
Alabama	199	4.7	45	1. New Hampshire
Alaska	n/a	n/a	n/a	2. Oregon
Arizona	390	9.6	8	3. Rhode Island
Arkansas	93	3.8	46	4. California
California	3,527	11.2	4	5. Connecticut
Colorado	326	8.9	10	6. Massachusetts
Connecticut	352	10.7	5	7. Utah
Delaware	60	8.5	14	8. Arizona
Florida	1,102	7.9	21	9. Maryland
Georgia	468	6.6	30	10. Colorado
Hawaii	n/a	n/a	n/a	11. Virginia
Idaho	69	6.1	34	12. Maine
Illinois	947	8.1	18	13. New Jersey
Indiana	309	5.4	41	14. Delaware
Iowa	207	7.3	25	15. Missouri
Kansas	150	5.9	37	16. North Dakota
Kentucky	187	4.9	43	17. Montana
Louisiana	210	4.9	44	18. Illinois
Maine	108	8.7	12	19. New York
Maryland	453	9.0	9	20. Ohio
Massachusetts	624	10.3	6	21. Florida
Michigan	591	6.2	32	22. New Mexico
Minnesota	334	7.3	26	23. Wisconsin
Mississippi	161	6.0	35	24. Texas
Missouri	440	8.3	15	25. Iowa
Montana	70	8.2	17	26. Minnesota
Nebraska	84	5.2	42	27. West Virginia
Nevada	81	5.6	40	28. North Carolina
New Hampshire	172	15.1	1	29. South Dakota
New Jersey	674	8.5	13	30. Georgia
New Mexico	130	7.9	22	31. Tennessee
New York	1,442	7.9	19	32. Michigan
North Carolina	492	7.0	28	33. Washington
North Dakota	53	8.3	16	34. Idaho
Ohio	877	7.9	20	35. Mississippi
Oklahoma	187	5.7	38	36. Pennsylvania
Oregon	440	14.3	2	37. Kansas
Pennsylvania	719	6.0	36	38. Oklahoma
Rhode Island	120	12.0	3	39. South Carolina
South Carolina	209	5.7	39	40. Nevada
South Dakota	49	6.8	29	41. Indiana
Tennessee	341	6.6	31	42. Nebraska
Texas	1,365	7.4	24	43. Kentucky
Utah	193	10.1	7	44. Louisiana
Vermont	21	3.6	47	45. Alabama
Virginia	584	8.9	11	46. Arkansas
Washington	326	6.1	33	47. Vermont
West Virginia	131	7.2	27	48. Wyoming
Wisconsin	380	7.5	23	
Wyoming	17	3.6	48	
50 States	20,464	7.9		
DC	n/a	n/a		
United States	20,411	7.8		

CQ State Fact Finder

C-6 Hunters With Firearms, 1994

State	Hunters with firearms (000)	% of population	Rank by %	Rank in order By %
Alabama	429	10.2	19	1. Montana
Alaska	n/a	n/a	n/a	2. Wyoming
Arizona	210	5.2	32	3. Idaho
Arkansas	368	15.0	10	4. Maine
California	716	2.3	45	5. South Dakota
Colorado	216	5.9	28	6. Wisconsin
Connecticut	158	4.8	34	7. West Virginia
Delaware	21	3.0	42	8. Nebraska
Florida	375	2.7	44	9. Mississippi
Georgia	429	6.1	27	10. Arkansas
Hawaii	n/a	n/a	n/a	11. North Dakota
Idaho	230	20.3	3	12. Vermont
Illinois	452	3.8	38	13. Minnesota
Indiana	337	5.9	30	14. Utah
Iowa	245	8.7	23	15. Pennsylvania
Kansas	138	5.4	31	16. Missouri
Kentucky	236	6.2	26	17. Louisiana
Louisiana	466	10.8	17	18. Oregon
Maine	243	19.6	4	19. Alabama
Maryland	173	3.5	39	20. South Carolina
Massachusetts	76	1.3	47	21. Oklahoma
Michigan	886	9.3	22	22. Michigan
Minnesota	609	13.3	13	23. Iowa
Mississippi	419	15.7	9	24. Texas
Missouri	571	10.8	16	25. Tennessee
Montana	303	35.4	1	26. Kentucky
Nebraska	266	16.4	8	27. Georgia
Nevada	50	3.4	40	28. Colorado
New Hampshire	12	1.1	48	29. North Carolina
New Jersey	241	3.0	41	30. Indiana
New Mexico	48	2.9	43	31. Kansas
New York	815	4.5	36	32. Arizona
North Carolina	417	5.9	29	33. Virginia
North Dakota	95	14.9	11	34. Connecticut
Ohio	514	4.6	35	35. Ohio
Oklahoma	306	9.4	21	36. New York
Oregon	324	10.5	18	37. Washington
Pennsylvania	1,344	11.2	15	38. Illinois
Rhode Island	17	1.7	46	39. Maryland
South Carolina	353	9.6	20	40. Nevada
South Dakota	139	19.3	5	41. New Jersey
Tennessee	374	7.2	25	42. Delaware
Texas	1,403	7.6	24	43. New Mexico
Utah	233	12.2	14	44. Florida
Vermont	79	13.6	12	45. California
Virginia	335	5.1	33	46. Rhode Island
Washington	212	4.0	37	47. Massachusetts
West Virginia	348	19.1	7	48. New Hampshire
Wisconsin	975	19.2	6	
Wyoming	168	35.3	2	
50 States	17,374	6.7		
DC	n/a	n/a		
United States	17,412	6.7		

State	registered boats	registered boats per 1,000 persons	Rank by total #	Rank in order By total #
Alabama	250,323	59.3	17	1. Michigan
Alaska	31,909	52.7	48	2. California
Arizona	137,968	33.9	29	3. Minnesota
Arkansas	161,344	65.8	27	4. Florida
California	838,541	26.7	2	5. Texas
Colorado	91,579	25.0	34	6. Wisconsin
Connecticut	97,617	29.8	32	7. New York
Delaware	40,985	58.1	44	8. Ohio
Florida	698,795	50.1	4	9. Illinois
Georgia	290,490	41.2	14	10. South Carolina
Hawaii	13,839	11.7	50	11. Pennsylvania
Idaho	77,285	68.2	36	12. North Carolina
Illinois	360,979	30.7	9	13. Missouri
Indiana	191,462	33.3	23	14. Georgia
Iowa	196,813	69.6	22	15. Louisiana
Kansas	97,481	38.2	33	16. Tennessee
Kentucky	146,006	38.2	28	17. Alabama
Louisiana	288,908	67.0	15	18. Washington
Maine	107,216	86.5	31	19. Mississippi
Maryland	179,263	35.8	25	20. Virginia
Massachusetts	129,250	21.4	30	21. Oklahoma
Michigan	898,265	94.6	1	22. Iowa
Minnesota	738,029	161.6	3	23. Indiana
Mississippi	218,317	81.8	19	24. Oregon
Missouri	298,152	56.5	13	25. Maryland
Montana	42,082	49.2	43	26. New Jersey
Nebraska	63,210	38.9	38	27. Arkansas
Nevada	47,897	32.9	40	28. Kentucky
New Hampshire	82,161	72.3	35	29. Arizona
New Jersey	173,979	22.0	26	30. Massachusetts
New Mexico	47,375	28.6	42	31. Maine
New York	441,897	24.3	7	32. Connecticut
North Carolina	300,827	42.5	12	33. Kansas
North Dakota	39,422	61.8	46	34. Colorado
Ohio	385,206	34.7	8	35. New Hampshire
Oklahoma	211,196	64.8	21	36. Idaho
Oregon	188,803	61.2	24	37. Utah
Pennsylvania	322,318	26.7	11	38. Nebraska
Rhode Island	35,766	35.9	47	39. West Virginia
South Carolina	333,218	90.9	10	40. Nevada
South Dakota	47,599	66.0	41	41. South Dakota
Tennessee	275,597	53.3	16	42. New Mexico
Texas	602,375	32.8	5	43. Montana
Utah	70,154	36.8	37	44. Delaware
Vermont	39,485	68.1	45	45. Vermont
Virginia	212,180	32.4	20	46. North Dakota
Washington	234,263	43.8	18	47. Rhode Island
West Virginia	48,352	26.5	39	48. Alaska
Wisconsin	526,973	103.7	6	49. Wyoming
Wyoming	27,269	57.3	49	50. Hawaii
50 States	11,380,420	43.8		
DC	6,614	11.6		
United States	11,429,585	43.9		

State	State spending for the arts $	Per capita in pennies	Rank by per capita	By per capita
Alabama	2,021,048	48	35	1. Hawaii
Alaska	1,058,100	177	5	2. Michigan
Arizona	2,425,600	62	30	3. Florida
Arkansas	1,023,073	42	41	4. Delaware
California	12,341,000	40	43	5. Alaska
Colorado	1,574,950	44	40	6. New York
Connecticut	2,161,703	66	27	7. New Jersey
Delaware	1,285,900	184	4	8. Minnesota
Florida	28,467,181	208	3	9. Maryland
Georgia	3,242,767	47	37	10. Utah
Hawaii	9,185,324	784	1	11. Massachusetts
Idaho	724,500	66	28	12. Montana
Illinois	6,657,200	57	31	13. Oklahoma
Indiana	2,749,705	48	36	14. South Carolina
Iowa	1,414,503	50	33	15. Ohio
Kansas	1,229,021	49	34	16. West Virginia
Kentucky	3,192,100	84	19	17. North Carolina
Louisiana	0	0	50	18. Tennessee
Maine	511,773	41	42	19. Kentucky
Maryland	6,213,751	125	9	20. Missouri
Massachusetts	6,309,470	105	11	21. New Mexico
Michigan	28,978,200	306	2	22. Pennsylvania
Minnesota	6,255,582	138	8	23. Nebraska
Mississippi	704,224	27	47	24. Rhode Island
Missouri	4,307,603	82	20	25. South Dakota
Montana	864,348	103	12	26. Vermont
Nebraska	1,151,704	72	23	27. Connecticut
Nevada	479,147	35	45	28. Idaho
New Hampshire	510,085	45	39	29. Wyoming
New Jersey	11,251,000	143	7	30. Arizona
New Mexico	1,305,200	81	21	31. Illinois
New York	29,378,800	161	6	32. Wisconsin
North Carolina	6,328,081	91	17	33. Iowa
North Dakota	297,609	47	38	34. Kansas
Ohio	10,440,686	94	15	35. Alabama
Oklahoma	3,100,565	96	13	36. Indiana
Oregon	1,032,802	34	46	37. Georgia
Pennsylvania	9,000,000	75	22	38. North Dakota
Rhode Island	723,442	72	24	39. New Hampshire
South Carolina	3,466,086	95	14	40. Colorado
South Dakota	491,701	69	25	41. Arkansas
Tennessee	4,387,400	86	18	42. Maine
Texas	3,350,769	19	49	43. California
Utah	2,062,800	111	10	44. Washington
Vermont	399,840	69	26	45. Nevada
Virginia	1,621,736	25	48	46. Oregon
Washington	1,993,927	38	44	47. Mississippi
West Virginia	1,712,317	94	16	48. Virginia
Wisconsin	2,792,000	55	32	49. Texas
Wyoming	296,281	63	29	50. Louisiana
50 States	232,472,604	94		
DC	3,382,000	n/a		
United States	246,230,880	94		

State	Energy consumption trillion btu's	BTUs per capita	Rank by per capita	By per capita
Alabama	1,669	399,187	12	1. Alaska
Alaska	599	1,001,672	1	2. Wyoming
Arizona	958	242,839	43	3. Louisiana
Arkansas	853	351,608	20	4. Texas
California	6,988	223,852	47	5. North Dakota
Colorado	1,023	287,037	39	6. West Virginia
Connecticut	762	232,459	45	7. Indiana
Delaware	257	368,195	14	8. Montana
Florida	3,128	227,889	46	9. Oklahoma
Georgia	2,237	324,109	24	10. Kansas
Hawaii	229	196,398	50	11. Kentucky
Idaho	399	362,727	17	12. Alabama
Illinois	3,582	306,521	30	13. Washington
Indiana	2,514	440,589	7	14. Delaware
Iowa	966	342,432	22	15. New Mexico
Kansas	1,057	416,963	10	16. Mississippi
Kentucky	1,577	415,656	11	17. Idaho
Louisiana	3,605	840,326	3	18. Tennessee
Maine	380	306,452	31	19. South Carolina
Maryland	1,246	251,311	40	20. Arkansas
Massachusetts	1,408	233,965	44	21. Ohio
Michigan	2,899	306,448	32	22. Iowa
Minnesota	1,432	316,534	26	23. Nebraska
Mississippi	963	364,773	16	24. Georgia
Missouri	1,597	305,062	34	25. Nevada
Montana	358	425,684	8	26. Minnesota
Nebraska	533	330,440	23	27. Oregon
Nevada	446	322,721	25	28. Utah
New Hampshire	246	218,861	48	29. New Jersey
New Jersey	2,422	308,182	29	30. Illinois
New Mexico	595	368,193	15	31. Maine
New York	3,702	203,933	49	32. Michigan
North Carolina	2,104	302,647	36	33. South Dakota
North Dakota	331	519,623	5	34. Missouri
Ohio	3,791	342,736	21	35. Pennsylvania
Oklahoma	1,355	419,115	9	36. North Carolina
Oregon	957	315,321	27	37. Virginia
Pennsylvania	3,666	304,738	35	38. Wisconsin
Rhode Island	245	245,000	42	39. Colorado
South Carolina	1,279	352,342	19	40. Maryland
South Dakota	219	305,866	33	41. Vermont
Tennessee	1,832	359,639	18	42. Rhode Island
Texas	10,081	559,372	4	43. Arizona
Utah	579	311,290	28	44. Massachusetts
Vermont	142	246,528	41	45. Connecticut
Virginia	1,911	295,226	37	46. Florida
Washington	1,944	369,652	13	47. California
West Virginia	826	454,345	6	48. New Hampshire
Wisconsin	1,465	290,444	38	49. New York
Wyoming	406	863,830	2	50. Hawaii
50 States	83,763	325,665		
DC	178	307,427		
United States	83,958	325,693		

C-10 Toxic Chemical Release, 1993

State	Toxic chemical release in pounds (000)	per capita release in pounds	Rank by per capita	Rank in order By %
Alabama	105,538	25.2	7	1. Louisiana
Alaska	8,287	13.9	14	2. Montana
Arizona	13,436	3.4	40	3. Utah
Arkansas	37,078	15.3	12	4. Mississippi
California	57,270	1.8	47	5. Tennessee
Colorado	4,912	1.4	48	6. Wyoming
Connecticut	13,195	4.0	37	7. Alabama
Delaware	4,813	6.9	29	8. Texas
Florida	69,145	5.0	34	9. Indiana
Georgia	49,887	7.2	26	10. South Carolina
Hawaii	704	0.6	50	11. Kansas
Idaho	8,018	7.3	25	12. Arkansas
Illinois	100,991	8.6	24	13. New Mexico
Indiana	97,844	17.1	9	14. Alaska
Iowa	31,516	11.2	18	15. West Virginia
Kansas	39,831	15.7	11	16. North Carolina
Kentucky	36,826	9.7	21	17. Ohio
Louisiana	450,681	105.1	1	18. Iowa
Maine	12,624	10.2	19	19. Maine
Maryland	13,230	2.7	42	20. Virginia
Massachusetts	11,638	1.9	46	21. Kentucky
Michigan	81,999	8.7	23	22. Missouri
Minnesota	24,980	5.5	33	23. Michigan
Mississippi	118,020	44.7	4	24. Illinois
Missouri	49,609	9.5	22	25. Idaho
Montana	45,212	53.8	2	26. Georgia
Nebraska	11,457	7.1	28	27. Wisconsin
Nevada	8,714	6.3	32	28. Nebraska
New Hampshire	4,004	3.6	39	29. Delaware
New Jersey	19,373	2.5	44	30. Oklahoma
New Mexico	23,830	14.7	13	31. Oregon
New York	47,759	2.6	43	32. Nevada
North Carolina	91,015	13.1	16	33. Minnesota
North Dakota	1,539	2.4	45	34. Florida
Ohio	138,035	12.5	17	35. Washington
Oklahoma	22,061	6.8	30	36. Pennsylvania
Oregon	19,436	6.4	31	37. Connecticut
Pennsylvania	54,082	4.5	36	38. Rhode Island
Rhode Island	3,659	3.7	38	39. New Hampshire
South Carolina	59,104	16.3	10	40. Arizona
South Dakota	2,007	2.8	41	41. South Dakota
Tennessee	188,208	36.9	5	42. Maryland
Texas	352,172	19.5	8	43. New York
Utah	91,851	49.4	3	44. New Jersey
Vermont	759	1.3	49	45. North Dakota
Virginia	65,093	10.1	20	46. Massachusetts
Washington	24,428	4.6	35	47. California
West Virginia	25,088	13.8	15	48. Colorado
Wisconsin	35,911	7.1	27	49. Vermont
Wyoming	16,594	35.3	6	50. Hawaii
50 States	2,793,462	10.9		
DC	n/a	n/a		
United States	2,793,462	10.8		

State	Hazordous Waste Sites	Rank	Rank in order By #
Alabama	13	29	1. New Jersey
Alaska	8	42	2. Pennsylvania
Arizona	10	38	3. California
Arkansas	12	31	4. New York
California	96	3	5. Michigan
Colorado	18	21	6. Florida
Connecticut	15	27	7. Washington
Delaware	19	20	8. Wisconsin
Florida	57	6	9. Ohio
Georgia	13	30	10. Illinois
Hawaii	4	45	11. Minnesota
Idaho	10	39	12. Indiana
Illinois	37	10	13. Massachusetts
Indiana	33	12	14. Texas
Iowa	18	22	15. South Carolina
Kansas	12	32	16. Virginia
Kentucky	20	19	17. North Carolina
Louisiana	17	24	18. Missouri
Maine	11	35	19. Kentucky
Maryland	14	28	20. Delaware
Massachusetts	30	13	21. Colorado
Michigan	76	5	22. Iowa
Minnesota	37	11	23. Tennessee
Mississippi	4	46	24. Louisiana
Missouri	22	18	25. New Hampshire
Montana	9	41	26. Utah
Nebraska	10	40	27. Connecticut
Nevada	1	50	28. Maryland
New Hampshire	17	25	29. Alabama
New Jersey	106	1	30. Georgia
New Mexico	11	36	31. Arkansas
New York	80	4	32. Kansas
North Carolina	23	17	33. Oregon
North Dakota	2	49	34. Rhode Island
Ohio	38	9	35. Maine
Oklahoma	11	37	36. New Mexico
Oregon	12	33	37. Oklahoma
Pennsylvania	102	2	38. Arizona
Rhode Island	12	34	39. Idaho
South Carolina	25	15	40. Nebraska
South Dakota	4	47	41. Montana
Tennessee	18	23	42. Alaska
Texas	29	14	43. Vermont
Utah	16	26	44. West Virginia
Vermont	8	43	45. Hawaii
Virginia	24	16	46. Mississippi
Washington	53	7	47. South Dakota
West Virginia	6	44	48. Wyoming
Wisconsin	40	8	49. North Dakota
Wyoming	3	48	50. Nevada
50 States	1,266		
DC	n/a		
United States	1,279		

State	Polluted miles #	Percent of river & stream miles polluted %	Rank by %
Alabama	3,491	28.4	36
Alaska	2,889	71.3	18
Arizona	3,645	81.7	12
Arkansas	3,825	51.3	28
California	4,966	87.4	8
Colorado	3,486	12.8	43
Connecticut	506	56.7	25
Delaware	716	89.2	7
Florida	2,885	36.4	33
Georgia	2,889	71.3	19
Hawaii	50	47.6	29
Idaho	12,354	95.1	2
Illinois	8,042	57.5	24
Indiana	2,101	30.7	35
Iowa	n/a	n/a	n/a
Kansas	16,205	94.7	3
Kentucky	3,250	33.4	34
Louisiana	6,702	73.7	16
Maine	472	1.5	48
Maryland	1,312	7.7	45
Massachusetts	1,184	75.3	15
Michigan	1,291	5.7	46
Minnesota	3,545	76.5	14
Mississippi	33,705	94.0	4
Missouri	9,975	47.5	30
Montana	17,141	26.5	38
Nebraska	5,943	73.7	17
Nevada	1,095	76.7	13
New Hampshire	227	2.1	47
New Jersey	n/a	n/a	n/a
New Mexico	3,276	91.3	6
New York	4,657	9.0	44
North Carolina	22,136	63.1	23
North Dakota	8,993	98.0	1
Ohio	5,291	66.9	22
Oklahoma	6,472	91.9	5
Oregon	16,457	56.5	26
Pennsylvania	4,610	18.6	41
Rhode Island	459	69.0	21
South Carolina	1,112	28.1	37
South Dakota	2,989	83.0	11
Tennessee	5,727	52.9	27
Texas	3,726	26.4	39
Utah	3,264	43.2	31
Vermont	2,152	40.9	32
Virginia	3,537	19.7	40
Washington	4,016	71.2	20
West Virginia	4,573	86.5	10
Wisconsin	2,003	17.7	42
Wyoming	5,251	87.3	9
50 States	276,090	43.4	
DC	n/a	n/a	
United States	282,598	44.0	

Rank in order
By %
1. North Dakota
2. Idaho
3. Kansas
4. Mississippi
5. Oklahoma
6. New Mexico
7. Delaware
8. California
9. Wyoming
10. West Virginia
11. South Dakota
12. Arizona
13. Nevada
14. Minnesota
15. Massachusetts
16. Louisiana
17. Nebraska
18. Alaska
19. Georgia
20. Washington
21. Rhode Island
22. Ohio
23. North Carolina
24. Illinois
25. Connecticut
26. Oregon
27. Tennessee
28. Arkansas
29. Hawaii
30. Missouri
31. Utah
32. Vermont
33. Florida
34. Kentucky
35. Indiana
36. Alabama
37. South Carolina
38. Montana
39. Texas
40. Virginia
41. Pennsylvania
42. Wisconsin
43. Colorado
44. New York
45. Maryland
46. Michigan
47. New Hampshire
48. Maine

C-13 Surface Water Pollution Discharges, 1994

State	Surface Water Discharge %	Rank		Rank in order By %
Alabama	6.88	27		1. Hawaii
Alaska	1.89	8		2. Montana
Arizona	5.00	16		3. New Mexico
Arkansas	8.00	29		4. North Dakota
California	1.21	6		5. Mississippi
Colorado	4.67	14		6. California
Connecticut	9.57	36		7. Idaho
Delaware	21.88	50		8. Alaska
Florida	5.24	18		9. Georgia
Georgia	2.76	9		10. Oregon
Hawaii	0.00	1		11. Wyoming
Idaho	1.45	7		12. Wisconsin
Illinois	4.48	13		13. Illinois
Indiana	14.36	46		14. Colorado
Iowa	9.57	36		15. North Carolina
Kansas	12.28	43		16. Arizona
Kentucky	13.11	44		17. Utah
Louisiana	8.70	32		18. Florida
Maine	8.16	31		19. Oklahoma
Maryland	6.19	24		20. Washington
Massachusetts	10.69	39		21. Vermont
Michigan	10.38	38		22. Nebraska
Minnesota	6.17	23		23. Minnesota
Mississippi	1.18	5		24. Maryland
Missouri	9.56	35		25. Texas
Montana	0.00	1		26. Virginia
Nebraska	5.97	22		27. Alabama
Nevada	9.09	34		28. Rhode Island
New Hampshire	8.82	33		29. Arkansas
New Jersey	14.00	45		30. Tennessee
New Mexico	0.00	1		31. Maine
New York	12.02	40		32. Louisiana
North Carolina	4.89	15		33. New Hampshire
North Dakota	0.00	1		34. Nevada
Ohio	16.78	48		35. Missouri
Oklahoma	5.26	19		36. Connecticut
Oregon	2.86	10		37. Iowa
Pennsylvania	12.19	42		38. Michigan
Rhode Island	6.90	28		39. Massachusetts
South Carolina	18.95	49		40. New York
South Dakota	12.12	41		41. South Dakota
Tennessee	8.05	30		42. Pennsylvania
Texas	6.39	25		43. Kansas
Utah	5.13	17		44. Kentucky
Vermont	5.88	21		45. New Jersey
Virginia	6.45	26		46. Indiana
Washington	5.38	20		47. West Virginia
West Virginia	15.69	47		48. Ohio
Wisconsin	4.38	12		49. South Carolina
Wyoming	3.45	11		50. Delaware
50 States	n/a			
DC	n/a			
United States	n/a			

State	Air Quality score low # equals high score	Rank
Alabama	0.18	15
Alaska	0.79	28
Arizona	1.57	38
Arkansas	0.00	1
California	5.35	50
Colorado	1.15	31
Connecticut	4.30	47
Delaware	2.73	42
Florida	0.72	27
Georgia	1.15	31
Hawaii	0.00	1
Idaho	0.00	1
Illinois	3.17	44
Indiana	0.81	29
Iowa	0.00	1
Kansas	0.00	1
Kentucky	0.65	21
Louisiana	0.45	17
Maine	1.24	35
Maryland	3.37	46
Massachusetts	3.32	45
Michigan	1.15	31
Minnesota	0.51	18
Mississippi	0.00	1
Missouri	0.69	26
Montana	0.05	14
Nebraska	0.00	1
Nevada	0.65	21
New Hampshire	0.68	25
New Jersey	5.03	49
New Mexico	0.30	16
New York	4.44	48
North Carolina	0.54	20
North Dakota	0.00	1
Ohio	1.23	34
Oklahoma	0.00	1
Oregon	0.66	23
Pennsylvania	2.07	41
Rhode Island	3.01	43
South Carolina	0.00	1
South Dakota	0.00	1
Tennessee	0.67	24
Texas	1.59	39
Utah	1.11	30
Vermont	0.00	1
Virginia	1.24	35
Washington	1.33	37
West Virginia	0.52	19
Wisconsin	1.78	40
Wyoming	0.00	1
50 States	n/a	
DC	n/a	
United States	n/a	

Rank in order

By score

1. Arkansas
1. Hawaii
1. Idaho
1. Iowa
1. Kansas
1. Mississippi
1. Nebraska
1. North Dakota
1. Oklahoma
1. South Carolina
1. South Dakota
1. Vermont
1. Wyoming
14. Montana
15. Alabama
16. New Mexico
17. Louisiana
18. Minnesota
19. West Virginia
20. North Carolina
21. Kentucky
21. Nevada
23. Oregon
24. Tennessee
25. New Hampshire
26. Missouri
27. Florida
28. Alaska
29. Indiana
30. Utah
31. Colorado
31. Georgia
31. Michigan
34. Ohio
35. Maine
35. Virginia
37. Washington
38. Arizona
39. Texas
40. Wisconsin
41. Pennsylvania
42. Delaware
43. Rhode Island
44. Illinois
45. Massachusetts
46. Maryland
47. Connecticut
48. New York
49. New Jersey
50. California

Government

State	House members	Rank
Alabama	7	21
Alaska	1	44
Arizona	6	23
Arkansas	4	32
California	52	1
Colorado	6	23
Connecticut	6	23
Delaware	1	44
Florida	23	4
Georgia	11	11
Hawaii	2	38
Idaho	2	38
Illinois	20	6
Indiana	10	13
Iowa	5	29
Kansas	4	32
Kentucky	6	23
Louisiana	7	21
Maine	2	38
Maryland	8	19
Massachusetts	10	13
Michigan	16	8
Minnesota	8	19
Mississippi	5	29
Missouri	9	15
Montana	1	44
Nebraska	3	34
Nevada	2	38
New Hampshire	2	38
New Jersey	13	9
New Mexico	3	34
New York	31	2
North Carolina	12	10
North Dakota	1	44
Ohio	19	7
Oklahoma	6	23
Oregon	5	29
Pennsylvania	21	5
Rhode Island	2	38
South Carolina	6	23
South Dakota	1	44
Tennessee	9	15
Texas	30	3
Utah	3	34
Vermont	1	44
Virginia	11	11
Washington	9	15
West Virginia	3	34
Wisconsin	9	15
Wyoming	1	44
50 States	**435**	
DC	n/a	
United States	**435**	

Rank in order

By #

1. California
2. New York
3. Texas
4. Florida
5. Pennsylvania
6. Illinois
7. Ohio
8. Michigan
9. New Jersey
10. North Carolina
11. Georgia
11. Virginia
13. Indiana
13. Massachusetts
15. Missouri
15. Tennessee
15. Washington
15. Wisconsin
19. Maryland
19. Minnesota
21. Alabama
21. Louisiana
23. Arizona
23. Colorado
23. Connecticut
23. Kentucky
23. Oklahoma
23. South Carolina
29. Iowa
29. Mississippi
29. Oregon
32. Arkansas
32. Kansas
34. Nebraska
34. New Mexico
34. Utah
34. West Virginia
38. Hawaii
38. Idaho
38. Maine
38. Nevada
38. New Hampshire
38. Rhode Island
44. Alaska
44. Delaware
44. Montana
44. North Dakota
44. South Dakota
44. Vermont
44. Wyoming

State	senate members	house members	total members	Rank by total members
Alabama	35	105	140	28
Alaska	20	40	60	49
Arizona	30	60	90	43
Arkansas	35	100	135	31
California	40	80	120	36
Colorado	35	65	100	42
Connecticut	36	151	187	9
Delaware	21	41	62	48
Florida	40	120	160	18
Georgia	56	180	236	3
Hawaii	25	51	76	46
Idaho	35	70	105	39
Illinois	59	118	177	13
Indiana	50	100	150	19
Iowa	50	100	150	20
Kansas	40	125	165	17
Kentucky	38	100	138	30
Louisiana	39	105	144	27
Maine	35	151	186	10
Maryland	47	141	188	8
Massachusetts	40	160	200	6
Michigan	38	110	148	24
Minnesota	67	134	201	5
Mississippi	52	122	174	14
Missouri	34	163	197	7
Montana	50	100	150	21
Nebraska	49	n/a	49	50
Nevada	21	42	63	47
New Hampshire	24	400	424	1
New Jersey	40	80	120	37
New Mexico	42	70	112	38
New York	61	150	211	4
North Carolina	50	120	170	15
North Dakota	49	98	147	25
Ohio	33	99	132	33
Oklahoma	48	101	149	23
Oregon	30	60	90	44
Pennsylvania	50	203	253	2
Rhode Island	50	100	150	22
South Carolina	46	124	170	16
South Dakota	35	70	105	40
Tennessee	33	99	132	34
Texas	31	150	181	11
Utah	29	75	104	41
Vermont	30	150	180	12
Virginia	40	100	140	29
Washington	49	98	147	26
West Virginia	34	100	134	32
Wisconsin	33	99	132	35
Wyoming	30	60	90	45
50 States	1984	5440	7424	
DC	n/a	n/a	n/a	
United States	1984	5440	7424	

Rank in order

By total

1. New Hampshire
2. Pennsylvania
3. Georgia
4. New York
5. Minnesota
6. Massachusetts
7. Missouri
8. Maryland
9. Connecticut
10. Maine
11. Texas
12. Vermont
13. Illinois
14. Mississippi
15. North Carolina
16. South Carolina
17. Kansas
18. Florida
19. Indiana
20. Iowa
21. Montana
22. Rhode Island
23. Oklahoma
24. Michigan
25. North Dakota
26. Washington
27. Louisiana
28. Alabama
29. Virginia
30. Kentucky
31. Arkansas
32. West Virginia
33. Ohio
34. Tennessee
35. Wisconsin
36. California
37. New Jersey
38. New Mexico
39. Idaho
40. South Dakota
41. Utah
42. Colorado
43. Arizona
44. Oregon
45. Wyoming
46. Hawaii
47. Nevada
48. Delaware
49. Alaska
50. Nebraska

State	Legislators per million population	Rank
Alabama	33	30
Alaska	99	9
Arizona	22	40
Arkansas	55	18
California	4	50
Colorado	27	35
Connecticut	57	17
Delaware	88	11
Florida	11	48
Georgia	33	28
Hawaii	64	16
Idaho	93	10
Illinois	15	45
Indiana	26	36
Iowa	53	20
Kansas	65	15
Kentucky	36	27
Louisiana	33	29
Maine	150	7
Maryland	38	25
Massachusetts	33	31
Michigan	16	43
Minnesota	44	23
Mississippi	65	14
Missouri	37	26
Montana	175	5
Nebraska	30	32
Nevada	43	24
New Hampshire	373	1
New Jersey	15	44
New Mexico	68	13
New York	12	47
North Carolina	24	39
North Dakota	230	3
Ohio	12	46
Oklahoma	46	22
Oregon	29	33
Pennsylvania	21	42
Rhode Island	150	6
South Carolina	46	21
South Dakota	146	8
Tennessee	26	38
Texas	10	49
Utah	55	19
Vermont	310	2
Virginia	21	41
Washington	28	34
West Virginia	74	12
Wisconsin	26	37
Wyoming	189	4
50 States	29	
DC	n/a	
United States	29	

Rank in order
By million
1. New Hampshire
2. Vermont
3. North Dakota
4. Wyoming
5. Montana
6. Rhode Island
7. Maine
8. South Dakota
9. Alaska
10. Idaho
11. Delaware
12. West Virginia
13. New Mexico
14. Mississippi
15. Kansas
16. Hawaii
17. Connecticut
18. Arkansas
19. Utah
20. Iowa
21. South Carolina
22. Oklahoma
23. Minnesota
24. Nevada
25. Maryland
26. Missouri
27. Kentucky
28. Georgia
29. Louisiana
30. Alabama
31. Massachusetts
32. Nebraska
33. Oregon
34. Washington
35. Colorado
36. Indiana
37. Wisconsin
38. Tennessee
39. North Carolina
40. Arizona
41. Virginia
42. Pennsylvania
43. Michigan
44. New Jersey
45. Illinois
46. Ohio
47. New York
48. Florida
49. Texas
50. California

State	Government units	Units per 10,000 population	Rank per 10,000	By per 10,000
Alabama	1,122	2.7	32	1. North Dakota
Alaska	175	3.0	29	2. South Dakota
Arizona	591	1.5	41	3. Nebraska
Arkansas	1,447	6.0	13	4. Montana
California	4,393	1.4	42	5. Kansas
Colorado	1,761	5.1	18	6. Vermont
Connecticut	564	1.7	39	7. Wyoming
Delaware	276	4.0	22	8. Idaho
Florida	1,014	0.8	48	9. Minnesota
Georgia	1,298	1.9	36	10. Iowa
Hawaii	21	0.2	50	11. Maine
Idaho	1,087	10.2	8	12. Missouri
Illinois	6,723	5.8	14	13. Arkansas
Indiana	2,899	5.1	17	14. Illinois
Iowa	1,881	6.7	10	15. Oklahoma
Kansas	3,892	15.4	5	16. Wisconsin
Kentucky	1,321	3.5	24	17. Indiana
Louisiana	459	1.1	46	18. Colorado
Maine	797	6.5	11	19. Oregon
Maryland	402	0.8	47	20. New Hampshire
Massachusetts	844	1.4	43	21. Pennsylvania
Michigan	2,722	2.9	30	22. Delaware
Minnesota	3,580	8.0	9	23. West Virginia
Mississippi	870	3.3	27	24. Kentucky
Missouri	3,310	6.4	12	25. Utah
Montana	1,276	15.5	4	26. Washington
Nebraska	2,924	18.2	3	27. Mississippi
Nevada	208	1.6	40	28. Ohio
New Hampshire	528	4.8	20	29. Alaska
New Jersey	1,513	1.9	34	30. Michigan
New Mexico	342	2.2	33	31. Texas
New York	3,299	1.8	38	32. Alabama
North Carolina	938	1.4	44	33. New Mexico
North Dakota	2,765	43.5	1	34. New Jersey
Ohio	3,524	3.2	28	35. South Carolina
Oklahoma	1,795	5.6	15	36. Georgia
Oregon	1,451	4.9	19	37. Tennessee
Pennsylvania	5,159	4.3	21	38. New York
Rhode Island	126	1.3	45	39. Connecticut
South Carolina	698	1.9	35	40. Nevada
South Dakota	1,786	25.1	2	41. Arizona
Tennessee	924	1.8	37	42. California
Texas	4,792	2.7	31	43. Massachusetts
Utah	627	3.5	25	44. North Carolina
Vermont	682	12.0	6	45. Rhode Island
Virginia	455	0.7	49	46. Louisiana
Washington	1,761	3.4	26	47. Maryland
West Virginia	692	3.8	23	48. Florida
Wisconsin	2,739	5.5	16	49. Virginia
Wyoming	550	11.8	7	50. Hawaii
50 States	85,004	3.3		
DC	2			
United States	85,006			

State	Salaries $	Per diem during session $	Rank by salary	Rank in order By salary
Alabama	1,050	2,280/month	48	1. California
Alaska	24,012	151/day	17	2. New York
Arizona	15,000	35/day	26	3. Michigan
Arkansas	12,500	82/day	30	4. Pennsylvania
California	72,000	109/day	1	5. Massachusetts
Colorado	17,500	45/day	21	6. Ohio
Connecticut	16,760	0	24	7. Illinois
Delaware	26,000	0	14	8. Wisconsin
Florida	23,244	75/day	18	9. New Jersey
Georgia	10,854	59/day	34	10. Hawaii
Hawaii	32,000	80/day	10	11. Oklahoma
Idaho	12,360	75/day	31	12. Minnesota
Illinois	42,265	81/day	7	13. Maryland
Indiana	11,600	105/day	33	14. Delaware
Iowa	18,800	60/day	19	15. Washington
Kansas	5,670	73/day	42	16. Missouri
Kentucky	6,000	75/day	41	17. Alaska
Louisiana	16,800	75/day	23	18. Florida
Maine	17,475	70/day	22	19. Iowa
Maryland	28,840	106/day	13	20. Virginia
Massachusetts	46,410	50/day	5	21. Colorado
Michigan	49,155	0	3	22. Maine
Minnesota	29,675	50	12	23. Louisiana
Mississippi	10,000	83/day	36	24. Connecticut
Missouri	24,313	35/day	16	25. Tennessee
Montana	5,130	50/day	43	26. Arizona
Nebraska	12,000	26-73/day	32	27. West Virginia
Nevada	7,800	66/day	39	28. North Carolina
New Hampshire	100	0	49	29. Oregon
New Jersey	35,000	0	9	30. Arkansas
New Mexico	0	75/day	50	31. Idaho
New York	57,500	89-130	2	32. Nebraska
North Carolina	13,951	104/day	28	33. Indiana
North Dakota	2,160	90/day	47	34. Georgia
Ohio	42,426	0	6	35. South Carolina
Oklahoma	32,000	35/day	11	36. Mississippi
Oregon	13,104	75/day	29	37. Rhode Island
Pennsylvania	47,000	109/day	4	38. Vermont
Rhode Island	10,000	5/day	37	39. Nevada
South Carolina	10,400	83/day	35	40. Texas
South Dakota	4,000	75/day	44	41. Kentucky
Tennessee	16,500	90/day	25	42. Kansas
Texas	7,200	95/day	40	43. Montana
Utah	3,825	35/day	45	44. South Dakota
Vermont	8,160	87/day	38	45. Utah
Virginia	17,820	93/day	20	46. Wyoming
Washington	25,900	66/day	15	47. North Dakota
West Virginia	15,000	85/day	27	48. Alabama
Wisconsin	38,056	75/day	8	49. New Hampshire
Wyoming	3,750	80/day	46	50. New Mexico
50 States	19,981			
DC	n/a			
United States	19,981			

State	% female legislators	Rank
Alabama	4	50
Alaska	23	21
Arizona	30	4
Arkansas	13	42
California	21	26
Colorado	31	3
Connecticut	27	11
Delaware	21	25
Florida	19	30
Georgia	18	32
Hawaii	20	29
Idaho	28	10
Illinois	24	20
Indiana	22	23
Iowa	18	35
Kansas	28	9
Kentucky	8	49
Louisiana	10	48
Maine	26	12
Maryland	29	8
Massachusetts	24	17
Michigan	22	22
Minnesota	25	13
Mississippi	12	45
Missouri	20	28
Montana	24	17
Nebraska	25	14
Nevada	35	2
New Hampshire	30	6
New Jersey	13	41
New Mexico	21	27
New York	18	34
North Carolina	17	36
North Dakota	15	37
Ohio	24	15
Oklahoma	11	47
Oregon	29	7
Pennsylvania	12	44
Rhode Island	24	17
South Carolina	12	43
South Dakota	18	33
Tennessee	14	40
Texas	18	31
Utah	14	39
Vermont	30	4
Virginia	11	46
Washington	40	1
West Virginia	15	38
Wisconsin	24	15
Wyoming	21	24
50 States	21	
DC	n/a	
United States	21	

Rank in order

By %

1. Washington
2. Nevada
3. Colorado
4. Arizona
5. Vermont
6. New Hampshire
7. Oregon
8. Maryland
9. Kansas
10. Idaho
11. Connecticut
12. Maine
13. Minnesota
14. Nebraska
15. Ohio
16. Wisconsin
17. Massachusetts
18. Montana
19. Rhode Island
20. Illinois
21. Alaska
22. Michigan
23. Indiana
24. Wyoming
25. Delaware
26. California
27. New Mexico
28. Missouri
29. Hawaii
30. Florida
31. Texas
32. Georgia
33. South Dakota
34. New York
35. Iowa
36. North Carolina
37. North Dakota
38. West Virginia
39. Utah
40. Tennessee
41. New Jersey
42. Arkansas
43. South Carolina
44. Pennsylvania
45. Mississippi
46. Virginia
47. Oklahoma
48. Louisiana
49. Kentucky
50. Alabama

State	Percentage of legislators new %	Rank
Alabama	37	5
Alaska	20	25
Arizona	32	9
Arkansas	27	15
California	28	12
Colorado	20	25
Connecticut	22	19
Delaware	18	32
Florida	22	20
Georgia	13	41
Hawaii	34	6
Idaho	19	29
Illinois	16	35
Indiana	13	41
Iowa	26	16
Kansas	21	23
Kentucky	18	31
Louisiana	1	47
Maine	47	1
Maryland	43	2
Massachusetts	16	34
Michigan	21	22
Minnesota	14	39
Mississippi	0	49
Missouri	19	28
Montana	37	4
Nebraska	12	43
Nevada	38	3
New Hampshire	33	8
New Jersey	1	48
New Mexico	19	30
New York	8	46
North Carolina	32	10
North Dakota	21	21
Ohio	15	37
Oklahoma	15	36
Oregon	29	11
Pennsylvania	11	44
Rhode Island	17	33
South Carolina	13	40
South Dakota	25	17
Tennessee	23	18
Texas	14	38
Utah	20	24
Vermont	28	13
Virginia	0	49
Washington	33	7
West Virginia	27	14
Wisconsin	10	45
Wyoming	20	25
50 States	21	
DC	n/a	
United States	21	

By %

1. Maine
2. Maryland
3. Nevada
4. Montana
5. Alabama
6. Hawaii
7. Washington
8. New Hampshire
9. Arizona
10. North Carolina
11. Oregon
12. California
13. Vermont
14. West Virginia
15. Arkansas
16. Iowa
17. South Dakota
18. Tennessee
19. Connecticut
20. Florida
21. North Dakota
22. Michigan
23. Kansas
24. Utah
25. Alaska
25. Colorado
25. Wyoming
28. Missouri
29. Idaho
30. New Mexico
31. Kentucky
32. Delaware
33. Rhode Island
34. Massachusetts
35. Illinois
36. Oklahoma
37. Ohio
38. Texas
39. Minnesota
40. South Carolina
41. Georgia
41. Indiana
43. Nebraska
44. Pennsylvania
45. Wisconsin
46. New York
47. Louisiana
48. New Jersey
49. Mississippi
49. Virginia

State	term limits governor	term limits house	term limits senate	Rank by house members
Alabama				n/a
Alaska				n/a
Arizona	8	8	8	2
Arkansas		6	8	1
California	8	6	8	1
Colorado		8	8	2
Connecticut				n/a
Delaware				n/a
Florida	8	8	8	2
Georgia				n/a
Hawaii				n/a
Idaho	8	8	8	2
Illinois				n/a
Indiana				n/a
Iowa				n/a
Kansas				n/a
Kentucky				n/a
Louisiana		8	8	2
Maine	8	8	8	2
Maryland				n/a
Massachusetts	8	8	8	2
Michigan	8	6	8	1
Minnesota				n/a
Mississippi				n/a
Missouri		16	16	4
Montana	8	8	8	2
Nebraska			8	n/a
Nevada	8	12	12	3
New Hampshire				n/a
New Jersey				n/a
New Mexico				n/a
New York				n/a
North Carolina				n/a
North Dakota				n/a
Ohio	8	8	8	2
Oklahoma		12	12	3
Oregon	8	6	8	1
Pennsylvania				n/a
Rhode Island				n/a
South Carolina				n/a
South Dakota	8	8	8	2
Tennessee				n/a
Texas				n/a
Utah	12	12	12	3
Vermont				n/a
Virginia				n/a
Washington	8	6	8	1
West Virginia				n/a
Wisconsin				n/a
Wyoming	8	6	12	1
50 States				
DC				
United States				

Rank in order

By house

1. Arkansas
1. California
1. Michigan
1. Oregon
1. Washington
1. Wyoming
2. Arizona
2. Colorado
2. Florida
2. Idaho
2. Louisiana
2. Maine
2. Massachusetts
2. Montana
2. Ohio
2. South Dakota
3. Nevada
3. Oklahoma
3. Utah
4. Missouri

State	legislative length in calendar days	Rank
Alabama	105	12
Alaska	120	8
Arizona	140	6
Arkansas	60	21
California	no limit	n/a
Colorado	120	8
Connecticut	140	6
Delaware	174	1
Florida	60	21
Georgia	48	27
Hawaii	62	20
Idaho	no limit	n/a
Illinois	no limit	n/a
Indiana	55	24
Iowa	indirect limitation	n/a
Kansas	45	29
Kentucky	36	34
Louisiana	85	15
Maine	76	17
Maryland	90	13
Massachusetts	no limit	n/a
Michigan	no limit	n/a
Minnesota	144	5
Mississippi	107	11
Missouri	157	3
Montana	54	25
Nebraska	90	13
Nevada	30	36
New Hampshire	54	25
New Jersey	no limit	n/a
New Mexico	45	29
New York	no limit	n/a
North Carolina	no limit	n/a
North Dakota	48	27
Ohio	no limit	n/a
Oklahoma	160	2
Oregon	no limit	n/a
Pennsylvania	no limit	n/a
Rhode Island	72	18
South Carolina	148	4
South Dakota	45	29
Tennessee	108	10
Texas	70	19
Utah	45	29
Vermont	indirect limitation	n/a
Virginia	45	29
Washington	82	16
West Virginia	60	21
Wisconsin	no limit	n/a
Wyoming	36	34
50 States	n/a	
DC	no limit	
United States	84	

Rank in order

By #

1. Delaware
2. Oklahoma
3. Missouri
4. South Carolina
5. Minnesota
6. Arizona
6. Connecticut
8. Alaska
8. Colorado
10. Tennessee
11. Mississippi
12. Alabama
13. Maryland
13. Nebraska
15. Louisiana
16. Washington
17. Maine
18. Rhode Island
19. Texas
20. Hawaii
21. Arkansas
21. Florida
21. West Virginia
24. Indiana
25. Montana
25. New Hampshire
27. Georgia
27. North Dakota
29. Kansas
29. New Mexico
29. South Dakota
29. Utah
29. Virginia
34. Kentucky
34. Wyoming
36. Nevada

D-10 Party Control of State Legislatures, 1995

State	# of democrats in combined houses	# of republicans in combined houses	legis-lative control	% of members democrats	Rank by % demo-cratic members	By %
Alabama	95	45	D	67.9	9	1. Hawaii
Alaska	24	35	R	40.7	38	2. Arkansas
Arizona	33	57	R	36.7	42	3. Rhode Island
Arkansas	116	19	D	85.9	2	4. Louisiana
California	60	58	S	50.8	22	5. Massachusetts
Colorado	40	60	R	40.0	39	6. Mississippi
Connecticut	109	78	S	58.3	14	7. West Virginia
Delaware	26	36	S	41.9	35	8. Maryland
Florida	81	79	S	50.6	23	9. Alabama
Georgia	148	87	D	63.0	12	10. Oklahoma
Hawaii	67	9	D	88.2	1	11. New Mexico
Idaho	21	84	R	20.0	49	12. Georgia
Illinois	80	97	R	45.2	31	13. Kentucky
Indiana	64	86	R	42.7	32	14. Connecticut
Iowa	63	87	S	42.0	34	15. Texas
Kansas	57	108	R	34.5	44	16. Tennessee
Kentucky	84	53	D	61.3	13	17. New York
Louisiana	120	23	D	83.9	4	18. Minnesota
Maine	92	93	S	49.7	24	19. Vermont
Maryland	132	56	D	70.2	8	20. Missouri
Massachusetts	151	44	D	77.4	5	21. Virginia
Michigan	70	78	R	47.3	28	22. California
Minnesota	112	89	D	55.7	18	23. Florida
Mississippi	127	45	D	73.8	6	24. Maine
Missouri	106	91	D	53.8	20	25. Pennsylvania
Montana	52	98	R	34.7	43	26. South Carolina
Nebraska	0	0	n/a	n/a	n/a	27. Wisconsin
Nevada	29	34	S	46.0	29	28. Michigan
New Hampshire	118	299	R	28.3	47	29. Nevada
New Jersey	46	74	R	38.3	40	30. North Carolina
New Mexico	73	39	D	65.2	11	31. Illinois
New York	119	92	S	56.4	17	32. Indiana
North Carolina	78	92	S	45.9	30	33. Ohio
North Dakota	43	104	R	29.3	45	34. Iowa
Ohio	56	76	R	42.4	33	35. Delaware
Oklahoma	100	49	D	67.1	10	36. Washington
Oregon	37	53	R	41.1	37	37. Oregon
Pennsylvania	122	131	R	48.2	25	38. Alaska
Rhode Island	126	24	D	84.0	3	39. Colorado
South Carolina	79	85	S	48.2	26	40. New Jersey
South Dakota	40	65	R	38.1	41	41. South Dakota
Tennessee	75	57	S	56.8	16	42. Arizona
Texas	103	78	D	56.9	15	43. Montana
Utah	30	74	R	28.8	46	44. Kansas
Vermont	98	79	S	55.4	19	45. North Dakota
Virginia	72	67	S	51.8	21	46. Utah
Washington	61	86	S	41.5	36	47. New Hampshire
West Virginia	95	39	D	70.9	7	48. Wyoming
Wisconsin	63	68	R	48.1	27	49. Idaho
Wyoming	23	67	R	25.6	48	
50 States	3816	3527		52.0		
DC	n/a	n/a	n/a	n/a		
United States	3816	3527	16D, 19R, 14S	52.0		

State	Governor	Performance Index	Rank
Alabama	Folsom	4.8	29
Alaska	Hickel	4.8	46
Arizona	Symington	4.8	42
Arkansas	Tucker	4.5	12
California	Wilson	4.5	37
Colorado	Romer	4.5	7
Connecticut	Weicker	4.3	29
Delaware	Carper	4.3	12
Florida	Chiles	4.3	34
Georgia	Miller	4.3	19
Hawaii	Wahiee	4.3	42
Idaho	Andrus	4.0	1
Illinois	Edgar	4.0	23
Indiana	Bayh	4.0	12
Iowa	Branstad	4.0	23
Kansas	Finney	4.0	50
Kentucky	Jones	4.0	37
Louisiana	Edwards	4.0	42
Maine	McKernan	3.8	42
Maryland	Schaefer	3.8	34
Massachusetts	Weld	3.8	23
Michigan	Engler	3.8	12
Minnesota	Carlson	3.5	23
Mississippi	Fordice	3.5	34
Missouri	Carnahan	3.5	7
Montana	Racicot	3.5	19
Nebraska	Nelson	3.5	7
Nevada	Miller	3.5	29
New Hampshire	Merrill	3.0	4
New Jersey	Whitman	3.0	12
New Mexico	King	3.0	37
New York	Cuomo	3.0	29
North Carolina	Hunt	3.0	4
North Dakota	Schafer	2.8	12
Ohio	Voinovich	2.8	7
Oklahoma	Walters	2.8	46
Oregon	Roberts	2.5	49
Pennsylvania	Casey	2.5	29
Rhode Island	Sundlun	2.5	46
South Carolina	Campbell	2.5	1
South Dakota	Miller	2.3	23
Tennessee	McWherter	2.0	7
Texas	Richards	2.0	19
Utah	Leavitt	2.0	1
Vermont	Dean	2.0	12
Virginia	Allen	1.8	23
Washington	Lowry	1.8	37
West Virginia	Caperton	1.8	41
Wisconsin	Thompson	1.5	4
Wyoming	Sullivan	1.3	19

50 States

DC

United States

Rank in order

By Index

1. Idaho
1. South Carolina
1. Utah
4. New Hampshire
4. North Carolina
4. Wisconsin
7. Colorado
7. Missouri
7. Nebraska
7. Ohio
7. Tennessee
12. Arkansas
12. Delaware
12. Indiana
12. Michigan
12. New Jersey
12. North Dakota
12. Vermont
19. Georgia
19. Montana
19. Texas
19. Wyoming
23. Illinois
23. Iowa
23. Massachusetts
23. Minnesota
23. South Dakota
23. Virginia
29. Alabama
29. Connecticut
29. Nevada
29. New York
29. Pennsylvania
34. Florida
34. Maryland
34. Mississippi
37. California
37. Kentucky
37. New Mexico
37. Washington
41. West Virginia
42. Arizona
42. Hawaii
42. Louisiana
42. Maine
46. Alaska
46. Oklahoma
46. Rhode Island
49. Oregon
50. Kansas

State	Elected officials	Rank
Alabama	7	11
Alaska	2	45
Arizona	5	35
Arkansas	6	16
California	8	7
Colorado	5	35
Connecticut	6	16
Delaware	6	16
Florida	8	7
Georgia	9	3
Hawaii	2	45
Idaho	7	11
Illinois	6	16
Indiana	6	16
Iowa	7	11
Kansas	6	16
Kentucky	7	11
Louisiana	8	7
Maine	1	48
Maryland	6	16
Massachusetts	6	16
Michigan	4	42
Minnesota	5	35
Mississippi	8	7
Missouri	6	16
Montana	5	35
Nebraska	6	16
Nevada	7	11
New Hampshire	1	48
New Jersey	1	48
New Mexico	6	16
New York	5	35
North Carolina	10	2
North Dakota	11	1
Ohio	6	16
Oklahoma	9	3
Oregon	6	16
Pennsylvania	5	35
Rhode Island	5	35
South Carolina	9	3
South Dakota	6	16
Tennessee	2	45
Texas	6	16
Utah	4	42
Vermont	6	16
Virginia	3	44
Washington	9	3
West Virginia	6	16
Wisconsin	6	16
Wyoming	6	16
50 States	5	
DC	1	
United States	5	

1. North Dakota
2. North Carolina
3. Georgia
3. Oklahoma
3. South Carolina
3. Washington
7. California
7. Florida
7. Louisiana
7. Mississippi
11. Alabama
11. Idaho
11. Iowa
11. Kentucky
11. Nevada
16. Arkansas
16. Connecticut
16. Delaware
16. Illinois
16. Indiana
16. Kansas
16. Maryland
16. Massachusetts
16. Missouri
16. Nebraska
16. New Mexico
16. Ohio
16. Oregon
16. South Dakota
16. Texas
16. Vermont
16. West Virginia
16. Wisconsin
16. Wyoming
35. Arizona
35. Colorado
35. Minnesota
35. Montana
35. New York
35. Pennsylvania
35. Rhode Island
42. Michigan
42. Utah
44. Virginia
45. Alaska
45. Hawaii
45. Tennessee
48. Maine
48. New Hampshire
48. New Jersey

State	Employees	per 10,000 population	Rank by per 10,000
Alabama	235,412	569	13
Alaska	46,027	784	2
Arizona	199,138	520	34
Arkansas	128,584	536	23
California	1,429,841	463	47
Colorado	185,140	534	28
Connecticut	151,167	461	49
Delaware	37,687	547	20
Florida	664,070	492	39
Georgia	397,053	588	10
Hawaii	64,539	556	17
Idaho	60,096	563	14
Illinois	567,178	488	41
Indiana	297,585	526	30
Iowa	155,793	554	18
Kansas	157,064	623	6
Kentucky	197,016	525	31
Louisiana	249,344	582	12
Maine	65,148	528	29
Maryland	239,627	488	41
Massachusetts	277,246	462	48
Michigan	460,471	488	41
Minnesota	239,943	536	23
Mississippi	155,159	594	8
Missouri	247,711	477	44
Montana	54,229	658	3
Nebraska	99,631	620	7
Nevada	66,001	497	38
New Hampshire	51,803	466	46
New Jersey	417,409	536	23
New Mexico	102,368	647	4
New York	1,151,077	635	5
North Carolina	368,847	539	22
North Dakota	37,515	590	9
Ohio	539,719	490	40
Oklahoma	187,811	585	11
Oregon	155,211	521	33
Pennsylvania	510,169	425	50
Rhode Island	47,629	474	45
South Carolina	201,698	560	15
South Dakota	39,172	551	19
Tennessee	253,944	505	37
Texas	987,993	560	15
Utah	92,955	513	35
Vermont	30,546	536	23
Virginia	344,975	541	21
Washington	275,419	536	23
West Virginia	92,232	509	36
Wisconsin	261,595	522	32
Wyoming	36,581	785	1
50 States	13,314,568	546	
DC	54,655	928	
United States	13,369,223	524	

Rank in order

By per 10,000

1. Wyoming
2. Alaska
3. Montana
4. New Mexico
5. New York
6. Kansas
7. Nebraska
8. Mississippi
9. North Dakota
10. Georgia
11. Oklahoma
12. Louisiana
13. Alabama
14. Idaho
15. South Carolina
15. Texas
17. Hawaii
18. Iowa
19. South Dakota
20. Delaware
21. Virginia
22. North Carolina
23. Arkansas
23. Minnesota
23. New Jersey
23. Vermont
23. Washington
28. Colorado
29. Maine
30. Indiana
31. Kentucky
32. Wisconsin
33. Oregon
34. Arizona
35. Utah
36. West Virginia
37. Tennessee
38. Nevada
39. Florida
40. Ohio
41. Illinois
41. Maryland
41. Michigan
44. Missouri
45. Rhode Island
46. New Hampshire
47. California
48. Massachusetts
49. Connecticut
50. Pennsylvania

State	Average Salary $	Rank
Alabama	23,616	45
Alaska	40,956	1
Arizona	30,048	20
Arkansas	22,704	49
California	39,744	2
Colorado	31,104	18
Connecticut	38,460	3
Delaware	30,744	19
Florida	27,264	27
Georgia	23,976	43
Hawaii	31,932	15
Idaho	24,600	39
Illinois	31,980	14
Indiana	27,480	26
Iowa	28,716	23
Kansas	25,812	35
Kentucky	25,356	37
Louisiana	23,364	48
Maine	26,592	29
Maryland	34,008	7
Massachusetts	32,832	13
Michigan	35,652	6
Minnesota	33,420	9
Mississippi	20,700	50
Missouri	25,380	36
Montana	25,080	38
Nebraska	26,340	30
Nevada	33,144	10
New Hampshire	29,328	22
New Jersey	36,876	5
New Mexico	24,132	42
New York	37,752	4
North Carolina	26,220	31
North Dakota	27,036	28
Ohio	29,820	21
Oklahoma	23,412	46
Oregon	31,212	17
Pennsylvania	31,704	16
Rhode Island	33,912	8
South Carolina	24,216	41
South Dakota	23,400	47
Tennessee	24,564	40
Texas	25,980	32
Utah	25,896	33
Vermont	28,284	24
Virginia	27,660	25
Washington	32,952	12
West Virginia	23,880	44
Wisconsin	33,048	11
Wyoming	25,872	34
50 States	28,963	
DC	38,100	
United States	30,744	

Rank in order

By $

1. Alaska
2. California
3. Connecticut
4. New York
5. New Jersey
6. Michigan
7. Maryland
8. Rhode Island
9. Minnesota
10. Nevada
11. Wisconsin
12. Washington
13. Massachusetts
14. Illinois
15. Hawaii
16. Pennsylvania
17. Oregon
18. Colorado
19. Delaware
20. Arizona
21. Ohio
22. New Hampshire
23. Iowa
24. Vermont
25. Virginia
26. Indiana
27. Florida
28. North Dakota
29. Maine
30. Nebraska
31. North Carolina
32. Texas
33. Utah
34. Wyoming
35. Kansas
36. Missouri
37. Kentucky
38. Montana
39. Idaho
40. Tennessee
41. South Carolina
42. New Mexico
43. Georgia
44. West Virginia
45. Alabama
46. Oklahoma
47. South Dakota
48. Louisiana
49. Arkansas
50. Mississippi

D-15 Local Employment, 1992

State	Local employees #	Local share of state & local employees %	Rank by %
Alabama	154,311	65.5	33
Alaska	21,781	47.3	48
Arizona	145,074	72.9	7
Arkansas	81,988	63.8	39
California	1,107,981	77.5	1
Colorado	132,136	71.4	12
Connecticut	97,013	64.2	38
Delaware	17,508	46.5	49
Florida	499,569	75.2	5
Georgia	282,589	71.2	13
Hawaii	13,882	21.5	50
Idaho	39,846	66.3	30
Illinois	430,555	75.9	3
Indiana	202,428	68.0	27
Iowa	108,439	69.6	20
Kansas	109,182	69.5	21
Kentucky	120,762	61.3	42
Louisiana	160,577	64.4	36
Maine	43,142	66.2	31
Maryland	157,555	65.8	32
Massachusetts	192,263	69.3	23
Michigan	322,618	70.1	19
Minnesota	172,611	71.9	10
Mississippi	107,726	69.4	22
Missouri	173,662	70.1	17
Montana	37,134	68.5	26
Nebraska	70,885	71.1	14
Nevada	46,859	71.0	15
New Hampshire	35,507	68.5	25
New Jersey	301,639	72.3	8
New Mexico	60,209	58.8	43
New York	883,648	76.8	2
North Carolina	259,801	70.4	16
North Dakota	21,047	56.1	47
Ohio	399,414	74.0	6
Oklahoma	120,740	64.3	37
Oregon	105,507	68.0	28
Pennsylvania	366,731	71.9	11
Rhode Island	27,739	58.2	44
South Carolina	123,944	61.5	41
South Dakota	25,655	65.5	34
Tennessee	178,014	70.1	18
Texas	748,291	75.7	4
Utah	53,337	57.4	46
Vermont	17,623	57.7	45
Virginia	229,158	66.4	29
Washington	177,403	64.4	35
West Virginia	58,635	63.6	40
Wisconsin	188,921	72.2	9
Wyoming	25,307	69.2	24
50 States	9,458,346	71.0	
DC	54,655	100.0	
United States	9,513,001	71.2	

Rank in order

By %

1. California
2. New York
3. Illinois
4. Texas
5. Florida
6. Ohio
7. Arizona
8. New Jersey
9. Wisconsin
10. Minnesota
11. Pennsylvania
12. Colorado
13. Georgia
14. Nebraska
15. Nevada
16. North Carolina
17. Missouri
18. Tennessee
19. Michigan
20. Iowa
21. Kansas
22. Mississippi
23. Massachusetts
24. Wyoming
25. New Hampshire
26. Montana
27. Indiana
28. Oregon
29. Virginia
30. Idaho
31. Maine
32. Maryland
33. Alabama
34. South Dakota
35. Washington
36. Louisiana
37. Oklahoma
38. Connecticut
39. Arkansas
40. West Virginia
41. South Carolina
42. Kentucky
43. New Mexico
44. Rhode Island
45. Vermont
46. Utah
47. North Dakota
48. Alaska
49. Delaware
50. Hawaii

D-16 Local Spending Accountability, 1992

State	Local spending raised by other gov't %	Local spending raised by local gov't %	Rank by % non-local	By % non-local
Alabama	40.0	60.0	19	1. New Mexico
Alaska	36.4	63.6	26	2. Delaware
Arizona	41.4	58.6	17	3. Wisconsin
Arkansas	46.1	53.9	6	4. West Virginia
California	45.4	54.6	8	5. Nevada
Colorado	32.6	67.4	36	6. Arkansas
Connecticut	34.6	65.4	31	7. North Carolina
Delaware	50.4	49.6	2	8. California
Florida	29.6	70.4	43	9. Montana
Georgia	28.3	71.7	47	10. Idaho
Hawaii	20.1	79.9	49	11. Kentucky
Idaho	44.9	55.1	10	12. Washington
Illinois	28.5	71.5	46	13. Minnesota
Indiana	39.7	60.3	21	14. Oklahoma
Iowa	37.4	62.6	23	15. Wyoming
Kansas	30.1	69.9	42	16. Mississippi
Kentucky	44.7	55.3	11	17. Arizona
Louisiana	36.8	63.2	24	18. North Dakota
Maine	38.3	61.7	22	19. Alabama
Maryland	29.4	70.6	44	20. South Carolina
Massachusetts	34.0	66.0	33	21. Indiana
Michigan	34.5	65.5	32	22. Maine
Minnesota	43.9	56.1	13	23. Iowa
Mississippi	42.2	57.8	16	24. Louisiana
Missouri	35.3	64.7	30	25. Pennsylvania
Montana	45.1	54.9	9	26. Alaska
Nebraska	28.7	71.3	45	27. New Jersey
Nevada	46.4	53.6	5	28. Utah
New Hampshire	9.6	90.4	50	29. Ohio
New Jersey	36.0	64.0	27	30. Missouri
New Mexico	56.0	44.0	1	31. Connecticut
New York	30.7	69.3	40	32. Michigan
North Carolina	45.7	54.3	7	33. Massachusetts
North Dakota	41.1	58.9	18	34. Oregon
Ohio	35.8	64.2	29	35. Virginia
Oklahoma	42.4	57.6	14	36. Colorado
Oregon	33.5	66.5	34	37. Vermont
Pennsylvania	36.7	63.3	25	38. Tennessee
Rhode Island	31.0	69.0	39	39. Rhode Island
South Carolina	39.8	60.2	20	40. New York
South Dakota	30.7	69.3	41	41. South Dakota
Tennessee	31.8	68.2	38	42. Kansas
Texas	28.2	71.8	48	43. Florida
Utah	35.9	64.1	28	44. Maryland
Vermont	31.9	68.1	37	45. Nebraska
Virginia	33.3	66.7	35	46. Illinois
Washington	44.1	55.9	12	47. Georgia
West Virginia	47.9	52.1	4	48. Texas
Wisconsin	49.0	51.0	3	49. Hawaii
Wyoming	42.3	57.7	15	50. New Hampshire
50 States	36.5	63.5		
DC	33.6	66.4		
United States	36.5	63.5		

State	% registered voters	Rank
Alabama	71	15
Alaska	72	12
Arizona	56	44
Arkansas	60	36
California	54	48
Colorado	64	24
Connecticut	68	18
Delaware	59	41
Florida	56	46
Georgia	55	47
Hawaii	52	49
Idaho	63	28
Illinois	63	28
Indiana	56	45
Iowa	72	12
Kansas	65	22
Kentucky	63	31
Louisiana	71	15
Maine	82	2
Maryland	63	30
Massachusetts	66	21
Michigan	74	6
Minnesota	81	3
Mississippi	73	9
Missouri	72	11
Montana	73	7
Nebraska	73	9
Nevada	50	50
New Hampshire	64	24
New Jersey	62	32
New Mexico	59	40
New York	57	43
North Carolina	61	33
North Dakota	93	1
Ohio	65	23
Oklahoma	66	19
Oregon	73	8
Pennsylvania	59	39
Rhode Island	64	26
South Carolina	61	33
South Dakota	75	5
Tennessee	64	27
Texas	58	42
Utah	59	38
Vermont	71	14
Virginia	60	36
Washington	67	19
West Virginia	61	33
Wisconsin	77	4
Wyoming	69	17
50 States	65	
DC	67	
United States	62	

Rank in order

By %

1. North Dakota
2. Maine
3. Minnesota
4. Wisconsin
5. South Dakota
6. Michigan
7. Montana
8. Oregon
9. Mississippi
10. Nebraska
11. Missouri
12. Alaska
13. Iowa
14. Vermont
15. Alabama
16. Louisiana
17. Wyoming
18. Connecticut
19. Washington
20. Oklahoma
21. Massachusetts
22. Kansas
23. Ohio
24. Colorado
25. New Hampshire
26. Rhode Island
27. Tennessee
28. Idaho
29. Illinois
30. Maryland
31. Kentucky
32. New Jersey
33. North Carolina
34. South Carolina
35. West Virginia
36. Arkansas
37. Virginia
38. Utah
39. Pennsylvania
40. New Mexico
41. Delaware
42. Texas
43. New York
44. Arizona
45. Indiana
46. Florida
47. Georgia
48. California
49. Hawaii
50. Nevada

State	Percent Voting	Rank
Alabama	46	27
Alaska	59	6
Arizona	42	38
Arkansas	42	39
California	45	30
Colorado	46	23
Connecticut	51	14
Delaware	41	40
Florida	42	37
Georgia	35	47
Hawaii	46	26
Idaho	51	15
Illinois	43	35
Indiana	39	44
Iowa	53	11
Kansas	51	17
Kentucky	35	48
Louisiana	34	49
Maine	58	8
Maryland	46	25
Massachusetts	52	13
Michigan	52	12
Minnesota	58	7
Mississippi	44	32
Missouri	55	9
Montana	61	5
Nebraska	54	10
Nevada	40	43
New Hampshire	41	41
New Jersey	40	42
New Mexico	47	20
New York	45	31
North Carolina	36	46
North Dakota	61	3
Ohio	47	22
Oklahoma	47	21
Oregon	61	4
Pennsylvania	43	36
Rhode Island	51	16
South Carolina	45	29
South Dakota	64	1
Tennessee	43	34
Texas	38	45
Utah	44	33
Vermont	49	19
Virginia	46	28
Washington	46	24
West Virginia	34	50
Wisconsin	50	18
Wyoming	64	2
50 States	47	
DC	56	
United States	45	

Rank in order

By %

1. South Dakota
2. Wyoming
3. North Dakota
4. Oregon
5. Montana
6. Alaska
7. Minnesota
8. Maine
9. Missouri
10. Nebraska
11. Iowa
12. Michigan
13. Massachusetts
14. Connecticut
15. Idaho
16. Rhode Island
17. Kansas
18. Wisconsin
19. Vermont
20. New Mexico
21. Oklahoma
22. Ohio
23. Colorado
24. Washington
25. Maryland
26. Hawaii
27. Alabama
28. Virginia
29. South Carolina
30. California
31. New York
32. Mississippi
33. Utah
34. Tennessee
35. Illinois
36. Pennsylvania
37. Florida
38. Arizona
39. Arkansas
40. Delaware
41. New Hampshire
42. New Jersey
43. Nevada
44. Indiana
45. Texas
46. North Carolina
47. Georgia
48. Kentucky
49. Louisiana
50. West Virginia

State	# of initiatives	initiatives approved by voters	Rank by # of initiatives
Alabama	0	0	n/a
Alaska	10	5	10
Arizona	16	5	3
Arkansas	10	5	10
California	58	27	1
Colorado	14	6	4
Connecticut	0	0	n/a
Delaware	0	0	n/a
Florida	4	2	21
Georgia	0	0	n/a
Hawaii	0	0	n/a
Idaho	5	4	17
Illinois	0	0	n/a
Indiana	0	0	n/a
Iowa	0	0	n/a
Kansas	0	0	n/a
Kentucky	0	0	n/a
Louisiana	0	0	n/a
Maine	12	6	8
Maryland	0	0	n/a
Massachusetts	11	5	9
Michigan	6	2	16
Minnesota	0	0	n/a
Mississippi	0	0	n/a
Missouri	7	3	14
Montana	13	5	7
Nebraska	5	2	17
Nevada	7	3	14
New Hampshire	0	0	n/a
New Jersey	0	0	n/a
New Mexico	0	0	n/a
New York	0	0	n/a
North Carolina	0	0	n/a
North Dakota	14	3	4
Ohio	8	0	13
Oklahoma	5	4	17
Oregon	37	16	2
Pennsylvania	0	0	n/a
Rhode Island	0	0	n/a
South Carolina	0	0	n/a
South Dakota	10	6	10
Tennessee	0	0	n/a
Texas	0	0	n/a
Utah	5	0	17
Vermont	0	0	n/a
Virginia	0	0	n/a
Washington	14	6	4
West Virginia	0	0	n/a
Wisconsin	0	0	n/a
Wyoming	0	0	n/a
50 States	271	115	
DC	0	0	
United States	271	115	

Rank in order

By #

1. California
2. Oregon
3. Arizona
4. Colorado
4. North Dakota
4. Washington
7. Montana
8. Maine
9. Massachusetts
10. Alaska
10. Arkansas
10. South Dakota
13. Ohio
14. Missouri
14. Nevada
16. Michigan
17. Idaho
17. Nebraska
17. Oklahoma
17. Utah
21. Florida

Federal Impacts

State	Total federal spending $ (millions)	per capita federal spending $	Rank by per capita		By per capita
Alabama	22,280	5,281	13		1. Alaska
Alaska	4,640	7,656	1		2. Maryland
Arizona	19,011	4,665	30		3. Virginia
Arkansas	11,376	4,638	31		4. New Mexico
California	155,391	4,944	23		5. Hawaii
Colorado	18,989	5,194	16		6. North Dakota
Connecticut	16,591	5,066	18		7. Missouri
Delaware	2,950	4,179	42		8. Massachusetts
Florida	71,092	5,095	17		9. Rhode Island
Georgia	32,067	4,545	35		10. Montana
Hawaii	7,603	6,449	5		11. Maine
Idaho	4,965	4,382	36		12. South Dakota
Illinois	49,936	4,249	39		13. Alabama
Indiana	22,104	3,843	50		14. Mississippi
Iowa	12,979	4,588	32		15. West Virginia
Kansas	12,506	4,897	25		16. Colorado
Kentucky	17,504	4,574	34		17. Florida
Louisiana	21,672	5,022	20		18. Connecticut
Maine	6,708	5,409	11		19. Pennsylvania
Maryland	36,576	7,306	2		20. Louisiana
Massachusetts	35,374	5,856	8		21. Washington
Michigan	38,975	4,104	45		22. New York
Minnesota	18,797	4,116	44		23. California
Mississippi	14,072	5,272	14		24. Wyoming
Missouri	31,766	6,019	7		25. Kansas
Montana	4,638	5,418	10		26. Tennessee
Nebraska	7,439	4,584	33		27. Oklahoma
Nevada	6,104	4,189	41		28. New Jersey
New Hampshire	4,636	4,078	47		29. South Carolina
New Jersey	37,328	4,723	28		30. Arizona
New Mexico	11,274	6,816	4		31. Arkansas
New York	90,346	4,973	22		32. Iowa
North Carolina	28,858	4,082	46		33. Nebraska
North Dakota	3,909	6,127	6		34. Kentucky
Ohio	48,023	4,326	37		35. Georgia
Oklahoma	15,718	4,824	27		36. Idaho
Oregon	13,057	4,231	40		37. Ohio
Pennsylvania	61,025	5,064	19		38. Texas
Rhode Island	5,473	5,489	9		39. Illinois
South Carolina	17,097	4,666	29		40. Oregon
South Dakota	3,814	5,289	12		41. Nevada
Tennessee	25,056	4,842	26		42. Delaware
Texas	79,308	4,315	38		43. Vermont
Utah	7,594	3,980	48		44. Minnesota
Vermont	2,411	4,157	43		45. Michigan
Virginia	45,890	7,004	3		46. North Carolina
Washington	26,644	4,987	21		47. New Hampshire
West Virginia	9,550	5,242	15		48. Utah
Wisconsin	19,670	3,870	49		49. Wisconsin
Wyoming	2,344	4,924	24		50. Indiana
50 States	1,263,130	4,991			
DC	21,766	38,186			
United States	1,320,132	4,996			

CQ State Fact Finder

State	% increase in federal spending %	Rank	Rank in order By %
Alabama	47.3	13	1. Maine
Alaska	54.5	5	2. Georgia
Arizona	41.9	23	3. Nevada
Arkansas	44.1	15	4. West Virginia
California	43.0	21	5. Alaska
Colorado	35.4	39	6. North Carolina
Connecticut	4.8	50	7. Florida
Delaware	39.8	28	8. Mississippi
Florida	52.1	7	9. Oregon
Georgia	57.1	2	10. Louisiana
Hawaii	40.2	27	11. Tennessee
Idaho	33.2	41	12. Michigan
Illinois	43.6	18	13. Alabama
Indiana	38.7	32	14. Maryland
Iowa	31.9	43	15. Arkansas
Kansas	35.8	36	16. Texas
Kentucky	41.5	24	17. Pennsylvania
Louisiana	50.9	10	18. Illinois
Maine	66.7	1	19. New Jersey
Maryland	46.1	14	20. Rhode Island
Massachusetts	23.6	48	21. California
Michigan	49.0	12	22. Virginia
Minnesota	29.3	45	23. Arizona
Mississippi	51.9	8	24. Kentucky
Missouri	35.7	37	25. Montana
Montana	41.3	25	26. Oklahoma
Nebraska	27.3	47	27. Hawaii
Nevada	56.6	3	28. Delaware
New Hampshire	35.6	38	29. New York
New Jersey	43.1	19	30. Vermont
New Mexico	38.5	33	31. South Carolina
New York	39.4	29	32. Indiana
North Carolina	52.6	6	33. New Mexico
North Dakota	28.5	46	34. Washington
Ohio	32.4	42	35. Wyoming
Oklahoma	41.1	26	36. Kansas
Oregon	51.8	9	37. Missouri
Pennsylvania	43.7	17	38. New Hampshire
Rhode Island	43.1	20	39. Colorado
South Carolina	38.8	31	40. Wisconsin
South Dakota	31.1	44	41. Idaho
Tennessee	49.5	11	42. Ohio
Texas	43.9	16	43. Iowa
Utah	22.3	49	44. South Dakota
Vermont	38.9	30	45. Minnesota
Virginia	42.9	22	46. North Dakota
Washington	38.1	34	47. Nebraska
West Virginia	55.5	4	48. Massachusetts
Wisconsin	35.3	40	49. Utah
Wyoming	38.0	35	50. Connecticut
50 States	40.9		
DC	36.9		
United States	41.2		

State	federal grants to state & local government $ (millions)	Per capita federal grants to st. & loc. govt $	Rank by per capita	By per capita
E-3 Federal Grants To State & Local Governments, 1994				Rank in order
Alabama	3,209	761	26	1. Alaska
Alaska	1,063	1,755	1	2. Wyoming
Arizona	2,996	735	31	3. New York
Arkansas	1,966	802	21	4. Louisiana
California	26,219	834	18	5. West Virginia
Colorado	2,102	575	47	6. Rhode Island
Connecticut	3,028	924	15	7. North Dakota
Delaware	472	669	43	8. Montana
Florida	8,018	575	48	9. Massachusetts
Georgia	5,028	713	36	10. New Mexico
Hawaii	1,088	923	16	11. Maine
Idaho	778	686	40	12. South Dakota
Illinois	8,506	724	35	13. Vermont
Indiana	3,553	618	46	14. Mississippi
Iowa	2,015	712	37	15. Connecticut
Kansas	1,666	652	44	16. Hawaii
Kentucky	3,096	809	19	17. New Hampshire
Louisiana	5,233	1,213	4	18. California
Maine	1,269	1,023	11	19. Kentucky
Maryland	3,637	727	33	20. Pennsylvania
Massachusetts	6,261	1,036	9	21. Arkansas
Michigan	7,117	749	29	22. New Jersey
Minnesota	3,515	770	23	23. Minnesota
Mississippi	2,507	939	14	24. Oregon
Missouri	3,971	752	28	25. Tennessee
Montana	906	1,059	8	26. Alabama
Nebraska	1,114	686	41	27. Ohio
Nevada	797	547	49	28. Missouri
New Hampshire	956	840	17	29. Michigan
New Jersey	6,163	780	22	30. South Carolina
New Mexico	1,714	1,036	10	31. Arizona
New York	22,445	1,235	3	32. Washington
North Carolina	4,862	688	39	33. Maryland
North Dakota	702	1,100	7	34. Oklahoma
Ohio	8,366	754	27	35. Illinois
Oklahoma	2,359	724	34	36. Georgia
Oregon	2,355	763	24	37. Iowa
Pennsylvania	9,705	805	20	38. Texas
Rhode Island	1,100	1,103	6	39. North Carolina
South Carolina	2,726	744	30	40. Idaho
South Dakota	724	1,004	12	41. Nebraska
Tennessee	3,940	761	25	42. Wisconsin
Texas	12,669	689	38	43. Delaware
Utah	1,209	634	45	44. Kansas
Vermont	546	942	13	45. Utah
Virginia	3,180	485	50	46. Indiana
Washington	3,924	734	32	47. Colorado
West Virginia	2,166	1,189	5	48. Florida
Wisconsin	3,450	679	42	49. Nevada
Wyoming	714	1,501	2	50. Virginia
50 States	207,105	814		
DC	2,222	3,898		
United States	214,239	811		

E-4 Federal Spending Per Capita On Procurement, 1994

State	Per capita Federal procurement spending $	Rank
Alabama	797	13
Alaska	1,661	3
Arizona	657	22
Arkansas	243	45
California	968	8
Colorado	1,223	6
Connecticut	840	11
Delaware	236	47
Florida	595	24
Georgia	680	21
Hawaii	768	14
Idaho	745	16
Illinois	274	38
Indiana	291	37
Iowa	225	48
Kansas	451	27
Kentucky	345	34
Louisiana	704	19
Maine	825	12
Maryland	1,644	4
Massachusetts	1,094	7
Michigan	261	41
Minnesota	394	30
Mississippi	860	10
Missouri	1,412	5
Montana	239	46
Nebraska	345	33
Nevada	717	18
New Hampshire	429	29
New Jersey	534	25
New Mexico	2,174	1
New York	338	35
North Carolina	268	40
North Dakota	329	36
Ohio	430	28
Oklahoma	350	32
Oregon	160	50
Pennsylvania	375	31
Rhode Island	501	26
South Carolina	743	17
South Dakota	273	39
Tennessee	865	9
Texas	699	20
Utah	624	23
Vermont	188	49
Virginia	1,784	2
Washington	765	15
West Virginia	244	44
Wisconsin	252	43
Wyoming	255	42
50 States	642	
DC	7,198	
United States	749	

Rank in order

By per capita

1. New Mexico
2. Virginia
3. Alaska
4. Maryland
5. Missouri
6. Colorado
7. Massachusetts
8. California
9. Tennessee
10. Mississippi
11. Connecticut
12. Maine
13. Alabama
14. Hawaii
15. Washington
16. Idaho
17. South Carolina
18. Nevada
19. Louisiana
20. Texas
21. Georgia
22. Arizona
23. Utah
24. Florida
25. New Jersey
26. Rhode Island
27. Kansas
28. Ohio
29. New Hampshire
30. Minnesota
31. Pennsylvania
32. Oklahoma
33. Nebraska
34. Kentucky
35. New York
36. North Dakota
37. Indiana
38. Illinois
39. South Dakota
40. North Carolina
41. Michigan
42. Wyoming
43. Wisconsin
44. West Virginia
45. Arkansas
46. Montana
47. Delaware
48. Iowa
49. Vermont
50. Oregon

E-5 Federal Spending On Payments To Individuals, 1994

State	Total federal payment to individuals $ (millions)	Per capita federal payment to individuals $	Rank by per capita	By per capita
Alabama	11,996	2,843	9	1. Florida
Alaska	924	1,525	50	2. West Virginia
Arizona	10,558	2,591	27	3. Pennsylvania
Arkansas	7,298	2,975	5	4. Rhode Island
California	75,466	2,401	38	5. Arkansas
Colorado	7,987	2,185	48	6. Massachusetts
Connecticut	8,902	2,718	14	7. New Jersey
Delaware	1,784	2,527	30	8. New York
Florida	46,381	3,324	1	9. Alabama
Georgia	15,486	2,195	47	10. Maine
Hawaii	2,898	2,458	35	11. Missouri
Idaho	2,520	2,224	45	12. Oklahoma
Illinois	31,367	2,669	21	13. Mississippi
Indiana	13,804	2,400	39	14. Connecticut
Iowa	7,590	2,683	18	15. Maryland
Kansas	6,914	2,707	16	16. Kansas
Kentucky	10,068	2,631	23	17. Michigan
Louisiana	10,656	2,470	34	18. Iowa
Maine	3,518	2,837	10	19. Oregon
Maryland	13,600	2,717	15	20. North Dakota
Massachusetts	17,672	2,925	6	21. Illinois
Michigan	25,535	2,689	17	22. Ohio
Minnesota	10,113	2,214	46	23. Kentucky
Mississippi	7,308	2,738	13	24. Montana
Missouri	14,889	2,821	11	25. Virginia
Montana	2,250	2,629	24	26. Tennessee
Nebraska	4,178	2,574	28	27. Arizona
Nevada	3,409	2,340	40	28. Nebraska
New Hampshire	2,648	2,329	42	29. South Dakota
New Jersey	22,685	2,870	7	30. Delaware
New Mexico	4,041	2,443	36	31. Washington
New York	51,909	2,857	8	32. Wisconsin
North Carolina	16,481	2,331	41	33. Vermont
North Dakota	1,704	2,671	20	34. Louisiana
Ohio	29,488	2,656	22	35. Hawaii
Oklahoma	8,943	2,745	12	36. New Mexico
Oregon	8,275	2,681	19	37. South Carolina
Pennsylvania	39,193	3,252	3	38. California
Rhode Island	3,109	3,118	4	39. Indiana
South Carolina	8,839	2,412	37	40. Nevada
South Dakota	1,848	2,563	29	41. North Carolina
Tennessee	13,461	2,601	26	42. New Hampshire
Texas	41,079	2,235	44	43. Wyoming
Utah	3,444	1,805	49	44. Texas
Vermont	1,435	2,474	33	45. Idaho
Virginia	17,168	2,620	25	46. Minnesota
Washington	13,381	2,504	31	47. Georgia
West Virginia	6,003	3,295	2	48. Colorado
Wisconsin	12,616	2,482	32	49. Utah
Wyoming	1,070	2,248	43	50. Alaska
50 States	683,891	2,633		
DC	2,523	4,426		
United States	691,666	2,657		

E-6 Federal Spending Per Capita On Social Security And Medicare, 1994

State	Per Capita Social Security & Medicare spending $	Rank	Rank in order By per capita
Alabama	1,872	24	1. Pennsylvania
Alaska	661	50	2. Florida
Arizona	1,790	30	3. West Virginia
Arkansas	2,090	12	4. Massachusetts
California	1,622	37	5. Rhode Island
Colorado	1,415	47	6. New Jersey
Connecticut	2,182	7	7. Connecticut
Delaware	1,863	25	8. New York
Florida	2,443	2	9. Iowa
Georgia	1,429	46	10. Michigan
Hawaii	1,415	48	11. Missouri
Idaho	1,547	41	12. Arkansas
Illinois	2,045	14	13. North Dakota
Indiana	1,918	21	14. Illinois
Iowa	2,166	9	15. Kansas
Kansas	2,032	15	16. Ohio
Kentucky	1,817	28	17. Maine
Louisiana	1,674	34	18. Wisconsin
Maine	2,012	17	19. Nebraska
Maryland	1,644	36	20. Oregon
Massachusetts	2,246	4	21. Indiana
Michigan	2,148	10	22. South Dakota
Minnesota	1,709	33	23. Oklahoma
Mississippi	1,787	31	24. Alabama
Missouri	2,126	11	25. Delaware
Montana	1,837	26	26. Montana
Nebraska	1,956	19	27. Tennessee
Nevada	1,536	42	28. Kentucky
New Hampshire	1,746	32	29. Vermont
New Jersey	2,213	6	30. Arizona
New Mexico	1,466	45	31. Mississippi
New York	2,179	8	32. New Hampshire
North Carolina	1,658	35	33. Minnesota
North Dakota	2,076	13	34. Louisiana
Ohio	2,026	16	35. North Carolina
Oklahoma	1,900	23	36. Maryland
Oregon	1,941	20	37. California
Pennsylvania	2,489	1	38. Washington
Rhode Island	2,235	5	39. South Carolina
South Carolina	1,590	39	40. Wyoming
South Dakota	1,913	22	41. Idaho
Tennessee	1,823	27	42. Nevada
Texas	1,478	44	43. Virginia
Utah	1,122	49	44. Texas
Vermont	1,815	29	45. New Mexico
Virginia	1,489	43	46. Georgia
Washington	1,603	38	47. Colorado
West Virginia	2,306	3	48. Hawaii
Wisconsin	2,011	18	49. Utah
Wyoming	1,553	40	50. Alaska
50 States	n/a		
DC	2,177		
United States	1,876		

E-7 Social Security Benefits Paid, 1993

State	Social Security amounts paid (000)	# of recipients #	SS average monthly benefit $	Rank by aver. benefit	By $
Alabama	412,057	752,836	547	46	1. Connecticut
Alaska	23,041	39,598	582	33	2. New Jersey
Arizona	409,793	660,973	620	22	3. New York
Arkansas	267,467	496,825	538	49	4. Illinois
California	2,422,001	3,891,546	622	18	5. Michigan
Colorado	279,093	469,766	594	30	6. Delaware
Connecticut	379,436	553,948	685	1	7. Pennsylvania
Delaware	73,202	113,582	644	6	8. Indiana
Florida	1,780,118	2,868,868	620	20	9. Washington
Georgia	541,317	964,901	561	43	10. Wisconsin
Hawaii	95,954	158,773	604	26	11. New Hampshire
Idaho	100,745	170,166	592	31	12. Nevada
Illinois	1,181,401	1,817,216	650	4	13. Oregon
Indiana	610,911	957,920	638	8	14. Kansas
Iowa	329,845	536,624	615	23	15. Rhode Island
Kansas	267,648	426,267	628	14	16. Massachusetts
Kentucky	374,612	684,801	547	47	17. Ohio
Louisiana	371,841	688,744	540	48	18. California
Maine	128,853	227,813	566	41	19. Maryland
Maryland	405,765	652,323	622	19	20. Florida
Massachusetts	640,351	1,023,498	626	16	21. Vermont
Michigan	1,018,943	1,569,530	649	5	22. Arizona
Minnesota	423,577	701,731	604	27	23. Iowa
Mississippi	244,412	477,229	512	50	24. Wyoming
Missouri	572,584	957,066	598	29	25. Nebraska
Montana	85,959	145,953	589	32	26. Hawaii
Nebraska	168,014	277,252	606	25	27. Minnesota
Nevada	129,394	205,729	629	12	28. Utah
New Hampshire	110,317	175,248	629	11	29. Missouri
New Jersey	879,425	1,291,165	681	2	30. Colorado
New Mexico	133,540	242,244	551	45	31. Idaho
New York	1,929,541	2,937,044	657	3	32. Montana
North Carolina	670,816	1,173,464	572	38	33. Alaska
North Dakota	65,188	114,753	568	39	34. West Virginia
Ohio	1,170,322	1,879,844	623	17	35. Virginia
Oklahoma	325,080	561,741	579	36	36. Oklahoma
Oregon	330,487	525,620	629	13	37. Texas
Pennsylvania	1,478,950	2,312,918	639	7	38. North Carolina
Rhode Island	117,181	187,009	627	15	39. North Dakota
South Carolina	335,212	591,982	566	40	40. South Carolina
South Dakota	73,592	132,640	555	44	41. Maine
Tennessee	499,943	890,469	561	42	42. Tennessee
Texas	1,372,763	2,378,744	577	37	43. Georgia
Utah	128,501	212,907	604	28	44. South Dakota
Vermont	58,694	94,622	620	21	45. New Mexico
Virginia	524,159	905,049	579	35	46. Alabama
Washington	486,833	763,414	638	9	47. Kentucky
West Virginia	222,516	382,858	581	34	48. Louisiana
Wisconsin	548,906	870,750	630	10	49. Arkansas
Wyoming	41,175	67,278	612	24	50. Mississippi
50 States	25,241,475	41,183,241	613		
DC	41,064	77,745	528		
United States	25,662,234	42,245,733	607		

E-8 Federal Spending On Employee Wages & Salaries, 1994

State	Total federal spending on wages & salaries $ (000)	Per capita spending on wages & salaries ($)	Rank by per capita
Alabama	3,124,963	741	15
Alaska	1,367,420	2,256	1
Arizona	2,268,568	557	27
Arkansas	1,019,962	416	42
California	18,829,975	599	24
Colorado	3,540,058	968	5
Connecticut	1,404,522	429	41
Delaware	455,420	645	20
Florida	7,262,593	521	31
Georgia	5,944,727	843	8
Hawaii	2,498,305	2,119	2
Idaho	611,479	540	29
Illinois	5,402,257	460	39
Indiana	2,100,938	365	46
Iowa	953,878	337	48
Kansas	1,892,117	741	14
Kentucky	2,607,970	681	19
Louisiana	2,135,549	495	34
Maine	772,946	623	23
Maryland	7,414,466	1,481	4
Massachusetts	3,112,100	515	33
Michigan	2,886,704	304	49
Minnesota	1,617,440	354	47
Mississippi	1,538,504	576	26
Missouri	3,331,943	631	22
Montana	610,638	713	16
Nebraska	971,440	599	25
Nevada	762,978	524	30
New Hampshire	432,384	380	45
New Jersey	3,738,702	473	36
New Mexico	1,590,247	961	6
New York	7,427,713	409	43
North Carolina	4,832,860	684	17
North Dakota	566,230	888	7
Ohio	4,466,688	402	44
Oklahoma	2,626,762	806	9
Oregon	1,418,829	460	38
Pennsylvania	5,802,343	481	35
Rhode Island	641,400	643	21
South Carolina	2,502,954	683	18
South Dakota	541,339	751	13
Tennessee	2,669,391	516	32
Texas	9,999,144	544	28
Utah	1,479,163	775	11
Vermont	267,897	462	37
Virginia	12,147,347	1,854	3
Washington	4,186,920	784	10
West Virginia	787,820	432	40
Wisconsin	1,395,848	275	50
Wyoming	357,727	752	12
50 States	156,319,568	689	
DC	11,415,021	20,026	
United States	168,951,181	639	

Rank in order

By per capita

1. Alaska
2. Hawaii
3. Virginia
4. Maryland
5. Colorado
6. New Mexico
7. North Dakota
8. Georgia
9. Oklahoma
10. Washington
11. Utah
12. Wyoming
13. South Dakota
14. Kansas
15. Alabama
16. Montana
17. North Carolina
18. South Carolina
19. Kentucky
20. Delaware
21. Rhode Island
22. Missouri
23. Maine
24. California
25. Nebraska
26. Mississippi
27. Arizona
28. Texas
29. Idaho
30. Nevada
31. Florida
32. Tennessee
33. Massachusetts
34. Louisiana
35. Pennsylvania
36. New Jersey
37. Vermont
38. Oregon
39. Illinois
40. West Virginia
41. Connecticut
42. Arkansas
43. New York
44. Ohio
45. New Hampshire
46. Indiana
47. Minnesota
48. Iowa
49. Michigan
50. Wisconsin

E-9 Federal Grant Spending Per Dollar Of State Tax Revenue, 1993

State	Federal aid per dollar of state tax revenue $	Rank
Alabama	0.63	12
Alaska	0.40	42
Arizona	0.41	40
Arkansas	0.62	14
California	0.48	28
Colorado	0.55	20
Connecticut	0.36	47
Delaware	0.33	49
Florida	0.43	37
Georgia	0.53	24
Hawaii	0.37	45
Idaho	0.43	38
Illinois	0.43	39
Indiana	0.54	22
Iowa	0.46	31
Kansas	0.50	26
Kentucky	0.53	25
Louisiana	0.99	2
Maine	0.59	16
Maryland	0.38	44
Massachusetts	0.45	32
Michigan	0.49	27
Minnesota	0.37	46
Mississippi	0.74	5
Missouri	0.58	18
Montana	0.67	10
Nebraska	0.48	29
Nevada	0.27	50
New Hampshire	0.79	4
New Jersey	0.44	33
New Mexico	0.44	34
New York	0.60	15
North Carolina	0.44	35
North Dakota	0.71	7
Ohio	0.54	23
Oklahoma	0.44	36
Oregon	0.63	13
Pennsylvania	0.47	30
Rhode Island	0.64	11
South Carolina	0.57	19
South Dakota	0.98	3
Tennessee	0.70	9
Texas	0.59	17
Utah	0.55	21
Vermont	0.71	8
Virginia	0.36	48
Washington	0.39	43
West Virginia	0.72	6
Wisconsin	0.41	41
Wyoming	1.02	1
50 States	n/a	
DC	n/a	
United States	0.50	

Rank in order

By $

1. Wyoming
2. Louisiana
3. South Dakota
4. New Hampshire
5. Mississippi
6. West Virginia
7. North Dakota
8. Vermont
9. Tennessee
10. Montana
11. Rhode Island
12. Alabama
13. Oregon
14. Arkansas
15. New York
16. Maine
17. Texas
18. Missouri
19. South Carolina
20. Colorado
21. Utah
22. Indiana
23. Ohio
24. Georgia
25. Kentucky
26. Kansas
27. Michigan
28. California
29. Nebraska
30. Pennsylvania
31. Iowa
32. Massachusetts
33. New Jersey
34. New Mexico
35. North Carolina
36. Oklahoma
37. Florida
38. Idaho
39. Illinois
40. Arizona
41. Wisconsin
42. Alaska
43. Washington
44. Maryland
45. Hawaii
46. Minnesota
47. Connecticut
48. Virginia
49. Delaware
50. Nevada

State	General revenue from federal government ($000)	% of Revenue from federal government %	Rank by total $
Alabama	2,929,047	22.8	22
Alaska	849,160	12.6	41
Arizona	2,160,807	16.8	28
Arkansas	1,719,560	25.0	32
California	24,211,907	18.9	1
Colorado	2,085,738	16.3	29
Connecticut	2,472,135	16.4	25
Delaware	437,497	14.5	50
Florida	6,354,625	13.8	8
Georgia	4,241,502	19.0	11
Hawaii	939,362	16.6	40
Idaho	667,901	19.4	46
Illinois	6,735,492	16.5	6
Indiana	3,327,380	18.0	16
Iowa	1,734,922	17.1	31
Kansas	1,418,133	16.7	34
Kentucky	2,792,097	22.8	23
Louisiana	4,017,741	25.8	13
Maine	998,706	21.3	38
Maryland	2,987,667	16.3	20
Massachusetts	4,848,898	18.9	10
Michigan	6,405,529	17.8	7
Minnesota	3,125,791	15.9	19
Mississippi	2,181,585	28.2	27
Missouri	3,205,573	20.7	18
Montana	772,907	25.1	43
Nebraska	987,192	17.1	39
Nevada	714,344	15.1	44
New Hampshire	784,340	19.6	42
New Jersey	5,374,269	14.8	9
New Mexico	1,238,107	20.6	35
New York	19,161,197	18.6	2
North Carolina	4,111,927	19.0	12
North Dakota	603,951	24.6	47
Ohio	7,083,038	19.0	5
Oklahoma	1,892,038	19.1	30
Oregon	2,416,049	20.1	26
Pennsylvania	8,798,896	19.3	4
Rhode Island	1,012,702	25.4	37
South Carolina	2,529,770	22.2	24
South Dakota	599,101	26.1	48
Tennessee	3,689,919	24.3	14
Texas	9,369,343	16.5	3
Utah	1,187,935	20.0	36
Vermont	517,956	22.1	49
Virginia	2,954,671	13.9	21
Washington	3,331,638	16.5	15
West Virginia	1,538,761	25.9	33
Wisconsin	3,211,840	16.8	17
Wyoming	676,964	26.7	45
50 States	177,407,610	19.5	
DC	1,776,195	26.5	
United States	179,183,805	18.4	

Rank in order

By $

1. California
2. New York
3. Texas
4. Pennsylvania
5. Ohio
6. Illinois
7. Michigan
8. Florida
9. New Jersey
10. Massachusetts
11. Georgia
12. North Carolina
13. Louisiana
14. Tennessee
15. Washington
16. Indiana
17. Wisconsin
18. Missouri
19. Minnesota
20. Maryland
21. Virginia
22. Alabama
23. Kentucky
24. South Carolina
25. Connecticut
26. Oregon
27. Mississippi
28. Arizona
29. Colorado
30. Oklahoma
31. Iowa
32. Arkansas
33. West Virginia
34. Kansas
35. New Mexico
36. Utah
37. Rhode Island
38. Maine
39. Nebraska
40. Hawaii
41. Alaska
42. New Hampshire
43. Montana
44. Nevada
45. Wyoming
46. Idaho
47. North Dakota
48. South Dakota
49. Vermont
50. Delaware

E-11 Federal Tax Burden Per Capita, 1995

State	Federal tax burden total ($million)	Federal tax burden per capita ($)	Rank by per capita
Alabama	16,660	3,922	41
Alaska	3,591	5,797	6
Arizona	16,578	3,981	40
Arkansas	9,248	3,751	46
California	163,851	5,130	17
Colorado	19,211	5,182	15
Connecticut	25,583	7,769	1
Delaware	4,261	5,969	5
Florida	70,770	4,974	20
Georgia	31,605	4,414	31
Hawaii	6,409	5,370	12
Idaho	4,569	3,986	39
Illinois	67,747	5,739	8
Indiana	26,121	4,518	28
Iowa	12,148	4,287	33
Kansas	12,272	4,773	24
Kentucky	14,755	3,836	44
Louisiana	16,631	3,848	43
Maine	5,115	4,094	36
Maryland	29,240	5,777	7
Massachusetts	37,129	6,113	4
Michigan	48,364	5,072	19
Minnesota	24,037	5,220	14
Mississippi	8,508	3,170	50
Missouri	24,356	4,585	25
Montana	3,499	4,060	37
Nebraska	7,473	4,583	27
Nevada	8,114	5,401	10
New Hampshire	6,265	5,441	9
New Jersey	54,793	6,889	2
New Mexico	6,128	3,654	47
New York	112,905	6,185	3
North Carolina	30,182	4,220	34
North Dakota	2,574	4,026	38
Ohio	53,924	4,836	22
Oklahoma	12,816	3,908	42
Oregon	14,296	4,585	26
Pennsylvania	62,586	5,173	16
Rhode Island	5,292	5,279	13
South Carolina	14,026	3,788	45
South Dakota	3,032	4,181	35
Tennessee	22,921	4,391	32
Texas	83,956	4,501	29
Utah	6,924	3,574	48
Vermont	2,629	4,493	30
Virginia	33,767	5,090	18
Washington	29,142	5,374	11
West Virginia	6,463	3,547	49
Wisconsin	24,466	4,783	23
Wyoming	2,314	4,844	21
50 States	1,309,246	4,762	
DC	4,207	7,396	
United States	1,313,454	4,996	

Rank in order

By per capita

1. Connecticut
2. New Jersey
3. New York
4. Massachusetts
5. Delaware
6. Alaska
7. Maryland
8. Illinois
9. New Hampshire
10. Nevada
11. Washington
12. Hawaii
13. Rhode Island
14. Minnesota
15. Colorado
16. Pennsylvania
17. California
18. Virginia
19. Michigan
20. Florida
21. Wyoming
22. Ohio
23. Wisconsin
24. Kansas
25. Missouri
26. Oregon
27. Nebraska
28. Indiana
29. Texas
30. Vermont
31. Georgia
32. Tennessee
33. Iowa
34. North Carolina
35. South Dakota
36. Maine
37. Montana
38. North Dakota
39. Idaho
40. Arizona
41. Alabama
42. Oklahoma
43. Louisiana
44. Kentucky
45. South Carolina
46. Arkansas
47. New Mexico
48. Utah
49. West Virginia
50. Mississippi

State	Spending per $ of taxes $	Rank	Rank in order By $
Alabama	1.37	6	1. New Mexico
Alaska	1.32	11	2. Mississippi
Arizona	1.17	19	3. North Dakota
Arkansas	1.26	14	4. West Virginia
California	0.97	33	5. Virginia
Colorado	1.01	30	6. Alabama
Connecticut	0.66	50	7. Montana
Delaware	0.71	48	8. Maine
Florida	1.03	28	9. Louisiana
Georgia	1.04	25	9. Missouri
Hawaii	1.21	17	11. Alaska
Idaho	1.11	22	12. South Dakota
Illinois	0.75	47	13. Maryland
Indiana	0.87	40	14. Arkansas
Iowa	1.09	23	14. Oklahoma
Kansas	1.04	25	16. South Carolina
Kentucky	1.21	17	17. Hawaii
Louisiana	1.33	9	17. Kentucky
Maine	1.34	8	19. Arizona
Maryland	1.28	13	20. Tennessee
Massachusetts	0.97	33	20. Utah
Michigan	0.82	41	22. Idaho
Minnesota	0.80	44	23. Iowa
Mississippi	1.69	2	24. Rhode Island
Missouri	1.33	9	25. Georgia
Montana	1.36	7	25. Kansas
Nebraska	1.02	29	25. Wyoming
Nevada	0.77	45	28. Florida
New Hampshire	0.76	46	29. Nebraska
New Jersey	0.70	49	30. Colorado
New Mexico	1.88	1	31. Pennsylvania
New York	0.82	41	32. North Carolina
North Carolina	0.98	32	33. California
North Dakota	1.55	3	33. Massachusetts
Ohio	0.91	39	33. Texas
Oklahoma	1.26	14	36. Vermont
Oregon	0.93	37	37. Oregon
Pennsylvania	1.00	31	37. Washington
Rhode Island	1.05	24	39. Ohio
South Carolina	1.25	16	40. Indiana
South Dakota	1.29	12	41. Michigan
Tennessee	1.12	20	41. New York
Texas	0.97	33	41. Wisconsin
Utah	1.12	20	44. Minnesota
Vermont	0.94	36	45. Nevada
Virginia	1.39	5	46. New Hampshire
Washington	0.93	37	47. Illinois
West Virginia	1.51	4	48. Delaware
Wisconsin	0.82	41	49. New Jersey
Wyoming	1.04	25	50. Connecticut
50 States	n/a		
DC	5.27		
United States	1.00		

State	Charges Returned %	Rank by highest to lowest	Rank in order By high to low
Alabama	98	46	1. Hawaii
Alaska	602	2	2. Alaska
Arizona	114	31	3. Massachusetts
Arkansas	123	28	4. Rhode Island
California	115	30	5. Montana
Colorado	128	26	6. North Dakota
Connecticut	206	8	7. South Dakota
Delaware	168	13	8. Connecticut
Florida	102	39	9. Wyoming
Georgia	96	49	10. Vermont
Hawaii	707	1	11. Idaho
Idaho	184	11	12. West Virginia
Illinois	130	25	13. Delaware
Indiana	101	41	14. Minnesota
Iowa	135	20	15. Washington
Kansas	126	27	16. New Mexico
Kentucky	112	33	17. Maine
Louisiana	112	33	18. Nebraska
Maine	143	17	19. New Hampshire
Maryland	108	37	20. Iowa
Massachusetts	362	3	20. New York
Michigan	100	43	22. Nevada
Minnesota	156	14	23. New Jersey
Mississippi	100	43	24. Pennsylvania
Missouri	106	38	25. Illinois
Montana	257	5	26. Colorado
Nebraska	141	18	27. Kansas
Nevada	133	22	28. Arkansas
New Hampshire	140	19	29. Oregon
New Jersey	132	23	30. California
New Mexico	150	16	31. Arizona
New York	135	20	31. Utah
North Carolina	102	39	33. Kentucky
North Dakota	226	6	33. Louisiana
Ohio	109	36	33. Wisconsin
Oklahoma	101	41	36. Ohio
Oregon	120	29	37. Maryland
Pennsylvania	131	24	38. Missouri
Rhode Island	260	4	39. Florida
South Carolina	83	50	39. North Carolina
South Dakota	220	7	41. Indiana
Tennessee	97	48	41. Oklahoma
Texas	98	46	43. Michigan
Utah	114	31	43. Mississippi
Vermont	187	10	43. Virginia
Virginia	100	43	46. Alabama
Washington	153	15	46. Texas
West Virginia	173	12	48. Tennessee
Wisconsin	112	33	49. Georgia
Wyoming	204	9	50. South Carolina
50 States	162		
DC	484		
United States	126		

State	Federal grants to state & local gov't $ (millions)	Terms Of Trade, Ratio of grants to federal taxes paid	Rank by ratio	Rank in order By ratio
Alabama	3,209	1.21	17	1. West Virginia
Alaska	1,063	1.86	4	2. Louisiana
Arizona	2,996	1.13	19	3. Wyoming
Arkansas	1,966	1.33	11	4. Alaska
California	26,219	1.00	29	5. Mississippi
Colorado	2,102	0.69	48	6. New Mexico
Connecticut	3,028	0.74	44	7. North Dakota
Delaware	472	0.70	47	8. Montana
Florida	8,018	0.71	45	9. Maine
Georgia	5,028	1.00	30	10. South Dakota
Hawaii	1,088	1.07	23	11. Arkansas
Idaho	778	1.07	22	12. Kentucky
Illinois	8,506	0.79	42	13. Rhode Island
Indiana	3,553	0.85	39	14. Vermont
Iowa	2,015	1.04	25	15. New York
Kansas	1,666	0.85	40	16. South Carolina
Kentucky	3,096	1.32	12	17. Alabama
Louisiana	5,233	1.97	2	18. Oklahoma
Maine	1,269	1.56	9	19. Arizona
Maryland	3,637	0.78	43	20. Utah
Massachusetts	6,261	1.06	24	21. Tennessee
Michigan	7,117	0.92	36	22. Idaho
Minnesota	3,515	0.92	37	23. Hawaii
Mississippi	2,507	1.85	5	24. Massachusetts
Missouri	3,971	1.02	27	25. Iowa
Montana	906	1.62	8	26. Oregon
Nebraska	1,114	0.94	35	27. Missouri
Nevada	797	0.62	49	28. North Carolina
New Hampshire	956	0.96	33	29. California
New Jersey	6,163	0.71	46	30. Georgia
New Mexico	1,714	1.76	6	31. Ohio
New York	22,445	1.25	15	32. Pennsylvania
North Carolina	4,862	1.01	28	33. New Hampshire
North Dakota	702	1.71	7	34. Texas
Ohio	8,366	0.97	31	35. Nebraska
Oklahoma	2,359	1.15	18	36. Michigan
Oregon	2,355	1.03	26	37. Minnesota
Pennsylvania	9,705	0.97	32	38. Wisconsin
Rhode Island	1,100	1.30	13	39. Indiana
South Carolina	2,726	1.22	16	40. Kansas
South Dakota	724	1.50	10	41. Washington
Tennessee	3,940	1.08	21	42. Illinois
Texas	12,669	0.95	34	43. Maryland
Utah	1,209	1.10	20	44. Connecticut
Vermont	546	1.30	14	45. Florida
Virginia	3,180	0.59	50	46. New Jersey
Washington	3,924	0.84	41	47. Delaware
West Virginia	2,166	2.10	1	48. Colorado
Wisconsin	3,450	0.88	38	49. Nevada
Wyoming	714	1.94	3	50. Virginia
50 States	207,105	0.99		
DC	2,222	3.31		
United States	214,239	1.00		

E-15 Federal Personal Income Taxes, 1993

State	Federal tax liability ($000)	Federal tax liability per capita $	Rank by per capita	By per capita
Alabama	6,448,324	1,542	39	1. Connecticut
Alaska	1,550,753	2,593	4	2. New Jersey
Arizona	6,701,498	1,699	35	3. Nevada
Arkansas	3,249,651	1,340	48	4. Alaska
California	63,907,920	2,047	18	5. Massachusetts
Colorado	8,136,012	2,283	11	6. New York
Connecticut	11,443,060	3,491	1	7. Illinois
Delaware	1,572,621	2,253	12	8. Maryland
Florida	29,539,064	2,152	14	9. New Hampshire
Georgia	12,946,742	1,876	26	10. Washington
Hawaii	2,506,998	2,150	15	11. Colorado
Idaho	1,719,483	1,563	38	12. Delaware
Illinois	28,529,617	2,441	7	13. Virginia
Indiana	10,882,796	1,907	24	14. Florida
Iowa	4,648,062	1,648	36	15. Hawaii
Kansas	4,749,185	1,873	27	16. Minnesota
Kentucky	5,602,738	1,477	44	17. Wyoming
Louisiana	6,345,386	1,479	42	18. California
Maine	1,895,543	1,529	40	19. Michigan
Maryland	11,904,130	2,401	8	20. Pennsylvania
Massachusetts	15,513,521	2,578	5	21. Rhode Island
Michigan	19,234,274	2,033	19	22. Texas
Minnesota	9,577,140	2,117	16	23. Wisconsin
Mississippi	3,090,173	1,171	50	24. Indiana
Missouri	9,501,307	1,815	30	25. Ohio
Montana	1,242,721	1,478	43	26. Georgia
Nebraska	2,814,450	1,745	31	27. Kansas
Nevada	3,831,695	2,773	3	28. Oregon
New Hampshire	2,696,979	2,399	9	29. Tennessee
New Jersey	23,616,357	3,005	2	30. Missouri
New Mexico	2,313,889	1,432	47	31. Nebraska
New York	45,164,525	2,488	6	32. North Carolina
North Carolina	11,991,677	1,725	32	33. South Dakota
North Dakota	1,029,510	1,616	37	34. Vermont
Ohio	20,993,250	1,898	25	35. Arizona
Oklahoma	4,701,419	1,454	46	36. Iowa
Oregon	5,584,004	1,840	28	37. North Dakota
Pennsylvania	24,176,133	2,010	20	38. Idaho
Rhode Island	1,974,642	1,975	21	39. Alabama
South Carolina	5,326,897	1,467	45	40. Maine
South Dakota	1,230,568	1,719	33	41. Utah
Tennessee	9,344,233	1,834	29	42. Louisiana
Texas	35,014,627	1,943	22	43. Montana
Utah	2,787,878	1,499	41	44. Kentucky
Vermont	987,530	1,714	34	45. South Carolina
Virginia	14,150,558	2,186	13	46. Oklahoma
Washington	12,132,328	2,307	10	47. New Mexico
West Virginia	2,327,956	1,281	49	48. Arkansas
Wisconsin	9,625,114	1,908	23	49. West Virginia
Wyoming	967,596	2,059	17	50. Mississippi
50 States	527,222,534	2,050		
DC	1,620,314	2,798		
United States	532,213,236	2,065		

State	Federal share of AFDC and medicaid %	Rank
Alabama	70.5	9
Alaska	50.0	38
Arizona	66.4	16
Arkansas	73.8	3
California	50.0	38
Colorado	53.1	36
Connecticut	50.0	38
Delaware	50.0	38
Florida	56.3	32
Georgia	62.2	24
Hawaii	50.0	38
Idaho	70.1	10
Illinois	50.0	38
Indiana	63.0	20
Iowa	62.6	22
Kansas	58.9	30
Kentucky	69.6	12
Louisiana	72.7	6
Maine	63.3	19
Maryland	50.0	38
Massachusetts	50.0	38
Michigan	56.8	31
Minnesota	54.3	34
Mississippi	78.6	1
Missouri	59.9	28
Montana	70.8	7
Nebraska	60.4	27
Nevada	50.0	38
New Hampshire	50.0	38
New Jersey	50.0	38
New Mexico	73.3	5
New York	50.0	38
North Carolina	64.7	17
North Dakota	68.7	13
Ohio	60.7	26
Oklahoma	70.1	11
Oregon	62.4	23
Pennsylvania	54.3	34
Rhode Island	55.5	33
South Carolina	70.7	8
South Dakota	68.1	14
Tennessee	66.5	15
Texas	63.3	18
Utah	73.5	4
Vermont	60.8	25
Virginia	50.0	38
Washington	52.0	37
West Virginia	74.6	2
Wisconsin	59.8	29
Wyoming	62.9	21
50 States	n/a	
DC	50.0	
United States	n/a	

Rank in order
By %
1. Mississippi
2. West Virginia
3. Arkansas
4. Utah
5. New Mexico
6. Louisiana
7. Montana
8. South Carolina
9. Alabama
10. Idaho
11. Oklahoma
12. Kentucky
13. North Dakota
14. South Dakota
15. Tennessee
16. Arizona
17. North Carolina
18. Texas
19. Maine
20. Indiana
21. Wyoming
22. Iowa
23. Oregon
24. Georgia
25. Vermont
26. Ohio
27. Nebraska
28. Missouri
29. Wisconsin
30. Kansas
31. Michigan
32. Florida
33. Rhode Island
34. Minnesota
34. Pennsylvania
36. Colorado
37. Washington
38. Alaska
38. California
38. Connecticut
38. Delaware
38. Hawaii
38. Illinois
38. Maryland
38. Massachusetts
38. Nevada
38. New Hampshire
38. New Jersey
38. New York
38. Virginia

Taxes

State	State & local taxes ($000)	State & local taxes as % of personal income %	Rank by %
Alabama	5,937,421	9.4	48
Alaska	2,254,758	18.8	1
Arizona	7,747,332	12.5	9
Arkansas	3,633,180	10.5	41
California	72,073,742	11.4	24
Colorado	7,013,534	10.7	34
Connecticut	10,036,231	11.7	17
Delaware	1,617,873	11.4	23
Florida	25,919,228	10.3	43
Georgia	12,369,401	10.7	35
Hawaii	3,392,340	14.1	3
Idaho	1,897,659	11.9	13
Illinois	25,609,314	10.7	36
Indiana	10,106,757	10.5	40
Iowa	5,694,685	11.8	15
Kansas	4,939,746	10.8	33
Kentucky	6,588,521	11.4	26
Louisiana	7,076,326	11.1	29
Maine	2,659,775	12.3	10
Maryland	11,467,141	10.6	38
Massachusetts	15,309,017	11.1	28
Michigan	20,503,351	11.7	16
Minnesota	11,081,160	13.1	5
Mississippi	3,458,601	10.0	45
Missouri	8,646,070	9.4	49
Montana	1,455,181	11.5	21
Nebraska	3,235,101	11.5	22
Nevada	2,712,857	10.7	37
New Hampshire	2,338,839	9.7	47
New Jersey	22,882,217	11.5	20
New Mexico	2,828,753	12.5	8
New York	63,993,572	15.8	2
North Carolina	12,397,236	10.9	32
North Dakota	1,117,937	11.3	27
Ohio	21,336,525	11.0	31
Oklahoma	5,240,594	10.6	39
Oregon	6,229,108	12.1	12
Pennsylvania	26,268,472	11.4	25
Rhode Island	2,244,870	11.6	19
South Carolina	5,706,939	10.4	42
South Dakota	1,108,157	9.8	46
Tennessee	7,393,684	9.1	50
Texas	32,838,328	11.0	30
Utah	3,080,795	11.9	14
Vermont	1,303,398	12.8	7
Virginia	12,684,150	10.0	44
Washington	11,944,237	12.2	11
West Virginia	3,003,188	11.7	18
Wisconsin	11,609,642	13.1	6
Wyoming	1,085,772	14.0	4
50 States	553,072,715	11.5	
DC	2,406,646	14.7	
United States	555,479,361	11.6	

F-1 State & Local Tax Revenue, 1992

Rank in order

By %

1. Alaska
2. New York
3. Hawaii
4. Wyoming
5. Minnesota
6. Wisconsin
7. Vermont
8. New Mexico
9. Arizona
10. Maine
11. Washington
12. Oregon
13. Idaho
14. Utah
15. Iowa
16. Michigan
17. Connecticut
18. West Virginia
19. Rhode Island
20. New Jersey
21. Montana
22. Nebraska
23. Delaware
24. California
25. Pennsylvania
26. Kentucky
27. North Dakota
28. Massachusetts
29. Louisiana
30. Texas
31. Ohio
32. North Carolina
33. Kansas
34. Colorado
35. Georgia
36. Illinois
37. Nevada
38. Maryland
39. Oklahoma
40. Indiana
41. Arkansas
42. South Carolina
43. Florida
44. Virginia
45. Mississippi
46. South Dakota
47. New Hampshire
48. Alabama
49. Missouri
50. Tennessee

F-2 Total State And Local Tax Revenue, Per Capita, 1992

State	State & local taxes per capita $	State taxes per capita $	Local taxes per capita $	Rank by state & local per capita	By state & local
Alabama	1,436	1,020	416	49	1. Alaska
Alaska	3,841	2,709	1,132	1	2. New York
Arizona	2,022	1,260	762	24	3. Connecticut
Arkansas	1,514	1,145	370	47	4. New Jersey
California	2,335	1,494	841	10	5. Hawaii
Colorado	2,021	1,015	1,007	25	6. Massachusetts
Connecticut	3,059	1,847	1,212	3	7. Minnesota
Delaware	2,348	1,946	402	8	8. Delaware
Florida	1,922	1,075	846	30	9. Maryland
Georgia	1,832	1,076	756	32	10. California
Hawaii	2,924	2,336	589	5	11. Wyoming
Idaho	1,778	1,314	465	36	12. Washington
Illinois	2,202	1,158	1,044	16	13. Wisconsin
Indiana	1,785	1,144	641	35	14. Vermont
Iowa	2,025	1,281	744	23	15. Rhode Island
Kansas	1,958	1,110	847	28	16. Illinois
Kentucky	1,755	1,353	401	39	17. Pennsylvania
Louisiana	1,651	991	659	43	18. Michigan
Maine	2,154	1,348	806	19	19. Maine
Maryland	2,336	1,325	1,012	9	20. New Hampshire
Massachusetts	2,552	1,651	901	6	21. Oregon
Michigan	2,173	1,195	977	18	22. Nevada
Minnesota	2,473	1,663	811	7	23. Iowa
Mississippi	1,323	954	369	50	24. Arizona
Missouri	1,665	988	677	41	25. Colorado
Montana	1,766	1,256	510	37	26. Nebraska
Nebraska	2,014	1,177	838	26	27. Virginia
Nevada	2,044	1,374	670	22	28. Kansas
New Hampshire	2,105	746	1,359	20	29. Ohio
New Jersey	2,938	1,644	1,294	4	30. Florida
New Mexico	1,789	1,419	371	34	31. Texas
New York	3,532	1,662	1,870	2	32. Georgia
North Carolina	1,812	1,317	495	33	33. North Carolina
North Dakota	1,758	1,186	571	38	34. New Mexico
Ohio	1,937	1,100	837	29	35. Indiana
Oklahoma	1,632	1,172	459	44	36. Idaho
Oregon	2,092	1,113	979	21	37. Montana
Pennsylvania	2,187	1,355	833	17	38. North Dakota
Rhode Island	2,234	1,301	933	15	39. Kentucky
South Carolina	1,584	1,092	492	45	40. Utah
South Dakota	1,559	795	764	46	41. Missouri
Tennessee	1,472	901	571	48	42. West Virginia
Texas	1,860	965	895	31	43. Louisiana
Utah	1,699	1,096	603	40	44. Oklahoma
Vermont	2,287	1,339	947	14	45. South Carolina
Virginia	1,989	1,102	887	27	46. South Dakota
Washington	2,326	1,650	675	12	47. Arkansas
West Virginia	1,657	1,298	359	42	48. Tennessee
Wisconsin	2,319	1,476	843	13	49. Alabama
Wyoming	2,330	1,386	944	11	50. Mississippi
50 States	2,080	1,290	883		
DC	4,222	n/a	4,107		
United States	2,183	1,290	892		

State	Tax effort %	Rank
Alabama	81	46
Alaska	119	2
Arizona	103	8
Arkansas	82	44
California	95	24
Colorado	86	39
Connecticut	99	17
Delaware	80	48
Florida	86	39
Georgia	95	24
Hawaii	95	24
Idaho	94	28
Illinois	100	13
Indiana	93	30
Iowa	100	13
Kansas	100	13
Kentucky	100	13
Louisiana	89	36
Maine	102	10
Maryland	103	8
Massachusetts	101	12
Michigan	107	7
Minnesota	112	5
Mississippi	92	32
Missouri	85	41
Montana	78	49
Nebraska	99	17
Nevada	73	50
New Hampshire	84	42
New Jersey	112	5
New Mexico	96	22
New York	156	1
North Carolina	87	37
North Dakota	92	32
Ohio	96	22
Oklahoma	93	30
Oregon	97	20
Pennsylvania	95	24
Rhode Island	115	4
South Carolina	90	35
South Dakota	83	43
Tennessee	82	44
Texas	87	37
Utah	94	28
Vermont	97	20
Virginia	91	34
Washington	99	17
West Virginia	102	10
Wisconsin	118	3
Wyoming	81	46
50 States	n/a	
DC	157	
United States	100	

Rank in order

By %

1. New York
2. Alaska
3. Wisconsin
4. Rhode Island
5. Minnesota
5. New Jersey
7. Michigan
8. Arizona
8. Maryland
10. Maine
10. West Virginia
12. Massachusetts
13. Illinois
13. Iowa
13. Kansas
13. Kentucky
17. Connecticut
17. Nebraska
17. Washington
20. Oregon
20. Vermont
22. New Mexico
22. Ohio
24. California
24. Georgia
24. Hawaii
24. Pennsylvania
28. Idaho
28. Utah
30. Indiana
30. Oklahoma
32. Mississippi
32. North Dakota
34. Virginia
35. South Carolina
36. Louisiana
37. North Carolina
37. Texas
39. Colorado
39. Florida
41. Missouri
42. New Hampshire
43. South Dakota
44. Arkansas
44. Tennessee
46. Alabama
46. Wyoming
48. Delaware
49. Montana
50. Nevada

F-4 State & Local Tax Capacity, 1991

State	Tax capacity %	Rank		Rank in order By %
Alabama	81	47		1. Alaska
Alaska	178	1		2. Hawaii
Arizona	94	25		3. Wyoming
Arkansas	78	48		4. Connecticut
California	115	9		5. Nevada
Colorado	109	11		6. Delaware
Connecticut	130	4		7. New Jersey
Delaware	125	6		8. Massachusetts
Florida	103	15		9. California
Georgia	91	31		10. New Hampshire
Hawaii	146	2		11. Colorado
Idaho	82	44		12. Washington
Illinois	102	18		13. Maryland
Indiana	90	35		14. Vermont
Iowa	93	27		15. Florida
Kansas	93	27		15. New York
Kentucky	83	42		15. Virginia
Louisiana	89	37		18. Illinois
Maine	95	23		19. Minnesota
Maryland	106	13		20. Oregon
Massachusetts	117	8		21. Texas
Michigan	94	25		22. Pennsylvania
Minnesota	101	19		23. Maine
Mississippi	68	50		23. Nebraska
Missouri	91	31		25. Arizona
Montana	91	31		25. Michigan
Nebraska	95	23		27. Iowa
Nevada	128	5		27. Kansas
New Hampshire	110	10		27. North Carolina
New Jersey	119	7		27. Ohio
New Mexico	87	39		31. Georgia
New York	103	15		31. Missouri
North Carolina	93	27		31. Montana
North Dakota	91	31		31. North Dakota
Ohio	93	27		35. Indiana
Oklahoma	87	39		35. Wisconsin
Oregon	100	20		37. Louisiana
Pennsylvania	96	22		37. Rhode Island
Rhode Island	89	37		39. New Mexico
South Carolina	83	42		39. Oklahoma
South Dakota	86	41		41. South Dakota
Tennessee	82	44		42. Kentucky
Texas	97	21		42. South Carolina
Utah	82	44		44. Idaho
Vermont	105	14		44. Tennessee
Virginia	103	15		44. Utah
Washington	108	12		47. Alabama
West Virginia	77	49		48. Arkansas
Wisconsin	90	35		49. West Virginia
Wyoming	134	3		50. Mississippi
50 States	n/a			
DC	123			
United States	100			

F-5 Change In State And Local Taxes, 1987-1992

State	% change in state & local taxes %	% change in s & I taxes per capita %	% change in s & I taxes as % of pers. inc %	Rank by % change in s & I taxes
Alabama	33.7	32.0	-3.2	32
Alaska	35.8	21.5	7.3	26
Arizona	43.5	26.8	3.2	13
Arkansas	46.8	46.1	11.1	8
California	35.3	21.2	-2.6	27
Colorado	32.8	26.2	1.1	35
Connecticut	41.0	38.0	2.9	19
Delaware	43.4	34.0	-3.8	14
Florida	57.9	40.8	7.1	5
Georgia	44.9	33.6	3.0	11
Hawaii	60.2	49.6	5.4	3
Idaho	61.4	50.9	13.9	2
Illinois	34.0	33.4	0.8	31
Indiana	40.1	36.9	5.1	20
Iowa	31.3	32.4	3.4	41
Kansas	32.3	29.9	4.4	37
Kentucky	46.1	45.0	5.5	9
Louisiana	29.3	34.5	1.8	46
Maine	38.8	33.4	-3.3	22
Maryland	32.8	22.7	-7.3	34
Massachusetts	24.2	21.2	-6.9	49
Michigan	25.5	22.4	-3.0	48
Minnesota	37.3	30.2	2.4	24
Mississippi	33.1	33.6	-1.7	33
Missouri	35.9	33.6	2.7	25
Montana	31.6	29.2	0.4	39
Nebraska	39.0	37.9	8.1	21
Nevada	66.1	26.1	-2.7	1
New Hampshire	59.3	51.5	8.3	4
New Jersey	42.1	39.9	1.2	15
New Mexico	44.2	36.8	7.5	12
New York	29.5	27.4	-3.0	45
North Carolina	41.8	32.9	-1.6	16
North Dakota	30.4	37.8	11.6	44
Ohio	31.1	28.3	1.0	42
Oklahoma	31.5	33.9	8.2	40
Oregon	41.8	29.8	-0.7	17
Pennsylvania	41.6	40.8	3.9	18
Rhode Island	32.4	29.9	-2.5	36
South Carolina	35.2	28.5	-6.3	28
South Dakota	30.9	30.6	-3.1	43
Tennessee	31.8	27.3	-7.0	38
Texas	47.2	39.9	10.7	7
Utah	34.9	25.0	-4.7	30
Vermont	45.9	40.2	3.3	10
Virginia	38.8	28.5	-2.0	23
Washington	55.1	37.0	6.2	6
West Virginia	28.6	36.2	1.3	47
Wisconsin	35.1	29.7	1.2	29
Wyoming	-3.4	1.6	-19.5	50
50 States	37.2	25.3	0.5	
DC	25.7	37.2	-6.6	
United States	37.1	31.1	0.8	

Rank in order

By % change

1. Nevada
2. Idaho
3. Hawaii
4. New Hampshire
5. Florida
6. Washington
7. Texas
8. Arkansas
9. Kentucky
10. Vermont
11. Georgia
12. New Mexico
13. Arizona
14. Delaware
15. New Jersey
16. North Carolina
17. Oregon
18. Pennsylvania
19. Connecticut
20. Indiana
21. Nebraska
22. Maine
23. Virginia
24. Minnesota
25. Missouri
26. Alaska
27. California
28. South Carolina
29. Wisconsin
30. Utah
31. Illinois
32. Alabama
33. Mississippi
34. Maryland
35. Colorado
36. Rhode Island
37. Kansas
38. Tennessee
39. Montana
40. Oklahoma
41. Iowa
42. Ohio
43. South Dakota
44. North Dakota
45. New York
46. Louisiana
47. West Virginia
48. Michigan
49. Massachusetts
50. Wyoming

State	Property Taxes ($000)	Per $1000 of personal income $	Rank by per $1000	Rank in order By per $1000
Alabama	720,288	11.4	50	1. New Hampshire
Alaska	628,802	52.3	5	2. Wyoming
Arizona	2,581,072	41.5	15	3. Vermont
Arkansas	625,923	18.0	46	4. New York
California	20,614,069	32.5	29	5. Alaska
Colorado	2,336,269	35.7	25	6. Michigan
Connecticut	3,927,937	45.9	13	7. Oregon
Delaware	228,326	16.1	47	8. New Jersey
Florida	9,948,598	39.5	21	9. Rhode Island
Georgia	3,659,903	31.7	32	10. Maine
Hawaii	556,461	23.1	39	11. Wisconsin
Idaho	475,986	29.9	34	12. Montana
Illinois	9,859,512	41.2	18	13. Connecticut
Indiana	3,214,093	33.4	27	14. Texas
Iowa	1,998,385	41.3	17	15. Arizona
Kansas	1,830,511	40.0	20	16. Nebraska
Kentucky	1,114,578	19.2	44	17. Iowa
Louisiana	1,184,115	18.5	45	18. Illinois
Maine	1,016,336	47.2	10	19. Minnesota
Maryland	3,210,082	29.8	35	20. Kansas
Massachusetts	5,253,394	38.1	23	21. Florida
Michigan	8,963,296	51.3	6	22. South Dakota
Minnesota	3,475,507	41.0	19	23. Massachusetts
Mississippi	933,227	27.0	37	24. Washington
Missouri	2,085,569	22.6	40	25. Colorado
Montana	581,541	45.9	12	26. North Dakota
Nebraska	1,166,764	41.3	16	27. Indiana
Nevada	652,265	25.7	38	28. Virginia
New Hampshire	1,498,907	62.4	1	29. California
New Jersey	9,913,791	49.8	8	30. Utah
New Mexico	343,809	15.2	49	31. Ohio
New York	21,335,082	52.6	4	32. Georgia
North Carolina	2,556,370	22.5	41	33. Pennsylvania
North Dakota	338,068	34.1	26	34. Idaho
Ohio	6,253,476	32.2	31	35. Maryland
Oklahoma	778,760	15.8	48	36. South Carolina
Oregon	2,568,376	50.0	7	37. Mississippi
Pennsylvania	7,300,522	31.6	33	38. Nevada
Rhode Island	944,183	48.9	9	39. Hawaii
South Carolina	1,623,969	29.5	36	40. Missouri
South Dakota	433,406	38.3	22	41. North Carolina
Tennessee	1,747,708	21.4	42	42. Tennessee
Texas	12,907,008	43.2	14	43. West Virginia
Utah	834,582	32.2	30	44. Kentucky
Vermont	544,873	53.4	3	45. Louisiana
Virginia	4,142,912	32.8	28	46. Arkansas
Washington	3,497,900	35.8	24	47. Delaware
West Virginia	531,702	20.6	43	48. Oklahoma
Wisconsin	4,103,127	46.2	11	49. New Mexico
Wyoming	461,066	59.2	2	50. Alabama
50 States	177,502,406	37.0		
DC	903,319	55.3		
United States	178,405,725	37.1		

State	Property tax per capita $	Rank
Alabama	174	50
Alaska	1,071	5
Arizona	674	23
Arkansas	261	47
California	668	25
Colorado	673	24
Connecticut	1,197	3
Delaware	331	43
Florida	738	16
Georgia	542	32
Hawaii	480	35
Idaho	446	38
Illinois	848	12
Indiana	568	31
Iowa	711	20
Kansas	726	19
Kentucky	297	44
Louisiana	276	46
Maine	823	13
Maryland	654	26
Massachusetts	876	10
Michigan	950	8
Minnesota	776	15
Mississippi	357	41
Missouri	402	39
Montana	706	21
Nebraska	727	18
Nevada	492	34
New Hampshire	1,349	1
New Jersey	1,273	2
New Mexico	217	49
New York	1,177	4
North Carolina	374	40
North Dakota	532	33
Ohio	568	30
Oklahoma	242	48
Oregon	863	11
Pennsylvania	608	29
Rhode Island	939	9
South Carolina	451	37
South Dakota	610	28
Tennessee	348	42
Texas	731	17
Utah	460	36
Vermont	956	7
Virginia	650	27
Washington	681	22
West Virginia	293	45
Wisconsin	819	14
Wyoming	989	6
50 States	651	
DC	1,542	
United States	701	

Rank in order

By per capita

1. New Hampshire
2. New Jersey
3. Connecticut
4. New York
5. Alaska
6. Wyoming
7. Vermont
8. Michigan
9. Rhode Island
10. Massachusetts
11. Oregon
12. Illinois
13. Maine
14. Wisconsin
15. Minnesota
16. Florida
17. Texas
18. Nebraska
19. Kansas
20. Iowa
21. Montana
22. Washington
23. Arizona
24. Colorado
25. California
26. Maryland
27. Virginia
28. South Dakota
29. Pennsylvania
30. Ohio
31. Indiana
32. Georgia
33. North Dakota
34. Nevada
35. Hawaii
36. Utah
37. South Carolina
38. Idaho
39. Missouri
40. North Carolina
41. Mississippi
42. Tennessee
43. Delaware
44. Kentucky
45. West Virginia
46. Louisiana
47. Arkansas
48. Oklahoma
49. New Mexico
50. Alabama

F-8 Property Tax Revenues As Percent Of Three-Tax Revenues, 1992			Rank in order
State	**Property tax as % of three-tax revenues** %	**Rank**	**By %**
Alabama	14.3	50	1. Alaska
Alaska	76.3	1	2. New Hampshire
Arizona	36.0	25	3. Wyoming
Arkansas	19.3	46	4. Montana
California	32.8	29	5. Michigan
Colorado	36.1	24	6. Oregon
Connecticut	44.3	12	7. New Jersey
Delaware	24.0	41	8. Vermont
Florida	43.3	13	9. Rhode Island
Georgia	31.7	32	10. South Dakota
Hawaii	17.4	48	11. Texas
Idaho	28.4	37	12. Connecticut
Illinois	42.2	14	13. Florida
Indiana	34.2	28	14. Illinois
Iowa	39.6	17	15. Kansas
Kansas	41.7	15	16. Maine
Kentucky	20.2	45	17. Iowa
Louisiana	20.4	44	18. Nebraska
Maine	41.3	16	19. Wisconsin
Maryland	30.7	34	20. Massachusetts
Massachusetts	38.2	20	21. New York
Michigan	50.9	5	22. North Dakota
Minnesota	35.0	26	23. Virginia
Mississippi	30.3	35	24. Colorado
Missouri	26.9	40	25. Arizona
Montana	52.6	4	26. Minnesota
Nebraska	39.5	18	27. Pennsylvania
Nevada	27.9	38	28. Indiana
New Hampshire	72.6	2	29. California
New Jersey	47.1	7	30. Ohio
New Mexico	14.7	49	31. Washington
New York	37.7	21	32. Georgia
North Carolina	23.3	42	33. South Carolina
North Dakota	36.8	22	34. Maryland
Ohio	32.3	30	35. Mississippi
Oklahoma	18.3	47	36. Utah
Oregon	48.1	6	37. Idaho
Pennsylvania	34.4	27	38. Nevada
Rhode Island	45.2	9	39. Tennessee
South Carolina	31.6	33	40. Missouri
South Dakota	44.6	10	41. Delaware
Tennessee	27.7	39	42. North Carolina
Texas	44.3	11	43. West Virginia
Utah	29.1	36	44. Louisiana
Vermont	45.9	8	45. Kentucky
Virginia	36.5	23	46. Arkansas
Washington	32.2	31	47. Oklahoma
West Virginia	22.2	43	48. Hawaii
Wisconsin	38.7	19	49. New Mexico
Wyoming	60.9	3	50. Alabama
50 States	36.4		
DC	41.0		
United States	36.4		

F-9 Sales Taxes And Per $1000 Of Personal Income, 1992

State	Sales taxes $	Per $1000 personal income $	Rank by per $1000
Alabama	3,019,254	47.6	15
Alaska	195,501	16.3	47
Arizona	3,349,396	53.9	8
Arkansas	1,774,821	51.2	10
California	25,275,457	39.9	25
Colorado	2,530,375	38.7	28
Connecticut	3,074,322	35.9	36
Delaware	196,893	13.9	49
Florida	13,020,719	51.6	9
Georgia	4,802,721	41.6	21
Hawaii	1,736,623	72.2	2
Idaho	664,987	41.7	20
Illinois	8,940,979	37.4	34
Indiana	3,621,229	37.6	33
Iowa	1,630,015	33.7	40
Kansas	1,726,203	37.8	31
Kentucky	2,346,949	40.4	23
Louisiana	3,746,509	58.6	5
Maine	854,631	39.7	26
Maryland	2,960,809	27.5	44
Massachusetts	3,149,053	22.8	45
Michigan	5,033,376	28.8	43
Minnesota	3,447,582	40.7	22
Mississippi	1,708,888	49.5	11
Missouri	3,602,829	39.0	27
Montana	202,305	16.0	48
Nebraska	1,132,545	40.1	24
Nevada	1,685,586	66.4	4
New Hampshire	530,469	22.1	46
New Jersey	7,017,939	35.2	37
New Mexico	1,553,635	68.5	3
New York	17,026,651	42.0	19
North Carolina	4,816,460	42.4	18
North Dakota	461,314	46.6	16
Ohio	6,724,997	34.6	39
Oklahoma	2,247,266	45.5	17
Oregon	549,433	10.7	50
Pennsylvania	7,383,468	32.0	41
Rhode Island	668,110	34.6	38
South Carolina	2,111,001	38.3	29
South Dakota	539,150	47.7	14
Tennessee	4,478,614	54.9	6
Texas	16,197,457	54.2	7
Utah	1,249,009	48.2	13
Vermont	369,780	36.3	35
Virginia	3,878,547	30.7	42
Washington	7,352,011	75.2	1
West Virginia	1,246,905	48.4	12
Wisconsin	3,349,426	37.7	32
Wyoming	295,837	38.0	30
50 States	195,478,036	40.7	
DC	671,832	41.1	
United States	196,149,868	40.7	

Rank in order

By per $1000

1. Washington
2. Hawaii
3. New Mexico
4. Nevada
5. Louisiana
6. Tennessee
7. Texas
8. Arizona
9. Florida
10. Arkansas
11. Mississippi
12. West Virginia
13. Utah
14. South Dakota
15. Alabama
16. North Dakota
17. Oklahoma
18. North Carolina
19. New York
20. Idaho
21. Georgia
22. Minnesota
23. Kentucky
24. Nebraska
25. California
26. Maine
27. Missouri
28. Colorado
29. South Carolina
30. Wyoming
31. Kansas
32. Wisconsin
33. Indiana
34. Illinois
35. Vermont
36. Connecticut
37. New Jersey
38. Rhode Island
39. Ohio
40. Iowa
41. Pennsylvania
42. Virginia
43. Michigan
44. Maryland
45. Massachusetts
46. New Hampshire
47. Alaska
48. Montana
49. Delaware
50. Oregon

	Sales Taxes Per capita $	Rank	By per capita
State			
Alabama	730	18	1. Hawaii
Alaska	333	47	2. Washington
Arizona	874	11	3. Nevada
Arkansas	740	17	4. New Mexico
California	819	13	5. Florida
Colorado	729	19	6. New York
Connecticut	937	7	7. Connecticut
Delaware	286	48	8. Texas
Florida	965	5	9. New Jersey
Georgia	711	21	10. Tennessee
Hawaii	1,497	1	11. Arizona
Idaho	623	37	12. Louisiana
Illinois	769	15	13. California
Indiana	640	34	14. Minnesota
Iowa	580	43	15. Illinois
Kansas	684	29	16. South Dakota
Kentucky	625	36	17. Arkansas
Louisiana	874	12	18. Alabama
Maine	692	26	19. Colorado
Maryland	603	41	20. North Dakota
Massachusetts	525	45	21. Georgia
Michigan	533	44	22. Nebraska
Minnesota	770	14	23. North Carolina
Mississippi	654	32	24. Oklahoma
Missouri	694	25	25. Missouri
Montana	246	49	26. Maine
Nebraska	705	22	27. Utah
Nevada	1,270	3	28. West Virginia
New Hampshire	477	46	29. Kansas
New Jersey	901	9	30. Wisconsin
New Mexico	983	4	31. Rhode Island
New York	940	6	32. Mississippi
North Carolina	704	23	33. Vermont
North Dakota	725	20	34. Indiana
Ohio	610	39	35. Wyoming
Oklahoma	700	24	36. Kentucky
Oregon	185	50	37. Idaho
Pennsylvania	615	38	38. Pennsylvania
Rhode Island	665	31	39. Ohio
South Carolina	586	42	40. Virginia
South Dakota	758	16	41. Maryland
Tennessee	891	10	42. South Carolina
Texas	917	8	43. Iowa
Utah	689	27	44. Michigan
Vermont	649	33	45. Massachusetts
Virginia	608	40	46. New Hampshire
Washington	1,431	2	47. Alaska
West Virginia	688	28	48. Delaware
Wisconsin	669	30	49. Montana
Wyoming	635	35	50. Oregon
50 States	723		
DC	1,146		
United States	771		

Rank in order

State	Sales tax as % of three-tax revenues %	Rank	Rank in order By %
Alabama	60.0	6	1. Nevada
Alaska	23.7	46	2. Tennessee
Arizona	46.7	16	3. Washington
Arkansas	54.6	11	4. New Mexico
California	40.2	23	5. Louisiana
Colorado	39.1	27	6. Alabama
Connecticut	34.7	35	7. Florida
Delaware	20.7	48	8. Texas
Florida	56.7	7	9. Mississippi
Georgia	41.6	21	10. South Dakota
Hawaii	54.3	12	11. Arkansas
Idaho	39.7	24	12. Hawaii
Illinois	38.2	30	13. Oklahoma
Indiana	38.6	28	14. West Virginia
Iowa	32.3	38	15. North Dakota
Kansas	39.3	25	16. Arizona
Kentucky	42.6	20	17. Missouri
Louisiana	64.6	5	18. North Carolina
Maine	34.7	33	19. Utah
Maryland	28.3	44	20. Kentucky
Massachusetts	22.9	47	21. Georgia
Michigan	28.6	43	22. South Carolina
Minnesota	34.7	32	23. California
Mississippi	55.5	9	24. Idaho
Missouri	46.5	17	25. Kansas
Montana	18.3	49	26. Wyoming
Nebraska	38.4	29	27. Colorado
Nevada	72.1	1	28. Indiana
New Hampshire	25.7	45	29. Nebraska
New Jersey	33.4	37	30. Illinois
New Mexico	66.3	4	31. Pennsylvania
New York	30.1	42	32. Minnesota
North Carolina	44.0	18	33. Maine
North Dakota	50.2	15	34. Ohio
Ohio	34.7	34	35. Connecticut
Oklahoma	52.9	13	36. Virginia
Oregon	10.3	50	37. New Jersey
Pennsylvania	34.8	31	38. Iowa
Rhode Island	32.0	39	39. Rhode Island
South Carolina	41.0	22	40. Wisconsin
South Dakota	55.4	10	41. Vermont
Tennessee	70.9	2	42. New York
Texas	55.7	8	43. Michigan
Utah	43.6	19	44. Maryland
Vermont	31.2	41	45. New Hampshire
Virginia	34.2	36	46. Alaska
Washington	67.8	3	47. Massachusetts
West Virginia	52.1	14	48. Delaware
Wisconsin	31.6	40	49. Montana
Wyoming	39.1	26	50. Oregon
50 States	40.1		
DC	30.5		
United States	40.1		

State	Services subject to Sales Tax #	Rank	By #
Alabama	32	28	1. Hawaii
Alaska	1	49	2. New Mexico
Arizona	60	19	3. Washington
Arkansas	52	21	4. Delaware
California	19	42	5. South Dakota
Colorado	15	46	6. West Virginia
Connecticut	84	8	7. Iowa
Delaware	141	4	8. Connecticut
Florida	65	15	9. Texas
Georgia	35	27	10. Kansas
Hawaii	155	1	11. New York
Idaho	29	31	12. Tennessee
Illinois	16	45	13. Mississippi
Indiana	24	38	14. Wisconsin
Iowa	95	7	15. Florida
Kansas	76	10	16. Wyoming
Kentucky	26	36	17. Minnesota
Louisiana	53	20	18. Pennsylvania
Maine	27	35	19. Arizona
Maryland	36	26	20. Louisiana
Massachusetts	20	41	21. Arkansas
Michigan	26	37	22. Utah
Minnesota	61	17	23. Nebraska
Mississippi	69	13	24. New Jersey
Missouri	28	33	25. Ohio
Montana	19	43	26. Maryland
Nebraska	48	23	27. Georgia
Nevada	11	47	28. Alabama
New Hampshire	11	48	29. South Carolina
New Jersey	45	24	30. Oklahoma
New Mexico	155	2	31. Idaho
New York	74	11	32. North Carolina
North Carolina	29	32	33. Missouri
North Dakota	21	40	34. Rhode Island
Ohio	42	25	35. Maine
Oklahoma	31	30	36. Kentucky
Oregon	0	50	37. Michigan
Pennsylvania	61	18	38. Indiana
Rhode Island	28	34	39. Vermont
South Carolina	32	29	40. North Dakota
South Dakota	130	5	41. Massachusetts
Tennessee	70	12	42. California
Texas	79	9	43. Montana
Utah	49	22	44. Virginia
Vermont	23	39	45. Illinois
Virginia	18	44	46. Colorado
Washington	152	3	47. Nevada
West Virginia	110	6	48. New Hampshire
Wisconsin	69	14	49. Alaska
Wyoming	64	16	50. Oregon
50 States	52		
DC	63		
United States	54		

F-13 Individual Income Taxes And Per $1000 Personal Income, 1992

State	Individual Income tax ($000)	Income tax per $1000 personal income $	Rank by per $1000
Alabama	1,291,053	20.3	34
Alaska	0	0.0	n/a
Arizona	1,240,372	20.0	35
Arkansas	850,131	24.5	27
California	17,029,575	26.9	17
Colorado	1,611,954	24.7	26
Connecticut	1,865,711	21.8	31
Delaware	524,299	37.0	6
Florida	0	0.0	n/a
Georgia	3,081,708	26.7	18
Hawaii	906,982	37.7	5
Idaho	535,482	33.6	10
Illinois	4,584,369	19.2	37
Indiana	2,552,465	26.5	20
Iowa	1,416,690	29.3	14
Kansas	833,756	18.2	38
Kentucky	2,052,399	35.4	8
Louisiana	867,929	13.6	39
Maine	591,615	27.5	16
Maryland	4,290,874	39.8	3
Massachusetts	5,336,957	38.7	4
Michigan	3,628,288	20.8	32
Minnesota	2,999,091	35.4	7
Mississippi	439,577	12.7	40
Missouri	2,061,674	22.3	30
Montana	321,538	25.4	23
Nebraska	652,638	23.1	29
Nevada	0	0.0	n/a
New Hampshire	34,958	1.5	42
New Jersey	4,101,895	20.6	33
New Mexico	445,309	19.6	36
New York	18,200,518	44.9	1
North Carolina	3,583,018	31.6	12
North Dakota	119,518	12.1	41
Ohio	6,405,831	33.0	11
Oklahoma	1,218,181	24.7	25
Oregon	2,221,297	43.3	2
Pennsylvania	6,532,830	28.3	15
Rhode Island	478,461	24.8	24
South Carolina	1,410,893	25.6	22
South Dakota	17	0.0	44
Tennessee	93,361	1.1	43
Texas	197	0.0	45
Utah	781,383	30.2	13
Vermont	271,430	26.6	19
Virginia	3,321,264	26.3	21
Washington	0	0.0	n/a
West Virginia	612,619	23.8	28
Wisconsin	3,142,211	35.3	9
Wyoming	0	0.0	n/a
50 States	114,542,318	23.9	
DC	627,800	38.4	
United States	115,170,118	23.9	

Rank in order

By per $1000

1. New York
2. Oregon
3. Maryland
4. Massachusetts
5. Hawaii
6. Delaware
7. Minnesota
8. Kentucky
9. Wisconsin
10. Idaho
11. Ohio
12. North Carolina
13. Utah
14. Iowa
15. Pennsylvania
16. Maine
17. California
18. Georgia
19. Vermont
20. Indiana
21. Virginia
22. South Carolina
23. Montana
24. Rhode Island
25. Oklahoma
26. Colorado
27. Arkansas
28. West Virginia
29. Nebraska
30. Missouri
31. Connecticut
32. Michigan
33. New Jersey
34. Alabama
35. Arizona
36. New Mexico
37. Illinois
38. Kansas
39. Louisiana
40. Mississippi
41. North Dakota
42. New Hampshire
43. Tennessee
44. South Dakota
45. Texas

State	Income tax per capita $	Rank
Alabama	312	37
Alaska	0	n/a
Arizona	324	36
Arkansas	354	33
California	552	11
Colorado	465	22
Connecticut	569	10
Delaware	761	5
Florida	0	n/a
Georgia	456	23
Hawaii	782	4
Idaho	502	18
Illinois	394	28
Indiana	451	24
Iowa	504	17
Kansas	330	35
Kentucky	547	12
Louisiana	202	39
Maine	479	19
Maryland	874	3
Massachusetts	890	2
Michigan	384	31
Minnesota	669	7
Mississippi	168	41
Missouri	397	27
Montana	390	30
Nebraska	406	26
Nevada	0	n/a
New Hampshire	31	42
New Jersey	527	14
New Mexico	282	38
New York	1,004	1
North Carolina	524	15
North Dakota	188	40
Ohio	582	9
Oklahoma	379	32
Oregon	746	6
Pennsylvania	544	13
Rhode Island	476	21
South Carolina	392	29
South Dakota	0	44
Tennessee	19	43
Texas	0	45
Utah	431	25
Vermont	476	20
Virginia	521	16
Washington	0	n/a
West Virginia	338	34
Wisconsin	628	8
Wyoming	0	n/a
50 States	405	
DC	1,071	
United States	453	

Rank in order

By per capita

1. New York
2. Massachusetts
3. Maryland
4. Hawaii
5. Delaware
6. Oregon
7. Minnesota
8. Wisconsin
9. Ohio
10. Connecticut
11. California
12. Kentucky
13. Pennsylvania
14. New Jersey
15. North Carolina
16. Virginia
17. Iowa
18. Idaho
19. Maine
20. Vermont
21. Rhode Island
22. Colorado
23. Georgia
24. Indiana
25. Utah
26. Nebraska
27. Missouri
28. Illinois
29. South Carolina
30. Montana
31. Michigan
32. Oklahoma
33. Arkansas
34. West Virginia
35. Kansas
36. Arizona
37. Alabama
38. New Mexico
39. Louisiana
40. North Dakota
41. Mississippi
42. New Hampshire
43. Tennessee
44. South Dakota
45. Texas

F-15 Individual Income Tax Revenues As Percent Of Three-Tax Revenues, 1992

State	Income tax as % of three-taxes %	Rank
Alabama	25.7	25
Alaska	0.0	46
Arizona	17.3	38
Arkansas	26.2	24
California	27.1	21
Colorado	24.9	27
Connecticut	21.0	32
Delaware	55.2	1
Florida	0.0	46
Georgia	26.7	22
Hawaii	28.3	16
Idaho	31.9	9
Illinois	19.6	34
Indiana	27.2	20
Iowa	28.1	17
Kansas	19.0	37
Kentucky	37.2	5
Louisiana	15.0	39
Maine	24.0	28
Maryland	41.0	3
Massachusetts	38.8	4
Michigan	20.6	33
Minnesota	30.2	11
Mississippi	14.3	40
Missouri	26.6	23
Montana	29.1	14
Nebraska	22.1	31
Nevada	0.0	46
New Hampshire	1.7	42
New Jersey	19.5	35
New Mexico	19.0	36
New York	32.2	8
North Carolina	32.7	7
North Dakota	13.0	41
Ohio	33.0	6
Oklahoma	28.7	15
Oregon	41.6	2
Pennsylvania	30.8	10
Rhode Island	22.9	29
South Carolina	27.4	18
South Dakota	0.0	44
Tennessee	1.5	43
Texas	0.0	45
Utah	27.3	19
Vermont	22.9	30
Virginia	29.3	13
Washington	0.0	46
West Virginia	25.6	26
Wisconsin	29.7	12
Wyoming	0.0	46
50 States	23.5	
DC	28.5	
United States	23.5	

Rank in order

By %

1. Delaware
2. Oregon
3. Maryland
4. Massachusetts
5. Kentucky
6. Ohio
7. North Carolina
8. New York
9. Idaho
10. Pennsylvania
11. Minnesota
12. Wisconsin
13. Virginia
14. Montana
15. Oklahoma
16. Hawaii
17. Iowa
18. South Carolina
19. Utah
20. Indiana
21. California
22. Georgia
23. Missouri
24. Arkansas
25. Alabama
26. West Virginia
27. Colorado
28. Maine
29. Rhode Island
30. Vermont
31. Nebraska
32. Connecticut
33. Michigan
34. Illinois
35. New Jersey
36. New Mexico
37. Kansas
38. Arizona
39. Louisiana
40. Mississippi
41. North Dakota
42. New Hampshire
43. Tennessee
44. South Dakota
45. Texas
46. Alaska
46. Florida
46. Nevada
46. Washington
46. Wyoming

State	Highest Rate %	Rank
Alabama	3	39
Alaska	No Tax	n/a
Arizona	7	19
Arkansas	7	15
California	11	1
Colorado	5	33
Connecticut	5	35
Delaware	8	13
Florida	No Tax	n/a
Georgia	6	25
Hawaii	10	3
Idaho	8	9
Illinois	3	40
Indiana	3	38
Iowa	6	24
Kansas	8	11
Kentucky	6	25
Louisiana	4	37
Maine	9	6
Maryland	6	25
Massachusetts	6	29
Michigan	4	36
Minnesota	9	6
Mississippi	5	33
Missouri	6	25
Montana	7	20
Nebraska	7	17
Nevada	No Tax	n/a
New Hampshire	No Tax	n/a
New Jersey	7	21
New Mexico	9	6
New York	8	10
North Carolina	8	11
North Dakota	6	32
Ohio	8	14
Oklahoma	6	23
Oregon	9	5
Pennsylvania	3	41
Rhode Island	11	2
South Carolina	7	15
South Dakota	No Tax	n/a
Tennessee	No Tax	n/a
Texas	No Tax	n/a
Utah	6	30
Vermont	10	4
Virginia	6	31
Washington	No Tax	n/a
West Virginia	7	22
Wisconsin	7	18
Wyoming	No Tax	n/a
50 States	n/a	
DC	10	
United States	n/a	

Rank in order

By %

1. California
2. Rhode Island
3. Hawaii
4. Vermont
5. Oregon
6. Maine
6. Minnesota
6. New Mexico
9. Idaho
10. New York
11. Kansas
11. North Carolina
13. Delaware
14. Ohio
15. Arkansas
15. South Carolina
17. Nebraska
18. Wisconsin
19. Arizona
20. Montana
21. New Jersey
22. West Virginia
23. Oklahoma
24. Iowa
25. Georgia
25. Kentucky
25. Maryland
25. Missouri
29. Massachusetts
30. Utah
31. Virginia
32. North Dakota
33. Colorado
33. Mississippi
35. Connecticut
36. Michigan
37. Louisiana
38. Indiana
39. Alabama
40. Illinois
41. Pennsylvania

State	Corporate income tax effort %	Rank	Rank in order By %
Alabama	84	24	1. Michigan
Alaska	130	10	2. New York
Arizona	67	31	3. Louisiana
Arkansas	71	30	4. Kentucky
California	144	6	5. West Virginia
Colorado	35	47	6. California
Connecticut	111	13	7. Pennsylvania
Delaware	104	16	8. Montana
Florida	55	43	9. Tennessee
Georgia	67	31	10. Alaska
Hawaii	103	17	11. New Hampshire
Idaho	78	26	12. North Dakota
Illinois	77	27	13. Connecticut
Indiana	60	37	14. Mississippi
Iowa	95	21	15. Massachusetts
Kansas	99	19	16. Delaware
Kentucky	154	4	17. Hawaii
Louisiana	163	3	17. New Jersey
Maine	72	29	19. Kansas
Maryland	58	38	20. Minnesota
Massachusetts	105	15	21. Iowa
Michigan	192	1	21. North Carolina
Minnesota	98	20	23. Wisconsin
Mississippi	108	14	24. Alabama
Missouri	56	41	25. South Dakota
Montana	138	8	26. Idaho
Nebraska	65	33	27. Illinois
Nevada	0	49	28. Oklahoma
New Hampshire	114	11	29. Maine
New Jersey	103	17	30. Arkansas
New Mexico	52	44	31. Arizona
New York	175	2	31. Georgia
North Carolina	95	21	33. Nebraska
North Dakota	112	12	34. Utah
Ohio	62	35	35. Ohio
Oklahoma	75	28	36. Oregon
Oregon	61	36	37. Indiana
Pennsylvania	139	7	38. Maryland
Rhode Island	56	41	38. South Carolina
South Carolina	58	38	40. Vermont
South Dakota	83	25	41. Missouri
Tennessee	131	9	41. Rhode Island
Texas	38	46	43. Florida
Utah	63	34	44. New Mexico
Vermont	57	40	45. Virginia
Virginia	46	45	46. Texas
Washington	0	49	47. Colorado
West Virginia	149	5	48. Wyoming
Wisconsin	93	23	49. Nevada
Wyoming	6	48	49. Washington
50 States	n/a		
DC	124		
United States	100		

F-18 Motor Fuel Taxes

State	Gasoline Tax 1995 Cents/Gal.	Motor fuel taxes 1992 ($000)	Fuel taxes per $1000 pers. income $	Rank by gas tax
Alabama	18	363,745	5.7	30
Alaska	8	43,247	3.6	48
Arizona	18	396,946	6.4	30
Arkansas	19	304,368	8.8	27
California	18	2,248,089	3.5	30
Colorado	22	360,502	5.5	13
Connecticut	32	361,770	4.2	1
Delaware	23	72,874	5.1	10
Florida	12	1,446,374	5.7	45
Georgia	8	449,782	3.9	50
Hawaii	16	128,298	5.3	39
Idaho	22	132,019	8.3	13
Illinois	19	1,198,597	5.0	25
Indiana	15	542,470	5.6	43
Iowa	20	333,425	6.9	20
Kansas	18	251,000	5.5	30
Kentucky	16	360,058	6.2	38
Louisiana	20	470,116	7.3	20
Maine	19	143,483	6.7	25
Maryland	24	462,777	4.3	8
Massachusetts	21	541,069	3.9	17
Michigan	15	745,000	4.3	43
Minnesota	20	464,916	5.5	20
Mississippi	18	323,390	9.4	29
Missouri	15	384,689	4.2	42
Montana	27	121,493	9.6	3
Nebraska	25	222,145	7.9	5
Nevada	24	169,498	6.7	6
New Hampshire	19	92,534	3.8	27
New Jersey	11	410,625	2.1	46
New Mexico	21	182,739	8.1	17
New York	8	495,216	1.2	48
North Carolina	21	861,487	7.6	16
North Dakota	18	75,245	7.6	30
Ohio	22	1,128,960	5.8	13
Oklahoma	17	341,114	6.9	37
Oregon	24	280,153	5.5	6
Pennsylvania	22	694,408	3.0	12
Rhode Island	28	94,074	4.9	2
South Carolina	16	287,393	5.2	39
South Dakota	18	82,685	7.3	30
Tennessee	21	656,573	8.0	17
Texas	20	1,953,467	6.5	20
Utah	20	136,352	5.3	24
Vermont	16	55,854	5.5	41
Virginia	18	629,125	5.0	36
Washington	23	627,136	6.4	10
West Virginia	25	207,992	8.1	4
Wisconsin	23	568,929	6.4	9
Wyoming	9	38,326	4.9	47
50 States	n/a	22,942,527	4.8	
DC	20	28,586	1.7	
United States	n/a	22,944,113	4.8	

By gas tax

1. Connecticut
2. Rhode Island
3. Montana
4. West Virginia
5. Nebraska
6. Nevada
6. Oregon
8. Maryland
9. Wisconsin
10. Delaware
10. Washington
12. Pennsylvania
13. Colorado
13. Idaho
13. Ohio
16. North Carolina
17. Massachusetts
17. New Mexico
17. Tennessee
20. Iowa
20. Louisiana
20. Minnesota
20. Texas
24. Utah
25. Illinois
25. Maine
27. Arkansas
27. New Hampshire
29. Mississippi
30. Alabama
30. Arizona
30. California
30. Kansas
30. North Dakota
30. South Dakota
36. Virginia
37. Oklahoma
38. Kentucky
39. Hawaii
39. South Carolina
41. Vermont
42. Missouri
43. Indiana
43. Michigan
45. Florida
46. New Jersey
47. Wyoming
48. Alaska
48. New York
50. Georgia

F-19 Tobacco Taxes					Rank in order

State	Cigarettee Tax Rates 1995 Cents/Pack	Tobacco taxes 1992 ($000)	Tobacco taxes Per $1000 pers. income $	Rank by tax rate	By tax rate
Alabama	17	81,703	1.3	42	1. Michigan
Alaska	29	16,972	1.4	24	2. Hawaii
Arizona	18	52,548	0.8	37	3. Washington
Arkansas	32	65,948	1.9	22	4. New York
California	37	717,624	1.1	16	4. Rhode Island
Colorado	20	61,689	0.9	34	6. Massachusetts
Connecticut	50	118,713	1.4	7	7. Connecticut
Delaware	24	19,662	1.4	28	8. Minnesota
Florida	34	435,947	1.7	21	9. Illinois
Georgia	12	84,261	0.7	45	9. North Dakota
Hawaii	60	27,384	1.1	2	11. Texas
Idaho	28	22,995	1.4	25	12. New Jersey
Illinois	44	378,386	1.6	9	13. Maine
Indiana	16	111,196	1.2	43	14. Oregon
Iowa	36	97,433	2.0	17	14. Wisconsin
Kansas	24	55,549	1.2	28	16. California
Kentucky	3	14,045	0.2	49	17. Iowa
Louisiana	20	86,878	1.4	34	17. Maryland
Maine	39	52,127	2.4	13	19. Nevada
Maryland	36	91,867	0.9	17	20. Nebraska
Massachusetts	51	139,856	1.0	6	21. Florida
Michigan	75	245,937	1.4	1	22. Arkansas
Minnesota	48	164,767	1.9	8	23. Pennsylvania
Mississippi	18	51,778	1.5	37	24. Alaska
Missouri	17	100,933	1.1	40	25. Idaho
Montana	18	13,397	1.1	37	26. Utah
Nebraska	34	38,751	1.4	20	27. New Hampshire
Nevada	35	48,292	1.9	19	28. Delaware
New Hampshire	25	38,140	1.6	27	28. Kansas
New Jersey	40	269,465	1.4	12	28. Ohio
New Mexico	21	18,408	0.8	33	31. Oklahoma
New York	56	637,850	1.6	4	31. South Dakota
North Carolina	5	40,363	0.4	48	33. New Mexico
North Dakota	44	13,772	1.4	9	34. Colorado
Ohio	24	224,201	1.2	28	34. Louisiana
Oklahoma	23	68,854	1.4	31	34. Vermont
Oregon	38	87,551	1.7	14	37. Arizona
Pennsylvania	31	336,244	1.5	23	37. Mississippi
Rhode Island	56	36,545	1.9	4	37. Montana
South Carolina	7	28,461	0.5	47	40. Missouri
South Dakota	23	13,952	1.2	31	40. West Virginia
Tennessee	13	80,326	1.0	44	42. Alabama
Texas	41	582,793	1.9	11	43. Indiana
Utah	27	26,100	1.0	26	44. Tennessee
Vermont	20	13,996	1.4	34	45. Georgia
Virginia	3	41,147	0.3	50	45. Wyoming
Washington	56	146,930	1.5	3	47. South Carolina
West Virginia	17	32,088	1.2	40	48. North Carolina
Wisconsin	38	153,564	1.7	14	49. Kentucky
Wyoming	12	5,632	0.7	45	50. Virginia
50 States	n/a	6,293,020	1.3		
DC	65	17,065	1.0		
United States	n/a	6,310,085	1.3		

State	Tax Burden ($)	Rank	Rank in order By $
Alabama	6,157	41	1. New York
Alaska	2,291	50	2. Maryland
Arizona	7,788	23	3. Rhode Island
Arkansas	7,761	26	4. Maine
California	8,496	15	5. Connecticut
Colorado	7,503	32	6. Wisconsin
Connecticut	9,996	5	7. Massachusetts
Delaware	6,781	36	8. Ohio
Florida	4,686	47	9. New Jersey
Georgia	8,378	18	10. Minnesota
Hawaii	8,471	16	11. Michigan
Idaho	8,448	17	12. Oregon
Illinois	7,755	27	13. Nebraska
Indiana	7,416	33	14. Montana
Iowa	7,723	28	15. California
Kansas	7,159	35	16. Hawaii
Kentucky	7,632	30	17. Idaho
Louisiana	6,625	39	18. Georgia
Maine	10,132	4	19. North Carolina
Maryland	10,471	2	20. Utah
Massachusetts	9,513	7	21. New Mexico
Michigan	8,793	11	22. West Virginia
Minnesota	8,822	10	23. Arizona
Mississippi	6,759	37	24. Vermont
Missouri	6,698	38	25. Pennsylvania
Montana	8,541	14	26. Arkansas
Nebraska	8,613	13	27. Illinois
Nevada	4,238	48	28. Iowa
New Hampshire	5,506	42	29. South Carolina
New Jersey	8,832	9	30. Kentucky
New Mexico	7,809	21	31. Oklahoma
New York	10,529	1	32. Colorado
North Carolina	8,308	19	33. Indiana
North Dakota	6,552	40	34. Virginia
Ohio	9,088	8	35. Kansas
Oklahoma	7,622	31	36. Delaware
Oregon	8,787	12	37. Mississippi
Pennsylvania	7,781	25	38. Missouri
Rhode Island	10,294	3	39. Louisiana
South Carolina	7,678	29	40. North Dakota
South Dakota	5,151	45	41. Alabama
Tennessee	5,073	46	42. New Hampshire
Texas	5,290	44	43. Washington
Utah	8,172	20	44. Texas
Vermont	7,788	24	45. South Dakota
Virginia	7,303	34	46. Tennessee
Washington	5,463	43	47. Florida
West Virginia	7,809	22	48. Nevada
Wisconsin	9,976	6	49. Wyoming
Wyoming	3,104	49	50. Alaska
50 States	7,551		
DC	9,632		
United States	7,592		

State	Taxes $	Percent of income %	Rank by $	Rank in order By $
Alabama	4,396	8.8	27	1. Connecticut
Alaska	1,514	3.0	50	2. New York
Arizona	4,021	8.0	31	3. New Jersey
Arkansas	4,428	8.9	26	4. Wisconsin
California	3,780	7.6	38	5. Pennsylvania
Colorado	4,301	8.6	28	6. Maine
Connecticut	7,657	15.3	1	7. Michigan
Delaware	4,664	9.3	17	8. Massachusetts
Florida	2,438	4.9	47	9. Maryland
Georgia	5,046	10.1	13	10. Illinois
Hawaii	4,453	8.9	25	11. Kentucky
Idaho	4,042	8.1	29	12. Rhode Island
Illinois	5,521	11.0	10	13. Georgia
Indiana	3,965	7.9	33	14. Nebraska
Iowa	4,673	9.3	16	15. South Carolina
Kansas	3,804	7.6	37	16. Iowa
Kentucky	5,417	10.8	11	17. Delaware
Louisiana	3,086	6.2	44	18. New Hampshire
Maine	6,158	12.3	6	19. Ohio
Maryland	5,522	11.0	9	20. North Carolina
Massachusetts	5,638	11.3	8	21. Virginia
Michigan	6,133	12.3	7	22. Utah
Minnesota	4,465	8.9	23	23. Minnesota
Mississippi	3,853	7.7	36	24. Missouri
Missouri	4,462	8.9	24	25. Hawaii
Montana	4,024	8.0	30	26. Arkansas
Nebraska	4,946	9.9	14	27. Alabama
Nevada	2,436	4.9	48	28. Colorado
New Hampshire	4,645	9.3	18	29. Idaho
New Jersey	6,694	13.4	3	30. Montana
New Mexico	3,758	7.5	39	31. Arizona
New York	6,731	13.5	2	32. West Virginia
North Carolina	4,601	9.2	20	33. Indiana
North Dakota	3,411	6.8	42	34. Vermont
Ohio	4,622	9.2	19	35. South Dakota
Oklahoma	3,700	7.4	40	36. Mississippi
Oregon	3,491	7.0	41	37. Kansas
Pennsylvania	6,181	12.4	5	38. California
Rhode Island	5,417	10.8	12	39. New Mexico
South Carolina	4,787	9.6	15	40. Oklahoma
South Dakota	3,934	7.9	35	41. Oregon
Tennessee	2,619	5.2	46	42. North Dakota
Texas	2,916	5.8	45	43. Washington
Utah	4,491	9.0	22	44. Louisiana
Vermont	3,937	7.9	34	45. Texas
Virginia	4,530	9.1	21	46. Tennessee
Washington	3,227	6.5	43	47. Florida
West Virginia	4,001	8.0	32	48. Nevada
Wisconsin	6,659	13.3	4	49. Wyoming
Wyoming	1,867	3.7	49	50. Alaska
50 States	4,421	8.8		
DC	4,737	9.5		
United States	4,427	8.9		

State	Progressivity Index	Rank
Alabama	0.712	44
Alaska	1.146	2
Arizona	0.991	12
Arkansas	0.818	33
California	0.612	49
Colorado	0.899	24
Connecticut	0.808	34
Delaware	0.783	37
Florida	0.858	28
Georgia	0.939	18
Hawaii	0.763	39
Idaho	0.666	48
Illinois	0.995	11
Indiana	1.011	10
Iowa	0.837	30
Kansas	0.821	32
Kentucky	0.936	20
Louisiana	0.533	50
Maine	0.853	29
Maryland	0.972	13
Massachusetts	0.968	14
Michigan	0.953	16
Minnesota	0.704	46
Mississippi	0.719	43
Missouri	0.964	15
Montana	0.690	47
Nebraska	0.912	22
Nevada	1.143	4
New Hampshire	1.100	7
New Jersey	0.942	17
New Mexico	0.747	41
New York	0.705	45
North Carolina	0.859	27
North Dakota	0.936	21
Ohio	0.883	26
Oklahoma	0.831	31
Oregon	0.776	38
Pennsylvania	1.042	9
Rhode Island	0.898	25
South Carolina	0.743	42
South Dakota	1.145	3
Tennessee	1.218	1
Texas	1.119	6
Utah	0.807	35
Vermont	0.753	40
Virginia	0.905	23
Washington	1.137	5
West Virginia	0.802	36
Wisconsin	0.939	19
Wyoming	1.076	8
50 States	0.887	
DC	0.770	
United States	0.869	

Rank in order

By Index

1. Tennessee
2. Alaska
3. South Dakota
4. Nevada
5. Washington
6. Texas
7. New Hampshire
8. Wyoming
9. Pennsylvania
10. Indiana
11. Illinois
12. Arizona
13. Maryland
14. Massachusetts
15. Missouri
16. Michigan
17. New Jersey
18. Georgia
19. Wisconsin
20. Kentucky
21. North Dakota
22. Nebraska
23. Virginia
24. Colorado
25. Rhode Island
26. Ohio
27. North Carolina
28. Florida
29. Maine
30. Iowa
31. Oklahoma
32. Kansas
33. Arkansas
34. Connecticut
35. Utah
36. West Virginia
37. Delaware
38. Oregon
39. Hawaii
40. Vermont
41. New Mexico
42. South Carolina
43. Mississippi
44. Alabama
45. New York
46. Minnesota
47. Montana
48. Idaho
49. California
50. Louisiana

State	Estate taxes above federal credit level	Inheritance taxes above federal credit level
Alabama		
Alaska		
Arizona		
Arkansas		
California		
Colorado		
Connecticut		Inheritance
Delaware		Inheritance
Florida		
Georgia		
Hawaii		
Idaho		
Illinois		
Indiana		Inheritance
Iowa		Inheritance
Kansas		Inheritance
Kentucky		Inheritance
Louisiana		Inheritance
Maine		
Maryland		Inheritance
Massachusetts	Estate	
Michigan		
Minnesota		
Mississippi	Estate	
Missouri		
Montana		Inheritance
Nebraska		Inheritance
Nevada		
New Hampshire		Inheritance
New Jersey		Inheritance
New Mexico		
New York	Estate	
North Carolina		Inheritance
North Dakota		
Ohio	Estate	
Oklahoma	Estate	
Oregon		
Pennsylvania		Inheritance
Rhode Island		
South Carolina		
South Dakota		Inheritance
Tennessee		Inheritance
Texas		
Utah		
Vermont		
Virginia		
Washington		
West Virginia		
Wisconsin		
Wyoming		
50 States		
DC		
United States		

Revenues and Finances

State	Total state & local revenue ($Bil)	Rank	Rank in order By $
Alabama	16.1	23	1. California
Alaska	7.9	34	2. New York
Arizona	16.1	24	3. Texas
Arkansas	8.0	33	4. Pennsylvania
California	162.2	1	5. Florida
Colorado	15.9	25	6. Ohio
Connecticut	17.6	22	7. Illinois
Delaware	3.6	46	8. New Jersey
Florida	53.4	5	9. Michigan
Georgia	27.3	11	10. Massachusetts
Hawaii	6.6	39	11. Georgia
Idaho	4.0	44	12. North Carolina
Illinois	48.2	7	13. Washington
Indiana	20.9	19	14. Wisconsin
Iowa	11.5	30	15. Virginia
Kansas	10.0	31	16. Minnesota
Kentucky	14.5	27	17. Maryland
Louisiana	18.2	21	18. Tennessee
Maine	5.4	41	19. Indiana
Maryland	22.1	17	20. Missouri
Massachusetts	30.8	10	21. Louisiana
Michigan	42.6	9	22. Connecticut
Minnesota	23.4	16	23. Alabama
Mississippi	9.1	32	24. Arizona
Missouri	18.3	20	25. Colorado
Montana	3.6	45	26. Oregon
Nebraska	7.7	35	27. Kentucky
Nevada	6.0	40	28. South Carolina
New Hampshire	4.5	43	29. Oklahoma
New Jersey	42.6	8	30. Iowa
New Mexico	7.0	38	31. Kansas
New York	125.8	2	32. Mississippi
North Carolina	27.1	12	33. Arkansas
North Dakota	2.8	48	34. Alaska
Ohio	50.2	6	35. Nebraska
Oklahoma	12.1	29	36. Utah
Oregon	15.2	26	37. West Virginia
Pennsylvania	54.8	4	38. New Mexico
Rhode Island	4.8	42	39. Hawaii
South Carolina	14.3	28	40. Nevada
South Dakota	2.6	50	41. Maine
Tennessee	20.9	18	42. Rhode Island
Texas	67.6	3	43. New Hampshire
Utah	7.6	36	44. Idaho
Vermont	2.7	49	45. Montana
Virginia	24.5	15	46. Delaware
Washington	27.0	13	47. Wyoming
West Virginia	7.1	37	48. North Dakota
Wisconsin	24.6	14	49. Vermont
Wyoming	2.9	47	50. South Dakota
50 States	1,179.7		
DC	5.4		
United States	1,185.1		

State	General Revenue ($Bil)	Per $1000 of pers. income $	per capita $	Rank by per capita
Alabama	12.8	202	3,103	45
Alaska	6.7	559	11,449	1
Arizona	12.8	206	3,350	33
Arkansas	6.9	199	2,871	50
California	127.9	202	4,144	10
Colorado	12.8	195	3,678	23
Connecticut	15.0	176	4,584	6
Delaware	3.0	213	4,379	7
Florida	46.0	182	3,409	30
Georgia	22.4	194	3,315	35
Hawaii	5.7	236	4,885	4
Idaho	3.4	216	3,221	41
Illinois	40.8	171	3,509	29
Indiana	18.4	191	3,257	39
Iowa	10.1	210	3,607	25
Kansas	8.5	186	3,363	32
Kentucky	12.2	211	3,257	38
Louisiana	15.6	243	3,632	24
Maine	4.7	218	3,799	20
Maryland	18.3	170	3,737	21
Massachusetts	25.7	186	4,281	9
Michigan	35.9	206	3,806	17
Minnesota	19.6	231	4,375	8
Mississippi	7.7	224	2,959	49
Missouri	15.5	167	2,975	48
Montana	3.1	243	3,734	22
Nebraska	5.8	205	3,601	27
Nevada	4.7	187	3,574	28
New Hampshire	4.0	166	3,602	26
New Jersey	36.4	183	4,677	5
New Mexico	6.0	265	3,805	18
New York	103.2	254	5,696	2
North Carolina	21.7	191	3,164	43
North Dakota	2.5	247	3,853	15
Ohio	37.3	192	3,388	31
Oklahoma	9.9	201	3,084	46
Oregon	12.0	234	4,035	12
Pennsylvania	45.6	198	3,801	19
Rhode Island	4.0	207	3,965	13
South Carolina	11.4	207	3,161	44
South Dakota	2.3	203	3,231	40
Tennessee	15.2	186	3,021	47
Texas	56.7	190	3,213	42
Utah	6.0	230	3,282	37
Vermont	2.3	230	4,118	11
Virginia	21.3	168	3,334	34
Washington	20.2	207	3,932	14
West Virginia	5.9	231	3,283	36
Wisconsin	19.1	215	3,819	16
Wyoming	2.5	326	5,437	3
50 States	967.7	202	3,803	
DC	4.7	288	8,041	
United States	972.5	202	3,812	

Rank in order

By per capita

1. Alaska
2. New York
3. Wyoming
4. Hawaii
5. New Jersey
6. Connecticut
7. Delaware
8. Minnesota
9. Massachusetts
10. California
11. Vermont
12. Oregon
13. Rhode Island
14. Washington
15. North Dakota
16. Wisconsin
17. Michigan
18. New Mexico
19. Pennsylvania
20. Maine
21. Maryland
22. Montana
23. Colorado
24. Louisiana
25. Iowa
26. New Hampshire
27. Nebraska
28. Nevada
29. Illinois
30. Florida
31. Ohio
32. Kansas
33. Arizona
34. Virginia
35. Georgia
36. West Virginia
37. Utah
38. Kentucky
39. Indiana
40. South Dakota
41. Idaho
42. Texas
43. North Carolina
44. South Carolina
45. Alabama
46. Oklahoma
47. Tennessee
48. Missouri
49. Mississippi
50. Arkansas

G-3 State And Local Own-Source General Revenue, 1992

State	State & local own-source general rev. ($Bil)	Per Capita $	Per $1000 pers. income $	Rank by per capita	By per capita
Alabama	9.9	2,395	156	45	1. Alaska
Alaska	5.9	10,003	489	1	2. New York
Arizona	10.7	2,786	172	32	3. Hawaii
Arkansas	5.2	2,155	149	49	4. New Jersey
California	103.7	3,360	164	10	5. Wyoming
Colorado	10.7	3,077	163	17	6. Connecticut
Connecticut	12.6	3,830	147	6	7. Delaware
Delaware	2.6	3,744	182	7	8. Minnesota
Florida	39.6	2,937	157	25	9. Massachusetts
Georgia	18.1	2,686	157	35	10. California
Hawaii	4.7	4,075	197	3	11. Washington
Idaho	2.8	2,595	174	39	12. Oregon
Illinois	34.1	2,930	142	26	13. Vermont
Indiana	15.1	2,669	157	37	14. Wisconsin
Iowa	8.4	2,990	174	22	15. Maryland
Kansas	7.1	2,801	155	30	16. Michigan
Kentucky	9.4	2,514	163	41	17. Colorado
Louisiana	11.6	2,695	181	34	18. Pennsylvania
Maine	3.7	2,990	171	21	19. Nevada
Maryland	15.4	3,129	142	15	20. New Mexico
Massachusetts	20.8	3,472	151	9	21. Maine
Michigan	29.5	3,127	169	16	22. Iowa
Minnesota	16.5	3,678	194	8	23. Nebraska
Mississippi	5.6	2,124	161	50	24. Rhode Island
Missouri	12.2	2,358	132	47	25. Florida
Montana	2.3	2,796	182	31	26. Illinois
Nebraska	4.8	2,986	170	23	27. North Dakota
Nevada	4.0	3,036	159	19	28. New Hampshire
New Hampshire	3.2	2,896	134	28	29. Virginia
New Jersey	31.1	3,987	156	4	30. Kansas
New Mexico	4.8	3,022	211	20	31. Montana
New York	84.1	4,639	207	2	32. Arizona
North Carolina	17.5	2,563	154	40	33. Ohio
North Dakota	1.8	2,903	186	27	34. Louisiana
Ohio	30.2	2,745	156	33	35. Georgia
Oklahoma	8.0	2,495	162	42	36. Texas
Oregon	9.6	3,224	187	12	37. Indiana
Pennsylvania	36.8	3,068	160	18	38. Utah
Rhode Island	3.0	2,958	154	24	39. Idaho
South Carolina	8.9	2,459	161	43	40. North Carolina
South Dakota	1.7	2,388	150	46	41. Kentucky
Tennessee	11.5	2,286	141	48	42. Oklahoma
Texas	47.4	2,682	158	36	43. South Carolina
Utah	4.8	2,627	184	38	44. West Virginia
Vermont	1.8	3,209	179	13	45. Alabama
Virginia	18.3	2,871	145	29	46. South Dakota
Washington	16.9	3,283	172	11	47. Missouri
West Virginia	4.4	2,434	171	44	48. Tennessee
Wisconsin	15.9	3,178	179	14	49. Arkansas
Wyoming	1.9	3,984	239	5	50. Mississippi
50 States	790.3	3,106	165		
DC	2.9	5,010	180		
United States	793.3	3,110	165		

State	Non-tax revenue $	non-tax revenue as % of personal income %	Rank by $
Alabama	3,969,131	6.3	20
Alaska	3,616,735	30.1	23
Arizona	2,928,235	4.7	27
Arkansas	1,535,969	4.4	37
California	31,632,001	5.0	1
Colorado	3,664,062	5.6	22
Connecticut	2,531,148	3.0	31
Delaware	961,717	6.8	42
Florida	13,700,074	5.4	4
Georgia	5,766,952	5.0	10
Hawaii	1,334,835	5.6	39
Idaho	870,767	5.5	44
Illinois	8,472,008	3.5	8
Indiana	5,006,596	5.2	15
Iowa	2,714,163	5.6	30
Kansas	2,126,105	4.7	32
Kentucky	2,850,576	4.9	28
Louisiana	4,477,662	7.0	17
Maine	1,033,357	4.8	41
Maryland	3,887,924	3.6	21
Massachusetts	5,516,565	4.0	12
Michigan	9,006,851	5.2	6
Minnesota	5,394,791	6.4	13
Mississippi	2,093,834	6.1	33
Missouri	3,599,150	3.9	24
Montana	848,621	6.7	45
Nebraska	1,560,802	5.5	36
Nevada	1,315,694	5.2	40
New Hampshire	879,101	3.7	43
New Jersey	8,169,447	4.1	9
New Mexico	1,949,465	8.6	34
New York	20,057,550	4.9	2
North Carolina	5,140,934	4.5	14
North Dakota	728,414	7.4	47
Ohio	8,898,894	4.6	7
Oklahoma	2,772,360	5.6	29
Oregon	3,368,444	6.6	25
Pennsylvania	10,573,584	4.6	5
Rhode Island	727,516	3.8	48
South Carolina	3,152,190	5.7	26
South Dakota	589,712	5.2	49
Tennessee	4,093,176	5.0	19
Texas	14,515,051	4.9	3
Utah	1,681,604	6.5	35
Vermont	525,633	5.2	50
Virginia	5,623,830	4.5	11
Washington	4,918,187	5.0	16
West Virginia	1,406,329	5.5	38
Wisconsin	4,301,843	4.8	18
Wyoming	770,676	9.9	46
50 States	237,260,265	4.9	
DC	528,970	3.2	
United States	237,789,235	4.9	

G-4 Non-Tax Revenue, 1992

Rank in order

By $

1. California
2. New York
3. Texas
4. Florida
5. Pennsylvania
6. Michigan
7. Ohio
8. Illinois
9. New Jersey
10. Georgia
11. Virginia
12. Massachusetts
13. Minnesota
14. North Carolina
15. Indiana
16. Washington
17. Louisiana
18. Wisconsin
19. Tennessee
20. Alabama
21. Maryland
22. Colorado
23. Alaska
24. Missouri
25. Oregon
26. South Carolina
27. Arizona
28. Kentucky
29. Oklahoma
30. Iowa
31. Connecticut
32. Kansas
33. Mississippi
34. New Mexico
35. Utah
36. Nebraska
37. Arkansas
38. West Virginia
39. Hawaii
40. Nevada
41. Maine
42. Delaware
43. New Hampshire
44. Idaho
45. Montana
46. Wyoming
47. North Dakota
48. Rhode Island
49. South Dakota
50. Vermont

State	State & Local total Expenditures ($Bil)	Per $1000 personal income $	Rank by total exp.
Alabama	15	238	25
Alaska	7	557	37
Arizona	16	256	23
Arkansas	7	211	34
California	163	257	1
Colorado	15	231	24
Connecticut	17	201	21
Delaware	3	231	46
Florida	54	215	4
Georgia	26	226	12
Hawaii	7	278	38
Idaho	4	229	44
Illinois	47	195	6
Indiana	20	206	18
Iowa	11	230	30
Kansas	10	210	31
Kentucky	14	234	28
Louisiana	18	275	20
Maine	5	243	41
Maryland	21	191	17
Massachusetts	31	222	10
Michigan	41	237	9
Minnesota	23	267	15
Mississippi	8	244	32
Missouri	17	184	22
Montana	3	262	45
Nebraska	7	263	33
Nevada	6	252	40
New Hampshire	5	190	43
New Jersey	42	213	8
New Mexico	7	291	39
New York	124	307	2
North Carolina	25	223	13
North Dakota	3	273	48
Ohio	46	234	7
Oklahoma	12	236	29
Oregon	14	268	27
Pennsylvania	53	230	5
Rhode Island	5	267	42
South Carolina	14	253	26
South Dakota	2	217	50
Tennessee	20	242	19
Texas	65	217	3
Utah	7	281	35
Vermont	3	254	49
Virginia	24	186	14
Washington	28	283	11
West Virginia	7	265	36
Wisconsin	22	248	16
Wyoming	3	351	47
50 States	1,145	238	
DC	6	356	
United States	1,150	239	

Rank in order

By $

1. California
2. New York
3. Texas
4. Florida
5. Pennsylvania
6. Illinois
7. Ohio
8. New Jersey
9. Michigan
10. Massachusetts
11. Washington
12. Georgia
13. North Carolina
14. Virginia
15. Minnesota
16. Wisconsin
17. Maryland
18. Indiana
19. Tennessee
20. Louisiana
21. Connecticut
22. Missouri
23. Arizona
24. Colorado
25. Alabama
26. South Carolina
27. Oregon
28. Kentucky
29. Oklahoma
30. Iowa
31. Kansas
32. Mississippi
33. Nebraska
34. Arkansas
35. Utah
36. West Virginia
37. Alaska
38. Hawaii
39. New Mexico
40. Nevada
41. Maine
42. Rhode Island
43. New Hampshire
44. Idaho
45. Montana
46. Delaware
47. Wyoming
48. North Dakota
49. Vermont
50. South Dakota

G-6 State And Local General Expenditures, 1992

State	State & Local General Exp ($Bil)	Per $1000 personal income $	Rank by total gen. exp.
Alabama	12.9	203	24
Alaska	5.8	483	37
Arizona	13.4	216	23
Arkansas	6.6	190	33
California	130.1	205	1
Colorado	12.8	196	25
Connecticut	15.1	176	21
Delaware	2.9	207	45
Florida	47.1	187	4
Georgia	22.4	194	11
Hawaii	6.0	251	34
Idaho	3.3	205	44
Illinois	40.3	169	6
Indiana	18.1	187	17
Iowa	10.1	209	29
Kansas	8.6	187	31
Kentucky	12.0	206	26
Louisiana	15.8	247	19
Maine	4.6	216	41
Maryland	17.9	166	18
Massachusetts	24.7	179	10
Michigan	35.6	204	9
Minnesota	20.1	238	15
Mississippi	7.5	217	32
Missouri	15.0	162	22
Montana	2.9	231	46
Nebraska	5.5	196	39
Nevada	5.3	209	40
New Hampshire	4.1	170	43
New Jersey	36.6	184	8
New Mexico	6.0	264	35
New York	102.2	252	2
North Carolina	21.3	187	13
North Dakota	2.5	250	47
Ohio	37.5	193	7
Oklahoma	10.0	203	30
Oregon	11.8	230	27
Pennsylvania	45.4	197	5
Rhode Island	4.4	228	42
South Carolina	11.7	212	28
South Dakota	2.3	200	50
Tennessee	15.1	185	20
Texas	55.6	186	3
Utah	5.8	224	38
Vermont	2.3	228	49
Virginia	21.1	167	14
Washington	21.6	221	12
West Virginia	5.8	226	36
Wisconsin	19.8	223	16
Wyoming	2.5	316	48
50 States	967.8	202	
DC	4.4	271	
United States	972.2	202	

Rank in order

By total gen. exp.

1. California
2. New York
3. Texas
4. Florida
5. Pennsylvania
6. Illinois
7. Ohio
8. New Jersey
9. Michigan
10. Massachusetts
11. Georgia
12. Washington
13. North Carolina
14. Virginia
15. Minnesota
16. Wisconsin
17. Indiana
18. Maryland
19. Louisiana
20. Tennessee
21. Connecticut
22. Missouri
23. Arizona
24. Alabama
25. Colorado
26. Kentucky
27. Oregon
28. South Carolina
29. Iowa
30. Oklahoma
31. Kansas
32. Mississippi
33. Arkansas
34. Hawaii
35. New Mexico
36. West Virginia
37. Alaska
38. Utah
39. Nebraska
40. Nevada
41. Maine
42. Rhode Island
43. New Hampshire
44. Idaho
45. Delaware
46. Montana
47. North Dakota
48. Wyoming
49. Vermont
50. South Dakota

State	State & local general exp. per capita $	State general exp. per capita $	Local general exp. per capita $	Rank by state & local per capita	Rank in order By st. & local
Alabama	3,111	2,125	1,504	44	1. Alaska
Alaska	9,893	8,157	3,523	1	2. New York
Arizona	3,509	2,149	2,142	28	3. Wyoming
Arkansas	2,751	2,110	1,251	50	4. Hawaii
California	4,215	2,701	2,834	10	5. New Jersey
Colorado	3,697	1,871	2,393	22	6. Connecticut
Connecticut	4,591	3,035	2,194	6	7. Minnesota
Delaware	4,250	3,253	1,563	9	8. Rhode Island
Florida	3,493	1,842	2,274	29	9. Delaware
Georgia	3,311	1,893	1,969	34	10. California
Hawaii	5,203	4,226	1,087	4	11. Washington
Idaho	3,060	2,170	1,622	46	12. Massachusetts
Illinois	3,467	2,032	2,011	30	13. Vermont
Indiana	3,189	2,065	1,773	39	14. Nevada
Iowa	3,587	2,387	2,013	26	15. Wisconsin
Kansas	3,392	2,002	1,960	33	16. Oregon
Kentucky	3,184	2,459	1,361	40	17. North Dakota
Louisiana	3,681	2,492	1,804	23	18. New Mexico
Maine	3,762	2,617	1,722	21	19. Pennsylvania
Maryland	3,656	2,244	1,934	25	20. Michigan
Massachusetts	4,117	2,970	1,823	12	21. Maine
Michigan	3,771	2,314	2,196	20	22. Colorado
Minnesota	4,494	2,750	2,800	7	23. Louisiana
Mississippi	2,870	1,996	1,549	49	24. New Hampshire
Missouri	2,884	1,832	1,586	48	25. Maryland
Montana	3,553	2,558	1,735	27	26. Iowa
Nebraska	3,443	2,201	1,894	31	27. Montana
Nevada	3,998	2,225	2,607	14	28. Arizona
New Hampshire	3,677	2,208	1,734	24	29. Florida
New Jersey	4,694	3,095	2,607	5	30. Illinois
New Mexico	3,788	2,905	1,772	18	31. Nebraska
New York	5,642	3,359	3,647	2	32. Ohio
North Carolina	3,108	2,144	1,771	45	33. Kansas
North Dakota	3,898	2,883	1,648	17	34. Georgia
Ohio	3,402	2,188	1,940	32	35. Virginia
Oklahoma	3,125	2,199	1,601	43	36. South Carolina
Oregon	3,959	2,298	2,203	16	37. West Virginia
Pennsylvania	3,781	2,526	1,972	19	38. Utah
Rhode Island	4,376	3,315	1,559	8	39. Indiana
South Carolina	3,235	2,212	1,587	36	40. Kentucky
South Dakota	3,179	2,095	1,478	41	41. South Dakota
Tennessee	3,005	1,917	1,544	47	42. Texas
Texas	3,151	1,741	1,940	42	43. Oklahoma
Utah	3,203	2,238	1,593	38	44. Alabama
Vermont	4,077	2,966	1,643	13	45. North Carolina
Virginia	3,311	1,991	1,868	35	46. Idaho
Washington	4,211	2,867	2,235	11	47. Tennessee
West Virginia	3,213	2,426	1,421	37	48. Missouri
Wisconsin	3,964	2,448	2,483	15	49. Mississippi
Wyoming	5,282	3,703	2,975	3	50. Arkansas
50 States	3,803	2,404	2,194		
DC	7,548	0	7,548		
United States	3,811	2,404	2,207		

State	% change	Rank	Rank in order By %
Alabama	51.8	18	1. Hawaii
Alaska	10.9	50	2. Nevada
Arizona	41.7	34	3. New Hampshire
Arkansas	44.9	26	4. Washington
California	50.8	19	5. Florida
Colorado	37.3	42	6. Pennsylvania
Connecticut	60.4	8	7. South Carolina
Delaware	52.0	17	8. Connecticut
Florida	66.7	5	9. North Carolina
Georgia	49.9	21	10. Rhode Island
Hawaii	96.6	1	11. Maine
Idaho	57.1	12	12. Idaho
Illinois	38.2	41	13. New Jersey
Indiana	50.8	20	14. Oregon
Iowa	41.4	35	15. Kentucky
Kansas	38.7	39	16. Vermont
Kentucky	53.7	15	17. Delaware
Louisiana	43.3	29	18. Alabama
Maine	57.7	11	19. California
Maryland	43.2	30	20. Indiana
Massachusetts	40.0	37	21. Georgia
Michigan	33.1	45	22. Tennessee
Minnesota	44.5	27	23. Virginia
Mississippi	41.0	36	24. New Mexico
Missouri	41.8	33	25. New York
Montana	25.5	47	26. Arkansas
Nebraska	39.9	38	27. Minnesota
Nevada	87.3	2	28. Wisconsin
New Hampshire	72.7	3	29. Louisiana
New Jersey	56.8	13	30. Maryland
New Mexico	48.2	24	31. Ohio
New York	46.4	25	32. Texas
North Carolina	59.6	9	33. Missouri
North Dakota	27.4	46	34. Arizona
Ohio	42.8	31	35. Iowa
Oklahoma	38.5	40	36. Mississippi
Oregon	54.0	14	37. Massachusetts
Pennsylvania	61.4	6	38. Nebraska
Rhode Island	59.4	10	39. Kansas
South Carolina	60.5	7	40. Oklahoma
South Dakota	25.3	48	41. Illinois
Tennessee	49.7	22	42. Colorado
Texas	42.6	32	43. Utah
Utah	35.8	43	44. West Virginia
Vermont	53.5	16	45. Michigan
Virginia	49.0	23	46. North Dakota
Washington	71.3	4	47. Montana
West Virginia	35.0	44	48. South Dakota
Wisconsin	44.3	28	49. Wyoming
Wyoming	13.5	49	50. Alaska
50 States	48.2		
DC	37.7		
United States	48.2		

G-9 State Government General Revenue, 1993

State	state govt general revenue ($000)	per capita $	Rank by per capita	Rank in order By per capita
Alabama	9,688,246	2,317	33	1. Alaska
Alaska	6,159,665	10,300	1	2. Hawaii
Arizona	8,808,186	2,233	40	3. Wyoming
Arkansas	5,626,556	2,319	32	4. Delaware
California	84,408,527	2,704	19	5. New York
Colorado	7,840,311	2,200	43	6. Connecticut
Connecticut	11,011,362	3,359	6	7. New Mexico
Delaware	2,532,084	3,628	4	8. Massachusetts
Florida	27,653,930	2,015	47	9. North Dakota
Georgia	14,076,646	2,040	46	10. New Jersey
Hawaii	4,837,650	4,149	2	11. Vermont
Idaho	2,745,624	2,496	25	12. Rhode Island
Illinois	24,971,077	2,137	45	13. Minnesota
Indiana	13,465,127	2,360	29	14. Montana
Iowa	7,123,434	2,525	24	15. Washington
Kansas	5,835,855	2,302	35	16. Maine
Kentucky	9,632,496	2,539	23	17. West Virginia
Louisiana	11,635,787	2,712	18	18. Louisiana
Maine	3,428,499	2,765	16	19. California
Maryland	12,070,672	2,435	27	20. Wisconsin
Massachusetts	19,251,683	3,199	8	21. Michigan
Michigan	24,638,379	2,604	21	22. Oregon
Minnesota	13,396,723	2,961	13	23. Kentucky
Mississippi	6,030,790	2,284	37	24. Iowa
Missouri	10,334,735	1,974	50	25. Idaho
Montana	2,407,806	2,863	14	26. Pennsylvania
Nebraska	3,712,109	2,301	36	27. Maryland
Nevada	3,185,186	2,305	34	28. Utah
New Hampshire	2,550,473	2,269	38	29. Indiana
New Jersey	23,816,234	3,030	10	30. North Carolina
New Mexico	5,375,922	3,327	7	31. South Carolina
New York	62,985,784	3,470	5	32. Arkansas
North Carolina	16,369,721	2,355	30	33. Alabama
North Dakota	2,009,521	3,155	9	34. Nevada
Ohio	24,483,360	2,213	42	35. Kansas
Oklahoma	7,274,678	2,250	39	36. Nebraska
Oregon	7,771,877	2,561	22	37. Mississippi
Pennsylvania	29,911,880	2,486	26	38. New Hampshire
Rhode Island	3,017,865	3,018	12	39. Oklahoma
South Carolina	8,429,365	2,322	31	40. Arizona
South Dakota	1,590,669	2,222	41	41. South Dakota
Tennessee	10,134,775	1,990	48	42. Ohio
Texas	35,688,184	1,980	49	43. Colorado
Utah	4,437,144	2,386	28	44. Virginia
Vermont	1,741,693	3,024	11	45. Illinois
Virginia	13,972,671	2,159	44	46. Georgia
Washington	14,587,491	2,774	15	47. Florida
West Virginia	5,016,409	2,759	17	48. Tennessee
Wisconsin	13,609,610	2,698	20	49. Texas
Wyoming	1,850,689	3,938	3	50. Missouri
50 States	653,135,160	2,539		
DC	n/a	n/a		
United States	653,135,160	2,534		

G-10 State Government Spending, 1993

State	State gov't general expenditure 1993 ($000)	Rank	Rank in order By $
Alabama	9,339,796	24	1. California
Alaska	4,933,907	36	2. New York
Arizona	8,782,381	26	3. Texas
Arkansas	5,455,006	32	4. Pennsylvania
California	89,037,012	1	5. Florida
Colorado	7,471,882	28	6. Ohio
Connecticut	10,582,334	20	7. Illinois
Delaware	2,319,842	45	8. New Jersey
Florida	27,688,696	5	9. Michigan
Georgia	14,061,084	13	10. Massachusetts
Hawaii	5,087,791	35	11. North Carolina
Idaho	2,441,966	44	12. Washington
Illinois	24,682,312	7	13. Georgia
Indiana	13,480,105	14	14. Indiana
Iowa	7,197,879	29	15. Virginia
Kansas	5,274,778	33	16. Wisconsin
Kentucky	9,550,437	23	17. Minnesota
Louisiana	11,725,998	18	18. Louisiana
Maine	3,405,338	41	19. Maryland
Maryland	11,406,315	19	20. Connecticut
Massachusetts	18,684,419	10	21. Tennessee
Michigan	23,357,795	9	22. Missouri
Minnesota	13,003,118	17	23. Kentucky
Mississippi	5,585,172	31	24. Alabama
Missouri	9,817,390	22	25. South Carolina
Montana	2,282,752	46	26. Arizona
Nebraska	3,717,214	39	27. Oregon
Nevada	3,150,967	42	28. Colorado
New Hampshire	2,583,651	43	29. Iowa
New Jersey	23,630,213	8	30. Oklahoma
New Mexico	5,189,922	34	31. Mississippi
New York	61,557,640	2	32. Arkansas
North Carolina	15,494,643	11	33. Kansas
North Dakota	1,919,490	47	34. New Mexico
Ohio	25,037,974	6	35. Hawaii
Oklahoma	7,057,834	30	36. Alaska
Oregon	7,684,558	27	37. West Virginia
Pennsylvania	28,704,733	4	38. Utah
Rhode Island	3,539,123	40	39. Nebraska
South Carolina	8,793,206	25	40. Rhode Island
South Dakota	1,603,543	50	41. Maine
Tennessee	10,287,797	21	42. Nevada
Texas	35,111,320	3	43. New Hampshire
Utah	4,370,101	38	44. Idaho
Vermont	1,696,410	48	45. Delaware
Virginia	13,398,381	15	46. Montana
Washington	15,141,261	12	47. North Dakota
West Virginia	4,832,665	37	48. Vermont
Wisconsin	13,272,436	16	49. Wyoming
Wyoming	1,657,030	49	50. South Dakota
50 States	646,087,617		
DC	n/a		
United States	646,087,617		

G-11 State Government Spending, 1994

State	State gov't spending ($mil)	Rank
Alabama	10,831	23
Alaska	4,980	36
Arizona	8,752	27
Arkansas	6,748	32
California	86,729	1
Colorado	7,861	29
Connecticut	13,677	17
Delaware	3,021	41
Florida	36,741	3
Georgia	16,403	12
Hawaii	6,256	34
Idaho	2,561	42
Illinois	25,676	7
Indiana	12,512	20
Iowa	8,651	28
Kansas	7,035	31
Kentucky	10,946	22
Louisiana	14,573	16
Maine	3,598	39
Maryland	12,541	19
Massachusetts	17,385	11
Michigan	22,524	8
Minnesota	13,267	18
Mississippi	6,428	33
Missouri	10,587	24
Montana	2,273	44
Nebraska	4,035	38
Nevada	n/a	n/a
New Hampshire	2,415	43
New Jersey	21,966	9
New Mexico	n/a	n/a
New York	57,907	2
North Carolina	17,515	10
North Dakota	1,651	46
Ohio	28,618	6
Oklahoma	7,419	30
Oregon	10,136	25
Pennsylvania	29,966	5
Rhode Island	3,326	40
South Carolina	10,093	26
South Dakota	1,603	47
Tennessee	11,740	21
Texas	35,768	4
Utah	4,360	37
Vermont	1,551	48
Virginia	15,382	13
Washington	15,229	14
West Virginia	5,365	35
Wisconsin	14,824	15
Wyoming	1,793	45
50 States	675,218	
DC		
United States	675,218	

Rank in order

By $

1. California
2. New York
3. Florida
4. Texas
5. Pennsylvania
6. Ohio
7. Illinois
8. Michigan
9. New Jersey
10. North Carolina
11. Massachusetts
12. Georgia
13. Virginia
14. Washington
15. Wisconsin
16. Louisiana
17. Connecticut
18. Minnesota
19. Maryland
20. Indiana
21. Tennessee
22. Kentucky
23. Alabama
24. Missouri
25. Oregon
26. South Carolina
27. Arizona
28. Iowa
29. Colorado
30. Oklahoma
31. Kansas
32. Arkansas
33. Mississippi
34. Hawaii
35. West Virginia
36. Alaska
37. Utah
38. Nebraska
39. Maine
40. Rhode Island
41. Delaware
42. Idaho
43. New Hampshire
44. Montana
45. Wyoming
46. North Dakota
47. South Dakota
48. Vermont

State	State & Local debt ($Bil)	State & local debt per capita $	Rank per capita	Rank in order By per capita
Alabama	11.1	2,688	40	1. Alaska
Alaska	9.0	15,306	1	2. Delaware
Arizona	18.9	4,941	8	3. New York
Arkansas	5.0	2,093	47	4. Rhode Island
California	114.2	3,698	24	5. Utah
Colorado	15.8	4,567	12	6. Washington
Connecticut	15.6	4,767	11	7. Hawaii
Delaware	4.6	6,613	2	8. Arizona
Florida	54.7	4,053	18	9. Nevada
Georgia	20.7	3,067	35	10. New Hampshire
Hawaii	6.0	5,214	7	11. Connecticut
Idaho	1.9	1,798	50	12. Colorado
Illinois	40.6	3,489	27	13. New Jersey
Indiana	12.5	2,205	46	14. Wyoming
Iowa	5.4	1,915	49	15. Louisiana
Kansas	7.2	2,838	38	16. Minnesota
Kentucky	15.7	4,186	17	17. Kentucky
Louisiana	18.9	4,405	15	18. Florida
Maine	4.1	3,295	31	19. Nebraska
Maryland	19.1	3,882	22	20. Massachusetts
Massachusetts	24.0	4,003	20	21. Pennsylvania
Michigan	23.9	2,534	41	22. Maryland
Minnesota	19.4	4,329	16	23. Texas
Mississippi	5.0	1,927	48	24. California
Missouri	11.8	2,277	45	25. Montana
Montana	2.9	3,565	25	26. Vermont
Nebraska	6.5	4,029	19	27. Illinois
Nevada	6.5	4,906	9	28. Oregon
New Hampshire	5.4	4,838	10	29. West Virginia
New Jersey	34.5	4,435	13	30. South Dakota
New Mexico	4.6	2,883	37	31. Maine
New York	116.1	6,406	3	32. Virginia
North Carolina	17.2	2,520	42	33. South Carolina
North Dakota	2.0	3,071	34	34. North Dakota
Ohio	25.8	2,338	44	35. Georgia
Oklahoma	8.9	2,774	39	36. Wisconsin
Oregon	10.4	3,480	28	37. New Mexico
Pennsylvania	47.4	3,948	21	38. Kansas
Rhode Island	5.9	5,902	4	39. Oklahoma
South Carolina	11.4	3,160	33	40. Alabama
South Dakota	2.4	3,382	30	41. Michigan
Tennessee	12.4	2,463	43	42. North Carolina
Texas	66.8	3,786	23	43. Tennessee
Utah	10.4	5,722	5	44. Ohio
Vermont	2.0	3,532	26	45. Missouri
Virginia	20.3	3,176	32	46. Indiana
Washington	28.0	5,461	6	47. Arkansas
West Virginia	6.3	3,479	29	48. Mississippi
Wisconsin	15.0	2,990	36	49. Iowa
Wyoming	2.1	4,420	14	50. Idaho
50 States	956.2	3,757		
DC	4.9	8,428		
United States	970.0	3,803		

G-13 State And Local Debt Related To Revenue, 1992

State	State & local debt as % of general revenue %	Rank
Alabama	86.6	33
Alaska	133.7	8
Arizona	147.5	4
Arkansas	72.9	44
California	89.2	31
Colorado	124.2	10
Connecticut	104.0	19
Delaware	151.0	2
Florida	118.9	12
Georgia	92.5	29
Hawaii	106.7	16
Idaho	55.8	49
Illinois	99.4	23
Indiana	67.7	46
Iowa	53.1	50
Kansas	84.4	36
Kentucky	128.5	9
Louisiana	121.3	11
Maine	86.7	32
Maryland	103.9	21
Massachusetts	93.5	28
Michigan	66.6	47
Minnesota	98.9	24
Mississippi	65.1	48
Missouri	76.5	42
Montana	95.5	25
Nebraska	111.9	15
Nevada	137.3	6
New Hampshire	134.3	7
New Jersey	94.8	27
New Mexico	75.8	43
New York	112.4	14
North Carolina	79.7	40
North Dakota	79.7	39
Ohio	69.0	45
Oklahoma	89.9	30
Oregon	86.2	34
Pennsylvania	103.9	20
Rhode Island	148.8	3
South Carolina	100.0	22
South Dakota	104.7	18
Tennessee	81.5	37
Texas	117.8	13
Utah	174.3	1
Vermont	85.8	35
Virginia	95.2	26
Washington	138.9	5
West Virginia	106.0	17
Wisconsin	78.3	41
Wyoming	81.3	38
50 States	98.8	
DC	104.8	
United States	99.8	

By %

1. Utah
2. Delaware
3. Rhode Island
4. Arizona
5. Washington
6. Nevada
7. New Hampshire
8. Alaska
9. Kentucky
10. Colorado
11. Louisiana
12. Florida
13. Texas
14. New York
15. Nebraska
16. Hawaii
17. West Virginia
18. South Dakota
19. Connecticut
20. Pennsylvania
21. Maryland
22. South Carolina
23. Illinois
24. Minnesota
25. Montana
26. Virginia
27. New Jersey
28. Massachusetts
29. Georgia
30. Oklahoma
31. California
32. Maine
33. Alabama
34. Oregon
35. Vermont
36. Kansas
37. Tennessee
38. Wyoming
39. North Dakota
40. North Carolina
41. Wisconsin
42. Missouri
43. New Mexico
44. Arkansas
45. Ohio
46. Indiana
47. Michigan
48. Mississippi
49. Idaho
50. Iowa

G-14 State And Local Full Faith And Credit Debt, 1992

State	Full faith & credit debt ($Bil)	Per capita $	Rank by per capita	Rank in order By per capita
Alabama	3.57	862	26	1. Alaska
Alaska	2.34	3,988	1	2. Hawaii
Arizona	5.04	1,315	17	3. Connecticut
Arkansas	0.93	389	44	4. Massachusetts
California	22.45	727	31	5. Oregon
Colorado	3.85	1,109	21	6. New York
Connecticut	9.09	2,770	3	7. Nevada
Delaware	0.88	1,279	20	8. Washington
Florida	8.32	617	36	9. Rhode Island
Georgia	5.61	831	28	10. Maryland
Hawaii	3.51	3,028	2	11. Wisconsin
Idaho	0.35	330	46	12. Louisiana
Illinois	16.55	1,423	15	13. Minnesota
Indiana	1.82	321	47	14. New Hampshire
Iowa	1.37	487	42	15. Illinois
Kansas	1.87	743	30	16. Pennsylvania
Kentucky	1.18	314	48	17. Arizona
Louisiana	6.67	1,556	12	18. Texas
Maine	1.30	1,052	23	19. New Jersey
Maryland	8.49	1,730	10	20. Delaware
Massachusetts	14.77	2,462	4	21. Colorado
Michigan	8.35	885	25	22. Vermont
Minnesota	6.58	1,469	13	23. Maine
Mississippi	1.76	673	33	24. Virginia
Missouri	2.53	487	41	25. Michigan
Montana	0.44	538	38	26. Alabama
Nebraska	0.76	470	43	27. Tennessee
Nevada	2.72	2,051	7	28. Georgia
New Hampshire	1.60	1,443	14	29. South Carolina
New Jersey	10.21	1,310	19	30. Kansas
New Mexico	0.81	512	39	31. California
New York	40.50	2,235	6	32. Ohio
North Carolina	4.32	631	35	33. Mississippi
North Dakota	0.32	500	40	34. Utah
Ohio	7.92	719	32	35. North Carolina
Oklahoma	0.96	300	49	36. Florida
Oregon	6.95	2,334	5	37. Wyoming
Pennsylvania	15.98	1,331	16	38. Montana
Rhode Island	1.78	1,769	9	39. New Mexico
South Carolina	2.78	772	29	40. North Dakota
South Dakota	0.18	247	50	41. Missouri
Tennessee	4.31	858	27	42. Iowa
Texas	23.18	1,313	18	43. Nebraska
Utah	1.15	635	34	44. Arkansas
Vermont	0.60	1,054	22	45. West Virginia
Virginia	6.24	979	24	46. Idaho
Washington	9.80	1,908	8	47. Indiana
West Virginia	0.66	367	45	48. Kentucky
Wisconsin	7.88	1,573	11	49. Oklahoma
Wyoming	0.26	556	37	50. South Dakota
50 States	291.50	1,145		
DC	3.32	5,658		
United States	294.81	1,156		

State	State Bond Ratings	Rank	By rating
Alabama	Aa	3	1. Georgia
Alaska	Aa	3	1. Maryland
Arizona	n/a	n/a	1. Missouri
Arkansas	Aa	3	1. North Carolina
California	A1	4	1. South Carolina
Colorado	n/a	n/a	1. Tennessee
Connecticut	Aa	3	1. Utah
Delaware	Aa1	2	1. Virginia
Florida	Aa	3	2. Delaware
Georgia	Aaa	1	2. Minnesota
Hawaii	Aa	3	2. New Jersey
Idaho	n/a	n/a	2. New Mexico
Illinois	A1	4	3. Alabama
Indiana	n/a	n/a	3. Alaska
Iowa	n/a	n/a	3. Arkansas
Kansas	n/a	n/a	3. Connecticut
Kentucky	n/a	n/a	3. Florida
Louisiana	Baa1	6	3. Hawaii
Maine	Aa	3	3. Maine
Maryland	Aaa	1	3. Michigan
Massachusetts	A1	4	3. Mississippi
Michigan	Aa	3	3. Montana
Minnesota	Aa1	2	3. Nevada
Mississippi	Aa	3	3. New Hampshire
Missouri	Aaa	1	3. North Dakota
Montana	Aa	3	3. Ohio
Nebraska	n/a	n/a	3. Oklahoma
Nevada	Aa	3	3. Oregon
New Hampshire	Aa	3	3. Texas
New Jersey	Aa1	2	3. Vermont
New Mexico	Aa1	2	3. Washington
New York	A	5	3. Wisconsin
North Carolina	Aaa	1	4. California
North Dakota	Aa	3	4. Illinois
Ohio	Aa	3	4. Massachusetts
Oklahoma	Aa	3	4. Pennsylvania
Oregon	Aa	3	4. Rhode Island
Pennsylvania	A1	4	4. West Virginia
Rhode Island	A1	4	5. New York
South Carolina	Aaa	1	6. Louisiana
South Dakota	n/a	n/a	
Tennessee	Aaa	1	
Texas	Aa	3	
Utah	Aaa	1	
Vermont	Aa	3	
Virginia	Aaa	1	
Washington	Aa	3	
West Virginia	A1	4	
Wisconsin	Aa	3	
Wyoming	n/a	n/a	

50 States

DC

United States

State	State Solvency Index	Rank
Alabama	46	23
Alaska	21,344	1
Arizona	97	22
Arkansas	483	12
California	-512	34
Colorado	784	6
Connecticut	-2,895	49
Delaware	200	17
Florida	-424	32
Georgia	139	20
Hawaii	-1,119	44
Idaho	137	21
Illinois	-854	38
Indiana	-233	27
Iowa	723	7
Kansas	582	8
Kentucky	-339	31
Louisiana	-2,206	48
Maine	-1,802	47
Maryland	-951	41
Massachusetts	-2,943	50
Michigan	-1,097	43
Minnesota	179	18
Mississippi	-256	28
Missouri	-19	24
Montana	259	15
Nebraska	498	11
Nevada	-319	30
New Hampshire	-624	35
New Jersey	-886	40
New Mexico	2,812	3
New York	-134	25
North Carolina	545	9
North Dakota	1,018	5
Ohio	-178	26
Oklahoma	-782	37
Oregon	1,138	4
Pennsylvania	-474	33
Rhode Island	-1,649	45
South Carolina	-877	39
South Dakota	527	10
Tennessee	142	19
Texas	352	14
Utah	359	13
Vermont	-1,061	42
Virginia	-292	29
Washington	-767	36
West Virginia	-1,657	46
Wisconsin	251	16
Wyoming	5,572	2
50 States	-304	
DC	n/a	
United States	-304	

Rank in order

By Index

1. Alaska
2. Wyoming
3. New Mexico
4. Oregon
5. North Dakota
6. Colorado
7. Iowa
8. Kansas
9. North Carolina
10. South Dakota
11. Nebraska
12. Arkansas
13. Utah
14. Texas
15. Montana
16. Wisconsin
17. Delaware
18. Minnesota
19. Tennessee
20. Georgia
21. Idaho
22. Arizona
23. Alabama
24. Missouri
25. New York
26. Ohio
27. Indiana
28. Mississippi
29. Virginia
30. Nevada
31. Kentucky
32. Florida
33. Pennsylvania
34. California
35. New Hampshire
36. Washington
37. Oklahoma
38. Illinois
39. South Carolina
40. New Jersey
41. Maryland
42. Vermont
43. Michigan
44. Hawaii
45. Rhode Island
46. West Virginia
47. Maine
48. Louisiana
49. Connecticut
50. Massachusetts

G-17 Assets Of State-Administered Pension Plans, 1992

State	total assets ($000)	total membership #	average assets per member $	Rank by average	By average
Alabama	10,740,955	197,829	54,294	24	1. Alaska
Alaska	5,402,558	49,796	108,494	1	2. California
Arizona	12,704,208	179,499	70,776	15	3. New York
Arkansas	4,987,106	123,077	40,520	40	4. Ohio
California	148,428,398	1,494,895	99,290	2	5. Wisconsin
Colorado	13,588,206	176,411	77,026	11	6. Hawaii
Connecticut	10,808,436	131,145	82,416	8	7. Missouri
Delaware	2,051,339	33,545	61,152	17	8. Connecticut
Florida	30,181,561	617,742	48,858	30	9. Maryland
Georgia	17,907,038	328,380	54,531	23	10. Pennsylvania
Hawaii	4,965,834	57,401	86,511	6	11. Colorado
Idaho	2,673,718	52,230	51,191	27	12. Nebraska
Illinois	36,991,838	622,787	59,397	20	13. Tennessee
Indiana	8,963,985	242,747	36,927	45	14. Rhode Island
Iowa	5,873,395	157,455	37,302	44	15. Arizona
Kansas	4,655,898	124,308	37,455	43	16. New Jersey
Kentucky	8,668,179	191,944	45,160	33	17. Delaware
Louisiana	11,492,004	285,689	40,226	41	18. Washington
Maine	2,088,021	49,899	41,845	38	19. Michigan
Maryland	15,900,923	200,758	79,204	9	20. Illinois
Massachusetts	13,022,838	309,158	42,124	37	21. Minnesota
Michigan	31,203,752	518,522	60,178	19	22. Texas
Minnesota	17,084,529	295,759	57,765	21	23. Georgia
Mississippi	5,821,563	189,981	30,643	50	24. Alabama
Missouri	16,656,409	200,986	82,873	7	25. Wyoming
Montana	1,916,815	57,803	33,161	47	26. South Carolina
Nebraska	3,880,304	51,224	75,752	12	27. Idaho
Nevada	4,367,417	107,256	40,720	39	28. South Dakota
New Hampshire	1,310,759	40,041	32,735	48	29. Oregon
New Jersey	27,172,643	435,981	62,325	16	30. Florida
New Mexico	5,028,781	116,542	43,150	36	31. North Carolina
New York	118,302,215	1,237,788	95,576	3	32. Oklahoma
North Carolina	19,399,609	401,154	48,360	31	33. Kentucky
North Dakota	1,088,786	28,003	38,881	42	34. Utah
Ohio	77,481,176	812,899	95,315	4	35. Virginia
Oklahoma	6,769,343	147,461	45,906	32	36. New Mexico
Oregon	8,173,345	162,969	50,153	29	37. Massachusetts
Pennsylvania	35,945,733	456,687	78,710	10	38. Maine
Rhode Island	2,666,381	36,092	73,877	14	39. Nevada
South Carolina	16,528,600	311,649	53,036	26	40. Arkansas
South Dakota	1,848,002	36,409	50,757	28	41. Louisiana
Tennessee	15,025,380	199,495	75,317	13	42. North Dakota
Texas	50,134,991	895,681	55,974	22	43. Kansas
Utah	4,662,771	104,093	44,794	34	44. Iowa
Vermont	785,601	24,936	31,505	49	45. Indiana
Virginia	15,927,377	358,653	44,409	35	46. West Virginia
Washington	17,104,317	283,137	60,410	18	47. Montana
West Virginia	2,674,620	74,269	36,013	46	48. New Hampshire
Wisconsin	27,285,071	313,878	86,929	5	49. Vermont
Wyoming	1,805,384	33,988	53,118	25	50. Mississippi
50 States	910,148,112	13,560,031	67,120		
DC	1,814,043	13,321	136,179		
United States	911,962,155	13,573,352	67,188		

State	Balances as % of expenditures %	Rank	Rank in order By %
Alabama	0.0	48	1. Alaska
Alaska	72.8	1	2. Delaware
Arizona	11.2	11	3. Indiana
Arkansas	0.0	48	4. Mississippi
California	1.6	44	4. Oregon
Colorado	10.9	12	6. South Carolina
Connecticut	0.9	45	7. Michigan
Delaware	24.3	2	8. Nevada
Florida	1.9	41	9. New Hampshire
Georgia	4.3	29	10. Nebraska
Hawaii	2.8	34	11. Arizona
Idaho	2.8	34	12. Colorado
Illinois	2.0	40	12. Kansas
Indiana	18.5	3	14. Minnesota
Iowa	9.0	15	15. Iowa
Kansas	10.9	12	15. Texas
Kentucky	7.2	20	17. North Carolina
Louisiana	2.3	38	18. West Virginia
Maine	0.7	46	19. Missouri
Maryland	6.0	24	20. Kentucky
Massachusetts	3.8	31	21. Oklahoma
Michigan	14.1	7	21. Washington
Minnesota	10.6	14	23. New Jersey
Mississippi	15.0	4	24. Maryland
Missouri	7.7	19	24. Ohio
Montana	5.0	26	26. Montana
Nebraska	11.7	10	27. North Dakota
Nevada	13.8	8	27. Utah
New Hampshire	12.5	9	29. Georgia
New Jersey	6.4	23	29. Wisconsin
New Mexico	2.2	39	31. Massachusetts
New York	0.5	47	32. Pennsylvania
North Carolina	8.9	17	33. Rhode Island
North Dakota	4.9	27	34. Hawaii
Ohio	6.0	24	34. Idaho
Oklahoma	7.0	21	34. Tennessee
Oregon	15.0	4	37. Wyoming
Pennsylvania	3.2	32	38. Louisiana
Rhode Island	3.1	33	39. New Mexico
South Carolina	14.5	6	40. Illinois
South Dakota	1.8	42	41. Florida
Tennessee	2.8	34	42. South Dakota
Texas	9.0	15	43. Virginia
Utah	4.9	27	44. California
Vermont	-2.1	50	45. Connecticut
Virginia	1.7	43	46. Maine
Washington	7.0	21	47. New York
West Virginia	8.6	18	48. Alabama
Wisconsin	4.3	29	48. Arkansas
Wyoming	2.6	37	50. Vermont
50 States	5.7		
DC	n/a		
United States	5.7		

G-19 State And Local Capital Outlays And Interest, 1992

State	Outlays & interest per capita $	Interest per capita $	Capital outlay per capita $	Rank by interest per capita	Rank in order by interest per capita
Alabama	513	178	334	40	1. Alaska
Alaska	2,436	1,323	1,113	1	2. Delaware
Arizona	881	349	532	6	3. New York
Arkansas	445	140	305	47	4. Utah
California	646	231	415	28	5. Oregon
Colorado	939	326	613	12	6. Arizona
Connecticut	832	293	539	18	7. Rhode Island
Delaware	1,023	428	595	2	8. Massachusetts
Florida	793	274	520	21	9. Wyoming
Georgia	643	195	448	38	10. New Hampshire
Hawaii	1,642	308	1,334	15	11. Nevada
Idaho	607	133	474	49	12. Colorado
Illinois	668	221	447	33	13. Louisiana
Indiana	508	132	376	50	14. Washington
Iowa	634	141	493	46	15. Hawaii
Kansas	670	199	471	36	16. Pennsylvania
Kentucky	674	285	389	20	17. Minnesota
Louisiana	704	323	381	13	18. Connecticut
Maine	589	225	365	31	19. New Jersey
Maryland	636	227	409	29	20. Kentucky
Massachusetts	744	343	401	8	21. Florida
Michigan	503	155	348	44	22. Texas
Minnesota	892	299	593	17	23. Nebraska
Mississippi	452	134	318	48	24. Vermont
Missouri	526	151	375	45	25. Montana
Montana	751	247	504	25	26. South Dakota
Nebraska	729	263	466	23	27. West Virginia
Nevada	1,114	332	782	11	28. California
New Hampshire	619	334	284	10	29. Maryland
New Jersey	756	292	464	19	30. South Carolina
New Mexico	671	209	463	34	31. Maine
New York	1,012	421	591	3	32. North Dakota
North Carolina	570	171	399	41	33. Illinois
North Dakota	795	222	574	32	34. New Mexico
Ohio	580	163	417	43	35. Virginia
Oklahoma	579	189	390	39	36. Kansas
Oregon	811	355	456	5	37. Wisconsin
Pennsylvania	716	300	416	16	38. Georgia
Rhode Island	778	348	430	7	39. Oklahoma
South Carolina	637	225	413	30	40. Alabama
South Dakota	708	243	465	26	41. North Carolina
Tennessee	609	169	440	42	42. Tennessee
Texas	685	269	416	22	43. Ohio
Utah	817	410	406	4	44. Michigan
Vermont	560	248	312	24	45. Missouri
Virginia	618	200	418	35	46. Iowa
Washington	1,062	308	755	14	47. Arkansas
West Virginia	568	240	328	27	48. Mississippi
Wisconsin	730	197	533	37	49. Idaho
Wyoming	1,322	343	980	9	50. Indiana
50 States	748	254	494		
DC	1,353	547	806		
United States	713	254	458		

State	Index	Rank
Alabama	59.3	32
Alaska	64.0	25
Arizona	73.0	13
Arkansas	47.0	43
California	46.7	44
Colorado	98.0	1
Connecticut	76.4	10
Delaware	72.0	15
Florida	70.9	17
Georgia	79.4	7
Hawaii	72.0	16
Idaho	58.0	35
Illinois	45.4	46
Indiana	39.0	47
Iowa	79.1	8
Kansas	54.0	38
Kentucky	60.0	31
Louisiana	62.0	28
Maine	35.6	49
Maryland	58.2	33
Massachusetts	82.3	4
Michigan	88.0	2
Minnesota	68.0	19
Mississippi	63.0	26
Missouri	80.5	5
Montana	66.0	23
Nebraska	50.0	39
Nevada	56.0	37
New Hampshire	37.7	48
New Jersey	87.0	3
New Mexico	58.1	34
New York	61.6	29
North Carolina	49.8	40
North Dakota	68.8	18
Ohio	66.7	21
Oklahoma	67.0	20
Oregon	80.0	6
Pennsylvania	66.6	22
Rhode Island	77.3	9
South Carolina	75.0	11
South Dakota	65.5	24
Tennessee	73.0	14
Texas	63.0	27
Utah	73.5	12
Vermont	18.6	50
Virginia	48.4	41
Washington	48.0	42
West Virginia	60.9	30
Wisconsin	45.6	45
Wyoming	58.0	36
50 States	**63.2**	
DC	n/a	
United States	**63.2**	

Rank in order

By Index

1. Colorado
2. Michigan
3. New Jersey
4. Massachusetts
5. Missouri
6. Oregon
7. Georgia
8. Iowa
9. Rhode Island
10. Connecticut
11. South Carolina
12. Utah
13. Arizona
14. Tennessee
15. Delaware
16. Hawaii
17. Florida
18. North Dakota
19. Minnesota
20. Oklahoma
21. Ohio
22. Pennsylvania
23. Montana
24. South Dakota
25. Alaska
26. Mississippi
27. Texas
28. Louisiana
29. New York
30. West Virginia
31. Kentucky
32. Alabama
33. Maryland
34. New Mexico
35. Idaho
36. Wyoming
37. Nevada
38. Kansas
39. Nebraska
40. North Carolina
41. Virginia
42. Washington
43. Arkansas
44. California
45. Wisconsin
46. Illinois
47. Indiana
48. New Hampshire
49. Maine
50. Vermont

State	Per capita additional spending needed to meet national average %	Rank by least "needed" spending to most "needed"	Rank in order By %, low to high
Alabama	10.83	41	1. New Hampshire
Alaska	-0.33	27	2. Connecticut
Arizona	7.49	38	3. New Jersey
Arkansas	14.34	46	4. Maryland
California	0.09	28	5. Massachusetts
Colorado	-4.55	20	6. Nevada
Connecticut	-16.00	2	7. Delaware
Delaware	-13.34	7	8. Hawaii
Florida	-8.46	12	9. Rhode Island
Georgia	4.24	33	10. Virginia
Hawaii	-13.16	8	11. Vermont
Idaho	7.18	37	12. Florida
Illinois	-1.39	26	13. Pennsylvania
Indiana	-5.74	16	14. Maine
Iowa	-4.25	21	15. Washington
Kansas	-2.51	23	16. Indiana
Kentucky	11.71	43	17. North Carolina
Louisiana	34.86	49	18. Oregon
Maine	-7.22	14	19. Minnesota
Maryland	-14.24	4	20. Colorado
Massachusetts	-14.07	5	21. Iowa
Michigan	3.75	32	22. New York
Minnesota	-5.10	19	23. Kansas
Mississippi	37.71	50	24. Wisconsin
Missouri	0.70	30	25. Nebraska
Montana	10.47	40	26. Illinois
Nebraska	-2.36	25	27. Alaska
Nevada	-13.35	6	28. California
New Hampshire	-17.48	1	29. Ohio
New Jersey	-15.55	3	30. Missouri
New Mexico	26.78	48	31. Tennessee
New York	-2.63	22	32. Michigan
North Carolina	-5.49	17	33. Georgia
North Dakota	5.20	35	34. Wyoming
Ohio	0.55	29	35. North Dakota
Oklahoma	10.00	39	36. South Carolina
Oregon	-5.17	18	37. Idaho
Pennsylvania	-7.78	13	38. Arizona
Rhode Island	-12.12	9	39. Oklahoma
South Carolina	5.50	36	40. Montana
South Dakota	13.51	45	41. Alabama
Tennessee	2.07	31	42. West Virginia
Texas	16.78	47	43. Kentucky
Utah	12.55	44	44. Utah
Vermont	-9.80	11	45. South Dakota
Virginia	-11.91	10	46. Arkansas
Washington	-6.18	15	47. Texas
West Virginia	11.25	42	48. New Mexico
Wisconsin	-2.42	24	49. Louisiana
Wyoming	4.28	34	50. Mississippi
50 States	0.00		
DC	-6.32		
United States	0.00		

Education

H-1 Average Proficiency In Math, Eighth Grade, 1992

State	Math Scores	Rank
Alabama	251	39
Alaska	n/a	n/a
Arizona	265	23
Arkansas	255	38
California	260	29
Colorado	272	12
Connecticut	273	11
Delaware	262	27
Florida	259	31
Georgia	259	31
Hawaii	257	37
Idaho	274	8
Illinois	n/a	n/a
Indiana	269	17
Iowa	283	1
Kansas	n/a	n/a
Kentucky	261	28
Louisiana	249	40
Maine	278	4
Maryland	264	25
Massachusetts	272	12
Michigan	267	18
Minnesota	282	3
Mississippi	246	41
Missouri	270	16
Montana	n/a	n/a
Nebraska	277	6
Nevada	n/a	n/a
New Hampshire	278	4
New Jersey	271	14
New Mexico	259	31
New York	266	22
North Carolina	258	34
North Dakota	283	1
Ohio	267	18
Oklahoma	267	18
Oregon	n/a	n/a
Pennsylvania	271	14
Rhode Island	265	23
South Carolina	260	29
South Dakota	n/a	n/a
Tennessee	258	34
Texas	264	25
Utah	274	8
Vermont	n/a	n/a
Virginia	267	18
Washington	n/a	n/a
West Virginia	258	34
Wisconsin	277	6
Wyoming	274	8
50 States	266	
DC	234	
United States	266	

Rank in order

By scores

1. Iowa
1. North Dakota
3. Minnesota
4. Maine
4. New Hampshire
6. Nebraska
6. Wisconsin
8. Idaho
8. Utah
8. Wyoming
11. Connecticut
12. Colorado
12. Massachusetts
14. New Jersey
14. Pennsylvania
16. Missouri
17. Indiana
18. Michigan
18. Ohio
18. Oklahoma
18. Virginia
22. New York
23. Arizona
23. Rhode Island
25. Maryland
25. Texas
27. Delaware
28. Kentucky
29. California
29. South Carolina
31. Florida
31. Georgia
31. New Mexico
34. North Carolina
34. Tennessee
34. West Virginia
37. Hawaii
38. Arkansas
39. Alabama
40. Louisiana
41. Mississippi

State	Math Score	Rank
Alabama	207	38
Alaska	n/a	n/a
Arizona	214	26
Arkansas	209	36
California	207	38
Colorado	220	15
Connecticut	226	7
Delaware	217	21
Florida	212	32
Georgia	214	26
Hawaii	213	31
Idaho	220	15
Illinois	n/a	n/a
Indiana	220	15
Iowa	229	2
Kansas	n/a	n/a
Kentucky	214	26
Louisiana	203	40
Maine	231	1
Maryland	216	25
Massachusetts	226	7
Michigan	219	19
Minnesota	227	6
Mississippi	200	41
Missouri	221	14
Montana	n/a	n/a
Nebraska	224	10
Nevada	n/a	n/a
New Hampshire	229	2
New Jersey	226	7
New Mexico	212	32
New York	217	21
North Carolina	211	34
North Dakota	228	4
Ohio	217	21
Oklahoma	219	19
Oregon	n/a	n/a
Pennsylvania	223	12
Rhode Island	214	26
South Carolina	211	34
South Dakota	n/a	n/a
Tennessee	209	36
Texas	217	21
Utah	223	12
Vermont	n/a	n/a
Virginia	220	15
Washington	n/a	n/a
West Virginia	214	26
Wisconsin	228	4
Wyoming	224	10
50 States	217	
DC	191	
United States	217	

Rank in order

By score

1. Maine
2. Iowa
2. New Hampshire
4. North Dakota
4. Wisconsin
6. Minnesota
7. Connecticut
7. Massachusetts
7. New Jersey
10. Nebraska
10. Wyoming
12. Pennsylvania
12. Utah
14. Missouri
15. Colorado
15. Idaho
15. Indiana
15. Virginia
19. Michigan
19. Oklahoma
21. Delaware
21. New York
21. Ohio
21. Texas
25. Maryland
26. Arizona
26. Georgia
26. Kentucky
26. Rhode Island
26. West Virginia
31. Hawaii
32. Florida
32. New Mexico
34. North Carolina
34. South Carolina
36. Arkansas
36. Tennessee
38. Alabama
38. California
40. Louisiana
41. Mississippi

H-3 Armed Forces Qualification Test Ranks, 1993

State	AFQT Rank	Rank
Alabama	58	47
Alaska	63	19
Arizona	63	18
Arkansas	58	45
California	61	35
Colorado	63	16
Connecticut	62	24
Delaware	62	23
Florida	62	25
Georgia	58	45
Hawaii	58	44
Idaho	64	9
Illinois	61	37
Indiana	62	20
Iowa	65	2
Kansas	63	17
Kentucky	60	41
Louisiana	57	49
Maine	63	14
Maryland	62	28
Massachusetts	61	30
Michigan	61	34
Minnesota	65	8
Mississippi	55	50
Missouri	62	27
Montana	65	3
Nebraska	64	11
Nevada	64	12
New Hampshire	65	7
New Jersey	62	28
New Mexico	60	39
New York	62	21
North Carolina	59	42
North Dakota	65	3
Ohio	61	36
Oklahoma	61	37
Oregon	66	1
Pennsylvania	62	21
Rhode Island	61	30
South Carolina	58	47
South Dakota	63	13
Tennessee	60	39
Texas	61	33
Utah	62	25
Vermont	63	14
Virginia	61	30
Washington	65	5
West Virginia	59	43
Wisconsin	64	10
Wyoming	65	5
50 States	62	
DC	56	
United States	61	

Rank in order

By rank

1. Oregon
2. Iowa
3. Montana
4. North Dakota
5. Washington
6. Wyoming
7. New Hampshire
8. Minnesota
9. Idaho
10. Wisconsin
11. Nebraska
12. Nevada
13. South Dakota
14. Maine
15. Vermont
16. Colorado
17. Kansas
18. Arizona
19. Alaska
20. Indiana
21. New York
22. Pennsylvania
23. Delaware
24. Connecticut
25. Florida
26. Utah
27. Missouri
28. Maryland
29. New Jersey
30. Massachusetts
31. Rhode Island
32. Virginia
33. Texas
34. Michigan
35. California
36. Ohio
37. Illinois
38. Oklahoma
39. New Mexico
40. Tennessee
41. Kentucky
42. North Carolina
43. West Virginia
44. Hawaii
45. Arkansas
46. Georgia
47. Alabama
48. South Carolina
49. Louisiana
50. Mississippi

State	SAT scores	% graduates tested %	Rank by score
Alabama	n/a		
Alaska	1,029	51	5
Arizona	n/a		
Arkansas	n/a		
California	934	48	13
Colorado	n/a		
Connecticut	946	70	12
Delaware	1,005	47	8
Florida	902	64	17
Georgia	980	81	10
Hawaii	908	80	15
Idaho	n/a		
Illinois	n/a		
Indiana	897	45	18
Iowa	n/a		
Kansas	n/a		
Kentucky	n/a		
Louisiana	n/a		
Maine	879	68	22
Maryland	854	70	23
Massachusetts	889	88	20
Michigan	n/a		
Minnesota	n/a		
Mississippi	n/a		
Missouri	n/a		
Montana	n/a		
Nebraska	n/a		
Nevada	n/a		
New Hampshire	971	68	11
New Jersey	1,025	65	6
New Mexico	n/a		
New York	882	47	21
North Carolina	1,109	74	1
North Dakota	n/a		
Ohio	n/a		
Oklahoma	n/a		
Oregon	1,060	57	3
Pennsylvania	999	70	9
Rhode Island	1,021	58	7
South Carolina	896	70	19
South Dakota	n/a		
Tennessee	n/a		
Texas	909	48	14
Utah	n/a		
Vermont	907	80	16
Virginia	1,033	85	4
Washington	1,084	58	2
West Virginia	n/a		
Wisconsin	n/a		
Wyoming	n/a		
50 States	n/a		
DC	879	53	
United States	896	41	

Rank in order

By score

1. North Carolina
2. Washington
3. Oregon
4. Virginia
5. Alaska
6. New Jersey
7. Rhode Island
8. Delaware
9. Pennsylvania
10. Georgia
11. New Hampshire
12. Connecticut
13. California
14. Texas
15. Hawaii
16. Vermont
17. Florida
18. Indiana
19. South Carolina
20. Massachusetts
21. New York
22. Maine
23. Maryland

H-5 ACT Test Scores, 1995

State	ACT composite scores	% graduates tested %	Rank by score	Rank in order By score
Alabama	20	60	24	1. Wisconsin
Alaska	n/a			2. Minnesota
Arizona	21	29	18	3. Iowa
Arkansas	20	63	21	3. Montana
California	n/a			5. Colorado
Colorado	21	63	5	5. Nebraska
Connecticut	n/a			5. Utah
Delaware	n/a			8. Missouri
Florida	n/a			8. Nevada
Georgia	n/a			8. Wyoming
Hawaii	n/a			11. Idaho
Idaho	21	61	11	11. Kansas
Illinois	21	67	16	11. North Dakota
Indiana	n/a			11. Ohio
Iowa	22	64	3	11. South Dakota
Kansas	21	72	11	16. Illinois
Kentucky	20	63	22	16. Michigan
Louisiana	19	75	26	18. Arizona
Maine	n/a			19. Oklahoma
Maryland	n/a			19. Tennessee
Massachusetts	n/a			21. Arkansas
Michigan	21	64	16	22. Kentucky
Minnesota	22	59	2	22. New Mexico
Mississippi	19	73	27	24. Alabama
Missouri	21	64	8	24. West Virginia
Montana	22	56	3	26. Louisiana
Nebraska	21	75	5	27. Mississippi
Nevada	21	42	8	
New Hampshire	n/a			
New Jersey	n/a			
New Mexico	20	59	22	
New York	n/a			
North Carolina	n/a			
North Dakota	21	75	11	
Ohio	21	59	11	
Oklahoma	20	65	19	
Oregon	n/a			
Pennsylvania	n/a			
Rhode Island	n/a			
South Carolina	n/a			
South Dakota	21	68	11	
Tennessee	20	68	19	
Texas	n/a			
Utah	21	67	5	
Vermont	n/a			
Virginia	n/a			
Washington	n/a			
West Virginia	20	56	24	
Wisconsin	23	64	1	
Wyoming	21	66	8	
50 States				
DC				
United States	21	37		

H-6 Percentage of Over 25 Population Without A High School Diploma, 1990

State	Percent of over 25 population without a high school diploma %	Rank by % lowest # equals 1	By low to high
Alabama	33.1	46	1. Alaska
Alaska	13.4	1	2. Utah
Arizona	21.3	20	3. Colorado
Arkansas	33.7	47	4. Washington
California	23.8	28	5. Wyoming
Colorado	15.6	3	6. Minnesota
Connecticut	20.8	17	7. New Hampshire
Delaware	22.5	23	8. Nebraska
Florida	25.6	37	9. Oregon
Georgia	29.1	41	10. Kansas
Hawaii	19.9	13	11. Montana
Idaho	20.3	16	12. Vermont
Illinois	23.8	29	13. Hawaii
Indiana	24.4	31	14. Iowa
Iowa	19.9	14	15. Massachusetts
Kansas	18.7	10	16. Idaho
Kentucky	35.4	49	17. Connecticut
Louisiana	31.7	43	18. Maine
Maine	21.2	18	19. Nevada
Maryland	21.6	22	20. Arizona
Massachusetts	20.0	15	21. Wisconsin
Michigan	23.2	25	22. Maryland
Minnesota	17.6	6	23. Delaware
Mississippi	35.7	50	24. South Dakota
Missouri	26.1	38	25. Michigan
Montana	19.0	11	26. New Jersey
Nebraska	18.2	8	27. North Dakota
Nevada	21.2	19	28. California
New Hampshire	17.8	7	29. Illinois
New Jersey	23.3	26	30. Ohio
New Mexico	24.9	33	31. Indiana
New York	25.2	34	32. Virginia
North Carolina	30.0	42	33. New Mexico
North Dakota	23.3	27	34. New York
Ohio	24.3	30	35. Pennsylvania
Oklahoma	25.4	36	36. Oklahoma
Oregon	18.5	9	37. Florida
Pennsylvania	25.3	35	38. Missouri
Rhode Island	28.0	40	39. Texas
South Carolina	31.7	44	40. Rhode Island
South Dakota	22.9	24	41. Georgia
Tennessee	32.9	45	42. North Carolina
Texas	27.9	39	43. Louisiana
Utah	14.9	2	44. South Carolina
Vermont	19.2	12	45. Tennessee
Virginia	24.8	32	46. Alabama
Washington	16.2	4	47. Arkansas
West Virginia	34.0	48	48. West Virginia
Wisconsin	21.4	21	49. Kentucky
Wyoming	17.0	5	50. Mississippi
50 States	n/a		
DC	26.9		
United States	24.8		

State	Private school enrollment (000)	As % of total enrollment %	Rank by %
Alabama	69	8.8	27
Alaska	6	4.4	45
Arizona	39	5.7	40
Arkansas	23	4.9	43
California	613	10.7	17
Colorado	57	8.8	26
Connecticut	67	12.3	14
Delaware	23	18.2	1
Florida	206	9.6	20
Georgia	97	7.6	29
Hawaii	36	17.2	3
Idaho	7	2.9	48
Illinois	301	14.0	8
Indiana	99	9.4	23
Iowa	51	9.5	22
Kansas	35	7.3	32
Kentucky	66	9.3	24
Louisiana	139	14.9	6
Maine	15	6.4	36
Maryland	114	13.4	9
Massachusetts	125	12.9	12
Michigan	187	10.5	18
Minnesota	93	10.8	16
Mississippi	59	10.4	19
Missouri	116	12.1	15
Montana	10	5.8	39
Nebraska	40	12.4	13
Nevada	8	3.9	47
New Hampshire	19	9.6	21
New Jersey	210	15.9	4
New Mexico	23	7.0	34
New York	499	15.9	5
North Carolina	63	5.4	42
North Dakota	8	6.0	37
Ohio	269	13.1	10
Oklahoma	34	5.5	41
Oregon	31	5.8	38
Pennsylvania	359	17.5	2
Rhode Island	21	13.0	11
South Carolina	46	6.8	35
South Dakota	11	7.4	30
Tennessee	83	9.1	25
Texas	171	4.7	44
Utah	10	2.1	49
Vermont	8	7.9	28
Virginia	81	7.4	31
Washington	67	7.1	33
West Virginia	13	3.9	46
Wisconsin	142	14.9	7
Wyoming	2	1.8	50
50 States	**4,872**	10.4	
DC	18	18.1	
United States	**4,890**	10.4	

By %

1. Delaware
2. Pennsylvania
3. Hawaii
4. New Jersey
5. New York
6. Louisiana
7. Wisconsin
8. Illinois
9. Maryland
10. Ohio
11. Rhode Island
12. Massachusetts
13. Nebraska
14. Connecticut
15. Missouri
16. Minnesota
17. California
18. Michigan
19. Mississippi
20. Florida
21. New Hampshire
22. Iowa
23. Indiana
24. Kentucky
25. Tennessee
26. Colorado
27. Alabama
28. Vermont
29. Georgia
30. South Dakota
31. Virginia
32. Kansas
33. Washington
34. New Mexico
35. South Carolina
36. Maine
37. North Dakota
38. Oregon
39. Montana
40. Arizona
41. Oklahoma
42. North Carolina
43. Arkansas
44. Texas
45. Alaska
46. West Virginia
47. Nevada
48. Idaho
49. Utah
50. Wyoming

State	Percent finishing high school %	Rank
Alabama	66.1	44
Alaska	74.1	29
Arizona	72.7	33
Arkansas	78.3	19
California	68.6	40
Colorado	75.1	28
Connecticut	80.4	16
Delaware	69.6	38
Florida	65.0	45
Georgia	63.7	46
Hawaii	78.1	20
Idaho	81.1	12
Illinois	78.6	18
Indiana	76.0	27
Iowa	87.6	2
Kansas	80.5	15
Kentucky	69.8	37
Louisiana	52.9	50
Maine	81.1	12
Maryland	76.1	25
Massachusetts	79.1	17
Michigan	70.9	35
Minnesota	89.2	1
Mississippi	62.1	47
Missouri	73.2	32
Montana	85.5	5
Nebraska	87.2	4
Nevada	70.7	36
New Hampshire	78.1	20
New Jersey	84.1	7
New Mexico	67.8	42
New York	66.6	43
North Carolina	68.5	41
North Dakota	87.5	3
Ohio	72.4	34
Oklahoma	76.3	24
Oregon	73.5	31
Pennsylvania	81.5	11
Rhode Island	76.8	23
South Carolina	58.1	49
South Dakota	85.3	6
Tennessee	68.7	39
Texas	61.3	48
Utah	81.1	12
Vermont	82.4	9
Virginia	74.0	30
Washington	76.1	25
West Virginia	77.0	22
Wisconsin	82.2	10
Wyoming	83.8	8
50 States	n/a	
DC	n/a	
United States	n/a	

Rank in order

By %

1. Minnesota
2. Iowa
3. North Dakota
4. Nebraska
5. Montana
6. South Dakota
7. New Jersey
8. Wyoming
9. Vermont
10. Wisconsin
11. Pennsylvania
12. Idaho
13. Maine
14. Utah
15. Kansas
16. Connecticut
17. Massachusetts
18. Illinois
19. Arkansas
20. Hawaii
21. New Hampshire
22. West Virginia
23. Rhode Island
24. Oklahoma
25. Maryland
26. Washington
27. Indiana
28. Colorado
29. Alaska
30. Virginia
31. Oregon
32. Missouri
33. Arizona
34. Ohio
35. Michigan
36. Nevada
37. Kentucky
38. Delaware
39. Tennessee
40. California
41. North Carolina
42. New Mexico
43. New York
44. Alabama
45. Florida
46. Georgia
47. Mississippi
48. Texas
49. South Carolina
50. Louisiana

State	Ratio	Rank	Rank in order — By ratio
Alabama	17.4	33	1. New Jersey
Alaska	16.8	24	2. Vermont
Arizona	18.7	42	3. Maine
Arkansas	17.0	28	4. Connecticut
California	24.1	49	5. Rhode Island
Colorado	18.3	40	6. Nebraska
Connecticut	14.3	4	7. Massachusetts
Delaware	16.7	22	8. Kansas
Florida	18.4	41	9. New York
Georgia	18.0	38	10. North Dakota
Hawaii	17.6	34	11. West Virginia
Idaho	19.6	47	12. South Dakota
Illinois	16.8	24	13. Oklahoma
Indiana	17.6	34	14. Wisconsin
Iowa	15.8	17	15. New Hampshire
Kansas	15.2	8	16. Texas
Kentucky	17.3	32	17. Iowa
Louisiana	16.6	21	18. Montana
Maine	14.1	3	19. Virginia
Maryland	16.9	26	20. Missouri
Massachusetts	15.0	7	21. Louisiana
Michigan	19.5	46	22. Delaware
Minnesota	17.6	34	23. North Carolina
Mississippi	18.2	39	24. Alaska
Missouri	16.2	20	25. Illinois
Montana	15.8	17	26. Maryland
Nebraska	14.6	6	27. Ohio
Nevada	18.7	42	28. Arkansas
New Hampshire	15.6	15	29. Pennsylvania
New Jersey	13.6	1	30. South Carolina
New Mexico	17.6	34	31. Wyoming
New York	15.2	8	32. Kentucky
North Carolina	16.7	22	33. Alabama
North Dakota	15.2	8	34. Hawaii
Ohio	16.9	26	35. Indiana
Oklahoma	15.5	13	36. Minnesota
Oregon	19.2	44	37. New Mexico
Pennsylvania	17.0	28	38. Georgia
Rhode Island	14.3	4	39. Mississippi
South Carolina	17.0	28	40. Colorado
South Dakota	15.3	12	41. Florida
Tennessee	19.4	45	42. Arizona
Texas	15.7	16	43. Nevada
Utah	24.2	50	44. Oregon
Vermont	14.0	2	45. Tennessee
Virginia	15.9	19	46. Michigan
Washington	20.2	48	47. Idaho
West Virginia	15.2	8	48. Washington
Wisconsin	15.5	13	49. California
Wyoming	17.2	31	50. Utah
50 States	17.0		
DC	13.3		
United States	17.4		

State	Enrollment ($000)	As % of total pop.	rank by %
Alabama	723.4	17.5	24
Alaska	122.5	20.9	4
Arizona	673.5	17.6	21
Arkansas	441.5	18.4	13
California	5,195.8	16.8	31
Colorado	612.6	17.7	17
Connecticut	488.5	14.9	44
Delaware	104.3	15.1	43
Florida	1,981.4	14.7	46
Georgia	1,207.2	17.9	15
Hawaii	177.4	15.3	42
Idaho	231.7	21.7	2
Illinois	1,873.6	16.1	40
Indiana	960.6	17.0	30
Iowa	494.8	17.6	18
Kansas	451.5	17.9	14
Kentucky	655.0	17.4	26
Louisiana	798.0	18.6	11
Maine	216.5	17.5	23
Maryland	751.9	15.3	41
Massachusetts	859.9	14.3	48
Michigan	1,603.6	17.0	29
Minnesota	793.7	17.7	16
Mississippi	506.7	19.4	8
Missouri	859.4	16.5	35
Montana	160.0	19.4	7
Nebraska	282.5	17.6	19
Nevada	223.0	16.8	33
New Hampshire	181.2	16.3	36
New Jersey	1,130.6	14.5	47
New Mexico	315.7	20.0	6
New York	2,689.7	14.8	45
North Carolina	1,114.1	16.3	38
North Dakota	118.7	18.7	10
Ohio	1,796.4	16.3	37
Oklahoma	597.1	18.6	12
Oregon	510.1	17.1	28
Pennsylvania	1,717.6	14.3	50
Rhode Island	143.8	14.3	49
South Carolina	633.4	17.6	20
South Dakota	134.6	18.9	9
Tennessee	845.6	16.8	32
Texas	3,535.9	20.0	5
Utah	463.9	25.6	1
Vermont	98.6	17.3	27
Virginia	1,031.9	16.2	39
Washington	896.5	17.5	25
West Virginia	318.3	17.6	22
Wisconsin	829.4	16.6	34
Wyoming	100.3	21.5	3
50 States	42,653.8	16.8	
DC	80.9	13.7	
United States	42,734.7	16.8	

Rank in order

By %

1. Utah
2. Idaho
3. Wyoming
4. Alaska
5. Texas
6. New Mexico
7. Montana
8. Mississippi
9. South Dakota
10. North Dakota
11. Louisiana
12. Oklahoma
13. Arkansas
14. Kansas
15. Georgia
16. Minnesota
17. Colorado
18. Iowa
19. Nebraska
20. South Carolina
21. Arizona
22. West Virginia
23. Maine
24. Alabama
25. Washington
26. Kentucky
27. Vermont
28. Oregon
29. Michigan
30. Indiana
31. California
32. Tennessee
33. Nevada
34. Wisconsin
35. Missouri
36. New Hampshire
37. Ohio
38. North Carolina
39. Virginia
40. Illinois
41. Maryland
42. Hawaii
43. Delaware
44. Connecticut
45. New York
46. Florida
47. New Jersey
48. Massachusetts
49. Rhode Island
50. Pennsylvania

State	Holdings per capita	Rank		Rank in order By per capita
Alabama	1.9	43		1. Maine
Alaska	3.1	21		1. Wyoming
Arizona	2.0	38		3. Vermont
Arkansas	2.1	36		4. Massachusetts
California	1.9	43		5. New Hampshire
Colorado	2.6	27		6. Kansas
Connecticut	4.2	7		7. Connecticut
Delaware	1.8	47		7. South Dakota
Florida	1.6	49		9. Rhode Island
Georgia	1.9	43		10. Iowa
Hawaii	2.3	33		10. Missouri
Idaho	3.3	19		12. Nebraska
Illinois	3.4	18		12. New Jersey
Indiana	3.7	15		12. New York
Iowa	3.9	10		15. Indiana
Kansas	4.3	6		16. Ohio
Kentucky	1.9	43		17. North Dakota
Louisiana	2.2	34		18. Illinois
Maine	4.9	1		19. Idaho
Maryland	2.7	25		20. Wisconsin
Massachusetts	4.7	4		21. Alaska
Michigan	2.5	28		21. New Mexico
Minnesota	2.8	24		23. Montana
Mississippi	2.0	38		24. Minnesota
Missouri	3.9	10		25. Maryland
Montana	3.0	23		25. Washington
Nebraska	3.8	12		27. Colorado
Nevada	2.0	38		28. Michigan
New Hampshire	4.6	5		28. Utah
New Jersey	3.8	12		28. Virginia
New Mexico	3.1	21		31. Oregon
New York	3.8	12		31. West Virginia
North Carolina	2.0	38		33. Hawaii
North Dakota	3.5	17		34. Louisiana
Ohio	3.6	16		34. Oklahoma
Oklahoma	2.2	34		36. Arkansas
Oregon	2.4	31		36. Pennsylvania
Pennsylvania	2.1	36		38. Arizona
Rhode Island	4.0	9		38. Mississippi
South Carolina	1.7	48		38. Nevada
South Dakota	4.2	7		38. North Carolina
Tennessee	1.6	49		38. Texas
Texas	2.0	38		43. Alabama
Utah	2.5	28		43. California
Vermont	4.8	3		43. Georgia
Virginia	2.5	28		43. Kentucky
Washington	2.7	25		47. Delaware
West Virginia	2.4	31		48. South Carolina
Wisconsin	3.2	20		49. Florida
Wyoming	4.9	1		49. Tennessee
50 States	3.0			
DC	3.1			
United States	2.7			

H-12 Children With Disabilities, 1992

State	children with disabilities	Rank
Alabama	96,975	17
Alaska	16,106	44
Arizona	61,076	29
Arkansas	49,018	33
California	494,058	1
Colorado	60,357	30
Connecticut	66,192	26
Delaware	14,435	46
Florida	253,606	4
Georgia	107,660	15
Hawaii	14,163	47
Idaho	22,755	39
Illinois	245,931	5
Indiana	118,924	13
Iowa	61,510	27
Kansas	47,063	34
Kentucky	81,681	22
Louisiana	78,760	24
Maine	27,891	38
Maryland	92,520	18
Massachusetts	156,633	10
Michigan	172,238	9
Minnesota	83,028	21
Mississippi	61,197	28
Missouri	105,521	16
Montana	18,038	43
Nebraska	35,975	37
Nevada	20,530	42
New Hampshire	21,047	41
New Jersey	184,621	8
New Mexico	38,207	36
New York	324,677	3
North Carolina	127,867	11
North Dakota	12,679	48
Ohio	210,268	7
Oklahoma	68,576	25
Oregon	56,702	31
Pennsylvania	214,035	6
Rhode Island	21,588	40
South Carolina	79,872	23
South Dakota	15,284	45
Tennessee	111,315	14
Texas	367,860	2
Utah	50,009	32
Vermont	11,101	50
Virginia	122,647	12
Washington	91,286	20
West Virginia	44,338	35
Wisconsin	91,742	19
Wyoming	11,935	49
50 States	4,941,497	
DC	7,104	
United States	4,948,601	

Rank in order

By #

1. California
2. Texas
3. New York
4. Florida
5. Illinois
6. Pennsylvania
7. Ohio
8. New Jersey
9. Michigan
10. Massachusetts
11. North Carolina
12. Virginia
13. Indiana
14. Tennessee
15. Georgia
16. Missouri
17. Alabama
18. Maryland
19. Wisconsin
20. Washington
21. Minnesota
22. Kentucky
23. South Carolina
24. Louisiana
25. Oklahoma
26. Connecticut
27. Iowa
28. Mississippi
29. Arizona
30. Colorado
31. Oregon
32. Utah
33. Arkansas
34. Kansas
35. West Virginia
36. New Mexico
37. Nebraska
38. Maine
39. Idaho
40. Rhode Island
41. New Hampshire
42. Nevada
43. Montana
44. Alaska
45. South Dakota
46. Delaware
47. Hawaii
48. North Dakota
49. Wyoming
50. Vermont

State	Per Capita $	Per $1000 personal income $	rank by per capita
Alabama	1,032	67.2	48
Alaska	2,325	113.6	1
Arizona	1,259	77.6	26
Arkansas	1,106	76.5	42
California	1,275	62.1	25
Colorado	1,348	71.5	19
Connecticut	1,411	54.0	13
Delaware	1,584	77.1	4
Florida	1,090	58.3	43
Georgia	1,084	63.4	44
Hawaii	1,159	55.9	39
Idaho	1,169	78.2	36
Illinois	1,148	55.8	40
Indiana	1,293	76.0	23
Iowa	1,419	82.5	12
Kansas	1,387	76.6	16
Kentucky	1,069	69.1	46
Louisiana	1,164	78.0	37
Maine	1,297	74.3	22
Maryland	1,275	58.0	24
Massachusetts	1,070	46.5	45
Michigan	1,468	79.3	11
Minnesota	1,495	79.0	9
Mississippi	1,019	77.1	49
Missouri	1,065	59.8	47
Montana	1,321	85.9	21
Nebraska	1,401	79.7	14
Nevada	1,206	63.0	31
New Hampshire	1,176	54.3	35
New Jersey	1,584	62.0	5
New Mexico	1,352	94.3	18
New York	1,570	70.1	6
North Carolina	1,200	72.3	33
North Dakota	1,483	95.2	10
Ohio	1,201	68.1	32
Oklahoma	1,161	75.6	38
Oregon	1,398	81.0	15
Pennsylvania	1,347	70.1	20
Rhode Island	1,255	65.4	27
South Carolina	1,198	78.4	34
South Dakota	1,129	71.0	41
Tennessee	942	58.0	50
Texas	1,239	73.2	29
Utah	1,366	95.6	17
Vermont	1,694	94.7	3
Virginia	1,241	62.7	28
Washington	1,512	79.4	7
West Virginia	1,234	86.8	30
Wisconsin	1,501	84.6	8
Wyoming	1,923	115.1	2
50 States	1,281	74.1	
DC	1,267	38.2	
United States	1,281	67.9	

Rank in order

By per capita

1. Alaska
2. Wyoming
3. Vermont
4. Delaware
5. New Jersey
6. New York
7. Washington
8. Wisconsin
9. Minnesota
10. North Dakota
11. Michigan
12. Iowa
13. Connecticut
14. Nebraska
15. Oregon
16. Kansas
17. Utah
18. New Mexico
19. Colorado
20. Pennsylvania
21. Montana
22. Maine
23. Indiana
24. Maryland
25. California
26. Arizona
27. Rhode Island
28. Virginia
29. Texas
30. West Virginia
31. Nevada
32. Ohio
33. North Carolina
34. South Carolina
35. New Hampshire
36. Idaho
37. Louisiana
38. Oklahoma
39. Hawaii
40. Illinois
41. South Dakota
42. Arkansas
43. Florida
44. Georgia
45. Massachusetts
46. Kentucky
47. Missouri
48. Alabama
49. Mississippi
50. Tennessee

State	Education Spending ($millions)	Educ. spending as % of general expenditure %	Rank by % gen exp
Alabama	4,268	33.2	36
Alaska	1,365	23.5	49
Arizona	4,825	35.9	24
Arkansas	2,654	40.2	6
California	39,348	30.2	44
Colorado	4,676	36.5	21
Connecticut	4,628	30.7	43
Delaware	1,092	37.3	16
Florida	14,704	31.2	42
Georgia	7,319	32.7	38
Hawaii	1,344	22.3	50
Idaho	1,247	38.2	12
Illinois	13,347	33.1	37
Indiana	7,319	40.5	5
Iowa	3,989	39.6	7
Kansas	3,500	40.9	3
Kentucky	4,012	33.6	34
Louisiana	4,990	31.6	40
Maine	1,602	34.5	32
Maryland	6,257	34.9	31
Massachusetts	6,416	26.0	48
Michigan	13,856	38.9	9
Minnesota	6,698	33.3	35
Mississippi	2,665	35.5	27
Missouri	5,532	36.9	20
Montana	1,088	37.2	17
Nebraska	2,250	40.7	4
Nevada	1,601	30.2	45
New Hampshire	1,306	32.0	39
New Jersey	12,340	33.8	33
New Mexico	2,137	35.7	25
New York	28,443	27.8	47
North Carolina	8,213	38.6	10
North Dakota	943	38.0	13
Ohio	13,232	35.3	29
Oklahoma	3,730	37.2	18
Oregon	4,161	35.3	30
Pennsylvania	16,180	35.6	26
Rhode Island	1,261	28.7	46
South Carolina	4,316	37.0	19
South Dakota	803	35.5	28
Tennessee	4,734	31.4	41
Texas	21,870	39.3	8
Utah	2,476	42.7	1
Vermont	965	41.5	2
Virginia	7,912	37.5	15
Washington	7,764	35.9	23
West Virginia	2,236	38.4	11
Wisconsin	7,516	37.9	14
Wyoming	896	36.4	22
50 States	326,027	33.5	
DC	7,429	16.8	
United States	326,770	33.6	

Rank in order

By %

1. Utah
2. Vermont
3. Kansas
4. Nebraska
5. Indiana
6. Arkansas
7. Iowa
8. Texas
9. Michigan
10. North Carolina
11. West Virginia
12. Idaho
13. North Dakota
14. Wisconsin
15. Virginia
16. Delaware
17. Montana
18. Oklahoma
19. South Carolina
20. Missouri
21. Colorado
22. Wyoming
23. Washington
24. Arizona
25. New Mexico
26. Pennsylvania
27. Mississippi
28. South Dakota
29. Ohio
30. Oregon
31. Maryland
32. Maine
33. New Jersey
34. Kentucky
35. Minnesota
36. Alabama
37. Illinois
38. Georgia
39. New Hampshire
40. Louisiana
41. Tennessee
42. Florida
43. Connecticut
44. California
45. Nevada
46. Rhode Island
47. New York
48. Massachusetts
49. Alaska
50. Hawaii

State	Spending per pupil $	Rank
Alabama	3,815	47
Alaska	8,254	2
Arizona	3,941	45
Arkansas	3,657	48
California	4,579	35
Colorado	4,872	28
Connecticut	7,991	3
Delaware	6,040	10
Florida	4,910	27
Georgia	4,174	41
Hawaii	5,550	16
Idaho	3,954	44
Illinois	4,924	26
Indiana	5,075	23
Iowa	4,939	25
Kansas	5,147	22
Kentucky	4,674	32
Louisiana	4,367	39
Maine	5,709	13
Maryland	6,028	11
Massachusetts	6,265	7
Michigan	6,015	12
Minnesota	5,360	20
Mississippi	3,297	49
Missouri	4,143	42
Montana	4,782	31
Nebraska	4,803	30
Nevada	4,606	34
New Hampshire	5,231	21
New Jersey	9,514	1
New Mexico	4,470	36
New York	7,872	4
North Carolina	4,634	33
North Dakota	4,263	40
Ohio	5,586	15
Oklahoma	3,886	46
Oregon	5,600	14
Pennsylvania	6,652	6
Rhode Island	6,223	9
South Carolina	4,407	38
South Dakota	4,436	37
Tennessee	4,053	43
Texas	4,829	29
Utah	3,203	50
Vermont	6,850	5
Virginia	5,012	24
Washington	5,385	18
West Virginia	5,360	19
Wisconsin	6,244	8
Wyoming	5,451	17
50 States	5,221	
DC	7,887	
United States	5,301	

Rank in order

By $

1. New Jersey
2. Alaska
3. Connecticut
4. New York
5. Vermont
6. Penn
7. Massachusetts
8. Wisconsin
9. Rhode Island
10. Delaware
11. Maryland
12. Michigan
13. Maine
14. Oregon
15. Ohio
16. Hawaii
17. Wyoming
18. Washington
19. West Virginia
20. Minnesota
21. New Hampshire
22. Kansas
23. Indiana
24. Virginia
25. Iowa
26. Illinois
27. Florida
28. Colorado
29. Texas
30. Nebraska
31. Montana
32. Kentucky
33. North Carolina
34. Nevada
35. California
36. New Mexico
37. South Dakota
38. South Carolina
39. Louisiana
40. North Dakota
41. Georgia
42. Missouri
43. Tennessee
44. Idaho
45. Arizona
46. Oklahoma
47. Alabama
48. Arkansas
49. Mississippi
50. Utah

State	Average teacher salary $	Rank	Rank in order By $
Alabama	28,705	40	1. Connecticut
Alaska	46,581	2	2. Alaska
Arizona	31,800	27	3. New York
Arkansas	27,873	44	4. New Jersey
California	40,289	8	5. Michigan
Colorado	33,826	24	6. Pennsylvania
Connecticut	49,910	1	7. Massachusetts
Delaware	37,469	13	8. California
Florida	31,944	26	9. Maryland
Georgia	30,527	33	10. Illinois
Hawaii	36,564	14	11. Rhode Island
Idaho	27,756	45	12. Oregon
Illinois	39,387	10	13. Delaware
Indiana	35,711	18	14. Hawaii
Iowa	30,760	31	15. Minnesota
Kansas	33,919	23	16. Wisconsin
Kentucky	31,640	28	17. Washington
Louisiana	26,285	47	18. Indiana
Maine	30,996	29	19. Ohio
Maryland	39,463	9	20. Vermont
Massachusetts	40,852	7	21. New Hampshire
Michigan	42,500	5	22. Nevada
Minnesota	36,146	15	23. Kansas
Mississippi	25,153	49	24. Colorado
Missouri	30,324	36	25. Virginia
Montana	28,200	41	26. Florida
Nebraska	29,564	39	27. Arizona
Nevada	33,955	22	28. Kentucky
New Hampshire	34,121	21	29. Maine
New Jersey	44,693	4	30. Wyoming
New Mexico	27,922	43	31. Iowa
New York	45,772	3	32. West Virginia
North Carolina	29,727	37	33. Georgia
North Dakota	25,506	48	34. Texas
Ohio	35,684	19	35. Tennessee
Oklahoma	27,009	46	36. Missouri
Oregon	37,590	12	37. North Carolina
Pennsylvania	42,411	6	38. South Carolina
Rhode Island	39,261	11	39. Nebraska
South Carolina	29,566	38	40. Alabama
South Dakota	25,059	50	41. Montana
Tennessee	30,514	35	42. Utah
Texas	30,519	34	43. New Mexico
Utah	28,056	42	44. Arkansas
Vermont	34,517	20	45. Idaho
Virginia	33,063	25	46. Oklahoma
Washington	35,855	17	47. Louisiana
West Virginia	30,549	32	48. North Dakota
Wisconsin	35,990	16	49. Mississippi
Wyoming	30,952	30	50. South Dakota
50 States	33,849		
DC	42,543		
United States	35,723		

State	% from federal %	% from state %	% from local %	Rank by % local
Alabama	12.7	65.7	21.6	48
Alaska	12.6	63.6	23.8	45
Arizona	8.9	42.3	48.9	22
Arkansas	9.4	62.7	27.9	41
California	8.8	54.8	36.4	36
Colorado	4.8	42.7	52.4	19
Connecticut	4.6	40.1	55.3	14
Delaware	8.3	66.4	25.3	44
Florida	9.3	47.9	42.8	32
Georgia	7.8	47.9	44.3	27
Hawaii	7.9	90.3	1.8	50
Idaho	8.3	62.4	29.4	39
Illinois	8.2	32.8	59.1	6
Indiana	5.2	52.1	42.6	33
Iowa	5.5	48.5	46.0	25
Kansas	5.5	49.7	44.9	26
Kentucky	9.9	68.3	21.7	47
Louisiana	11.7	55.4	32.9	37
Maine	7.6	48.3	44.1	28
Maryland	5.6	39.0	55.4	13
Massachusetts	5.5	36.0	58.5	8
Michigan	5.7	32.1	62.2	3
Minnesota	5.1	46.5	48.5	23
Mississippi	17.7	51.8	30.5	38
Missouri	6.8	36.7	56.5	11
Montana	9.4	36.7	53.9	17
Nebraska	4.8	39.1	56.1	12
Nevada	4.9	36.2	58.9	7
New Hampshire	3.1	8.1	88.8	1
New Jersey	4.2	41.6	54.2	16
New Mexico	12.8	75.3	11.9	49
New York	5.9	39.5	54.7	15
North Carolina	8.7	64.2	27.1	42
North Dakota	12.3	43.6	44.1	28
Ohio	6.0	40.1	53.9	17
Oklahoma	7.4	63.3	29.4	39
Oregon	7.3	41.0	51.7	20
Pennsylvania	6.1	42.3	51.6	21
Rhode Island	5.2	36.5	58.3	9
South Carolina	9.4	47.1	43.5	31
South Dakota	11.9	27.5	60.6	5
Tennessee	10.0	49.0	41.0	34
Texas	8.5	43.4	48.1	24
Utah	6.8	55.6	37.5	35
Vermont	5.2	32.4	62.5	2
Virginia	4.8	34.2	60.9	4
Washington	5.8	71.5	22.6	46
West Virginia	8.0	66.7	25.4	43
Wisconsin	4.6	37.1	58.3	9
Wyoming	5.8	50.2	43.9	30
50 States	7.6	48.1	44.2	
DC	12.9	n/a	87.1	
United States	7.2	45.8	47.0	

Rank in order

By % local

1. New Hampshire
2. Vermont
3. Michigan
4. Virginia
5. South Dakota
6. Illinois
7. Nevada
8. Massachusetts
9. Rhode Island
9. Wisconsin
11. Missouri
12. Nebraska
13. Maryland
14. Connecticut
15. New York
16. New Jersey
17. Montana
17. Ohio
19. Colorado
20. Oregon
21. Pennsylvania
22. Arizona
23. Minnesota
24. Texas
25. Iowa
26. Kansas
27. Georgia
28. Maine
28. North Dakota
30. Wyoming
31. South Carolina
32. Florida
33. Indiana
34. Tennessee
35. Utah
36. California
37. Louisiana
38. Mississippi
39. Idaho
39. Oklahoma
41. Arkansas
42. North Carolina
43. West Virginia
44. Delaware
45. Alaska
46. Washington
47. Kentucky
48. Alabama
49. New Mexico
50. Hawaii

State	State aid per pupil ($000)	Rank	Rank in order By $
Alabama	2,678	27	1. Alaska
Alaska	6,190	1	2. Hawaii
Arizona	2,253	39	3. Delaware
Arkansas	2,864	22	4. Washington
California	2,931	20	5. New Jersey
Colorado	2,347	36	6. West Virginia
Connecticut	3,617	12	7. Pennsylvania
Delaware	4,714	3	8. Kentucky
Florida	3,057	16	9. New York
Georgia	2,273	38	10. New Mexico
Hawaii	6,172	2	11. North Carolina
Idaho	2,733	26	12. Connecticut
Illinois	2,138	43	13. Indiana
Indiana	3,463	13	14. Minnesota
Iowa	2,877	21	15. Wyoming
Kansas	2,970	19	16. Florida
Kentucky	3,849	8	17. Maine
Louisiana	2,846	23	18. Oklahoma
Maine	3,053	17	19. Kansas
Maryland	2,743	25	20. California
Massachusetts	2,289	37	21. Iowa
Michigan	2,387	35	22. Arkansas
Minnesota	3,354	14	23. Louisiana
Mississippi	2,065	45	24. Wisconsin
Missouri	2,173	42	25. Maryland
Montana	2,098	44	26. Idaho
Nebraska	2,580	30	27. Alabama
Nevada	2,037	46	28. Texas
New Hampshire	577	48	29. Ohio
New Jersey	4,517	5	30. Nebraska
New Mexico	3,783	10	31. Rhode Island
New York	3,827	9	32. South Carolina
North Carolina	3,636	11	33. Oregon
North Dakota	2,217	41	34. Vermont
Ohio	2,615	29	35. Michigan
Oklahoma	2,973	18	36. Colorado
Oregon	2,467	33	37. Massachusetts
Pennsylvania	3,876	7	38. Georgia
Rhode Island	2,555	31	39. Arizona
South Carolina	2,485	32	40. Utah
South Dakota	1,367	47	41. North Dakota
Tennessee	403	49	42. Missouri
Texas	2,649	28	43. Illinois
Utah	2,226	40	44. Montana
Vermont	2,442	34	45. Mississippi
Virginia	280	50	46. Nevada
Washington	4,624	4	47. South Dakota
West Virginia	4,325	6	48. New Hampshire
Wisconsin	2,790	24	49. Tennessee
Wyoming	3,267	15	50. Virginia
50 States	2,893		
DC	n/a		
United States	2,936		

State	Higher education spending ($000)	higher ed. spending per capita $	higher ed. spending as a % of pers. inc. %	Rank by per capita		Rank in order By per capita
Alabama	1,437,777	348	2.27	23		1. North Dakota
Alaska	296,194	505	2.47	4		2. Delaware
Arizona	1,476,923	385	2.38	18		3. Wyoming
Arkansas	766,433	319	2.21	32		4. Alaska
California	11,066,561	359	1.75	21		5. Utah
Colorado	1,457,300	420	2.23	13		6. Kansas
Connecticut	765,691	233	0.89	47		7. New Mexico
Delaware	389,319	565	2.75	2		8. Vermont
Florida	3,070,761	228	1.22	49		9. Iowa
Georgia	1,569,866	233	1.36	48		10. Hawaii
Hawaii	511,473	441	2.13	10		11. Nebraska
Idaho	364,119	341	2.29	25		12. Wisconsin
Illinois	3,350,096	288	1.40	39		13. Colorado
Indiana	2,186,764	386	2.27	17		14. Michigan
Iowa	1,251,000	445	2.59	9		15. Oregon
Kansas	1,223,224	485	2.68	6		16. Washington
Kentucky	1,191,749	317	2.05	33		17. Indiana
Louisiana	1,240,036	289	1.94	37		18. Arizona
Maine	356,489	289	1.65	38		19. North Carolina
Maryland	1,704,009	347	1.58	24		20. Minnesota
Massachusetts	1,297,082	216	0.94	50		21. California
Michigan	3,935,126	417	2.25	14		22. South Carolina
Minnesota	1,663,828	371	1.96	20		23. Alabama
Mississippi	851,873	326	2.47	29		24. Maryland
Missouri	1,289,465*	248	1.39	45		25. Idaho
Montana	247,328	300	1.95	35		26. Oklahoma
Nebraska	690,948	430	2.45	11		27. Pennsylvania
Nevada	377,052	284	1.48	41		28. Virginia
New Hampshire	274,113	247	1.14	46		29. Mississippi
New Jersey	2,179,094	280	1.09	43		30. Texas
New Mexico	751,025	475	3.31	7		31. Ohio
New York	5,080,801	280	1.25	42		32. Arkansas
North Carolina	2,555,980	374	2.25	19		33. Kentucky
North Dakota	370,252	582	3.74	1		34. West Virginia
Ohio	3,555,905	323	1.83	31		35. Montana
Oklahoma	1,085,060	338	2.20	26		36. Tennessee
Oregon	1,174,281	394	2.29	15		37. Louisiana
Pennsylvania	3,992,643	332	1.73	27		38. Maine
Rhode Island	288,397	287	1.50	40		39. Illinois
South Carolina	1,257,832	349	2.28	22		40. Rhode Island
South Dakota	183,681	258	1.63	44		41. Nevada
Tennessee	1,507,955	300	1.85	36		42. New York
Texas	5,733,321	325	1.92	30		43. New Jersey
Utah	880,025	485	3.40	5		44. South Dakota
Vermont	268,608	471	2.63	8		45. Missouri
Virginia	2,086,107	327	1.65	28		46. New Hampshire
Washington	2,023,231	394	2.07	16		47. Connecticut
West Virginia	551,272	304	2.14	34		48. Georgia
Wisconsin	2,137,310	427	2.40	12		49. Florida
Wyoming	244,354	524	3.14	3		50. Massachusetts
50 States	84,209,733	331	1.75			
DC	119,143	202	0.73			
United States	84,328,876	331	1.75			

H-20 State And Local Higher Education Spending As A % Of Total Spending, 1992

State	Higher education spending as a % of general spending %	Rank
Alabama	11.18	14
Alaska	5.10	48
Arizona	10.98	17
Arkansas	11.62	10
California	8.51	33
Colorado	11.36	12
Connecticut	5.08	49
Delaware	13.30	4
Florida	6.52	45
Georgia	7.02	42
Hawaii	8.47	34
Idaho	11.15	15
Illinois	8.31	36
Indiana	12.11	8
Iowa	12.40	7
Kansas	14.30	3
Kentucky	9.97	23
Louisiana	7.86	39
Maine	7.67	40
Maryland	9.50	27
Massachusetts	5.25	47
Michigan	11.06	16
Minnesota	8.26	37
Mississippi	11.36	13
Missouri	8.61	32
Montana	8.45	35
Nebraska	12.50	6
Nevada	7.11	41
New Hampshire	6.71	43
New Jersey	5.96	46
New Mexico	12.54	5
New York	4.97	50
North Carolina	12.02	9
North Dakota	14.94	2
Ohio	9.49	28
Oklahoma	10.81	18
Oregon	9.96	24
Pennsylvania	8.79	31
Rhode Island	6.56	44
South Carolina	10.79	19
South Dakota	8.13	38
Tennessee	9.99	22
Texas	10.31	21
Utah	15.16	1
Vermont	11.56	11
Virginia	9.88	26
Washington	9.36	30
West Virginia	9.47	29
Wisconsin	10.77	20
Wyoming	9.93	25
50 States	8.66	
DC	2.69	
United States	8.67	

By %

1. Utah
2. North Dakota
3. Kansas
4. Delaware
5. New Mexico
6. Nebraska
7. Iowa
8. Indiana
9. North Carolina
10. Arkansas
11. Vermont
12. Colorado
13. Mississippi
14. Alabama
15. Idaho
16. Michigan
17. Arizona
18. Oklahoma
19. South Carolina
20. Wisconsin
21. Texas
22. Tennessee
23. Kentucky
24. Oregon
25. Wyoming
26. Virginia
27. Maryland
28. Ohio
29. West Virginia
30. Washington
31. Pennsylvania
32. Missouri
33. California
34. Hawaii
35. Montana
36. Illinois
37. Minnesota
38. South Dakota
39. Louisiana
40. Maine
41. Nevada
42. Georgia
43. New Hampshire
44. Rhode Island
45. Florida
46. New Jersey
47. Massachusetts
48. Alaska
49. Connecticut
50. New York

State	Higher education Enrollment (000)	As % of total pop %	Rank by %		Rank in order By %
Alabama	206	5.0	13		1. Arizona
Alaska	29	4.9	15		2. Wyoming
Arizona	256	6.7	1		3. Nebraska
Arkansas	86	3.6	42		4. Colorado
California	1,748	5.7	8		5. Kansas
Colorado	211	6.1	4		6. New Mexico
Connecticut	108	3.3	47		7. North Dakota
Delaware	35	5.1	11		8. California
Florida	511	3.8	40		9. Utah
Georgia	233	3.4	44		10. Wisconsin
Hawaii	50	4.3	29		11. Delaware
Idaho	47	4.4	27		12. Michigan
Illinois	566	4.9	17		13. Alabama
Indiana	235	4.1	33		14. Oklahoma
Iowa	128	4.5	25		15. Alaska
Kansas	153	6.1	5		16. Oregon
Kentucky	158	4.2	32		17. Illinois
Louisiana	177	4.1	34		18. Nevada
Maine	41	3.3	46		19. Minnesota
Maryland	228	4.6	23		20. Texas
Massachusetts	183	3.1	49		21. Virginia
Michigan	473	5.0	12		22. Washington
Minnesota	212	4.7	19		23. Maryland
Mississippi	110	4.2	31		24. North Carolina
Missouri	199	3.8	39		25. Iowa
Montana	34	4.1	35		26. West Virginia
Nebraska	103	6.4	3		27. Idaho
Nevada	63	4.8	18		28. Rhode Island
New Hampshire	35	3.2	48		29. Hawaii
New Jersey	278	3.6	43		30. South Dakota
New Mexico	95	6.0	6		31. Mississippi
New York	611	3.4	45		32. Kentucky
North Carolina	316	4.6	24		33. Indiana
North Dakota	37	5.8	7		34. Louisiana
Ohio	437	4.0	37		35. Montana
Oklahoma	159	5.0	14		36. South Carolina
Oregon	145	4.9	16		37. Ohio
Pennsylvania	363	3.0	50		38. Tennessee
Rhode Island	43	4.3	28		39. Missouri
South Carolina	146	4.0	36		40. Florida
South Dakota	30	4.3	30		41. Vermont
Tennessee	192	3.8	38		42. Arkansas
Texas	832	4.7	20		43. New Jersey
Utah	97	5.3	9		44. Georgia
Vermont	21	3.8	41		45. New York
Virginia	298	4.7	21		46. Maine
Washington	239	4.6	22		47. Connecticut
West Virginia	79	4.4	26		48. New Hampshire
Wisconsin	257	5.1	10		49. Massachusetts
Wyoming	31	6.6	2		50. Pennsylvania
50 States	11,323	4.4			
DC	12	2.1			
United States	11,388	4.5			

State	Per pupil support $	Rank	By $
Alabama	10,665	5	1. Iowa
Alaska	11,227	3	2. Arkansas
Arizona	2,962	46	3. Alaska
Arkansas	11,904	2	4. South Carolina
California	3,148	44	5. Alabama
Colorado	5,236	29	6. Connecticut
Connecticut	10,113	6	7. Oregon
Delaware	4,474	34	8. Kentucky
Florida	4,151	36	9. Georgia
Georgia	8,640	9	10. Hawaii
Hawaii	8,628	10	11. North Carolina
Idaho	4,828	32	12. Wisconsin
Illinois	3,734	40	13. Nebraska
Indiana	4,220	35	14. Louisiana
Iowa	14,760	1	15. Rhode Island
Kansas	6,943	17	16. Tennessee
Kentucky	8,718	8	17. Kansas
Louisiana	7,414	14	18. South Dakota
Maine	3,966	37	19. Maryland
Maryland	6,632	19	20. Minnesota
Massachusetts	2,982	45	21. West Virginia
Michigan	3,281	42	22. New York
Minnesota	6,552	20	23. Oklahoma
Mississippi	5,741	25	24. Virginia
Missouri	3,253	43	25. Mississippi
Montana	5,598	27	26. Texas
Nebraska	7,713	13	27. Montana
Nevada	n/a	n/a	28. North Dakota
New Hampshire	2,950	47	29. Colorado
New Jersey	3,437	41	30. Washington
New Mexico	n/a	n/a	31. Utah
New York	6,465	22	32. Idaho
North Carolina	8,209	11	33. Wyoming
North Dakota	5,383	28	34. Delaware
Ohio	3,757	38	35. Indiana
Oklahoma	5,866	23	36. Florida
Oregon	9,310	7	37. Maine
Pennsylvania	3,752	39	38. Ohio
Rhode Island	7,327	15	39. Pennsylvania
South Carolina	10,791	4	40. Illinois
South Dakota	6,690	18	41. New Jersey
Tennessee	7,228	16	42. Michigan
Texas	5,701	26	43. Missouri
Utah	4,909	31	44. California
Vermont	2,570	48	45. Massachusetts
Virginia	5,754	24	46. Arizona
Washington	5,009	30	47. New Hampshire
West Virginia	6,546	21	48. Vermont
Wisconsin	8,000	12	
Wyoming	4,823	33	
50 States	5,351		
DC	n/a		
United States	5,320		

State	Average tuition $	Rank		Rank in order By $
Alabama	1,983	30		1. Vermont
Alaska	1,908	35		2. Pennsylvania
Arizona	1,819	39		3. Massachusetts
Arkansas	1,808	40		4. New Hampshire
California	2,378	21		5. Delaware
Colorado	2,262	27		6. Virginia
Connecticut	3,479	9		7. New Jersey
Delaware	3,684	5		8. Michigan
Florida	1,784	42		9. Connecticut
Georgia	1,894	36		10. Rhode Island
Hawaii	1,455	49		11. Ohio
Idaho	1,498	48		12. Maine
Illinois	3,029	14		13. Maryland
Indiana	2,621	19		14. Illinois
Iowa	2,352	23		15. New York
Kansas	1,921	33		16. South Carolina
Kentucky	1,913	34		17. Oregon
Louisiana	2,182	28		18. Minnesota
Maine	3,139	12		19. Indiana
Maryland	3,120	13		20. Missouri
Massachusetts	4,142	3		21. California
Michigan	3,481	8		22. Mississippi
Minnesota	2,780	18		23. Iowa
Mississippi	2,370	22		24. Washington
Missouri	2,475	20		25. Wisconsin
Montana	1,890	37		26. South Dakota
Nebraska	1,939	32		27. Colorado
Nevada	1,538	46		28. Louisiana
New Hampshire	3,833	4		29. North Dakota
New Jersey	3,518	7		30. Alabama
New Mexico	1,731	43		31. Utah
New York	2,921	15		32. Nebraska
North Carolina	1,409	50		33. Kansas
North Dakota	2,128	29		34. Kentucky
Ohio	3,259	11		35. Alaska
Oklahoma	1,645	45		36. Georgia
Oregon	2,833	17		37. Montana
Pennsylvania	4,316	2		38. West Virginia
Rhode Island	3,402	10		39. Arizona
South Carolina	2,891	16		40. Arkansas
South Dakota	2,288	26		41. Tennessee
Tennessee	1,797	41		42. Florida
Texas	1,503	47		43. New Mexico
Utah	1,964	31		44. Wyoming
Vermont	5,536	1		45. Oklahoma
Virginia	3,639	6		46. Nevada
Washington	2,337	24		47. Texas
West Virginia	1,875	38		48. Idaho
Wisconsin	2,318	25		49. Hawaii
Wyoming	1,648	44		50. North Carolina
50 States	2,513			
DC	974			
United States	2,543			

State	Average salary ($000)	Rank
Alabama	47.6	30
Alaska	55.5	4
Arizona	48.8	23
Arkansas	44.5	40
California	52.9	9
Colorado	52.3	12
Connecticut	58.9	2
Delaware	54.8	5
Florida	45.8	36
Georgia	46.7	32
Hawaii	55.7	3
Idaho	42.4	47
Illinois	45.0	38
Indiana	49.1	21
Iowa	51.8	14
Kansas	44.7	39
Kentucky	48.7	26
Louisiana	43.7	45
Maine	43.4	46
Maryland	49.9	17
Massachusetts	53.4	8
Michigan	50.7	15
Minnesota	49.9	17
Mississippi	46.1	35
Missouri	48.8	23
Montana	37.0	50
Nebraska	48.4	28
Nevada	48.8	23
New Hampshire	49.6	19
New Jersey	67.1	1
New Mexico	46.5	34
New York	53.7	7
North Carolina	53.9	6
North Dakota	39.8	48
Ohio	50.7	15
Oklahoma	44.5	40
Oregon	44.4	42
Pennsylvania	52.6	11
Rhode Island	49.6	19
South Carolina	47.4	31
South Dakota	37.7	49
Tennessee	49.1	21
Texas	48.5	27
Utah	45.5	37
Vermont	46.7	32
Virginia	52.9	9
Washington	48.2	29
West Virginia	44.2	43
Wisconsin	52.3	12
Wyoming	43.8	44
50 States	48.7	
DC	56.0	
United States	48.8	

Rank in order

By $

1. New Jersey
2. Connecticut
3. Hawaii
4. Alaska
5. Delaware
6. North Carolina
7. New York
8. Massachusetts
9. California
9. Virginia
11. Pennsylvania
12. Colorado
12. Wisconsin
14. Iowa
15. Michigan
15. Ohio
17. Maryland
17. Minnesota
19. New Hampshire
19. Rhode Island
21. Indiana
21. Tennessee
23. Arizona
23. Missouri
23. Nevada
26. Kentucky
27. Texas
28. Nebraska
29. Washington
30. Alabama
31. South Carolina
32. Georgia
32. Vermont
34. New Mexico
35. Mississippi
36. Florida
37. Utah
38. Illinois
39. Kansas
40. Arkansas
40. Oklahoma
42. Oregon
43. West Virginia
44. Wyoming
45. Louisiana
46. Maine
47. Idaho
48. North Dakota
49. South Dakota
50. Montana

State	Education employees per 10,000 pop	Rank	Rank in order By per 10,000
Alabama	198	29	1. Montana
Alaska	252	3	2. Wyoming
Arizona	192	34	3. Alaska
Arkansas	224	15	4. Kansas
California	151	50	5. Texas
Colorado	195	32	6. Maine
Connecticut	187	36	7. South Dakota
Delaware	175	43	8. Vermont
Florida	172	48	9. Mississippi
Georgia	226	12	10. Oklahoma
Hawaii	187	37	11. New Mexico
Idaho	216	18	12. Georgia
Illinois	180	40	13. West Virginia
Indiana	201	27	14. Nebraska
Iowa	217	17	15. Arkansas
Kansas	246	4	16. Louisiana
Kentucky	215	21	17. Iowa
Louisiana	224	16	18. Idaho
Maine	244	6	19. Virginia
Maryland	174	45	20. New York
Massachusetts	176	42	21. Kentucky
Michigan	202	26	22. New Jersey
Minnesota	196	30	23. North Dakota
Mississippi	237	9	24. South Carolina
Missouri	189	35	25. North Carolina
Montana	313	1	26. Michigan
Nebraska	224	14	27. Indiana
Nevada	178	41	28. New Hampshire
New Hampshire	201	28	29. Alabama
New Jersey	213	22	30. Minnesota
New Mexico	230	11	31. Wisconsin
New York	215	20	32. Colorado
North Carolina	202	25	33. Oregon
North Dakota	210	23	34. Arizona
Ohio	183	39	35. Missouri
Oklahoma	235	10	36. Connecticut
Oregon	193	33	37. Hawaii
Pennsylvania	171	49	38. Utah
Rhode Island	174	47	39. Ohio
South Carolina	207	24	40. Illinois
South Dakota	239	7	41. Nevada
Tennessee	175	44	42. Massachusetts
Texas	245	5	43. Delaware
Utah	185	38	44. Tennessee
Vermont	237	8	45. Maryland
Virginia	215	19	46. Washington
Washington	174	46	47. Rhode Island
West Virginia	225	13	48. Florida
Wisconsin	196	31	49. Pennsylvania
Wyoming	295	2	50. California
50 States	196		
DC	191		
United States	196		

State	Federal R&D spending ($000)	Per capita $	Rank by per capita
Alabama	2,149,352	514	5
Alaska	92,692	155	20
Arizona	535,274	136	24
Arkansas	79,185	33	49
California	14,883,737	477	7
Colorado	1,343,392	377	9
Connecticut	522,181	159	19
Delaware	56,160	80	37
Florida	2,775,255	202	14
Georgia	3,035,313	440	8
Hawaii	113,005	97	33
Idaho	303,689	276	11
Illinois	963,774	82	36
Indiana	513,647	90	35
Iowa	215,777	76	39
Kansas	87,858	35	48
Kentucky	86,668	23	50
Louisiana	152,635	36	47
Maine	65,239	53	42
Maryland	7,238,624	1,460	1
Massachusetts	3,551,660	590	3
Michigan	877,983	93	34
Minnesota	445,536	98	31
Mississippi	259,827	98	32
Missouri	726,344	139	23
Montana	89,050	106	28
Nebraska	78,477	49	43
Nevada	406,159	294	10
New Hampshire	237,604	211	13
New Jersey	1,422,848	181	15
New Mexico	2,309,611	1,429	2
New York	2,538,016	140	22
North Carolina	719,115	103	29
North Dakota	50,329	79	38
Ohio	1,921,720	174	16
Oklahoma	117,908	36	46
Oregon	229,375	76	40
Pennsylvania	2,566,507	213	12
Rhode Island	495,591	496	6
South Carolina	173,173	48	44
South Dakota	26,896	38	45
Tennessee	674,420	132	25
Texas	2,546,244	141	21
Utah	298,829	161	18
Vermont	62,143	108	27
Virginia	3,402,556	526	4
Washington	878,074	167	17
West Virginia	206,208	113	26
Wisconsin	350,775	70	41
Wyoming	48,234	103	30
50 States	62,924,669	245	
DC	2,488,923	4,299	
United States	65,744,145	255	

Rank in order

By per capita

1. Maryland
2. New Mexico
3. Massachusetts
4. Virginia
5. Alabama
6. Rhode Island
7. California
8. Georgia
9. Colorado
10. Nevada
11. Idaho
12. Pennsylvania
13. New Hampshire
14. Florida
15. New Jersey
16. Ohio
17. Washington
18. Utah
19. Connecticut
20. Alaska
21. Texas
22. New York
23. Missouri
24. Arizona
25. Tennessee
26. West Virginia
27. Vermont
28. Montana
29. North Carolina
30. Wyoming
31. Minnesota
32. Mississippi
33. Hawaii
34. Michigan
35. Indiana
36. Illinois
37. Delaware
38. North Dakota
39. Iowa
40. Oregon
41. Wisconsin
42. Maine
43. Nebraska
44. South Carolina
45. South Dakota
46. Oklahoma
47. Louisiana
48. Kansas
49. Arkansas
50. Kentucky

State	Library spending ($000)	library spending per capita $	Rank by per capita	Rank in order By per capita
Alabama	41,535	9.9	43	1. New York
Alaska	17,668	29.5	3	2. Ohio
Arizona	59,603	15.1	27	3. Alaska
Arkansas	17,767	7.3	50	4. New Jersey
California	550,300	17.6	21	5. Connecticut
Colorado	75,722	21.2	13	6. Washington
Connecticut	86,346	26.3	5	7. Indiana
Delaware	7,588	10.9	40	8. Maryland
Florida	207,131	15.1	28	9. Illinois
Georgia	88,778	12.9	34	10. Minnesota
Hawaii	24,918	21.4	12	11. Wyoming
Idaho	13,407	12.2	37	12. Hawaii
Illinois	262,601	22.5	9	13. Colorado
Indiana	137,575	24.1	7	14. Massachusetts
Iowa	46,153	16.4	25	15. Wisconsin
Kansas	43,384	17.1	23	16. Rhode Island
Kentucky	37,332	9.8	44	17. Oregon
Louisiana	58,479	13.6	29	18. Virginia
Maine	16,537	13.3	32	19. New Hampshire
Maryland	113,681	22.9	8	20. Nevada
Massachusetts	126,343	21.0	14	21. California
Michigan	163,996	17.3	22	22. Michigan
Minnesota	101,067	22.3	10	23. Kansas
Mississippi	20,396	7.7	49	24. Utah
Missouri	81,192	15.5	26	25. Iowa
Montana	8,879	10.6	41	26. Missouri
Nebraska	21,953	13.6	30	27. Arizona
Nevada	25,061	18.1	20	28. Florida
New Hampshire	20,515	18.3	19	29. Louisiana
New Jersey	227,330	28.9	4	30. Nebraska
New Mexico	17,682	10.9	39	31. Vermont
New York	569,616	31.4	1	32. Maine
North Carolina	88,452	12.7	35	33. Pennsylvania
North Dakota	5,917	9.3	47	34. Georgia
Ohio	335,890	30.4	2	35. North Carolina
Oklahoma	32,585	10.1	42	36. South Dakota
Oregon	55,844	18.4	17	37. Idaho
Pennsylvania	160,126	13.3	33	38. South Carolina
Rhode Island	19,168	19.2	16	39. New Mexico
South Carolina	41,035	11.3	38	40. Delaware
South Dakota	8,954	12.5	36	41. Montana
Tennessee	49,715	9.8	46	42. Oklahoma
Texas	176,390	9.8	45	43. Alabama
Utah	30,768	16.5	24	44. Kentucky
Vermont	7,820	13.6	31	45. Texas
Virginia	118,319	18.3	18	46. Tennessee
Washington	129,830	24.7	6	47. North Dakota
West Virginia	16,836	9.3	48	48. West Virginia
Wisconsin	105,285	20.9	15	49. Mississippi
Wyoming	10,321	22.0	11	50. Arkansas
50 States	4,683,790	18.2		
DC	20,909	36.1		
United States	4,704,700	18.3		

Health

State	Divorces per 1,000 population	Rank
Alabama	6.2	6
Alaska	5.5	14
Arizona	5.8	10
Arkansas	7.1	2
California	n/a	n/a
Colorado	5.1	18
Connecticut	2.8	46
Delaware	4.8	23
Florida	5.9	9
Georgia	5.2	17
Hawaii	4.2	30
Idaho	6.2	6
Illinois	3.7	37
Indiana	n/a	n/a
Iowa	3.9	36
Kansas	4.7	24
Kentucky	5.8	10
Louisiana	n/a	n/a
Maine	4.4	28
Maryland	3.5	39
Massachusetts	2.4	47
Michigan	4.1	33
Minnesota	3.6	38
Mississippi	5.7	12
Missouri	5.0	20
Montana	4.9	22
Nebraska	4.0	34
Nevada	9.0	1
New Hampshire	4.4	28
New Jersey	3.0	45
New Mexico	6.0	8
New York	3.3	42
North Carolina	5.1	18
North Dakota	3.4	40
Ohio	4.5	27
Oklahoma	6.7	3
Oregon	5.3	16
Pennsylvania	3.3	42
Rhode Island	3.2	44
South Carolina	4.2	30
South Dakota	4.2	30
Tennessee	6.6	4
Texas	5.4	15
Utah	4.7	24
Vermont	4.0	34
Virginia	4.6	26
Washington	5.6	13
West Virginia	5.0	20
Wisconsin	3.4	40
Wyoming	6.5	5
50 States (unweighted average)	4.5	
DC	3.9	
United States (unweighted average)	4.5	

Rank in order

By rate

1. Nevada
2. Arkansas
3. Oklahoma
4. Tennessee
5. Wyoming
6. Alabama
6. Idaho
8. New Mexico
9. Florida
10. Arizona
10. Kentucky
12. Mississippi
13. Washington
14. Alaska
15. Texas
16. Oregon
17. Georgia
18. Colorado
18. North Carolina
20. Missouri
20. West Virginia
22. Montana
23. Delaware
24. Kansas
24. Utah
26. Virginia
27. Ohio
28. Maine
28. New Hampshire
30. Hawaii
30. South Carolina
30. South Dakota
33. Michigan
34. Nebraska
34. Vermont
36. Iowa
37. Illinois
38. Minnesota
39. Maryland
40. North Dakota
40. Wisconsin
42. New York
42. Pennsylvania
44. Rhode Island
45. New Jersey
46. Connecticut
47. Massachusetts

I-2 Infant Mortality Rate, 1994

State	Infant deaths per 1,000 live births	Rank
Alabama	9.9	4
Alaska	5.9	48
Arizona	8.6	15
Arkansas	8.0	22
California	6.7	35
Colorado	6.6	38
Connecticut	6.5	40
Delaware	7.0	31
Florida	8.1	20
Georgia	9.7	5
Hawaii	6.5	40
Idaho	7.3	29
Illinois	9.1	9
Indiana	9.5	6
Iowa	7.0	31
Kansas	8.8	14
Kentucky	7.7	27
Louisiana	9.5	6
Maine	6.3	42
Maryland	8.9	10
Massachusetts	5.7	49
Michigan	8.6	15
Minnesota	6.7	35
Mississippi	10.1	2
Missouri	8.1	20
Montana	8.2	19
Nebraska	7.9	25
Nevada	6.2	44
New Hampshire	6.6	38
New Jersey	7.9	25
New Mexico	8.9	10
New York	8.5	17
North Carolina	10.0	3
North Dakota	6.3	42
Ohio	8.9	10
Oklahoma	9.4	8
Oregon	7.0	31
Pennsylvania	7.6	28
Rhode Island	6.0	45
South Carolina	8.9	10
South Dakota	11.8	1
Tennessee	8.3	18
Texas	7.2	30
Utah	6.0	45
Vermont	6.7	35
Virginia	8.0	22
Washington	5.4	50
West Virginia	6.8	34
Wisconsin	8.0	22
Wyoming	6.0	45
50 States	7.8	
DC	20.1	
United States	7.9	

Rank in order

By rate

1. South Dakota
2. Mississippi
3. North Carolina
4. Alabama
5. Georgia
6. Indiana
6. Louisiana
8. Oklahoma
9. Illinois
10. Maryland
10. New Mexico
10. Ohio
10. South Carolina
14. Kansas
15. Arizona
15. Michigan
17. New York
18. Tennessee
19. Montana
20. Florida
20. Missouri
22. Arkansas
22. Virginia
22. Wisconsin
25. Nebraska
25. New Jersey
27. Kentucky
28. Pennsylvania
29. Idaho
30. Texas
31. Delaware
31. Iowa
31. Oregon
34. West Virginia
35. California
35. Minnesota
35. Vermont
38. Colorado
38. New Hampshire
40. Connecticut
40. Hawaii
42. Maine
42. North Dakota
44. Nevada
45. Rhode Island
45. Utah
45. Wyoming
48. Alaska
49. Massachusetts
50. Washington

State	State health Rankings	Rank
Alabama	-13	45
Alaska	-8	38
Arizona	1	25
Arkansas	-14	46
California	0	28
Colorado	12	10
Connecticut	19	3
Delaware	0	28
Florida	-8	38
Georgia	-4	36
Hawaii	18	5
Idaho	1	25
Illinois	-1	30
Indiana	4	22
Iowa	14	8
Kansas	12	10
Kentucky	-8	38
Louisiana	-19	50
Maine	10	14
Maryland	8	16
Massachusetts	15	7
Michigan	2	24
Minnesota	20	2
Mississippi	-18	49
Missouri	-3	33
Montana	1	25
Nebraska	12	10
Nevada	-10	43
New Hampshire	21	1
New Jersey	9	15
New Mexico	-10	43
New York	-8	38
North Carolina	-1	30
North Dakota	8	16
Ohio	7	19
Oklahoma	-3	33
Oregon	4	22
Pennsylvania	5	21
Rhode Island	7	19
South Carolina	-14	46
South Dakota	-3	33
Tennessee	-9	42
Texas	-2	32
Utah	19	3
Vermont	16	6
Virginia	13	9
Washington	8	16
West Virginia	-16	48
Wisconsin	11	13
Wyoming	-4	36
50 States	n/a	
DC	n/a	
United States	n/a	

Rank in order

By ranking

1. New Hampshire
2. Minnesota
3. Connecticut
4. Utah
5. Hawaii
6. Vermont
7. Massachusetts
8. Iowa
9. Virginia
10. Colorado
11. Kansas
12. Nebraska
13. Wisconsin
14. Maine
15. New Jersey
16. Maryland
17. North Dakota
18. Washington
19. Ohio
20. Rhode Island
21. Pennsylvania
22. Indiana
23. Oregon
24. Michigan
25. Arizona
26. Idaho
27. Montana
28. California
29. Delaware
30. Illinois
31. North Carolina
32. Texas
33. Missouri
34. Oklahoma
35. South Dakota
36. Georgia
37. Wyoming
38. Alaska
39. Florida
40. Kentucky
41. New York
42. Tennessee
43. Nevada
44. New Mexico
45. Alabama
46. Arkansas
47. South Carolina
48. West Virginia
49. Mississippi
50. Louisiana

I-4 Percentage Of Non-Elderly Population Without Health Insurance, 1993

State	% without health insurance %	Rank
Alabama	20.7	13
Alaska	15.8	25
Arizona	24.1	5
Arkansas	23.5	6
California	22.7	7
Colorado	15.2	29
Connecticut	12.1	47
Delaware	15.6	27
Florida	14.1	37
Georgia	22.0	9
Hawaii	13.7	40
Idaho	17.0	19
Illinois	14.9	30
Indiana	14.3	34
Iowa	10.9	49
Kansas	14.6	32
Kentucky	14.7	31
Louisiana	27.0	2
Maine	13.1	42
Maryland	17.2	17
Massachusetts	14.1	38
Michigan	13.1	43
Minnesota	12.7	45
Mississippi	21.1	11
Missouri	14.2	36
Montana	18.4	15
Nebraska	14.3	35
Nevada	21.5	10
New Hampshire	14.1	39
New Jersey	16.2	23
New Mexico	26.0	3
New York	16.5	22
North Carolina	17.0	20
North Dakota	16.6	21
Ohio	13.1	44
Oklahoma	27.4	1
Oregon	17.2	18
Pennsylvania	13.4	41
Rhode Island	12.1	48
South Carolina	19.9	14
South Dakota	15.8	26
Tennessee	15.6	28
Texas	25.1	4
Utah	12.4	46
Vermont	14.6	33
Virginia	15.9	24
Washington	21.0	12
West Virginia	22.5	8
Wisconsin	10.0	50
Wyoming	17.7	16
50 States	n/a	
DC	23.5	
United States	18.1	

Rank in order

By %

1. Oklahoma
2. Louisiana
3. New Mexico
4. Texas
5. Arizona
6. Arkansas
7. California
8. West Virginia
9. Georgia
10. Nevada
11. Mississippi
12. Washington
13. Alabama
14. South Carolina
15. Montana
16. Wyoming
17. Maryland
18. Oregon
19. Idaho
20. North Carolina
21. North Dakota
22. New York
23. New Jersey
24. Virginia
25. Alaska
26. South Dakota
27. Delaware
28. Tennessee
29. Colorado
30. Illinois
31. Kentucky
32. Kansas
33. Vermont
34. Indiana
35. Nebraska
36. Missouri
37. Florida
38. Massachusetts
39. New Hampshire
40. Hawaii
41. Pennsylvania
42. Maine
43. Michigan
44. Ohio
45. Minnesota
46. Utah
47. Connecticut
48. Rhode Island
49. Iowa
50. Wisconsin

State	Abortions #	Per 1,000 births ratio	rank by ratio	By ratio
Alabama	14,097	224	31	1. California
Alaska	1,718	147	45	2. New York
Arizona	15,491	228	28	3. Rhode Island
Arkansas	6,211	175	42	4. Delaware
California	350,983	576	1	5. Massachusetts
Colorado	11,402	212	34	6. Connecticut
Connecticut	18,534	382	6	7. Washington
Delaware	5,547	496	4	8. Vermont
Florida	71,254	368	9	9. Florida
Georgia	38,407	348	11	10. North Carolina
Hawaii	5,714	286	18	11. Georgia
Idaho	1,647	98	47	12. Nevada
Illinois	46,502	239	25	13. Oregon
Indiana	13,493	158	44	14. Virginia
Iowa	7,029	181	39	15. New Jersey
Kansas	7,318	194	37	16. Pennsylvania
Kentucky	9,590	179	41	17. Texas
Louisiana	12,190	169	43	18. Hawaii
Maine	3,827	228	29	19. Montana
Maryland	18,994	240	24	20. Tennessee
Massachusetts	37,071	420	5	21. Nebraska
Michigan	34,556	231	27	22. Ohio
Minnesota	16,177	241	23	23. Minnesota
Mississippi	8,184	190	38	24. Maryland
Missouri	15,473	197	36	25. Illinois
Montana	3,226	281	19	26. New Hampshire
Nebraska	6,194	259	21	27. Michigan
Nevada	7,484	337	12	28. Arizona
New Hampshire	3,842	235	26	29. Maine
New Jersey	37,541	309	15	30. Wisconsin
New Mexico	5,745	207	35	31. Alabama
New York	158,761	553	2	32. Oklahoma
North Carolina	36,420	356	10	33. South Carolina
North Dakota	1,602	180	40	34. Colorado
Ohio	41,705	257	22	35. New Mexico
Oklahoma	10,533	220	32	36. Missouri
Oregon	14,310	337	13	37. Kansas
Pennsylvania	50,988	304	16	38. Mississippi
Rhode Island	7,412	503	3	39. Iowa
South Carolina	12,538	218	33	40. North Dakota
South Dakota	984	90	48	41. Kentucky
Tennessee	19,779	266	20	42. Arkansas
Texas	91,947	289	17	43. Louisiana
Utah	4,213	117	46	44. Indiana
Vermont	3,015	379	8	45. Alaska
Virginia	31,943	330	14	46. Utah
Washington	30,243	380	7	47. Idaho
West Virginia	2,598	71	49	48. South Dakota
Wisconsin	16,237	225	30	49. West Virginia
Wyoming	369	55	50	50. Wyoming
50 States	1,371,038	n/a		
DC	18,899	n/a		
United States	1,388,937	339		

CQ State Fact Finder

State	Per capita consumption in gallons	Rank
Alabama	1.80	46
Alaska	3.05	3
Arizona	2.77	5
Arkansas	1.92	42
California	2.55	12
Colorado	2.54	13
Connecticut	2.31	26
Delaware	2.75	7
Florida	2.80	4
Georgia	2.25	30
Hawaii	2.64	8
Idaho	2.22	33
Illinois	2.45	17
Indiana	1.96	41
Iowa	1.92	43
Kansas	1.80	47
Kentucky	1.72	48
Louisiana	2.53	14
Maine	2.23	31
Maryland	2.26	29
Massachusetts	2.40	21
Michigan	2.23	32
Minnesota	2.37	22
Mississippi	2.09	37
Missouri	2.28	27
Montana	2.61	9
Nebraska	2.19	34
Nevada	4.33	1
New Hampshire	4.30	2
New Jersey	2.36	24
New Mexico	2.50	15
New York	2.11	35
North Carolina	1.99	39
North Dakota	2.41	20
Ohio	1.99	40
Oklahoma	1.82	45
Oregon	2.43	19
Pennsylvania	2.00	38
Rhode Island	2.37	23
South Carolina	2.35	25
South Dakota	2.28	28
Tennessee	1.92	44
Texas	2.46	16
Utah	1.37	50
Vermont	2.57	11
Virginia	2.11	36
Washington	2.45	18
West Virginia	1.67	49
Wisconsin	2.77	6
Wyoming	2.58	10
50 States	2.36	
DC	4.15	
United States	2.31	

By per capita

1. Nevada
2. New Hampshire
3. Alaska
4. Florida
5. Arizona
6. Wisconsin
7. Delaware
8. Hawaii
9. Montana
10. Wyoming
11. Vermont
12. California
13. Colorado
14. Louisiana
15. New Mexico
16. Texas
17. Illinois
18. Washington
19. Oregon
20. North Dakota
21. Massachusetts
22. Minnesota
23. Rhode Island
24. New Jersey
25. South Carolina
26. Connecticut
27. Missouri
28. South Dakota
29. Maryland
30. Georgia
31. Maine
32. Michigan
33. Idaho
34. Nebraska
35. New York
36. Virginia
37. Mississippi
38. Pennsylvania
39. North Carolina
40. Ohio
41. Indiana
42. Arkansas
43. Iowa
44. Tennessee
45. Oklahoma
46. Alabama
47. Kansas
48. Kentucky
49. West Virginia
50. Utah

State	Adult smokers %	Rank by lowest % (1) to highest % (48)	Rank in order By %
Alabama	21.8	17	1. Utah
Alaska	28.0	47	2. Nebraska
Arizona	19.2	6	3. Montana
Arkansas	n/a	n/a	4. Idaho
California	19.4	8	5. Georgia
Colorado	23.1	30	6. Arizona
Connecticut	22.1	21	7. Iowa
Delaware	26.5	42	8. California
Florida	22.1	21	9. Hawaii
Georgia	19.1	5	10. New Mexico
Hawaii	19.5	9	11. Maryland
Idaho	18.7	4	12. New Jersey
Illinois	23.6	35	13. Oregon
Indiana	27.0	45	14. Washington
Iowa	19.3	7	15. Minnesota
Kansas	22.3	25	16. Vermont
Kentucky	27.9	46	17. Alabama
Louisiana	24.2	36	18. North Dakota
Maine	23.2	31	18. South Dakota
Maryland	19.9	11	20. Texas
Massachusetts	22.9	29	21. Connecticut
Michigan	25.1	39	21. Florida
Minnesota	21.4	15	21. New York
Mississippi	23.5	34	24. Rhode Island
Missouri	23.3	32	25. Kansas
Montana	18.0	3	26. Wisconsin
Nebraska	17.4	2	27. New Hampshire
Nevada	30.5	48	27. Virginia
New Hampshire	22.8	27	29. Massachusetts
New Jersey	20.1	12	30. Colorado
New Mexico	19.6	10	31. Maine
New York	22.1	21	32. Missouri
North Carolina	26.4	41	33. Ohio
North Dakota	21.9	18	34. Mississippi
Ohio	23.4	33	35. Illinois
Oklahoma	25.6	40	36. Louisiana
Oregon	20.8	13	37. Pennsylvania
Pennsylvania	24.4	37	38. West Virginia
Rhode Island	22.2	24	39. Michigan
South Carolina	26.7	44	40. Oklahoma
South Dakota	21.9	18	41. North Carolina
Tennessee	26.6	43	42. Delaware
Texas	22.0	20	43. Tennessee
Utah	15.6	1	44. South Carolina
Vermont	21.7	16	45. Indiana
Virginia	22.8	27	46. Kentucky
Washington	21.2	14	47. Alaska
West Virginia	24.5	38	48. Nevada
Wisconsin	22.5	26	
Wyoming	n/a	n/a	
50 States	n/a		
DC	18.7		
United States	22.2		

I-8 Percent Of Population Obese, 1991

State	Obese population %	Rank by %
Alabama	30.1	9
Alaska	30.1	9
Arizona	24.5	39
Arkansas	27.9	23
California	25.7	33
Colorado	21.3	47
Connecticut	24.5	39
Delaware	32.3	3
Florida	26.4	31
Georgia	25.8	32
Hawaii	23.5	44
Idaho	26.5	30
Illinois	27.7	24
Indiana	31.0	6
Iowa	29.6	11
Kansas	n/a	n/a
Kentucky	30.6	8
Louisiana	31.7	5
Maine	27.7	24
Maryland	24.7	38
Massachusetts	25.2	35
Michigan	34.1	1
Minnesota	27.5	26
Mississippi	30.9	7
Missouri	28.0	21
Montana	24.3	42
Nebraska	28.7	17
Nevada	n/a	n/a
New Hampshire	25.0	36
New Jersey	25.3	34
New Mexico	22.3	45
New York	28.0	21
North Carolina	27.5	26
North Dakota	28.6	18
Ohio	28.1	20
Oklahoma	28.5	19
Oregon	27.1	28
Pennsylvania	32.5	2
Rhode Island	25.0	36
South Carolina	29.1	14
South Dakota	28.8	15
Tennessee	28.8	15
Texas	29.5	12
Utah	24.4	41
Vermont	26.7	29
Virginia	22.3	45
Washington	24.1	43
West Virginia	32.1	4
Wisconsin	29.2	13
Wyoming	n/a	n/a
50 States	27.5	
DC	n/a	
United States	27.8	

Rank in order

By %

1. Michigan
2. Pennsylvania
3. Delaware
4. West Virginia
5. Louisiana
6. Indiana
7. Mississippi
8. Kentucky
9. Alabama
9. Alaska
11. Iowa
12. Texas
13. Wisconsin
14. South Carolina
15. South Dakota
15. Tennessee
17. Nebraska
18. North Dakota
19. Oklahoma
20. Ohio
21. Missouri
21. New York
23. Arkansas
24. Illinois
24. Maine
26. Minnesota
26. North Carolina
28. Oregon
29. Vermont
30. Idaho
31. Florida
32. Georgia
33. California
34. New Jersey
35. Massachusetts
36. New Hampshire
36. Rhode Island
38. Maryland
39. Arizona
39. Connecticut
41. Utah
42. Montana
43. Washington
44. Hawaii
45. New Mexico
45. Virginia
47. Colorado

I-9 AIDS Cases, 1994-1995

State	AIDS cases #	Per 100,000 residents rate	Rank by rate
Alabama	566	13.4	27
Alaska	79	13.0	29
Arizona	559	13.7	26
Arkansas	288	11.7	30
California	10,989	35.0	6
Colorado	718	19.6	18
Connecticut	1,086	32.5	7
Delaware	313	44.3	5
Florida	9,377	67.2	2
Georgia	2,284	32.4	8
Hawaii	263	22.3	16
Idaho	57	5.0	46
Illinois	2,785	23.7	14
Indiana	524	9.1	36
Iowa	145	5.1	45
Kansas	284	11.1	33
Kentucky	311	8.1	39
Louisiana	1,124	26.0	13
Maine	139	11.2	32
Maryland	2,951	58.9	4
Massachusetts	1,396	23.1	15
Michigan	1,071	11.3	31
Minnesota	413	9.0	37
Mississippi	414	15.5	23
Missouri	696	13.2	28
Montana	24	2.8	47
Nebraska	111	6.8	42
Nevada	413	28.3	10
New Hampshire	116	10.2	35
New Jersey	4,764	60.3	3
New Mexico	228	13.8	25
New York	12,578	69.2	1
North Carolina	1,015	14.4	24
North Dakota	7	1.1	50
Ohio	1,188	10.7	34
Oklahoma	266	8.2	38
Oregon	506	16.4	22
Pennsylvania	2,678	22.2	17
Rhode Island	291	29.2	9
South Carolina	995	27.2	12
South Dakota	20	2.8	48
Tennessee	883	17.1	21
Texas	5,153	28.0	11
Utah	153	8.0	40
Vermont	32	5.5	44
Virginia	1,150	17.6	19
Washington	993	17.5	20
West Virginia	114	6.3	43
Wisconsin	366	7.2	41
Wyoming	13	2.7	49
50 States	72,889	19.4	
DC	1,220	214.0	
United States	74,029	28.4	

Rank in order

By rate

1. New York
2. Florida
3. New Jersey
4. Maryland
5. Delaware
6. California
7. Connecticut
8. Georgia
9. Rhode Island
10. Nevada
11. Texas
12. South Carolina
13. Louisiana
14. Illinois
15. Massachusetts
16. Hawaii
17. Pennsylvania
18. Colorado
19. Virginia
20. Washington
21. Tennessee
22. Oregon
23. Mississippi
24. North Carolina
25. New Mexico
26. Arizona
27. Alabama
28. Missouri
29. Alaska
30. Arkansas
31. Michigan
32. Maine
33. Kansas
34. Ohio
35. New Hampshire
36. Indiana
37. Minnesota
38. Oklahoma
39. Kentucky
40. Utah
41. Wisconsin
42. Nebraska
43. West Virginia
44. Vermont
45. Iowa
46. Idaho
47. Montana
48. South Dakota
49. Wyoming
50. North Dakota

State	physicians per 100,000 pop	Rank
Alabama	168	39
Alaska	133	49
Arizona	196	25
Arkansas	161	42
California	241	10
Colorado	217	13
Connecticut	318	4
Delaware	207	20
Florida	212	16
Georgia	179	34
Hawaii	249	9
Idaho	129	50
Illinois	228	12
Indiana	165	41
Iowa	157	43
Kansas	183	33
Kentucky	178	37
Louisiana	201	23
Maine	189	29
Maryland	342	2
Massachusetts	353	1
Michigan	194	27
Minnesota	232	11
Mississippi	136	48
Missouri	207	20
Montana	166	40
Nebraska	187	30
Nevada	145	46
New Hampshire	209	18
New Jersey	260	7
New Mexico	191	28
New York	333	3
North Carolina	198	24
North Dakota	185	32
Ohio	206	22
Oklahoma	153	44
Oregon	210	17
Pennsylvania	251	8
Rhode Island	269	5
South Carolina	172	38
South Dakota	151	45
Tennessee	208	19
Texas	179	34
Utah	187	30
Vermont	263	6
Virginia	215	15
Washington	217	13
West Virginia	179	34
Wisconsin	195	26
Wyoming	140	47
50 States	205	
DC	677	
United States	224	

Rank in order

By per 100,000

1. Massachusetts
2. Maryland
3. New York
4. Connecticut
5. Rhode Island
6. Vermont
7. New Jersey
8. Pennsylvania
9. Hawaii
10. California
11. Minnesota
12. Illinois
13. Colorado
13. Washington
15. Virginia
16. Florida
17. Oregon
18. New Hampshire
19. Tennessee
20. Delaware
20. Missouri
22. Ohio
23. Louisiana
24. North Carolina
25. Arizona
26. Wisconsin
27. Michigan
28. New Mexico
29. Maine
30. Nebraska
30. Utah
32. North Dakota
33. Kansas
34. Georgia
34. Texas
34. West Virginia
37. Kentucky
38. South Carolina
39. Alabama
40. Montana
41. Indiana
42. Arkansas
43. Iowa
44. Oklahoma
45. South Dakota
46. Nevada
47. Wyoming
48. Mississippi
49. Alaska
50. Idaho

State	Hospital beds per 1,000 population	Rank	Rank in order By per 1,000
Alabama	4.5	13	1. North Dakota
Alaska	2.2	50	2. South Dakota
Arizona	2.5	47	3. Montana
Arkansas	4.6	8	4. Nebraska
California	2.6	44	5. Iowa
Colorado	2.9	39	6. Mississippi
Connecticut	2.8	40	7. Wyoming
Delaware	3.0	37	8. Arkansas
Florida	3.8	23	9. Missouri
Georgia	3.9	20	10. Tennessee
Hawaii	2.5	46	11. Kansas
Idaho	3.2	33	12. West Virginia
Illinois	3.9	21	13. Alabama
Indiana	3.7	24	14. Louisiana
Iowa	4.9	5	15. Pennsylvania
Kansas	4.6	11	16. Kentucky
Kentucky	4.3	16	17. Minnesota
Louisiana	4.4	14	18. New York
Maine	3.6	27	19. New Jersey
Maryland	2.7	42	20. Georgia
Massachusetts	3.6	28	21. Illinois
Michigan	3.3	29	22. Ohio
Minnesota	4.2	17	23. Florida
Mississippi	4.8	6	24. Indiana
Missouri	4.6	9	25. Oklahoma
Montana	5.3	3	26. Wisconsin
Nebraska	5.3	4	27. Maine
Nevada	2.7	41	28. Massachusetts
New Hampshire	3.1	36	29. Michigan
New Jersey	4.0	19	30. Texas
New Mexico	2.7	43	31. North Carolina
New York	4.2	18	32. South Carolina
North Carolina	3.3	31	33. Idaho
North Dakota	6.9	1	34. Rhode Island
Ohio	3.8	22	35. Virginia
Oklahoma	3.7	25	36. New Hampshire
Oregon	2.5	45	37. Delaware
Pennsylvania	4.3	15	38. Vermont
Rhode Island	3.1	34	39. Colorado
South Carolina	3.2	32	40. Connecticut
South Dakota	6.0	2	41. Nevada
Tennessee	4.6	10	42. Maryland
Texas	3.3	30	43. New Mexico
Utah	2.4	48	44. California
Vermont	3.0	38	45. Oregon
Virginia	3.1	35	46. Hawaii
Washington	2.3	49	47. Arizona
West Virginia	4.5	12	48. Utah
Wisconsin	3.7	26	49. Washington
Wyoming	4.7	7	50. Alaska
50 States	3.6		
DC	7.5	.	
United States	3.6		

State	Recipients #	As % of population %	Rank	Rank in order By %
Alabama	466,918	11.3	22	1. Rhode Island
Alaska	57,540	9.8	29	2. Mississippi
Arizona	402,212	10.5	26	3. West Virginia
Arkansas	320,875	13.4	11	4. Louisiana
California	4,485,743	14.5	7	5. Tennessee
Colorado	258,690	7.5	47	6. Kentucky
Connecticut	316,278	9.6	31	7. California
Delaware	60,696	8.8	40	8. New York
Florida	1,537,926	11.4	20	9. Vermont
Georgia	863,670	12.8	14	10. New Mexico
Hawaii	99,666	8.6	42	11. Arkansas
Idaho	86,924	8.1	43	12. Maine
Illinois	1,313,140	11.3	21	13. Ohio
Indiana	506,829	9.0	38	14. Georgia
Iowa	278,828	9.9	28	15. South Carolina
Kansas	226,991	9.0	36	16. Michigan
Kentucky	583,089	15.5	6	17. North Carolina
Louisiana	702,264	16.4	4	18. Texas
Maine	162,441	13.2	12	19. Massachusetts
Maryland	377,075	7.7	45	20. Florida
Massachusetts	686,235	11.4	19	21. Illinois
Michigan	1,129,023	12.0	16	22. Alabama
Minnesota	406,491	9.1	34	23. Oklahoma
Mississippi	486,861	18.6	2	24. Washington
Missouri	554,477	10.7	25	25. Missouri
Montana	60,186	7.3	48	26. Arizona
Nebraska	150,791	9.4	32	27. Oregon
Nevada	77,525	5.8	50	28. Iowa
New Hampshire	71,179	6.4	49	29. Alaska
New Jersey	697,083	8.9	39	30. Pennsylvania
New Mexico	211,805	13.4	10	31. Connecticut
New York	2,557,701	14.1	8	32. Nebraska
North Carolina	785,043	11.5	17	33. Wyoming
North Dakota	57,068	9.0	37	34. Minnesota
Ohio	1,442,289	13.1	13	35. South Dakota
Oklahoma	360,039	11.2	23	36. Kansas
Oregon	295,320	9.9	27	37. North Dakota
Pennsylvania	1,174,779	9.8	30	38. Indiana
Rhode Island	213,388	21.2	1	39. New Jersey
South Carolina	431,083	12.0	15	40. Delaware
South Dakota	64,230	9.0	35	41. Wisconsin
Tennessee	785,231	15.6	5	42. Hawaii
Texas	2,024,554	11.5	18	43. Idaho
Utah	137,264	7.6	46	44. Virginia
Vermont	77,502	13.6	9	45. Maryland
Virginia	515,064	8.1	44	46. Utah
Washington	568,673	11.1	24	47. Colorado
West Virginia	308,034	17.0	3	48. Montana
Wisconsin	440,136	8.8	41	49. New Hampshire
Wyoming	42,401	9.1	33	50. Nevada
50 States	29,919,250	11.8		
DC	108,514	18.5		
United States	30,027,764	11.8		

State	Recipients as % of poverty population %	Rank
Alabama	51	45
Alaska	83	19
Arizona	59	40
Arkansas	67	33
California	83	19
Colorado	64	36
Connecticut	95	8
Delaware	96	6
Florida	60	38
Georgia	69	30
Hawaii	101	4
Idaho	49	47
Illinois	72	29
Indiana	48	48
Iowa	96	6
Kansas	66	34
Kentucky	77	24
Louisiana	81	21
Maine	88	12
Maryland	84	18
Massachusetts	102	3
Michigan	85	15
Minnesota	75	25
Mississippi	74	26
Missouri	68	32
Montana	50	46
Nebraska	85	15
Nevada	42	50
New Hampshire	74	26
New Jersey	81	21
New Mexico	46	49
New York	90	11
North Carolina	69	30
North Dakota	57	43
Ohio	87	13
Oklahoma	56	44
Oregon	66	34
Pennsylvania	95	8
Rhode Island	165	1
South Carolina	64	36
South Dakota	60	38
Tennessee	94	10
Texas	58	41
Utah	58	41
Vermont	97	5
Virginia	73	28
Washington	107	2
West Virginia	87	13
Wisconsin	85	15
Wyoming	78	23
50 States	76	
DC	n/a	
United States	76	

Rank in order

By %

1. Rhode Island
2. Washington
3. Massachusetts
4. Hawaii
5. Vermont
6. Delaware
6. Iowa
8. Connecticut
8. Pennsylvania
10. Tennessee
11. New York
12. Maine
13. Ohio
13. West Virginia
15. Michigan
15. Nebraska
15. Wisconsin
18. Maryland
19. Alaska
19. California
21. Louisiana
21. New Jersey
23. Wyoming
24. Kentucky
25. Minnesota
26. Mississippi
26. New Hampshire
28. Virginia
29. Illinois
30. Georgia
30. North Carolina
32. Missouri
33. Arkansas
34. Kansas
34. Oregon
36. Colorado
36. South Carolina
38. Florida
38. South Dakota
40. Arizona
41. Texas
41. Utah
43. North Dakota
44. Oklahoma
45. Alabama
46. Montana
47. Idaho
48. Indiana
49. New Mexico
50. Nevada

I-14 State And Local Spending For Health And Hospitals, 1992

State	Per capita $	Per $1000 personal income $	Rank by per capita
Alabama	566	36.9	2
Alaska	375	18.3	14
Arizona	193	11.9	44
Arkansas	227	15.7	36
California	424	20.7	8
Colorado	244	13.0	33
Connecticut	346	13.3	20
Delaware	229	11.2	35
Florida	339	18.1	22
Georgia	530	31.0	4
Hawaii	350	16.9	19
Idaho	266	17.8	30
Illinois	227	11.0	37
Indiana	345	20.3	21
Iowa	387	22.5	10
Kansas	292	16.1	27
Kentucky	217	14.0	42
Louisiana	444	29.7	6
Maine	168	9.6	46
Maryland	183	8.3	45
Massachusetts	358	15.6	16
Michigan	381	20.6	12
Minnesota	417	22.1	9
Mississippi	432	32.7	7
Missouri	237	13.3	34
Montana	207	13.4	43
Nebraska	304	17.3	23
Nevada	302	15.8	25
New Hampshire	136	6.3	48
New Jersey	222	8.7	40
New Mexico	353	24.7	17
New York	550	24.6	3
North Carolina	377	22.7	13
North Dakota	134	8.6	49
Ohio	290	16.5	29
Oklahoma	351	22.9	18
Oregon	302	17.5	24
Pennsylvania	220	11.4	41
Rhode Island	252	13.1	31
South Carolina	504	33.0	5
South Dakota	164	10.3	47
Tennessee	367	22.6	15
Texas	294	17.3	26
Utah	222	15.6	39
Vermont	118	6.6	50
Virginia	291	14.7	28
Washington	384	20.2	11
West Virginia	224	15.7	38
Wisconsin	250	14.1	32
Wyoming	585	35.1	1
50 States	n/a	n/a	
DC	913	32.8	
United States	345	18.3	

Rank in order

By per capita

1. Wyoming
2. Alabama
3. New York
4. Georgia
5. South Carolina
6. Louisiana
7. Mississippi
8. California
9. Minnesota
10. Iowa
11. Washington
12. Michigan
13. North Carolina
14. Alaska
15. Tennessee
16. Massachusetts
17. New Mexico
18. Oklahoma
19. Hawaii
20. Connecticut
21. Indiana
22. Florida
23. Nebraska
24. Oregon
25. Nevada
26. Texas
27. Kansas
28. Virginia
29. Ohio
30. Idaho
31. Rhode Island
32. Wisconsin
33. Colorado
34. Missouri
35. Delaware
36. Arkansas
37. Illinois
38. West Virginia
39. Utah
40. New Jersey
41. Pennsylvania
42. Kentucky
43. Montana
44. Arizona
45. Maryland
46. Maine
47. South Dakota
48. New Hampshire
49. North Dakota
50. Vermont

State	Health & Hospital spending as % of total spending %	Rank	Rank in order By %
Alabama	18.2	1	1. Alabama
Alaska	3.8	47	2. Georgia
Arizona	5.5	41	3. South Carolina
Arkansas	8.3	26	4. Mississippi
California	10.1	13	5. Tennessee
Colorado	6.6	35	6. North Carolina
Connecticut	7.5	30	7. Louisiana
Delaware	5.4	42	8. Oklahoma
Florida	9.7	15	9. Wyoming
Georgia	16.0	2	10. Indiana
Hawaii	6.7	34	11. Iowa
Idaho	8.7	22	12. Michigan
Illinois	6.5	36	13. California
Indiana	10.8	10	14. New York
Iowa	10.8	11	15. Florida
Kansas	8.6	24	16. New Mexico
Kentucky	6.8	33	17. Texas
Louisiana	12.1	7	18. Minnesota
Maine	4.5	46	19. Washington
Maryland	5.0	44	20. Nebraska
Massachusetts	8.7	23	21. Virginia
Michigan	10.1	12	22. Idaho
Minnesota	9.3	18	23. Massachusetts
Mississippi	15.1	4	24. Kansas
Missouri	8.2	27	25. Ohio
Montana	5.8	38	26. Arkansas
Nebraska	8.8	20	27. Missouri
Nevada	7.5	29	28. Oregon
New Hampshire	3.7	48	29. Nevada
New Jersey	4.7	45	30. Connecticut
New Mexico	9.3	16	31. West Virginia
New York	9.7	14	32. Utah
North Carolina	12.1	6	33. Kentucky
North Dakota	3.4	49	34. Hawaii
Ohio	8.5	25	35. Colorado
Oklahoma	11.2	8	36. Illinois
Oregon	7.6	28	37. Wisconsin
Pennsylvania	5.8	39	38. Montana
Rhode Island	5.8	40	39. Pennsylvania
South Carolina	15.6	3	40. Rhode Island
South Dakota	5.1	43	41. Arizona
Tennessee	12.2	5	42. Delaware
Texas	9.3	17	43. South Dakota
Utah	6.9	32	44. Maryland
Vermont	2.9	50	45. New Jersey
Virginia	8.8	21	46. Maine
Washington	9.1	19	47. Alaska
West Virginia	7.0	31	48. New Hampshire
Wisconsin	6.3	37	49. North Dakota
Wyoming	11.1	9	50. Vermont
50 States	n/a		
DC	12.1		
United States	9.1		

State	Per capita medicaid spending $	Rank
Alabama	255	40
Alaska	319	23
Arizona	55	50
Arkansas	369	14
California	282	34
Colorado	235	46
Connecticut	507	6
Delaware	318	25
Florida	261	37
Georgia	318	24
Hawaii	233	47
Idaho	258	39
Illinois	350	16
Indiana	393	10
Iowa	304	29
Kansas	246	43
Kentucky	411	8
Louisiana	578	3
Maine	520	5
Maryland	328	20
Massachusetts	542	4
Michigan	297	31
Minnesota	391	12
Mississippi	337	18
Missouri	260	38
Montana	263	35
Nebraska	291	33
Nevada	213	48
New Hampshire	306	27
New Jersey	360	15
New Mexico	302	30
New York	843	1
North Carolina	304	28
North Dakota	398	9
Ohio	391	11
Oklahoma	313	26
Oregon	251	41
Pennsylvania	295	32
Rhode Island	770	2
South Carolina	319	22
South Dakota	325	21
Tennessee	345	17
Texas	250	42
Utah	201	49
Vermont	389	13
Virginia	237	45
Washington	262	36
West Virginia	439	7
Wisconsin	335	19
Wyoming	245	44
50 States	n/a	
DC	852	
United States	355	

Rank in order

By per capita

1. New York
2. Rhode Island
3. Louisiana
4. Massachusetts
5. Maine
6. Connecticut
7. West Virginia
8. Kentucky
9. North Dakota
10. Indiana
11. Ohio
12. Minnesota
13. Vermont
14. Arkansas
15. New Jersey
16. Illinois
17. Tennessee
18. Mississippi
19. Wisconsin
20. Maryland
21. South Dakota
22. South Carolina
23. Alaska
24. Georgia
25. Delaware
26. Oklahoma
27. New Hampshire
28. North Carolina
29. Iowa
30. New Mexico
31. Michigan
32. Pennsylvania
33. Nebraska
34. California
35. Montana
36. Washington
37. Florida
38. Missouri
39. Idaho
40. Alabama
41. Oregon
42. Texas
43. Kansas
44. Wyoming
45. Virginia
46. Colorado
47. Hawaii
48. Nevada
49. Utah
50. Arizona

State	Average spending $	Rank	By $
Alabama	5,042	45	1. New York
Alaska	10,934	8	2. Connecticut
Arizona	579	50	3. Minnesota
Arkansas	5,163	43	4. New Hampshire
California	4,579	47	5. Massachusetts
Colorado	7,618	25	6. New Jersey
Connecticut	14,458	2	7. Delaware
Delaware	11,515	7	8. Alaska
Florida	5,770	38	9. Wyoming
Georgia	5,405	40	10. Maine
Hawaii	8,115	23	11. Indiana
Idaho	8,154	22	12. Ohio
Illinois	8,233	21	13. Pennsylvania
Indiana	10,627	11	14. Wisconsin
Iowa	6,206	34	15. Montana
Kansas	7,410	26	16. North Dakota
Kentucky	5,908	37	17. Maryland
Louisiana	5,514	39	18. South Dakota
Maine	10,751	10	19. Nebraska
Maryland	8,942	17	20. Washington
Massachusetts	11,925	5	21. Illinois
Michigan	7,674	24	22. Idaho
Minnesota	12,339	3	23. Hawaii
Mississippi	4,005	49	24. Michigan
Missouri	5,975	36	25. Colorado
Montana	9,500	15	26. Kansas
Nebraska	8,421	19	27. Utah
Nevada	7,035	29	28. Rhode Island
New Hampshire	12,040	4	29. Nevada
New Jersey	11,592	6	30. Vermont
New Mexico	6,622	32	31. Oregon
New York	18,288	1	32. New Mexico
North Carolina	5,368	41	33. West Virginia
North Dakota	9,275	16	34. Iowa
Ohio	10,090	12	35. Virginia
Oklahoma	5,156	44	36. Missouri
Oregon	6,906	31	37. Kentucky
Pennsylvania	10,038	13	38. Florida
Rhode Island	7,128	28	39. Louisiana
South Carolina	4,549	48	40. Georgia
South Dakota	8,755	18	41. North Carolina
Tennessee	4,723	46	42. Texas
Texas	5,284	42	43. Arkansas
Utah	7,318	27	44. Oklahoma
Vermont	7,013	30	45. Alabama
Virginia	6,204	35	46. Tennessee
Washington	8,301	20	47. California
West Virginia	6,312	33	48. South Carolina
Wisconsin	9,922	14	49. Mississippi
Wyoming	10,894	9	50. Arizona
50 States	n/a		
DC	12,171		
United States	8,039		

State	Average spending $	Rank
Alabama	746	47
Alaska	1,640	1
Arizona	406	50
Arkansas	896	38
California	652	49
Colorado	1,033	20
Connecticut	1,111	13
Delaware	1,014	22
Florida	932	30
Georgia	865	40
Hawaii	929	31
Idaho	955	28
Illinois	972	26
Indiana	1,585	2
Iowa	1,015	21
Kansas	928	32
Kentucky	1,085	19
Louisiana	1,541	4
Maine	1,094	17
Maryland	1,512	6
Massachusetts	1,259	8
Michigan	811	44
Minnesota	1,007	23
Mississippi	899	37
Missouri	906	35
Montana	832	42
Nebraska	926	33
Nevada	1,343	7
New Hampshire	986	24
New Jersey	950	29
New Mexico	1,153	10
New York	1,547	3
North Carolina	1,121	11
North Dakota	1,238	9
Ohio	1,098	15
Oklahoma	1,521	5
Oregon	905	36
Pennsylvania	912	34
Rhode Island	825	43
South Carolina	1,097	16
South Dakota	1,109	14
Tennessee	964	27
Texas	887	39
Utah	985	25
Vermont	653	48
Virginia	1,116	12
Washington	791	45
West Virginia	844	41
Wisconsin	768	46
Wyoming	1,093	18
50 States	n/a	
DC	1,658	
United States	998	

By $

1. Alaska
2. Indiana
3. New York
4. Louisiana
5. Oklahoma
6. Maryland
7. Nevada
8. Massachusetts
9. North Dakota
10. New Mexico
11. North Carolina
12. Virginia
13. Connecticut
14. South Dakota
15. Ohio
16. South Carolina
17. Maine
18. Wyoming
19. Kentucky
20. Colorado
21. Iowa
22. Delaware
23. Minnesota
24. New Hampshire
25. Utah
26. Illinois
27. Tennessee
28. Idaho
29. New Jersey
30. Florida
31. Hawaii
32. Kansas
33. Nebraska
34. Pennsylvania
35. Missouri
36. Oregon
37. Mississippi
38. Arkansas
39. Texas
40. Georgia
41. West Virginia
42. Montana
43. Rhode Island
44. Michigan
45. Washington
46. Wisconsin
47. Alabama
48. Vermont
49. California
50. Arizona

State	Average cost of a hospital-day $	Rank
Alabama	1,877	13
Alaska	2,036	7
Arizona	2,366	3
Arkansas	1,382	45
California	2,966	2
Colorado	2,228	5
Connecticut	1,801	16
Delaware	1,768	21
Florida	2,133	6
Georgia	1,698	27
Hawaii	2,245	4
Idaho	1,792	19
Illinois	1,951	10
Indiana	1,581	33
Iowa	1,452	41
Kansas	1,766	23
Kentucky	1,469	38
Louisiana	1,803	15
Maine	1,462	39
Maryland	1,260	49
Massachusetts	1,508	37
Michigan	1,757	25
Minnesota	1,793	18
Mississippi	1,313	48
Missouri	1,767	22
Montana	1,617	30
Nebraska	1,721	26
Nevada	2,975	1
New Hampshire	1,535	36
New Jersey	1,641	29
New Mexico	1,786	20
New York	1,251	50
North Carolina	1,605	32
North Dakota	1,366	47
Ohio	1,801	17
Oklahoma	1,457	40
Oregon	1,908	12
Pennsylvania	1,927	11
Rhode Island	1,413	43
South Carolina	1,673	28
South Dakota	1,405	44
Tennessee	1,549	34
Texas	1,958	9
Utah	1,999	8
Vermont	1,448	42
Virginia	1,611	31
Washington	1,817	14
West Virginia	1,381	46
Wisconsin	1,536	35
Wyoming	1,763	24
50 States	n/a	
DC	1,949	
United States	1,756	

1. Nevada
2. California
3. Arizona
4. Hawaii
5. Colorado
6. Florida
7. Alaska
8. Utah
9. Texas
10. Illinois
11. Pennsylvania
12. Oregon
13. Alabama
14. Washington
15. Louisiana
16. Connecticut
17. Ohio
18. Minnesota
19. Idaho
20. New Mexico
21. Delaware
22. Missouri
23. Kansas
24. Wyoming
25. Michigan
26. Nebraska
27. Georgia
28. South Carolina
29. New Jersey
30. Montana
31. Virginia
32. North Carolina
33. Indiana
34. Tennessee
35. Wisconsin
36. New Hampshire
37. Massachusetts
38. Kentucky
39. Maine
40. Oklahoma
41. Iowa
42. Vermont
43. Rhode Island
44. South Dakota
45. Arkansas
46. West Virginia
47. North Dakota
48. Mississippi
49. Maryland
50. New York

State	Allowed costs per hospital-day $	Rank
Alabama	1,438	17
Alaska	1,277	24
Arizona	1,637	8
Arkansas	1,293	22
California	1,920	2
Colorado	1,212	31
Connecticut	1,549	12
Delaware	1,529	13
Florida	2,127	1
Georgia	1,452	16
Hawaii	1,260	28
Idaho	1,003	47
Illinois	1,482	15
Indiana	1,181	33
Iowa	1,029	44
Kansas	1,301	21
Kentucky	1,302	20
Louisiana	1,592	9
Maine	1,124	38
Maryland	1,727	6
Massachusetts	1,568	11
Michigan	1,592	10
Minnesota	923	50
Mississippi	1,267	26
Missouri	1,251	29
Montana	1,057	42
Nebraska	1,048	43
Nevada	1,891	3
New Hampshire	1,141	36
New Jersey	1,775	5
New Mexico	1,141	37
New York	1,790	4
North Carolina	1,121	39
North Dakota	1,015	45
Ohio	1,365	19
Oklahoma	1,272	25
Oregon	1,092	40
Pennsylvania	1,673	7
Rhode Island	1,423	18
South Carolina	1,151	35
South Dakota	999	49
Tennessee	1,281	23
Texas	1,512	14
Utah	1,007	46
Vermont	1,002	48
Virginia	1,264	27
Washington	1,238	30
West Virginia	1,204	32
Wisconsin	1,088	41
Wyoming	1,170	34
50 States	n/a	
DC	1,950	
United States	1,508	

Rank in order

By $

1. Florida
2. California
3. Nevada
4. New York
5. New Jersey
6. Maryland
7. Pennsylvania
8. Arizona
9. Louisiana
10. Michigan
11. Massachusetts
12. Connecticut
13. Delaware
14. Texas
15. Illinois
16. Georgia
17. Alabama
18. Rhode Island
19. Ohio
20. Kentucky
21. Kansas
22. Arkansas
23. Tennessee
24. Alaska
25. Oklahoma
26. Mississippi
27. Virginia
28. Hawaii
29. Missouri
30. Washington
31. Colorado
32. West Virginia
33. Indiana
34. Wyoming
35. South Carolina
36. New Hampshire
37. New Mexico
38. Maine
39. North Carolina
40. Oregon
41. Wisconsin
42. Montana
43. Nebraska
44. Iowa
45. North Dakota
46. Utah
47. Idaho
48. Vermont
49. South Dakota
50. Minnesota

State	% of population in HMOs %	Rank	By %
Alabama	10.0	30	1. California
Alaska	0.0	48	2. Oregon
Arizona	35.8	4	3. Maryland
Arkansas	3.8	42	4. Arizona
California	38.3	1	5. Massachusetts
Colorado	24.4	9	6. Rhode Island
Connecticut	27.4	7	7. Connecticut
Delaware	20.5	14	8. Minnesota
Florida	20.1	16	9. Colorado
Georgia	8.8	33	10. New York
Hawaii	23.2	12	11. Wisconsin
Idaho	1.2	45	12. Hawaii
Illinois	16.9	21	13. Pennsylvania
Indiana	7.4	36	14. Delaware
Iowa	4.1	41	15. Michigan
Kansas	10.9	29	16. Florida
Kentucky	12.1	28	17. Ohio
Louisiana	7.0	38	18. Utah
Maine	6.2	39	19. New Mexico
Maryland	36.2	3	20. New Hampshire
Massachusetts	35.2	5	21. Illinois
Michigan	20.2	15	22. New Jersey
Minnesota	26.6	8	23. Washington
Mississippi	0.3	47	24. Tennessee
Missouri	14.7	25	25. Missouri
Montana	1.5	44	26. Nevada
Nebraska	9.5	32	27. Vermont
Nevada	14.7	26	28. Kentucky
New Hampshire	17.0	20	29. Kansas
New Jersey	16.9	22	30. Alabama
New Mexico	17.4	19	31. Texas
New York	24.3	10	32. Nebraska
North Carolina	8.3	35	33. Georgia
North Dakota	1.1	46	34. Virginia
Ohio	19.2	17	35. North Carolina
Oklahoma	7.3	37	36. Indiana
Oregon	37.5	2	37. Oklahoma
Pennsylvania	21.5	13	38. Louisiana
Rhode Island	28.8	6	39. Maine
South Carolina	4.2	40	40. South Carolina
South Dakota	2.9	43	41. Iowa
Tennessee	16.2	24	42. Arkansas
Texas	9.7	31	43. South Dakota
Utah	19.2	18	44. Montana
Vermont	12.6	27	45. Idaho
Virginia	8.4	34	46. North Dakota
Washington	16.4	23	47. Mississippi
West Virginia	0.0	48	48. Alaska
Wisconsin	24.2	11	48. West Virginia
Wyoming	0.0	48	48. Wyoming
50 States	n/a		
DC	25.6		
United States	19.5		

Crime and Law Enforcement

J-1 Total Crime Rate, 1993

State	Crime rate (per 100,000)	Rank	By rate
Alabama	4,879	26	1. Florida
Alaska	5,568	16	2. Arizona
Arizona	7,432	2	3. Louisiana
Arkansas	4,811	28	4. California
California	6,457	4	5. Texas
Colorado	5,527	18	6. Hawaii
Connecticut	4,650	31	7. New Mexico
Delaware	4,872	27	8. Georgia
Florida	8,351	1	9. Nevada
Georgia	6,193	8	10. Maryland
Hawaii	6,277	6	11. Washington
Idaho	3,845	43	12. South Carolina
Illinois	5,618	15	13. Oregon
Indiana	4,465	34	14. North Carolina
Iowa	3,846	42	15. Illinois
Kansas	4,975	24	16. Alaska
Kentucky	3,260	45	17. New York
Louisiana	6,847	3	18. Colorado
Maine	3,154	46	19. Michigan
Maryland	6,107	10	20. Oklahoma
Massachusetts	4,894	25	21. Tennessee
Michigan	5,453	19	22. Utah
Minnesota	4,386	36	23. Missouri
Mississippi	4,418	35	24. Kansas
Missouri	5,095	23	25. Massachusetts
Montana	4,790	30	26. Alabama
Nebraska	4,117	38	27. Delaware
Nevada	6,180	9	28. Arkansas
New Hampshire	2,905	48	29. New Jersey
New Jersey	4,801	29	30. Montana
New Mexico	6,266	7	31. Connecticut
New York	5,551	17	32. Rhode Island
North Carolina	5,652	14	33. Ohio
North Dakota	2,820	49	34. Indiana
Ohio	4,485	33	35. Mississippi
Oklahoma	5,294	20	36. Minnesota
Oregon	5,766	13	37. Wyoming
Pennsylvania	3,271	44	38. Nebraska
Rhode Island	4,499	32	39. Virginia
South Carolina	5,903	12	40. Wisconsin
South Dakota	2,958	47	41. Vermont
Tennessee	5,240	21	42. Iowa
Texas	6,439	5	43. Idaho
Utah	5,237	22	44. Pennsylvania
Vermont	3,972	41	45. Kentucky
Virginia	4,116	39	46. Maine
Washington	5,952	11	47. South Dakota
West Virginia	2,533	50	48. New Hampshire
Wisconsin	4,054	40	49. North Dakota
Wyoming	4,163	37	50. West Virginia
50 States	n/a		
DC	11,761		
United States	5,483		

State	Violent crime rate (per 100,000)	Rank
Alabama	780	12
Alaska	761	15
Arizona	715	18
Arkansas	593	23
California	1,078	2
Colorado	567	24
Connecticut	456	31
Delaware	686	19
Florida	1,206	1
Georgia	723	17
Hawaii	261	43
Idaho	282	41
Illinois	960	7
Indiana	489	29
Iowa	326	38
Kansas	496	28
Kentucky	463	30
Louisiana	1,062	4
Maine	126	48
Maryland	998	6
Massachusetts	805	10
Michigan	792	11
Minnesota	327	37
Mississippi	434	32
Missouri	744	16
Montana	178	46
Nebraska	339	36
Nevada	875	9
New Hampshire	138	47
New Jersey	627	22
New Mexico	930	8
New York	1,074	3
North Carolina	679	20
North Dakota	82	50
Ohio	504	26
Oklahoma	635	21
Oregon	503	27
Pennsylvania	418	33
Rhode Island	402	34
South Carolina	1,023	5
South Dakota	208	44
Tennessee	766	13
Texas	762	14
Utah	301	39
Vermont	114	49
Virginia	372	35
Washington	515	25
West Virginia	208	45
Wisconsin	264	42
Wyoming	286	40
50 States	n/a	
DC	2,922	
United States	746	

Rank in order

By rate

1. Florida
2. California
3. New York
4. Louisiana
5. South Carolina
6. Maryland
7. Illinois
8. New Mexico
9. Nevada
10. Massachusetts
11. Michigan
12. Alabama
13. Tennessee
14. Texas
15. Alaska
16. Missouri
17. Georgia
18. Arizona
19. Delaware
20. North Carolina
21. Oklahoma
22. New Jersey
23. Arkansas
24. Colorado
25. Washington
26. Ohio
27. Oregon
28. Kansas
29. Indiana
30. Kentucky
31. Connecticut
32. Mississippi
33. Pennsylvania
34. Rhode Island
35. Virginia
36. Nebraska
37. Minnesota
38. Iowa
39. Utah
40. Wyoming
41. Idaho
42. Wisconsin
43. Hawaii
44. South Dakota
45. West Virginia
46. Montana
47. New Hampshire
48. Maine
49. Vermont
50. North Dakota

State	Murder rate (per 100,000)	Rape rate (per 100,000)	Rank by murder rate
Alabama	12	35	7
Alaska	9	84	17
Arizona	9	38	19
Arkansas	10	42	14
California	13	38	4
Colorado	6	46	30
Connecticut	6	24	28
Delaware	5	77	33
Florida	9	54	18
Georgia	11	35	8
Hawaii	4	34	39
Idaho	3	35	46
Illinois	11	35	9
Indiana	8	39	23
Iowa	2	24	47
Kansas	6	40	27
Kentucky	7	34	26
Louisiana	20	42	1
Maine	2	27	50
Maryland	13	44	5
Massachusetts	4	33	36
Michigan	10	71	16
Minnesota	3	35	41
Mississippi	14	43	2
Missouri	11	36	10
Montana	3	28	45
Nebraska	4	28	37
Nevada	10	61	12
New Hampshire	2	44	48
New Jersey	5	28	31
New Mexico	8	52	22
New York	13	28	3
North Carolina	11	34	11
North Dakota	2	24	49
Ohio	6	49	29
Oklahoma	8	49	20
Oregon	5	51	34
Pennsylvania	7	27	25
Rhode Island	4	29	38
South Carolina	10	52	13
South Dakota	3	45	42
Tennessee	10	50	15
Texas	12	55	6
Utah	3	45	44
Vermont	4	40	40
Virginia	8	32	21
Washington	5	64	32
West Virginia	7	20	24
Wisconsin	4	25	35
Wyoming	3	34	43
50 States	n/a	n/a	
DC	79	56	
United States	10	41	

Rank in order

By murder rate

1. Louisiana
2. Mississippi
3. New York
4. California
5. Maryland
6. Texas
7. Alabama
8. Georgia
9. Illinois
10. Missouri
11. North Carolina
12. Nevada
13. South Carolina
14. Arkansas
15. Tennessee
16. Michigan
17. Alaska
18. Florida
19. Arizona
20. Oklahoma
21. Virginia
22. New Mexico
23. Indiana
24. West Virginia
25. Pennsylvania
26. Kentucky
27. Kansas
28. Connecticut
29. Ohio
30. Colorado
31. New Jersey
32. Washington
33. Delaware
34. Oregon
35. Wisconsin
36. Massachusetts
37. Nebraska
38. Rhode Island
39. Hawaii
40. Vermont
41. Minnesota
42. South Dakota
43. Wyoming
44. Utah
45. Montana
46. Idaho
47. Iowa
48. New Hampshire
49. North Dakota
50. Maine

J-4 Property Crime Rate, 1993			Rank in order

State	Property crime rate (per 100,000)	Rank	By rate
Alabama	4,098	30	1. Florida
Alaska	4,807	17	2. Arizona
Arizona	6,717	2	3. Hawaii
Arkansas	4,218	26	4. Louisiana
California	5,379	8	5. Texas
Colorado	4,960	14	6. Georgia
Connecticut	4,194	27	7. Washington
Delaware	4,186	28	8. California
Florida	7,145	1	9. New Mexico
Georgia	5,470	6	10. Nevada
Hawaii	6,016	3	11. Oregon
Idaho	3,563	42	12. Maryland
Illinois	4,658	20	13. North Carolina
Indiana	3,976	36	14. Colorado
Iowa	3,521	43	15. Utah
Kansas	4,479	22	16. South Carolina
Kentucky	2,797	46	17. Alaska
Louisiana	5,785	4	18. Michigan
Maine	3,028	44	19. Oklahoma
Maryland	5,109	12	20. Illinois
Massachusetts	4,089	32	21. Montana
Michigan	4,661	18	22. Kansas
Minnesota	4,059	33	23. New York
Mississippi	3,984	34	24. Tennessee
Missouri	4,351	25	25. Missouri
Montana	4,613	21	26. Arkansas
Nebraska	3,778	40	27. Connecticut
Nevada	5,305	10	28. Delaware
New Hampshire	2,767	47	29. New Jersey
New Jersey	4,174	29	30. Alabama
New Mexico	5,336	9	31. Rhode Island
New York	4,478	23	32. Massachusetts
North Carolina	4,973	13	33. Minnesota
North Dakota	2,738	49	34. Mississippi
Ohio	3,981	35	35. Ohio
Oklahoma	4,659	19	36. Indiana
Oregon	5,263	11	37. Wyoming
Pennsylvania	2,854	45	38. Vermont
Rhode Island	4,097	31	39. Wisconsin
South Carolina	4,880	16	40. Nebraska
South Dakota	2,750	48	41. Virginia
Tennessee	4,474	24	42. Idaho
Texas	5,677	5	43. Iowa
Utah	4,936	15	44. Maine
Vermont	3,858	38	45. Pennsylvania
Virginia	3,743	41	46. Kentucky
Washington	5,438	7	47. New Hampshire
West Virginia	2,324	50	48. South Dakota
Wisconsin	3,790	39	49. North Dakota
Wyoming	3,877	37	50. West Virginia
50 States	n/a		
DC	8,839		
United States	4,737		

J-5 Motor Vehicle Theft Rate, 1993

State	Motor vehicle theft rate (per 100,000)	Rank	Rank in order By rate
Alabama	338	31	1. California
Alaska	451	21	2. Florida
Arizona	864	3	3. Arizona
Arkansas	323	34	4. New York
California	1,023	1	5. Massachusetts
Colorado	450	23	6. Nevada
Connecticut	596	13	7. New Jersey
Delaware	315	35	8. Texas
Florida	896	2	9. Maryland
Georgia	594	14	10. Rhode Island
Hawaii	451	22	11. Michigan
Idaho	183	44	12. Louisiana
Illinois	559	17	13. Connecticut
Indiana	428	26	14. Georgia
Iowa	191	43	15. Tennessee
Kansas	323	33	16. Oregon
Kentucky	216	40	17. Illinois
Louisiana	614	12	18. Missouri
Maine	134	48	19. Oklahoma
Maryland	683	9	20. Washington
Massachusetts	816	5	21. Alaska
Michigan	615	11	22. Hawaii
Minnesota	343	30	23. Colorado
Mississippi	335	32	24. Pennsylvania
Missouri	548	18	25. Ohio
Montana	246	38	26. Indiana
Nebraska	202	41	27. New Mexico
Nevada	738	6	28. Wisconsin
New Hampshire	194	42	29. South Carolina
New Jersey	714	7	30. Minnesota
New Mexico	405	27	31. Alabama
New York	835	4	32. Mississippi
North Carolina	289	36	33. Kansas
North Dakota	149	47	34. Arkansas
Ohio	435	25	35. Delaware
Oklahoma	481	19	36. North Carolina
Oregon	581	16	37. Virginia
Pennsylvania	440	24	38. Montana
Rhode Island	646	10	39. Utah
South Carolina	344	29	40. Kentucky
South Dakota	115	50	41. Nebraska
Tennessee	591	15	42. New Hampshire
Texas	692	8	43. Iowa
Utah	242	39	44. Idaho
Vermont	133	49	45. West Virginia
Virginia	286	37	46. Wyoming
Washington	456	20	47. North Dakota
West Virginia	162	45	48. Maine
Wisconsin	365	28	49. Vermont
Wyoming	155	46	50. South Dakota
50 States	n/a		
DC	1,395		
United States	605		

State	1989 Violent crime rate (per 100,000)	% change in violent crime 89-93 %	Rank by %
Alabama	559	39.6	12
Alaska	523	45.5	6
Arizona	610	17.2	30
Arkansas	423	40.3	10
California	930	15.9	32
Colorado	473	19.9	27
Connecticut	455	0.3	44
Delaware	452	51.7	3
Florida	1,118	7.9	39
Georgia	665	8.7	38
Hawaii	257	1.6	42
Idaho	235	19.9	28
Illinois	810	18.5	29
Indiana	380	28.7	20
Iowa	257	26.7	21
Kansas	365	36.0	15
Kentucky	330	40.2	11
Louisiana	717	48.1	4
Maine	157	-19.9	50
Maryland	807	23.6	25
Massachusetts	620	29.8	19
Michigan	742	6.7	41
Minnesota	290	12.8	34
Mississippi	325	33.5	18
Missouri	553	34.6	17
Montana	123	44.3	7
Nebraska	273	24.2	23
Nevada	781	12.1	35
New Hampshire	148	-6.9	46
New Jersey	583	7.5	40
New Mexico	658	41.3	9
New York	1,097	-2.1	45
North Carolina	502	35.3	16
North Dakota	59	39.3	13
Ohio	452	11.5	36
Oklahoma	435	45.9	5
Oregon	546	-7.9	47
Pennsylvania	362	15.3	33
Rhode Island	397	1.2	43
South Carolina	741	38.1	14
South Dakota	114	82.8	1
Tennessee	533	43.7	8
Texas	653	16.7	31
Utah	243	23.9	24
Vermont	142	-19.6	49
Virginia	299	24.5	22
Washington	466	10.4	37
West Virginia	131	59.1	2
Wisconsin	214	23.6	26
Wyoming	314	-8.9	48
50 States	n/a	n/a	
DC	n/a	n/a	
United States	610	22.3	

J-6 Violent Crime Rate Change, 1989-1993

Rank in order

By %

1. South Dakota
2. West Virginia
3. Delaware
4. Louisiana
5. Oklahoma
6. Alaska
7. Montana
8. Tennessee
9. New Mexico
10. Arkansas
11. Kentucky
12. Alabama
13. North Dakota
14. South Carolina
15. Kansas
16. North Carolina
17. Missouri
18. Mississippi
19. Massachusetts
20. Indiana
21. Iowa
22. Virginia
23. Nebraska
24. Utah
25. Maryland
26. Wisconsin
27. Colorado
28. Idaho
29. Illinois
30. Arizona
31. Texas
32. California
33. Pennsylvania
34. Minnesota
35. Nevada
36. Ohio
37. Washington
38. Georgia
39. Florida
40. New Jersey
41. Michigan
42. Hawaii
43. Rhode Island
44. Connecticut
45. New York
46. New Hampshire
47. Oregon
48. Wyoming
49. Vermont
50. Maine

State	Incarceration rate (per 100,000 residents)	Rank
Alabama	450	8
Alaska	317	22
Arizona	459	6
Arkansas	353	18
California	384	15
Colorado	289	25
Connecticut	321	21
Delaware	393	14
Florida	406	11
Georgia	456	7
Hawaii	202	35
Idaho	258	28
Illinois	310	23
Indiana	258	29
Iowa	192	38
Kansas	249	31
Kentucky	288	26
Louisiana	530	2
Maine	118	47
Maryland	395	12
Massachusetts	171	43
Michigan	428	9
Minnesota	100	49
Mississippi	408	10
Missouri	338	19
Montana	194	37
Nebraska	159	45
Nevada	460	5
New Hampshire	177	41
New Jersey	310	24
New Mexico	220	34
New York	367	17
North Carolina	322	20
North Dakota	78	50
Ohio	377	16
Oklahoma	508	3
Oregon	175	42
Pennsylvania	235	33
Rhode Island	186	40
South Carolina	494	4
South Dakota	240	32
Tennessee	277	27
Texas	636	1
Utah	155	46
Vermont	168	44
Virginia	395	13
Washington	201	36
West Virginia	106	48
Wisconsin	187	39
Wyoming	254	30
50 States	n/a	
DC	1,583	
United States	387	

Rank in order

By rate

1. Texas
2. Louisiana
3. Oklahoma
4. South Carolina
5. Nevada
6. Arizona
7. Georgia
8. Alabama
9. Michigan
10. Mississippi
11. Florida
12. Maryland
13. Virginia
14. Delaware
15. California
16. Ohio
17. New York
18. Arkansas
19. Missouri
20. North Carolina
21. Connecticut
22. Alaska
23. Illinois
24. New Jersey
25. Colorado
26. Kentucky
27. Tennessee
28. Idaho
29. Indiana
30. Wyoming
31. Kansas
32. South Dakota
33. Pennsylvania
34. New Mexico
35. Hawaii
36. Washington
37. Montana
38. Iowa
39. Wisconsin
40. Rhode Island
41. New Hampshire
42. Oregon
43. Massachusetts
44. Vermont
45. Nebraska
46. Utah
47. Maine
48. West Virginia
49. Minnesota
50. North Dakota

J-8 Change In Incarceration Rate, 1989-1994			Rank in order

State	% change in incarceration rate %	Rank	By %
Alabama	40.5	17	1. New Hampshire
Alaska	1.4	47	2. Connecticut
Arizona	49.3	10	3. Georgia
Arkansas	33.1	27	4. Texas
California	43.6	13	5. Virginia
Colorado	55.1	8	6. Vermont
Connecticut	66.4	2	7. Washington
Delaware	22.1	40	8. Colorado
Florida	42.9	15	9. Iowa
Georgia	65.8	3	10. Arizona
Hawaii	36.1	24	11. Illinois
Idaho	n/a	n/a	12. Minnesota
Illinois	47.8	11	13. California
Indiana	22.1	40	14. Oklahoma
Iowa	51.7	9	15. Florida
Kansas	13.5	45	16. Mississippi
Kentucky	33.5	26	17. Alabama
Louisiana	33.0	28	17. Wisconsin
Maine	2.2	46	19. Pennsylvania
Maryland	29.1	30	20. North Carolina
Massachusetts	n/a	n/a	21. South Dakota
Michigan	28.9	31	22. Ohio
Minnesota	47.3	12	23. Tennessee
Mississippi	42.2	16	24. Hawaii
Missouri	28.6	32	25. Nevada
Montana	26.5	34	26. Kentucky
Nebraska	13.7	44	27. Arkansas
Nevada	34.5	25	28. Louisiana
New Hampshire	73.3	1	29. New York
New Jersey	26.3	35	30. Maryland
New Mexico	17.9	43	31. Michigan
New York	30.3	29	32. Missouri
North Carolina	38.2	20	33. Utah
North Dakota	24.0	38	34. Montana
Ohio	37.2	22	35. New Jersey
Oklahoma	43.3	14	36. Rhode Island
Oregon	n/a	n/a	37. West Virginia
Pennsylvania	38.3	19	38. North Dakota
Rhode Island	26.1	36	39. South Carolina
South Carolina	22.7	39	40. Delaware
South Dakota	38.1	21	40. Indiana
Tennessee	36.2	23	42. Wyoming
Texas	60.5	4	43. New Mexico
Utah	26.6	33	44. Nebraska
Vermont	56.7	6	45. Kansas
Virginia	59.9	5	46. Maine
Washington	56.4	7	47. Alaska
West Virginia	25.7	37	
Wisconsin	40.5	17	
Wyoming	18.6	42	
50 States	n/a		
DC	34.8		
United States	42.5		

CQ State Fact Finder

State	Prisoners #	Rank
Alabama	19,573	16
Alaska	3,292	38
Arizona	19,746	15
Arkansas	8,836	29
California	125,605	1
Colorado	10,717	27
Connecticut	14,380	22
Delaware	4,411	35
Florida	57,139	4
Georgia	33,425	8
Hawaii	3,333	37
Idaho	2,964	40
Illinois	36,531	7
Indiana	15,014	20
Iowa	5,437	33
Kansas	6,373	32
Kentucky	11,066	25
Louisiana	24,092	12
Maine	1,537	47
Maryland	20,998	14
Massachusetts	11,282	23
Michigan	40,775	6
Minnesota	4,572	34
Mississippi	11,274	24
Missouri	17,898	18
Montana	1,680	46
Nebraska	2,633	42
Nevada	7,122	30
New Hampshire	2,021	43
New Jersey	24,632	11
New Mexico	3,866	36
New York	66,750	3
North Carolina	23,639	13
North Dakota	536	50
Ohio	41,913	5
Oklahoma	16,631	19
Oregon	6,936	31
Pennsylvania	28,302	9
Rhode Island	2,919	41
South Carolina	18,999	17
South Dakota	1,734	45
Tennessee	14,474	21
Texas	118,195	2
Utah	3,016	39
Vermont	1,301	48
Virginia	26,192	10
Washington	10,833	26
West Virginia	1,930	44
Wisconsin	10,020	28
Wyoming	1,217	49
50 States	947,761	
DC	10,943	
United States	1,053,738	

Rank in order

By

1. California
2. Texas
3. New York
4. Florida
5. Ohio
6. Michigan
7. Illinois
8. Georgia
9. Pennsylvania
10. Virginia
11. New Jersey
12. Louisiana
13. North Carolina
14. Maryland
15. Arizona
16. Alabama
17. South Carolina
18. Missouri
19. Oklahoma
20. Indiana
21. Tennessee
22. Connecticut
23. Massachusetts
24. Mississippi
25. Kentucky
26. Washington
27. Colorado
28. Wisconsin
29. Arkansas
30. Nevada
31. Oregon
32. Kansas
33. Iowa
34. Minnesota
35. Delaware
36. New Mexico
37. Hawaii
38. Alaska
39. Utah
40. Idaho
41. Rhode Island
42. Nebraska
43. New Hampshire
44. West Virginia
45. South Dakota
46. Montana
47. Maine
48. Vermont
49. Wyoming
50. North Dakota

J-10 Juvenile Arrest Rate, 1992

State	Juvenile arrest rate (per 100,000 youths)	Rank	By rate
Alabama	209	11	1. Vermont
Alaska	250	14	2. North Dakota
Arizona	522	41	3. West Virginia
Arkansas	274	17	4. Wyoming
California	634	46	5. Montana
Colorado	518	40	6. New Hampshire
Connecticut	501	39	7. Maine
Delaware	430	36	8. Nebraska
Florida	751	49	9. South Dakota
Georgia	345	24	10. Iowa
Hawaii	241	13	11. Alabama
Idaho	322	21	12. Virginia
Illinois	376	32	13. Hawaii
Indiana	446	37	14. Alaska
Iowa	186	10	15. Minnesota
Kansas	346	25	16. Mississippi
Kentucky	341	23	17. Arkansas
Louisiana	552	43	18. Tennessee
Maine	108	7	19. South Carolina
Maryland	653	47	20. Oregon
Massachusetts	559	44	21. Idaho
Michigan	379	34	22. Oklahoma
Minnesota	250	15	23. Kentucky
Mississippi	273	16	24. Georgia
Missouri	539	42	25. Kansas
Montana	88	5	26. Ohio
Nebraska	129	8	27. Nevada
Nevada	357	27	28. New Mexico
New Hampshire	102	6	29. Utah
New Jersey	717	48	30. Wisconsin
New Mexico	358	28	31. Washington
New York	1,025	50	32. Illinois
North Carolina	404	35	33. Texas
North Dakota	64	2	34. Michigan
Ohio	351	26	35. North Carolina
Oklahoma	339	22	36. Delaware
Oregon	314	20	37. Indiana
Pennsylvania	478	38	38. Pennsylvania
Rhode Island	579	45	39. Connecticut
South Carolina	301	19	40. Colorado
South Dakota	140	9	41. Arizona
Tennessee	296	18	42. Missouri
Texas	379	33	43. Louisiana
Utah	361	29	44. Massachusetts
Vermont	49	1	45. Rhode Island
Virginia	228	12	46. California
Washington	372	31	47. Maryland
West Virginia	72	3	48. New Jersey
Wisconsin	368	30	49. Florida
Wyoming	87	4	50. New York
50 States	n/a		
DC	1,487		
United States	483		

State	Proportion of sentence served %	Rank
Alabama	n/a	n/a
Alaska	65	7
Arizona	82	2
Arkansas	36	34
California	86	1
Colorado	52	14
Connecticut	n/a	n/a
Delaware	59	8
Florida	47	18
Georgia	48	17
Hawaii	42	24
Idaho	67	5
Illinois	43	23
Indiana	n/a	n/a
Iowa	32	37
Kansas	n/a	n/a
Kentucky	38	29
Louisiana	57	9
Maine	n/a	n/a
Maryland	54	11
Massachusetts	77	3
Michigan	n/a	n/a
Minnesota	73	4
Mississippi	40	27
Missouri	51	15
Montana	37	31
Nebraska	45	21
Nevada	n/a	n/a
New Hampshire	41	26
New Jersey	37	31
New Mexico	n/a	n/a
New York	54	11
North Carolina	30	38
North Dakota	46	20
Ohio	17	39
Oklahoma	36	34
Oregon	42	24
Pennsylvania	49	16
Rhode Island	n/a	n/a
South Carolina	37	31
South Dakota	n/a	n/a
Tennessee	35	36
Texas	39	28
Utah	45	21
Vermont	56	10
Virginia	n/a	n/a
Washington	67	5
West Virginia	54	11
Wisconsin	38	29
Wyoming	47	18
50 States	n/a	
DC	67	
United States	46	

By %

1. California
2. Arizona
3. Massachusetts
4. Minnesota
5. Idaho
5. Washington
7. Alaska
8. Delaware
9. Louisiana
10. Vermont
11. Maryland
11. New York
11. West Virginia
14. Colorado
15. Missouri
16. Pennsylvania
17. Georgia
18. Florida
18. Wyoming
20. North Dakota
21. Nebraska
21. Utah
23. Illinois
24. Hawaii
24. Oregon
26. New Hampshire
27. Mississippi
28. Texas
29. Kentucky
29. Wisconsin
31. Montana
31. New Jersey
31. South Carolina
34. Arkansas
34. Oklahoma
36. Tennessee
37. Iowa
38. North Carolina
39. Ohio

State	Law enforcement employees per 10,000 population	Rank	Rank in order By per 10,000
Alabama	25.6	27	1. New Jersey
Alaska	27.2	24	2. New York
Arizona	29.2	10	3. Illinois
Arkansas	22.4	40	4. Florida
California	27.7	17	4. Wyoming
Colorado	27.3	21	6. Nevada
Connecticut	28.2	15	7. Rhode Island
Delaware	28.2	15	8. Maryland
Florida	33.6	4	9. Hawaii
Georgia	27.7	17	10. Arizona
Hawaii	29.6	9	11. Missouri
Idaho	25.6	27	11. New Mexico
Illinois	35.0	3	13. Louisiana
Indiana	23.3	37	14. Massachusetts
Iowa	21.6	44	15. Connecticut
Kansas	27.3	21	15. Delaware
Kentucky	20.4	49	17. California
Louisiana	28.6	13	17. Georgia
Maine	23.8	36	19. Texas
Maryland	29.8	8	20. Oklahoma
Massachusetts	28.5	14	21. Colorado
Michigan	22.6	39	21. Kansas
Minnesota	20.9	47	21. New Hampshire
Mississippi	22.9	38	24. Alaska
Missouri	28.7	11	25. Wisconsin
Montana	24.3	33	26. North Carolina
Nebraska	24.5	32	27. Alabama
Nevada	32.9	6	27. Idaho
New Hampshire	27.3	21	29. Ohio
New Jersey	39.7	1	30. South Carolina
New Mexico	28.7	11	30. Tennessee
New York	37.4	2	32. Nebraska
North Carolina	25.8	26	33. Montana
North Dakota	21.0	46	34. Pennsylvania
Ohio	25.1	29	34. Virginia
Oklahoma	27.4	20	36. Maine
Oregon	22.3	41	37. Indiana
Pennsylvania	24.1	34	38. Mississippi
Rhode Island	29.9	7	39. Michigan
South Carolina	25.0	30	40. Arkansas
South Dakota	21.4	45	41. Oregon
Tennessee	25.0	30	42. Washington
Texas	27.6	19	43. Vermont
Utah	20.6	48	44. Iowa
Vermont	21.8	43	45. South Dakota
Virginia	24.1	34	46. North Dakota
Washington	21.9	42	47. Minnesota
West Virginia	16.7	50	48. Utah
Wisconsin	26.1	25	49. Kentucky
Wyoming	33.6	4	50. West Virginia
50 States	n/a		
DC	86.3		
United States	28.0		

State	Corrections employees per 10,000 population	Rank	By per 10,000
Alabama	14.2	42	1. New York
Alaska	21.7	15	2. Florida
Arizona	26.4	5	3. Georgia
Arkansas	15.9	33	4. Nevada
California	19.7	18	5. Arizona
Colorado	17.8	23	6. Texas
Connecticut	16.5	31	7. Delaware
Delaware	24.3	7	8. South Carolina
Florida	31.0	2	9. New Mexico
Georgia	27.8	3	10. New Jersey
Hawaii	17.5	26	11. Louisiana
Idaho	15.5	35	12. Maryland
Illinois	16.9	27	13. North Carolina
Indiana	16.6	29	14. Virginia
Iowa	9.9	49	15. Alaska
Kansas	19.4	19	16. Tennessee
Kentucky	18.1	20	17. Michigan
Louisiana	22.9	11	18. California
Maine	15.1	40	19. Kansas
Maryland	22.3	12	20. Kentucky
Massachusetts	16.1	32	20. Rhode Island
Michigan	20.6	17	22. Oregon
Minnesota	12.4	44	23. Colorado
Mississippi	13.5	43	23. Washington
Missouri	16.6	29	25. Oklahoma
Montana	15.4	38	26. Hawaii
Nebraska	15.9	33	27. Illinois
Nevada	26.9	4	28. Wyoming
New Hampshire	12.4	44	29. Indiana
New Jersey	23.3	10	29. Missouri
New Mexico	23.6	9	31. Connecticut
New York	32.6	1	32. Massachusetts
North Carolina	22.1	13	33. Arkansas
North Dakota	10.6	48	33. Nebraska
Ohio	15.2	39	35. Idaho
Oklahoma	17.6	25	35. Pennsylvania
Oregon	18.0	22	35. Utah
Pennsylvania	15.5	35	38. Montana
Rhode Island	18.1	20	39. Ohio
South Carolina	24.0	8	40. Maine
South Dakota	11.5	47	41. Wisconsin
Tennessee	21.1	16	42. Alabama
Texas	26.3	6	43. Mississippi
Utah	15.5	35	44. Minnesota
Vermont	12.2	46	44. New Hampshire
Virginia	21.9	14	46. Vermont
Washington	17.8	23	47. South Dakota
West Virginia	7.8	50	48. North Dakota
Wisconsin	14.6	41	49. Iowa
Wyoming	16.7	28	50. West Virginia
50 States	n/a		
DC	85.9		
United States	20.9		

State	Cost per inmate per day $	Rank
Alabama	25.74	50
Alaska	106.56	1
Arizona	43.87	35
Arkansas	32.95	46
California	57.33	19
Colorado	56.98	20
Connecticut	63.09	12
Delaware	57.39	18
Florida	43.75	36
Georgia	51.66	26
Hawaii	81.06	2
Idaho	45.07	33
Illinois	43.75	37
Indiana	43.18	38
Iowa	52.42	24
Kansas	56.39	21
Kentucky	34.92	43
Louisiana	33.02	45
Maine	76.51	3
Maryland	50.02	29
Massachusetts	63.01	13
Michigan	53.43	23
Minnesota	72.30	7
Mississippi	29.85	48
Missouri	25.94	49
Montana	69.34	10
Nebraska	57.68	16
Nevada	40.76	39
New Hampshire	46.21	32
New Jersey	74.84	6
New Mexico	75.21	4
New York	70.00	8
North Carolina	58.51	14
North Dakota	50.60	27
Ohio	37.49	42
Oklahoma	31.81	47
Oregon	50.06	28
Pennsylvania	58.17	15
Rhode Island	75.00	5
South Carolina	34.10	44
South Dakota	39.85	40
Tennessee	48.49	30
Texas	44.40	34
Utah	57.53	17
Vermont	69.49	9
Virginia	46.61	31
Washington	64.40	11
West Virginia	39.73	41
Wisconsin	55.39	22
Wyoming	52.05	25
50 States	n/a	
DC	62.12	
United States	Federal 58.5	

Rank in order

By $

1. Alaska
2. Hawaii
3. Maine
4. New Mexico
5. Rhode Island
6. New Jersey
7. Minnesota
8. New York
9. Vermont
10. Montana
11. Washington
12. Connecticut
13. Massachusetts
14. North Carolina
15. Pennsylvania
16. Nebraska
17. Utah
18. Delaware
19. California
20. Colorado
21. Kansas
22. Wisconsin
23. Michigan
24. Iowa
25. Wyoming
26. Georgia
27. North Dakota
28. Oregon
29. Maryland
30. Tennessee
31. Virginia
32. New Hampshire
33. Idaho
34. Texas
35. Arizona
36. Florida
37. Illinois
38. Indiana
39. Nevada
40. South Dakota
41. West Virginia
42. Ohio
43. Kentucky
44. South Carolina
45. Louisiana
46. Arkansas
47. Oklahoma
48. Mississippi
49. Missouri
50. Alabama

State	Corrections spending ($mil)	per prisoner $	Rank by per prisoner		By per prisoner
Alabama	150	7,664	48		1. Minnesota
Alaska	136	41,312	2		2. Alaska
Arizona	318	16,105	39		3. Maine
Arkansas	90	10,186	46		4. Utah
California	3,099	24,673	22		5. Rhode Island
Colorado	348	32,472	6		6. Colorado
Connecticut	362	25,174	18		7. Washington
Delaware	85	19,270	30		8. Wisconsin
Florida	1,120	19,601	28		9. Vermont
Georgia	563	16,844	37		10. New York
Hawaii	90	27,003	11		11. Hawaii
Idaho	56	18,893	33		12. Tennessee
Illinois	669	18,313	34		13. North Dakota
Indiana	305	20,314	27		14. New Jersey
Iowa	139	25,566	15		15. Iowa
Kansas	159	24,949	19		16. Michigan
Kentucky	178	16,085	40		17. Oregon
Louisiana	328	13,614	43		18. Connecticut
Maine	60	39,037	3		19. Kansas
Maryland	404	19,240	31		20. Massachusetts
Massachusetts	281	24,907	20		21. North Carolina
Michigan	1,041	25,530	16		22. California
Minnesota	202	44,182	1		23. Nebraska
Mississippi	95	8,426	47		24. Virginia
Missouri	184	10,280	45		25. Pennsylvania
Montana	35	20,833	26		26. Montana
Nebraska	59	22,408	23		27. Indiana
Nevada	n/a	n/a	n/a		28. Florida
New Hampshire	39	19,297	29		29. New Hampshire
New Jersey	643	26,104	14		30. Delaware
New Mexico	n/a	n/a	n/a		31. Maryland
New York	1,864	27,925	10		32. Ohio
North Carolina	587	24,832	21		33. Idaho
North Dakota	14	26,119	13		34. Illinois
Ohio	800	19,087	32		35. Wyoming
Oklahoma	174	10,462	44		36. West Virginia
Oregon	176	25,375	17		37. Georgia
Pennsylvania	604	21,341	25		38. South Dakota
Rhode Island	101	34,601	5		39. Arizona
South Carolina	264	13,895	42		40. Kentucky
South Dakota	28	16,148	38		41. Texas
Tennessee	387	26,738	12		42. South Carolina
Texas	1,856	15,703	41		43. Louisiana
Utah	113	37,467	4		44. Oklahoma
Vermont	37	28,440	9		45. Missouri
Virginia	579	22,106	24		46. Arkansas
Washington	330	30,462	7		47. Mississippi
West Virginia	34	17,617	36		48. Alabama
Wisconsin	294	29,341	8		
Wyoming	22	18,077	35		
50 States	19,502	20,577			
DC	n/a	n/a			
United States	19,502	18,507			

State	% increase in state corrections spending %	Rank
Alabama	9.3	20
Alaska	1.4	43
Arizona	15.4	11
Arkansas	9.1	21
California	15.4	11
Colorado	76.1	1
Connecticut	26.6	5
Delaware	4.9	34
Florida	23.3	6
Georgia	9.0	23
Hawaii	0.0	45
Idaho	7.7	28
Illinois	9.1	21
Indiana	2.9	36
Iowa	1.3	44
Kansas	9.0	23
Kentucky	2.7	37
Louisiana	11.7	18
Maine	1.7	42
Maryland	3.5	35
Massachusetts	1.8	41
Michigan	7.1	30
Minnesota	11.9	17
Mississippi	12.6	16
Missouri	5.7	32
Montana	2.6	38
Nebraska	-8.6	48
Nevada	n/a	n/a
New Hampshire	7.7	28
New Jersey	6.5	31
New Mexico	n/a	n/a
New York	5.2	33
North Carolina	19.3	8
North Dakota	0.0	45
Ohio	15.5	10
Oklahoma	2.1	39
Oregon	8.0	26
Pennsylvania	37.8	2
Rhode Island	1.9	40
South Carolina	9.8	19
South Dakota	14.8	15
Tennessee	8.4	25
Texas	27.1	4
Utah	15.0	14
Vermont	19.4	7
Virginia	8.0	26
Washington	33.6	3
West Virginia	16.1	9
Wisconsin	15.2	13
Wyoming	-8.3	47
50 States	11.2	
DC	n/a	
United States	14.0	

Rank in order

By %

1. Colorado
2. Pennsylvania
3. Washington
4. Texas
5. Connecticut
6. Florida
7. Vermont
8. North Carolina
9. West Virginia
10. Ohio
11. Arizona
11. California
13. Wisconsin
14. Utah
15. South Dakota
16. Mississippi
17. Minnesota
18. Louisiana
19. South Carolina
20. Alabama
21. Arkansas
21. Illinois
23. Georgia
23. Kansas
25. Tennessee
26. Oregon
26. Virginia
28. Idaho
28. New Hampshire
30. Michigan
31. New Jersey
32. Missouri
33. New York
34. Delaware
35. Maryland
36. Indiana
37. Kentucky
38. Montana
39. Oklahoma
40. Rhode Island
41. Massachusetts
42. Maine
43. Alaska
44. Iowa
45. Hawaii
45. North Dakota
47. Wyoming
48. Nebraska

State	Law enforcement spending ($000)	Per capita $	Rank by per capita
Alabama	636,967	154	41
Alaska	259,605	442	1
Arizona	1,084,451	283	8
Arkansas	298,026	124	46
California	10,842,069	351	4
Colorado	849,665	245	13
Connecticut	886,751	270	10
Delaware	206,829	300	6
Florida	4,175,040	310	5
Georgia	1,511,969	224	21
Hawaii	270,906	234	18
Idaho	183,659	172	34
Illinois	2,656,874	228	20
Indiana	828,529	146	43
Iowa	303,520	108	49
Kansas	477,642	189	30
Kentucky	565,024	150	42
Louisiana	892,577	208	25
Maine	204,474	166	36
Maryland	1,370,270	279	9
Massachusetts	1,434,530	239	15
Michigan	2,380,639	252	12
Minnesota	808,066	180	32
Mississippi	290,695	111	47
Missouri	811,229	156	38
Montana	118,990	144	44
Nebraska	248,485	155	40
Nevada	486,770	367	3
New Hampshire	198,087	178	33
New Jersey	2,249,281	289	7
New Mexico	378,719	240	14
New York	7,178,576	396	2
North Carolina	1,350,369	197	28
North Dakota	69,297	109	48
Ohio	2,231,411	203	27
Oklahoma	510,215	159	37
Oregon	661,775	222	22
Pennsylvania	2,273,624	189	29
Rhode Island	230,243	229	19
South Carolina	744,997	207	26
South Dakota	95,132	134	45
Tennessee	925,824	184	31
Texas	3,773,854	214	24
Utah	309,757	171	35
Vermont	88,473	155	39
Virginia	1,405,479	220	23
Washington	1,357,680	264	11
West Virginia	150,528	83	50
Wisconsin	1,180,979	236	17
Wyoming	110,798	238	16
50 States	62,559,349	246	
DC	591,065	1,009	
United States	63,150,414	248	

Rank in order

By per capita

1. Alaska
2. New York
3. Nevada
4. California
5. Florida
6. Delaware
7. New Jersey
8. Arizona
9. Maryland
10. Connecticut
11. Washington
12. Michigan
13. Colorado
14. New Mexico
15. Massachusetts
16. Wyoming
17. Wisconsin
18. Hawaii
19. Rhode Island
20. Illinois
21. Georgia
22. Oregon
23. Virginia
24. Texas
25. Louisiana
26. South Carolina
27. Ohio
28. North Carolina
29. Pennsylvania
30. Kansas
31. Tennessee
32. Minnesota
33. New Hampshire
34. Idaho
35. Utah
36. Maine
37. Oklahoma
38. Missouri
39. Vermont
40. Nebraska
41. Alabama
42. Kentucky
43. Indiana
44. Montana
45. South Dakota
46. Arkansas
47. Mississippi
48. North Dakota
49. Iowa
50. West Virginia

State	Law enforcement spending as % of total %	Rank		Rank in order By %
Alabama	4.95	33		1. Nevada
Alaska	4.47	41		2. Florida
Arizona	8.06	4		3. California
Arkansas	4.52	37		4. Arizona
California	8.33	3		5. Maryland
Colorado	6.62	12		6. Delaware
Connecticut	5.89	22		7. New York
Delaware	7.06	6		8. Texas
Florida	8.86	2		9. Georgia
Georgia	6.76	9		10. Michigan
Hawaii	4.49	40		11. Virginia
Idaho	5.62	25		12. Colorado
Illinois	6.59	13		13. Illinois
Indiana	4.59	36		14. South Carolina
Iowa	3.01	48		15. North Carolina
Kansas	5.58	27		16. New Mexico
Kentucky	4.73	35		17. Washington
Louisiana	5.66	24		18. New Jersey
Maine	4.40	42		19. Tennessee
Maryland	7.64	5		20. Ohio
Massachusetts	5.81	23		21. Wisconsin
Michigan	6.69	10		22. Connecticut
Minnesota	4.01	45		23. Massachusetts
Mississippi	3.88	46		24. Louisiana
Missouri	5.42	28		25. Idaho
Montana	4.06	44		26. Oregon
Nebraska	4.49	39		27. Kansas
Nevada	9.18	1		28. Missouri
New Hampshire	4.85	34		29. Utah
New Jersey	6.15	18		30. Rhode Island
New Mexico	6.32	16		31. Oklahoma
New York	7.02	7		32. Pennsylvania
North Carolina	6.35	15		33. Alabama
North Dakota	2.80	49		34. New Hampshire
Ohio	5.95	20		35. Kentucky
Oklahoma	5.08	31		36. Indiana
Oregon	5.61	26		37. Arkansas
Pennsylvania	5.01	32		38. Wyoming
Rhode Island	5.24	30		39. Nebraska
South Carolina	6.39	14		40. Hawaii
South Dakota	4.21	43		41. Alaska
Tennessee	6.13	19		42. Maine
Texas	6.78	8		43. South Dakota
Utah	5.33	29		44. Montana
Vermont	3.81	47		45. Minnesota
Virginia	6.66	11		46. Mississippi
Washington	6.28	17		47. Vermont
West Virginia	2.59	50		48. Iowa
Wisconsin	5.95	21		49. North Dakota
Wyoming	4.50	38		50. West Virginia
50 States	6.46			
DC	13.36			
United States	6.50			

Transportation

State	Annual vehicle-miles interstate millions	% of travel on interstates	Rank by %	Rank in order By %
Alabama	9,089	19.2	39	1. Utah
Alaska	1,165	29.7	3	2. Connecticut
Arizona	8,866	22.6	25	3. Alaska
Arkansas	5,203	21.7	30	4. Wyoming
California	67,502	25.3	14	5. Maryland
Colorado	7,943	24.3	19	6. Massachusetts
Connecticut	8,238	30.5	2	7. Missouri
Delaware	1,009	14.6	50	8. Washington
Florida	22,501	18.7	42	9. Georgia
Georgia	21,025	26.8	9	10. New Mexico
Hawaii	1,526	18.9	41	11. Tennessee
Idaho	2,456	21.4	33	12. Illinois
Illinois	23,435	26.1	12	13. West Virginia
Indiana	13,106	21.7	31	14. California
Iowa	5,233	20.8	35	15. Ohio
Kansas	4,944	20.5	36	16. Oregon
Kentucky	9,382	23.7	23	17. Virginia
Louisiana	8,890	24.5	18	18. Louisiana
Maine	2,215	18.2	44	19. Colorado
Maryland	12,377	28.6	5	20. South Carolina
Massachusetts	13,052	28.0	6	21. Montana
Michigan	18,957	22.1	28	22. Rhode Island
Minnesota	9,037	21.4	32	23. Kentucky
Mississippi	4,422	16.5	48	24. South Dakota
Missouri	15,142	27.6	7	25. Arizona
Montana	2,096	24.1	21	26. Nevada
Nebraska	2,814	19.0	40	27. Texas
Nevada	2,631	22.6	26	28. Michigan
New Hampshire	2,106	20.4	37	29. Vermont
New Jersey	10,408	17.4	47	30. Arkansas
New Mexico	5,050	26.7	10	31. Indiana
New York	19,969	17.8	45	32. Minnesota
North Carolina	12,267	17.7	46	33. Idaho
North Dakota	1,244	20.2	38	34. Oklahoma
Ohio	24,531	25.3	15	35. Iowa
Oklahoma	7,435	20.9	34	36. Kansas
Oregon	7,078	25.0	16	37. New Hampshire
Pennsylvania	16,498	18.2	43	38. North Dakota
Rhode Island	1,735	24.0	22	39. Alabama
South Carolina	8,713	24.1	20	40. Nebraska
South Dakota	1,718	23.2	24	41. Hawaii
Tennessee	13,847	26.6	11	42. Florida
Texas	37,189	22.2	27	43. Pennsylvania
Utah	5,918	34.7	1	44. Maine
Vermont	1,313	22.0	29	45. New York
Virginia	15,799	24.6	17	46. North Carolina
Washington	12,407	26.9	8	47. New Jersey
West Virginia	4,284	25.5	13	48. Mississippi
Wisconsin	7,615	15.5	49	49. Wisconsin
Wyoming	2,001	29.6	4	50. Delaware
50 States	523,381	22.8		
DC	477	13.7		
United States	523,858	22.8		

K-1 Travel On Interstate Highways, 1993

K-2 Percent Of Mileage On Interstates In Poor Or Mediocre Condition, 1993

State	interstate mileage in poor or mediocre condition %	rank by %	By %
Alabama	4.3	45	1. Mississippi
Alaska	56.4	7	2. Wyoming
Arizona	10.8	36	3. Minnesota
Arkansas	77.2	4	4. Arkansas
California	7.6	38	5. South Dakota
Colorado	47.4	12	6. Connecticut
Connecticut	57.4	6	7. Alaska
Delaware	n/a	n/a	8. Texas
Florida	14.0	32	9. Nebraska
Georgia	0.0	48	10. West Virginia
Hawaii	n/a	n/a	11. Idaho
Idaho	47.7	11	12. Colorado
Illinois	16.1	29	13. Michigan
Indiana	11.0	35	14. Washington
Iowa	5.0	42	15. Pennsylvania
Kansas	34.5	17	16. Montana
Kentucky	34.3	18	17. Kansas
Louisiana	22.2	26	18. Kentucky
Maine	16.0	30	19. North Dakota
Maryland	25.1	25	20. Wisconsin
Massachusetts	4.9	43	21. Rhode Island
Michigan	44.0	13	22. New Mexico
Minnesota	78.9	3	23. North Carolina
Mississippi	93.0	1	24. Virginia
Missouri	6.1	39	25. Maryland
Montana	40.3	16	26. Louisiana
Nebraska	53.3	9	27. New Jersey
Nevada	4.3	46	28. South Carolina
New Hampshire	5.1	40	29. Illinois
New Jersey	17.7	27	30. Maine
New Mexico	28.6	22	31. New York
New York	15.5	31	32. Florida
North Carolina	28.0	23	33. Oklahoma
North Dakota	33.0	19	34. Tennessee
Ohio	10.6	37	35. Indiana
Oklahoma	13.6	33	36. Arizona
Oregon	4.8	44	37. Ohio
Pennsylvania	41.9	15	38. California
Rhode Island	28.6	21	39. Missouri
South Carolina	17.5	28	40. New Hampshire
South Dakota	60.7	5	41. Utah
Tennessee	11.6	34	42. Iowa
Texas	53.7	8	43. Massachusetts
Utah	5.1	41	44. Oregon
Vermont	3.2	47	45. Alabama
Virginia	25.4	24	46. Nevada
Washington	43.7	14	47. Vermont
West Virginia	52.0	10	48. Georgia
Wisconsin	29.3	20	
Wyoming	80.7	2	
50 States	31.4		
DC	n/a		
United States	31.4		

K-3 Deficient Bridges, 1994

State	Total deficient bridges #	% of bridges deficient %	Rank by %
Alabama	2,270	29.0	18
Alaska	136	20.3	35
Arizona	434	8.5	50
Arkansas	1,510	19.8	37
California	4,313	26.8	25
Colorado	824	19.8	38
Connecticut	846	29.8	17
Delaware	130	25.0	27
Florida	1,640	22.3	32
Georgia	1,932	23.3	29
Hawaii	439	53.7	3
Idaho	403	19.7	39
Illinois	2,626	23.7	28
Indiana	1,548	20.3	36
Iowa	1,361	18.7	41
Kansas	2,124	19.4	40
Kentucky	1,620	31.0	15
Louisiana	1,907	30.7	16
Maine	552	35.5	10
Maryland	720	27.4	23
Massachusetts	2,292	60.0	2
Michigan	2,103	32.6	13
Minnesota	851	15.7	45
Mississippi	3,441	35.8	9
Missouri	3,059	33.5	12
Montana	536	20.7	34
Nebraska	771	14.8	46
Nevada	162	18.3	42
New Hampshire	343	28.8	19
New Jersey	2,051	45.3	5
New Mexico	354	13.5	47
New York	5,798	62.3	1
North Carolina	2,058	33.5	11
North Dakota	173	9.8	49
Ohio	3,260	27.1	24
Oklahoma	2,255	22.7	30
Oregon	1,243	27.9	22
Pennsylvania	4,671	40.4	7
Rhode Island	287	46.4	4
South Carolina	1,031	22.5	31
South Dakota	360	13.3	48
Tennessee	2,578	28.0	21
Texas	4,675	15.8	44
Utah	472	28.0	20
Vermont	501	38.4	8
Virginia	1,830	25.3	26
Washington	1,355	31.7	14
West Virginia	1,489	44.6	6
Wisconsin	1,467	21.7	33
Wyoming	310	16.0	43
50 States	79,111	26.8	
DC	116	57.7	
United States	79,853	26.9	

Rank in order

By %

1. New York
2. Massachusetts
3. Hawaii
4. Rhode Island
5. New Jersey
6. West Virginia
7. Pennsylvania
8. Vermont
9. Mississippi
10. Maine
11. North Carolina
12. Missouri
13. Michigan
14. Washington
15. Kentucky
16. Louisiana
17. Connecticut
18. Alabama
19. New Hampshire
20. Utah
21. Tennessee
22. Oregon
23. Maryland
24. Ohio
25. California
26. Virginia
27. Delaware
28. Illinois
29. Georgia
30. Oklahoma
31. South Carolina
32. Florida
33. Wisconsin
34. Montana
35. Alaska
36. Indiana
37. Arkansas
38. Colorado
39. Idaho
40. Kansas
41. Iowa
42. Nevada
43. Wyoming
44. Texas
45. Minnesota
46. Nebraska
47. New Mexico
48. South Dakota
49. North Dakota
50. Arizona

traffic deaths

State	rate	Rank
Alabama	2.20	11
Alaska	3.01	2
Arizona	2.05	14
Arkansas	2.43	4
California	1.56	35
Colorado	1.71	29
Connecticut	1.27	46
Delaware	1.61	33
Florida	2.19	13
Georgia	1.78	23
Hawaii	1.66	31
Idaho	1.98	16
Illinois	1.55	36
Indiana	1.47	40
Iowa	1.83	21
Kansas	1.77	25
Kentucky	2.20	11
Louisiana	2.42	5
Maine	1.52	39
Maryland	1.54	37
Massachusetts	1.02	49
Michigan	1.64	32
Minnesota	1.27	46
Mississippi	3.03	1
Missouri	1.73	27
Montana	2.24	10
Nebraska	1.72	28
Nevada	2.26	8
New Hampshire	1.17	48
New Jersey	1.32	45
New Mexico	2.28	7
New York	1.59	34
North Carolina	2.00	15
North Dakota	1.45	41
Ohio	1.53	38
Oklahoma	1.89	17
Oregon	1.85	19
Pennsylvania	1.69	30
Rhode Island	1.02	49
South Carolina	2.34	6
South Dakota	1.89	17
Tennessee	2.25	9
Texas	1.81	22
Utah	1.78	23
Vermont	1.84	20
Virginia	1.37	44
Washington	1.43	43
West Virginia	2.56	3
Wisconsin	1.45	41
Wyoming	1.77	25
50 States	1.82	
DC	1.64	
United States	1.75	

Rank in order

By rate

1. Mississippi
2. Alaska
3. West Virginia
4. Arkansas
5. Louisiana
6. South Carolina
7. New Mexico
8. Nevada
9. Tennessee
10. Montana
11. Alabama
11. Kentucky
13. Florida
14. Arizona
15. North Carolina
16. Idaho
17. Oklahoma
17. South Dakota
19. Oregon
20. Vermont
21. Iowa
22. Texas
23. Georgia
23. Utah
25. Kansas
25. Wyoming
27. Missouri
28. Nebraska
29. Colorado
30. Pennsylvania
31. Hawaii
32. Michigan
33. Delaware
34. New York
35. California
36. Illinois
37. Maryland
38. Ohio
39. Maine
40. Indiana
41. North Dakota
41. Wisconsin
43. Washington
44. Virginia
45. New Jersey
46. Connecticut
46. Minnesota
48. New Hampshire
49. Massachusetts
49. Rhode Island

State	Drivers using seatbelts %	Rank by %	Rank in order By %
Alabama	55	38	1. Hawaii
Alaska	69	15	2. California
Arizona	60	30	3. North Carolina
Arkansas	51	42	3. Washington
California	83	2	5. New Mexico
Colorado	54	39	6. Oregon
Connecticut	72	8	7. Iowa
Delaware	63	25	8. Connecticut
Florida	61	28	8. New York
Georgia	57	35	8. Pennsylvania
Hawaii	84	1	8. Virginia
Idaho	61	28	12. Nevada
Illinois	68	18	12. Texas
Indiana	56	37	14. Kansas
Iowa	73	7	15. Alaska
Kansas	70	14	15. Maryland
Kentucky	58	32	15. Montana
Louisiana	50	43	18. Illinois
Maine	36	48	18. Missouri
Maryland	69	15	18. Vermont
Massachusetts	47	44	21. Michigan
Michigan	66	21	22. New Jersey
Minnesota	57	35	22. South Carolina
Mississippi	43	46	22. Wisconsin
Missouri	68	18	25. Delaware
Montana	69	15	25. Nebraska
Nebraska	63	25	27. Ohio
Nevada	71	12	28. Florida
New Hampshire	54	39	28. Idaho
New Jersey	64	22	30. Arizona
New Mexico	79	5	30. Tennessee
New York	72	8	32. Kentucky
North Carolina	81	3	32. Rhode Island
North Dakota	32	49	32. West Virginia
Ohio	62	27	35. Georgia
Oklahoma	45	45	35. Minnesota
Oregon	77	6	37. Indiana
Pennsylvania	72	8	38. Alabama
Rhode Island	58	32	39. Colorado
South Carolina	64	22	39. New Hampshire
South Dakota	40	47	41. Utah
Tennessee	60	30	42. Arkansas
Texas	71	12	43. Louisiana
Utah	53	41	44. Massachusetts
Vermont	68	18	45. Oklahoma
Virginia	72	8	46. Mississippi
Washington	81	3	47. South Dakota
West Virginia	58	32	48. Maine
Wisconsin	64	22	49. North Dakota
Wyoming	n/a	n/a	
50 States	n/a		
DC	62		
United States	67		

State	Vehicle miles travelled millions	Vehicle miles travelled per capita	Rank by per capita	Rank in order By per capita
Alabama	47,337	11,322	4	1. Wyoming
Alaska	3,918	6,552	49	2. New Mexico
Arizona	39,150	9,924	17	3. Georgia
Arkansas	23,995	9,891	19	4. Alabama
California	266,408	8,534	39	5. Oklahoma
Colorado	32,718	9,180	30	6. Indiana
Connecticut	27,001	8,237	42	7. Missouri
Delaware	6,895	9,878	20	8. Idaho
Florida	120,467	8,777	35	9. Kentucky
Georgia	78,426	11,363	3	10. Vermont
Hawaii	8,074	6,925	48	11. South Dakota
Idaho	11,481	10,437	8	12. Montana
Illinois	89,693	7,675	44	13. Tennessee
Indiana	60,461	10,596	6	14. Mississippi
Iowa	25,118	8,904	34	15. North Carolina
Kansas	24,115	9,513	24	16. South Carolina
Kentucky	39,598	10,437	9	17. Arizona
Louisiana	36,351	8,473	40	18. Virginia
Maine	12,182	9,824	21	19. Arkansas
Maryland	43,311	8,736	38	20. Delaware
Massachusetts	46,684	7,757	43	21. Maine
Michigan	85,686	9,058	33	22. Wisconsin
Minnesota	42,214	9,331	26	23. North Dakota
Mississippi	26,864	10,176	14	24. Kansas
Missouri	54,821	10,472	7	25. Oregon
Montana	8,707	10,353	12	26. Minnesota
Nebraska	14,777	9,161	32	27. Texas
Nevada	11,624	8,411	41	28. West Virginia
New Hampshire	10,342	9,201	29	29. New Hampshire
New Jersey	59,726	7,600	45	30. Colorado
New Mexico	18,945	11,723	2	31. Utah
New York	112,240	6,183	50	32. Nebraska
North Carolina	69,493	9,996	15	33. Michigan
North Dakota	6,158	9,667	23	34. Iowa
Ohio	96,992	8,769	37	35. Florida
Oklahoma	35,529	10,989	5	36. Washington
Oregon	28,352	9,342	25	37. Ohio
Pennsylvania	90,706	7,540	46	38. Maryland
Rhode Island	7,227	7,227	47	39. California
South Carolina	36,125	9,952	16	40. Louisiana
South Dakota	7,413	10,353	11	41. Nevada
Tennessee	52,112	10,230	13	42. Connecticut
Texas	167,611	9,300	27	43. Massachusetts
Utah	17,056	9,170	31	44. Illinois
Vermont	5,976	10,375	10	45. New Jersey
Virginia	64,171	9,914	18	46. Pennsylvania
Washington	46,135	8,773	36	47. Rhode Island
West Virginia	16,778	9,229	28	48. Hawaii
Wisconsin	49,167	9,748	22	49. Alaska
Wyoming	6,770	14,404	1	50. New York
50 States	2,293,100	8,915		
DC	3,485	6,019		
United States	2,296,585	8,909		

State	Workers using public transportation %	Rank by %
Alabama	0.8	41
Alaska	2.4	21
Arizona	2.1	25
Arkansas	0.5	49
California	4.9	8
Colorado	2.9	15
Connecticut	3.9	11
Delaware	2.4	21
Florida	2.0	26
Georgia	2.8	16
Hawaii	7.4	6
Idaho	1.9	28
Illinois	10.1	2
Indiana	1.3	32
Iowa	1.2	34
Kansas	0.7	43
Kentucky	1.6	29
Louisiana	3.0	14
Maine	0.9	40
Maryland	8.1	5
Massachusetts	8.3	4
Michigan	1.6	29
Minnesota	3.6	12
Mississippi	0.8	41
Missouri	2.0	26
Montana	0.6	46
Nebraska	1.2	34
Nevada	2.7	17
New Hampshire	0.7	43
New Jersey	8.8	3
New Mexico	1.0	38
New York	24.8	1
North Carolina	1.0	38
North Dakota	0.6	46
Ohio	2.5	18
Oklahoma	0.6	46
Oregon	3.4	13
Pennsylvania	6.4	7
Rhode Island	2.5	18
South Carolina	1.1	36
South Dakota	0.3	50
Tennessee	1.3	32
Texas	2.2	24
Utah	2.3	23
Vermont	0.7	43
Virginia	4.0	10
Washington	4.5	9
West Virginia	1.1	36
Wisconsin	2.5	18
Wyoming	1.4	31
50 States	3.1	
DC	36.6	
United States	5.3	

Rank in order

By %

1. New York
2. Illinois
3. New Jersey
4. Massachusetts
5. Maryland
6. Hawaii
7. Pennsylvania
8. California
9. Washington
10. Virginia
11. Connecticut
12. Minnesota
13. Oregon
14. Louisiana
15. Colorado
16. Georgia
17. Nevada
18. Ohio
18. Rhode Island
18. Wisconsin
21. Alaska
21. Delaware
23. Utah
24. Texas
25. Arizona
26. Florida
26. Missouri
28. Idaho
29. Kentucky
29. Michigan
31. Wyoming
32. Indiana
32. Tennessee
34. Iowa
34. Nebraska
36. South Carolina
36. West Virginia
38. New Mexico
38. North Carolina
40. Maine
41. Alabama
41. Mississippi
43. Kansas
43. New Hampshire
43. Vermont
46. Montana
46. North Dakota
46. Oklahoma
49. Arkansas
50. South Dakota

K-8 Road And Street Miles, 1993

State	Total road & street miles	Total miles under state control	% under state control %	Rank
Alabama	165,037	11,032	6.7	35
Alaska	25,956	5,319	20.5	7
Arizona	95,186	6,144	6.5	36
Arkansas	146,789	16,234	11.1	19
California	257,341	18,653	7.2	30
Colorado	144,539	9,225	6.4	37
Connecticut	29,171	3,975	13.6	16
Delaware	9,219	4,887	53.0	1
Florida	176,438	11,932	6.8	34
Georgia	195,484	17,867	9.1	24
Hawaii	6,413	1,027	16.0	11
Idaho	114,254	5,124	4.5	48
Illinois	238,749	17,305	7.2	31
Indiana	165,486	11,363	6.9	33
Iowa	216,198	10,166	4.7	46
Kansas	256,932	10,672	4.2	50
Kentucky	135,125	27,606	20.4	8
Louisiana	105,432	16,634	15.8	12
Maine	42,437	8,550	20.1	9
Maryland	44,955	5,417	12.0	18
Massachusetts	41,490	3,656	8.8	27
Michigan	207,144	9,637	4.7	47
Minnesota	245,032	13,351	5.4	44
Mississippi	137,764	10,480	7.6	29
Missouri	227,424	32,202	14.2	15
Montana	137,156	8,176	6.0	42
Nebraska	180,350	10,253	5.7	43
Nevada	86,959	5,271	6.1	40
New Hampshire	27,007	4,023	14.9	14
New Jersey	46,165	3,273	7.1	32
New Mexico	115,773	11,527	10.0	22
New York	184,471	16,264	8.8	26
North Carolina	170,333	78,044	45.8	4
North Dakota	171,636	7,409	4.3	49
Ohio	196,078	20,527	10.5	21
Oklahoma	212,140	13,107	6.2	38
Oregon	182,044	11,215	6.2	39
Pennsylvania	201,460	44,363	22.0	6
Rhode Island	7,391	1,371	18.5	10
South Carolina	117,795	41,680	35.4	5
South Dakota	164,750	7,895	4.8	45
Tennessee	153,553	13,905	9.1	25
Texas	509,152	76,851	15.1	13
Utah	74,910	5,779	7.7	28
Vermont	27,008	2,839	10.5	20
Virginia	121,277	56,441	46.5	3
Washington	141,638	18,889	13.3	17
West Virginia	66,953	31,953	47.7	2
Wisconsin	206,365	12,440	6.0	41
Wyoming	72,898	6,728	9.2	23
50 States	7,005,257	798,681	11.4	
DC	1,107	1,039	93.9	
United States	7,006,364	799,720	11.4	

Rank in order

By %

1. Delaware
2. West Virginia
3. Virginia
4. North Carolina
5. South Carolina
6. Pennsylvania
7. Alaska
8. Kentucky
9. Maine
10. Rhode Island
11. Hawaii
12. Louisiana
13. Texas
14. New Hampshire
15. Missouri
16. Connecticut
17. Washington
18. Maryland
19. Arkansas
20. Vermont
21. Ohio
22. New Mexico
23. Wyoming
24. Georgia
25. Tennessee
26. New York
27. Massachusetts
28. Utah
29. Mississippi
30. California
31. Illinois
32. New Jersey
33. Indiana
34. Florida
35. Alabama
36. Arizona
37. Colorado
38. Oklahoma
39. Oregon
40. Nevada
41. Wisconsin
42. Montana
43. Nebraska
44. Minnesota
45. South Dakota
46. Iowa
47. Michigan
48. Idaho
49. North Dakota
50. Kansas

CQ State Fact Finder

State	Highway employees per 10,000 population	Rank	By per 10,000
Alabama	27.5	20	1. Alaska
Alaska	61.7	1	2. Wyoming
Arizona	18.1	43	3. South Dakota
Arkansas	30.7	11	4. Montana
California	13.1	50	5. West Virginia
Colorado	22.3	30	6. Maine
Connecticut	22.2	31	7. Vermont
Delaware	28.4	16	8. Kansas
Florida	18.4	41	9. North Dakota
Georgia	19.6	37	10. Nebraska
Hawaii	16.6	48	11. Arkansas
Idaho	30.2	12	12. Idaho
Illinois	17.1	46	13. Mississippi
Indiana	18.9	39	14. New Hampshire
Iowa	30.0	15	15. Iowa
Kansas	34.9	8	16. Delaware
Kentucky	23.2	28	17. Minnesota
Louisiana	24.8	23	18. New York
Maine	36.1	6	19. Oklahoma
Maryland	20.8	34	20. Alabama
Massachusetts	17.0	47	21. New Mexico
Michigan	13.5	49	22. Oregon
Minnesota	28.0	17	23. Louisiana
Mississippi	30.2	13	24. Washington
Missouri	23.7	27	25. New Jersey
Montana	38.4	4	26. Virginia
Nebraska	34.5	10	27. Missouri
Nevada	18.6	40	28. Kentucky
New Hampshire	30.2	14	29. Tennessee
New Jersey	24.0	25	30. Colorado
New Mexico	27.0	21	31. Connecticut
New York	27.8	18	32. North Carolina
North Carolina	22.2	32	33. Wisconsin
North Dakota	34.9	9	34. Maryland
Ohio	19.9	36	35. South Carolina
Oklahoma	27.7	19	36. Ohio
Oregon	25.6	22	37. Georgia
Pennsylvania	19.3	38	38. Pennsylvania
Rhode Island	18.3	42	39. Indiana
South Carolina	20.1	35	40. Nevada
South Dakota	39.3	3	41. Florida
Tennessee	22.8	29	42. Rhode Island
Texas	17.9	44	43. Arizona
Utah	17.8	45	44. Texas
Vermont	35.9	7	45. Utah
Virginia	23.9	26	46. Illinois
Washington	24.5	24	47. Massachusetts
West Virginia	36.6	5	48. Hawaii
Wisconsin	21.7	33	49. Michigan
Wyoming	56.7	2	50. California
50 States	n/a		
DC	14.9		
United States	21.3		

State	transit employees per 10,000 pop	Rank	Rank in order By per 10,000
Alabama	1.0	34	1. New York
Alaska	14.3	3	2. Illinois
Arizona	0.2	47	3. Alaska
Arkansas	0.7	38	4. Washington
California	9.0	7	5. Massachusetts
Colorado	6.1	10	6. Pennsylvania
Connecticut	1.2	30	7. California
Delaware	4.9	18	8. Oregon
Florida	3.8	21	9. Maryland
Georgia	6.0	11	10. Colorado
Hawaii	0.5	43	11. Georgia
Idaho	0.2	47	12. Utah
Illinois	14.5	2	13. Ohio
Indiana	2.0	27	14. Minnesota
Iowa	2.2	25	15. Missouri
Kansas	0.8	36	15. Texas
Kentucky	2.4	22	17. Rhode Island
Louisiana	0.8	36	18. Delaware
Maine	0.7	38	19. Wisconsin
Maryland	7.0	9	20. Michigan
Massachusetts	11.8	5	21. Florida
Michigan	4.4	20	22. Kentucky
Minnesota	5.3	14	22. Nebraska
Mississippi	0.4	45	24. New Mexico
Missouri	5.2	15	25. Iowa
Montana	1.2	30	26. West Virginia
Nebraska	2.4	22	27. Indiana
Nevada	0.4	45	27. Virginia
New Hampshire	0.9	35	29. Vermont
New Jersey	1.2	30	30. Connecticut
New Mexico	2.3	24	30. Montana
New York	36.1	1	30. New Jersey
North Carolina	0.7	38	30. South Carolina
North Dakota	0.6	41	34. Alabama
Ohio	5.5	13	35. New Hampshire
Oklahoma	0.6	41	36. Kansas
Oregon	7.4	8	36. Louisiana
Pennsylvania	11.2	6	38. Arkansas
Rhode Island	5.0	17	38. Maine
South Carolina	1.2	30	38. North Carolina
South Dakota	0.0	50	41. North Dakota
Tennessee	0.5	43	41. Oklahoma
Texas	5.2	15	43. Hawaii
Utah	5.9	12	43. Tennessee
Vermont	1.4	29	45. Mississippi
Virginia	2.0	27	45. Nevada
Washington	12.9	4	47. Arizona
West Virginia	2.1	26	47. Idaho
Wisconsin	4.5	19	49. Wyoming
Wyoming	0.1	49	50. South Dakota
50 States	n/a		
DC	141.1		
United States	7.9		

State	Per capita spending on highways $	Spending on highways per $1000 of personal income $	Rank by per capita
Alabama	223	14.5	42
Alaska	1,043	50.9	1
Arizona	276	17.0	27
Arkansas	263	18.2	32
California	202	9.8	48
Colorado	299	15.9	22
Connecticut	329	12.6	14
Delaware	396	19.3	9
Florida	250	13.4	35
Georgia	204	12.0	47
Hawaii	373	18.0	11
Idaho	318	21.3	17
Illinois	307	14.9	19
Indiana	210	12.3	46
Iowa	441	25.6	4
Kansas	372	20.6	12
Kentucky	283	18.3	24
Louisiana	282	18.9	25
Maine	315	18.1	18
Maryland	227	10.3	40
Massachusetts	220	9.6	45
Michigan	200	10.8	49
Minnesota	378	20.0	10
Mississippi	275	20.8	29
Missouri	246	13.8	37
Montana	428	27.9	7
Nebraska	350	19.9	13
Nevada	327	17.1	15
New Hampshire	255	11.8	34
New Jersey	323	12.6	16
New Mexico	462	32.2	3
New York	282	12.6	26
North Carolina	231	13.9	38
North Dakota	439	28.2	5
Ohio	247	14.0	36
Oklahoma	293	19.1	23
Oregon	265	15.4	31
Pennsylvania	222	11.6	44
Rhode Island	226	11.8	41
South Carolina	174	11.4	50
South Dakota	433	27.2	6
Tennessee	262	16.1	33
Texas	223	13.2	43
Utah	228	16.0	39
Vermont	423	23.6	8
Virginia	276	13.9	28
Washington	271	14.2	30
West Virginia	301	21.2	21
Wisconsin	303	17.1	20
Wyoming	745	44.6	2
50 States	n/a	n/a	
DC	208	7.4	
United States	261	13.9	

K-11 State And Local Spending For Highways, 1992

Rank in order

By per capita

1. Alaska
2. Wyoming
3. New Mexico
4. Iowa
5. North Dakota
6. South Dakota
7. Montana
8. Vermont
9. Delaware
10. Minnesota
11. Hawaii
12. Kansas
13. Nebraska
14. Connecticut
15. Nevada
16. New Jersey
17. Idaho
18. Maine
19. Illinois
20. Wisconsin
21. West Virginia
22. Colorado
23. Oklahoma
24. Kentucky
25. Louisiana
26. New York
27. Arizona
28. Virginia
29. Mississippi
30. Washington
31. Oregon
32. Arkansas
33. Tennessee
34. New Hampshire
35. Florida
36. Ohio
37. Missouri
38. North Carolina
39. Utah
40. Maryland
41. Rhode Island
42. Alabama
43. Texas
44. Pennsylvania
45. Massachusetts
46. Indiana
47. Georgia
48. California
49. Michigan
50. South Carolina

K-12 State And Local Highway Spending As Percent Of Total Spending, 1992

State	Highway spending as % of total spending %	Rank by %	By %
Alabama	7.17	31	1. Wyoming
Alaska	10.54	8	2. South Dakota
Arizona	7.87	26	3. Iowa
Arkansas	9.57	13	4. New Mexico
California	4.78	50	5. Montana
Colorado	8.08	25	6. North Dakota
Connecticut	7.17	32	7. Kansas
Delaware	9.31	16	8. Alaska
Florida	7.16	34	9. Idaho
Georgia	6.17	43	10. Vermont
Hawaii	7.17	33	11. Nebraska
Idaho	10.40	9	12. Mississippi
Illinois	8.85	18	13. Arkansas
Indiana	6.57	40	14. West Virginia
Iowa	12.29	3	15. Oklahoma
Kansas	10.98	7	16. Delaware
Kentucky	8.89	17	17. Kentucky
Louisiana	7.66	27	18. Illinois
Maine	8.39	22	19. Tennessee
Maryland	6.21	42	20. Missouri
Massachusetts	5.34	46	21. Minnesota
Michigan	5.31	47	22. Maine
Minnesota	8.40	21	23. Virginia
Mississippi	9.58	12	24. Nevada
Missouri	8.52	20	25. Colorado
Montana	12.06	5	26. Arizona
Nebraska	10.18	11	27. Louisiana
Nevada	8.19	24	28. Wisconsin
New Hampshire	6.93	37	29. North Carolina
New Jersey	6.88	38	30. Ohio
New Mexico	12.20	4	31. Alabama
New York	4.99	49	32. Connecticut
North Carolina	7.44	29	33. Hawaii
North Dakota	11.26	6	34. Florida
Ohio	7.27	30	35. Utah
Oklahoma	9.37	15	36. Texas
Oregon	6.70	39	37. New Hampshire
Pennsylvania	5.88	44	38. New Jersey
Rhode Island	5.16	48	39. Oregon
South Carolina	5.39	45	40. Indiana
South Dakota	13.62	2	41. Washington
Tennessee	8.73	19	42. Maryland
Texas	7.07	36	43. Georgia
Utah	7.13	35	44. Pennsylvania
Vermont	10.38	10	45. South Carolina
Virginia	8.33	23	46. Massachusetts
Washington	6.43	41	47. Michigan
West Virginia	9.37	14	48. Rhode Island
Wisconsin	7.65	28	49. New York
Wyoming	14.11	1	50. California
50 States	n/a		
DC	2.75		
United States	6.86		

Welfare/Families/Social Services

L-1 Percent Of Births To Unwed Mothers, 1993

State	# of births	% of births	Rank by %
Alabama	20,680	33.5	14
Alaska	3,101	28.0	28
Arizona	26,151	37.9	4
Arkansas	10,878	31.7	20
California	206,376	35.3	8
Colorado	13,373	24.8	41
Connecticut	13,919	29.8	23
Delaware	3,577	33.8	12
Florida	67,431	35.0	9
Georgia	39,575	35.8	7
Hawaii	5,328	27.2	31
Idaho	3,268	18.7	48
Illinois	65,130	34.1	10
Indiana	25,844	30.8	22
Iowa	9,297	24.6	42
Kansas	9,696	25.9	39
Kentucky	14,401	27.2	32
Louisiana	29,179	42.0	2
Maine	4,061	27.0	35
Maryland	24,335	32.5	16
Massachusetts	22,380	26.4	36
Michigan	36,326	26.0	38
Minnesota	15,099	23.4	45
Mississippi	18,718	44.4	1
Missouri	24,353	32.4	17
Montana	3,104	27.3	30
Nebraska	5,449	23.5	44
Nevada	7,614	34.0	11
New Hampshire	3,179	20.6	47
New Jersey	31,949	27.1	33
New Mexico	11,526	41.4	3
New York	105,101	37.2	5
North Carolina	32,586	32.1	19
North Dakota	1,999	23.0	46
Ohio	52,385	33.0	15
Oklahoma	13,441	29.1	24
Oregon	11,730	28.2	27
Pennsylvania	51,783	32.2	18
Rhode Island	4,436	31.7	21
South Carolina	19,359	36.0	6
South Dakota	2,968	27.7	29
Tennessee	24,556	33.6	13
Texas	54,670	17.0	49
Utah	5,744	15.5	50
Vermont	1,805	24.2	43
Virginia	27,532	29.0	25
Washington	20,670	26.3	37
West Virginia	6,328	29.0	26
Wisconsin	18,882	27.1	34
Wyoming	1,689	25.8	40
50 States	1,232,961	n/a	
DC	7,211	67.8	
United States	1,240,172	31.0	

Rank in order

By %

1. Mississippi
2. Louisiana
3. New Mexico
4. Arizona
5. New York
6. South Carolina
7. Georgia
8. California
9. Florida
10. Illinois
11. Nevada
12. Delaware
13. Tennessee
14. Alabama
15. Ohio
16. Maryland
17. Missouri
18. Pennsylvania
19. North Carolina
20. Arkansas
21. Rhode Island
22. Indiana
23. Connecticut
24. Oklahoma
25. Virginia
26. West Virginia
27. Oregon
28. Alaska
29. South Dakota
30. Montana
31. Hawaii
32. Kentucky
33. New Jersey
34. Wisconsin
35. Maine
36. Massachusetts
37. Washington
38. Michigan
39. Kansas
40. Wyoming
41. Colorado
42. Iowa
43. Vermont
44. Nebraska
45. Minnesota
46. North Dakota
47. New Hampshire
48. Idaho
49. Texas
50. Utah

State	Average monthly # of recipients #	Recipients as % of population %	Rank by %	Rank in order By %
Alabama	132,067	3.0	41	1. California
Alaska	37,998	6.2	5	2. New York
Arizona	200,809	4.9	21	3. Michigan
Arkansas	69,333	2.8	43	4. New Mexico
California	2,639,214	8.5	1	5. Alaska
Colorado	118,986	3.2	40	5. Rhode Island
Connecticut	165,928	5.1	17	7. Illinois
Delaware	27,488	3.6	36	8. Ohio
Florida	669,419	4.7	24	8. West Virginia
Georgia	393,499	5.5	12	10. Mississippi
Hawaii	62,016	5.4	15	11. Tennessee
Idaho	23,170	2.0	50	12. Georgia
Illinois	712,295	6.1	7	12. Louisiana
Indiana	216,038	3.7	34	12. Washington
Iowa	110,268	3.9	33	15. Hawaii
Kansas	86,686	3.4	38	16. Kentucky
Kentucky	208,033	5.3	16	17. Connecticut
Louisiana	248,163	5.5	12	17. Maine
Maine	64,333	5.1	17	17. Pennsylvania
Maryland	221,793	4.5	26	20. Missouri
Massachusetts	307,082	4.9	21	21. Arizona
Michigan	665,785	6.8	3	21. Massachusetts
Minnesota	186,987	4.0	30	23. Vermont
Mississippi	158,743	5.8	10	24. Florida
Missouri	263,452	5.0	20	25. North Carolina
Montana	34,852	4.0	30	26. Maryland
Nebraska	45,277	2.7	44	27. Wisconsin
Nevada	37,710	2.6	46	28. New Jersey
New Hampshire	30,345	2.7	44	28. Texas
New Jersey	335,414	4.2	28	30. Minnesota
New Mexico	102,248	6.3	4	30. Montana
New York	1,254,739	7.0	2	30. Oklahoma
North Carolina	332,594	4.6	25	33. Iowa
North Dakota	16,458	2.5	49	34. Indiana
Ohio	684,519	6.0	8	34. South Carolina
Oklahoma	131,208	4.0	30	36. Delaware
Oregon	114,043	3.6	36	36. Oregon
Pennsylvania	619,642	5.1	17	38. Kansas
Rhode Island	62,843	6.2	5	39. Wyoming
South Carolina	139,694	3.7	34	40. Colorado
South Dakota	19,105	2.6	46	41. Alabama
Tennessee	299,686	5.7	11	42. Virginia
Texas	787,504	4.2	28	43. Arkansas
Utah	49,882	2.6	46	44. Nebraska
Vermont	27,815	4.8	23	44. New Hampshire
Virginia	194,603	2.9	42	46. Nevada
Washington	291,534	5.5	12	46. South Dakota
West Virginia	114,314	6.0	8	46. Utah
Wisconsin	226,147	4.3	27	49. North Dakota
Wyoming	16,354	3.3	39	50. Idaho
50 States	13,958,115	5.3		
DC	73,953	13.0		
United States	14,225,591	5.8		

State	Food stamp recipients #	as % of population %	Rank by %	Rank in order By %
Alabama	547,731	13.0	8	1. Mississippi
Alaska	45,871	7.6	34	2. West Virginia
Arizona	511,739	12.6	9	3. Louisiana
Arkansas	282,521	11.5	13	4. Texas
California	3,154,602	10.0	22	5. New Mexico
Colorado	268,256	7.3	37	6. Tennessee
Connecticut	222,618	6.8	46	7. Kentucky
Delaware	59,242	8.4	30	8. Alabama
Florida	1,474,426	10.6	19	9. Arizona
Georgia	830,360	11.8	11	10. New York
Hawaii	114,576	9.7	24	11. Georgia
Idaho	81,504	7.2	39	12. Oklahoma
Illinois	1,188,760	10.1	21	13. Arkansas
Indiana	517,939	9.0	27	14. Missouri
Iowa	195,706	6.9	43	15. Ohio
Kansas	191,749	7.5	35	16. Vermont
Kentucky	522,339	13.6	7	17. Maine
Louisiana	756,438	17.5	3	18. Michigan
Maine	135,784	11.0	17	19. Florida
Maryland	390,204	7.8	33	20. South Carolina
Massachusetts	441,794	7.3	38	21. Illinois
Michigan	1,030,671	10.9	18	22. California
Minnesota	317,904	7.0	42	23. Pennsylvania
Mississippi	510,539	19.1	1	24. Hawaii
Missouri	593,071	11.2	14	25. Rhode Island
Montana	71,377	8.3	32	26. Oregon
Nebraska	110,750	6.8	45	27. Indiana
Nevada	96,742	6.6	48	28. North Carolina
New Hampshire	61,565	5.4	50	29. Washington
New Jersey	545,315	6.9	44	30. Delaware
New Mexico	244,266	14.8	5	31. Virginia
New York	2,153,627	11.9	10	32. Montana
North Carolina	629,880	8.9	28	33. Maryland
North Dakota	45,408	7.1	41	34. Alaska
Ohio	1,245,214	11.2	15	35. Kansas
Oklahoma	376,002	11.5	12	36. South Dakota
Oregon	286,342	9.3	26	37. Colorado
Pennsylvania	1,208,314	10.0	23	38. Massachusetts
Rhode Island	93,784	9.4	25	39. Idaho
South Carolina	385,410	10.5	20	40. Wyoming
South Dakota	53,283	7.4	36	41. North Dakota
Tennessee	734,566	14.2	6	42. Minnesota
Texas	2,725,788	14.8	4	43. Iowa
Utah	127,771	6.7	47	44. New Jersey
Vermont	64,557	11.1	16	45. Nebraska
Virginia	547,120	8.4	31	46. Connecticut
Washington	467,617	8.8	29	47. Utah
West Virginia	321,360	17.6	2	48. Nevada
Wisconsin	329,807	6.5	49	49. Wisconsin
Wyoming	34,035	7.2	40	50. New Hampshire
50 States	27,346,244	10.5		
DC	90,697	15.9		
United States	27,472,148	10.6		

L-4 SSI Recipients As A Percent Of Population, 1994

State	SSI recipients #	% of pop %	Rank by %
Alabama	161,673	3.8	4
Alaska	6,389	1.1	48
Arizona	58,559	1.4	39
Arkansas	93,841	3.8	5
California	1,014,150	3.2	8
Colorado	54,591	1.5	34
Connecticut	42,707	1.3	44
Delaware	10,271	1.5	37
Florida	317,040	2.3	17
Georgia	194,093	2.8	11
Hawaii	18,043	1.5	33
Idaho	15,728	1.4	42
Illinois	260,289	2.2	19
Indiana	85,777	1.5	35
Iowa	40,788	1.4	38
Kansas	35,550	1.4	41
Kentucky	155,846	4.1	3
Louisiana	178,758	4.1	2
Maine	28,567	2.3	15
Maryland	78,658	1.6	31
Massachusetts	156,914	2.6	12
Michigan	206,585	2.2	21
Minnesota	59,587	1.3	43
Mississippi	139,618	5.2	1
Missouri	109,842	2.1	26
Montana	13,292	1.6	32
Nebraska	20,501	1.3	46
Nevada	18,952	1.3	45
New Hampshire	9,654	0.8	50
New Jersey	140,377	1.8	29
New Mexico	42,613	2.6	14
New York	563,965	3.1	9
North Carolina	182,385	2.6	13
North Dakota	8,888	1.4	40
Ohio	235,883	2.1	23
Oklahoma	72,354	2.2	18
Oregon	45,404	1.5	36
Pennsylvania	252,179	2.1	25
Rhode Island	22,823	2.3	16
South Carolina	108,478	3.0	10
South Dakota	13,196	1.8	28
Tennessee	174,643	3.4	7
Texas	390,351	2.1	24
Utah	19,808	1.0	49
Vermont	12,681	2.2	20
Virginia	124,859	1.9	27
Washington	87,787	1.6	30
West Virginia	64,365	3.5	6
Wisconsin	108,686	2.1	22
Wyoming	5,512	1.2	47
50 States	6,263,500	2.4	
DC	19,852	3.5	
United States	6,295,786	2.4	

Rank in order

By %

1. Mississippi
2. Louisiana
3. Kentucky
4. Alabama
5. Arkansas
6. West Virginia
7. Tennessee
8. California
9. New York
10. South Carolina
11. Georgia
12. Massachusetts
13. North Carolina
14. New Mexico
15. Maine
16. Rhode Island
17. Florida
18. Oklahoma
19. Illinois
20. Vermont
21. Michigan
22. Wisconsin
23. Ohio
24. Texas
25. Pennsylvania
26. Missouri
27. Virginia
28. South Dakota
29. New Jersey
30. Washington
31. Maryland
32. Montana
33. Hawaii
34. Colorado
35. Indiana
36. Oregon
37. Delaware
38. Iowa
39. Arizona
40. North Dakota
41. Kansas
42. Idaho
43. Minnesota
44. Connecticut
45. Nevada
46. Nebraska
47. Wyoming
48. Alaska
49. Utah
50. New Hampshire

State	Average monthly AFDC recipients 1989 (000)	% change 1989-1994	Rank by %
Alabama	129	2.4	45
Alaska	19	95.9	3
Arizona	105	90.5	4
Arkansas	70	-0.4	47
California	1,763	49.7	11
Colorado	97	22.3	31
Connecticut	106	56.2	8
Delaware	19	43.2	16
Florida	327	104.8	2
Georgia	266	48.0	12
Hawaii	43	44.9	15
Idaho	17	37.9	18
Illinois	632	12.7	38
Indiana	147	46.6	13
Iowa	98	13.0	37
Kansas	74	17.3	34
Kentucky	156	33.6	20
Louisiana	277	-10.3	49
Maine	51	26.6	28
Maryland	176	25.9	29
Massachusetts	242	27.1	27
Michigan	640	4.0	44
Minnesota	164	14.4	36
Mississippi	179	-11.2	50
Missouri	203	29.7	24
Montana	28	25.8	30
Nebraska	41	10.4	40
Nevada	20	87.6	5
New Hampshire	13	138.9	1
New Jersey	298	12.6	39
New Mexico	59	74.2	6
New York	979	28.2	25
North Carolina	200	66.0	7
North Dakota	15	7.6	42
Ohio	629	8.8	41
Oklahoma	103	27.4	26
Oregon	87	30.6	22
Pennsylvania	523	18.5	33
Rhode Island	42	50.0	10
South Carolina	108	29.9	23
South Dakota	19	1.1	46
Tennessee	196	53.3	9
Texas	540	45.9	14
Utah	44	14.4	35
Vermont	20	41.2	17
Virginia	146	33.7	19
Washington	219	32.9	21
West Virginia	109	4.6	43
Wisconsin	245	-7.7	48
Wyoming	14	19.4	32
50 States	10,693	30.5	
DC	48	54.4	
United States	10,741	32.4	

Rank in order

By %

1. New Hampshire
2. Florida
3. Alaska
4. Arizona
5. Nevada
6. New Mexico
7. North Carolina
8. Connecticut
9. Tennessee
10. Rhode Island
11. California
12. Georgia
13. Indiana
14. Texas
15. Hawaii
16. Delaware
17. Vermont
18. Idaho
19. Virginia
20. Kentucky
21. Washington
22. Oregon
23. South Carolina
24. Missouri
25. New York
26. Oklahoma
27. Massachusetts
28. Maine
29. Maryland
30. Montana
31. Colorado
32. Wyoming
33. Pennsylvania
34. Kansas
35. Utah
36. Minnesota
37. Iowa
38. Illinois
39. New Jersey
40. Nebraska
41. Ohio
42. North Dakota
43. West Virginia
44. Michigan
45. Alabama
46. South Dakota
47. Arkansas
48. Wisconsin
49. Louisiana
50. Mississippi

Condition Of Children Index
"Child well-being" ranked from 1 (highest) to 51 (lowest)

State		By Index Ranked highest (1) to lowest (50)
Alabama	44	1. New Hampshire
Alaska	26	2. Iowa
Arizona	45	3. North Dakota
Arkansas	39	4. Maine
California	35	5. Nebraska
Colorado	27	6. Utah
Connecticut	10	7. Vermont
Delaware	24	8. Minnesota
Florida	47	9. Wisconsin
Georgia	43	10. Connecticut
Hawaii	17	11. Massachusetts
Idaho	25	12. Washington
Illinois	38	13. South Dakota
Indiana	32	14. Kansas
Iowa	2	15. Virginia
Kansas	14	16. Rhode Island
Kentucky	33	17. Hawaii
Louisiana	50	18. Oregon
Maine	4	19. New Jersey
Maryland	30	20. Pennsylvania
Massachusetts	11	21. Montana
Michigan	31	22. Ohio
Minnesota	8	23. Wyoming
Mississippi	49	24. Delaware
Missouri	36	25. Idaho
Montana	21	26. Alaska
Nebraska	5	27. Colorado
Nevada	34	28. Texas
New Hampshire	1	29. Oklahoma
New Jersey	19	30. Maryland
New Mexico	40	31. Michigan
New York	37	32. Indiana
North Carolina	42	33. Kentucky
North Dakota	3	34. Nevada
Ohio	22	35. California
Oklahoma	29	36. Missouri
Oregon	18	37. New York
Pennsylvania	20	38. Illinois
Rhode Island	16	39. Arkansas
South Carolina	46	40. New Mexico
South Dakota	13	41. West Virginia
Tennessee	48	42. North Carolina
Texas	28	43. Georgia
Utah	6	44. Alabama
Vermont	7	45. Arizona
Virginia	15	46. South Carolina
Washington	12	47. Florida
West Virginia	41	48. Tennessee
Wisconsin	9	49. Mississippi
Wyoming	23	50. Louisiana
50 States	n/a	
DC	51	
United States	n/a	

State	% of families %	Rank		Rank in order By %
Alabama	25.9	15		1. Louisiana
Alaska	27.7	10		2. Mississippi
Arizona	25.4	20		3. Tennessee
Arkansas	22.7	36		4. Indiana
California	25.3	21		5. Georgia
Colorado	25.6	18		6. Florida
Connecticut	23.9	27		7. New York
Delaware	25.5	19		8. Michigan
Florida	28.6	6		9. Maryland
Georgia	28.8	5		10. Alaska
Hawaii	22.0	39		11. Nevada
Idaho	17.7	49		12. Illinois
Illinois	26.2	12		13. Rhode Island
Indiana	29.0	4		14. Massachusetts
Iowa	19.6	46		15. Alabama
Kansas	21.0	43		16. South Carolina
Kentucky	24.0	26		17. Missouri
Louisiana	30.8	1		18. Colorado
Maine	22.1	38		19. Delaware
Maryland	27.9	9		20. Arizona
Massachusetts	26.1	14		21. California
Michigan	27.9	8		22. Minnesota
Minnesota	25.1	22		23. North Carolina
Mississippi	29.9	2		24. Washington
Missouri	25.6	17		25. Oregon
Montana	23.1	31		26. Kentucky
Nebraska	18.5	47		27. Connecticut
Nevada	26.3	11		28. Ohio
New Hampshire	20.0	44		29. New Mexico
New Jersey	23.0	33		30. Wisconsin
New Mexico	23.5	29		31. Montana
New York	28.5	7		32. Texas
North Carolina	24.8	23		33. New Jersey
North Dakota	18.3	48		34. Oklahoma
Ohio	23.5	28		35. West Virginia
Oklahoma	22.9	34		36. Arkansas
Oregon	24.2	25		37. Virginia
Pennsylvania	21.4	41		38. Maine
Rhode Island	26.1	13		39. Hawaii
South Carolina	25.9	16		40. South Dakota
South Dakota	21.6	40		41. Pennsylvania
Tennessee	29.7	3		42. Vermont
Texas	23.0	32		43. Kansas
Utah	16.0	50		44. New Hampshire
Vermont	21.1	42		45. Wyoming
Virginia	22.2	37		46. Iowa
Washington	24.7	24		47. Nebraska
West Virginia	22.7	35		48. North Dakota
Wisconsin	23.4	30		49. Idaho
Wyoming	19.9	45		50. Utah
50 States	n/a			
DC	56.6			
United States	25.3			

L-8 Typical Monthly AFDC Payments, Family Of Three, 1994

State	Typical monthly AFDC payment $	Rank	By $
Alabama	164	49	1. Alaska
Alaska	923	1	2. Hawaii
Arizona	347	31	3. Vermont
Arkansas	204	44	4. California
California	607	4	5. Connecticut
Colorado	356	29	6. Massachusetts
Connecticut	581	5	7. New York
Delaware	338	33	8. Rhode Island
Florida	303	36	9. New Hampshire
Georgia	280	40	10. Washington
Hawaii	712	2	11. Minnesota
Idaho	317	35	12. Wisconsin
Illinois	377	25	13. Oregon
Indiana	288	39	14. Michigan
Iowa	426	17	15. North Dakota
Kansas	403	22	16. South Dakota
Kentucky	228	43	17. Iowa
Louisiana	190	46	18. New Jersey
Maine	418	19	19. Maine
Maryland	373	26	20. Montana
Massachusetts	579	6	21. Utah
Michigan	459	14	22. Kansas
Minnesota	532	11	23. Pennsylvania
Mississippi	120	50	24. New Mexico
Missouri	292	37	25. Illinois
Montana	416	20	26. Maryland
Nebraska	364	27	27. Nebraska
Nevada	348	30	28. Wyoming
New Hampshire	549	9	29. Colorado
New Jersey	424	18	30. Nevada
New Mexico	381	24	31. Arizona
New York	577	7	32. Ohio
North Carolina	272	41	33. Delaware
North Dakota	431	15	34. Oklahoma
Ohio	341	32	35. Idaho
Oklahoma	324	34	36. Florida
Oregon	460	13	37. Missouri
Pennsylvania	403	23	38. Virginia
Rhode Island	554	8	39. Indiana
South Carolina	200	45	40. Georgia
South Dakota	430	16	41. North Carolina
Tennessee	185	48	42. West Virginia
Texas	188	47	43. Kentucky
Utah	414	21	44. Arkansas
Vermont	638	3	45. South Carolina
Virginia	291	38	46. Louisiana
Washington	546	10	47. Texas
West Virginia	253	42	48. Tennessee
Wisconsin	518	12	49. Alabama
Wyoming	360	28	50. Mississippi
50 States	n/a		
DC	420		
United States	n/a		

L-9 Welfare As Percentage Of Poverty Level Income, 1994

State	Welfare as % of poverty level income %	Rank
Alabama	48	49
Alaska	101	2
Arizona	67	28
Arkansas	52	44
California	86	5
Colorado	67	28
Connecticut	91	3
Delaware	66	33
Florida	62	37
Georgia	60	40
Hawaii	103	1
Idaho	64	36
Illinois	69	24
Indiana	61	38
Iowa	72	17
Kansas	74	15
Kentucky	55	43
Louisiana	51	46
Maine	72	17
Maryland	69	24
Massachusetts	83	9
Michigan	75	14
Minnesota	80	11
Mississippi	43	50
Missouri	61	38
Montana	71	22
Nebraska	68	26
Nevada	67	28
New Hampshire	81	10
New Jersey	73	16
New Mexico	67	28
New York	85	7
North Carolina	59	41
North Dakota	71	22
Ohio	66	33
Oklahoma	65	35
Oregon	78	13
Pennsylvania	72	17
Rhode Island	86	5
South Carolina	52	44
South Dakota	72	17
Tennessee	50	47
Texas	50	47
Utah	72	17
Vermont	88	4
Virginia	67	28
Washington	84	8
West Virginia	57	42
Wisconsin	79	12
Wyoming	68	26
50 States	n/a	
DC	72	
United States	69	

Rank in order

By %

1. Hawaii
2. Alaska
3. Connecticut
4. Vermont
5. Rhode Island
5. California
7. New York
8. Washington
9. Massachusetts
10. New Hampshire
11. Minnesota
12. Wisconsin
13. Oregon
14. Michigan
15. Kansas
16. New Jersey
17. Utah
17. South Dakota
17. Pennsylvania
17. Maine
17. Iowa
22. North Dakota
22. Montana
24. Maryland
24. Illinois
26. Wyoming
26. Nebraska
28. Virginia
28. New Mexico
28. Nevada
28. Colorado
28. Arizona
33. Ohio
33. Delaware
35. Oklahoma
36. Idaho
37. Florida
38. Missouri
38. Indiana
40. Georgia
41. North Carolina
42. West Virginia
43. Kentucky
44. South Carolina
44. Arkansas
46. Louisiana
47. Texas
47. Tennessee
49. Alabama
50. Mississippi

State	SSI state supplements per recipient $	Rank
Alabama	10	37
Alaska	2,030	2
Arizona	7	40
Arkansas	0	41
California	1,957	4
Colorado	992	8
Connecticut	2,329	1
Delaware	81	31
Florida	58	34
Georgia	0	42
Hawaii	628	13
Idaho	267	23
Illinois	280	22
Indiana	45	36
Iowa	73	33
Kansas	0	45
Kentucky	110	30
Louisiana	0	47
Maine	260	24
Maryland	80	32
Massachusetts	1,050	6
Michigan	393	19
Minnesota	898	9
Mississippi	0	44
Missouri	0	47
Montana	1,974	3
Nebraska	287	21
Nevada	199	26
New Hampshire	1,010	7
New Jersey	533	15
New Mexico	7	38
New York	884	10
North Carolina	603	14
North Dakota	208	25
Ohio	0	43
Oklahoma	529	16
Oregon	445	18
Pennsylvania	517	17
Rhode Island	777	11
South Carolina	115	28
South Dakota	54	35
Tennessee	0	46
Texas	0	47
Utah	7	39
Vermont	765	12
Virginia	146	27
Washington	323	20
West Virginia	0	47
Wisconsin	1,131	5
Wyoming	114	29
50 States	595	
DC	260	
United States	588	

By $

1. Connecticut
2. Alaska
3. Montana
4. California
5. Wisconsin
6. Massachusetts
7. New Hampshire
8. Colorado
9. Minnesota
10. New York
11. Rhode Island
12. Vermont
13. Hawaii
14. North Carolina
15. New Jersey
16. Oklahoma
17. Pennsylvania
18. Oregon
19. Michigan
20. Washington
21. Nebraska
22. Illinois
23. Idaho
24. Maine
25. North Dakota
26. Nevada
27. Virginia
28. South Carolina
29. Wyoming
30. Kentucky
31. Delaware
32. Maryland
33. Iowa
34. Florida
35. South Dakota
36. Indiana
37. Alabama
38. New Mexico
39. Utah
40. Arizona
41. Arkansas
42. Georgia
43. Ohio
44. Mississippi
45. Kansas
46. Tennessee
47. Louisiana
47. Missouri
47. Texas
47. West Virginia

L-11 State Income Tax Liability Of Typical Family In Poverty, 1994

State	Income Tax liability	Rank
Alabama	273	5
Alaska	n/a	n/a
Arizona	0	22
Arkansas	85	14
California	0	22
Colorado	0	22
Connecticut	0	22
Delaware	185	10
Florida	n/a	n/a
Georgia	58	18
Hawaii	331	1
Idaho	0	22
Illinois	265	6
Indiana	300	3
Iowa	0	22
Kansas	0	22
Kentucky	307	2
Louisiana	35	20
Maine	0	22
Maryland	0	22
Massachusetts	293	4
Michigan	247	7
Minnesota	-357	39
Mississippi	0	22
Missouri	74	17
Montana	160	12
Nebraska	0	22
Nevada	n/a	n/a
New Hampshire	n/a	n/a
New Jersey	149	13
New Mexico	n/a	n/a
New York	-156	37
North Carolina	85	14
North Dakota	0	22
Ohio	49	19
Oklahoma	81	16
Oregon	212	8
Pennsylvania	0	22
Rhode Island	0	22
South Carolina	0	22
South Dakota	n/a	n/a
Tennessee	n/a	n/a
Texas	n/a	n/a
Utah	19	21
Vermont	-596	40
Virginia	191	9
Washington	n/a	n/a
West Virginia	176	11
Wisconsin	-312	38
Wyoming	n/a	n/a
50 States	n/a	
DC	n/a	
United States	n/a	

Rank in order

By

1. Hawaii
2. Kentucky
3. Indiana
4. Massachusetts
5. Alabama
6. Illinois
7. Michigan
8. Oregon
9. Virginia
10. Delaware
11. West Virginia
12. Montana
13. New Jersey
14. Arkansas
14. North Carolina
16. Oklahoma
17. Missouri
18. Georgia
19. Ohio
20. Louisiana
21. Utah
22. Arizona
22. California
22. Colorado
22. Connecticut
22. Idaho
22. Iowa
22. Kansas
22. Maine
22. Maryland
22. Mississippi
22. Nebraska
22. North Dakota
22. Pennsylvania
22. Rhode Island
22. South Carolina
37. New York
38. Wisconsin
39. Minnesota
40. Vermont

L-12 Child Support Collections, 1993

State	Total colections ($000)	Per capita collections $	Rank by per capita	
Alabama	87,824	21.0	29	1. Michigan
Alaska	39,946	66.8	2	2. Alaska
Arizona	60,658	15.4	41	3. Wisconsin
Arkansas	37,757	15.6	40	4. Ohio
California	436,077	14.0	43	5. Pennsylvania
Colorado	61,234	17.2	38	6. New Jersey
Connecticut	82,520	25.2	17	7. Delaware
Delaware	30,702	44.0	7	8. Maryland
Florida	282,006	20.5	30	9. Washington
Georgia	153,515	22.2	27	10. Minnesota
Hawaii	39,180	33.6	11	11. Hawaii
Idaho	24,383	22.2	28	12. Nebraska
Illinois	208,851	17.9	36	13. Maine
Indiana	n/a	n/a	n/a	14. Oregon
Iowa	56,115	19.9	31	15. New York
Kansas	48,493	19.1	34	16. Nevada
Kentucky	91,297	24.1	19	17. Connecticut
Louisiana	3,888	0.9	47	18. Massachusetts
Maine	38,149	30.8	13	19. Kentucky
Maryland	180,503	36.4	8	20. North Carolina
Massachusetts	149,439	24.8	18	21. Utah
Michigan	655,060	69.2	1	22. South Dakota
Minnesota	159,685	35.3	10	23. North Dakota
Mississippi	38,617	14.6	42	24. West Virginia
Missouri	120,207	23.0	25	25. Missouri
Montana	14,531	17.3	37	26. Tennessee
Nebraska	52,553	32.6	12	27. Georgia
Nevada	39,152	28.3	16	28. Idaho
New Hampshire	n/a	n/a	n/a	29. Alabama
New Jersey	372,977	47.5	6	30. Florida
New Mexico	15,812	9.8	44	31. Iowa
New York	515,376	28.4	15	32. South Carolina
North Carolina	166,842	24.0	20	33. Vermont
North Dakota	15,121	23.7	23	34. Kansas
Ohio	628,174	56.8	4	35. Rhode Island
Oklahoma	5,277	1.6	46	36. Illinois
Oregon	91,490	30.1	14	37. Montana
Pennsylvania	634,044	52.7	5	38. Colorado
Rhode Island	17,936	17.9	35	39. Texas
South Carolina	72,181	19.9	32	40. Arkansas
South Dakota	17,046	23.8	22	41. Arizona
Tennessee	115,068	22.6	26	42. Mississippi
Texas	298,568	16.6	39	43. California
Utah	44,430	23.9	21	44. New Mexico
Vermont	11,037	19.2	33	45. Wyoming
Virginia	n/a	n/a	n/a	46. Oklahoma
Washington	188,973	35.9	9	47. Louisiana
West Virginia	42,233	23.2	24	
Wisconsin	325,529	64.5	3	
Wyoming	3,971	8.4	45	
50 States	6,774,425	26.3		
DC	24,145	41.7		
United States	6,874,436	26.7		

State	Collections per dollar of costs $	Rank
Alabama	3.27	27
Alaska	3.71	23
Arizona	1.79	50
Arkansas	3.20	28
California	2.54	43
Colorado	2.47	44
Connecticut	3.19	30
Delaware	2.39	45
Florida	3.78	22
Georgia	4.47	12
Hawaii	3.79	21
Idaho	3.43	24
Illinois	2.36	47
Indiana	5.45	5
Iowa	5.14	7
Kansas	3.18	32
Kentucky	3.05	38
Louisiana	3.19	30
Maine	3.39	26
Maryland	4.56	10
Massachusetts	4.30	14
Michigan	8.29	2
Minnesota	4.20	16
Mississippi	2.20	49
Missouri	4.30	14
Montana	2.76	42
Nebraska	4.17	17
Nevada	2.39	45
New Hampshire	2.87	39
New Jersey	4.02	19
New Mexico	3.08	36
New York	3.10	34
North Carolina	3.20	28
North Dakota	4.05	18
Ohio	5.48	4
Oklahoma	3.13	33
Oregon	4.95	8
Pennsylvania	9.09	1
Rhode Island	4.35	13
South Carolina	3.88	20
South Dakota	4.90	9
Tennessee	5.42	6
Texas	2.31	48
Utah	2.86	40
Vermont	3.06	37
Virginia	4.50	11
Washington	3.09	35
West Virginia	3.42	25
Wisconsin	2.77	41
Wyoming	7.15	3
50 States	2.34	
DC	2.51	
United States	3.97	

By #

1. Pennsylvania
2. Michigan
3. Wyoming
4. Ohio
5. Indiana
6. Tennessee
7. Iowa
8. Oregon
9. South Dakota
10. Maryland
11. Virginia
12. Georgia
13. Rhode Island
14. Massachusetts
14. Missouri
16. Minnesota
17. Nebraska
18. North Dakota
19. New Jersey
20. South Carolina
21. Hawaii
22. Florida
23. Alaska
24. Idaho
25. West Virginia
26. Maine
27. Alabama
28. Arkansas
28. North Carolina
30. Connecticut
30. Louisiana
32. Kansas
33. Oklahoma
34. New York
35. Washington
36. New Mexico
37. Vermont
38. Kentucky
39. New Hampshire
40. Utah
41. Wisconsin
42. Montana
43. California
44. Colorado
45. Delaware
45. Nevada
47. Illinois
48. Texas
49. Mississippi
50. Arizona

State	Children in foster care #	% of children in foster care	Rank by %
Alabama	810	0.075	47
Alaska	303	0.160	37
Arizona	1,771	0.166	36
Arkansas	715	0.113	42
California	48,526	0.565	4
Colorado	2,521	0.269	15
Connecticut	1,482	0.191	26
Delaware	183	0.105	45
Florida	4,191	0.132	39
Georgia	3,254	0.177	31
Hawaii	368	0.123	40
Idaho	225	0.068	50
Illinois	11,349	0.370	8
Indiana	2,541	0.173	35
Iowa	1,502	0.205	24
Kansas	1,371	0.200	25
Kentucky	1,797	0.185	28
Louisiana	2,784	0.224	22
Maine	1,000	0.326	11
Maryland	3,073	0.248	16
Massachusetts	7,904	0.567	3
Michigan	8,672	0.346	9
Minnesota	3,607	0.294	13
Mississippi	868	0.115	41
Missouri	4,555	0.334	10
Montana	557	0.240	18
Nebraska	1,291	0.294	12
Nevada	621	0.176	32
New Hampshire	526	0.186	27
New Jersey	4,115	0.217	23
New Mexico	875	0.182	29
New York	53,475	1.197	1
North Carolina	2,985	0.175	33
North Dakota	402	0.234	20
Ohio	6,546	0.229	21
Oklahoma	1,379	0.159	38
Oregon	1,882	0.241	17
Pennsylvania	15,020	0.523	5
Rhode Island	673	0.286	14
South Carolina	1,652	0.174	34
South Dakota	225	0.108	44
Tennessee	6,533	0.515	6
Texas	4,920	0.095	46
Utah	454	0.068	49
Vermont	1,145	0.795	2
Virginia	1,778	0.112	43
Washington	2,484	0.178	30
West Virginia	1,017	0.234	19
Wisconsin	5,987	0.446	7
Wyoming	97	0.070	48
50 States	232,011	0.346	
DC	593	0.516	
United States	232,668	0.347	

Rank in order

By %

1. New York
2. Vermont
3. Massachusetts
4. California
5. Pennsylvania
6. Tennessee
7. Wisconsin
8. Illinois
9. Michigan
10. Missouri
11. Maine
12. Nebraska
13. Minnesota
14. Rhode Island
15. Colorado
16. Maryland
17. Oregon
18. Montana
19. West Virginia
20. North Dakota
21. Ohio
22. Louisiana
23. New Jersey
24. Iowa
25. Kansas
26. Connecticut
27. New Hampshire
28. Kentucky
29. New Mexico
30. Washington
31. Georgia
32. Nevada
33. North Carolina
34. South Carolina
35. Indiana
36. Arizona
37. Alaska
38. Oklahoma
39. Florida
40. Hawaii
41. Mississippi
42. Arkansas
43. Virginia
44. South Dakota
45. Delaware
46. Texas
47. Alabama
48. Wyoming
49. Utah
50. Idaho

State	Welfare spending per capita $	Welfare spending per $1000 personal income $	Rank per capita	Rank in order — By per capita
Alabama	451	25.6	34	1. New York
Alaska	707	30.5	10	2. New Hampshire
Arizona	479	25.8	29	3. Massachusetts
Arkansas	486	29.4	28	4. Maine
California	647	29.2	12	5. Minnesota
Colorado	427	19.3	39	6. Pennsylvania
Connecticut	756	26.3	7	7. Connecticut
Delaware	418	18.9	42	8. Rhode Island
Florida	394	18.4	45	9. New Jersey
Georgia	487	24.6	27	10. Alaska
Hawaii	511	21.7	24	11. Wisconsin
Idaho	347	19.0	50	12. California
Illinois	530	22.9	21	13. Vermont
Indiana	473	24.1	30	14. Kentucky
Iowa	497	26.4	25	15. Ohio
Kansas	359	17.4	47	16. West Virginia
Kentucky	635	36.1	14	17. Michigan
Louisiana	590	34.6	18	18. Louisiana
Maine	811	42.0	4	19. North Dakota
Maryland	547	22.3	20	20. Maryland
Massachusetts	843	33.4	3	21. Illinois
Michigan	595	28.2	17	22. Washington
Minnesota	802	37.1	5	23. Tennessee
Mississippi	443	28.9	37	24. Hawaii
Missouri	491	24.7	26	25. Iowa
Montana	426	24.2	40	26. Missouri
Nebraska	463	22.6	31	27. Georgia
Nevada	349	14.9	49	28. Arkansas
New Hampshire	872	37.5	2	29. Arizona
New Jersey	742	27.0	9	30. Indiana
New Mexico	458	27.3	33	31. Nebraska
New York	1,146	45.5	1	32. Oklahoma
North Carolina	431	22.4	38	33. New Mexico
North Dakota	575	32.2	19	34. Alabama
Ohio	629	31.3	15	35. Oregon
Oklahoma	463	26.8	32	36. South Carolina
Oregon	447	22.5	35	37. Mississippi
Pennsylvania	767	35.1	6	38. North Carolina
Rhode Island	752	34.9	8	39. Colorado
South Carolina	443	25.7	36	40. Montana
South Dakota	420	23.0	41	41. South Dakota
Tennessee	515	27.3	23	42. Delaware
Texas	408	20.8	44	43. Wyoming
Utah	365	21.9	46	44. Texas
Vermont	643	32.4	13	45. Florida
Virginia	359	16.3	48	46. Utah
Washington	528	23.7	22	47. Kansas
West Virginia	602	36.4	16	48. Virginia
Wisconsin	656	32.3	11	49. Nevada
Wyoming	415	20.8	43	50. Idaho
50 States	n/a	n/a		
DC	1,488	53.4		
United States	598	28.1		

State	Welfare Spending as % of total spending %	Rank	Rank in order By %
Alabama	14.7	28	1. New Hampshire
Alaska	7.3	50	2. Maine
Arizona	14.0	30	3. Massachusetts
Arkansas	17.9	10	4. New York
California	15.5	21	5. Pennsylvania
Colorado	11.9	39	6. Kentucky
Connecticut	16.5	15	7. West Virginia
Delaware	10.0	46	8. Ohio
Florida	11.4	43	9. Minnesota
Georgia	15.1	24	10. Arkansas
Hawaii	9.9	47	11. Tennessee
Idaho	11.7	41	12. Missouri
Illinois	15.4	22	13. Rhode Island
Indiana	15.0	25	14. Wisconsin
Iowa	13.9	31	15. Connecticut
Kansas	10.6	45	16. Louisiana
Kentucky	20.1	6	17. New Jersey
Louisiana	16.1	16	18. Vermont
Maine	21.6	2	19. Michigan
Maryland	15.1	23	20. Mississippi
Massachusetts	20.5	3	21. California
Michigan	15.8	19	22. Illinois
Minnesota	18.0	9	23. Maryland
Mississippi	15.6	20	24. Georgia
Missouri	17.2	12	25. Indiana
Montana	12.2	38	26. Oklahoma
Nebraska	13.5	33	27. North Dakota
Nevada	9.1	48	28. Alabama
New Hampshire	24.0	1	29. North Carolina
New Jersey	16.0	17	30. Arizona
New Mexico	12.4	37	31. Iowa
New York	20.4	4	32. South Carolina
North Carolina	14.1	29	33. Nebraska
North Dakota	14.7	27	34. South Dakota
Ohio	18.6	8	35. Texas
Oklahoma	14.9	26	36. Washington
Oregon	11.5	42	37. New Mexico
Pennsylvania	20.3	5	38. Montana
Rhode Island	17.1	13	39. Colorado
South Carolina	13.9	32	40. Utah
South Dakota	13.3	34	41. Idaho
Tennessee	17.4	11	42. Oregon
Texas	13.2	35	43. Florida
Utah	11.7	40	44. Virginia
Vermont	15.9	18	45. Kansas
Virginia	11.0	44	46. Delaware
Washington	12.8	36	47. Hawaii
West Virginia	18.8	7	48. Nevada
Wisconsin	16.7	14	49. Wyoming
Wyoming	7.9	49	50. Alaska
50 States	n/a		
DC	19.7		
United States	15.9		

State	Costs per case $	Rank	Rank in order By $
Alabama	468	37	1. New York
Alaska	759	13	2. New Jersey
Arizona	575	26	3. Oregon
Arkansas	498	34	4. Kansas
California	628	22	5. Minnesota
Colorado	575	27	6. Maryland
Connecticut	528	30	7. Idaho
Delaware	583	25	8. Nevada
Florida	657	19	9. Utah
Georgia	427	40	10. Oklahoma
Hawaii	455	38	11. Washington
Idaho	985	7	12. Rhode Island
Illinois	409	42	13. Alaska
Indiana	506	33	14. Wisconsin
Iowa	527	31	15. Montana
Kansas	1,045	4	16. New Hampshire
Kentucky	413	41	17. Michigan
Louisiana	236	49	18. Massachusetts
Maine	255	47	19. Florida
Maryland	1,033	6	20. North Dakota
Massachusetts	667	18	21. New Mexico
Michigan	676	17	22. California
Minnesota	1,037	5	23. Nebraska
Mississippi	249	48	24. South Dakota
Missouri	395	43	25. Delaware
Montana	721	15	26. Arizona
Nebraska	621	23	27. Colorado
Nevada	948	8	28. Vermont
New Hampshire	697	16	29. Virginia
New Jersey	1,263	2	30. Connecticut
New Mexico	629	21	31. Iowa
New York	1,280	1	32. Wyoming
North Carolina	483	36	33. Indiana
North Dakota	650	20	34. Arkansas
Ohio	351	44	35. Pennsylvania
Oklahoma	829	10	36. North Carolina
Oregon	1,232	3	37. Alabama
Pennsylvania	487	35	38. Hawaii
Rhode Island	771	12	39. Texas
South Carolina	331	45	40. Georgia
South Dakota	590	24	41. Kentucky
Tennessee	295	46	42. Illinois
Texas	454	39	43. Missouri
Utah	846	9	44. Ohio
Vermont	566	28	45. South Carolina
Virginia	532	29	46. Tennessee
Washington	792	11	47. Maine
West Virginia	160	50	48. Mississippi
Wisconsin	739	14	49. Louisiana
Wyoming	518	32	50. West Virginia
50 States	n/a		
DC	1,196		
United States	641		

Source Notes

POPULATION

A-1 Population, 1994: The U.S. population is counted every ten years by the U.S. Census Bureau. The last such count was in 1990. For all other years, the Census Bureau prepares estimates for July 1 of each year.

The 1994 estimates were released as a Census Bureau press release (CB 94-204) dated December 28, 1994. The estimates of 1995 population have been delayed because of the shutdown of federal offices in late 1995 and early 1996 because of debates over the federal budget.

Outside experts and the Census Bureau agree that the 1990 Census probably undercounted the nation's population by approximately five million people. This undercount was concentrated in low-income areas in major cities. The understatement of population is greatest for these communities and the states that contain them. Because population estimates are used to determine representation in Congress and how much state and local governments get from federal aid programs, some states and cities have gone to court seeking to force the federal government to use more correct estimates. The Census Bureau has resisted this because, while it agrees the official count is inaccurate, it does not know what data might be substituted for that count.

A-2 Population Change, 1993-1994: When the Census Bureau makes its annual estimates of population each year, it often changes the estimates for previous years. For example, the population changes shown are calculated from the 1994 and 1993 population estimates made in late 1994 (see source for A-1), not those made in late 1993.

A-3 Population Change, 1980-1994: The 1980 Census estimates are those of the 1980 Census, reflecting the count as of April 1, 1980.

A-4 Population Change, 1993-2005: The projections shown were made by the U.S. Department of Commerce in the *Survey of Current Business* (July 1995). Many private market research and economic forecasting firms also make population projections. The projections reflect recent trends, so Western states are predicted to gain population rapidly while the slowest growth appears in the Northeast and Midwest.

Projections for short periods are quite reliable because they are based on events that are predictable for large groups, such as the percentage of persons who will die each year and the percentage of women of child-bearing age who will have babies. Over longer periods, more guesswork is involved. Major economic shifts can be caused by changes in defense spending, fluctuations in oil and gas prices, and success or failure of particular firms or industries. Those shifts affect migration of workers and ultimately where they have children and die.

A-5 Population Estimate for the Year 2000: These estimates, from the same source as Table A-4, show major changes in the population ranking of states when compared with the 1994 estimates shown in Table A-1. If the estimates prove accurate, many southern and western states will gain seats in the House of Representatives when it is reapportioned after the Census taken in the year 2000.

A-6 Percentage of Population Over 65 Years Old, 1994: These Census Bureau estimates were provided to *State Fact Finder* in a Census Bureau tabulation on September 26, 1995.

Two kinds of states have the largest percentage of elderly citizens. First, there are states, like Florida and Arkansas, that draw large numbers of retirees from other states. Second, there are states with slow population growth, such as Pennsylvania, that lose many of their working-age younger people through migration to other states.

A-7 Percent of Population Aged 17 and Under, 1994: These estimates, from the same source as Table A-6, show the flip side of the high concentrations of elderly citizens shown in Table A-6. The highest ranking states, typified by Utah, have a large percentage of adults of child-bearing age and high birth rates.

A-8 Median Age, 1994: In each state, half the population was older than the age shown, while half was younger. This statistic, from the same source as Table

A-6, is a way to capture age differences among states in a single number for each state. The rankings are based on unrounded numbers.

A-9 African-American Population and Percent of State Population, 1992: Census takers ask citizens to identify their race. Nearly every respondent does this, using the Census Bureau categories, but not everyone classifies the same way the Census Bureau does. For example, "Hispanic" is not considered a race, so Hispanics are asked to classify themselves as "black" or "white." Regardless of how they classify themselves, most Americans are of mixed races, but this category is not recognized in the federal statistics.

The 1992 estimates come from the Census Bureau (press release CB 91-100, March 11, 1991). Estimates for other federally recognized racial groups are available from the Census Bureau. The "undercount" (see notes to Table A-1) means that statistics by race probably undercount African-Americans and Hispanics.

A-10 Hispanic Population and Percent of State Population, 1992: See notes to Table A-9. While the Census theoretically accounts for everyone resident in the country, illegal immigrants (many of whom are Hispanic) have an understandable fear of being identified by any government agency. Therefore, the count of this group is probably not very accurate.

A-11 Population in Poverty, 1994: The federal government has a uniform definition of the income families need to avoid poverty. The amount considered necessary varies with family size but not with rural or urban location or from state to state. The income used to calculate whether households are living in poverty does not include the value of noncash benefits, such as free medical care, provided to the poor under government programs.

The estimates shown are from a special Census Bureau tabulation provided to *State Fact Finder* on November 8, 1995. They are based in part on monthly household surveys of a small sample of the nation's population, not a full count. They reflect possible sampling errors, particularly for less populous states.

A-12 Poverty Rate for Related Children Aged 5-17, 1994: These statistics are from the same source, and subject to the same caveats, as similar data for persons of all ages in Table A-11. The percentage of children in poverty exceeds the percentage of all persons in poverty because households with children are often headed by a parent or parents in their early earning years and the income needed to avoid the poverty standard is higher for families with children than adults without children. Children not related to heads of households, such as foster children, are not included in this count.

A-13 Female Population, 1994: More than half of newly born children are male, but women tend to outlive men. The result is about equal numbers of each in the population as a whole, but disproportionate numbers of women in states with more aged population (see Table A-8). These data come from the Census

Bureau's Population Division Home Page on the Internet: *http://www.census.gov*

A-14 Birth Rates, 1994: These data show that 1.5 children are born each year for every 100 people. The birth rate is nearly 7 per 100 when only women of child-bearing age are considered. The data are Census Bureau estimates (press release CB 94-204, December 28, 1994).

A-15 Death Rates, 1994: These data show that there is just under one death each year for every 100 people. As would be expected, death rates are highest for the states with the oldest populations (see Table A-8). The data are from the same source as Table A-14.

A-16 Estimated Population Density, 1994: Although the Census Bureau only reports population density for Census years, the land area of states does not change. *State Fact Finder* calculated this table by taking the land area estimate from the 1990 Census (p. 360 of the *United States Summary*) and relating it to the 1994 population. The result is a rough measure of urban-rural characteristics of each state and is often cited as a proxy for possible crowding. However, in many states much of the land area is unusable for settlement because of lack of water, extraordinary low or high elevation, and other factors. Consequently, much of the population of a low-density state may in fact be densely packed in a few small areas.

A-17 Illegal Immigrant Population, 1994: Counting illegal immigrants, many of whom fear being counted, is inherently difficult. These estimates come from a Census Bureau working paper (*Illustrative Ranges of the Distribution of Undocumented Immigrants by State, 1994*). While the estimates may not be accurate, they are useful in illustrating the large differences among states.

ECONOMIES

B-1 Personal Income, 1994: These data reflect income of residents of each state, including pensions, dividends, interest, and rent as well as amount received from employers as wages and salaries. These estimates are made by the Department of Commerce each quarter. The calendar year 1994 estimates in the table first appeared in the *Survey of Current Business* (August 1995).

B-2 Gross State Product, 1992: The gross state product is the state counterpart of the gross national product (now called the gross domestic product). It is the sum of all the value of production of goods and services. While estimates of national data are released on a current basis, state-by-state estimates are made by the Department of Commerce only with a substantial lag. These 1992 data appeared in the *Survey of Current Business* (July 1995). This is the single best measure of the size of a state's economy.

B-3 Per Capita Personal Income, 1994: These data, from the same source as Table B-1, reflect personal income in relation to population. They are a common measure of the relative affluence of each state. The data are also used to determine what percentage the federal government pays of each state's welfare and Medicaid costs.

B-4 Percent of Personal Income from Wages and Salaries, 1994: These data show the portion of personal income (Table B-1) that comes from wages and salaries. The percentages indicate relative reliance of states' economies on current work, as distinct from investments and government payments.

B-5 Average Annual Pay, 1994: These data reflect the average pay of workers in each state. They are prepared by the Department of Labor. These were released in September 1995 as *Average Annual Pay by State and Industry, 1994*.

B-6 Average Hourly Earnings, 1994: These data are often used to compare wage costs of the states. They are prepared by the Department of Labor monthly and released in the publication *Employment and Earnings*. These October 1994 data appeared in the January 1995 edition. These data only cover production workers, excluding service and retailing employees as well as government employees.

B-7 Value Added in Manufacturing, 1991: This table measures the value that is added by manufacturing operations in each state. Value added is calculated by subtracting the value of inputs to production from the value of the outputs. For example, the value of manufacturing a car is the value of the car minus the value of components, such as engines, purchased to manufacture it. These data are available from the Census Bureau in the Annual Survey of Manufacturers. Value added per worker is sometimes used to compare the productivity of state work forces but is a misleading statistic because capital investments in machinery make massive contributions to adding values in highly automated operations such as chemical manufacturing.

B-8 Cost of Living, 1994: The federal government has not attempted to produce measures that compare living costs since the 1980s and, even then, provided the data only for selected large metropolitan areas, not states. Some researchers periodically try to produce such indices, but they are of doubtful statistical validity. The one shown is used in the 1995 report *The Federal Budget and the States, Fiscal Year 1994*, published jointly in 1995 by the offices of Sen. Daniel Patrick Moynihan (D-N.Y.) and the John F. Kennedy School of Government at Harvard.

B-9 Average Annual Pay in Manufacturing, 1994: This is the manufacturing component of the data described for Table B-5, from the same source. States with many jobs in high-wage industries, like chemical or vehicle manufacturing, rank highest.

B-10 Average Annual Pay in Retailing, 1994: This is the retailing component of the data described for Table B-5, from the same source. Because most retailing jobs are entry-level positions requiring little experience or formal training, these data are a good measure of the costs of obtaining new workers in the states.

B-11 Labor Force, 1995: The Department of Labor publishes these estimates in several different forms, including a monthly series covering the fifty states called *State and Metropolitan Area Employment and Unemployment*. The August 1995 publication of data for July 1995 was used for this table.

The labor force consists of all persons available for work, including those who are holding jobs and those who report they are seeking work but have not found it (the unemployed). It does not include another category of possible workers (called "discouraged workers") who say they want to work but have given up hope of finding a job. Labor force as a percentage of population varies with the percentage of population at working age and differences in the percentage of people who want to work (the labor force participation rate). Population data is for 1994 and comes from the Census Bureau (see Table A-1).

National estimates of the labor force, employment, and unemployment rates come from monthly surveys of a sample of the national population. For its estimates for smaller states, the Department of Labor has been using a different estimating method. As a result, the totals of state data (including those reflected in this table) are not always identical to reported national data.

B-12 Unemployed and Unemployment Rate, 1995: These data, using the same source and concepts as Table B-11, show the number of unemployed persons and the percentage of the labor force unemployed.

B-13 Employment and Employment Rate, 1995: These data, using the same source as Table B-11, show the number of employed persons on nonfarm payrolls and the percentage of the nonfarm labor force employed. Because farmers are not counted in the employment numbers, the figures in this table do not combine perfectly with the figures in Table B-12 to equal the total labor force in Table B-11.

B-14 Government Employment, 1995: Statistics on government employment for particular functions, such as education, and on number and pay of government workers come from the Department of Commerce based on surveys of governments. They lag reality by a considerable period. For example, the latest available data from this source in early 1996 covered October of 1992.

To count employment for the report described in B-11, the Labor Department must estimate employment in each field, including government. The data show the result. All levels of government—state, federal, and local—are covered by these estimates.

B-15 Manufacturing Employment, 1995: These data are comparable to those shown in Table B-14, but cover manufacturing.

B-16 Fortune 500 Companies, 1995: The three major business magazines—*Business Week, Fortune,* and *Forbes*—provide annual listings of the largest companies in America, using somewhat different criteria. This table reflects the list as published in *Fortune*

(May 15, 1995). Because large states tend to have the most large companies, the rankings are based on a calculation of the representation of these companies' headquarters in each state in relation to population of that state.

B-17 Business Week 1000 Companies, 1995: This table is the counterpart of Table B-17, relying on an unpublished compilation of states where these companies are located that was provided by *Business Week*.

B-18 Tourism Spending, 1993: The travel industry is unquestionably a major factor in the economies of all states and a dominant factor in a few. However, data on it are elusive. Many trips combine business and pleasure, so separating tourism from business is difficult. Other trips combine an activity, such as coming home for Christmas, with a tourist activity, such as visiting a museum. Restaurants and gift shops do not normally know whether their customers are tourists or local customers. Consequently, estimates of tourism spending have more guesswork than most of the statistics in *State Fact Finder*. The 1993 data shown in the table are estimates provided by the Travel Industry Association of America.

B-19 Export-Related Jobs, 1991: National estimates of exports are made currently and quarterly by the Department of Commerce to develop estimates of gross domestic product and balance of payments with other nations. Relatively current estimates by state are also made by the Commerce Department but are of doubtful reliability because of data-gathering limitations and conceptual problems. For example, does a shipment from a New York port of a product from an Ohio plant of items made from components from Ohio and Mississippi contained in boxes produced in South Carolina constitute an export from New York, Ohio, or where? The data shown come from the Census Bureau's special report, *Exports From Manufacturing Establishments,* and cover only exports of manufactured products, not exports of services.

B-20 Housing Permits, 1994: No state-by-state reporting system exists to report completion of single-family houses and apartment and condominium units, but there are good data on the issuance of permits for such construction. Although some builders will obtain permits and then not build the units, permits are expensive so most permits are followed by construction. The data shown were compiled by the National Association of Home Builders. The relationship to population shows which states have rapidly growing populations and which are more stagnant.

B-21 Change in Price of Existing Homes, 1991-1994: Most people who are interested in changes in housing prices are interested because of interest in the implications of the changes for a specific existing home—usually the one they own. The data often cited in the media, which come from realtors' sales records, come from averages of homes sold. As a result, they include large percentages of new (and typically larger,

better equipped, and more expensive) homes in fast-growing states than in other states. A preferable way to measure price changes is to examine prices for successive sales of the same homes. This has recently become possible with improvements in computing capacity and the increasing importance of secondary mortgage lenders, who buy massive numbers of mortgages from banks and other lenders. The data in the table reflect this approach, which cannot be followed reliably for states with few home sales. The information comes from the federally sponsored agency, known in the industry as Freddie Mac, in its *Mortgage Market Review 1995.*

B-22 Net Farm Income, 1994: These data reflect the net income derived from farming—the value of farm sales minus the cost of production. They are estimates made by the Department of Agriculture and published in *Agricultural Income & Finance* (September 1995). The *State Fact Finder* calculation of per capita amounts provides an excellent basis for comparing the importance of agriculture to the economies of each state.

B-23 Financial Institution Assets, 1994: This table shows total assets of banks and trust companies. These data, from the Federal Deposit Insurance Corporation's *Statistics on Banking: 1994,* provide a good measure of the importance of banking in each state. However, they provide no indication of the wealth of individuals in a state as deposits flow freely across state lines. States that have successfully tried to draw financial institutions, like Delaware and South Dakota, show large per capita amounts, as do regional banking centers, such as the Boston banks that serve customers throughout New England.

B-24 Bankruptcy Filings, 1994: These data, from the Administrative Office of the U.S. Courts, show how the over 800,000 new bankruptcy cases (mostly individuals rather than businesses) were distributed among the states.

B-25 Patents Issued, 1994: The U.S. Patent Office issued about 65,000 new patents in 1994 to residents (both corporations and individuals) in the states shown. When related to population, this statistic is often used to compare states in the degree to which they are on the forefront of new technology.

B-26 Workers' Compensation Temporary Total Disability Payments, 1995: All states maintain a program that provides compensation for workers who are injured on the job. These programs differ massively from state to state in how much money is paid for certain injuries, how hard it is to prove disability and its relationship to the job, and how employers are forced to pay program costs. These differences, set by state policy, are not captured by aggregate statistics on Workers' Compensation costs because some industries (like construction and logging) are inherently more hazardous than others (like banking), so state-by-state costs will vary with the mix of industries. This table compares one major dimension of benefit generosity/parsimony, the maximum payment per month to a worker who is temporarily unable to work because of a job-related injury. The data come from the Department of Labor publication, *State Workers' Compensation Laws*.

B-27 Average Weekly Unemployment Compensation Benefit, 1994: All states maintain a federally supervised program of Unemployment Compensation. States have wide discretion in determining how large unemployment compensation payments will be, how long they will last, and how costs are distributed among employers. This table, from a computer run furnished by the Department of Labor, shows the average weekly benefit payable in each state.

B-28 Index of State Economic Momentum, 1995: Each quarter *State Policy Reports* publishes its Index of State Economic Momentum as a way to compare the recent economic performance of each state in relation to the national average. A state growing at the national average rate would show an Index of 0.0 while one growing roughly 1 percent faster would show an Index of 1.0. Negative numbers show states lagging behind national average growth. The index combines (with equal weights) the most recent known one-year changes in (1) employment, (2) personal income, and (3) population.

B-29 Employment Change, 1994-1995: This table uses Department of Labor data from June of 1994 and 1995 to show the change in the number of jobs in each state. The data, from the July 1995 edition of *State and Metropolitan Area Unemployment and Unemployment*, are one component of the momentum index shown in Table B-28.

B-30 Manufacturing Employment Change, 1994-1995: This table uses Department of Labor data from August 1994 to August 1995 (not seasonally adjusted) to show the states experiencing job loss and those experiencing job growth in manufacturing. These data are released monthly and revised often, but differences in state economic performance tend to persist from month to month.

B-31 Home Ownership, 1990: These data show the percentage of households living in homes they own. The data come from the 1990 Census. No reliable update will be available until the next Census is taken in 2000.

B-32 Gambling, 1994: Legal gambling establishments in the United States received bets of $36 billion in 1994—$139 per person, including people who do not gamble at all. The distribution of these revenues among the states is shown in the table, reflecting estimates made in *International Gaming & Wagering Business* (August 1995).

These statistics dealing with the revenues of gaming establishments provide one indication of the amount of gambling activity. However, they should not be confused with amounts bet. While gamblers lose, on average, about 55 cents for every dollar spent on state lotteries and 20 cents for every dollar at horse tracks, they only lose about 2 cents of what they bet at casino table games and about 5 cents at slot machines. So, the same dollar is, in effect, bet many times before it is lost. *Gaming & Wagering* has much more detailed estimates of gambling by state and type of gambling, as well as information on gambling taxes and revenues of gambling establishments.

B-33 Average Annual Electricity Use Per Residential Customer, 1993: These data from the Edison Electric Institute show differences in electricity use among the states. The results are heavily influenced by the relative importance of heating and air conditioning and the mix of fuels used for heating.

B-34 Average Revenue Per Kilowatt Hour, 1993: These data also come from the Edison Electric Institute, which maintains additional details on other years, types of consumers, and more. The data have many uses. The revenue per kilowatt hour permits comparisons among states of electricity costs for households and businesses. The residential rate as a percentage of industrial rate is a useful indicator of the extent to which state regulatory policy (which controls rate charged by private companies) is tilted toward providing low industrial rates to stimulate economic development or low residential rates to keep prices low for voter/consumers at the potential expense of loss of industry. Based on costs of service, industrial users should pay less because they are cheaper per kilowatt to bill and often agree to have service curtailed when there is a shortage of power.

B-35 New Companies, 1993: These data show the number of companies that applied for new account numbers from state employment services related to the total number of workers in each state. It is collected by the U.S. Department of Labor and reported by the Corporation for Enterprise Development in its *1995 Economic Development Report Card for the States*.

GEOGRAPHY/ENVIRONMENT/ RECREATION

C-1 Total Land Area, 1990: This statistic comes from the geography division of the Bureau of the Census. It can be combined with population to calculate the population "density" of each state (see Table A-16).

C-2 Land Owned by Federal Government, 1991: The federal government owns land for its buildings, military installations, and other facilities in every state, but these holdings are not major factors in the land use patterns of most states. The federal government also owns massive areas as part of the National Park Service and the Forest Service, and public lands managed by the U.S. Department of the Interior, primarily arid lands in Western states. These federal land holdings, measured in land area—not land usefulness—are more than half of the land in some states. The data are maintained by the individual federal agencies that own the land and appear in the *Statistical Abstract of the United States*.

C-3 State Park Acreage, 1993: These statistics show the acres of state parks and the number of acres of state parks per 1,000 people. The areas are reported by the

National Association of State Park Directors. The ratio was calculated for *State Fact Finder*.

C-4 State Park Visitors, 1993: State park agencies make estimates of the number of visitors to state parks maintained by the National Association of State Park Directors. *State Fact Finder* related these visits to population using Census data. The data can be viewed as indicating that the average person visits a state park about 2.8 times a year.

C-5 Exercisers at Clubs, 1994: There are few reliable data on a state level on the participation of citizens in various forms of recreational activities, as no one maintains records of who hikes, plays tennis, or fishes except when they use facilities requiring admission. Estimates by state are made by the National Sporting Goods Association (Mt. Prospect, Illinois 60056) for all major recreation activities. This table, covering those who participated in some form of exercise (for example, on exercise machines) at clubs, is indicative of such data. It shows the estimated number of participants and relates the number to the population of each state.

C-6 Hunters with Firearms, 1994: These data, from the same source as Table C-5, show the sharp differences among states in the use of firearms for hunting—statistics highly relevant to debates over use and control of firearms. Note that participants in hunting in a particular state may not be residents of that state.

C-7 Registered Boats, 1994: All states require registration of motorboats and some require registration of other boats, such as canoes and sailboats. These data, collected from state authorities by the U.S. Coast Guard, show the number of registered boats and the relationship between the number of boats and population.

C-8 State Spending for the Arts, 1994: The federal government subsidizes arts programs in the states and encourages states to do the same. This table measures state support in fiscal 1994 using data collected by the National Assembly of State Arts Agencies, as published in *State Legislatures* (May 1995).

C-9 Energy Consumption Total and Per Capita, 1993: At the time of the "energy crisis" of the 1970s, the federal government established a Department of Energy (DOE) and a vast data collection mechanism covering production and consumption of all forms of energy, including coal, oil, gas, and nuclear power. This table from the Energy Information Administration (EIA) of the DOE shows total energy consumption and relates it to the population of each state.

These data show consumption by all users, including businesses, by the state where energy is used, not necessarily where it was produced. States with relatively small populations and intensive energy use for mining and petrochemical manufacturing show the largest use. The EIA has detailed data by state on sources of energy and use in categories, such as residential and industrial.

C-10 Toxic Chemical Release, 1993: The U.S. Environmental Protection Administration requires detailed reporting of what it defines as "toxic" chemical releases into the atmosphere. These data, from the *1993 Toxics Release Inventory*, are frequently cited by the media as indicators of health risks and air pollution in particular states. They are of little value for this purpose. The effects of releases in a particular state often are not felt in that state because they are carried to an adjacent state or the oceans. High totals are generally associated with a few plants, whose owners argue that their releases are not hazardous to health.

C-11 Hazardous Waste Sites, 1995: This table shows the number of sites the Environmental Protection Administration has designated for cleanup under the Superfund program. The program and the designations are highly controversial, but the data are often cited as indicators of the relative prevalence of hazardous waste problems in particular states.

C-12 Miles of Polluted Rivers and Streams, 1992: Under federal water pollution laws, each state reports to the Environmental Protection Agency on the status of its rivers, specifically whether they are safe for fishing (and eating the catch) and swimming. Because this assessment includes the total river-miles assessed and the number of miles not suitable for such uses, State Policy Research could make the arithmetic calculation of the percentage of river miles polluted, which is used to rank states in the table. The data come from the EPA's *National Water Quality Inventory: 1992 Report to Congress*.

This table and other available measures of the pollution of rivers are not particularly useful for many purposes. Any compilation of river-miles includes many stretches in remote locations that are of little use for swimming or fishing because of inaccessibility, low flows, few fish, and insufficient depth for swimming. There is no statistic that allows comparing states on a basis more reflective of the extent to which pollution prevents safe fishing and swimming in relation to the fishing and swimming that would occur if there were no pollution at all.

C-13 Surface Water Pollution Discharges, 1994: This statistic, prepared by the Environmental Protection Agency and compiled by the Corporation for Enterprise Development for its *1995 Development Report Card for the States*, provides a measure of pollution discharged into surface waters, such as lakes and streams, without compliance with established water quality standards.

C-14 Air Quality Scores, 1995: Based on information from the Environmental Protection Agency Office of Air Quality Planning and Standards, these scores were developed by the Corporation for Enterprise Development for its *1995 Development Report Card for the States*. The underlying data cover a variety of years of observation. The scores and ranks represent about the best summary measure of air quality that can be used to compare states. However, for purposes of locating new sites or finding a nonpolluted state in which to live, the relevant concept is an airshed, not a state. Within each state, there are dramatic differences in pollution levels associated with such factors as proximity to prevailing winds and pollution sources and elevation.

GOVERNMENT

D-1 Members of U.S. House, 1992: Each state is allocated two senators and representation in the House of Representatives based on population, as determined by the Census, which is taken in every year ending in zero (for example, 1990, 2000). The data in the table list the number of House seats as of 1992. This allocation will prevail for the remainder of the decade.

D-2 Members of State Legislatures, 1995: Like the Congress, state legislatures—except Nebraska's one-House legislature—have an upper and lower house, generally called senates and assemblies. These data come from the organization of legislators nationwide, the National Conference of State Legislatures.

D-3 Legislators Per 100,000 Population: Some small population states, like New Hampshire, have large legislatures. Some large states, like California, have relatively small ones. This table highlights the differences.

D-4 Units of Government, 1992: There are more than 80,000 units of government in the United States, including counties, cities, towns, townships, school districts, and special districts that provide water, maintain sewage systems, build and maintain roads, control mosquitoes, and more. There are so many that they are only counted every five years in the Census Bureau's Census of Governments, the most recent of which was in 1992.

D-5 Legislators' Compensation, 1995: These data show the major sources of cash compensation of legislators, annual salaries and per diem amounts. The data are drawn from the National Conference of State Legislatures' extensive compilation *Compensation and Benefits for State Legislators.* Comparisons of legislative pay from state-to-state are nearly impossible. Some states pay their legislators like most employers pay their employees—a regular salary plus reimbursement of employment-related travel expenses while on official business away from the normal place of work. In addition, because most legislators live in their districts, they are paid expenses when staying overnight in the state capitol. Some states compensate legislators at a per diem rate, often adding an expense allowance that can exceed expenses actually incurred. Additionally, some legislatures provide extra pay for committee chairpersons and legislative leaders.

Pensions for legislative service are nonexistent or negligible in some states, while pension and other benefits, such as employer-paid health care, are an important part of legislative compensation in other states.

D-6 Percentage of Legislators Who Are Female, 1995: The percentage of legislators who are women passed 20 percent in 1993 from less than 10 percent in the 1970s and less than 5 percent in the 1960s. The percentages for each state were calculated by the Center for the American Woman and Politics, Eagleton Institute of Politics, at Rutgers University.

D-7 Turnover in Legislatures, 1995: This table, from the National Conference of State Legislatures, shows the percentage of state legislators taking office after the November 1994 election who were newly elected. Nationwide about 80 percent of legislators in the 1995 sessions were in their second or subsequent terms. This percentage is likely to drop as limits on legislative terms take effect in an increasing number of states. A few states with low percentages did not have legislative elections in 1994.

D-8 Term Limits, 1995: This table, from the National Conference of State Legislatures, shows the maximum number of consecutive years governors and legislators can serve. The states shown with no limits allow elected officials to serve as long as voters approve. The states are ranked, with many ties, somewhat arbitrarily; those with the shortest allowable terms for members of their lower house are ranked highest.

D-9 Legislative Session Length: Many states have constitutional limits on the length of time the legislature meets in its regular sessions. Those shown in the table show the two principal forms of limits: those on calendar days (for example, a sixty-day limit would be about two months) and those on legislative days (days actually in session, so a sixty-day limit could result in three months in session, meeting four days a week). Many of the states with short sessions exercise the option of having special sessions called by the legislative leadership or governor. These data were compiled from reviews of state constitutions by the Council of State Governments and printed in the Council's volume *The Book of The States, 1994-1995.*

It is difficult to compare the varying practices of the states. To make this comparison, *State Fact Finder* used the average of two years for states with different limits on odd and even numbered years and assumed that every five legislative days equals seven calendar days.

D-10 Party Control of State Legislatures, 1995: These data, developed by the National Conference of State Legislatures shortly after the 1994 election, show the party affiliation of legislators taking office in 1995. The states are ranked by the percentage of Democrats (reading top to bottom) or Republicans (bottom to top) in the combined legislative houses. S represents a split in party control.

D-11 Governors' Performance Ratings, 1994: This table presents the results of a special study by Dr. Thad Beyle of the University of North Carolina (Chapel Hill), published in the Winter 1995 edition of *State and Local Government Review.* The ranking is an equally weighted composite of governors' performance ratings in public opinion polls and assessments by experts identified in each state by Beyle. These ratings are not necessarily ''right'' because not everyone agrees on what governors should and should not be doing.

D-12 Number of Statewide Elected Officials, 1994: The federal pattern of holding nationwide elections for only the chief executive and running mate (president and vice president) is not followed by the states. States often elect the attorneys general, secretaries of state, comptrollers, treasurers, and auditors. The count in the table, made from *The Book of the States*, excludes judges, who are also elected in many states.

D-13 State and Local Government Employees, 1992: These statistics, from the Census Bureau's *Public Employment 1992*, express the full-time equivalent of part-time workers plus full-time workers in state and local governments and relate the totals to population.

D-14 State and Local Average Salaries, 1992: These statistics, from the Census Bureau's *Public Employment 1992*, show annual average state and local government salaries, which were obtained by multiplying compensation in October 1992 by twelve.

D-15 Local Employment, 1992: The count of local employees identified in the Census Bureau's *Public Employment 1992* is substantially larger than the number of state employees. The table shows the percentage of local employees.

D-16 Local Spending Accountability, 1992: Since 1970 there has been a massive growth in both federal and state aid to local governments. As a result, local officials finance over one-third of what they spend with money they do not raise by their own local taxes and fees. Critics say this encourages government spending to be excessive because the elected officials who spend the money do not have to account to taxpayers for raising it. The Wisconsin Taxpayers Association has dubbed this difference "the accountability gap." The table shows a measure of this gap, as calculated by State Policy Research using data from the Census Bureau.

The numbers reflect (1) the percentage of their spending local officials raised and (2) the percentage they did not raise. New Hampshire ranks last by this measure because it has uniquely low state taxes (with no state sales or income tax) and only minor state aid programs by comparison with other states.

D-17 Percentage of Eligible Voters Registered, November 1994: These data, collected from the Census Bureau through the Internet, show the percentage of persons presumably eligible to vote in each state, based on the voting age population in relation to the number who have complied with that state's requirements to vote (that is, becoming and staying registered as voters).

D-18 Percentage of Population Voting in November 1994: Not all persons legally old enough to vote actually do so. The table shows the percentage who actually voted in the elections of November 1994. It comes from a Census Bureau tabulation available on the Internet.

D-19 Statewide Initiatives, 1981-1990: In most states, voters select candidates to make policy for them as legislators but never vote directly on policy except when changes in the state constitution are being made. Some states allow "direct democracy," including allowing voters to put up a measure for popular vote by collecting a minimum number of signatures (voter initiatives). This tabulation shows the number of such initiatives on state ballots between 1981 and 1990. The numbers reflect (1) whether initiatives are permitted in the state; (2) the difficulty of putting measures on the ballot, as affected by the number for signatures required and other factors in the constitutions of each state; and (3) voter interest in making state policy by this direct democracy approach.

FEDERAL IMPACTS

E-1 Federal Spending, 1994: The federal government affects state economies and state finances through its massive spending, accounting for nearly one-quarter of all economic activity in the United States. The primary components of that spending are grants to state and local governments; payments to individuals, such as Social Security; wages and salaries of federal employees; and purchases of goods and services, such as weapons for the Defense Department. Details of where these funds are spent are compiled by federal agencies and summarized by the Census Bureau in *Federal Government Expenditures by State*. Many tables in this section reflect the latest version of this report, covering federal spending in fiscal 1994, which for the federal government ended in September 1994.

This table reflects total federal spending of $1.3 trillion, along with the results of dividing each state's total by its population to permit meaningful comparisons among states. The federal figures exclude certain forms of federal spending that cannot reasonably be associated with particular states, primarily interest on the federal debt and money spent in other countries.

E-2 Increase in Total Federal Spending, 1989-1994: This table uses the Census reports for federal fiscal years 1989 and 1994 to show the percentage change in total federal spending in each state over a five-year period.

E-3 Federal Grants to State and Local Governments, 1994: This table reflects the federal spending for grants that help state and local governments finance welfare, Medicaid, highway construction, and other activities. The data come from the federal report described in the notes to Table E-1.

E-4 Federal Spending Per Capita on Procurement, 1994: This table reflects the federal spending for purchases ranging from tanks and space shuttles to gasoline for federal vehicles. The data come from the federal report described in the notes to Table E-1.

E-5 Federal Spending on Payments to Individuals, 1994: This table reflects the federal spending for payments to individuals. The primary components are Social Security pensions, Medicare payments to health care providers, pensions for retired federal workers, and Food Stamps. The data come from the federal report described in the notes to Table E-1.

E-6 Federal Spending Per Capita on Social Security and Medicare, 1994: This table reflects the federal spending for Social Security pensions and Medicare payments to health care providers. This spending is a part of the total covered by Table E-5. The per capita amounts suggest the massive impact that this flow of funds has among states. While revenues from payroll taxes are concentrated in states that are showing strong economic growth, states with slower growth (primarily those in the Northeast) receive large portions of personal income from these retirement-related federal payments and private pensions.

E-7 Social Security Benefits Paid, December 1993: This table provides another perspective on Social Security payments, using tabulations for December 1993 payments prepared by the Social Security Administration. This agency can provide additional details on benefits paid in each state, such as the amounts paid to retired workers, to deceased workers' beneficiaries, and to workers and their families based on disability. Besides the amounts paid and number of recipient households, the table shows the average benefit per household. This amount is appreciably higher in states where salaries have been high (such as in the Northeast) than where they have been low (such as in the South).

E-8 Federal Spending on Employee Wages and Salaries, 1994: This table reflects the federal spending on payments for salaries of civilian and military federal employees. The largest amounts are found in states with major federal installations, such as military bases. Because the Postal Service is included and some agencies, such as the Department of Agriculture, operate in every state, even states without major installations show substantial federal spending.

E-9 Federal Grant Spending Per Dollar of State Tax Revenue, 1993: Most federal grant spending is now concentrated on state administered programs, such as welfare and Medicaid. The amounts are substantial when compared with the amount that states raise from state taxes, as shown by the table, which relates the amounts provided by federal grants to the amounts states raised from taxes. The data from fiscal 1993 are collected by the Census Bureau for publication in *State Government Finances, 1993*. The numbers in the table were calculated from preliminary Census data by the Center for the Study of the States.

E-10 State and Local General Revenue from Federal Government, 1992: These data, covering both state and local government, show the amount of federal aid contributing to "general revenue" as defined by the Census Bureau in its annual survey of government finances. It excludes certain trust funds, such as Unemployment Insurance, but includes others, such as those used for highway construction. The data are calculated from *Government Finances in 1992*.

E-11 Federal Tax Burden, Per Capita, 1995: This table shows where the burdens of federal taxes fell in federal fiscal year 1995. The data come from the Tax Foundation, which uses formulas to spread the burden of certain taxes, such as the corporate income tax, among states and actual data from federal tax collectors to show the sources of major tax revenues, such as those from personal income and payroll taxes.

E-12 Federal Spending Per Dollar of Taxes Paid, 1994: These data relate how much taxpayers in each state pay in federal taxes to the amounts the federal government spends in each state. The information comes from calculations by the Tax Foundation using allocations of tax burdens (see Table E-11) and the Census Bureau report on federal spending (see Table E-1). Many states get more than a dollar back in federal spending for every dollar sent to the federal government in taxes. This occurs primarily in states where federal installations and/or purchasing is concentrated. Because a substantial portion of federal spending is financed by borrowing (deficit spending), the nationwide total would show more money returned as spending than paid as taxes, so the Tax Foundation adjusted spending to eliminate the deficit-financed portion.

E-13 Percent Highway Charges Returned to States, 1993: Federal spending for highways is financed by special "user charges," such as federal taxes on gasoline and diesel fuel. This table is parallel to Table E-12 but covers only highway spending. It was developed by the Federal Highway Administration in its *1993 Highway Statistics*.

E-14 Terms of Trade with the Federal Government, 1994: This table was developed by State Policy Research to show the relationship between amounts paid by taxpayers in each state to the federal grants to state and local government financed by their federal taxes. The table shows federal grants, identical to the amounts shown in Table E-3. Because all grants, even those paid currently out of money the federal government raises by borrowing, are ultimately paid for by taxpayers, the total federal tax revenue to pay for grants was stipulated as equal to the grants for the fifty states and the District of Columbia. To determine how this tax burden to pay for grants was distributed among states, the total tax burden for grants was allocated based on the percentage of all federal taxes paid by citizens and corporations in each state, using the Tax Foundation's logic (also used to prepare Table E-11). The result is that the sum of grants and of taxes are identical for the fifty states plus the District of Columbia.

However, the amounts are by no means equal for individual states. States with relatively high personal incomes (and thus federal tax liabilities) but low grants will show ratios below one. Conceptually, for example, 0.95 can be considered as getting 95 cents back in grants for every dollar in federal taxes paid, or a 95 percent return. Conversely, states with lower incomes and high grants will show a ratio above one.

E-15 Federal Personal Income Taxes, 1993: This table shows how much households in each state were required to pay in federal income taxes on their income during 1993, as reported in tax returns filed in early 1994. The data are from the Internal Revenue Service as reported in the *SOI Bulletin* (Summer 1995).

E-16 Federal Share of Welfare and Medicaid, 1995: The federal grants to states for welfare (AFDC) and Medicaid are based on multiplying the total costs of these programs by the federal cost-sharing percentages shown in the table. The formula used to determine each state's share provides the largest federal shares for the states with the lowest per capita incomes. A special rule overrides the calculation for more affluent states, so no state has less than 50 percent of these costs paid by the federal government. The information comes from the federal agencies that administer these grants.

TAXES

F-1 State and Local Tax Revenue, 1992: This is the most common definition of the tax burdens of state and local governments. It is the tax component of "general revenue" used by the Census Bureau in its annual survey of government finances. It excludes taxes used to finance certain trust funds, such as Unemployment Insurance taxes, but includes other earmarked revenues, such as gasoline tax revenues for highway construction. Tax revenues are related to personal income as a common proxy for tax base or "ability to pay."

F-2 Total State and Local Tax Revenue, Per Capita, 1992: This table relates total tax revenue (see F-1) to population, providing another measure of relative tax burdens. It also shows the division of tax revenues between state and local governments in each state.

F-3 State and Local Tax Effort, 1991: The revenue-raising ability of states and their local governments varies markedly among the states. For example, Alaska and Texas get massive revenues by taxing oil and gas exploration and Nevada gets large revenues from taxing casino gambling, but most states get no revenue from these sources. What states will collect from particular tax rates applied to property, sales, and income is higher in states with more affluent citizens. Because of these differences, the revenue collected (see F-1 and F-2) is not a good indicator of how high tax rates are in each state.

A more appropriate way to compare the relative burden of state and local taxes, or what is often called "tax effort," is to consider what each state would raise if it and its local government applied national average tax rates to their own tax bases. This approach, known as the "representative tax system," has been pioneered by the Advisory Commission on Intergovernmental Relations. Its most recent publication, *State Revenue Capacity and Tax Effort,* was based on Census data for 1991.

The values reflect differences in tax effort. For example, New York state and local governments have taxes that raise 56 percent more than would be raised

if tax rates in that state were equal to the national average.

F-4 State and Local Tax Capacity, 1991: The representative tax system (see F-3) also permits a comparison of the tax base, or fiscal capacity, of individual states. This is presented in what can be viewed either as percentages of the national average or as index numbers. Either way, the table indicates, for example, that if it applied national average tax rates, Alabama would raise only 81 percent of the amount that those same rates would in the average state.

F-5 Change in State and Local Taxes, 1987-1992: In the five years covered by the table, the Census Bureau reports for each year indicate that state and local tax revenues have increased by about 37 percent. However, growth has been much faster in some states than others.

F-6 Property Taxes and Per $1000 Personal Income, 1992: This and subsequent tables deal with the total revenues raised by particular state and local taxes. They start with the revenues from that tax as indicated by the Census Bureau report, *Government Finances in 1992.* That revenue is then related to both population and personal income to provide the two most common measures of the level, or burdens, of that tax in each state.

F-7 Property Taxes, Per Capita, 1992: See note for Table F-6.

F-8 Property Tax Revenues as Percent of Three-Tax Revenues, 1992: Some people feel that their total state and local taxes are too high while others may not be sure about total tax burdens but feel that a particular revenue source, such as property taxes, is too heavily used in their state. This table, using Census data, relates the amount raised from taxing property with the amounts raised from the other two major tax bases — sales and income.

F-9 Sales Taxes and Per $1000 of Personal Income, 1992: See note for Table F-6.

F-10 Sales Taxes, Per Capita, 1992: See note for Table F-6.

F-11 Sales Tax Revenues as Percent of Three-Tax Revenues, 1992: See note for Table F-8.

F-12 Number of Services Reached by Sales Tax, 1992: Sales taxes of state and local governments typically apply to goods, such as cars and clothing, but not to services, such as barbering and landscaping. Many experts suggest that the sales tax would be fairer and a more productive revenue source if it applied equally to both sales and services. This table summarizes a comprehensive study by the Federation of Tax Administrators (*Sales Taxation of Services: An Update, 1994*) showing the number of services taxed by the sales tax in each state. It includes states, such as Oregon, that have no general sales tax and ones, such as Alaska, that may have special excise taxes on a few services.

F-13 Individual Income Taxes and Per $1000 Personal Income, 1992: See note for Table F-6.

F-14 Individual Income Taxes, Per Capita, 1992: See note for Table F-6.

F-15 Individual Income Tax Revenues as Percent of Three-Tax Revenues, 1992: See note for Table F-8.

F-16 Highest Personal Income Tax Rate, 1994: While some states have no income taxes at all, the rates paid by high-income households can go as high as 10 percent in a few. This table, developed by State Policy Research from compilations of state tax laws, shows the highest state personal income rate. In most states, this "marginal" or "top bracket" rate is paid only on income above a certain threshold, not on all income. The rates shown were those in effect on income earned in 1994 and state income tax returns filed in early 1995. *Note:* Tables F-13, F-14, and F-15 show income tax receipts for some states that are listed here as having no tax. The amounts shown in those tables, which are quite small compared to other states, arise from unearned income such as investment income and rents.

F-17 Corporate Income Tax "Effort," 1991: This statistic measures the relative costs of state corporate income taxes, taking into account differences among states both in tax rates and how taxable corporate income is calculated. It is one component of the aggregate tax burdens under the representative tax system (see F-3). Even though the data have not been updated recently by the agency that prepares them, this statistic is the most meaningful way to answer the question, "Which states tax corporate income the most?"

F-18 Motor Fuel Taxes: States tax motor fuels, such as gasoline and diesel fuel, mostly to provide funds for road construction and maintenance. The table shows the tax rate on gasoline from a special compilation prepared by the Federation of Tax Administrators, covering rates in effect at the beginning of 1995. It also includes total state and local revenues from motor fuel taxes in fiscal 1992 and those revenues related to personal income as calculated by the Census Bureau.

F-19 Tobacco Taxes: These data come from the same sources as those of Table F-18 but cover cigarette and related tobacco taxes.

F-20 Tax Burden on High Income Family, 1994: The amounts shown are the liability to be faced by a typical higher income family for state and local income, sales, property, and gasoline taxes in 1994. The calculation was made by *Money* magazine from a variety of sources, including state-by-state calculations of income tax liability by the accounting firm of Ernst & Young. The tax liability reflects the average income of readers of the magazine ($79,029). *Money* published these results in its January 1995 issue.

F-21 State and Local Taxes in the Largest City in Each State, 1993: These data show the costs of state and local taxes in the largest city in each state to typical families with incomes of $50,000, as calculated by the District of Columbia Department of Finance and Reve-

nue in *Tax Rates and Tax Burdens in the District of Columbia: A Nationwide Comparison.* The calculations for each state's largest city are not necessarily representative of statewide averages.

F-22 Progressivity of Major State and Local Taxes, 1993: These data compare the tax burdens as a percentage of income on households of two income levels ($25,000 and $100,000), using data from the analysis described in Table F-21. Low ratios indicate that the percentage paid by higher income households is significantly higher than the percentage paid by low-income households, making the state and local tax structure "progressive." States with no personal income tax and high reliance on sales and property taxes, such as Nevada, have tax systems that can be called regressive. Their progressivity scores of more than one indicate that poorer households pay a larger percentage of their income on state and local taxes than do higher income households.

F-23 Estate and Inheritance Taxes Above Federal Credit Level, 1995: The federal government levies taxes on the estates of persons when they die. State governments also tax estates either directly by taxing the amount left to heirs (estate taxes) or by taxing the amounts received by particular heirs (inheritance taxes). Some of the state tax liability is allowed by the federal government as a 100 percent credit against federal taxes owed. This means that states can levy taxes up to the amount of the credit without making taxpayers pay more, so all states levy such "pick-up" taxes. Some states levy additional taxes, though the trend has been to eliminate the extra taxes out of fear that they encourage affluent older residents to take up residence in other states. The table shows which states levy these extra taxes and the type of tax they use.

REVENUES AND FINANCES

G-1 Total State and Local Revenue, 1992: This is the most inclusive definition of the financial size of state and local governments used by the Census Bureau in its annual survey of government finances. It includes utilities run by state and local governments and many categories of trust funds. Such funds typically collect revenues, such as Unemployment Insurance taxes, for a particular purpose, such as paying Unemployment Compensation benefits, and are not commingled with other public funds. The revenues included come from state and local taxes, fees such as hospital charges and university tuition, and from the federal government.

G-2 State and Local General Revenue, 1992: This table relates general revenue to population and personal income in each state. It excludes utility and trust fund revenues.

G-3 State and Local "Own Source" General Revenue, 1992: These data reflect the concept often used to measure the fiscal burdens associated with state and local activity. Revenues from federal aid are excluded, along with the revenues of trust funds and utilities.

G-4 Non-Tax Revenue, 1992: The principal sources of non-tax revenues are (1) fees related to use of state facilities and services, such as those charged by public hospitals and universities, and (2) interest earned on money held by governments in anticipation of spending.

G-5 State and Local Expenditure, 1992: This is the spending counterpart of the revenues shown on Table G-1.

G-6 State and Local General Expenditure, 1992: This concept of "general" spending (see G-3) is the most appropriate for comparing spending among states.

G-7 State and Local General Expenditure, Per Capita, 1992: This table relates general expenditure to population with separate totals for state governments and local governments. Because state aid to local governments is included as both state spending and again when local officials spend the resources, the total is less than the sum of its two parts.

G-8 Percentage Change in State and Local General Expenditure, 1987-1992: This statistic shows the differences among states in the five-year growth of state and local spending. The changes shown are not adjusted for factors that might account for some of the differences in growth rates, such as growth in population and other factors affecting needs for government service.

G-9 State Government General Revenue, 1993: Unlike Tables G-1 through G-8, these data deal with state governments alone, not state and local governments combined. Unlike data in those tables, these data cover fiscal year 1993. They are from the preliminary version of *State Government Finances in 1993,* which has been made available by the Census Bureau for electronic retrieval only. The corresponding data for 1993 for local governments are not yet available.

For most purposes, comparisons of finances among states need to include state and local revenues and spending because of major differences in the division of state and local responsibilities between states. For example, New York local governments pay nearly half of all state and local welfare costs, but local governments in most states have almost no responsibility for paying these costs. Comparisons of states alone would make New York spending look artificially small. In Hawaii, the state alone pays for schools, while in other states local governments pay half these costs. Comparisons of states alone would make Hawaii's spending look artificially large.

However, comparisons of state governments alone are useful for those attempting to evaluate state office holders and aspirants and for discussions of state government spending priorities and tax burdens.

G-10 State Government Spending, 1993: See notes to Table G-9.

G-11 State Government Spending, 1994: These data reflect more current estimates of state government spending. They come from a survey of state executive branch budget offices reported in the *1994 State Expenditure Report* by the National Association of State Budget Officers (NASBO). They reflect state fiscal 1994 definitions. The year ended on June 30, 1994, for forty-six states, while one state ended the fiscal year in the spring and three ended in the fall.

The NASBO report differs from Census reports in many ways. The Census Bureau reports include all funds, while the NASBO report covers primarily funds subject to appropriation by legislatures and therefore excludes for most states funds of quasi-independent entities such as toll highway authorities. The Census Bureau does not distinguish among funds within state government, while the NASBO report presents data separately for state general funds, federal funds, and other state funds. The data shown in the table reflect the total of all reported funds. The NASBO data use different definitions of spending categories than the Census Bureau data.

G-12 State and Local Debt, 1992: These data, from the Census Bureau's *Government Finances in 1992,* reflect the total debt of all state and local governments at the end of fiscal 1992, including debt of special authorities.

G-13 State and Local Debt Related to Revenue, 1992: This table relates total debt (see G-12) to total revenue. Consequently, it offers a measure of how state and local budgets are strained by the costs of paying principal and interest on past obligations.

G-14 State and Local Full Faith and Credit Debt, 1992: These data reflect the component of total debt (see Table G-12) that is backed by the "full faith and credit" of the governments that issued the debt. This debt, commonly known as "general obligation" debt, is backed by all revenue sources of the issuing government. The debt not included in these totals, often known as revenue bonds, is backed only by specified revenues, not general taxes.

G-15 State Government Bond Ratings, 1995: Because thousands of individual state and local governments issue bonds, purchasers such as individuals and mutual funds find it difficult to analyze the risks associated with each individual issue. As a result, three rating agencies (Fitch, Moody's, and Standard & Poor's) evaluate the quality of individual bond issues. The ratings of revenue bonds are unique to the bonds and the revenue sources that back them. The ratings of general obligation bonds shown in this table are reflections of the fiscal soundness of state governments overall. As a result, they affect perceptions of fiscal soundness of states by voters as well as by potential bond purchasers.

The ratings shown come from Moody's. Ratings from the other two agencies would show about the same ranking of states. Moody's system considers AAA highest, followed by AA, etc., down to lower ratings, which are awarded some local governments but no states that are generally considered good credit risks. Some states have so little general obligation debt that they have no recent ratings.

G-16 State Solvency Index, 1993: While state financial reports and Census Bureau data provide substantial detail about state finances, they do not provide answers to some common sense questions about state financial status. One of these questions is equivalent to "net worth," a fundamental concept in viewing the finances of individuals and companies. This table reflects a special study by State Policy Research, reported in its *State Policy Reports* (September 1993), using data from a variety of dates as close to late 1993 as possible.

Conceptually, the number shown is an answer to the question: If each state were to cease operations tomorrow and pay off all debts (including pension promises to employees), how much money would be left over? For most states, the answer is that nothing would be left. Instead, they would have to levy a special assessment on every citizen (the amounts shown as negative numbers) in order to cease operations. Some states, particularly Alaska with its large reserves built from oil revenues, would have money left over that could be distributed to taxpayers. The calculations exclude the value of physical assets, such as state park lands and buildings, and property, such as trucks and computers.

G-17 Assets of State-Administered Pension Plans, 1992: State and local governments have more than 10 million employees, most of whom are covered by pension plans. States run these plans for their own employees and, in most states, for local employees, teachers, and city workers, as well. To be considered actuarially sound, these plans must have built up enough assets from contributions of employees and their government employers to be able to cover the amounts needed to pay retired workers plus current workers when they retire. How much this amounts to depends on many factors, such as the exact benefits promised and the life expectancy of workers. There is no substitute for actuarial studies of each plan for determining the right amount each plan should have to cover future obligations.

The data in the table, from the Census Bureau's *1992 Census of Governments,* provide the data on the assets of state-administered plans and the persons who are considered members of these plans—retirees and active workers accruing retirement benefits. Dividing these two numbers produces average assets per member, which is a rough measure of the relative solvency of the public pension plans in each state.

G-18 State Reserves, 1995: These data reflect the cash reserves of state governments as they finished fiscal year 1995, generally in the summer of 1995. These reserves come in two primary forms—balances (equivalent to the balances people show in their checkbooks) and "rainy day" or stabilization funds (formal reserves, somewhat akin to the savings accounts maintained by individuals). The data come from the survey of state budget officers by the National Association of State Budget Officers published in late 1995.

Relating balances to spending provides a basis for comparisons among states of different size and financial responsibilities. Nationwide, this table indicates that states have enough in reserve to pay their normal bills for about 5 percent of their fiscal years, or roughly twelve working days, with no additional revenue coming in.

G-19 State and Local Capital Outlays and Interest, 1992: This table, drawn from the Census Bureau's *Government Finances in 1992,* shows the total annual interest bill of state and local governments and per capita amounts of spending in fiscal 1992 for interest and capital outlays. The outlays reflect the pace of activity in financing new facilities, such as roads and schools. The interest reflects the extent to which taxpayers of each state are seeing their tax funds used to pay interest on past spending, normally borrowing to finance capital outlays.

G-20 Index of State Budget Process Quality, 1994: Experts in public administration and budgeting generally agree on criteria of best budgeting practices, such as considering the impacts of spending and tax decisions over a longer period than one year. The numbers shown in the table are scores, with a perfect score being 100, developed by State Policy Research by comparing these criteria with actual state budget practices, as reported by the National Association of State Budget Officers in its special report, *Budget Processes in the States.* This special study appeared in *State Policy Reports* (Volume 13, Issue 5).

G-21 Relative State Spending "Needs": Individual states have quite different population characteristics, as shown by many of the tables in *State Fact Finder.* For example, school-age children are an extraordinarily large proportion of the population of Utah, but a smaller-than-average proportion of Pennsylvania's population. As a result, some states would have higher per capita spending than others, even if all states spent identical amounts per pupil, had identical welfare payments, and identical levels of other services. These differences are important to consider in viewing differences in per capita spending among states.

A special study by State Policy Research, which appeared in *State Policy Reports* (Vol. 13, Issue 20), calculated what state and local governments in each state would have to spend if they applied national average spending (for example, spending per pupil) to their own particular mix of population using government services. The study, sometimes called the "representative expenditure system," can be expressed as differences in per capita amounts like those shown in the table. For example, to match national average spending patterns, Mississippi would have to spend 37.7 percent more per capita than the national average. Why? Because the state has extra burdens associated with large percentages of welfare recipients and school children.

EDUCATION

H-1 Average Proficiency in Math, Eighth Grade, 1992: These statistics, while not available for all states, reflect scores on national tests administered to eighth graders to determine their ability to deal with basic concepts of mathematics. The statistics are representative of those being developed through the National Assessment of Educational Progress, as administered by the U.S. Department of Education and cooperating states. They were printed in the *Digest of Education Statistics, 1994.*

Statistics comparing the educational achievements of students in individual states, school districts, and schools are a response to the widespread criticism that taxpayers and parents have few ways to assess how well schools are performing their mission of educating children. Many states have established their own tests and print comparisons, often called "report cards," that permit comparisons among school districts and schools within the state. Supporters of these statistics and tests argue that it is much more appropriate to compare results in education programs than the common statistics that just compare costs, such as how much is spent per pupil.

Statistics on test results measure achievement of pupils, not that of teachers or school systems. Experts disagree on the relative influence of factors affecting student achievement, but all agree that it is heavily influenced by such out-of-school factors as early childhood training in the home, children's physical and mental health, and participation of parents in the educational process.

H-2 Average Proficiency in Math, Fourth Grade, 1992: These data are comparable to those shown in Table H-1, except they cover a younger group of children.

H-3 Armed Forces Qualification Test Ranks, 1993: Many employers test potential employees to determine their suitability for work, as indicated by such factors as ability to read and understand instructions and perform simple calculations. One of the most widely used tests is offered nationwide to persons seeking to enlist in the armed forces. These data reflect average scores of test-takers in the period from October 1992 to the end of September 1993.

These data are prepared by the Department of Defense and published annually, along with other information about persons in uniform, in *Population Representation in the Military Services.* The Defense Department, which does not want to become an arbitrator of which states prepare students best for jobs, tries to discourage the use of these results to rank states. Regardless, the results provide the best single measure of performance of high school graduates being tested by an employer using criteria approximating aptitude for work.

H-4 Scholastic Aptitude Test Scores, 1995: College-bound students are generally required to take an achievement test to gain admission to the college or university of their choice. There are two major tests used for this purpose, the Scholastic Aptitude Test (SAT), which is administered by the College Board, and the ACT test, which is administered by the American College Testing Program. Both organizations seek to discourage the use of their test scores as a way to compare education systems of states, but they are commonly used for lack of other comparisons indicating how well states and individual school districts and schools compare in meeting this standard for college admissions.

The test scores are presented here and in Table H-5, with neither table including all states. Each state's results are for the test that is most often taken in that state. Failure to do this would produce highly misleading results. For example, many southern states rely primarily on the ACT, but their students who seek admission to exclusive private universities in the Northeast and California must take the SAT to gain admission. As a result, the SAT test is taken by a small fraction of high school graduates, but those who take it score extraordinarily high.

H-5 ACT Test Scores, 1995: See notes for Table H-4.

H-6 Percentage of Over-25 Population Without a High School Degree, 1990: These data from the 1990 Census, published in the *Digest of Education Statistics,* reflect the percentage of the total population over age twenty-five that does not have a high school degree.

H-7 Students in Private Schools, 1991: Almost five million students in kindergarten through the twelfth grade attend private schools. The enrollment statistics are gathered by the Department of Education and published in the *Digest of Education Statistics.*

H-8 Percent of Students Finishing High School, 1992: Nationwide, persons graduating from high school in 1992 equaled about 84 percent of those who entered high school in 1988, according to the Department of Education report *Number of Public High School Graduates by State.* Subtracting this figure from a 100 percent graduation rate suggests a "dropout" rate of 16 percent. This approach is one of several ways of comparing dropout rates among the states.

H-9 Pupil-Teacher Ratio, 1992: Small classes are generally believed to be more beneficial to students than large ones, so pupil-teacher ratios are commonly used as a proxy measure of educational quality. The statistic shows a lower ratio than typical class sizes because some specialized teachers, such as those teaching art or special education, are included. These data come from the Department of Education as published in the *Digest of Education Statistics.*

For these and other commonly used educational statistics comparing states, there are three primary sources: the Department of Education, the National Education Association (NEA), and the American Federation of Teachers (which, like the NEA, represents teachers). These organizations produce somewhat different data, using different concepts and different schedules. However, the rankings of states on any particular indicator are about the same regardless of the source used.

H-10 Public School Enrollment, 1992: These statistics, from the Department of Education, show how the nation's 42.6 million public school pupils are distributed among the states. The comparison with each state's population is a rough indicator of the differences among states in the financial burdens of providing free public education.

H-11 Public Library Holdings Per Capita, 1993: These data, from the American Library Association, relate the holdings of books (and related materials) to the population of each state. Nationally, public libraries hold about three books for every person. The reports exclude significant sources of reading materials not in public libraries, such as collections of private and university libraries and certain public school systems.

H-12 Children with Disabilities, 1992: A substantial percentage of the nation's public school students are given special financing by state and federal programs because of something unique about them. The table reflects a Department of Education count of students in the 1991-1992 school year classified as disabled or receiving extra school money because of poverty.

H-13 Spending for Education, 1992: This table relates spending data from *Government Finances in 1992* to population and personal income in each state.

H-14 State and Local Education Spending as Percent of Total Spending, 1992: This table shows the relative importance of education spending in state and local budgets. It is derived by comparing this spending with total "general" spending. General spending includes essentially all other spending, except municipal electric and other utilities and trust funds, such as those for Workers' Compensation.

H-15 Spending Per Pupil, 1994: This table, from the National Education Association's *Rankings of the States, 1994*, shows spending in public schools for operations (excluding capital outlays) in relation to the number of pupils enrolled.

H-16 Average Teacher Salary, 1994: These average salary calculations, from the National Education Association's *Rankings of the States, 1994*, show the average gross wage of teachers, not including special pay for leading student activities or teaching in summer sessions.

H-17 Sources of School Funds, 1994: Except in a few states, federal aid covers less than 10 percent of public school costs. State and local governments divide the remainder in proportions that vary considerably from state to state, as shown in the table. The data come from the National Education Association's *Rankings of the States, 1994*.

H-18 State Aid Per Pupil in Average Daily Attendance, 1994: These data, calculated from attendance

and expenditure data in the National Education Association's *Rankings of the States, 1994*, show the amount each state government spends on supporting local public schools, expressed in relation to the number of pupils enrolled.

H-19 State and Local Spending for Higher Education, 1992: This table relates spending data from the Census Bureau's *Government Finances in 1992* to population and personal income in each state.

H-20 State and Local Higher Education Spending as Percent of Total Spending, 1992: This table, from the same source as H-19, shows the relative importance of higher education in state and local budgets. It is derived by comparing this spending with total "general" spending. General spending includes essentially all other spending excepting municipal electric and other utilities and trust funds, such as those for Workers' Compensation.

H-21 Public Higher Education Enrollment, 1992: This table shows the total number of students enrolled in public universities and colleges in the fall of 1992 and relates this number to the total population of each state. This percentage is an indicator of the relative costs of supporting public higher education in each state. The data are from the Department of Education's *Digest of Educational Statistics*.

H-22 State Per Pupil Support of Higher Education, 1992: There are a variety of different statistics seeking to measure state outlays for higher education on a per pupil basis. None are totally satisfactory for complex reasons, such as difficulty in classifying pupils as private or public in institutions that receive public support for some of their programs but are truly private in financing other programs. This table relates fiscal 1993 state government spending (including construction funds) from the National Association of State Budget Officers' *State Expenditure Report* to fall 1992 enrollment as reported by the U.S. Department of Education.

H-23 Average Tuition and Fees at Public Universities, 1993-1994: These data, from the *Digest of Education Statistics*, reflect a composite of average tuition and general fees charged by public four-year institutions of higher education in the 1993-1994 academic year.

H-24 Average Salary of Associate Professors at "Flagship" State Universities, 1994-1995: These statistics were developed for *State Fact Finder* based on detailed salary surveys by the American Association of University Professors as printed in its magazine *Academe* (March/April 1995). To make the comparisons, the "flagship" university salary was used. Usually the "flagship" is the largest, oldest state university, but in some states several institutions can be considered flagships, such as the University of Michigan and Michigan State. In those cases, *State Fact Finder* generally selected the university originally constituted as the general land-grant institution (e.g., the University of Michigan) rather than the one initially designated as an agricultural and mechanical school (e.g., Michigan State).

H-25 State and Local Education Employees Per 10,000 Population, 1992: This statistic comes from a Census Bureau survey of state and local government employment, *Public Employment in 1992.* It covers employees of public schools, from janitors to principals, but it does not include higher education employees.

H-26 Federal Research and Development Spending, 1993: The federal government is a major supplier of funds for research and development of new products and processes. This federally supported research provides an important source of income for state and private universities and a base from which state economies can develop in high technology industries. The table shows how federal R&D spending in fiscal 1993 was distributed among the states and relates that spending to the population of each state. The data were developed by the National Science Foundation in its *Survey of Federal Funds for Research and Development.*

H-27 Total Library Operating Expenditures, 1993: These data were developed by the Census Bureau and published by the Department of Education as *Public Libraries in the United States: 1993.*

HEALTH

I-1 Divorce Rates, 1994: Some observers like to think of the health of a state's population as including more than the presence or absence of physical illness or death rates (see A-15). They look for other indicators, which are scarce, such as general happiness of the population and incidence of suicide and divorce. Relating divorces to resident population produces divorces per 1,000 population, the statistic shown in the table. The data were collected by the Department of Health and Human Services and reported in *Monthly Vital Statistics* (October 1995).

I-2 Infant Mortality Rate, 1994: These data, from the same source as I-1, cover deaths of all children under one year of age, expressed in relation to each 1,000 live births. This statistic is considered one of the best indicators with which to compare health among states and local areas. Higher death rates are associated with poor health of the mother, absence of medical care during pregnancy, and lack of medical treatment for infants.

I-3 State Health Rankings, 1994: These scores and rankings are developed annually for Northwestern National Life Insurance Company by T. E. Eckstein & Associates, Inc. (1926 Fairmouth Ave., St. Paul, Minnesota 55105). The results are from *An Analysis of the Relative Healthiness of the Population in All Fifty States.* They reflect a composite of indicators, including unemployment, health practices (such as smoking), the availability of health services, and outcomes (such as death rates). Probably no two researchers would use identical

lists to produce such rankings, but the state rankings would likely be similar. While decisions by states have some impact on health rankings, decisions on health practices by individual citizens have more of an impact.

I-4 Percentage of Nonelderly Population Without Health Insurance, 1993: Most Americans get health insurance coverage through family members who are offered coverage by their employers. All Americans over age sixty-four are covered by Medicare. About 13 percent of the nonelderly, including all welfare recipients, get coverage paid for by state and federal governments through Medicaid. About 18 percent of nonelderly citizens have no health insurance. These data come from the Employee Benefits Research Institute in Washington, D.C.

I-5 Abortions, 1991: There are about 1.4 million legal abortions performed each year. The numbers in each state are collected by the Department of Health and Human Services (Centers for Disease Control), which furnished the data to *State Fact Finder* from a 1995 report, *Abortion Surveillance, United States, 1991.* The abortion ratio shown compares the number of abortions with the number of live births.

I-6 Alcohol Consumption Per Capita, 1992: Some public health authorities consider high levels of alcoholic beverage consumption an indicator of poor health of a state's population. The data show the number of gallons of pure ethanol (typical liquor is about 43 percent ethanol or ethanol alcohol, wine 14 percent, and beer about 6 percent) consumed per resident age fourteen and over.

The data are derived by dividing sales of alcoholic beverages by population. Those shown were developed by the Department of Health and Human Services (National Institute on Alcohol Abuse and Alcoholism). They are called "apparent" alcohol consumption because some alcoholic beverages are bought in one state for consumption by residents of another. This raises the apparent consumption of tourist-destination states, like Nevada, and states with low prices, like New Hampshire, that draw purchasers from other states.

I-7 Percent Adult Smokers, 1992: These estimates are developed by the Department of Health and Human Services for inclusion in the special report, *Surveillance for Selected Tobacco-Use Behaviors, United States, 1990-1994.*

I-8 Percent of Population Obese, 1991: These data, like those on tobacco use, were developed as part of the Centers for Disease Control behavioral risk factor surveillance system. Different definitions of how much people can weigh without being considered to have health risks would produce different percentages for every state, but not appreciably affect the rankings.

I-9 AIDS Cases, 1994-1995: These data are developed by the Centers for Disease Control and reported in the *HIV/AIDS Surveillance Report.* They cover cases newly reported between July 1994 and June 1995. The rate shown is cases per 100,000 residents. Because persons at most risk of contracting AIDS are predominately found in larger metropolitan areas, states containing those areas typically show the highest rates.

I-10 Physicians Per 100,000 Population, 1992:
This table shows the number of physicians in relation to population. Rural states will show below-average numbers in part because intensive medical care, such as that received from major hospitals, is often sought in nearby states with large metropolitan areas. The statistics are based on American Medical Association data.

I-11 Hospital Beds Per 1,000 Population, 1992:
This table shows the number of hospital beds in relation to population. Rural states will show below-average numbers in part because hospital care is often sought in nearby states with large metropolitan areas.

I-12 Medicaid Recipients, 1992: About 30 million people receive health care through the Medicaid program each year. The federal government sets minimum standards for this program and pays about 57 percent of the costs nationwide through a formula that provides 50 percent of the costs in the most affluent states and up to 80 percent in the poorest states. Within federal guidelines, states set the rules for eligibility, the health services covered, and the amount of reimbursements to the providers of care.

The primary recipients are families that receive cash assistance from states through Aid to Families with Dependent Children or from the federal government through Supplemental Security Income. These data come from tabulations of the Department of Health and Human Services furnished to the U.S. House of Representatives, Committee on Ways and Means, appearing in the committee's *Overview of Entitlement Programs*.

I-13 Medicaid Recipients as Percentage of Poverty Population, 1991: These data, from the same source as Table I-12, relate the number of Medicaid recipients to the number of persons in households with income below federally defined poverty levels. The differences among states are a good indication of how inclusive are the eligibility criteria set by the individual states.

I-14 State and Local Spending for Health and Hospitals, 1992: This table relates spending data from the Census Bureau's *Government Finances in 1992* to population in each state. The spending includes public health activities plus the gross outlays of hospitals and nursing homes run by state and local governments, including costs defrayed by the charges such hospitals make to patients and their health insurance providers. The largest outlays appear in states that rely heavily on government-owned hospitals.

I-15 State and Local Health and Hospitals Spending as Percent of Total Spending, 1992: This table shows the relative importance of health and hospitals outlays in state and local budgets. It is derived by comparing this spending (see Table I-14) with total "general" spending. General spending includes essentially all other spending except municipal electric and other utilities and trust funds, such as those for Workers' Compensation.

I-16 Per Capita Medicaid Spending, 1992: These data, from the same source as the number of recipients in Table I-12, reflect the major impact that Medicaid costs are having on government budgets. The amounts shown reflect primarily federal grants spent by states, about 57 percent of the total with differences among the states, and state government matching funds. In a few states, particularly New York, some of the federally required state match is provided by local governments.

I-17 Average Medicaid Spending Per Aged Recipient, 1992: These data, from the same source as Table I-12, illustrate differences among the states in this component of Medicaid costs. Over half of the nursing home residents in the United States are having their bills paid by Medicaid. States differ in the extent and success of programs designed to encourage people to live at home and with relatives rather than enter nursing homes. Those programs typically provide visiting nurses and homemakers who assist frail elderly persons in their homes, thereby reducing the need for institutionalization. A compilation of Department of Health and Human Services data, they relate total spending on all Medicaid recipients age sixty-five and over to the number of recipients.

I-18 Average Medicaid Spending Per AFDC Child, 1992: These data reflect the same concepts and come from the same source as those shown in Table I-17. Differences among states primarily reflect differences in how much doctors and other providers of health care are compensated for providing services.

I-19 Medicare Payment Per Hospital Day, 1994: These data are one way to measure health care cost differences among states. They reflect the cost of a day in short-stay hospitals as reimbursed by the federal Medicare program. The data were reported in the 1995 annual statistical supplement to the *Social Security Bulletin*.

I-20 Medicare Average Service Payment, 1992: While actual charges (see I-19) reflect services provided to individual patients based on their medical needs, federal guidelines set the ceiling on basic per-day changes. The data shown in this table reflect lower costs per day than those shown on Table I-19. In setting allowable charges, federal authorities consider a variety of factors, including different wages for hospital workers in the states.

I-21 Percentage of Population in Health Maintenance Organizations, 1994: Most Americans receive their health care by purchasing it from individual doctors, hospitals, pharmacies, and others. However, a growing percentage are served by health maintenance organizations that provide complete packages of care for one monthly fee. Many people believe that this approach to buying care will reduce health care costs because the service providers cannot increase their incomes by providing additional services. Many companies providing health insurance to their employees and government programs have been shifting to this approach.

The statistics, reflecting enrollment in December 1994 as a percentage of population, come from the Group Health Association of America, the trade association of health maintenance organizations.

CRIME AND LAW ENFORCEMENT

J-1 Total Crime Rate, 1993: This table reflects the total crime rate as defined by the uniform crime reporting system of the U.S. Department of Justice (Federal Bureau of Investigation). The reports are compiled by individual law enforcement agencies throughout the nation and summarized in the Justice Department publication *Crime in the United States, 1993.*

These statistics inherently cover only crime known to law enforcement agencies, so they are often cited as "crime reported to the police." Certain crimes, such as murder and thefts where victims seek insurance reimbursement, are almost always reported to police. Victims often fail to report other categories of crime, ranging from rape to thefts of small items. To capture information on crimes actually committed, the Justice Department does a survey of households known as the "victimization survey." Because that survey is based on nationwide samples, data from it are not available on a state-by-state basis.

The FBI has worked for years to make the statistics reported from different states and cities more comparable. However, some significant differences remain. Some reflect differences among states in their criminal laws and crime reporting systems. Some reflect inherent differences among citizens in reporting crime that are in turn related to differences in perceptions of whether law enforcement authorities will be able to solve the crimes. Small thefts, for example, are often not reported in large cities but commonly reported in some smaller communities.

J-2 Violent Crime Rates, 1993: Crimes fall into two major classes. Some, such as murder and assault, involve violence or the threat of violence. Others, such as auto theft and burglary, do not. This table, from the same source as Table J-1, shows the rates for all violent crimes combined.

J-3 Murder and Rape Rates, 1993: This table, from the same source as Table J-1, shows the rates for two specific crimes.

J-4 Property Crime, 1993: This table, from the same source as Table J-1, shows the rates for crimes against property, such as burglary and auto theft.

J-5 Motor Vehicle Theft, 1993: This table combines auto theft with theft of other vehicles, such as pickup trucks, using the same source as Table J-1.

J-6 Violent Crime Rate Change, 1989-1993: Although there have recently been some signs that the crime rate is decreasing, the trend from 1989 to 1993 shows a 21 percent increase in violent crime nationwide. The increase is measured by comparing the crime rate (crimes per 100,000 people) from the 1989 and 1993 uniform crime reports.

J-7 Incarceration Rate, 1994: This table measures the relationship between prison populations (see J-9) and total population. It is developed by the Department of Justice from statistical reports of state and federal corrections agencies. The data shown are from *Prisoners in 1994.* They reflect both state and federal prisoners. Federal prisoners constitute about 10 percent of all prisoners. The count of total prisoners covers only those sentenced for more than a year and thus excludes persons who are being held for short periods in local jails. The statistics show the number of prisoners per 100,000 population. While the national rate is equivalent to having 0.4 percent of the population in prison, the percentages are much higher for certain age and ethnic groups and for males.

J-8 Change in Incarceration Rate, 1989-1994: This table, from the same source as Table J-7, shows the percentage change in incarceration rates, reflecting an increase of about 42 percent over this five-year period.

J-9 Prisoners, 1994: This table shows the total number of prisoners held in state (90 percent) and federal (10 percent) penal institutions at the end of 1994.

J-10 Juvenile Arrest Rate, 1992: This table, from the Annie E. Casey Foundation's *Kids Count Data Booklet,* reflects the number of arrests during 1992 of youths between the ages of ten and seventeen per 100,000 youths in the population of each state.

J-11 Proportion of Sentence Served, 1994: Because of parole and time off for good behavior, violent offenders typically serve only about half of the time they are sentenced to serve. These statistics, not available for all states, show the proportion of time served based on data reported in the Department of Justice publication *Violent Offenders in State Prison: Sentences and Time Served.* The United States total reflects only the states participating in the survey.

The states with high percentages are not necessarily the toughest on criminals. They may have shorter sentences but force prisoners to serve a longer percentage of their sentences.

J-12 State and Local Law Enforcement Employees Per 10,000 Population, 1992: This statistic comes from a Census Bureau survey of state and local government employment, *Public Employment in 1992.*

J-13 State and Local Corrections Employees Per 10,000 Population, 1992: This statistic comes from the same source as Table J-12.

J-14 Costs Per Inmate-Day, 1994: These estimates of daily costs of keeping an inmate in prison for a day were developed by the Criminal Justice Institute, Inc. (South Salem, New York 10590) for its publication *The Corrections Yearbook 1995.* The data are reprinted with the permission of the Institute. Copies or other use of the data in this table may not be made without the written permission of the Institute.

These data primarily reflect variable costs of holding an inmate, such as food, clothing, and health care, as well as categories of operating costs known to the corrections agencies that supply the data. These include, for example, the salaries of prison guards. However, the data understate substantially the full costs, which include constructing and rehabilitating prisons as well as operating them and certain overhead costs often not included in corrections agency budgets (insurance, employee retirement benefits, and central operations, such as personnel and purchasing management, etc.).

J-15 State Corrections Spending, 1994: These data provide another approach to the costs of maintaining prison systems in each state. The total spending shown is the general fund spending reported by state budget offices in the National Association of State Budget Officers' *1994 State Expenditure Report.* The per-inmate spending is the result of dividing the spending in fiscal 1994 by the number of inmates in prison at the end of 1994.

The resulting calculation is somewhat arbitrary as it includes some federal prisoners and does not separately account for the supervision of inmates on parole, which is another major function of corrections agencies not associated directly with inmates in prison. However, it provides a useful contrast with the comparisons shown in Table J-14, reflecting both a higher total and somewhat different state comparisons.

J-16 Percentage Increase, State Corrections Spending, 1993-1994: These data, from the same source as the spending in Table J-15, reflect the major impact that growing prison populations are having on state government budgets.

J-17 State and Local Spending for Law Enforcement, 1992: This table relates spending on police and corrections, as obtained from the Census Bureau's *Government Finances in 1992,* to population in each state.

J-18 State and Local Law Enforcement Spending as Percent of Total Spending, 1992: This table shows the relative importance of law enforcement outlays in state and local budgets. It is derived by comparing this spending with total "general" spending. General spending includes essentially all other spending except municipal electric and other utilities and trust funds, such as those for Workers' Compensation.

TRANSPORTATION

K-1 Travel on Interstate Highways, 1993: Use of highways is measured by vehicle miles—travel by one vehicle for one mile. By this measure, interstate highways account for nearly one-fourth of the nation's highway travel, according to calculations based on the U.S. Department of Transportation's *1993 Highway Statistics* (1994). The federal government provides 90 percent of the money used to build interstates, but lower percentages for other highways. Having a large percentage of travel on interstates is good fiscal news as well as an indication of highway quality.

K-2 Percent of Mileage on Interstates in Poor or Mediocre Condition, 1993: The Federal Highway

Administration and the states, which are responsible for highway maintenance, maintain a rating system for interstate highways. This table from the U.S. Department of Transportation's *1993 Highway Statistics* shows the percentage of interstates in the worst two categories of conditions.

K-3 Deficient Bridges, 1994: This table shows the total number of deficient bridges on major highways in each state. Details appear in the complete inventory, *The Status of the Nation's Highway Bridges,* published by the Department of Transportation. Bridges can be classified as deficient as a result of deterioration, poor maintenance, or by original design (for example, too narrow for modern traffic).

K-4 Traffic Deaths Per 100 Million Vehicle Miles, 1993: Relating deaths to total urban and rural miles traveled is a common way of measuring the safety of highways. Many factors could affect the totals, including weather conditions, highway designs, congestion, and traffic law enforcement by the states. The figures come from the Department of Transportation.

K-5 Percentage of Drivers Using Seat Belts, 1994: These data come from periodic checks of safety belt usage, as reported by the Department of Transportation in an unpublished tabulation furnished to *State Fact Finder.*

K-6 Vehicle Miles Traveled Per Capita, 1993: Vehicle miles of travel, as reported by the U.S. Department of Transportation in *1993 Highway Statistics,* show the intensity of use of state highway systems. Vehicle miles per capita show that the average American travels nearly 9,000 miles a year by car. Short distances between homes, shopping, and offices plus mass transit make usage lowest in northern urban areas.

K-7 Percentage of Workers Using Public Transportation, 1990: This table shows the percentage of workers who used public transportation systems for their journey to work in 1990. The data come from questions about transportation usage from the 1990 Census, so the next update will not come until the next Census is taken in the year 2000.

K-8 Road and Street Miles, 1993: These data, from the U.S. Department of Transportation's *1993 Highway Statistics,* reflect total road and street (as distinct from highway) miles. They show the percentage of these miles that are controlled and maintained by state governments. Some states, such as Delaware and Virginia, maintain many local service roads that are controlled and maintained by counties and municipalities in other states.

K-9 State and Local Highway Employees Per 10,000 Population, 1992: This statistic comes from a Census Bureau survey of state and local government employment, *Public Employment in 1992.* It shows the higher levels of employees, and thus costs, associated with maintaining highways in rural states.

K-10 State and Local Transit Employees Per 10,000 Population, 1992: This statistic, from the same source as K-9, shows the higher levels of employees, and thus costs, associated with transit in urbanized states.

K-11 State and Local Spending for Highways, 1992: This table, from the Census Bureau's *Government Finances in 1992*, relates spending data to population and personal income in each state.

K-12 State and Local Highway Spending as Percent of Total Spending, 1992: This table shows the relative importance of highway outlays in state and local budgets. It is derived by comparing highway spending with total "general" spending. General spending includes essentially all other spending excepting municipal electric and other utilities and trust funds, such as those for Workers' Compensation.

WELFARE

L-1 Percent of Births to Unwed Mothers, 1993: These data come from state reports summarized by the National Center for Health Statistics in *Advance Report of Final Natality Statistics, 1993,* provided as a September 1995 supplement to the Center's *Monthly Vital Statistics.* The birth data, which come from hospitals, are highly reliable, but some states report the marital status of mothers somewhat differently.

L-2 AFDC Recipients as a Percent of Population, 1994: The primary federal welfare program is Aid to Families with Dependent Children (AFDC), which is available to households with children and income below stipulated levels. The table, from a special tabulation of data the U.S. Department of Health and Human Services provided to *State Fact Finder* on October 20, 1995, expresses the total number of people in households receiving AFDC during fiscal year 1994 as a percentage of population on July 1, 1994. Because states set their own eligibility standards, states with high percentages of persons in poverty do not necessarily have a larger-than-average percentage.

L-3 Food Stamp Recipients as a Percent of Population, 1994: Unlike Aid to Families with Dependent Children, Food Stamp standards of eligibility are uniform nationwide, so participation in this program tends to resemble closely the percentage of state population in poverty. The data are from a special Department of Agriculture tabulation provided to *State Fact Finder* on November 8, 1995.

L-4 SSI Recipients as a Percent of Population, 1994: The Supplemental Security Income (SSI) program provides federal cash payments to persons eligible by reason of a combination of low incomes and disability, blindness, or age over sixty-five. The eligibility standards are uniform nationwide, as are the cash payments, except in about half the states that supplement the federal payments with state money (see Table L-10). The data were calculated from information on recipients provided in the *Social Security Bulletin, Annual Statistical Supplement* (1995).

L-5 Change in AFDC Recipients, 1989-1994: This table compares the 1989 recipient population of each

state from a special tabulation of the Department of Health and Human Services with the 1994 recipient population (see Table L-2) to show growth in welfare recipients over the past five years.

L-6 Condition of Children Index, 1995: This is a ranking of states (1 highest, 50 lowest) prepared by the Annie E. Casey Foundation based on a wide variety of indicators of health, income, education, and other factors. The details behind the rankings are found in *Kids Count Data Booklet,* the foundation's annual comprehensive publication.

L-7 Percent of Families with Children Headed by Single Parent, 1992: A large and growing number of American children do not live in households with two parents. These statistics (from *Kids Count;* see Table L-6) include only children in households with a single parent present.

L-8 Typical Monthly AFDC Payments, Family of Three, 1994: These data (reflecting the situation on July 1, 1994), from a special tabulation of the Department of Health and Human Services, reflect what a welfare family of three (usually a mother and two children) would receive in cash each month. Each state sets its own level of benefits. A few states have cut their benefits recently, while a few have raised them. In addition to these cash payments, a typical welfare household would receive Food Stamps, assistance in paying heating and cooling bills, and free medical care under the Medicaid program. Some households would also receive additional cash as "emergency assistance" and reduced rents under various federal housing subsidy programs.

L-9 Welfare as Percentage of Poverty Level Income, 1994: These data, from a special compilation of the Ways and Means Committee of the U.S. House of Representatives, compare the combined value of AFDC cash payments and Food Stamps of a typical welfare family with the poverty level for that family. The AFDC cash payments are set by the states (see Table L-8). Federally determined Food Stamp values differ from state to state, as greater amounts are provided in states with low cash welfare payments. The poverty level is uniform nationwide.

The table indicates that the typical welfare recipient receives enough in cash and the cash-equivalent of Food Stamps to bring him or her up to 69 percent of the poverty level, assuming no income from any other sources and not counting noncash benefits, such as housing and Medicaid care.

L-10 State Supplements of SSI, 1994: These data compare the extent to which states supplement benefits under the federal SSI program. For a description of the program, see the notes to Table L-4. The calculation was made by comparing data appearing in the *Annual Statistical Supplement, 1995* to the *Social Security Bulletin.* The complex rules for determining who receives supplements and how large they are mean that the statistics shown are not necessarily indicative of the average supplement received. Some states provide relatively large supplements to some beneficiaries and none to the rest. However, the extreme differences among states show marked differences in their willingness to add to federally funded benefits using their own funds.

L-11 State Income Tax Liability of Typical Poverty Family, 1994: States have quite different approaches toward taxes on poor working families. The table illustrates these by showing how much state income tax a family of three making the poverty level income ($11,817) would have to pay in tax on their 1994 income. A few states, like the federal government, supplement their income with a refundable credit indicated by the minus amounts shown in the table. Some states do not have income taxes (n/a on the table) or have a tax but do not make such families pay it (shown as zeroes on the table). The others charge the taxes shown.

The calculations were performed by the Center on Budget and Policy Priorities in a paper entitled "State Income Tax Burdens on Low-Income Families and Opportunities for Relief," which appeared in *State Tax Notes* (August 21, 1995).

L-12 Child Support Collections, 1993: Because large numbers of families on welfare consist of mothers and children who receive little or no child support from fathers, state and federal officials are intensifying efforts to ensure that fathers pay the support amounts they owe. The table provides an indication of the relative significance of the resulting child support payments in each state. The collections are those reported by the Department of Health and Human Services for fiscal year 1993. The per capita amounts are those collections divided by states' population on July 1, 1993. While most differences among states are real, some reflect the different degrees to which individual states enforce child support requirements through centralized systems.

L-13 Child Support Collections Per Dollar of Administrative Cost, 1993: Nationwide, it costs about a quarter to collect every dollar of child support. These data, from the same source as Table L-12, indicate that the effectiveness of collections efforts show considerable variation among the states.

L-14 Children in Foster Care, 1993: In 1993, nearly 250,000 children were in foster care during some part of the year. Most commonly, these are children who have been removed from their natural parent(s) because of suspected abuse or neglect. The count is from a special calculation furnished to the U.S. House of Representatives, Committee on Ways and Means.

High rankings are not necessarily good or bad. Having large numbers of children in foster care for long periods is generally viewed as undesirable because the alternatives (adoption, return to natural parents) provide more stability for the child than temporary homes with strangers. However, having small numbers may indicate that child welfare authorities are leaving abused and neglected children in homes where they should not be left.

L-15 State and Local Welfare Spending, 1992: These data come from the Census Bureau publication *Government Finances in 1992*. Each state's state and local spending (including spending of federal funds) is expressed in relation to population and personal income. The definition of welfare spending includes administrative costs and welfare-related social services in addition to cash payments.

L-16 Welfare Spending as Percentage of State and Local Spending, 1992: These data (see note to L-15) show the importance of welfare spending relative to total spending of state and local governments for "general" activities, a category that excludes spending for certain trust funds such as Unemployment Compensation and municipal utilities.

L-17 Administrative Costs Per AFDC Case, 1994: The costs of administering welfare run about $640 per case, with substantial variation among the states. The information was calculated for *State Fact Finder* from unpublished tabulations by the Department of Health and Human Services. The cases reflect the average number of cases open in each month in FY 1994, so costs per case opened anytime during the year would be somewhat lower than the numbers shown.

State Rankings

Population

Population	22
Percent Population Change	26
Population 2000	23
Median Age	20
Percent Population African-American	5
Percent Population in Poverty	10
Percent Population Female	2
Birth Rates	25
Death Rates	12
Illegal Immigrant Population	43

Economies

Personal Income	25
Per Capita Personal Income	40
Percent of Personal Income from Wages & Salaries	22
Average Annual Pay	30
Cost Of Living	40
Average Annual Pay in Manufacturing	44
Average Annual Pay in Retailing	33
Unemployment Rate	7
Government Employment	22
Manufacturing Employment	19
Fortune 500 Companies	37
Tourism Spending	28
Export-related Jobs	22
Change in Price of Existing Homes	20
Net Farm Income	16
Bankruptcy Filings	3
Patents Issued	47
WC Disability Payments	28
UC Average Weekly Benefit	48
Economic Momentum	30
Employment Change	38
Manufacturing Employment Change	43
Home Ownership	6
Gambling Losses	36
Electricity Use Per Residential Customer	7
Revenue Per Kwh	31
New Companies	37

Geography

Total Land Area	28
Federally-Owned Land	27
State Park Visitors	34
State Park Acreage	39
Hunters With Firearms	19
Registered Boats	17
Per Capita State Spending For the Arts	35
Energy Consumption Per Capita	12
Toxic Chemical Release Per Capita	7
Hazardous Waste Sites	29
Polluted Rivers	36
Air Quality	15

Government

Members Of US House	21
Legislators Per Million Population	30
Units Of Government	32
Female Legislators	50
Turnover In Legislatures	5
Democrats in State Legislatures	9
Number Of Statewide Elected Officials	11
State And Local Government Employees	13
State And Local Average Salaries	45
Local Employment	33
Registered Voters	15
Statewide Initiatives	n/a

Federal

Per Capita Federal Spending	13
Increase In Federal Spending	13
Federal Grants To State And Local Government	26
Per Capita Federal Spending On Procurement	13
Per Capita Federal Spending On Social Security And Medicare	24
Social Security Benefits	46

Federal Spending On Employee Wages & Salaries	15
Federal Grant Spending Per $ Of State Tax Revenue	12
General Revenue From Federal Government	22
Federal Tax Burden Per Capita	41
Highway Charges Returned To States	46
Terms Of Trade	17
Per Capita Federal Income Tax Liability	39

Taxes

Tax Revenue	48
Per Capita Tax Revenue	49
Tax Effort	46
Tax Capacity	47
Percent Change In Taxes	32
Property Taxes Per Capita	50
Property Tax Revenue As Percent Of Three-Tax Revenue	50
Sales Taxes Per Capita	18
Sales Tax Revenue As Percent Of Three-Tax Revenue	6
Services With Sales Tax	28
Income Taxes Per Capita	37
Income Tax Revenue As Percent Of Three-Tax Revenue	25
Highest Personal Income Tax Rate	39
Motor Fuel Taxes	30
Tobacco Taxes	42
Tax Burden On High Income Family	41
Progressivity Of Taxes	44

Revenues And Finances

State And Local Revenue	23
Non-Tax Revenue	20
State And Local Expenditures	25
Per Capita State And Local General Expenditures	44
Change In General Expenditures	44
State Government General Spending	24

Debt As Percent Of Revenue	33
Full Faith And Credit Debt	26
Bond Ratings	3
State Solvency Index	23
Pension Plan Assets	24
State Reserves	48
State Budget Process Quality	32
Relative State Spending "Needs"	41

Education

Math Proficiency, Grade Eight	39
AFQT Ranks	47
SAT Scores	n/a
ACT Scores	24
Over-25 Population Without High School Diploma	46
Private School Students	27
Percent Students Finishing High School	44
Pupil-Teacher Ratio	33
Public School Enrollment	24
Library Holdings Per Capita	43
Education Spending As Percent Of Total	36
Spending Per Pupil	47
Average Teacher Salary	40
State Aid Per Pupil	27
State And Local Spending For Higher Education	23
Higher Education Spending As Percent Of Total	14
Public Higher Education Enrollment	13
State Per Pupil Support Of Higher Education	5
Tuition And Fees	30
Average Professor Salary	30
Education Employees	29
R&D Spending	5

Health

Infant Mortality Rates	4
State Health Rankings	45
Population Without Health Insurance	13
Abortions	31

Alcohol Consumption	46
Percent Non-Smokers	17
Percent Obese	9
AIDS Cases	27
Physicians Per 100,000 Population	39
Medicaid Recipients Related To Poverty Population	45
Health/Hospital Spending As Percent Of Total	1
Per Capita Medicaid Spending	40
Medicaid Spending Per Aged Recipient	45
Medicaid Spending Per AFDC Child	47
Medicare Payment Per Hospital-Day	13
Population In HMOs	30

Crime And Law Enforcement

Crime Rate	26
Violent Crime Rate	12
Murder Rate	
Property Crime Rate	30
Motor Vehicle Theft Rate	31
Violent Crime Rate Change	12
Incarceration Rate	8
Juvenile Arrest Rate	11
Proportion Of Sentence Served	n/a
Law Enforcement Employees	27
Corrections Employees	42
Costs Per Inmate-Day	50
State Corrections Spending	48
Spending For Law Enforcement	41
Law Enforcement Spending As Percent Of Total	33

Transportation

Percent Of Travel On Interstates	39
Interstate Mileage In Poor Condition	45

Deficient Bridges	18
Traffic Deaths Per 100 Million Vehicle-miles	11
Seat Belt Use	38
Vehicle Miles Traveled Per Capita	4
Workers Using Public Transportation	41
Road And Street Miles Under State Control	35
Highway Employees	20
Public Transit Employees	34
State And Local Spending For Highways	42
Highway Spending As Percent Of Total	31

Welfare

Percent Of Births To Unwed Mothers	14
AFDC Recipients As Percent Of Population	41
Food Stamp Recipients As Percent Of Population	8
SSI Recipients As Percent Of Population	4
Change In AFDC Recipients	45
Condition Of Children Index	44
Percent Of Families With Single Parent	15
Typical Monthly AFDC Payments	49
Welfare As Percent Of Poverty Level Income	49
Average SSI State Supplements Per Recipient	37
State Income Tax Liability Of Typical Family In Poverty	5
Child Support Collections Per $ Of Administrative Costs	27
Percent Of Children In Foster Care	47
State And Local Welfare Spending Per Capita	34
Welfare Spending As Percent Of Total	28
Administrative Costs Per AFDC Case	37

Alaska

Population

Population	48
Percent Population Change	15
Population 2000	47
Median Age	49
Percent Population African-American	30
Percent Population in Poverty	38
Percent Population Female	50
Birth Rates	3
Death Rates	50
Illegal Immigrant Population	23

Economies

Personal Income	46
Per Capita Personal Income	10
Percent of Personal Income from Wages & Salaries	1
Average Annual Pay	4
Cost Of Living	3
Average Annual Pay in Manufacturing	30
Average Annual Pay in Retailing	2
Unemployment Rate	5
Government Employment	44
Manufacturing Employment	48
Fortune 500 Companies	n/a
Tourism Spending	45
Export-related Jobs	43
Change in Price of Existing Homes	n/a
Net Farm Income	50
Bankruptcy Filings	48
Patents Issued	43
WC Disability Payments	4
UC Average Weekly Benefit	25
Economic Momentum	41
Employment Change	42
Manufacturing Employment Change	29
Home Ownership	46
Gambling Losses	43
Electricity Use Per Residential Customer	35
Revenue Per Kwh	29
New Companies	5

Geography

Total Land Area	1
Federally-Owned Land	1
State Park Visitors	32
State Park Acreage	1
Hunters With Firearms	n/a
Registered Boats	48
Per Capita State Spending For the Arts	5
Energy Consumption Per Capita	1
Toxic Chemical Release Per Capita	14
Hazardous Waste Sites	42
Polluted Rivers	18
Air Quality	28

Government

Members Of US House	44
Legislators Per Million Population	9
Units Of Government	29
Female Legislators	21
Turnover In Legislatures	25
Democrats in State Legislatures	38
Number Of Statewide Elected Officials	45
State And Local Government Employees	2
State And Local Average Salaries	1
Local Employment	48
Registered Voters	12
Statewide Initiatives	10

Federal

Per Capita Federal Spending	1
Increase In Federal Spending	5
Federal Grants To State And Local Government	1
Per Capita Federal Spending On Procurement	3
Per Capita Federal Spending On Social Security And Medicare	50
Social Security Benefits	33
Federal Spending On Employee Wages & Salaries	1
Federal Grant Spending Per $ Of State Tax Revenue	42
General Revenue From Federal Government	41
Federal Tax Burden Per Capita	6
Highway Charges Returned To States	2
Terms Of Trade	4
Per Capita Federal Income Tax Liability	4

Taxes

Tax Revenue	1
Per Capita Tax Revenue	1
Tax Effort	2
Tax Capacity	1
Percent Change In Taxes	26
Property Taxes Per Capita	5
Property Tax Revenue As Percent Of Three-Tax Revenue	1
Sales Taxes Per Capita	47
Sales Tax Revenue As Percent Of Three-Tax Revenue	46
Services With Sales Tax	49
Income Taxes Per Capita	n/a
Income Tax Revenue As Percent Of Three-Tax Revenue	46
Highest Personal Income Tax Rate	n/a
Motor Fuel Taxes	48
Tobacco Taxes	24
Tax Burden On High Income Family	50
Progressivity Of Taxes	2

Revenues And Finances

State And Local Revenue	34
Non-Tax Revenue	23
State And Local Expenditures	37
Per Capita State And Local General Expenditures	1
Change In General Expenditures	1
State Government General Spending	36

Debt As Percent Of Revenue	8
Full Faith And Credit Debt	1
Bond Ratings	3
State Solvency Index	1
Pension Plan Assets	1
State Reserves	1
State Budget Process Quality	25
Relative State Spending "Needs"	27

Education

Math Proficiency, 8th Grade	n/a
AFQT Ranks	19
SAT Scores	5
ACT Scores	n/a
Over-25 Population Without High School Diploma	1
Private School Students	45
Percent Students Finishing High School	29
Pupil-Teacher Ratio	24
Public School Enrollment	4
Library Holdings Per Capita	21
Education Spending As Percent Of Total	49
Spending Per Pupil	2
Average Teacher Salary	2
State Aid Per Pupil	1
State And Local Spending For Higher Education	4
Higher Education Spending As Percent Of Total	48
Public Higher Education Enrollment	15
State Per Pupil Support Of Higher Education	3
Tuition And Fees	35
Average Professor Salary	4
Education Employees	3
R&D Spending	20

Health

Infant Mortality Rates	48
State Health Rankings	38
Population Without Health Insurance	25
Abortions	45

Alcohol Consumption	3
Percent Non-Smokers	47
Percent Obese	9
AIDS Cases	29
Physicians Per 100,000 Population	49
Medicaid Recipients Related To Poverty Population	19
Health/Hospital Spending As Percent Of Total	47
Per Capita Medicaid Spending	23
Medicaid Spending Per Aged Recipient	8
Medicaid Spending Per AFDC Child	1
Medicare Payment Per Hospital-Day	7
Population In HMOs	48

Crime And Law Enforcement

Crime Rate	16
Violent Crime Rate	15
Murder Rate	
Property Crime Rate	17
Motor Vehicle Theft Rate	21
Violent Crime Rate Change	6
Incarceration Rate	22
Juvenile Arrest Rate	14
Proportion Of Sentence Served	7
Law Enforcement Employees	24
Corrections Employees	15
Costs Per Inmate-Day	1
State Corrections Spending	2
Spending For Law Enforcement	1
Law Enforcement Spending As Percent Of Total	41

Transportation

Percent Of Travel On Interstates	3
Interstate Mileage In Poor Condition	7

Deficient Bridges	35
Traffic Deaths Per 100 Million Vehicle-miles	2
Seat Belt Use	15
Vehicle Miles Traveled Per Capita	49
Workers Using Public Transportation	21
Road And Street Miles Under State Control	7
Highway Employees	1
Public Transit Employees	3
State And Local Spending For Highways	1
Highway Spending As Percent Of Total	8

Welfare

Percent Of Births To Unwed Mothers	28
AFDC Recipients As Percent Of Population	5
Food Stamp Recipients As Percent Of Population	34
SSI Recipients As Percent Of Population	48
Change In AFDC Recipients	3
Condition Of Children Index	26
Percent Of Families With Single Parent	10
Typical Monthly AFDC Payments	1
Welfare As Percent Of Poverty Level Income	2
Average SSI State Supplements Per Recipient	2
State Income Tax Liability Of Typical Family In Poverty	n/a
Child Support Collections Per $ Of Administrative Costs	23
Percent Of Children In Foster Care	37
State And Local Welfare Spending Per Capita	10
Welfare Spending As Percent Of Total	50
Administrative Costs Per AFDC Case	13

Population

Population	23
Percent Population Change	2
Population 2000	21
Median Age	41
Percent Population African-American	36
Percent Population in Poverty	11
Percent Population Female	39
Birth Rates	7
Death Rates	33
Illegal Immigrant Population	7

Economies

Personal Income	23
Per Capita Personal Income	37
Percent of Personal Income from Wages & Salaries	25
Average Annual Pay	27
Cost Of Living	17
Average Annual Pay in Manufacturing	13
Average Annual Pay in Retailing	15
Unemployment Rate	17
Government Employment	25
Manufacturing Employment	28
Fortune 500 Companies	27
Tourism Spending	19
Export-related Jobs	25
Change in Price of Existing Homes	9
Net Farm Income	30
Bankruptcy Filings	6
Patents Issued	18
WC Disability Payments	44
UC Average Weekly Benefit	42
Economic Momentum	2
Employment Change	3
Manufacturing Employment Change	4
Home Ownership	38
Gambling Losses	29
Electricity Use Per Residential Customer	23
Revenue Per Kwh	18
New Companies	23

Geography

Total Land Area	6
Federally-Owned Land	4
State Park Visitors	46
State Park Acreage	41
Hunters With Firearms	32
Registered Boats	29
Per Capita State Spending For the Arts	30
Energy Consumption Per Capita	43
Toxic Chemical Release Per Capita	40
Hazardous Waste Sites	38
Polluted Rivers	12
Air Quality	38

Government

Members Of US House	23
Legislators Per Million Population	40
Units Of Government	41
Female Legislators	4
Turnover In Legislatures	9
Democrats in State Legislatures	42
Number Of Statewide Elected Officials	35
State And Local Government Employees	34
State And Local Average Salaries	20
Local Employment	7
Registered Voters	44
Statewide Initiatives	3

Federal

Per Capita Federal Spending	30
Increase In Federal Spending	23
Federal Grants To State And Local Government	31
Per Capita Federal Spending On Procurement	22
Per Capita Federal Spending On Social Security And Medicare	30
Social Security Benefits	22
Federal Spending On Employee Wages & Salaries	27
Federal Grant Spending Per $ Of State Tax Revenue	40
General Revenue From Federal Government	28
Federal Tax Burden Per Capita	40
Highway Charges Returned To States	31
Terms Of Trade	19
Per Capita Federal Income Tax Liability	35

Taxes

Tax Revenue	9
Per Capita Tax Revenue	24
Tax Effort	8
Tax Capacity	25
Percent Change In Taxes	13
Property Taxes Per Capita	23
Property Tax Revenue As Percent Of Three-Tax Revenue	25
Sales Taxes Per Capita	11
Sales Tax Revenue As Percent Of Three-Tax Revenue	16
Services With Sales Tax	19
Income Taxes Per Capita	36
Income Tax Revenue As Percent Of Three-Tax Revenue	38
Highest Personal Income Tax Rate	19
Motor Fuel Taxes	30
Tobacco Taxes	37
Tax Burden On High Income Family	23
Progressivity Of Taxes	12

Revenues And Finances

State And Local Revenue	24
Non-Tax Revenue	27
State And Local Expenditures	23
Per Capita State And Local General Expenditures	28
Change In General Expenditures	28
State Government General Spending	26

Debt As Percent Of Revenue	4	
Full Faith And Credit Debt	17	
Bond Ratings	n/a	
State Solvency Index	22	
Pension Plan Assets	15	
State Reserves	11	
State Budget Process Quality	13	
Relative State Spending "Needs"	38	

Education

Math Proficiency, 8th Grade	23
AFQT Ranks	18
SAT Scores	n/a
ACT Scores	18
Over-25 Population Without High School Diploma	20
Private School Students	40
Percent Students Finishing High School	33
Pupil-Teacher Ratio	42
Public School Enrollment	21
Library Holdings Per Capita	38
Education Spending As Percent Of Total	24
Spending Per Pupil	45
Average Teacher Salary	27
State Aid Per Pupil	39
State And Local Spending For Higher Education	18
Higher Education Spending As Percent Of Total	17
Public Higher Education Enrollment	1
State Per Pupil Support Of Higher Education	46
Tuition And Fees	39
Average Professor Salary	23
Education Employees	34
R&D Spending	24

Health

Infant Mortality Rates	15
State Health Rankings	25
Population Without Health Insurance	5
Abortions	28

Alcohol Consumption	5
Percent Non-Smokers	6
Percent Obese	39
AIDS Cases	26
Physicians Per 100,000 Population	25
Medicaid Recipients Related To Poverty Population	40
Health/Hospital Spending As Percent Of Total	41
Per Capita Medicaid Spending	50
Medicaid Spending Per Aged Recipient	50
Medicaid Spending Per AFDC Child	50
Medicare Payment Per Hospital-Day	3
Population In HMOs	4

Crime And Law Enforcement

Crime Rate	2
Violent Crime Rate	18
Murder Rate	
Property Crime Rate	2
Motor Vehicle Theft Rate	3
Violent Crime Rate Change	30
Incarceration Rate	6
Juvenile Arrest Rate	41
Proportion Of Sentence Served	2
Law Enforcement Employees	10
Corrections Employees	5
Costs Per Inmate-Day	35
State Corrections Spending	39
Spending For Law Enforcement	8
Law Enforcement Spending As Percent Of Total	4

Transportation

Percent Of Travel On Interstates	25
Interstate Mileage In Poor Condition	36

Deficient Bridges	50
Traffic Deaths Per 100 Million Vehicle-miles	14
Seat Belt Use	30
Vehicle Miles Traveled Per Capita	17
Workers Using Public Transportation	25
Road And Street Miles Under State Control	36
Highway Employees	43
Public Transit Employees	47
State And Local Spending For Highways	27
Highway Spending As Percent Of Total	26

Welfare

Percent Of Births To Unwed Mothers	4
AFDC Recipients As Percent Of Population	21
Food Stamp Recipients As Percent Of Population	9
SSI Recipients As Percent Of Population	39
Change In AFDC Recipients	4
Condition Of Children Index	45
Percent Of Families With Single Parent	20
Typical Monthly AFDC Payments	31
Welfare As Percent Of Poverty Level Income	28
Average SSI State Supplements Per Recipient	40
State Income Tax Liability Of Typical Family In Poverty	22
Child Support Collections Per $ Of Administrative Costs	50
Percent Of Children In Foster Care	36
State And Local Welfare Spending Per Capita	29
Welfare Spending As Percent Of Total	30
Administrative Costs Per AFDC Case	26

Population

Population	33
Percent Population Change	21
Population 2000	33
Median Age	12
Percent Population African-American	11
Percent Population in Poverty	13
Percent Population Female	10
Birth Rates	39
Death Rates	3
Illegal Immigrant Population	41

Economies

Personal Income	33
Per Capita Personal Income	49
Percent of Personal Income from Wages & Salaries	32
Average Annual Pay	46
Cost Of Living	49
Average Annual Pay in Manufacturing	48
Average Annual Pay in Retailing	31
Unemployment Rate	34
Government Employment	33
Manufacturing Employment	24
Fortune 500 Companies	22
Tourism Spending	32
Export-related Jobs	27
Change in Price of Existing Homes	n/a
Net Farm Income	10
Bankruptcy Filings	28
Patents Issued	49
WC Disability Payments	49
UC Average Weekly Benefit	32
Economic Momentum	12
Employment Change	8
Manufacturing Employment Change	17
Home Ownership	13
Gambling Losses	41
Electricity Use Per Residential Customer	18
Revenue Per Kwh	20
New Companies	33

Geography

Total Land Area	27
Federally-Owned Land	18
State Park Visitors	30
State Park Acreage	40
Hunters With Firearms	10
Registered Boats	27
Per Capita State Spending For the Arts	41
Energy Consumption Per Capita	20
Toxic Chemical Release Per Capita	12
Hazardous Waste Sites	31
Polluted Rivers	28
Air Quality	1

Government

Members Of US House	32
Legislators Per Million Population	18
Units Of Government	13
Female Legislators	42
Turnover In Legislatures	15
Democrats in State Legislatures	2
Number Of Statewide Elected Officials	16
State And Local Government Employees	23
State And Local Average Salaries	49
Local Employment	39
Registered Voters	36
Statewide Initiatives	10

Federal

Per Capita Federal Spending	31
Increase In Federal Spending	15
Federal Grants To State And Local Government	21
Per Capita Federal Spending On Procurement	45
Per Capita Federal Spending On Social Security And Medicare	12
Social Security Benefits	49

Federal Spending On Employee Wages & Salaries	42
Federal Grant Spending Per $ Of State Tax Revenue	14
General Revenue From Federal Government	32
Federal Tax Burden Per Capita	46
Highway Charges Returned To States	28
Terms Of Trade	11
Per Capita Federal Income Tax Liability	48

Taxes

Tax Revenue	41
Per Capita Tax Revenue	47
Tax Effort	44
Tax Capacity	48
Percent Change In Taxes	8
Property Taxes Per Capita	47
Property Tax Revenue As Percent Of Three-Tax Revenue	46
Sales Taxes Per Capita	17
Sales Tax Revenue As Percent Of Three-Tax Revenue	11
Services With Sales Tax	21
Income Taxes Per Capita	33
Income Tax Revenue As Percent Of Three-Tax Revenue	24
Highest Personal Income Tax Rate	15
Motor Fuel Taxes	27
Tobacco Taxes	22
Tax Burden On High Income Family	26
Progressivity Of Taxes	33

Revenues And Finances

State And Local Revenue	33
Non-Tax Revenue	37
State And Local Expenditures	34
Per Capita State And Local General Expenditures	50
Change In General Expenditures	50
State Government General Spending	32

Debt As Percent Of Revenue	44
Full Faith And Credit Debt	44
Bond Ratings	3
State Solvency Index	12
Pension Plan Assets	40
State Reserves	48
State Budget Process Quality	43
Relative State Spending "Needs"	46

Education

Math Proficiency, 8th Grade	38
AFQT Ranks	45
SAT Scores	n/a
ACT Scores	21
Over-25 Population Without High School Diploma	47
Private School Students	43
Percent Students Finishing High School	19
Pupil-Teacher Ratio	28
Public School Enrollment	13
Library Holdings Per Capita	36
Education Spending As Percent Of Total	6
Spending Per Pupil	48
Average Teacher Salary	44
State Aid Per Pupil	22
State And Local Spending For Higher Education	32
Higher Education Spending As Percent Of Total	10
Public Higher Education Enrollment	42
State Per Pupil Support Of Higher Education	2
Tuition And Fees	40
Average Professor Salary	40
Education Employees	15
R&D Spending	49

Health

Infant Mortality Rates	22
State Health Rankings	46
Population Without Health Insurance	6
Abortions	42

Alcohol Consumption	42
Percent Non-Smokers	n/a
Percent Obese	23
AIDS Cases	30
Physicians Per 100,000 Population	42
Medicaid Recipients Related To Poverty Population	33
Health/Hospital Spending As Percent Of Total	26
Per Capita Medicaid Spending	14
Medicaid Spending Per Aged Recipient	43
Medicaid Spending Per AFDC Child	38
Medicare Payment Per Hospital-Day	45
Population In HMOs	42

Crime And Law Enforcement

Crime Rate	28
Violent Crime Rate	23
Murder Rate	
Property Crime Rate	26
Motor Vehicle Theft Rate	34
Violent Crime Rate Change	10
Incarceration Rate	18
Juvenile Arrest Rate	17
Proportion Of Sentence Served	34
Law Enforcement Employees	40
Corrections Employees	33
Costs Per Inmate-Day	46
State Corrections Spending	46
Spending For Law Enforcement	46
Law Enforcement Spending As Percent Of Total	37

Transportation

Percent Of Travel On Interstates	30
Interstate Mileage In Poor Condition	4

Deficient Bridges	37
Traffic Deaths Per 100 Million Vehicle-miles	4
Seat Belt Use	42
Vehicle Miles Traveled Per Capita	19
Workers Using Public Transportation	49
Road And Street Miles Under State Control	19
Highway Employees	11
Public Transit Employees	38
State And Local Spending For Highways	32
Highway Spending As Percent Of Total	13

Welfare

Percent Of Births To Unwed Mothers	20
AFDC Recipients As Percent Of Population	43
Food Stamp Recipients As Percent Of Population	13
SSI Recipients As Percent Of Population	5
Change In AFDC Recipients	47
Condition Of Children Index	39
Percent Of Families With Single Parent	36
Typical Monthly AFDC Payments	44
Welfare As Percent Of Poverty Level Income	44
Average SSI State Supplements Per Recipient	41
State Income Tax Liability Of Typical Family In Poverty	14
Child Support Collections Per $ Of Administrative Costs	28
Percent Of Children In Foster Care	42
State And Local Welfare Spending Per Capita	28
Welfare Spending As Percent Of Total	10
Administrative Costs Per AFDC Case	34

Population

Population	1
Percent Population Change	35
Population 2000	1
Median Age	47
Percent Population African-American	25
Percent Population in Poverty	7
Percent Population Female	46
Birth Rates	2
Death Rates	43
Illegal Immigrant Population	1

Economies

Personal Income	1
Per Capita Personal Income	14
Percent of Personal Income from Wages & Salaries	26
Average Annual Pay	6
Cost Of Living	13
Average Annual Pay in Manufacturing	7
Average Annual Pay in Retailing	4
Unemployment Rate	2
Government Employment	1
Manufacturing Employment	1
Fortune 500 Companies	2
Tourism Spending	1
Export-related Jobs	1
Change in Price of Existing Homes	35
Net Farm Income	1
Bankruptcy Filings	5
Patents Issued	8
WC Disability Payments	34
UC Average Weekly Benefit	38
Economic Momentum	26
Employment Change	36
Manufacturing Employment Change	35
Home Ownership	47
Gambling Losses	3
Electricity Use Per Residential Customer	49
Revenue Per Kwh	30
New Companies	11

Geography

Total Land Area	3
Federally-Owned Land	3
State Park Visitors	1
State Park Acreage	2
Hunters With Firearms	45
Registered Boats	2
Per Capita State Spending For the Arts	43
Energy Consumption Per Capita	47
Toxic Chemical Release Per Capita	47
Hazardous Waste Sites	3
Polluted Rivers	8
Air Quality	50

Government

Members Of US House	1
Legislators Per Million Population	50
Units Of Government	42
Female Legislators	26
Turnover In Legislatures	12
Democrats in State Legislatures	22
Number Of Statewide Elected Officials	7
State And Local Government Employees	47
State And Local Average Salaries	2
Local Employment	1
Registered Voters	48
Statewide Initiatives	1

Federal

Per Capita Federal Spending	23
Increase In Federal Spending	21
Federal Grants To State And Local Government	18
Per Capita Federal Spending On Procurement	8
Per Capita Federal Spending On Social Security And Medicare	37
Social Security Benefits	18

Federal Spending On Employee Wages & Salaries	24
Federal Grant Spending Per $ Of State Tax Revenue	28
General Revenue From Federal Government	1
Federal Tax Burden Per Capita	17
Highway Charges Returned To States	30
Terms Of Trade	29
Per Capita Federal Income Tax Liability	18

Taxes

Tax Revenue	24
Per Capita Tax Revenue	10
Tax Effort	24
Tax Capacity	9
Percent Change In Taxes	27
Property Taxes Per Capita	25
Property Tax Revenue As Percent Of Three-Tax Revenue	29
Sales Taxes Per Capita	13
Sales Tax Revenue As Percent Of Three-Tax Revenue	23
Services With Sales Tax	42
Income Taxes Per Capita	11
Income Tax Revenue As Percent Of Three-Tax Revenue	21
Highest Personal Income Tax Rate	1
Motor Fuel Taxes	30
Tobacco Taxes	16
Tax Burden On High Income Family	15
Progressivity Of Taxes	49

Revenues And Finances

State And Local Revenue	1
Non-Tax Revenue	1
State And Local Expenditures	1
Per Capita State And Local General Expenditures	10
Change In General Expenditures	10
State Government General Spending	1

Debt As Percent Of Revenue	31
Full Faith And Credit Debt	31
Bond Ratings	4
State Solvency Index	34
Pension Plan Assets	2
State Reserves	44
State Budget Process Quality	44
Relative State Spending "Needs"	28

Education

Math Proficiency, 8th Grade	29
AFQT Ranks	35
SAT Scores	13
ACT Scores	n/a
Over-25 Population Without High School Diploma	28
Private School Students	17
Percent Students Finishing High School	40
Pupil-Teacher Ratio	49
Public School Enrollment	31
Library Holdings Per Capita	43
Education Spending As Percent Of Total	44
Spending Per Pupil	35
Average Teacher Salary	8
State Aid Per Pupil	20
State And Local Spending For Higher Education	21
Higher Education Spending As Percent Of Total	33
Public Higher Education Enrollment	8
State Per Pupil Support Of Higher Education	44
Tuition And Fees	21
Average Professor Salary	9
Education Employees	50
R&D Spending	7

Health

Infant Mortality Rates	35
State Health Rankings	28
Population Without Health Insurance	7
Abortions	1

Alcohol Consumption	12
Percent Non-Smokers	8
Percent Obese	33
AIDS Cases	6
Physicians Per 100,000 Population	10
Medicaid Recipients Related To Poverty Population	19
Health/Hospital Spending As Percent Of Total	13
Per Capita Medicaid Spending	34
Medicaid Spending Per Aged Recipient	47
Medicaid Spending Per AFDC Child	49
Medicare Payment Per Hospital-Day	2
Population In HMOs	1

Crime And Law Enforcement

Crime Rate	4
Violent Crime Rate	2
Murder Rate	
Property Crime Rate	8
Motor Vehicle Theft Rate	1
Violent Crime Rate Change	32
Incarceration Rate	15
Juvenile Arrest Rate	46
Proportion Of Sentence Served	1
Law Enforcement Employees	17
Corrections Employees	18
Costs Per Inmate-Day	19
State Corrections Spending	22
Spending For Law Enforcement	4
Law Enforcement Spending As Percent Of Total	3

Transportation

Percent Of Travel On Interstates	14
Interstate Mileage In Poor Condition	38

Deficient Bridges	25
Traffic Deaths Per 100 Million Vehicle-miles	35
Seat Belt Use	2
Vehicle Miles Traveled Per Capita	39
Workers Using Public Transportation	8
Road And Street Miles Under State Control	30
Highway Employees	50
Public Transit Employees	7
State And Local Spending For Highways	48
Highway Spending As Percent Of Total	50

Welfare

Percent Of Births To Unwed Mothers	8
AFDC Recipients As Percent Of Population	1
Food Stamp Recipients As Percent Of Population	22
SSI Recipients As Percent Of Population	8
Change In AFDC Recipients	11
Condition Of Children Index	35
Percent Of Families With Single Parent	21
Typical Monthly AFDC Payments	4
Welfare As Percent Of Poverty Level Income	5
Average SSI State Supplements Per Recipient	4
State Income Tax Liability Of Typical Family In Poverty	22
Child Support Collections Per $ Of Administrative Costs	43
Percent Of Children In Foster Care	4
State And Local Welfare Spending Per Capita	12
Welfare Spending As Percent Of Total	21
Administrative Costs Per AFDC Case	22

Population

Population	26
Percent Population Change	4
Population 2000	24
Median Age	32
Percent Population African-American	31
Percent Population in Poverty	43
Percent Population Female	40
Birth Rates	19
Death Rates	47
Illegal Immigrant Population	18

Economies

Personal Income	22
Per Capita Personal Income	15
Percent of Personal Income from Wages & Salaries	9
Average Annual Pay	15
Cost Of Living	19
Average Annual Pay in Manufacturing	15
Average Annual Pay in Retailing	16
Unemployment Rate	40
Government Employment	23
Manufacturing Employment	29
Fortune 500 Companies	26
Tourism Spending	17
Export-related Jobs	28
Change in Price of Existing Homes	2
Net Farm Income	27
Bankruptcy Filings	12
Patents Issued	9
WC Disability Payments	24
UC Average Weekly Benefit	12
Economic Momentum	8
Employment Change	25
Manufacturing Employment Change	23
Home Ownership	42
Gambling Losses	16
Electricity Use Per Residential Customer	41
Revenue Per Kwh	23
New Companies	3

Geography

Total Land Area	8
Federally-Owned Land	11
State Park Visitors	22
State Park Acreage	6
Hunters With Firearms	28
Registered Boats	34
Per Capita State Spending For the Arts	40
Energy Consumption Per Capita	39
Toxic Chemical Release Per Capita	48
Hazardous Waste Sites	21
Polluted Rivers	43
Air Quality	31

Government

Members Of US House	23
Legislators Per Million Population	35
Units Of Government	18
Female Legislators	3
Turnover In Legislatures	25
Democrats in State Legislatures	39
Number Of Statewide Elected Officials	35
State And Local Government Employees	28
State And Local Average Salaries	18
Local Employment	12
Registered Voters	24
Statewide Initiatives	4

Federal

Per Capita Federal Spending	16
Increase In Federal Spending	39
Federal Grants To State And Local Government	47
Per Capita Federal Spending On Procurement	6
Per Capita Federal Spending On Social Security And Medicare	47
Social Security Benefits	30

Federal Spending On

Employee Wages & Salaries	5
Federal Grant Spending Per $ Of State Tax Revenue	20
General Revenue From Federal Government	29
Federal Tax Burden Per Capita	15
Highway Charges Returned To States	26
Terms Of Trade	48
Per Capita Federal Income Tax Liability	11

Taxes

Tax Revenue	34
Per Capita Tax Revenue	25
Tax Effort	39
Tax Capacity	11
Percent Change In Taxes	35
Property Taxes Per Capita	24
Property Tax Revenue As Percent Of Three-Tax Revenue	24
Sales Taxes Per Capita	19
Sales Tax Revenue As Percent Of Three-Tax Revenue	27
Services With Sales Tax	46
Income Taxes Per Capita	22
Income Tax Revenue As Percent Of Three-Tax Revenue	27
Highest Personal Income Tax Rate	33
Motor Fuel Taxes	13
Tobacco Taxes	34
Tax Burden On High Income Family	32
Progressivity Of Taxes	24

Revenues And Finances

State And Local Revenue	25
Non-Tax Revenue	22
State And Local Expenditures	24
Per Capita State And Local General Expenditures	22
Change In General Expenditures	22
State Government General Spending	28

Debt As Percent Of Revenue	10
Full Faith And Credit Debt	21
Bond Ratings	n/a
State Solvency Index	6
Pension Plan Assets	11
State Reserves	12
State Budget Process Quality	1
Relative State Spending "Needs"	20

Education

Math Proficiency, 8th Grade	12
AFQT Ranks	16
SAT Scores	n/a
ACT Scores	5
Over-25 Population Without High School Diploma	3
Private School Students	26
Percent Students Finishing High School	28
Pupil-Teacher Ratio	40
Public School Enrollment	17
Library Holdings Per Capita	27
Education Spending As Percent Of Total	21
Spending Per Pupil	28
Average Teacher Salary	24
State Aid Per Pupil	36
State And Local Spending For Higher Education	13
Higher Education Spending As Percent Of Total	12
Public Higher Education Enrollment	4
State Per Pupil Support Of Higher Education	29
Tuition And Fees	27
Average Professor Salary	12
Education Employees	32
R&D Spending	9

Health

Infant Mortality Rates	38
State Health Rankings	10
Population Without Health Insurance	29
Abortions	34

Alcohol Consumption	13
Percent Non-Smokers	30
Percent Obese	47
AIDS Cases	18
Physicians Per 100,000 Population	13
Medicaid Recipients Related To Poverty Population	36
Health/Hospital Spending As Percent Of Total	35
Per Capita Medicaid Spending	46
Medicaid Spending Per Aged Recipient	25
Medicaid Spending Per AFDC Child	20
Medicare Payment Per Hospital-Day	5
Population In HMOs	9

Crime And Law Enforcement

Crime Rate	18
Violent Crime Rate	24
Murder Rate	
Property Crime Rate	14
Motor Vehicle Theft Rate	23
Violent Crime Rate Change	27
Incarceration Rate	25
Juvenile Arrest Rate	40
Proportion Of Sentence Served	14
Law Enforcement Employees	21
Corrections Employees	23
Costs Per Inmate-Day	20
State Corrections Spending	6
Spending For Law Enforcement	13
Law Enforcement Spending As Percent Of Total	12

Transportation

Percent Of Travel On Interstates	19
Interstate Mileage In Poor Condition	12

Deficient Bridges	38
Traffic Deaths Per 100 Million Vehicle-miles	29
Seat Belt Use	39
Vehicle Miles Traveled Per Capita	30
Workers Using Public Transportation	15
Road And Street Miles Under State Control	37
Highway Employees	30
Public Transit Employees	10
State And Local Spending For Highways	22
Highway Spending As Percent Of Total	25

Welfare

Percent Of Births To Unwed Mothers	41
AFDC Recipients As Percent Of Population	40
Food Stamp Recipients As Percent Of Population	37
SSI Recipients As Percent Of Population	34
Change In AFDC Recipients	31
Condition Of Children Index	27
Percent Of Families With Single Parent	18
Typical Monthly AFDC Payments	29
Welfare As Percent Of Poverty Level Income	28
Average SSI State Supplements Per Recipient	8
State Income Tax Liability Of Typical Family In Poverty	22
Child Support Collections Per $ Of Administrative Costs	44
Percent Of Children In Foster Care	15
State And Local Welfare Spending Per Capita	39
Welfare Spending As Percent Of Total	39
Administrative Costs Per AFDC Case	27

Population

Population	27
Percent Population Change	49
Population 2000	27
Median Age	6
Percent Population African-American	21
Percent Population in Poverty	32
Percent Population Female	16
Birth Rates	35
Death Rates	28
Illegal Immigrant Population	14

Economies

Personal Income	21
Per Capita Personal Income	1
Percent of Personal Income from Wages & Salaries	24
Average Annual Pay	1
Cost Of Living	6
Average Annual Pay in Manufacturing	3
Average Annual Pay in Retailing	3
Unemployment Rate	18
Government Employment	32
Manufacturing Employment	23
Fortune 500 Companies	8
Tourism Spending	30
Export-related Jobs	19
Change in Price of Existing Homes	33
Net Farm Income	39
Bankruptcy Filings	29
Patents Issued	2
WC Disability Payments	5
UC Average Weekly Benefit	4
Economic Momentum	50
Employment Change	47
Manufacturing Employment Change	45
Home Ownership	33
Gambling Losses	22
Electricity Use Per Residential Customer	36
Revenue Per Kwh	42
New Companies	32

Geography

Total Land Area	48
Federally-Owned Land	49
State Park Visitors	29
State Park Acreage	18
Hunters With Firearms	34
Registered Boats	32
Per Capita State Spending For the Arts	27
Energy Consumption Per Capita	45
Toxic Chemical Release Per Capita	37
Hazardous Waste Sites	27
Polluted Rivers	25
Air Quality	47

Government

Members Of US House	23
Legislators Per Million Population	17
Units Of Government	39
Female Legislators	11
Turnover In Legislatures	19
Democrats in State Legislatures	14
Number Of Statewide Elected Officials	16
State And Local Government Employees	49
State And Local Average Salaries	3
Local Employment	38
Registered Voters	18
Statewide Initiatives	n/a

Federal

Per Capita Federal Spending	18
Increase In Federal Spending	50
Federal Grants To State And Local Government	15
Per Capita Federal Spending On Procurement	11
Per Capita Federal Spending On Social Security And Medicare	7
Social Security Benefits	1
Federal Spending On Employee Wages & Salaries	41
Federal Grant Spending Per $ Of State Tax Revenue	47
General Revenue From Federal Government	25
Federal Tax Burden Per Capita	1
Highway Charges Returned To States	8
Terms Of Trade	44
Per Capita Federal Income Tax Liability	1

Taxes

Tax Revenue	17
Per Capita Tax Revenue	3
Tax Effort	17
Tax Capacity	4
Percent Change In Taxes	19
Property Taxes Per Capita	3
Property Tax Revenue As Percent Of Three-Tax Revenue	12
Sales Taxes Per Capita	7
Sales Tax Revenue As Percent Of Three-Tax Revenue	35
Services With Sales Tax	8
Income Taxes Per Capita	10
Income Tax Revenue As Percent Of Three-Tax Revenue	32
Highest Personal Income Tax Rate	35
Motor Fuel Taxes	1
Tobacco Taxes	7
Tax Burden On High Income Family	5
Progressivity Of Taxes	34

Revenues And Finances

State And Local Revenue	22
Non-Tax Revenue	31
State And Local Expenditures	21
Per Capita State And Local General Expenditures	6
Change In General Expenditures	6
State Government General Spending	20

Debt As Percent Of Revenue	19
Full Faith And Credit Debt	3
Bond Ratings	3
State Solvency Index	49
Pension Plan Assets	8
State Reserves	45
State Budget Process Quality	10
Relative State Spending "Needs"	2

Education

Math Proficiency, 8th Grade	11
AFQT Ranks	24
SAT Scores	12
ACT Scores	n/a
Over-25 Population Without High School Diploma	17
Private School Students	14
Percent Students Finishing High School	16
Pupil-Teacher Ratio	4
Public School Enrollment	44
Library Holdings Per Capita	7
Education Spending As Percent Of Total	43
Spending Per Pupil	3
Average Teacher Salary	1
State Aid Per Pupil	12
State And Local Spending For Higher Education	47
Higher Education Spending As Percent Of Total	49
Public Higher Education Enrollment	47
State Per Pupil Support Of Higher Education	6
Tuition And Fees	9
Average Professor Salary	2
Education Employees	36
R&D Spending	19

Health

Infant Mortality Rates	40
State Health Rankings	3
Population Without Health Insurance	47
Abortions	6

Alcohol Consumption	26
Percent Non-Smokers	21
Percent Obese	39
AIDS Cases	7
Physicians Per 100,000 Population	4
Medicaid Recipients Related To Poverty Population	8
Health/Hospital Spending As Percent Of Total	30
Per Capita Medicaid Spending	6
Medicaid Spending Per Aged Recipient	2
Medicaid Spending Per AFDC Child	13
Medicare Payment Per Hospital-Day	16
Population In HMOs	7

Crime And Law Enforcement

Crime Rate	31
Violent Crime Rate	31
Murder Rate	
Property Crime Rate	27
Motor Vehicle Theft Rate	13
Violent Crime Rate Change	44
Incarceration Rate	21
Juvenile Arrest Rate	39
Proportion Of Sentence Served	n/a
Law Enforcement Employees	15
Corrections Employees	31
Costs Per Inmate-Day	12
State Corrections Spending	18
Spending For Law Enforcement	10
Law Enforcement Spending As Percent Of Total	22

Transportation

Percent Of Travel On Interstates	2
Interstate Mileage In Poor Condition	6

Deficient Bridges	17
Traffic Deaths Per 100 Million Vehicle-miles	46
Seat Belt Use	8
Vehicle Miles Traveled Per Capita	42
Workers Using Public Transportation	11
Road And Street Miles Under State Control	16
Highway Employees	31
Public Transit Employees	30
State And Local Spending For Highways	14
Highway Spending As Percent Of Total	32

Welfare

Percent Of Births To Unwed Mothers	23
AFDC Recipients As Percent Of Population	17
Food Stamp Recipients As Percent Of Population	46
SSI Recipients As Percent Of Population	44
Change In AFDC Recipients	8
Condition Of Children Index	10
Percent Of Families With Single Parent	27
Typical Monthly AFDC Payments	5
Welfare As Percent Of Poverty Level Income	3
Average SSI State Supplements Per Recipient	1
State Income Tax Liability Of Typical Family In Poverty	22
Child Support Collections Per $ Of Administrative Costs	30
Percent Of Children In Foster Care	26
State And Local Welfare Spending Per Capita	7
Welfare Spending As Percent Of Total	15
Administrative Costs Per AFDC Case	30

Population

Population	46
Percent Population Change	19
Population 2000	46
Median Age	26
Percent Population African-American	9
Percent Population in Poverty	47
Percent Population Female	23
Birth Rates	31
Death Rates	13
Illegal Immigrant Population	24

Economies

Personal Income	44
Per Capita Personal Income	11
Percent of Personal Income from Wages & Salaries	2
Average Annual Pay	10
Cost Of Living	11
Average Annual Pay in Manufacturing	1
Average Annual Pay in Retailing	20
Unemployment Rate	41
Government Employment	49
Manufacturing Employment	41
Fortune 500 Companies	28
Tourism Spending	47
Export-related Jobs	41
Change in Price of Existing Homes	n/a
Net Farm Income	41
Bankruptcy Filings	46
Patents Issued	1
WC Disability Payments	42
UC Average Weekly Benefit	20
Economic Momentum	34
Employment Change	44
Manufacturing Employment Change	46
Home Ownership	8
Gambling Losses	37
Electricity Use Per Residential Customer	27
Revenue Per Kwh	3
New Companies	19

Geography

Total Land Area	49
Federally-Owned Land	48
State Park Visitors	41
State Park Acreage	49
Hunters With Firearms	42
Registered Boats	44
Per Capita State Spending For the Arts	4
Energy Consumption Per Capita	14
Toxic Chemical Release Per Capita	29
Hazardous Waste Sites	20
Polluted Rivers	7
Air Quality	42

Government

Members Of US House	44
Legislators Per Million Population	11
Units Of Government	22
Female Legislators	25
Turnover In Legislatures	32
Democrats in State Legislatures	35
Number Of Statewide Elected Officials	16
State And Local Government Employees	20
State And Local Average Salaries	19
Local Employment	49
Registered Voters	41
Statewide Initiatives	n/a

Federal

Per Capita Federal Spending	42
Increase In Federal Spending	28
Federal Grants To State And Local Government	43
Per Capita Federal Spending On Procurement	47
Per Capita Federal Spending On Social Security And Medicare	25
Social Security Benefits	6
Federal Spending On Employee Wages & Salaries	20
Federal Grant Spending Per $ Of State Tax Revenue	49
General Revenue From Federal Government	50
Federal Tax Burden Per Capita	5
Highway Charges Returned To States	13
Terms Of Trade	47
Per Capita Federal Income Tax Liability	12

Taxes

Tax Revenue	23
Per Capita Tax Revenue	8
Tax Effort	48
Tax Capacity	6
Percent Change In Taxes	14
Property Taxes Per Capita	43
Property Tax Revenue As Percent Of Three-Tax Revenue	41
Sales Taxes Per Capita	48
Sales Tax Revenue As Percent Of Three-Tax Revenue	48
Services With Sales Tax	4
Income Taxes Per Capita	5
Income Tax Revenue As Percent Of Three-Tax Revenue	1
Highest Personal Income Tax Rate	13
Motor Fuel Taxes	10
Tobacco Taxes	28
Tax Burden On High Income Family	36
Progressivity Of Taxes	37

Revenues And Finances

State And Local Revenue	46
Non-Tax Revenue	42
State And Local Expenditures	46
Per Capita State And Local General Expenditures	9
Change In General Expenditures	9
State Government General Spending	45

Debt As Percent Of Revenue	2
Full Faith And Credit Debt	20
Bond Ratings	2
State Solvency Index	17
Pension Plan Assets	17
State Reserves	2
State Budget Process Quality	15
Relative State Spending "Needs"	7

Education

Math Proficiency, 8th Grade	27
AFQT Ranks	23
SAT Scores	8
ACT Scores	n/a
Over-25 Population Without High School Diploma	23
Private School Students	1
Percent Students Finishing High School	38
Pupil-Teacher Ratio	22
Public School Enrollment	43
Library Holdings Per Capita	47
Education Spending As Percent Of Total	16
Spending Per Pupil	10
Average Teacher Salary	13
State Aid Per Pupil	3
State And Local Spending For Higher Education	2
Higher Education Spending As Percent Of Total	4
Public Higher Education Enrollment	11
State Per Pupil Support Of Higher Education	34
Tuition And Fees	5
Average Professor Salary	5
Education Employees	43
R&D Spending	37

Health

Infant Mortality Rates	31
State Health Rankings	28
Population Without Health Insurance	27
Abortions	4

Alcohol Consumption	7
Percent Non-Smokers	42
Percent Obese	3
AIDS Cases	5
Physicians Per 100,000 Population	20
Medicaid Recipients Related To Poverty Population	6
Health/Hospital Spending As Percent Of Total	42
Per Capita Medicaid Spending	25
Medicaid Spending Per Aged Recipient	7
Medicaid Spending Per AFDC Child	22
Medicare Payment Per Hospital-Day	21
Population In HMOs	14

Crime And Law Enforcement

Crime Rate	27
Violent Crime Rate	19
Murder Rate	
Property Crime Rate	28
Motor Vehicle Theft Rate	35
Violent Crime Rate Change	3
Incarceration Rate	14
Juvenile Arrest Rate	36
Proportion Of Sentence Served	8
Law Enforcement Employees	15
Corrections Employees	7
Costs Per Inmate-Day	18
State Corrections Spending	30
Spending For Law Enforcement	6
Law Enforcement Spending As Percent Of Total	6

Transportation

Percent Of Travel On Interstates	50
Interstate Mileage In Poor Condition	n/a

Deficient Bridges	27
Traffic Deaths Per 100 Million Vehicle-miles	33
Seat Belt Use	25
Vehicle Miles Traveled Per Capita	20
Workers Using Public Transportation	21
Road And Street Miles Under State Control	1
Highway Employees	16
Public Transit Employees	18
State And Local Spending For Highways	9
Highway Spending As Percent Of Total	16

Welfare

Percent Of Births To Unwed Mothers	12
AFDC Recipients As Percent Of Population	36
Food Stamp Recipients As Percent Of Population	30
SSI Recipients As Percent Of Population	37
Change In AFDC Recipients	16
Condition Of Children Index	24
Percent Of Families With Single Parent	19
Typical Monthly AFDC Payments	33
Welfare As Percent Of Poverty Level Income	33
Average SSI State Supplements Per Recipient	31
State Income Tax Liability Of Typical Family In Poverty	10
Child Support Collections Per $ Of Administrative Costs	45
Percent Of Children In Foster Care	45
State And Local Welfare Spending Per Capita	42
Welfare Spending As Percent Of Total	46
Administrative Costs Per AFDC Case	25

Population

Population	4
Percent Population Change	12
Population 2000	4
Median Age	1
Percent Population African-American	15
Percent Population in Poverty	14
Percent Population Female	15
Birth Rates	40
Death Rates	6
Illegal Immigrant Population	3

Economies

Personal Income	4
Per Capita Personal Income	20
Percent of Personal Income from Wages & Salaries	48
Average Annual Pay	29
Cost Of Living	30
Average Annual Pay in Manufacturing	27
Average Annual Pay in Retailing	14
Unemployment Rate	21
Government Employment	4
Manufacturing Employment	14
Fortune 500 Companies	14
Tourism Spending	2
Export-related Jobs	14
Change in Price of Existing Homes	23
Net Farm Income	6
Bankruptcy Filings	21
Patents Issued	29
WC Disability Payments	23
UC Average Weekly Benefit	27
Economic Momentum	7
Employment Change	9
Manufacturing Employment Change	30
Home Ownership	27
Gambling Losses	6
Electricity Use Per Residential Customer	13
Revenue Per Kwh	37
New Companies	10

Geography

Total Land Area	26
Federally-Owned Land	16
State Park Visitors	20
State Park Acreage	4
Hunters With Firearms	44
Registered Boats	4
Per Capita State Spending For the Arts	3
Energy Consumption Per Capita	46
Toxic Chemical Release Per Capita	34
Hazardous Waste Sites	6
Polluted Rivers	33
Air Quality	27

Government

Members Of US House	4
Legislators Per Million Population	48
Units Of Government	48
Female Legislators	30
Turnover In Legislatures	20
Democrats in State Legislatures	23
Number Of Statewide Elected Officials	7
State And Local Government Employees	39
State And Local Average Salaries	27
Local Employment	5
Registered Voters	46
Statewide Initiatives	21

Federal

Per Capita Federal Spending	17
Increase In Federal Spending	7
Federal Grants To State And Local Government	48
Per Capita Federal Spending On Procurement	24
Per Capita Federal Spending On Social Security And Medicare	2
Social Security Benefits	20
Federal Spending On Employee Wages & Salaries	31
Federal Grant Spending Per $ Of State Tax Revenue	37
General Revenue From Federal Government	8
Federal Tax Burden Per Capita	20
Highway Charges Returned To States	39
Terms Of Trade	45
Per Capita Federal Income Tax Liability	14

Taxes

Tax Revenue	43
Per Capita Tax Revenue	30
Tax Effort	39
Tax Capacity	15
Percent Change In Taxes	5
Property Taxes Per Capita	16
Property Tax Revenue As Percent Of Three-Tax Revenue	13
Sales Taxes Per Capita	5
Sales Tax Revenue As Percent Of Three-Tax Revenue	7
Services With Sales Tax	15
Income Taxes Per Capita	n/a
Income Tax Revenue As Percent Of Three-Tax Revenue	46
Highest Personal Income Tax Rate	n/a
Motor Fuel Taxes	45
Tobacco Taxes	21
Tax Burden On High Income Family	47
Progressivity Of Taxes	28

Revenues And Finances

State And Local Revenue	5
Non-Tax Revenue	4
State And Local Expenditures	4
Per Capita State And Local General Expenditures	29
Change In General Expenditures	29
State Government General Spending	5

Debt As Percent Of Revenue	12
Full Faith And Credit Debt	36
Bond Ratings	3
State Solvency Index	32
Pension Plan Assets	30
State Reserves	41
State Budget Process Quality	17
Relative State Spending "Needs"	12

Education

Math Proficiency, 8th Grade	31
AFQT Ranks	25
SAT Scores	17
ACT Scores	n/a
Over-25 Population Without High School Diploma	37
Private School Students	20
Percent Students Finishing High School	45
Pupil-Teacher Ratio	41
Public School Enrollment	46
Library Holdings Per Capita	49
Education Spending As Percent Of Total	42
Spending Per Pupil	27
Average Teacher Salary	26
State Aid Per Pupil	16
State And Local Spending For Higher Education	49
Higher Education Spending As Percent Of Total	45
Public Higher Education Enrollment	40
State Per Pupil Support Of Higher Education	36
Tuition And Fees	42
Average Professor Salary	36
Education Employees	48
R&D Spending	14

Health

Infant Mortality Rates	20
State Health Rankings	38
Population Without Health Insurance	37
Abortions	9

Alcohol Consumption	4
Percent Non-Smokers	21
Percent Obese	31
AIDS Cases	2
Physicians Per 100,000 Population	16
Medicaid Recipients Related To Poverty Population	38
Health/Hospital Spending As Percent Of Total	15
Per Capita Medicaid Spending	37
Medicaid Spending Per Aged Recipient	38
Medicaid Spending Per AFDC Child	30
Medicare Payment Per Hospital-Day	6
Population In HMOs	16

Crime And Law Enforcement

Crime Rate	1
Violent Crime Rate	1
Murder Rate	
Property Crime Rate	1
Motor Vehicle Theft Rate	2
Violent Crime Rate Change	39
Incarceration Rate	11
Juvenile Arrest Rate	49
Proportion Of Sentence Served	18
Law Enforcement Employees	4
Corrections Employees	2
Costs Per Inmate-Day	36
State Corrections Spending	28
Spending For Law Enforcement	5
Law Enforcement Spending As Percent Of Total	2

Transportation

Percent Of Travel On Interstates	42
Interstate Mileage In Poor Condition	32

Deficient Bridges	32
Traffic Deaths Per 100 Million Vehicle-miles	13
Seat Belt Use	28
Vehicle Miles Traveled Per Capita	35
Workers Using Public Transportation	26
Road And Street Miles Under State Control	34
Highway Employees	41
Public Transit Employees	21
State And Local Spending For Highways	35
Highway Spending As Percent Of Total	34

Welfare

Percent Of Births To Unwed Mothers	9
AFDC Recipients As Percent Of Population	24
Food Stamp Recipients As Percent Of Population	19
SSI Recipients As Percent Of Population	17
Change In AFDC Recipients	2
Condition Of Children Index	47
Percent Of Families With Single Parent	6
Typical Monthly AFDC Payments	36
Welfare As Percent Of Poverty Level Income	37
Average SSI State Supplements Per Recipient	34
State Income Tax Liability Of Typical Family In Poverty	n/a
Child Support Collections Per $ Of Administrative Costs	22
Percent Of Children In Foster Care	39
State And Local Welfare Spending Per Capita	45
Welfare Spending As Percent Of Total	43
Administrative Costs Per AFDC Case	19

Population

Population	11
Percent Population Change	7
Population 2000	11
Median Age	42
Percent Population African-American	4
Percent Population in Poverty	21
Percent Population Female	22
Birth Rates	13
Death Rates	41
Illegal Immigrant Population	21

Economies

Personal Income	12
Per Capita Personal Income	29
Percent of Personal Income from Wages & Salaries	5
Average Annual Pay	22
Cost Of Living	46
Average Annual Pay in Manufacturing	40
Average Annual Pay in Retailing	22
Unemployment Rate	26
Government Employment	11
Manufacturing Employment	11
Fortune 500 Companies	12
Tourism Spending	9
Export-related Jobs	15
Change in Price of Existing Homes	26
Net Farm Income	7
Bankruptcy Filings	2
Patents Issued	35
WC Disability Payments	48
UC Average Weekly Benefit	40
Economic Momentum	4
Employment Change	7
Manufacturing Employment Change	26
Home Ownership	36
Gambling Losses	15
Electricity Use Per Residential Customer	14
Revenue Per Kwh	22
New Companies	7

Geography

Total Land Area	21
Federally-Owned Land	24
State Park Visitors	14
State Park Acreage	36
Hunters With Firearms	27
Registered Boats	14
Per Capita State Spending For the Arts	37
Energy Consumption Per Capita	24
Toxic Chemical Release Per Capita	26
Hazardous Waste Sites	30
Polluted Rivers	19
Air Quality	31

Government

Members Of US House	11
Legislators Per Million Population	28
Units Of Government	36
Female Legislators	32
Turnover In Legislatures	41
Democrats in State Legislatures	12
Number Of Statewide Elected Officials	3
State And Local Government Employees	10
State And Local Average Salaries	43
Local Employment	13
Registered Voters	47
Statewide Initiatives	n/a

Federal

Per Capita Federal Spending	35
Increase In Federal Spending	2
Federal Grants To State And Local Government	36
Per Capita Federal Spending On Procurement	21
Per Capita Federal Spending On Social Security And Medicare	46
Social Security Benefits	43

Federal Spending On Employee Wages & Salaries	8
Federal Grant Spending Per $ Of State Tax Revenue	24
General Revenue From Federal Government	11
Federal Tax Burden Per Capita	31
Highway Charges Returned To States	49
Terms Of Trade	30
Per Capita Federal Income Tax Liability	26

Taxes

Tax Revenue	35
Per Capita Tax Revenue	32
Tax Effort	24
Tax Capacity	31
Percent Change In Taxes	11
Property Taxes Per Capita	32
Property Tax Revenue As Percent Of Three-Tax Revenue	32
Sales Taxes Per Capita	21
Sales Tax Revenue As Percent Of Three-Tax Revenue	21
Services With Sales Tax	27
Income Taxes Per Capita	23
Income Tax Revenue As Percent Of Three-Tax Revenue	22
Highest Personal Income Tax Rate	25
Motor Fuel Taxes	50
Tobacco Taxes	45
Tax Burden On High Income Family	18
Progressivity Of Taxes	18

Revenues And Finances

State And Local Revenue	11
Non-Tax Revenue	10
State And Local Expenditures	12
Per Capita State And Local General Expenditures	34
Change In General Expenditures	34
State Government General Spending	13

Debt As Percent Of Revenue	29
Full Faith And Credit Debt	28
Bond Ratings	1
State Solvency Index	20
Pension Plan Assets	23
State Reserves	29
State Budget Process Quality	7
Relative State Spending "Needs"	33

Education

Math Proficiency, 8th Grade	31
AFQT Ranks	45
SAT Scores	10
ACT Scores	n/a
Over-25 Population Without High School Diploma	41
Private School Students	29
Percent Students Finishing High School	46
Pupil-Teacher Ratio	38
Public School Enrollment	15
Library Holdings Per Capita	43
Education Spending As Percent Of Total	38
Spending Per Pupil	41
Average Teacher Salary	33
State Aid Per Pupil	38
State And Local Spending For Higher Education	48
Higher Education Spending As Percent Of Total	42
Public Higher Education Enrollment	44
State Per Pupil Support Of Higher Education	9
Tuition And Fees	36
Average Professor Salary	32
Education Employees	12
R&D Spending	8

Health

Infant Mortality Rates	5
State Health Rankings	36
Population Without Health Insurance	9
Abortions	11

Alcohol Consumption	30
Percent Non-Smokers	5
Percent Obese	32
AIDS Cases	8
Physicians Per 100,000 Population	34
Medicaid Recipients Related To Poverty Population	30
Health/Hospital Spending As Percent Of Total	2
Per Capita Medicaid Spending	24
Medicaid Spending Per Aged Recipient	40
Medicaid Spending Per AFDC Child	40
Medicare Payment Per Hospital-Day	27
Population In HMOs	33

Crime And Law Enforcement

Crime Rate	8
Violent Crime Rate	17
Murder Rate	
Property Crime Rate	6
Motor Vehicle Theft Rate	14
Violent Crime Rate Change	38
Incarceration Rate	7
Juvenile Arrest Rate	24
Proportion Of Sentence Served	17
Law Enforcement Employees	17
Corrections Employees	3
Costs Per Inmate-Day	26
State Corrections Spending	37
Spending For Law Enforcement	21
Law Enforcement Spending As Percent Of Total	9

Transportation

Percent Of Travel On Interstates	9
Interstate Mileage In Poor Condition	48

Deficient Bridges	29
Traffic Deaths Per 100 Million Vehicle-miles	23
Seat Belt Use	35
Vehicle Miles Traveled Per Capita	3
Workers Using Public Transportation	16
Road And Street Miles Under State Control	24
Highway Employees	37
Public Transit Employees	11
State And Local Spending For Highways	47
Highway Spending As Percent Of Total	43

Welfare

Percent Of Births To Unwed Mothers	7
AFDC Recipients As Percent Of Population	12
Food Stamp Recipients As Percent Of Population	11
SSI Recipients As Percent Of Population	11
Change In AFDC Recipients	12
Condition Of Children Index	43
Percent Of Families With Single Parent	5
Typical Monthly AFDC Payments	40
Welfare As Percent Of Poverty Level Income	40
Average SSI State Supplements Per Recipient	42
State Income Tax Liability Of Typical Family In Poverty	18
Child Support Collections Per $ Of Administrative Costs	12
Percent Of Children In Foster Care	31
State And Local Welfare Spending Per Capita	27
Welfare Spending As Percent Of Total	24
Administrative Costs Per AFDC Case	40

Population

Population	40
Percent Population Change	20
Population 2000	40
Median Age	27
Percent Population African-American	38
Percent Population in Poverty	46
Percent Population Female	48
Birth Rates	5
Death Rates	48
Illegal Immigrant Population	9

Economies

Personal Income	38
Per Capita Personal Income	6
Percent of Personal Income from Wages & Salaries	12
Average Annual Pay	12
Cost Of Living	1
Average Annual Pay in Manufacturing	34
Average Annual Pay in Retailing	6
Unemployment Rate	22
Government Employment	38
Manufacturing Employment	49
Fortune 500 Companies	n/a
Tourism Spending	18
Export-related Jobs	48
Change in Price of Existing Homes	n/a
Net Farm Income	49
Bankruptcy Filings	50
Patents Issued	44
WC Disability Payments	14
UC Average Weekly Benefit	1
Economic Momentum	49
Employment Change	49
Manufacturing Employment Change	50
Home Ownership	49
Gambling Losses	n/a
Electricity Use Per Residential Customer	42
Revenue Per Kwh	41
New Companies	35

Geography

Total Land Area	47
Federally-Owned Land	36
State Park Visitors	15
State Park Acreage	46
Hunters With Firearms	n/a
Registered Boats	50
Per Capita State Spending For the Arts	1
Energy Consumption Per Capita	50
Toxic Chemical Release Per Capita	50
Hazardous Waste Sites	45
Polluted Rivers	29
Air Quality	1

Government

Members Of US House	38
Legislators Per Million Population	16
Units Of Government	50
Female Legislators	29
Turnover In Legislatures	6
Democrats in State Legislatures	1
Number Of Statewide Elected Officials	45
State And Local Government Employees	17
State And Local Average Salaries	15
Local Employment	50
Registered Voters	49
Statewide Initiatives	n/a

Federal

Per Capita Federal Spending	5
Increase In Federal Spending	27
Federal Grants To State And Local Government	16
Per Capita Federal Spending On Procurement	14
Per Capita Federal Spending On Social Security And Medicare	48
Social Security Benefits	26
Federal Spending On Employee Wages & Salaries	2
Federal Grant Spending Per $ Of State Tax Revenue	45
General Revenue From Federal Government	40
Federal Tax Burden Per Capita	12
Highway Charges Returned To States	1
Terms Of Trade	23
Per Capita Federal Income Tax Liability	15

Taxes

Tax Revenue	3
Per Capita Tax Revenue	5
Tax Effort	24
Tax Capacity	2
Percent Change In Taxes	3
Property Taxes Per Capita	35
Property Tax Revenue As Percent Of Three-Tax Revenue	48
Sales Taxes Per Capita	1
Sales Tax Revenue As Percent Of Three-Tax Revenue	12
Services With Sales Tax	1
Income Taxes Per Capita	4
Income Tax Revenue As Percent Of Three-Tax Revenue	16
Highest Personal Income Tax Rate	3
Motor Fuel Taxes	39
Tobacco Taxes	2
Tax Burden On High Income Family	16
Progressivity Of Taxes	39

Revenues And Finances

State And Local Revenue	39
Non-Tax Revenue	39
State And Local Expenditures	38
Per Capita State And Local General Expenditures	4
Change In General Expenditures	4
State Government General Spending	35

Debt As Percent Of Revenue	16
Full Faith And Credit Debt	2
Bond Ratings	3
State Solvency Index	44
Pension Plan Assets	6
State Reserves	34
State Budget Process Quality	16
Relative State Spending "Needs"	8

Education

Math Proficiency, 8th Grade	37
AFQT Ranks	44
SAT Scores	15
ACT Scores	n/a
Over-25 Population Without High School Diploma	13
Private School Students	3
Percent Students Finishing High School	20
Pupil-Teacher Ratio	34
Public School Enrollment	42
Library Holdings Per Capita	33
Education Spending As Percent Of Total	50
Spending Per Pupil	16
Average Teacher Salary	14
State Aid Per Pupil	2
State And Local Spending For Higher Education	10
Higher Education Spending As Percent Of Total	34
Public Higher Education Enrollment	29
State Per Pupil Support Of Higher Education	10
Tuition And Fees	49
Average Professor Salary	3
Education Employees	37
R&D Spending	33

Health

Infant Mortality Rates	40
State Health Rankings	5
Population Without Health Insurance	40
Abortions	18

Alcohol Consumption	8
Percent Non-Smokers	9
Percent Obese	44
AIDS Cases	16
Physicians Per 100,000 Population	9
Medicaid Recipients Related To Poverty Population	4
Health/Hospital Spending As Percent Of Total	34
Per Capita Medicaid Spending	47
Medicaid Spending Per Aged Recipient	23
Medicaid Spending Per AFDC Child	31
Medicare Payment Per Hospital-Day	4
Population In HMOs	12

Crime And Law Enforcement

Crime Rate	6
Violent Crime Rate	43
Murder Rate	
Property Crime Rate	3
Motor Vehicle Theft Rate	22
Violent Crime Rate Change	42
Incarceration Rate	35
Juvenile Arrest Rate	13
Proportion Of Sentence Served	24
Law Enforcement Employees	9
Corrections Employees	26
Costs Per Inmate-Day	2
State Corrections Spending	11
Spending For Law Enforcement	18
Law Enforcement Spending As Percent Of Total	40

Transportation

Percent Of Travel On Interstates	41
Interstate Mileage In Poor Condition	n/a

Deficient Bridges	3
Traffic Deaths Per 100 Million Vehicle-miles	31
Seat Belt Use	1
Vehicle Miles Traveled Per Capita	48
Workers Using Public Transportation	6
Road And Street Miles Under State Control	11
Highway Employees	48
Public Transit Employees	43
State And Local Spending For Highways	11
Highway Spending As Percent Of Total	33

Welfare

Percent Of Births To Unwed Mothers	31
AFDC Recipients As Percent Of Population	15
Food Stamp Recipients As Percent Of Population	24
SSI Recipients As Percent Of Population	33
Change In AFDC Recipients	15
Condition Of Children Index	17
Percent Of Families With Single Parent	39
Typical Monthly AFDC Payments	2
Welfare As Percent Of Poverty Level Income	1
Average SSI State Supplements Per Recipient	13
State Income Tax Liability Of Typical Family In Poverty	1
Child Support Collections Per $ Of Administrative Costs	21
Percent Of Children In Foster Care	40
State And Local Welfare Spending Per Capita	24
Welfare Spending As Percent Of Total	47
Administrative Costs Per AFDC Case	38

Population

Population	42
Percent Population Change	3
Population 2000	42
Median Age	43
Percent Population African-American	49
Percent Population in Poverty	26
Percent Population Female	45
Birth Rates	17
Death Rates	45
Illegal Immigrant Population	19

Economies

Personal Income	43
Per Capita Personal Income	39
Percent of Personal Income from Wages & Salaries	41
Average Annual Pay	44
Cost Of Living	29
Average Annual Pay in Manufacturing	25
Average Annual Pay in Retailing	35
Unemployment Rate	19
Government Employment	40
Manufacturing Employment	40
Fortune 500 Companies	29
Tourism Spending	40
Export-related Jobs	40
Change in Price of Existing Homes	n/a
Net Farm Income	23
Bankruptcy Filings	24
Patents Issued	10
WC Disability Payments	39
UC Average Weekly Benefit	29
Economic Momentum	10
Employment Change	18
Manufacturing Employment Change	10
Home Ownership	10
Gambling Losses	44
Electricity Use Per Residential Customer	2
Revenue Per Kwh	12
New Companies	2

Geography

Total Land Area	12
Federally-Owned Land	6
State Park Visitors	42
State Park Acreage	44
Hunters With Firearms	3
Registered Boats	36
Per Capita State Spending For the Arts	28
Energy Consumption Per Capita	17
Toxic Chemical Release Per Capita	25
Hazardous Waste Sites	39
Polluted Rivers	2
Air Quality	1

Government

Members Of US House	38
Legislators Per Million Population	10
Units Of Government	8
Female Legislators	10
Turnover In Legislatures	29
Democrats in State Legislatures	49
Number Of Statewide Elected Officials	11
State And Local Government Employees	14
State And Local Average Salaries	39
Local Employment	30
Registered Voters	28
Statewide Initiatives	17

Federal

Per Capita Federal Spending	36
Increase In Federal Spending	41
Federal Grants To State And Local Government	40
Per Capita Federal Spending On Procurement	16
Per Capita Federal Spending On Social Security And Medicare	41
Social Security Benefits	31

Federal Spending On Employee Wages & Salaries	29
Federal Grant Spending Per $ Of State Tax Revenue	38
General Revenue From Federal Government	46
Federal Tax Burden Per Capita	39
Highway Charges Returned To States	11
Terms Of Trade	22
Per Capita Federal Income Tax Liability	38

Taxes

Tax Revenue	13
Per Capita Tax Revenue	36
Tax Effort	28
Tax Capacity	44
Percent Change In Taxes	2
Property Taxes Per Capita	38
Property Tax Revenue As Percent Of Three-Tax Revenue	37
Sales Taxes Per Capita	37
Sales Tax Revenue As Percent Of Three-Tax Revenue	24
Services With Sales Tax	31
Income Taxes Per Capita	18
Income Tax Revenue As Percent Of Three-Tax Revenue	9
Highest Personal Income Tax Rate	9
Motor Fuel Taxes	13
Tobacco Taxes	25
Tax Burden On High Income Family	17
Progressivity Of Taxes	48

Revenues And Finances

State And Local Revenue	44
Non-Tax Revenue	44
State And Local Expenditures	44
Per Capita State And Local General Expenditures	46
Change In General Expenditures	46
State Government General Spending	44

Debt As Percent Of Revenue	49
Full Faith And Credit Debt	46
Bond Ratings	n/a
State Solvency Index	21
Pension Plan Assets	27
State Reserves	34
State Budget Process Quality	35
Relative State Spending "Needs"	37

Education

Math Proficiency, 8th Grade	8
AFQT Ranks	9
SAT Scores	n/a
ACT Scores	11
Over-25 Population Without High School Diploma	16
Private School Students	48
Percent Students Finishing High School	12
Pupil-Teacher Ratio	47
Public School Enrollment	2
Library Holdings Per Capita	19
Education Spending As Percent Of Total	12
Spending Per Pupil	44
Average Teacher Salary	45
State Aid Per Pupil	26
State And Local Spending For Higher Education	25
Higher Education Spending As Percent Of Total	15
Public Higher Education Enrollment	27
State Per Pupil Support Of Higher Education	32
Tuition And Fees	48
Average Professor Salary	47
Education Employees	18
R&D Spending	11

Health

Infant Mortality Rates	29
State Health Rankings	25
Population Without Health Insurance	19
Abortions	47

Alcohol Consumption	33
Percent Non-Smokers	4
Percent Obese	30
AIDS Cases	46
Physicians Per 100,000 Population	50
Medicaid Recipients Related To Poverty Population	47
Health/Hospital Spending As Percent Of Total	22
Per Capita Medicaid Spending	39
Medicaid Spending Per Aged Recipient	22
Medicaid Spending Per AFDC Child	28
Medicare Payment Per Hospital-Day	19
Population In HMOs	45

Crime And Law Enforcement

Crime Rate	43
Violent Crime Rate	41
Murder Rate	
Property Crime Rate	42
Motor Vehicle Theft Rate	44
Violent Crime Rate Change	28
Incarceration Rate	28
Juvenile Arrest Rate	21
Proportion Of Sentence Served	5
Law Enforcement Employees	27
Corrections Employees	35
Costs Per Inmate-Day	33
State Corrections Spending	33
Spending For Law Enforcement	34
Law Enforcement Spending As Percent Of Total	25

Transportation

Percent Of Travel On Interstates	33
Interstate Mileage In Poor Condition	11

Deficient Bridges	39
Traffic Deaths Per 100 Million Vehicle-miles	16
Seat Belt Use	28
Vehicle Miles Traveled Per Capita	8
Workers Using Public Transportation	28
Road And Street Miles Under State Control	48
Highway Employees	12
Public Transit Employees	47
State And Local Spending For Highways	17
Highway Spending As Percent Of Total	9

Welfare

Percent Of Births To Unwed Mothers	48
AFDC Recipients As Percent Of Population	50
Food Stamp Recipients As Percent Of Population	39
SSI Recipients As Percent Of Population	42
Change In AFDC Recipients	18
Condition Of Children Index	25
Percent Of Families With Single Parent	49
Typical Monthly AFDC Payments	35
Welfare As Percent Of Poverty Level Income	36
Average SSI State Supplements Per Recipient	23
State Income Tax Liability Of Typical Family In Poverty	22
Child Support Collections Per $ Of Administrative Costs	24
Percent Of Children In Foster Care	50
State And Local Welfare Spending Per Capita	50
Welfare Spending As Percent Of Total	41
Administrative Costs Per AFDC Case	7

Population

Population	6
Percent Population Change	39
Population 2000	6
Median Age	34
Percent Population African-American	12
Percent Population in Poverty	25
Percent Population Female	25
Birth Rates	8
Death Rates	24
Illegal Immigrant Population	6

Economies

Personal Income	5
Per Capita Personal Income	9
Percent of Personal Income from Wages & Salaries	13
Average Annual Pay	8
Cost Of Living	18
Average Annual Pay in Manufacturing	9
Average Annual Pay in Retailing	13
Unemployment Rate	27
Government Employment	5
Manufacturing Employment	5
Fortune 500 Companies	3
Tourism Spending	5
Export-related Jobs	5
Change in Price of Existing Homes	14
Net Farm Income	8
Bankruptcy Filings	15
Patents Issued	13
WC Disability Payments	2
UC Average Weekly Benefit	11
Economic Momentum	40
Employment Change	41
Manufacturing Employment Change	27
Home Ownership	39
Gambling Losses	4
Electricity Use Per Residential Customer	38
Revenue Per Kwh	4
New Companies	39

Geography

Total Land Area	24
Federally-Owned Land	30
State Park Visitors	6
State Park Acreage	5
Hunters With Firearms	38
Registered Boats	9
Per Capita State Spending For the Arts	31
Energy Consumption Per Capita	30
Toxic Chemical Release Per Capita	24
Hazardous Waste Sites	10
Polluted Rivers	24
Air Quality	44

Government

Members Of US House	6
Legislators Per Million Population	45
Units Of Government	14
Female Legislators	20
Turnover In Legislatures	35
Democrats in State Legislatures	31
Number Of Statewide Elected Officials	16
State And Local Government Employees	41
State And Local Average Salaries	14
Local Employment	3
Registered Voters	28
Statewide Initiatives	n/a

Federal

Per Capita Federal Spending	39
Increase In Federal Spending	18
Federal Grants To State And Local Government	35
Per Capita Federal Spending On Procurement	38
Per Capita Federal Spending On Social Security And Medicare	14
Social Security Benefits	4
Federal Spending On Employee Wages & Salaries	39
Federal Grant Spending Per $ Of State Tax Revenue	39
General Revenue From Federal Government	6
Federal Tax Burden Per Capita	8
Highway Charges Returned To States	25
Terms Of Trade	42
Per Capita Federal Income Tax Liability	7

Taxes

Tax Revenue	36
Per Capita Tax Revenue	16
Tax Effort	13
Tax Capacity	18
Percent Change In Taxes	31
Property Taxes Per Capita	12
Property Tax Revenue As Percent Of Three-Tax Revenue	14
Sales Taxes Per Capita	15
Sales Tax Revenue As Percent Of Three-Tax Revenue	30
Services With Sales Tax	45
Income Taxes Per Capita	28
Income Tax Revenue As Percent Of Three-Tax Revenue	34
Highest Personal Income Tax Rate	40
Motor Fuel Taxes	25
Tobacco Taxes	9
Tax Burden On High Income Family	27
Progressivity Of Taxes	11

Revenues And Finances

State And Local Revenue	7
Non-Tax Revenue	8
State And Local Expenditures	6
Per Capita State And Local General Expenditures	30
Change In General Expenditures	30
State Government General Spending	7

Debt As Percent Of Revenue	23
Full Faith And Credit Debt	15
Bond Ratings	4
State Solvency Index	38
Pension Plan Assets	20
State Reserves	40
State Budget Process Quality	46
Relative State Spending "Needs"	26

Education

Math Proficiency, 8th Grade	n/a
AFQT Ranks	37
SAT Scores	n/a
ACT Scores	16
Over-25 Population Without High School Diploma	29
Private School Students	8
Percent Students Finishing High School	18
Pupil-Teacher Ratio	24
Public School Enrollment	40
Library Holdings Per Capita	18
Education Spending As Percent Of Total	37
Spending Per Pupil	26
Average Teacher Salary	10
State Aid Per Pupil	43
State And Local Spending For Higher Education	39
Higher Education Spending As Percent Of Total	36
Public Higher Education Enrollment	17
State Per Pupil Support Of Higher Education	40
Tuition And Fees	14
Average Professor Salary	38
Education Employees	40
R&D Spending	36

Health

Infant Mortality Rates	9
State Health Rankings	30
Population Without Health Insurance	30
Abortions	25

Alcohol Consumption	17
Percent Non-Smokers	35
Percent Obese	24
AIDS Cases	14
Physicians Per 100,000 Population	12
Medicaid Recipients Related To Poverty Population	29
Health/Hospital Spending As Percent Of Total	36
Per Capita Medicaid Spending	16
Medicaid Spending Per Aged Recipient	21
Medicaid Spending Per AFDC Child	26
Medicare Payment Per Hospital-Day	10
Population In HMOs	21

Crime And Law Enforcement

Crime Rate	15
Violent Crime Rate	7
Murder Rate	
Property Crime Rate	20
Motor Vehicle Theft Rate	17
Violent Crime Rate Change	29
Incarceration Rate	23
Juvenile Arrest Rate	32
Proportion Of Sentence Served	23
Law Enforcement Employees	3
Corrections Employees	27
Costs Per Inmate-Day	37
State Corrections Spending	34
Spending For Law Enforcement	20
Law Enforcement Spending As Percent Of Total	13

Transportation

Percent Of Travel On Interstates	12
Interstate Mileage In Poor Condition	29

Deficient Bridges	28
Traffic Deaths Per 100 Million Vehicle-miles	36
Seat Belt Use	18
Vehicle Miles Traveled Per Capita	44
Workers Using Public Transportation	2
Road And Street Miles Under State Control	31
Highway Employees	46
Public Transit Employees	2
State And Local Spending For Highways	19
Highway Spending As Percent Of Total	18

Welfare

Percent Of Births To Unwed Mothers	10
AFDC Recipients As Percent Of Population	7
Food Stamp Recipients As Percent Of Population	21
SSI Recipients As Percent Of Population	19
Change In AFDC Recipients	38
Condition Of Children Index	38
Percent Of Families With Single Parent	12
Typical Monthly AFDC Payments	25
Welfare As Percent Of Poverty Level Income	24
Average SSI State Supplements Per Recipient	22
State Income Tax Liability Of Typical Family In Poverty	6
Child Support Collections Per $ Of Administrative Costs	47
Percent Of Children In Foster Care	8
State And Local Welfare Spending Per Capita	21
Welfare Spending As Percent Of Total	22
Administrative Costs Per AFDC Case	42

Population

Population	14
Percent Population Change	29
Population 2000	14
Median Age	21
Percent Population African-American	22
Percent Population in Poverty	23
Percent Population Female	20
Birth Rates	26
Death Rates	23
Illegal Immigrant Population	38

Economies

Personal Income	16
Per Capita Personal Income	28
Percent of Personal Income from Wages & Salaries	14
Average Annual Pay	23
Cost Of Living	25
Average Annual Pay in Manufacturing	14
Average Annual Pay in Retailing	38
Unemployment Rate	32
Government Employment	17
Manufacturing Employment	9
Fortune 500 Companies	18
Tourism Spending	26
Export-related Jobs	11
Change in Price of Existing Homes	10
Net Farm Income	20
Bankruptcy Filings	9
Patents Issued	24
WC Disability Payments	27
UC Average Weekly Benefit	36
Economic Momentum	35
Employment Change	33
Manufacturing Employment Change	15
Home Ownership	9
Gambling Losses	25
Electricity Use Per Residential Customer	22
Revenue Per Kwh	25
New Companies	44

Geography

Total Land Area	38
Federally-Owned Land	39
State Park Visitors	21
State Park Acreage	37
Hunters With Firearms	30
Registered Boats	23
Per Capita State Spending For the Arts	36
Energy Consumption Per Capita	7
Toxic Chemical Release Per Capita	9
Hazardous Waste Sites	12
Polluted Rivers	35
Air Quality	29

Government

Members Of US House	13
Legislators Per Million Population	36
Units Of Government	17
Female Legislators	23
Turnover In Legislatures	41
Democrats in State Legislatures	32
Number Of Statewide Elected Officials	16
State And Local Government Employees	30
State And Local Average Salaries	26
Local Employment	27
Registered Voters	45
Statewide Initiatives	n/a

Federal

Per Capita Federal Spending	50
Increase In Federal Spending	32
Federal Grants To State And Local Government	46
Per Capita Federal Spending On Procurement	37
Per Capita Federal Spending On Social Security And Medicare	21
Social Security Benefits	8
Federal Spending On Employee Wages & Salaries	46
Federal Grant Spending Per $ Of State Tax Revenue	22
General Revenue From Federal Government	16
Federal Tax Burden Per Capita	28
Highway Charges Returned To States	41
Terms Of Trade	39
Per Capita Federal Income Tax Liability	24

Taxes

Tax Revenue	40
Per Capita Tax Revenue	35
Tax Effort	30
Tax Capacity	35
Percent Change In Taxes	20
Property Taxes Per Capita	31
Property Tax Revenue As Percent Of Three-Tax Revenue	28
Sales Taxes Per Capita	34
Sales Tax Revenue As Percent Of Three-Tax Revenue	28
Services With Sales Tax	38
Income Taxes Per Capita	24
Income Tax Revenue As Percent Of Three-Tax Revenue	20
Highest Personal Income Tax Rate	38
Motor Fuel Taxes	43
Tobacco Taxes	43
Tax Burden On High Income Family	33
Progressivity Of Taxes	10

Revenues And Finances

State And Local Revenue	19
Non-Tax Revenue	15
State And Local Expenditures	18
Per Capita State And Local General Expenditures	39
Change In General Expenditures	39
State Government General Spending	14

Debt As Percent Of Revenue	46
Full Faith And Credit Debt	47
Bond Ratings	n/a
State Solvency Index	27
Pension Plan Assets	45
State Reserves	3
State Budget Process Quality	47
Relative State Spending "Needs"	16

Education

Math Proficiency, 8th Grade	17
AFQT Ranks	20
SAT Scores	18
ACT Scores	n/a
Over-25 Population Without High School Diploma	31
Private School Students	23
Percent Students Finishing High School	27
Pupil-Teacher Ratio	34
Public School Enrollment	30
Library Holdings Per Capita	15
Education Spending As Percent Of Total	5
Spending Per Pupil	23
Average Teacher Salary	18
State Aid Per Pupil	13
State And Local Spending For Higher Education	17
Higher Education Spending As Percent Of Total	8
Public Higher Education Enrollment	33
State Per Pupil Support Of Higher Education	35
Tuition And Fees	19
Average Professor Salary	21
Education Employees	27
R&D Spending	35

Health

Infant Mortality Rates	6
State Health Rankings	22
Population Without Health Insurance	34
Abortions	44

Alcohol Consumption	41
Percent Non-Smokers	45
Percent Obese	6
AIDS Cases	36
Physicians Per 100,000 Population	41
Medicaid Recipients Related To Poverty Population	48
Health/Hospital Spending As Percent Of Total	10
Per Capita Medicaid Spending	10
Medicaid Spending Per Aged Recipient	11
Medicaid Spending Per AFDC Child	2
Medicare Payment Per Hospital-Day	33
Population In HMOs	36

Crime And Law Enforcement

Crime Rate	34
Violent Crime Rate	29
Murder Rate	
Property Crime Rate	36
Motor Vehicle Theft Rate	26
Violent Crime Rate Change	20
Incarceration Rate	29
Juvenile Arrest Rate	37
Proportion Of Sentence Served	n/a
Law Enforcement Employees	37
Corrections Employees	29
Costs Per Inmate-Day	38
State Corrections Spending	27
Spending For Law Enforcement	43
Law Enforcement Spending As Percent Of Total	36

Transportation

Percent Of Travel On Interstates	31
Interstate Mileage In Poor Condition	35

Deficient Bridges	36
Traffic Deaths Per 100 Million Vehicle-miles	40
Seat Belt Use	37
Vehicle Miles Traveled Per Capita	6
Workers Using Public Transportation	32
Road And Street Miles Under State Control	33
Highway Employees	39
Public Transit Employees	27
State And Local Spending For Highways	46
Highway Spending As Percent Of Total	40

Welfare

Percent Of Births To Unwed Mothers	22
AFDC Recipients As Percent Of Population	34
Food Stamp Recipients As Percent Of Population	27
SSI Recipients As Percent Of Population	35
Change In AFDC Recipients	13
Condition Of Children Index	32
Percent Of Families With Single Parent	4
Typical Monthly AFDC Payments	39
Welfare As Percent Of Poverty Level Income	38
Average SSI State Supplements Per Recipient	36
State Income Tax Liability Of Typical Family In Poverty	3
Child Support Collections Per $ Of Administrative Costs	5
Percent Of Children In Foster Care	35
State And Local Welfare Spending Per Capita	30
Welfare Spending As Percent Of Total	25
Administrative Costs Per AFDC Case	33

Population

Population	30
Percent Population Change	43
Population 2000	30
Median Age	8
Percent Population African-American	40
Percent Population in Poverty	33
Percent Population Female	21
Birth Rates	45
Death Rates	8
Illegal Immigrant Population	36

Economies

Personal Income	30
Per Capita Personal Income	30
Percent of Personal Income from Wages & Salaries	39
Average Annual Pay	42
Cost Of Living	34
Average Annual Pay in Manufacturing	28
Average Annual Pay in Retailing	46
Unemployment Rate	47
Government Employment	30
Manufacturing Employment	26
Fortune 500 Companies	32
Tourism Spending	31
Export-related Jobs	26
Change in Price of Existing Homes	6
Net Farm Income	4
Bankruptcy Filings	41
Patents Issued	27
WC Disability Payments	1
UC Average Weekly Benefit	19
Economic Momentum	27
Employment Change	28
Manufacturing Employment Change	19
Home Ownership	11
Gambling Losses	27
Electricity Use Per Residential Customer	29
Revenue Per Kwh	11
New Companies	47

Geography

Total Land Area	23
Federally-Owned Land	42
State Park Visitors	23
State Park Acreage	38
Hunters With Firearms	23
Registered Boats	22
Per Capita State Spending For the Arts	33
Energy Consumption Per Capita	22
Toxic Chemical Release Per Capita	18
Hazardous Waste Sites	22
Polluted Rivers	n/a
Air Quality	1

Government

Members Of US House	29
Legislators Per Million Population	20
Units Of Government	10
Female Legislators	35
Turnover In Legislatures	16
Democrats in State Legislatures	34
Number Of Statewide Elected Officials	11
State And Local Government Employees	18
State And Local Average Salaries	23
Local Employment	20
Registered Voters	12
Statewide Initiatives	n/a

Federal

Per Capita Federal Spending	32
Increase In Federal Spending	43
Federal Grants To State And Local Government	37
Per Capita Federal Spending On Procurement	48
Per Capita Federal Spending On Social Security And Medicare	9
Social Security Benefits	23
Federal Spending On Employee Wages & Salaries	48
Federal Grant Spending Per $ Of State Tax Revenue	31
General Revenue From Federal Government	31
Federal Tax Burden Per Capita	33
Highway Charges Returned To States	20
Terms Of Trade	25
Per Capita Federal Income Tax Liability	36

Taxes

Tax Revenue	15
Per Capita Tax Revenue	23
Tax Effort	13
Tax Capacity	27
Percent Change In Taxes	41
Property Taxes Per Capita	20
Property Tax Revenue As Percent Of Three-Tax Revenue	17
Sales Taxes Per Capita	43
Sales Tax Revenue As Percent Of Three-Tax Revenue	38
Services With Sales Tax	7
Income Taxes Per Capita	17
Income Tax Revenue As Percent Of Three-Tax Revenue	17
Highest Personal Income Tax Rate	24
Motor Fuel Taxes	20
Tobacco Taxes	17
Tax Burden On High Income Family	28
Progressivity Of Taxes	30

Revenues And Finances

State And Local Revenue	30
Non-Tax Revenue	30
State And Local Expenditures	30
Per Capita State And Local General Expenditures	26
Change In General Expenditures	26
State Government General Spending	29

Debt As Percent Of Revenue	50
Full Faith And Credit Debt	42
Bond Ratings	n/a
State Solvency Index	7
Pension Plan Assets	44
State Reserves	15
State Budget Process Quality	8
Relative State Spending "Needs"	21

Education

Math Proficiency, 8th Grade	1
AFQT Ranks	2
SAT Scores	n/a
ACT Scores	3
Over-25 Population Without High School Diploma	14
Private School Students	22
Percent Students Finishing High School	2
Pupil-Teacher Ratio	17
Public School Enrollment	18
Library Holdings Per Capita	10
Education Spending As Percent Of Total	7
Spending Per Pupil	25
Average Teacher Salary	31
State Aid Per Pupil	21
State And Local Spending For Higher Education	9
Higher Education Spending As Percent Of Total	7
Public Higher Education Enrollment	25
State Per Pupil Support Of Higher Education	1
Tuition And Fees	23
Average Professor Salary	14
Education Employees	17
R&D Spending	39

Health

Infant Mortality Rates	31
State Health Rankings	8
Population Without Health Insurance	49
Abortions	39
Alcohol Consumption	43
Percent Non-Smokers	7
Percent Obese	11
AIDS Cases	45
Physicians Per 100,000 Population	43
Medicaid Recipients Related To Poverty Population	6
Health/Hospital Spending As Percent Of Total	11
Per Capita Medicaid Spending	29
Medicaid Spending Per Aged Recipient	34
Medicaid Spending Per AFDC Child	21
Medicare Payment Per Hospital-Day	41
Population In HMOs	41

Crime And Law Enforcement

Crime Rate	42
Violent Crime Rate	38
Murder Rate	
Property Crime Rate	43
Motor Vehicle Theft Rate	43
Violent Crime Rate Change	21
Incarceration Rate	38
Juvenile Arrest Rate	10
Proportion Of Sentence Served	37
Law Enforcement Employees	44
Corrections Employees	49
Costs Per Inmate-Day	24
State Corrections Spending	15
Spending For Law Enforcement	49
Law Enforcement Spending As Percent Of Total	48

Transportation

Percent Of Travel On Interstates	35
Interstate Mileage In Poor Condition	42
Deficient Bridges	41
Traffic Deaths Per 100 Million Vehicle-miles	21
Seat Belt Use	7
Vehicle Miles Traveled Per Capita	34
Workers Using Public Transportation	34
Road And Street Miles Under State Control	46
Highway Employees	15
Public Transit Employees	25
State And Local Spending For Highways	4
Highway Spending As Percent Of Total	3

Welfare

Percent Of Births To Unwed Mothers	42
AFDC Recipients As Percent Of Population	33
Food Stamp Recipients As Percent Of Population	43
SSI Recipients As Percent Of Population	38
Change In AFDC Recipients	37
Condition Of Children Index	2
Percent Of Families With Single Parent	46
Typical Monthly AFDC Payments	17
Welfare As Percent Of Poverty Level Income	17
Average SSI State Supplements Per Recipient	33
State Income Tax Liability Of Typical Family In Poverty	22
Child Support Collections Per $ Of Administrative Costs	7
Percent Of Children In Foster Care	24
State And Local Welfare Spending Per Capita	25
Welfare Spending As Percent Of Total	31
Administrative Costs Per AFDC Case	31

Population

Population	32
Percent Population Change	32
Population 2000	32
Median Age	33
Percent Population African-American	27
Percent Population in Poverty	15
Percent Population Female	33
Birth Rates	24
Death Rates	18
Illegal Immigrant Population	25

Economies

Personal Income	31
Per Capita Personal Income	24
Percent of Personal Income from Wages & Salaries	35
Average Annual Pay	35
Cost Of Living	38
Average Annual Pay in Manufacturing	26
Average Annual Pay in Retailing	37
Unemployment Rate	35
Government Employment	28
Manufacturing Employment	30
Fortune 500 Companies	33
Tourism Spending	36
Export-related Jobs	32
Change in Price of Existing Homes	10
Net Farm Income	9
Bankruptcy Filings	18
Patents Issued	36
WC Disability Payments	46
UC Average Weekly Benefit	13
Economic Momentum	23
Employment Change	15
Manufacturing Employment Change	5
Home Ownership	22
Gambling Losses	32
Electricity Use Per Residential Customer	31
Revenue Per Kwh	38
New Companies	29

Geography

Total Land Area	13
Federally-Owned Land	38
State Park Visitors	37
State Park Acreage	7
Hunters With Firearms	31
Registered Boats	33
Per Capita State Spending For the Arts	34
Energy Consumption Per Capita	10
Toxic Chemical Release Per Capita	11
Hazardous Waste Sites	32
Polluted Rivers	3
Air Quality	1

Government

Members Of US House	32
Legislators Per Million Population	15
Units Of Government	5
Female Legislators	9
Turnover In Legislatures	23
Democrats in State Legislatures	44
Number Of Statewide Elected Officials	16
State And Local Government Employees	6
State And Local Average Salaries	35
Local Employment	21
Registered Voters	22
Statewide Initiatives	n/a

Federal

Per Capita Federal Spending	25
Increase In Federal Spending	36
Federal Grants To State And Local Government	44
Per Capita Federal Spending On Procurement	27
Per Capita Federal Spending On Social Security And Medicare	15
Social Security Benefits	14
Federal Spending On Employee Wages & Salaries	14
Federal Grant Spending Per $ Of State Tax Revenue	26
General Revenue From Federal Government	34
Federal Tax Burden Per Capita	24
Highway Charges Returned To States	27
Terms Of Trade	40
Per Capita Federal Income Tax Liability	27

Taxes

Tax Revenue	33
Per Capita Tax Revenue	28
Tax Effort	13
Tax Capacity	27
Percent Change In Taxes	37
Property Taxes Per Capita	19
Property Tax Revenue As Percent Of Three-Tax Revenue	15
Sales Taxes Per Capita	29
Sales Tax Revenue As Percent Of Three-Tax Revenue	25
Services With Sales Tax	10
Income Taxes Per Capita	35
Income Tax Revenue As Percent Of Three-Tax Revenue	37
Highest Personal Income Tax Rate	11
Motor Fuel Taxes	30
Tobacco Taxes	28
Tax Burden On High Income Family	35
Progressivity Of Taxes	32

Revenues And Finances

State And Local Revenue	31
Non-Tax Revenue	32
State And Local Expenditures	31
Per Capita State And Local General Expenditures	33
Change In General Expenditures	33
State Government General Spending	33

Debt As Percent Of Revenue	36	Alcohol Consumption	47	Deficient Bridges	40
Full Faith And Credit Debt	30	Percent Non-Smokers	25	Traffic Deaths Per	
Bond Ratings	n/a	Percent Obese	n/a	100 Million Vehicle-miles	25
State Solvency Index	8	AIDS Cases	33	Seat Belt Use	14
Pension Plan Assets	43	Physicians Per 100,000		Vehicle Miles Traveled	
State Reserves	12	Population	33	Per Capita	24
State Budget Process Quality	38	Medicaid Recipients Related		Workers Using Public	
Relative State Spending "Needs"	23	To Poverty Population	34	Transportation	43

Education

Math Proficiency, 8th Grade	n/a
AFQT Ranks	17
SAT Scores	n/a
ACT Scores	11
Over-25 Population Without High School Diploma	10
Private School Students	32
Percent Students Finishing High School	15
Pupil-Teacher Ratio	8
Public School Enrollment	14
Library Holdings Per Capita	6
Education Spending As Percent Of Total	3
Spending Per Pupil	22
Average Teacher Salary	23
State Aid Per Pupil	19
State And Local Spending For Higher Education	6
Higher Education Spending As Percent Of Total	3
Public Higher Education Enrollment	5
State Per Pupil Support Of Higher Education	17
Tuition And Fees	33
Average Professor Salary	39
Education Employees	4
R&D Spending	48

Health

Infant Mortality Rates	14
State Health Rankings	10
Population Without Health Insurance	32
Abortions	37

Medicaid Recipients Related To Poverty Population — 34
Health/Hospital Spending As Percent Of Total — 24
Per Capita Medicaid Spending — 43
Medicaid Spending Per Aged Recipient — 26
Medicaid Spending Per AFDC Child — 32
Medicare Payment Per Hospital-Day — 23
Population In HMOs — 29

Crime And Law Enforcement

Crime Rate	24
Violent Crime Rate	28
Murder Rate	
Property Crime Rate	22
Motor Vehicle Theft Rate	33
Violent Crime Rate Change	15
Incarceration Rate	31
Juvenile Arrest Rate	25
Proportion Of Sentence Served	n/a
Law Enforcement Employees	21
Corrections Employees	19
Costs Per Inmate-Day	21
State Corrections Spending	19
Spending For Law Enforcement	30
Law Enforcement Spending As Percent Of Total	27

Transportation

Percent Of Travel On Interstates	36
Interstate Mileage In Poor Condition	17

Road And Street Miles Under State Control — 50
Highway Employees — 8
Public Transit Employees — 36
State And Local Spending For Highways — 12
Highway Spending As Percent Of Total — 7

Welfare

Percent Of Births To Unwed Mothers	39
AFDC Recipients As Percent Of Population	38
Food Stamp Recipients As Percent Of Population	35
SSI Recipients As Percent Of Population	41
Change In AFDC Recipients	34
Condition Of Children Index	14
Percent Of Families With Single Parent	43
Typical Monthly AFDC Payments	22
Welfare As Percent Of Poverty Level Income	15
Average SSI State Supplements Per Recipient	45
State Income Tax Liability Of Typical Family In Poverty	22
Child Support Collections Per $ Of Administrative Costs	32
Percent Of Children In Foster Care	25
State And Local Welfare Spending Per Capita	47
Welfare Spending As Percent Of Total	45
Administrative Costs Per AFDC Case	4

Population

Population	24
Percent Population Change	27
Population 2000	25
Median Age	18
Percent Population African-American	24
Percent Population in Poverty	6
Percent Population Female	17
Birth Rates	41
Death Rates	15
Illegal Immigrant Population	46

Economies

Personal Income	26
Per Capita Personal Income	42
Percent of Personal Income from Wages & Salaries	28
Average Annual Pay	37
Cost Of Living	48
Average Annual Pay in Manufacturing	32
Average Annual Pay in Retailing	41
Unemployment Rate	28
Government Employment	26
Manufacturing Employment	22
Fortune 500 Companies	30
Tourism Spending	29
Export-related Jobs	23
Change in Price of Existing Homes	10
Net Farm Income	13.
Bankruptcy Filings	17
Patents Issued	45
WC Disability Payments	33
UC Average Weekly Benefit	35
Economic Momentum	25
Employment Change	27
Manufacturing Employment Change	24
Home Ownership	14
Gambling Losses	21
Electricity Use Per Residential Customer	12
Revenue Per Kwh	44
New Companies	45

Geography

Total Land Area	36
Federally-Owned Land	26
State Park Visitors	9
State Park Acreage	43
Hunters With Firearms	26
Registered Boats	28
Per Capita State Spending For the Arts	19
Energy Consumption Per Capita	11
Toxic Chemical Release Per Capita	21
Hazardous Waste Sites	19
Polluted Rivers	34
Air Quality	21

Government

Members Of US House	23
Legislators Per Million Population	27
Units Of Government	24
Female Legislators	49
Turnover In Legislatures	31
Democrats in State Legislatures	13
Number Of Statewide Elected Officials	11
State And Local Government Employees	31
State And Local Average Salaries	37
Local Employment	42
Registered Voters	31
Statewide Initiatives	n/a

Federal

Per Capita Federal Spending	34
Increase In Federal Spending	24
Federal Grants To State And Local Government	19
Per Capita Federal Spending On Procurement	34
Per Capita Federal Spending On Social Security And Medicare	28
Social Security Benefits	47
Federal Spending On Employee Wages & Salaries	19
Federal Grant Spending Per $ Of State Tax Revenue	25
General Revenue From Federal Government	23
Federal Tax Burden Per Capita	44
Highway Charges Returned To States	33
Terms Of Trade	12
Per Capita Federal Income Tax Liability	44

Taxes

Tax Revenue	26
Per Capita Tax Revenue	39
Tax Effort	13
Tax Capacity	42
Percent Change In Taxes	9
Property Taxes Per Capita	44
Property Tax Revenue As Percent Of Three-Tax Revenue	45
Sales Taxes Per Capita	36
Sales Tax Revenue As Percent Of Three-Tax Revenue	20
Services With Sales Tax	36
Income Taxes Per Capita	12
Income Tax Revenue As Percent Of Three-Tax Revenue	5
Highest Personal Income Tax Rate	25
Motor Fuel Taxes	38
Tobacco Taxes	49
Tax Burden On High Income Family	30
Progressivity Of Taxes	20

Revenues And Finances

State And Local Revenue	27
Non-Tax Revenue	28
State And Local Expenditures	28
Per Capita State And Local General Expenditures	40
Change In General Expenditures	40
State Government General Spending	23

Debt As Percent Of Revenue	9
Full Faith And Credit Debt	48
Bond Ratings	n/a
State Solvency Index	31
Pension Plan Assets	33
State Reserves	20
State Budget Process Quality	31
Relative State Spending "Needs"	43

Education

Math Proficiency, 8th Grade	28
AFQT Ranks	41
SAT Scores	n/a
ACT Scores	22
Over-25 Population Without High School Diploma	49
Private School Students	24
Percent Students Finishing High School	37
Pupil-Teacher Ratio	32
Public School Enrollment	26
Library Holdings Per Capita	43
Education Spending As Percent Of Total	34
Spending Per Pupil	32
Average Teacher Salary	28
State Aid Per Pupil	8
State And Local Spending For Higher Education	33
Higher Education Spending As Percent Of Total	23
Public Higher Education Enrollment	32
State Per Pupil Support Of Higher Education	8
Tuition And Fees	34
Average Professor Salary	26
Education Employees	21
R&D Spending	50

Health

Infant Mortality Rates	27
State Health Rankings	38
Population Without Health Insurance	31
Abortions	41

Alcohol Consumption	48
Percent Non-Smokers	46
Percent Obese	8
AIDS Cases	39
Physicians Per 100,000 Population	37
Medicaid Recipients Related To Poverty Population	24
Health/Hospital Spending As Percent Of Total	33
Per Capita Medicaid Spending	8
Medicaid Spending Per Aged Recipient	37
Medicaid Spending Per AFDC Child	19
Medicare Payment Per Hospital-Day	38
Population In HMOs	28

Crime And Law Enforcement

Crime Rate	45
Violent Crime Rate	30
Murder Rate	
Property Crime Rate	46
Motor Vehicle Theft Rate	40
Violent Crime Rate Change	11
Incarceration Rate	26
Juvenile Arrest Rate	23
Proportion Of Sentence Served	29
Law Enforcement Employees	49
Corrections Employees	20
Costs Per Inmate-Day	43
State Corrections Spending	40
Spending For Law Enforcement	42
Law Enforcement Spending As Percent Of Total	35

Transportation

Percent Of Travel On Interstates	23
Interstate Mileage In Poor Condition	18

Deficient Bridges	15
Traffic Deaths Per 100 Million Vehicle-miles	11
Seat Belt Use	32
Vehicle Miles Traveled Per Capita	9
Workers Using Public Transportation	29
Road And Street Miles Under State Control	8
Highway Employees	28
Public Transit Employees	22
State And Local Spending For Highways	24
Highway Spending As Percent Of Total	17

Welfare

Percent Of Births To Unwed Mothers	32
AFDC Recipients As Percent Of Population	16
Food Stamp Recipients As Percent Of Population	7
SSI Recipients As Percent Of Population	3
Change In AFDC Recipients	20
Condition Of Children Index	33
Percent Of Families With Single Parent	26
Typical Monthly AFDC Payments	43
Welfare As Percent Of Poverty Level Income	43
Average SSI State Supplements Per Recipient	30
State Income Tax Liability Of Typical Family In Poverty	2
Child Support Collections Per $ Of Administrative Costs	38
Percent Of Children In Foster Care	28
State And Local Welfare Spending Per Capita	14
Welfare Spending As Percent Of Total	6
Administrative Costs Per AFDC Case	41

Population

Population	21
Percent Population Change	37
Population 2000	22
Median Age	44
Percent Population African-American	2
Percent Population in Poverty	1
Percent Population Female	6
Birth Rates	9
Death Rates	20
Illegal Immigrant Population	32

Economies

Personal Income	24
Per Capita Personal Income	44
Percent of Personal Income from Wages & Salaries	31
Average Annual Pay	32
Cost Of Living	39
Average Annual Pay in Manufacturing	19
Average Annual Pay in Retailing	39
Unemployment Rate	4
Government Employment	21
Manufacturing Employment	31
Fortune 500 Companies	38
Tourism Spending	22
Export-related Jobs	31
Change in Price of Existing Homes	6
Net Farm Income	29
Bankruptcy Filings	25
Patents Issued	38
WC Disability Payments	45
UC Average Weekly Benefit	50
Economic Momentum	17
Employment Change	5
Manufacturing Employment Change	22
Home Ownership	32
Gambling Losses	9
Electricity Use Per Residential Customer	3
Revenue Per Kwh	15
New Companies	38

Geography

Total Land Area	33
Federally-Owned Land	31
State Park Visitors	47
State Park Acreage	45
Hunters With Firearms	17
Registered Boats	15
Per Capita State Spending For the Arts	50
Energy Consumption Per Capita	3
Toxic Chemical Release Per Capita	1
Hazardous Waste Sites	24
Polluted Rivers	16
Air Quality	17

Government

Members Of US House	21
Legislators Per Million Population	29
Units Of Government	46
Female Legislators	48
Turnover In Legislatures	47
Democrats in State Legislatures	4
Number Of Statewide Elected Officials	7
State And Local Government Employees	12
State And Local Average Salaries	48
Local Employment	36
Registered Voters	15
Statewide Initiatives	n/a

Federal

Per Capita Federal Spending	20
Increase In Federal Spending	10
Federal Grants To State And Local Government	4
Per Capita Federal Spending On Procurement	19
Per Capita Federal Spending On Social Security And Medicare	34
Social Security Benefits	48
Federal Spending On Employee Wages & Salaries	34
Federal Grant Spending Per $ Of State Tax Revenue	2
General Revenue From Federal Government	13
Federal Tax Burden Per Capita	43
Highway Charges Returned To States	33
Terms Of Trade	2
Per Capita Federal Income Tax Liability	42

Taxes

Tax Revenue	29
Per Capita Tax Revenue	43
Tax Effort	36
Tax Capacity	37
Percent Change In Taxes	46
Property Taxes Per Capita	46
Property Tax Revenue As Percent Of Three-Tax Revenue	44
Sales Taxes Per Capita	12
Sales Tax Revenue As Percent Of Three-Tax Revenue	5
Services With Sales Tax	20
Income Taxes Per Capita	39
Income Tax Revenue As Percent Of Three-Tax Revenue	39
Highest Personal Income Tax Rate	37
Motor Fuel Taxes	20
Tobacco Taxes	34
Tax Burden On High Income Family	39
Progressivity Of Taxes	50

Revenues And Finances

State And Local Revenue	21
Non-Tax Revenue	17
State And Local Expenditures	20
Per Capita State And Local General Expenditures	23
Change In General Expenditures	23
State Government General Spending	18

Debt As Percent Of Revenue	11
Full Faith And Credit Debt	12
Bond Ratings	6
State Solvency Index	48
Pension Plan Assets	41
State Reserves	38
State Budget Process Quality	28
Relative State Spending "Needs"	49

Education

Math Proficiency, 8th Grade	40
AFQT Ranks	49
SAT Scores	n/a
ACT Scores	26
Over-25 Population Without High School Diploma	43
Private School Students	6
Percent Students Finishing High School	50
Pupil-Teacher Ratio	21
Public School Enrollment	11
Library Holdings Per Capita	34
Education Spending As Percent Of Total	40
Spending Per Pupil	39
Average Teacher Salary	47
State Aid Per Pupil	23
State And Local Spending For Higher Education	37
Higher Education Spending As Percent Of Total	39
Public Higher Education Enrollment	34
State Per Pupil Support Of Higher Education	14
Tuition And Fees	28
Average Professor Salary	45
Education Employees	16
R&D Spending	47

Health

Infant Mortality Rates	6
State Health Rankings	50
Population Without Health Insurance	2
Abortions	43

Alcohol Consumption	14
Percent Non-Smokers	36
Percent Obese	5
AIDS Cases	13
Physicians Per 100,000 Population	23
Medicaid Recipients Related To Poverty Population	21
Health/Hospital Spending As Percent Of Total	7
Per Capita Medicaid Spending	3
Medicaid Spending Per Aged Recipient	39
Medicaid Spending Per AFDC Child	4
Medicare Payment Per Hospital-Day	15
Population In HMOs	38

Crime And Law Enforcement

Crime Rate	3
Violent Crime Rate	4
Murder Rate	
Property Crime Rate	4
Motor Vehicle Theft Rate	12
Violent Crime Rate Change	4
Incarceration Rate	2
Juvenile Arrest Rate	43
Proportion Of Sentence Served	9
Law Enforcement Employees	13
Corrections Employees	11
Costs Per Inmate-Day	45
State Corrections Spending	43
Spending For Law Enforcement	25
Law Enforcement Spending As Percent Of Total	24

Transportation

Percent Of Travel On Interstates	18
Interstate Mileage In Poor Condition	26

Deficient Bridges	16
Traffic Deaths Per 100 Million Vehicle-miles	5
Seat Belt Use	43
Vehicle Miles Traveled Per Capita	40
Workers Using Public Transportation	14
Road And Street Miles Under State Control	12
Highway Employees	23
Public Transit Employees	36
State And Local Spending For Highways	25
Highway Spending As Percent Of Total	27

Welfare

Percent Of Births To Unwed Mothers	2
AFDC Recipients As Percent Of Population	12
Food Stamp Recipients As Percent Of Population	3
SSI Recipients As Percent Of Population	2
Change In AFDC Recipients	49
Condition Of Children Index	50
Percent Of Families With Single Parent	1
Typical Monthly AFDC Payments	46
Welfare As Percent Of Poverty Level Income	46
Average SSI State Supplements Per Recipient	47
State Income Tax Liability Of Typical Family In Poverty	20
Child Support Collections Per $ Of Administrative Costs	30
Percent Of Children In Foster Care	22
State And Local Welfare Spending Per Capita	18
Welfare Spending As Percent Of Total	16
Administrative Costs Per AFDC Case	49

Population

Population	39
Percent Population Change	48
Population 2000	39
Median Age	5
Percent Population African-American	47
Percent Population in Poverty	40
Percent Population Female	26
Birth Rates	48
Death Rates	14
Illegal Immigrant Population	34

Economies

Personal Income	41
Per Capita Personal Income	35
Percent of Personal Income from Wages & Salaries	45
Average Annual Pay	39
Cost Of Living	10
Average Annual Pay in Manufacturing	35
Average Annual Pay in Retailing	26
Unemployment Rate	8
Government Employment	41
Manufacturing Employment	37
Fortune 500 Companies	34
Tourism Spending	39
Export-related Jobs	36
Change in Price of Existing Homes	n/a
Net Farm Income	44
Bankruptcy Filings	47
Patents Issued	37
WC Disability Payments	25
UC Average Weekly Benefit	33
Economic Momentum	37
Employment Change	22
Manufacturing Employment Change	31
Home Ownership	7
Gambling Losses	35
Electricity Use Per Residential Customer	46
Revenue Per Kwh	19
New Companies	18

Geography

Total Land Area	39
Federally-Owned Land	45
State Park Visitors	45
State Park Acreage	31
Hunters With Firearms	4
Registered Boats	31
Per Capita State Spending For the Arts	42
Energy Consumption Per Capita	31
Toxic Chemical Release Per Capita	19
Hazardous Waste Sites	35
Polluted Rivers	48
Air Quality	35

Government

Members Of US House	38
Legislators Per Million Population	7
Units Of Government	11
Female Legislators	12
Turnover In Legislatures	1
Democrats in State Legislatures	24
Number Of Statewide Elected Officials	48
State And Local Government Employees	29
State And Local Average Salaries	29
Local Employment	31
Registered Voters	2
Statewide Initiatives	8

Federal

Per Capita Federal Spending	11
Increase In Federal Spending	1
Federal Grants To State And Local Government	11
Per Capita Federal Spending On Procurement	12
Per Capita Federal Spending On Social Security And Medicare	17
Social Security Benefits	41
Federal Spending On Employee Wages & Salaries	23
Federal Grant Spending Per $ Of State Tax Revenue	16
General Revenue From Federal Government	38
Federal Tax Burden Per Capita	36
Highway Charges Returned To States	17
Terms Of Trade	9
Per Capita Federal Income Tax Liability	40

Taxes

Tax Revenue	10
Per Capita Tax Revenue	19
Tax Effort	10
Tax Capacity	23
Percent Change In Taxes	22
Property Taxes Per Capita	13
Property Tax Revenue As Percent Of Three-Tax Revenue	16
Sales Taxes Per Capita	26
Sales Tax Revenue As Percent Of Three-Tax Revenue	33
Services With Sales Tax	35
Income Taxes Per Capita	19
Income Tax Revenue As Percent Of Three-Tax Revenue	28
Highest Personal Income Tax Rate	6
Motor Fuel Taxes	25
Tobacco Taxes	13
Tax Burden On High Income Family	4
Progressivity Of Taxes	29

Revenues And Finances

State And Local Revenue	41
Non-Tax Revenue	41
State And Local Expenditures	41
Per Capita State And Local General Expenditures	21
Change In General Expenditures	21
State Government General Spending	41

Debt As Percent Of Revenue	32
Full Faith And Credit Debt	23
Bond Ratings	3
State Solvency Index	47
Pension Plan Assets	38
State Reserves	46
State Budget Process Quality	49
Relative State Spending "Needs"	14

Education

Math Proficiency, 8th Grade	4
AFQT Ranks	14
SAT Scores	22
ACT Scores	n/a
Over-25 Population Without High School Diploma	18
Private School Students	36
Percent Students Finishing High School	12
Pupil-Teacher Ratio	3
Public School Enrollment	23
Library Holdings Per Capita	1
Education Spending As Percent Of Total	32
Spending Per Pupil	13
Average Teacher Salary	29
State Aid Per Pupil	17
State And Local Spending For Higher Education	38
Higher Education Spending As Percent Of Total	40
Public Higher Education Enrollment	46
State Per Pupil Support Of Higher Education	37
Tuition And Fees	12
Average Professor Salary	46
Education Employees	6
R&D Spending	42

Health

Infant Mortality Rates	42
State Health Rankings	14
Population Without Health Insurance	42
Abortions	29

Alcohol Consumption	31
Percent Non-Smokers	31
Percent Obese	24
AIDS Cases	32
Physicians Per 100,000 Population	29
Medicaid Recipients Related To Poverty Population	12
Health/Hospital Spending As Percent Of Total	46
Per Capita Medicaid Spending	5
Medicaid Spending Per Aged Recipient	10
Medicaid Spending Per AFDC Child	17
Medicare Payment Per Hospital-Day	39
Population In HMOs	39

Crime And Law Enforcement

Crime Rate	46
Violent Crime Rate	48
Murder Rate	
Property Crime Rate	44
Motor Vehicle Theft Rate	48
Violent Crime Rate Change	50
Incarceration Rate	47
Juvenile Arrest Rate	7
Proportion Of Sentence Served	n/a
Law Enforcement Employees	36
Corrections Employees	40
Costs Per Inmate-Day	3
State Corrections Spending	3
Spending For Law Enforcement	36
Law Enforcement Spending As Percent Of Total	42

Transportation

Percent Of Travel On Interstates	44
Interstate Mileage In Poor Condition	30

Deficient Bridges	10
Traffic Deaths Per 100 Million Vehicle-miles	39
Seat Belt Use	48
Vehicle Miles Traveled Per Capita	21
Workers Using Public Transportation	40
Road And Street Miles Under State Control	9
Highway Employees	6
Public Transit Employees	38
State And Local Spending For Highways	18
Highway Spending As Percent Of Total	22

Welfare

Percent Of Births To Unwed Mothers	35
AFDC Recipients As Percent Of Population	17
Food Stamp Recipients As Percent Of Population	17
SSI Recipients As Percent Of Population	15
Change In AFDC Recipients	28
Condition Of Children Index	4
Percent Of Families With Single Parent	38
Typical Monthly AFDC Payments	19
Welfare As Percent Of Poverty Level Income	17
Average SSI State Supplements Per Recipient	24
State Income Tax Liability Of Typical Family In Poverty	22
Child Support Collections Per $ Of Administrative Costs	26
Percent Of Children In Foster Care	11
State And Local Welfare Spending Per Capita	4
Welfare Spending As Percent Of Total	2
Administrative Costs Per AFDC Case	47

Population

Population	19
Percent Population Change	23
Population 2000	18
Median Age	28
Percent Population African-American	6
Percent Population in Poverty	34
Percent Population Female	19
Birth Rates	14
Death Rates	35
Illegal Immigrant Population	13

Economies

Personal Income	14
Per Capita Personal Income	5
Percent of Personal Income from Wages & Salaries	43
Average Annual Pay	9
Cost Of Living	20
Average Annual Pay in Manufacturing	11
Average Annual Pay in Retailing	8
Unemployment Rate	29
Government Employment	14
Manufacturing Employment	32
Fortune 500 Companies	19
Tourism Spending	21
Export-related Jobs	29
Change in Price of Existing Homes	32
Net Farm Income	35
Bankruptcy Filings	16
Patents Issued	21
WC Disability Payments	9
UC Average Weekly Benefit	21
Economic Momentum	43
Employment Change	45
Manufacturing Employment Change	40
Home Ownership	35
Gambling Losses	14
Electricity Use Per Residential Customer	15
Revenue Per Kwh	34
New Companies	30

Geography

Total Land Area	42
Federally-Owned Land	44
State Park Visitors	24
State Park Acreage	14
Hunters With Firearms	39
Registered Boats	25
Per Capita State Spending For the Arts	9
Energy Consumption Per Capita	40
Toxic Chemical Release Per Capita	42
Hazardous Waste Sites	28
Polluted Rivers	45
Air Quality	46

Government

Members Of US House	19
Legislators Per Million Population	25
Units Of Government	47
Female Legislators	8
Turnover In Legislatures	2
Democrats in State Legislatures	8
Number Of Statewide Elected Officials	16
State And Local Government Employees	41
State And Local Average Salaries	7
Local Employment	32
Registered Voters	30
Statewide Initiatives	n/a

Federal

Per Capita Federal Spending	2
Increase In Federal Spending	14
Federal Grants To State And Local Government	33
Per Capita Federal Spending On Procurement	4
Per Capita Federal Spending On Social Security And Medicare	36
Social Security Benefits	19
Federal Spending On Employee Wages & Salaries	4
Federal Grant Spending Per $ Of State Tax Revenue	44
General Revenue From Federal Government	20
Federal Tax Burden Per Capita	7
Highway Charges Returned To States	37
Terms Of Trade	43
Per Capita Federal Income Tax Liability	8

Taxes

Tax Revenue	38
Per Capita Tax Revenue	9
Tax Effort	8
Tax Capacity	13
Percent Change In Taxes	34
Property Taxes Per Capita	26
Property Tax Revenue As Percent Of Three-Tax Revenue	34
Sales Taxes Per Capita	41
Sales Tax Revenue As Percent Of Three-Tax Revenue	44
Services With Sales Tax	26
Income Taxes Per Capita	3
Income Tax Revenue As Percent Of Three-Tax Revenue	3
Highest Personal Income Tax Rate	25
Motor Fuel Taxes	8
Tobacco Taxes	17
Tax Burden On High Income Family	2
Progressivity Of Taxes	13

Revenues And Finances

State And Local Revenue	17
Non-Tax Revenue	21
State And Local Expenditures	17
Per Capita State And Local General Expenditures	25
Change In General Expenditures	25
State Government General Spending	19

Debt As Percent Of Revenue	21	
Full Faith And Credit Debt	10	
Bond Ratings	1	
State Solvency Index	41	
Pension Plan Assets	9	
State Reserves	24	
State Budget Process Quality	33	
Relative State Spending "Needs"	4	

Education

Math Proficiency, 8th Grade	25
AFQT Ranks	28
SAT Scores	23
ACT Scores	n/a
Over-25 Population Without High School Diploma	22
Private School Students	9
Percent Students Finishing High School	25
Pupil-Teacher Ratio	26
Public School Enrollment	41
Library Holdings Per Capita	25
Education Spending As Percent Of Total	31
Spending Per Pupil	11
Average Teacher Salary	9
State Aid Per Pupil	25
State And Local Spending For Higher Education	24
Higher Education Spending As Percent Of Total	27
Public Higher Education Enrollment	23
State Per Pupil Support Of Higher Education	19
Tuition And Fees	13
Average Professor Salary	17
Education Employees	45
R&D Spending	1

Health

Infant Mortality Rates	10
State Health Rankings	16
Population Without Health Insurance	17
Abortions	24

Alcohol Consumption	29
Percent Non-Smokers	11
Percent Obese	38
AIDS Cases	4
Physicians Per 100,000 Population	2
Medicaid Recipients Related To Poverty Population	18
Health/Hospital Spending As Percent Of Total	44
Per Capita Medicaid Spending	20
Medicaid Spending Per Aged Recipient	17
Medicaid Spending Per AFDC Child	6
Medicare Payment Per Hospital-Day	49
Population In HMOs	3

Crime And Law Enforcement

Crime Rate	10
Violent Crime Rate	6
Murder Rate	
Property Crime Rate	12
Motor Vehicle Theft Rate	9
Violent Crime Rate Change	25
Incarceration Rate	12
Juvenile Arrest Rate	47
Proportion Of Sentence Served	11
Law Enforcement Employees	8
Corrections Employees	12
Costs Per Inmate-Day	29
State Corrections Spending	31
Spending For Law Enforcement	9
Law Enforcement Spending As Percent Of Total	5

Transportation

Percent Of Travel On Interstates	5
Interstate Mileage In Poor Condition	25

Deficient Bridges	23
Traffic Deaths Per 100 Million Vehicle-miles	37
Seat Belt Use	15
Vehicle Miles Traveled Per Capita	38
Workers Using Public Transportation	5
Road And Street Miles Under State Control	18
Highway Employees	34
Public Transit Employees	9
State And Local Spending For Highways	40
Highway Spending As Percent Of Total	42

Welfare

Percent Of Births To Unwed Mothers	16
AFDC Recipients As Percent Of Population	26
Food Stamp Recipients As Percent Of Population	33
SSI Recipients As Percent Of Population	31
Change In AFDC Recipients	29
Condition Of Children Index	30
Percent Of Families With Single Parent	9
Typical Monthly AFDC Payments	26
Welfare As Percent Of Poverty Level Income	24
Average SSI State Supplements Per Recipient	32
State Income Tax Liability Of Typical Family In Poverty	22
Child Support Collections Per $ Of Administrative Costs	10
Percent Of Children In Foster Care	16
State And Local Welfare Spending Per Capita	20
Welfare Spending As Percent Of Total	23
Administrative Costs Per AFDC Case	6

Massachusetts

Population

Population	13
Percent Population Change	40
Population 2000	13
Median Age	13
Percent Population African-American	29
Percent Population in Poverty	39
Percent Population Female	7
Birth Rates	38
Death Rates	17
Illegal Immigrant Population	10

Economies

Personal Income	10
Per Capita Personal Income	4
Percent of Personal Income from Wages & Salaries	8
Average Annual Pay	5
Cost Of Living	4
Average Annual Pay in Manufacturing	5
Average Annual Pay in Retailing	9
Unemployment Rate	14
Government Employment	16
Manufacturing Employment	15
Fortune 500 Companies	9
Tourism Spending	14
Export-related Jobs	9
Change in Price of Existing Homes	30
Net Farm Income	40
Bankruptcy Filings	32
Patents Issued	3
WC Disability Payments	7
UC Average Weekly Benefit	3
Economic Momentum	32
Employment Change	31
Manufacturing Employment Change	33
Home Ownership	45
Gambling Losses	11
Electricity Use Per Residential Customer	45
Revenue Per Kwh	49
New Companies	42

Geography

Total Land Area	45
Federally-Owned Land	47
State Park Visitors	16
State Park Acreage	9
Hunters With Firearms	47
Registered Boats	30
Per Capita State Spending For the Arts	11
Energy Consumption Per Capita	44
Toxic Chemical Release Per Capita	46
Hazardous Waste Sites	13
Polluted Rivers	15
Air Quality	45

Government

Members Of US House	13
Legislators Per Million Population	31
Units Of Government	43
Female Legislators	17
Turnover In Legislatures	34
Democrats in State Legislatures	5
Number Of Statewide Elected Officials	16
State And Local Government Employees	48
State And Local Average Salaries	13
Local Employment	23
Registered Voters	21
Statewide Initiatives	9

Federal

Per Capita Federal Spending	8
Increase In Federal Spending	48
Federal Grants To State And Local Government	9
Per Capita Federal Spending On Procurement	7
Per Capita Federal Spending On Social Security And Medicare	4
Social Security Benefits	16
Federal Spending On Employee Wages & Salaries	33
Federal Grant Spending Per $ Of State Tax Revenue	32
General Revenue From Federal Government	10
Federal Tax Burden Per Capita	4
Highway Charges Returned To States	3
Terms Of Trade	24
Per Capita Federal Income Tax Liability	5

Taxes

Tax Revenue	28
Per Capita Tax Revenue	6
Tax Effort	12
Tax Capacity	8
Percent Change In Taxes	49
Property Taxes Per Capita	10
Property Tax Revenue As Percent Of Three-Tax Revenue	20
Sales Taxes Per Capita	45
Sales Tax Revenue As Percent Of Three-Tax Revenue	47
Services With Sales Tax	41
Income Taxes Per Capita	2
Income Tax Revenue As Percent Of Three-Tax Revenue	4
Highest Personal Income Tax Rate	29
Motor Fuel Taxes	17
Tobacco Taxes	6
Tax Burden On High Income Family	7
Progressivity Of Taxes	14

Revenues And Finances

State And Local Revenue	10
Non-Tax Revenue	12
State And Local Expenditures	10
Per Capita State And Local General Expenditures	12
Change In General Expenditures	12
State Government General Spending	10

Debt As Percent Of Revenue	28
Full Faith And Credit Debt	4
Bond Ratings	4
State Solvency Index	50
Pension Plan Assets	37
State Reserves	31
State Budget Process Quality	4
Relative State Spending "Needs"	5

Education

Math Proficiency, 8th Grade	12
AFQT Ranks	30
SAT Scores	20
ACT Scores	n/a
Over-25 Population Without High School Diploma	15
Private School Students	12
Percent Students Finishing High School	17
Pupil-Teacher Ratio	7
Public School Enrollment	48
Library Holdings Per Capita	4
Education Spending As Percent Of Total	48
Spending Per Pupil	7
Average Teacher Salary	7
State Aid Per Pupil	37
State And Local Spending For Higher Education	50
Higher Education Spending As Percent Of Total	47
Public Higher Education Enrollment	49
State Per Pupil Support Of Higher Education	45
Tuition And Fees	3
Average Professor Salary	8
Education Employees	42
R&D Spending	3

Health

Infant Mortality Rates	49
State Health Rankings	7
Population Without Health Insurance	38
Abortions	5

Alcohol Consumption	21
Percent Non-Smokers	29
Percent Obese	35
AIDS Cases	15
Physicians Per 100,000 Population	1
Medicaid Recipients Related To Poverty Population	3
Health/Hospital Spending As Percent Of Total	23
Per Capita Medicaid Spending	4
Medicaid Spending Per Aged Recipient	5
Medicaid Spending Per AFDC Child	8
Medicare Payment Per Hospital-Day	37
Population In HMOs	5

Crime And Law Enforcement

Crime Rate	25
Violent Crime Rate	10
Murder Rate	
Property Crime Rate	32
Motor Vehicle Theft Rate	5
Violent Crime Rate Change	19
Incarceration Rate	43
Juvenile Arrest Rate	44
Proportion Of Sentence Served	3
Law Enforcement Employees	14
Corrections Employees	32
Costs Per Inmate-Day	13
State Corrections Spending	20
Spending For Law Enforcement	15
Law Enforcement Spending As Percent Of Total	23

Transportation

Percent Of Travel On Interstates	6
Interstate Mileage In Poor Condition	43

Deficient Bridges	2
Traffic Deaths Per 100 Million Vehicle-miles	49
Seat Belt Use	44
Vehicle Miles Traveled Per Capita	43
Workers Using Public Transportation	4
Road And Street Miles Under State Control	27
Highway Employees	47
Public Transit Employees	5
State And Local Spending For Highways	45
Highway Spending As Percent Of Total	46

Welfare

Percent Of Births To Unwed Mothers	36
AFDC Recipients As Percent Of Population	21
Food Stamp Recipients As Percent Of Population	38
SSI Recipients As Percent Of Population	12
Change In AFDC Recipients	27
Condition Of Children Index	11
Percent Of Families With Single Parent	14
Typical Monthly AFDC Payments	6
Welfare As Percent Of Poverty Level Income	9
Average SSI State Supplements Per Recipient	6
State Income Tax Liability Of Typical Family In Poverty	4
Child Support Collections Per $ Of Administrative Costs	14
Percent Of Children In Foster Care	3
State And Local Welfare Spending Per Capita	3
Welfare Spending As Percent Of Total	3
Administrative Costs Per AFDC Case	18

Population

Population	8
Percent Population Change	41
Population 2000	8
Median Age	35
Percent Population African-American	14
Percent Population in Poverty	19
Percent Population Female	24
Birth Rates	23
Death Rates	30
Illegal Immigrant Population	26

Economies

Personal Income	9
Per Capita Personal Income	18
Percent of Personal Income from Wages & Salaries	11
Average Annual Pay	7
Cost Of Living	31
Average Annual Pay in Manufacturing	2
Average Annual Pay in Retailing	24
Unemployment Rate	30
Government Employment	8
Manufacturing Employment	4
Fortune 500 Companies	10
Tourism Spending	13
Export-related Jobs	6
Change in Price of Existing Homes	17
Net Farm Income	38
Bankruptcy Filings	33
Patents Issued	7
WC Disability Payments	12
UC Average Weekly Benefit	7
Economic Momentum	20
Employment Change	19
Manufacturing Employment Change	21
Home Ownership	4
Gambling Losses	13
Electricity Use Per Residential Customer	43
Revenue Per Kwh	39
New Companies	46

Geography

Total Land Area	22
Federally-Owned Land	14
State Park Visitors	11
State Park Acreage	10
Hunters With Firearms	22
Registered Boats	1
Per Capita State Spending For the Arts	2
Energy Consumption Per Capita	32
Toxic Chemical Release Per Capita	23
Hazardous Waste Sites	5
Polluted Rivers	46
Air Quality	31

Government

Members Of US House	8
Legislators Per Million Population	43
Units Of Government	30
Female Legislators	22
Turnover In Legislatures	22
Democrats in State Legislatures	28
Number Of Statewide Elected Officials	42
State And Local Government Employees	41
State And Local Average Salaries	6
Local Employment	19
Registered Voters	6
Statewide Initiatives	16

Federal

Per Capita Federal Spending	45
Increase In Federal Spending	12
Federal Grants To State And Local Government	29
Per Capita Federal Spending On Procurement	41
Per Capita Federal Spending On Social Security And Medicare	10
Social Security Benefits	5
Federal Spending On Employee Wages & Salaries	49
Federal Grant Spending Per $ Of State Tax Revenue	27
General Revenue From Federal Government	7
Federal Tax Burden Per Capita	19
Highway Charges Returned To States	43
Terms Of Trade	36
Per Capita Federal Income Tax Liability	19

Taxes

Tax Revenue	16
Per Capita Tax Revenue	18
Tax Effort	7
Tax Capacity	25
Percent Change In Taxes	48
Property Taxes Per Capita	8
Property Tax Revenue As Percent Of Three-Tax Revenue	5
Sales Taxes Per Capita	44
Sales Tax Revenue As Percent Of Three-Tax Revenue	43
Services With Sales Tax	37
Income Taxes Per Capita	31
Income Tax Revenue As Percent Of Three-Tax Revenue	33
Highest Personal Income Tax Rate	36
Motor Fuel Taxes	43
Tobacco Taxes	1
Tax Burden On High Income Family	11
Progressivity Of Taxes	16

Revenues And Finances

State And Local Revenue	9
Non-Tax Revenue	6
State And Local Expenditures	9
Per Capita State And Local General Expenditures	20
Change In General Expenditures	20
State Government General Spending	9

Debt As Percent Of Revenue	47
Full Faith And Credit Debt	25
Bond Ratings	3
State Solvency Index	43
Pension Plan Assets	19
State Reserves	7
State Budget Process Quality	2
Relative State Spending "Needs"	32

Education

Math Proficiency, 8th Grade	18
AFQT Ranks	34
SAT Scores	n/a
ACT Scores	16
Over-25 Population Without High School Diploma	25
Private School Students	18
Percent Students Finishing High School	35
Pupil-Teacher Ratio	46
Public School Enrollment	29
Library Holdings Per Capita	28
Education Spending As Percent Of Total	9
Spending Per Pupil	12
Average Teacher Salary	5
State Aid Per Pupil	35
State And Local Spending For Higher Education	14
Higher Education Spending As Percent Of Total	16
Public Higher Education Enrollment	12
State Per Pupil Support Of Higher Education	42
Tuition And Fees	8
Average Professor Salary	15
Education Employees	26
R&D Spending	34

Health

Infant Mortality Rates	15
State Health Rankings	24
Population Without Health Insurance	43
Abortions	27

Alcohol Consumption	32
Percent Non-Smokers	39
Percent Obese	1
AIDS Cases	31
Physicians Per 100,000 Population	27
Medicaid Recipients Related To Poverty Population	15
Health/Hospital Spending As Percent Of Total	12
Per Capita Medicaid Spending	31
Medicaid Spending Per Aged Recipient	24
Medicaid Spending Per AFDC Child	44
Medicare Payment Per Hospital-Day	25
Population In HMOs	15

Crime And Law Enforcement

Crime Rate	19
Violent Crime Rate	11
Murder Rate	
Property Crime Rate	18
Motor Vehicle Theft Rate	11
Violent Crime Rate Change	41
Incarceration Rate	9
Juvenile Arrest Rate	34
Proportion Of Sentence Served	n/a
Law Enforcement Employees	39
Corrections Employees	17
Costs Per Inmate-Day	23
State Corrections Spending	16
Spending For Law Enforcement	12
Law Enforcement Spending As Percent Of Total	10

Transportation

Percent Of Travel On Interstates	28
Interstate Mileage In Poor Condition	13

Deficient Bridges	13
Traffic Deaths Per 100 Million Vehicle-miles	32
Seat Belt Use	21
Vehicle Miles Traveled Per Capita	33
Workers Using Public Transportation	29
Road And Street Miles Under State Control	47
Highway Employees	49
Public Transit Employees	20
State And Local Spending For Highways	49
Highway Spending As Percent Of Total	47

Welfare

Percent Of Births To Unwed Mothers	38
AFDC Recipients As Percent Of Population	3
Food Stamp Recipients As Percent Of Population	18
SSI Recipients As Percent Of Population	21
Change In AFDC Recipients	44
Condition Of Children Index	31
Percent Of Families With Single Parent	8
Typical Monthly AFDC Payments	14
Welfare As Percent Of Poverty Level Income	14
Average SSI State Supplements Per Recipient	19
State Income Tax Liability Of Typical Family In Poverty	7
Child Support Collections Per $ Of Administrative Costs	2
Percent Of Children In Foster Care	9
State And Local Welfare Spending Per Capita	17
Welfare Spending As Percent Of Total	19
Administrative Costs Per AFDC Case	17

Population

Population	20
Percent Population Change	24
Population 2000	20
Median Age	36
Percent Population African-American	37
Percent Population in Poverty	28
Percent Population Female	34
Birth Rates	37
Death Rates	38
Illegal Immigrant Population	31

Economies

Personal Income	19
Per Capita Personal Income	16
Percent of Personal Income from Wages & Salaries	4
Average Annual Pay	13
Cost Of Living	32
Average Annual Pay in Manufacturing	12
Average Annual Pay in Retailing	25
Unemployment Rate	44
Government Employment	19
Manufacturing Employment	16
Fortune 500 Companies	11
Tourism Spending	24
Export-related Jobs	17
Change in Price of Existing Homes	14
Net Farm Income	11
Bankruptcy Filings	22
Patents Issued	5
WC Disability Payments	10
UC Average Weekly Benefit	6
Economic Momentum	18
Employment Change	23
Manufacturing Employment Change	11
Home Ownership	2
Gambling Losses	23
Electricity Use Per Residential Customer	33
Revenue Per Kwh	21
New Companies	41

Geography

Total Land Area	14
Federally-Owned Land	13
State Park Visitors	28
State Park Acreage	15
Hunters With Firearms	13
Registered Boats	3
Per Capita State Spending For the Arts	8
Energy Consumption Per Capita	26
Toxic Chemical Release Per Capita	33
Hazardous Waste Sites	11
Polluted Rivers	14
Air Quality	18

Government

Members Of US House	19
Legislators Per Million Population	23
Units Of Government	9
Female Legislators	13
Turnover In Legislatures	39
Democrats in State Legislatures	18
Number Of Statewide Elected Officials	35
State And Local Government Employees	23
State And Local Average Salaries	9
Local Employment	10
Registered Voters	3
Statewide Initiatives	n/a

Federal

Per Capita Federal Spending	44
Increase In Federal Spending	45
Federal Grants To State And Local Government	23
Per Capita Federal Spending On Procurement	30
Per Capita Federal Spending On Social Security And Medicare	33
Social Security Benefits	27
Federal Spending On Employee Wages & Salaries	47
Federal Grant Spending Per $ Of State Tax Revenue	46
General Revenue From Federal Government	19
Federal Tax Burden Per Capita	14
Highway Charges Returned To States	14
Terms Of Trade	37
Per Capita Federal Income Tax Liability	16

Taxes

Tax Revenue	5
Per Capita Tax Revenue	7
Tax Effort	5
Tax Capacity	19
Percent Change In Taxes	24
Property Taxes Per Capita	15
Property Tax Revenue As Percent Of Three-Tax Revenue	26
Sales Taxes Per Capita	14
Sales Tax Revenue As Percent Of Three-Tax Revenue	32
Services With Sales Tax	17
Income Taxes Per Capita	7
Income Tax Revenue As Percent Of Three-Tax Revenue	11
Highest Personal Income Tax Rate	6
Motor Fuel Taxes	20
Tobacco Taxes	8
Tax Burden On High Income Family	10
Progressivity Of Taxes	46

Revenues And Finances

State And Local Revenue	16
Non-Tax Revenue	13
State And Local Expenditures	15
Per Capita State And Local General Expenditures	7
Change In General Expenditures	7
State Government General Spending	17

Debt As Percent Of Revenue	24
Full Faith And Credit Debt	13
Bond Ratings	2
State Solvency Index	18
Pension Plan Assets	21
State Reserves	14
State Budget Process Quality	19
Relative State Spending "Needs"	19

Education

Math Proficiency, 8th Grade	3
AFQT Ranks	8
SAT Scores	n/a
ACT Scores	2
Over-25 Population Without High School Diploma	6
Private School Students	16
Percent Students Finishing High School	1
Pupil-Teacher Ratio	34
Public School Enrollment	16
Library Holdings Per Capita	24
Education Spending As Percent Of Total	35
Spending Per Pupil	20
Average Teacher Salary	15
State Aid Per Pupil	14
State And Local Spending For Higher Education	20
Higher Education Spending As Percent Of Total	37
Public Higher Education Enrollment	19
State Per Pupil Support Of Higher Education	20
Tuition And Fees	18
Average Professor Salary	17
Education Employees	30
R&D Spending	31

Health

Infant Mortality Rates	35
State Health Rankings	2
Population Without Health Insurance	45
Abortions	23

Alcohol Consumption	22
Percent Non-Smokers	15
Percent Obese	26
AIDS Cases	37
Physicians Per 100,000 Population	11
Medicaid Recipients Related To Poverty Population	25
Health/Hospital Spending As Percent Of Total	18
Per Capita Medicaid Spending	12
Medicaid Spending Per Aged Recipient	3
Medicaid Spending Per AFDC Child	23
Medicare Payment Per Hospital-Day	18
Population In HMOs	8

Crime And Law Enforcement

Crime Rate	36
Violent Crime Rate	37
Murder Rate	
Property Crime Rate	33
Motor Vehicle Theft Rate	30
Violent Crime Rate Change	34
Incarceration Rate	49
Juvenile Arrest Rate	15
Proportion Of Sentence Served	4
Law Enforcement Employees	47
Corrections Employees	44
Costs Per Inmate-Day	7
State Corrections Spending	1
Spending For Law Enforcement	32
Law Enforcement Spending As Percent Of Total	45

Transportation

Percent Of Travel On Interstates	32
Interstate Mileage In Poor Condition	3

Deficient Bridges	45
Traffic Deaths Per 100 Million Vehicle-miles	46
Seat Belt Use	35
Vehicle Miles Traveled Per Capita	26
Workers Using Public Transportation	12
Road And Street Miles Under State Control	44
Highway Employees	17
Public Transit Employees	14
State And Local Spending For Highways	10
Highway Spending As Percent Of Total	21

Welfare

Percent Of Births To Unwed Mothers	45
AFDC Recipients As Percent Of Population	30
Food Stamp Recipients As Percent Of Population	42
SSI Recipients As Percent Of Population	43
Change In AFDC Recipients	36
Condition Of Children Index	8
Percent Of Families With Single Parent	22
Typical Monthly AFDC Payments	11
Welfare As Percent Of Poverty Level Income	11
Average SSI State Supplements Per Recipient	9
State Income Tax Liability Of Typical Family In Poverty	39
Child Support Collections Per $ Of Administrative Costs	16
Percent Of Children In Foster Care	13
State And Local Welfare Spending Per Capita	5
Welfare Spending As Percent Of Total	9
Administrative Costs Per AFDC Case	5

Population

Population	31
Percent Population Change	22
Population 2000	31
Median Age	45
Percent Population African-American	1
Percent Population in Poverty	3
Percent Population Female	1
Birth Rates	12
Death Rates	10
Illegal Immigrant Population	44

Economies

Personal Income	32
Per Capita Personal Income	50
Percent of Personal Income from Wages & Salaries	34
Average Annual Pay	47
Cost Of Living	50
Average Annual Pay in Manufacturing	49
Average Annual Pay in Retailing	43
Unemployment Rate	15
Government Employment	31
Manufacturing Employment	25
Fortune 500 Companies	39
Tourism Spending	37
Export-related Jobs	30
Change in Price of Existing Homes	n/a
Net Farm Income	22
Bankruptcy Filings	10
Patents Issued	50
WC Disability Payments	50
UC Average Weekly Benefit	49
Economic Momentum	44
Employment Change	50
Manufacturing Employment Change	49
Home Ownership	3
Gambling Losses	8
Electricity Use Per Residential Customer	9
Revenue Per Kwh	33
New Companies	24

Geography

Total Land Area	31
Federally-Owned Land	25
State Park Visitors	38
State Park Acreage	47
Hunters With Firearms	9
Registered Boats	19
Per Capita State Spending For the Arts	47
Energy Consumption Per Capita	16
Toxic Chemical Release Per Capita	4
Hazardous Waste Sites	46
Polluted Rivers	4
Air Quality	1

Government

Members Of US House	29
Legislators Per Million Population	14
Units Of Government	27
Female Legislators	45
Turnover In Legislatures	49
Democrats in State Legislatures	6
Number Of Statewide Elected Officials	7
State And Local Government Employees	8
State And Local Average Salaries	50
Local Employment	22
Registered Voters	9
Statewide Initiatives	n/a

Federal

Per Capita Federal Spending	14
Increase In Federal Spending	8
Federal Grants To State And Local Government	14
Per Capita Federal Spending On Procurement	10
Per Capita Federal Spending On Social Security And Medicare	31
Social Security Benefits	50
Federal Spending On Employee Wages & Salaries	26
Federal Grant Spending Per $ Of State Tax Revenue	5
General Revenue From Federal Government	27
Federal Tax Burden Per Capita	50
Highway Charges Returned To States	43
Terms Of Trade	5
Per Capita Federal Income Tax Liability	50

Taxes

Tax Revenue	45
Per Capita Tax Revenue	50
Tax Effort	32
Tax Capacity	50
Percent Change In Taxes	33
Property Taxes Per Capita	41
Property Tax Revenue As Percent Of Three-Tax Revenue	35
Sales Taxes Per Capita	32
Sales Tax Revenue As Percent Of Three-Tax Revenue	9
Services With Sales Tax	13
Income Taxes Per Capita	41
Income Tax Revenue As Percent Of Three-Tax Revenue	40
Highest Personal Income Tax Rate	33
Motor Fuel Taxes	29
Tobacco Taxes	37
Tax Burden On High Income Family	37
Progressivity Of Taxes	43

Revenues And Finances

State And Local Revenue	32
Non-Tax Revenue	33
State And Local Expenditures	32
Per Capita State And Local General Expenditures	49
Change In General Expenditures	49
State Government General Spending	31

Debt As Percent Of Revenue	48
Full Faith And Credit Debt	33
Bond Ratings	3
State Solvency Index	28
Pension Plan Assets	50
State Reserves	4
State Budget Process Quality	26
Relative State Spending "Needs"	50

Education

Math Proficiency, 8th Grade	41
AFQT Ranks	50
SAT Scores	n/a
ACT Scores	27
Over-25 Population Without High School Diploma	50
Private School Students	19
Percent Students Finishing High School	47
Pupil-Teacher Ratio	39
Public School Enrollment	8
Library Holdings Per Capita	38
Education Spending As Percent Of Total	27
Spending Per Pupil	49
Average Teacher Salary	49
State Aid Per Pupil	45
State And Local Spending For Higher Education	29
Higher Education Spending As Percent Of Total	13
Public Higher Education Enrollment	31
State Per Pupil Support Of Higher Education	25
Tuition And Fees	22
Average Professor Salary	35
Education Employees	9
R&D Spending	32

Health

Infant Mortality Rates	2
State Health Rankings	49
Population Without Health Insurance	11
Abortions	38

Alcohol Consumption	37
Percent Non-Smokers	34
Percent Obese	7
AIDS Cases	23
Physicians Per 100,000 Population	48
Medicaid Recipients Related To Poverty Population	26
Health/Hospital Spending As Percent Of Total	4
Per Capita Medicaid Spending	18
Medicaid Spending Per Aged Recipient	49
Medicaid Spending Per AFDC Child	37
Medicare Payment Per Hospital-Day	48
Population In HMOs	47

Crime And Law Enforcement

Crime Rate	35
Violent Crime Rate	32
Murder Rate	
Property Crime Rate	34
Motor Vehicle Theft Rate	32
Violent Crime Rate Change	18
Incarceration Rate	10
Juvenile Arrest Rate	16
Proportion Of Sentence Served	27
Law Enforcement Employees	38
Corrections Employees	43
Costs Per Inmate-Day	48
State Corrections Spending	47
Spending For Law Enforcement	47
Law Enforcement Spending As Percent Of Total	46

Transportation

Percent Of Travel On Interstates	48
Interstate Mileage In Poor Condition	1

Deficient Bridges	9
Traffic Deaths Per 100 Million Vehicle-miles	1
Seat Belt Use	46
Vehicle Miles Traveled Per Capita	14
Workers Using Public Transportation	41
Road And Street Miles Under State Control	29
Highway Employees	13
Public Transit Employees	45
State And Local Spending For Highways	29
Highway Spending As Percent Of Total	12

Welfare

Percent Of Births To Unwed Mothers	1
AFDC Recipients As Percent Of Population	10
Food Stamp Recipients As Percent Of Population	1
SSI Recipients As Percent Of Population	1
Change In AFDC Recipients	50
Condition Of Children Index	49
Percent Of Families With Single Parent	2
Typical Monthly AFDC Payments	50
Welfare As Percent Of Poverty Level Income	50
Average SSI State Supplements Per Recipient	44
State Income Tax Liability Of Typical Family In Poverty	22
Child Support Collections Per $ Of Administrative Costs	49
Percent Of Children In Foster Care	41
State And Local Welfare Spending Per Capita	37
Welfare Spending As Percent Of Total	20
Administrative Costs Per AFDC Case	48

Debt As Percent Of Revenue	42	Alcohol Consumption	27	Deficient Bridges	12
Full Faith And Credit Debt	41	Percent Non-Smokers	32	Traffic Deaths Per	
Bond Ratings	1	Percent Obese	21	100 Million Vehicle-miles	27
State Solvency Index	24	AIDS Cases	28	Seat Belt Use	18
Pension Plan Assets	7	Physicians Per 100,000		Vehicle Miles Traveled	
State Reserves	19	Population	20	Per Capita	7
State Budget Process Quality	5	Medicaid Recipients Related		Workers Using Public	
Relative State Spending "Needs"	30	To Poverty Population	32	Transportation	26

Education

Math Proficiency, 8th Grade	16	Health/Hospital Spending		Road And Street Miles	
AFQT Ranks	27	As Percent Of Total	27	Under State Control	15
SAT Scores	n/a	Per Capita Medicaid		Highway Employees	27
ACT Scores	8	Spending	38	Public Transit Employees	15
Over-25 Population Without		Medicaid Spending Per		State And Local Spending	
High School Diploma	38	Aged Recipient	36	For Highways	37
Private School Students	15	Medicaid Spending Per		Highway Spending As	
Percent Students Finishing		AFDC Child	35	Percent Of Total	20
High School	32	Medicare Payment Per			
Pupil-Teacher Ratio	20	Hospital-Day	22		
Public School Enrollment	35	Population In HMOs	25		
Library Holdings Per Capita	10				
Education Spending As					
Percent Of Total	20				
Spending Per Pupil	42				
Average Teacher Salary	36				
State Aid Per Pupil	42	**Crime And Law Enforcement**		**Welfare**	
State And Local Spending		Crime Rate	23	Percent Of Births To	
For Higher Education	45	Violent Crime Rate	16	Unwed Mothers	17
Higher Education Spending		Murder Rate		AFDC Recipients As	
As Percent Of Total	32	Property Crime Rate	25	Percent Of Population	20
Public Higher Education		Motor Vehicle Theft Rate	18	Food Stamp Recipients As	
Enrollment	39	Violent Crime Rate Change	17	Percent Of Population	14
State Per Pupil Support Of		Incarceration Rate	19	SSI Recipients As	
Higher Education	43	Juvenile Arrest Rate	42	Percent Of Population	26
Tuition And Fees	20	Proportion Of Sentence		Change In AFDC Recipients	24
Average Professor Salary	23	Served	15	Condition Of Children Index	36
Education Employees	35	Law Enforcement		Percent Of Families With	
R&D Spending	23	Employees	11	Single Parent	17
		Corrections Employees	29	Typical Monthly AFDC	
		Costs Per Inmate-Day	49	Payments	37
		State Corrections Spending	45	Welfare As Percent Of	
		Spending For Law		Poverty Level Income	38
		Enforcement	38	Average SSI State Supplements	
		Law Enforcement Spending		Per Recipient	47
		As Percent Of Total	28	State Income Tax Liability Of	
				Typical Family In Poverty	17
				Child Support Collections Per $	
				Of Administrative Costs	14
				Percent Of Children In	
				Foster Care	10
Health				State And Local Welfare	
Infant Mortality Rates	20	**Transportation**		Spending Per Capita	26
State Health Rankings	33	Percent Of Travel On		Welfare Spending As	
Population Without Health		Interstates	7	Percent Of Total	12
Insurance	36	Interstate Mileage In		Administrative Costs Per	
Abortions	36	Poor Condition	39	AFDC Case	43

Population

Population	44
Percent Population Change	9
Population 2000	44
Median Age	9
Percent Population African-American	50
Percent Population in Poverty	30
Percent Population Female	42
Birth Rates	46
Death Rates	37
Illegal Immigrant Population	49

Economies

Personal Income	45
Per Capita Personal Income	41
Percent of Personal Income from Wages & Salaries	49
Average Annual Pay	48
Cost Of Living	28
Average Annual Pay in Manufacturing	46
Average Annual Pay in Retailing	44
Unemployment Rate	20
Government Employment	43
Manufacturing Employment	46
Fortune 500 Companies	n/a
Tourism Spending	41
Export-related Jobs	47
Change in Price of Existing Homes	n/a
Net Farm Income	32
Bankruptcy Filings	36
Patents Issued	39
WC Disability Payments	37
UC Average Weekly Benefit	37
Economic Momentum	29
Employment Change	14
Manufacturing Employment Change	6
Home Ownership	26
Gambling Losses	28
Electricity Use Per Residential Customer	24
Revenue Per Kwh	5
New Companies	6

Geography

Total Land Area	4
Federally-Owned Land	9
State Park Visitors	36
State Park Acreage	42
Hunters With Firearms	1
Registered Boats	43
Per Capita State Spending For the Arts	12
Energy Consumption Per Capita	8
Toxic Chemical Release Per Capita	2
Hazardous Waste Sites	41
Polluted Rivers	38
Air Quality	14

Government

Members Of US House	44
Legislators Per Million Population	5
Units Of Government	4
Female Legislators	17
Turnover In Legislatures	4
Democrats in State Legislatures	43
Number Of Statewide Elected Officials	35
State And Local Government Employees	3
State And Local Average Salaries	38
Local Employment	26
Registered Voters	7
Statewide Initiatives	7

Federal

Per Capita Federal Spending	10
Increase In Federal Spending	25
Federal Grants To State And Local Government	8
Per Capita Federal Spending On Procurement	46
Per Capita Federal Spending On Social Security And Medicare	26
Social Security Benefits	32

Federal Spending On Employee Wages & Salaries	16
Federal Grant Spending Per $ Of State Tax Revenue	10
General Revenue From Federal Government	43
Federal Tax Burden Per Capita	37
Highway Charges Returned To States	5
Terms Of Trade	8
Per Capita Federal Income Tax Liability	43

Taxes

Tax Revenue	21
Per Capita Tax Revenue	37
Tax Effort	49
Tax Capacity	31
Percent Change In Taxes	39
Property Taxes Per Capita	21
Property Tax Revenue As Percent Of Three-Tax Revenue	4
Sales Taxes Per Capita	49
Sales Tax Revenue As Percent Of Three-Tax Revenue	49
Services With Sales Tax	43
Income Taxes Per Capita	30
Income Tax Revenue As Percent Of Three-Tax Revenue	14
Highest Personal Income Tax Rate	20
Motor Fuel Taxes	3
Tobacco Taxes	37
Tax Burden On High Income Family	14
Progressivity Of Taxes	47

Revenues And Finances

State And Local Revenue	45
Non-Tax Revenue	45
State And Local Expenditures	45
Per Capita State And Local General Expenditures	27
Change In General Expenditures	27
State Government General Spending	46

Debt As Percent Of Revenue	25
Full Faith And Credit Debt	38
Bond Ratings	3
State Solvency Index	15
Pension Plan Assets	47
State Reserves	26
State Budget Process Quality	23
Relative State Spending "Needs"	40

Education

Math Proficiency, 8ᵗʰ Grade	n/a
AFQT Ranks	3
SAT Scores	n/a
ACT Scores	3
Over-25 Population Without High School Diploma	11
Private School Students	39
Percent Students Finishing High School	5
Pupil-Teacher Ratio	17
Public School Enrollment	7
Library Holdings Per Capita	23
Education Spending As Percent Of Total	17
Spending Per Pupil	31
Average Teacher Salary	41
State Aid Per Pupil	44
State And Local Spending For Higher Education	35
Higher Education Spending As Percent Of Total	35
Public Higher Education Enrollment	35
State Per Pupil Support Of Higher Education	27
Tuition And Fees	37
Average Professor Salary	50
Education Employees	1
R&D Spending	28

Health

Infant Mortality Rates	19
State Health Rankings	25
Population Without Health Insurance	15
Abortions	19

Alcohol Consumption	9
Percent Non-Smokers	3
Percent Obese	42
AIDS Cases	47
Physicians Per 100,000 Population	40
Medicaid Recipients Related To Poverty Population	46
Health/Hospital Spending As Percent Of Total	38
Per Capita Medicaid Spending	35
Medicaid Spending Per Aged Recipient	15
Medicaid Spending Per AFDC Child	42
Medicare Payment Per Hospital-Day	30
Population In HMOs	44

Crime And Law Enforcement

Crime Rate	30
Violent Crime Rate	46
Murder Rate	
Property Crime Rate	21
Motor Vehicle Theft Rate	38
Violent Crime Rate Change	7
Incarceration Rate	37
Juvenile Arrest Rate	5
Proportion Of Sentence Served	31
Law Enforcement Employees	33
Corrections Employees	38
Costs Per Inmate-Day	10
State Corrections Spending	26
Spending For Law Enforcement	44
Law Enforcement Spending As Percent Of Total	44

Transportation

Percent Of Travel On Interstates	21
Interstate Mileage In Poor Condition	16

Deficient Bridges	34
Traffic Deaths Per 100 Million Vehicle-miles	10
Seat Belt Use	15
Vehicle Miles Traveled Per Capita	12
Workers Using Public Transportation	46
Road And Street Miles Under State Control	42
Highway Employees	4
Public Transit Employees	30
State And Local Spending For Highways	7
Highway Spending As Percent Of Total	5

Welfare

Percent Of Births To Unwed Mothers	30
AFDC Recipients As Percent Of Population	30
Food Stamp Recipients As Percent Of Population	32
SSI Recipients As Percent Of Population	32
Change In AFDC Recipients	30
Condition Of Children Index	21
Percent Of Families With Single Parent	31
Typical Monthly AFDC Payments	20
Welfare As Percent Of Poverty Level Income	22
Average SSI State Supplements Per Recipient	3
State Income Tax Liability Of Typical Family In Poverty	12
Child Support Collections Per $ Of Administrative Costs	42
Percent Of Children In Foster Care	18
State And Local Welfare Spending Per Capita	40
Welfare Spending As Percent Of Total	38
Administrative Costs Per AFDC Case	15

Population

Population	37
Percent Population Change	36
Population 2000	37
Median Age	22
Percent Population African-American	32
Percent Population in Poverty	45
Percent Population Female	28
Birth Rates	30
Death Rates	21
Illegal Immigrant Population	27

Economies

Personal Income	35
Per Capita Personal Income	23
Percent of Personal Income from Wages & Salaries	33
Average Annual Pay	45
Cost Of Living	33
Average Annual Pay in Manufacturing	42
Average Annual Pay in Retailing	48
Unemployment Rate	50
Government Employment	36
Manufacturing Employment	35
Fortune 500 Companies	23
Tourism Spending	38
Export-related Jobs	39
Change in Price of Existing Homes	6
Net Farm Income	5
Bankruptcy Filings	37
Patents Issued	42
WC Disability Payments	40
UC Average Weekly Benefit	46
Economic Momentum	15
Employment Change	30
Manufacturing Employment Change	9
Home Ownership	29
Gambling Losses	38
Electricity Use Per Residential Customer	25
Revenue Per Kwh	27
New Companies	17

Geography

Total Land Area	15
Federally-Owned Land	34
State Park Visitors	25
State Park Acreage	20
Hunters With Firearms	8
Registered Boats	38
Per Capita State Spending For the Arts	23
Energy Consumption Per Capita	23
Toxic Chemical Release Per Capita	28
Hazardous Waste Sites	40
Polluted Rivers	17
Air Quality	1

Government

Members Of US House	34
Legislators Per Million Population	32
Units Of Government	3
Female Legislators	14
Turnover In Legislatures	43
Democrats in State Legislatures	n/a
Number Of Statewide Elected Officials	16
State And Local Government Employees	7
State And Local Average Salaries	30
Local Employment	14
Registered Voters	9
Statewide Initiatives	17

Federal

Per Capita Federal Spending	33
Increase In Federal Spending	47
Federal Grants To State And Local Government	41
Per Capita Federal Spending On Procurement	33
Per Capita Federal Spending On Social Security And Medicare	19
Social Security Benefits	25

Federal Spending On Employee Wages & Salaries	25
Federal Grant Spending Per $ Of State Tax Revenue	29
General Revenue From Federal Government	39
Federal Tax Burden Per Capita	27
Highway Charges Returned To States	18
Terms Of Trade	35
Per Capita Federal Income Tax Liability	31

Taxes

Tax Revenue	22
Per Capita Tax Revenue	26
Tax Effort	17
Tax Capacity	23
Percent Change In Taxes	21
Property Taxes Per Capita	18
Property Tax Revenue As Percent Of Three-Tax Revenue	18
Sales Taxes Per Capita	22
Sales Tax Revenue As Percent Of Three-Tax Revenue	29
Services With Sales Tax	23
Income Taxes Per Capita	26
Income Tax Revenue As Percent Of Three-Tax Revenue	31
Highest Personal Income Tax Rate	17
Motor Fuel Taxes	5
Tobacco Taxes	20
Tax Burden On High Income Family	13
Progressivity Of Taxes	22

Revenues And Finances

State And Local Revenue	35
Non-Tax Revenue	36
State And Local Expenditures	33
Per Capita State And Local General Expenditures	31
Change In General Expenditures	31
State Government General Spending	39

Debt As Percent Of Revenue	15
Full Faith And Credit Debt	43
Bond Ratings	n/a
State Solvency Index	11
Pension Plan Assets	12
State Reserves	10
State Budget Process Quality	39
Relative State Spending "Needs"	25

Education

Math Proficiency, 8th Grade	6
AFQT Ranks	11
SAT Scores	n/a
ACT Scores	5
Over-25 Population Without High School Diploma	8
Private School Students	13
Percent Students Finishing High School	4
Pupil-Teacher Ratio	6
Public School Enrollment	19
Library Holdings Per Capita	12
Education Spending As Percent Of Total	4
Spending Per Pupil	30
Average Teacher Salary	39
State Aid Per Pupil	30
State And Local Spending For Higher Education	11
Higher Education Spending As Percent Of Total	6
Public Higher Education Enrollment	3
State Per Pupil Support Of Higher Education	13
Tuition And Fees	32
Average Professor Salary	28
Education Employees	14
R&D Spending	43

Health

Infant Mortality Rates	25
State Health Rankings	10
Population Without Health Insurance	35
Abortions	21

Alcohol Consumption	34
Percent Non-Smokers	2
Percent Obese	17
AIDS Cases	42
Physicians Per 100,000 Population	30
Medicaid Recipients Related To Poverty Population	15
Health/Hospital Spending As Percent Of Total	20
Per Capita Medicaid Spending	33
Medicaid Spending Per Aged Recipient	19
Medicaid Spending Per AFDC Child	33
Medicare Payment Per Hospital-Day	26
Population In HMOs	32

Crime And Law Enforcement

Crime Rate	38
Violent Crime Rate	36
Murder Rate	
Property Crime Rate	40
Motor Vehicle Theft Rate	41
Violent Crime Rate Change	23
Incarceration Rate	45
Juvenile Arrest Rate	8
Proportion Of Sentence Served	21
Law Enforcement Employees	32
Corrections Employees	33
Costs Per Inmate-Day	16
State Corrections Spending	23
Spending For Law Enforcement	40
Law Enforcement Spending As Percent Of Total	39

Transportation

Percent Of Travel On Interstates	40
Interstate Mileage In Poor Condition	9

Deficient Bridges	46
Traffic Deaths Per 100 Million Vehicle-miles	28
Seat Belt Use	25
Vehicle Miles Traveled Per Capita	32
Workers Using Public Transportation	34
Road And Street Miles Under State Control	43
Highway Employees	10
Public Transit Employees	22
State And Local Spending For Highways	13
Highway Spending As Percent Of Total	11

Welfare

Percent Of Births To Unwed Mothers	44
AFDC Recipients As Percent Of Population	44
Food Stamp Recipients As Percent Of Population	45
SSI Recipients As Percent Of Population	46
Change In AFDC Recipients	40
Condition Of Children Index	5
Percent Of Families With Single Parent	47
Typical Monthly AFDC Payments	27
Welfare As Percent Of Poverty Level Income	26
Average SSI State Supplements Per Recipient	21
State Income Tax Liability Of Typical Family In Poverty	22
Child Support Collections Per $ Of Administrative Costs	17
Percent Of Children In Foster Care	12
State And Local Welfare Spending Per Capita	31
Welfare Spending As Percent Of Total	33
Administrative Costs Per AFDC Case	23

Population

Population	38
Percent Population Change	1
Population 2000	38
Median Age	29
Percent Population African-American	26
Percent Population in Poverty	31
Percent Population Female	49
Birth Rates	10
Death Rates	34
Illegal Immigrant Population	8

Economies

Personal Income	34
Per Capita Personal Income	7
Percent of Personal Income from Wages & Salaries	7
Average Annual Pay	19
Cost Of Living	15
Average Annual Pay in Manufacturing	31
Average Annual Pay in Retailing	5
Unemployment Rate	13
Government Employment	39
Manufacturing Employment	45
Fortune 500 Companies	n/a
Tourism Spending	6
Export-related Jobs	46
Change in Price of Existing Homes	24
Net Farm Income	46
Bankruptcy Filings	4
Patents Issued	30
WC Disability Payments	26
UC Average Weekly Benefit	18
Economic Momentum	1
Employment Change	1
Manufacturing Employment Change	3
Home Ownership	48
Gambling Losses	1
Electricity Use Per Residential Customer	19
Revenue Per Kwh	47
New Companies	13

Geography

Total Land Area	7
Federally-Owned Land	2
State Park Visitors	43
State Park Acreage	19
Hunters With Firearms	40
Registered Boats	40
Per Capita State Spending For the Arts	45
Energy Consumption Per Capita	25
Toxic Chemical Release Per Capita	32
Hazardous Waste Sites	50
Polluted Rivers	13
Air Quality	21

Government

Members Of US House	38
Legislators Per Million Population	24
Units Of Government	40
Female Legislators	2
Turnover In Legislatures	3
Democrats in State Legislatures	29
Number Of Statewide Elected Officials	11
State And Local Government Employees	38
State And Local Average Salaries	10
Local Employment	15
Registered Voters	50
Statewide Initiatives	14

Federal

Per Capita Federal Spending	41
Increase In Federal Spending	3
Federal Grants To State And Local Government	49
Per Capita Federal Spending On Procurement	18
Per Capita Federal Spending On Social Security And Medicare	42
Social Security Benefits	12
Federal Spending On Employee Wages & Salaries	30
Federal Grant Spending Per $ Of State Tax Revenue	50
General Revenue From Federal Government	44
Federal Tax Burden Per Capita	10
Highway Charges Returned To States	22
Terms Of Trade	49
Per Capita Federal Income Tax Liability	3

Taxes

Tax Revenue	37
Per Capita Tax Revenue	22
Tax Effort	50
Tax Capacity	5
Percent Change In Taxes	1
Property Taxes Per Capita	34
Property Tax Revenue As Percent Of Three-Tax Revenue	38
Sales Taxes Per Capita	3
Sales Tax Revenue As Percent Of Three-Tax Revenue	1
Services With Sales Tax	47
Income Taxes Per Capita	n/a
Income Tax Revenue As Percent Of Three-Tax Revenue	46
Highest Personal Income Tax Rate	n/a
Motor Fuel Taxes	6
Tobacco Taxes	19
Tax Burden On High Income Family	48
Progressivity Of Taxes	4

Revenues And Finances

State And Local Revenue	40
Non-Tax Revenue	40
State And Local Expenditures	40
Per Capita State And Local General Expenditures	14
Change In General Expenditures	14
State Government General Spending	42

Debt As Percent Of Revenue	6
Full Faith And Credit Debt	7
Bond Ratings	3
State Solvency Index	30
Pension Plan Assets	39
State Reserves	8
State Budget Process Quality	37
Relative State Spending "Needs"	6

Education

Math Proficiency, 8th Grade	n/a
AFQT Ranks	12
SAT Scores	n/a
ACT Scores	8
Over-25 Population Without High School Diploma	19
Private School Students	47
Percent Students Finishing High School	36
Pupil-Teacher Ratio	42
Public School Enrollment	33
Library Holdings Per Capita	38
Education Spending As Percent Of Total	45
Spending Per Pupil	34
Average Teacher Salary	22
State Aid Per Pupil	46
State And Local Spending For Higher Education	41
Higher Education Spending As Percent Of Total	41
Public Higher Education Enrollment	18
State Per Pupil Support Of Higher Education	n/a
Tuition And Fees	46
Average Professor Salary	23
Education Employees	41
R&D Spending	10

Health

Infant Mortality Rates	44
State Health Rankings	43
Population Without Health Insurance	10
Abortions	12

Alcohol Consumption	1
Percent Non-Smokers	48
Percent Obese	n/a
AIDS Cases	10
Physicians Per 100,000 Population	46
Medicaid Recipients Related To Poverty Population	50
Health/Hospital Spending As Percent Of Total	29
Per Capita Medicaid Spending	48
Medicaid Spending Per Aged Recipient	29
Medicaid Spending Per AFDC Child	7
Medicare Payment Per Hospital-Day	1
Population In HMOs	26

Crime And Law Enforcement

Crime Rate	9
Violent Crime Rate	9
Murder Rate	
Property Crime Rate	10
Motor Vehicle Theft Rate	6
Violent Crime Rate Change	35
Incarceration Rate	5
Juvenile Arrest Rate	27
Proportion Of Sentence Served	n/a
Law Enforcement Employees	6
Corrections Employees	4
Costs Per Inmate-Day	39
State Corrections Spending	n/a
Spending For Law Enforcement	3
Law Enforcement Spending As Percent Of Total	1

Transportation

Percent Of Travel On Interstates	26
Interstate Mileage In Poor Condition	46

Deficient Bridges	42
Traffic Deaths Per 100 Million Vehicle-miles	8
Seat Belt Use	12
Vehicle Miles Traveled Per Capita	41
Workers Using Public Transportation	17
Road And Street Miles Under State Control	40
Highway Employees	40
Public Transit Employees	45
State And Local Spending For Highways	15
Highway Spending As Percent Of Total	24

Welfare

Percent Of Births To Unwed Mothers	11
AFDC Recipients As Percent Of Population	46
Food Stamp Recipients As Percent Of Population	48
SSI Recipients As Percent Of Population	45
Change In AFDC Recipients	5
Condition Of Children Index	34
Percent Of Families With Single Parent	11
Typical Monthly AFDC Payments	30
Welfare As Percent Of Poverty Level Income	28
Average SSI State Supplements Per Recipient	26
State Income Tax Liability Of Typical Family In Poverty	n/a
Child Support Collections Per $ Of Administrative Costs	45
Percent Of Children In Foster Care	32
State And Local Welfare Spending Per Capita	49
Welfare Spending As Percent Of Total	48
Administrative Costs Per AFDC Case	8

Population

Population	41
Percent Population Change	18
Population 2000	41
Median Age	19
Percent Population African-American	45
Percent Population in Poverty	49
Percent Population Female	31
Birth Rates	34
Death Rates	39
Illegal Immigrant Population	28

Economies

Personal Income	40
Per Capita Personal Income	8
Percent of Personal Income from Wages & Salaries	46
Average Annual Pay	20
Cost Of Living	8
Average Annual Pay in Manufacturing	16
Average Annual Pay in Retailing	12
Unemployment Rate	43
Government Employment	42
Manufacturing Employment	36
Fortune 500 Companies	40
Tourism Spending	42
Export-related Jobs	34
Change in Price of Existing Homes	34
Net Farm Income	47
Bankruptcy Filings	26
Patents Issued	6
WC Disability Payments	3
UC Average Weekly Benefit	43
Economic Momentum	22
Employment Change	40
Manufacturing Employment Change	39
Home Ownership	17
Gambling Losses	33
Electricity Use Per Residential Customer	44
Revenue Per Kwh	45
New Companies	9

Geography

Total Land Area	44
Federally-Owned Land	32
State Park Visitors	48
State Park Acreage	32
Hunters With Firearms	48
Registered Boats	35
Per Capita State Spending For the Arts	39
Energy Consumption Per Capita	48
Toxic Chemical Release Per Capita	39
Hazardous Waste Sites	25
Polluted Rivers	47
Air Quality	25

Government

Members Of US House	38
Legislators Per Million Population	1
Units Of Government	20
Female Legislators	6
Turnover In Legislatures	8
Democrats in State Legislatures	47
Number Of Statewide Elected Officials	48
State And Local Government Employees	46
State And Local Average Salaries	22
Local Employment	25
Registered Voters	24
Statewide Initiatives	n/a

Federal

Per Capita Federal Spending	47
Increase In Federal Spending	38
Federal Grants To State And Local Government	17
Per Capita Federal Spending On Procurement	29
Per Capita Federal Spending On Social Security And Medicare	32
Social Security Benefits	11
Federal Spending On Employee Wages & Salaries	45
Federal Grant Spending Per $ Of State Tax Revenue	4
General Revenue From Federal Government	42
Federal Tax Burden Per Capita	9
Highway Charges Returned To States	19
Terms Of Trade	33
Per Capita Federal Income Tax Liability	9

Taxes

Tax Revenue	47
Per Capita Tax Revenue	20
Tax Effort	42
Tax Capacity	10
Percent Change In Taxes	4
Property Taxes Per Capita	1
Property Tax Revenue As Percent Of Three-Tax Revenue	2
Sales Taxes Per Capita	46
Sales Tax Revenue As Percent Of Three-Tax Revenue	45
Services With Sales Tax	48
Income Taxes Per Capita	42
Income Tax Revenue As Percent Of Three-Tax Revenue	42
Highest Personal Income Tax Rate	n/a
Motor Fuel Taxes	27
Tobacco Taxes	27
Tax Burden On High Income Family	42
Progressivity Of Taxes	7

Revenues And Finances

State And Local Revenue	43
Non-Tax Revenue	43
State And Local Expenditures	43
Per Capita State And Local General Expenditures	24
Change In General Expenditures	24
State Government General Spending	43

Debt As Percent Of Revenue	7
Full Faith And Credit Debt	14
Bond Ratings	3
State Solvency Index	35
Pension Plan Assets	48
State Reserves	9
State Budget Process Quality	48
Relative State Spending "Needs"	1

Education

Math Proficiency, 8th Grade	4
AFQT Ranks	7
SAT Scores	11
ACT Scores	n/a
Over-25 Population Without High School Diploma	7
Private School Students	21
Percent Students Finishing High School	20
Pupil-Teacher Ratio	15
Public School Enrollment	36
Library Holdings Per Capita	5
Education Spending As Percent Of Total	39
Spending Per Pupil	21
Average Teacher Salary	21
State Aid Per Pupil	48
State And Local Spending For Higher Education	46
Higher Education Spending As Percent Of Total	43
Public Higher Education Enrollment	48
State Per Pupil Support Of Higher Education	47
Tuition And Fees	4
Average Professor Salary	19
Education Employees	28
R&D Spending	13

Health

Infant Mortality Rates	38
State Health Rankings	1
Population Without Health Insurance	39
Abortions	26

Alcohol Consumption	2
Percent Non-Smokers	27
Percent Obese	36
AIDS Cases	35
Physicians Per 100,000 Population	18
Medicaid Recipients Related To Poverty Population	26
Health/Hospital Spending As Percent Of Total	48
Per Capita Medicaid Spending	27
Medicaid Spending Per Aged Recipient	4
Medicaid Spending Per AFDC Child	24
Medicare Payment Per Hospital-Day	36
Population In HMOs	20

Crime And Law Enforcement

Crime Rate	48
Violent Crime Rate	47
Murder Rate	47
Property Crime Rate	47
Motor Vehicle Theft Rate	42
Violent Crime Rate Change	46
Incarceration Rate	41
Juvenile Arrest Rate	6
Proportion Of Sentence Served	26
Law Enforcement Employees	21
Corrections Employees	44
Costs Per Inmate-Day	32
State Corrections Spending	29
Spending For Law Enforcement	33
Law Enforcement Spending As Percent Of Total	34

Transportation

Percent Of Travel On Interstates	37
Interstate Mileage In Poor Condition	40

Deficient Bridges	19
Traffic Deaths Per 100 Million Vehicle-miles	48
Seat Belt Use	39
Vehicle Miles Traveled Per Capita	29
Workers Using Public Transportation	43
Road And Street Miles Under State Control	14
Highway Employees	14
Public Transit Employees	35
State And Local Spending For Highways	34
Highway Spending As Percent Of Total	37

Welfare

Percent Of Births To Unwed Mothers	47
AFDC Recipients As Percent Of Population	44
Food Stamp Recipients As Percent Of Population	50
SSI Recipients As Percent Of Population	50
Change In AFDC Recipients	1
Condition Of Children Index	1
Percent Of Families With Single Parent	44
Typical Monthly AFDC Payments	9
Welfare As Percent Of Poverty Level Income	10
Average SSI State Supplements Per Recipient	7
State Income Tax Liability Of Typical Family In Poverty	n/a
Child Support Collections Per $ Of Administrative Costs	39
Percent Of Children In Foster Care	27
State And Local Welfare Spending Per Capita	2
Welfare Spending As Percent Of Total	1
Administrative Costs Per AFDC Case	16

Population

Population	9
Percent Population Change	38
Population 2000	9
Median Age	7
Percent Population African-American	16
Percent Population in Poverty	42
Percent Population Female	14
Birth Rates	21
Death Rates	22
Illegal Immigrant Population	5

Economies

Personal Income	8
Per Capita Personal Income	2
Percent of Personal Income from Wages & Salaries	30
Average Annual Pay	2
Cost Of Living	2
Average Annual Pay in Manufacturing	4
Average Annual Pay in Retailing	1
Unemployment Rate	6
Government Employment	12
Manufacturing Employment	13
Fortune 500 Companies	7
Tourism Spending	7
Export-related Jobs	12
Change in Price of Existing Homes	29
Net Farm Income	36
Bankruptcy Filings	23
Patents Issued	4
WC Disability Payments	21
UC Average Weekly Benefit	2
Economic Momentum	36
Employment Change	34
Manufacturing Employment Change	48
Home Ownership	37
Gambling Losses	2
Electricity Use Per Residential Customer	40
Revenue Per Kwh	40
New Companies	20

Geography

Total Land Area	46
Federally-Owned Land	46
State Park Visitors	18
State Park Acreage	8
Hunters With Firearms	41
Registered Boats	26
Per Capita State Spending For the Arts	7
Energy Consumption Per Capita	29
Toxic Chemical Release Per Capita	44
Hazardous Waste Sites	1
Polluted Rivers	n/a
Air Quality	49

Government

Members Of US House	9
Legislators Per Million Population	44
Units Of Government	34
Female Legislators	41
Turnover In Legislatures	48
Democrats in State Legislatures	40
Number Of Statewide Elected Officials	48
State And Local Government Employees	23
State And Local Average Salaries	5
Local Employment	8
Registered Voters	32
Statewide Initiatives	n/a

Federal

Per Capita Federal Spending	28
Increase In Federal Spending	19
Federal Grants To State And Local Government	22
Per Capita Federal Spending On Procurement	25
Per Capita Federal Spending On Social Security And Medicare	6
Social Security Benefits	2
Federal Spending On Employee Wages & Salaries	36
Federal Grant Spending Per $ Of State Tax Revenue	33
General Revenue From Federal Government	9
Federal Tax Burden Per Capita	2
Highway Charges Returned To States	23
Terms Of Trade	46
Per Capita Federal Income Tax Liability	2

Taxes

Tax Revenue	20
Per Capita Tax Revenue	4
Tax Effort	5
Tax Capacity	7
Percent Change In Taxes	15
Property Taxes Per Capita	2
Property Tax Revenue As Percent Of Three-Tax Revenue	7
Sales Taxes Per Capita	9
Sales Tax Revenue As Percent Of Three-Tax Revenue	37
Services With Sales Tax	24
Income Taxes Per Capita	14
Income Tax Revenue As Percent Of Three-Tax Revenue	35
Highest Personal Income Tax Rate	21
Motor Fuel Taxes	46
Tobacco Taxes	12
Tax Burden On High Income Family	9
Progressivity Of Taxes	17

Revenues And Finances

State And Local Revenue	8
Non-Tax Revenue	9
State And Local Expenditures	8
Per Capita State And Local General Expenditures	5
Change In General Expenditures	5
State Government General Spending	8

Debt As Percent Of Revenue	27
Full Faith And Credit Debt	19
Bond Ratings	2
State Solvency Index	40
Pension Plan Assets	16
State Reserves	23
State Budget Process Quality	3
Relative State Spending "Needs"	3

Education

Math Proficiency, 8th Grade	14
AFQT Ranks	28
SAT Scores	6
ACT Scores	n/a
Over-25 Population Without High School Diploma	26
Private School Students	4
Percent Students Finishing High School	7
Pupil-Teacher Ratio	1
Public School Enrollment	47
Library Holdings Per Capita	12
Education Spending As Percent Of Total	33
Spending Per Pupil	1
Average Teacher Salary	4
State Aid Per Pupil	5
State And Local Spending For Higher Education	43
Higher Education Spending As Percent Of Total	46
Public Higher Education Enrollment	43
State Per Pupil Support Of Higher Education	41
Tuition And Fees	7
Average Professor Salary	1
Education Employees	22
R&D Spending	15

Health

Infant Mortality Rates	25
State Health Rankings	15
Population Without Health Insurance	23
Abortions	15

Alcohol Consumption	24
Percent Non-Smokers	12
Percent Obese	34
AIDS Cases	3
Physicians Per 100,000 Population	7
Medicaid Recipients Related To Poverty Population	21
Health/Hospital Spending As Percent Of Total	45
Per Capita Medicaid Spending	15
Medicaid Spending Per Aged Recipient	6
Medicaid Spending Per AFDC Child	29
Medicare Payment Per Hospital-Day	29
Population In HMOs	22

Crime And Law Enforcement

Crime Rate	29
Violent Crime Rate	22
Murder Rate	
Property Crime Rate	29
Motor Vehicle Theft Rate	7
Violent Crime Rate Change	40
Incarceration Rate	24
Juvenile Arrest Rate	48
Proportion Of Sentence Served	31
Law Enforcement Employees	1
Corrections Employees	10
Costs Per Inmate-Day	6
State Corrections Spending	14
Spending For Law Enforcement	7
Law Enforcement Spending As Percent Of Total	18

Transportation

Percent Of Travel On Interstates	47
Interstate Mileage In Poor Condition	27

Deficient Bridges	5
Traffic Deaths Per 100 Million Vehicle-miles	45
Seat Belt Use	22
Vehicle Miles Traveled Per Capita	45
Workers Using Public Transportation	3
Road And Street Miles Under State Control	32
Highway Employees	25
Public Transit Employees	30
State And Local Spending For Highways	16
Highway Spending As Percent Of Total	38

Welfare

Percent Of Births To Unwed Mothers	33
AFDC Recipients As Percent Of Population	28
Food Stamp Recipients As Percent Of Population	44
SSI Recipients As Percent Of Population	29
Change In AFDC Recipients	39
Condition Of Children Index	19
Percent Of Families With Single Parent	33
Typical Monthly AFDC Payments	18
Welfare As Percent Of Poverty Level Income	16
Average SSI State Supplements Per Recipient	15
State Income Tax Liability Of Typical Family In Poverty	13
Child Support Collections Per $ Of Administrative Costs	19
Percent Of Children In Foster Care	23
State And Local Welfare Spending Per Capita	9
Welfare Spending As Percent Of Total	17
Administrative Costs Per AFDC Case	2

Population

Population	36
Percent Population Change	6
Population 2000	36
Median Age	46
Percent Population African-American	39
Percent Population in Poverty	2
Percent Population Female	36
Birth Rates	6
Death Rates	46
Illegal Immigrant Population	11

Economies

Personal Income	39
Per Capita Personal Income	48
Percent of Personal Income from Wages & Salaries	23
Average Annual Pay	40
Cost Of Living	23
Average Annual Pay in Manufacturing	41
Average Annual Pay in Retailing	32
Unemployment Rate	12
Government Employment	34
Manufacturing Employment	42
Fortune 500 Companies	n/a
Tourism Spending	35
Export-related Jobs	44
Change in Price of Existing Homes	3
Net Farm Income	33
Bankruptcy Filings	39
Patents Issued	28
WC Disability Payments	43
UC Average Weekly Benefit	45
Economic Momentum	5
Employment Change	4
Manufacturing Employment Change	7
Home Ownership	25
Gambling Losses	42
Electricity Use Per Residential Customer	50
Revenue Per Kwh	8
New Companies	12

Geography

Total Land Area	5
Federally-Owned Land	10
State Park Visitors	35
State Park Acreage	25
Hunters With Firearms	43
Registered Boats	42
Per Capita State Spending For the Arts	21
Energy Consumption Per Capita	15
Toxic Chemical Release Per Capita	13
Hazardous Waste Sites	36
Polluted Rivers	6
Air Quality	16

Government

Members Of US House	34
Legislators Per Million Population	13
Units Of Government	33
Female Legislators	27
Turnover In Legislatures	30
Democrats in State Legislatures	11
Number Of Statewide Elected Officials	16
State And Local Government Employees	4
State And Local Average Salaries	42
Local Employment	43
Registered Voters	40
Statewide Initiatives	n/a

Federal

Per Capita Federal Spending	4
Increase In Federal Spending	33
Federal Grants To State And Local Government	10
Per Capita Federal Spending On Procurement	1
Per Capita Federal Spending On Social Security And Medicare	45
Social Security Benefits	45

Federal Spending On Employee Wages & Salaries	6
Federal Grant Spending Per $ Of State Tax Revenue	34
General Revenue From Federal Government	35
Federal Tax Burden Per Capita	47
Highway Charges Returned To States	16
Terms Of Trade	6
Per Capita Federal Income Tax Liability	47

Taxes

Tax Revenue	8
Per Capita Tax Revenue	34
Tax Effort	22
Tax Capacity	39
Percent Change In Taxes	12
Property Taxes Per Capita	49
Property Tax Revenue As Percent Of Three-Tax Revenue	49
Sales Taxes Per Capita	4
Sales Tax Revenue As Percent Of Three-Tax Revenue	4
Services With Sales Tax	2
Income Taxes Per Capita	38
Income Tax Revenue As Percent Of Three-Tax Revenue	36
Highest Personal Income Tax Rate	6
Motor Fuel Taxes	17
Tobacco Taxes	33
Tax Burden On High Income Family	21
Progressivity Of Taxes	41

Revenues And Finances

State And Local Revenue	38
Non-Tax Revenue	34
State And Local Expenditures	39
Per Capita State And Local General Expenditures	18
Change In General Expenditures	18
State Government General Spending	34

Debt As Percent Of Revenue	43
Full Faith And Credit Debt	39
Bond Ratings	2
State Solvency Index	3
Pension Plan Assets	36
State Reserves	39
State Budget Process Quality	34
Relative State Spending "Needs"	48

Education

Math Proficiency, 8th Grade	31
AFQT Ranks	39
SAT Scores	n/a
ACT Scores	22
Over-25 Population Without High School Diploma	33
Private School Students	34
Percent Students Finishing High School	42
Pupil-Teacher Ratio	34
Public School Enrollment	6
Library Holdings Per Capita	21
Education Spending As Percent Of Total	25
Spending Per Pupil	36
Average Teacher Salary	43
State Aid Per Pupil	10
State And Local Spending For Higher Education	7
Higher Education Spending As Percent Of Total	5
Public Higher Education Enrollment	6
State Per Pupil Support Of Higher Education	n/a
Tuition And Fees	43
Average Professor Salary	34
Education Employees	11
R&D Spending	2

Health

Infant Mortality Rates	10
State Health Rankings	43
Population Without Health Insurance	3
Abortions	35

Alcohol Consumption	15
Percent Non-Smokers	10
Percent Obese	45
AIDS Cases	25
Physicians Per 100,000 Population	28
Medicaid Recipients Related To Poverty Population	49
Health/Hospital Spending As Percent Of Total	16
Per Capita Medicaid Spending	30
Medicaid Spending Per Aged Recipient	32
Medicaid Spending Per AFDC Child	10
Medicare Payment Per Hospital-Day	20
Population In HMOs	19

Crime And Law Enforcement

Crime Rate	7
Violent Crime Rate	8
Murder Rate	
Property Crime Rate	9
Motor Vehicle Theft Rate	27
Violent Crime Rate Change	9
Incarceration Rate	34
Juvenile Arrest Rate	28
Proportion Of Sentence Served	n/a
Law Enforcement Employees	11
Corrections Employees	9
Costs Per Inmate-Day	4
State Corrections Spending	n/a
Spending For Law Enforcement	14
Law Enforcement Spending As Percent Of Total	16

Transportation

Percent Of Travel On Interstates	10
Interstate Mileage In Poor Condition	22

Deficient Bridges	47
Traffic Deaths Per 100 Million Vehicle-miles	7
Seat Belt Use	5
Vehicle Miles Traveled Per Capita	2
Workers Using Public Transportation	38
Road And Street Miles Under State Control	22
Highway Employees	21
Public Transit Employees	24
State And Local Spending For Highways	3
Highway Spending As Percent Of Total	4

Welfare

Percent Of Births To Unwed Mothers	3
AFDC Recipients As Percent Of Population	4
Food Stamp Recipients As Percent Of Population	5
SSI Recipients As Percent Of Population	14
Change In AFDC Recipients	6
Condition Of Children Index	40
Percent Of Families With Single Parent	29
Typical Monthly AFDC Payments	24
Welfare As Percent Of Poverty Level Income	28
Average SSI State Supplements Per Recipient	38
State Income Tax Liability Of Typical Family In Poverty	n/a
Child Support Collections Per $ Of Administrative Costs	36
Percent Of Children In Foster Care	29
State And Local Welfare Spending Per Capita	33
Welfare Spending As Percent Of Total	37
Administrative Costs Per AFDC Case	21

Population

Population	3
Percent Population Change	47
Population 2000	3
Median Age	17
Percent Population African-American	13
Percent Population in Poverty	8
Percent Population Female	5
Birth Rates	11
Death Rates	16
Illegal Immigrant Population	2

Economies

Personal Income	2
Per Capita Personal Income	3
Percent of Personal Income from Wages & Salaries	20
Average Annual Pay	3
Cost Of Living	5
Average Annual Pay in Manufacturing	6
Average Annual Pay in Retailing	7
Unemployment Rate	9
Government Employment	3
Manufacturing Employment	6
Fortune 500 Companies	1
Tourism Spending	4
Export-related Jobs	4
Change in Price of Existing Homes	30
Net Farm Income	34
Bankruptcy Filings	30
Patents Issued	11
WC Disability Payments	35
UC Average Weekly Benefit	10
Economic Momentum	47
Employment Change	43
Manufacturing Employment Change	36
Home Ownership	50
Gambling Losses	5
Electricity Use Per Residential Customer	47
Revenue Per Kwh	1
New Companies	22

Geography

Total Land Area	30
Federally-Owned Land	43
State Park Visitors	2
State Park Acreage	12
Hunters With Firearms	36
Registered Boats	7
Per Capita State Spending For the Arts	6
Energy Consumption Per Capita	49
Toxic Chemical Release Per Capita	43
Hazardous Waste Sites	4
Polluted Rivers	44
Air Quality	48

Government

Members Of US House	2
Legislators Per Million Population	47
Units Of Government	38
Female Legislators	34
Turnover In Legislatures	46
Democrats in State Legislatures	17
Number Of Statewide Elected Officials	35
State And Local Government Employees	5
State And Local Average Salaries	4
Local Employment	2
Registered Voters	43
Statewide Initiatives	n/a

Federal

Per Capita Federal Spending	22
Increase In Federal Spending	29
Federal Grants To State And Local Government	3
Per Capita Federal Spending On Procurement	35
Per Capita Federal Spending On Social Security And Medicare	8
Social Security Benefits	3
Federal Spending On Employee Wages & Salaries	43
Federal Grant Spending Per $ Of State Tax Revenue	15
General Revenue From Federal Government	2
Federal Tax Burden Per Capita	3
Highway Charges Returned To States	20
Terms Of Trade	15
Per Capita Federal Income Tax Liability	6

Taxes

Tax Revenue	2
Per Capita Tax Revenue	2
Tax Effort	1
Tax Capacity	15
Percent Change In Taxes	45
Property Taxes Per Capita	4
Property Tax Revenue As Percent Of Three-Tax Revenue	21
Sales Taxes Per Capita	6
Sales Tax Revenue As Percent Of Three-Tax Revenue	42
Services With Sales Tax	11
Income Taxes Per Capita	1
Income Tax Revenue As Percent Of Three-Tax Revenue	8
Highest Personal Income Tax Rate	10
Motor Fuel Taxes	48
Tobacco Taxes	4
Tax Burden On High Income Family	1
Progressivity Of Taxes	45

Revenues And Finances

State And Local Revenue	2
Non-Tax Revenue	2
State And Local Expenditures	2
Per Capita State And Local General Expenditures	2
Change In General Expenditures	2
State Government General Spending	2

Debt As Percent Of Revenue	14
Full Faith And Credit Debt	6
Bond Ratings	5
State Solvency Index	25
Pension Plan Assets	3
State Reserves	47
State Budget Process Quality	29
Relative State Spending "Needs"	22

Education

Math Proficiency, 8th Grade	22
AFQT Ranks	21
SAT Scores	21
ACT Scores	n/a
Over-25 Population Without High School Diploma	34
Private School Students	5
Percent Students Finishing High School	43
Pupil-Teacher Ratio	8
Public School Enrollment	45
Library Holdings Per Capita	12
Education Spending As Percent Of Total	47
Spending Per Pupil	4
Average Teacher Salary	3
State Aid Per Pupil	9
State And Local Spending For Higher Education	42
Higher Education Spending As Percent Of Total	50
Public Higher Education Enrollment	45
State Per Pupil Support Of Higher Education	22
Tuition And Fees	15
Average Professor Salary	7
Education Employees	20
R&D Spending	22

Health

Infant Mortality Rates	17
State Health Rankings	38
Population Without Health Insurance	22
Abortions	2

Alcohol Consumption	35
Percent Non-Smokers	21
Percent Obese	21
AIDS Cases	1
Physicians Per 100,000 Population	3
Medicaid Recipients Related To Poverty Population	11
Health/Hospital Spending As Percent Of Total	14
Per Capita Medicaid Spending	1
Medicaid Spending Per Aged Recipient	1
Medicaid Spending Per AFDC Child	3
Medicare Payment Per Hospital-Day	50
Population In HMOs	10

Crime And Law Enforcement

Crime Rate	17
Violent Crime Rate	3
Murder Rate	
Property Crime Rate	23
Motor Vehicle Theft Rate	4
Violent Crime Rate Change	45
Incarceration Rate	17
Juvenile Arrest Rate	50
Proportion Of Sentence Served	11
Law Enforcement Employees	2
Corrections Employees	1
Costs Per Inmate-Day	8
State Corrections Spending	10
Spending For Law Enforcement	2
Law Enforcement Spending As Percent Of Total	7

Transportation

Percent Of Travel On Interstates	45
Interstate Mileage In Poor Condition	31

Deficient Bridges	1
Traffic Deaths Per 100 Million Vehicle-miles	34
Seat Belt Use	8
Vehicle Miles Traveled Per Capita	50
Workers Using Public Transportation	1
Road And Street Miles Under State Control	26
Highway Employees	18
Public Transit Employees	1
State And Local Spending For Highways	26
Highway Spending As Percent Of Total	49

Welfare

Percent Of Births To Unwed Mothers	5
AFDC Recipients As Percent Of Population	2
Food Stamp Recipients As Percent Of Population	10
SSI Recipients As Percent Of Population	9
Change In AFDC Recipients	25
Condition Of Children Index	37
Percent Of Families With Single Parent	7
Typical Monthly AFDC Payments	7
Welfare As Percent Of Poverty Level Income	7
Average SSI State Supplements Per Recipient	10
State Income Tax Liability Of Typical Family In Poverty	37
Child Support Collections Per $ Of Administrative Costs	34
Percent Of Children In Foster Care	1
State And Local Welfare Spending Per Capita	1
Welfare Spending As Percent Of Total	4
Administrative Costs Per AFDC Case	1

Population

Population	10
Percent Population Change	10
Population 2000	10
Median Age	30
Percent Population African-American	7
Percent Population in Poverty	18
Percent Population Female	18
Birth Rates	27
Death Rates	27
Illegal Immigrant Population	29

Economies

Personal Income	13
Per Capita Personal Income	34
Percent of Personal Income from Wages & Salaries	6
Average Annual Pay	31
Cost Of Living	43
Average Annual Pay in Manufacturing	43
Average Annual Pay in Retailing	28
Unemployment Rate	42
Government Employment	10
Manufacturing Employment	8
Fortune 500 Companies	16
Tourism Spending	12
Export-related Jobs	8
Change in Price of Existing Homes	17
Net Farm Income	3
Bankruptcy Filings	42
Patents Issued	26
WC Disability Payments	17
UC Average Weekly Benefit	23
Economic Momentum	14
Employment Change	29
Manufacturing Employment Change	37
Home Ownership	20
Gambling Losses	46
Electricity Use Per Residential Customer	11
Revenue Per Kwh	24
New Companies	27

Geography

Total Land Area	29
Federally-Owned Land	21
State Park Visitors	17
State Park Acreage	21
Hunters With Firearms	29
Registered Boats	12
Per Capita State Spending For the Arts	17
Energy Consumption Per Capita	36
Toxic Chemical Release Per Capita	16
Hazardous Waste Sites	17
Polluted Rivers	23
Air Quality	20

Government

Members Of US House	10
Legislators Per Million Population	39
Units Of Government	44
Female Legislators	36
Turnover In Legislatures	10
Democrats in State Legislatures	30
Number Of Statewide Elected Officials	2
State And Local Government Employees	22
State And Local Average Salaries	31
Local Employment	16
Registered Voters	33
Statewide Initiatives	n/a

Federal

Per Capita Federal Spending	46
Increase In Federal Spending	6
Federal Grants To State And Local Government	39
Per Capita Federal Spending On Procurement	40
Per Capita Federal Spending On Social Security And Medicare	35
Social Security Benefits	38
Federal Spending On Employee Wages & Salaries	17
Federal Grant Spending Per $ Of State Tax Revenue	35
General Revenue From Federal Government	12
Federal Tax Burden Per Capita	34
Highway Charges Returned To States	39
Terms Of Trade	28
Per Capita Federal Income Tax Liability	32

Taxes

Tax Revenue	32
Per Capita Tax Revenue	33
Tax Effort	37
Tax Capacity	27
Percent Change In Taxes	16
Property Taxes Per Capita	40
Property Tax Revenue As Percent Of Three-Tax Revenue	42
Sales Taxes Per Capita	23
Sales Tax Revenue As Percent Of Three-Tax Revenue	18
Services With Sales Tax	32
Income Taxes Per Capita	15
Income Tax Revenue As Percent Of Three-Tax Revenue	7
Highest Personal Income Tax Rate	11
Motor Fuel Taxes	16
Tobacco Taxes	48
Tax Burden On High Income Family	19
Progressivity Of Taxes	27

Revenues And Finances

State And Local Revenue	12
Non-Tax Revenue	14
State And Local Expenditures	13
Per Capita State And Local General Expenditures	45
Change In General Expenditures	45
State Government General Spending	11

Debt As Percent Of Revenue	40
Full Faith And Credit Debt	35
Bond Ratings	1
State Solvency Index	9
Pension Plan Assets	31
State Reserves	17
State Budget Process Quality	40
Relative State Spending "Needs"	17

Education

Math Proficiency, 8th Grade	34
AFQT Ranks	42
SAT Scores	1
ACT Scores	n/a
Over-25 Population Without High School Diploma	42
Private School Students	42
Percent Students Finishing High School	41
Pupil-Teacher Ratio	22
Public School Enrollment	38
Library Holdings Per Capita	38
Education Spending As Percent Of Total	10
Spending Per Pupil	33
Average Teacher Salary	37
State Aid Per Pupil	11
State And Local Spending For Higher Education	19
Higher Education Spending As Percent Of Total	9
Public Higher Education Enrollment	24
State Per Pupil Support Of Higher Education	11
Tuition And Fees	50
Average Professor Salary	6
Education Employees	25
R&D Spending	29

Health

Infant Mortality Rates	3
State Health Rankings	30
Population Without Health Insurance	20
Abortions	10

Alcohol Consumption	39
Percent Non-Smokers	41
Percent Obese	26
AIDS Cases	24
Physicians Per 100,000 Population	24
Medicaid Recipients Related To Poverty Population	30
Health/Hospital Spending As Percent Of Total	6
Per Capita Medicaid Spending	28
Medicaid Spending Per Aged Recipient	41
Medicaid Spending Per AFDC Child	11
Medicare Payment Per Hospital-Day	32
Population In HMOs	35

Crime And Law Enforcement

Crime Rate	14
Violent Crime Rate	20
Murder Rate	
Property Crime Rate	13
Motor Vehicle Theft Rate	36
Violent Crime Rate Change	16
Incarceration Rate	20
Juvenile Arrest Rate	35
Proportion Of Sentence Served	38
Law Enforcement Employees	26
Corrections Employees	13
Costs Per Inmate-Day	14
State Corrections Spending	21
Spending For Law Enforcement	28
Law Enforcement Spending As Percent Of Total	15

Transportation

Percent Of Travel On Interstates	46
Interstate Mileage In Poor Condition	23

Deficient Bridges	11
Traffic Deaths Per 100 Million Vehicle-miles	15
Seat Belt Use	3
Vehicle Miles Traveled Per Capita	15
Workers Using Public Transportation	38
Road And Street Miles Under State Control	4
Highway Employees	32
Public Transit Employees	38
State And Local Spending For Highways	38
Highway Spending As Percent Of Total	29

Welfare

Percent Of Births To Unwed Mothers	19
AFDC Recipients As Percent Of Population	25
Food Stamp Recipients As Percent Of Population	28
SSI Recipients As Percent Of Population	13
Change In AFDC Recipients	7
Condition Of Children Index	42
Percent Of Families With Single Parent	23
Typical Monthly AFDC Payments	41
Welfare As Percent Of Poverty Level Income	41
Average SSI State Supplements Per Recipient	14
State Income Tax Liability Of Typical Family In Poverty	14
Child Support Collections Per $ Of Administrative Costs	28
Percent Of Children In Foster Care	33
State And Local Welfare Spending Per Capita	38
Welfare Spending As Percent Of Total	29
Administrative Costs Per AFDC Case	36

Population

Population	47
Percent Population Change	46
Population 2000	48
Median Age	31
Percent Population African-American	44
Percent Population in Poverty	36
Percent Population Female	44
Birth Rates	32
Death Rates	4
Illegal Immigrant Population	48

Economies

Personal Income	48
Per Capita Personal Income	38
Percent of Personal Income from Wages & Salaries	44
Average Annual Pay	49
Cost Of Living	36
Average Annual Pay in Manufacturing	47
Average Annual Pay in Retailing	50
Unemployment Rate	48
Government Employment	46
Manufacturing Employment	47
Fortune 500 Companies	n/a
Tourism Spending	49
Export-related Jobs	49
Change in Price of Existing Homes	n/a
Net Farm Income	19
Bankruptcy Filings	43
Patents Issued	40
WC Disability Payments	38
UC Average Weekly Benefit	34
Economic Momentum	45
Employment Change	24
Manufacturing Employment Change	28
Home Ownership	34
Gambling Losses	39
Electricity Use Per Residential Customer	16
Revenue Per Kwh	43
New Companies	43

Geography

Total Land Area	17
Federally-Owned Land	22
State Park Visitors	49
State Park Acreage	48
Hunters With Firearms	11
Registered Boats	46
Per Capita State Spending For the Arts	38
Energy Consumption Per Capita	5
Toxic Chemical Release Per Capita	45
Hazardous Waste Sites	49
Polluted Rivers	1
Air Quality	1

Government

Members Of US House	44
Legislators Per Million Population	3
Units Of Government	1
Female Legislators	37
Turnover In Legislatures	21
Democrats in State Legislatures	45
Number Of Statewide Elected Officials	1
State And Local Government Employees	9
State And Local Average Salaries	28
Local Employment	47
Registered Voters	1
Statewide Initiatives	4

Federal

Per Capita Federal Spending	6
Increase In Federal Spending	46
Federal Grants To State And Local Government	7
Per Capita Federal Spending On Procurement	36
Per Capita Federal Spending On Social Security And Medicare	13
Social Security Benefits	39

Federal Spending On Employee Wages & Salaries	7
Federal Grant Spending Per $ Of State Tax Revenue	7
General Revenue From Federal Government	47
Federal Tax Burden Per Capita	38
Highway Charges Returned To States	6
Terms Of Trade	7
Per Capita Federal Income Tax Liability	37

Taxes

Tax Revenue	27
Per Capita Tax Revenue	38
Tax Effort	32
Tax Capacity	31
Percent Change In Taxes	44
Property Taxes Per Capita	33
Property Tax Revenue As Percent Of Three-Tax Revenue	22
Sales Taxes Per Capita	20
Sales Tax Revenue As Percent Of Three-Tax Revenue	15
Services With Sales Tax	40
Income Taxes Per Capita	40
Income Tax Revenue As Percent Of Three-Tax Revenue	41
Highest Personal Income Tax Rate	32
Motor Fuel Taxes	30
Tobacco Taxes	9
Tax Burden On High Income Family	40
Progressivity Of Taxes	21

Revenues And Finances

State And Local Revenue	48
Non-Tax Revenue	47
State And Local Expenditures	48
Per Capita State And Local General Expenditures	17
Change In General Expenditures	17
State Government General Spending	47

Debt As Percent Of Revenue	39
Full Faith And Credit Debt	40
Bond Ratings	3
State Solvency Index	5
Pension Plan Assets	42
State Reserves	27
State Budget Process Quality	18
Relative State Spending "Needs"	35

Education

Math Proficiency, 8ᵗʰ Grade	1
AFQT Ranks	3
SAT Scores	n/a
ACT Scores	11
Over-25 Population Without High School Diploma	27
Private School Students	37
Percent Students Finishing High School	3
Pupil-Teacher Ratio	8
Public School Enrollment	10
Library Holdings Per Capita	17
Education Spending As Percent Of Total	13
Spending Per Pupil	40
Average Teacher Salary	48
State Aid Per Pupil	41
State And Local Spending For Higher Education	1
Higher Education Spending As Percent Of Total	2
Public Higher Education Enrollment	7
State Per Pupil Support Of Higher Education	28
Tuition And Fees	29
Average Professor Salary	48
Education Employees	23
R&D Spending	38

Health

Infant Mortality Rates	42
State Health Rankings	16
Population Without Health Insurance	21
Abortions	40

Alcohol Consumption	20
Percent Non-Smokers	18
Percent Obese	18
AIDS Cases	50
Physicians Per 100,000 Population	32
Medicaid Recipients Related To Poverty Population	43
Health/Hospital Spending As Percent Of Total	49
Per Capita Medicaid Spending	9
Medicaid Spending Per Aged Recipient	16
Medicaid Spending Per AFDC Child	9
Medicare Payment Per Hospital-Day	47
Population In HMOs	46

Crime And Law Enforcement

Crime Rate	49
Violent Crime Rate	50
Murder Rate	
Property Crime Rate	49
Motor Vehicle Theft Rate	47
Violent Crime Rate Change	13
Incarceration Rate	50
Juvenile Arrest Rate	2
Proportion Of Sentence Served	20
Law Enforcement Employees	46
Corrections Employees	48
Costs Per Inmate-Day	27
State Corrections Spending	13
Spending For Law Enforcement	48
Law Enforcement Spending As Percent Of Total	49

Transportation

Percent Of Travel On Interstates	38
Interstate Mileage In Poor Condition	19

Deficient Bridges	49
Traffic Deaths Per 100 Million Vehicle-miles	41
Seat Belt Use	49
Vehicle Miles Traveled Per Capita	23
Workers Using Public Transportation	46
Road And Street Miles Under State Control	49
Highway Employees	9
Public Transit Employees	41
State And Local Spending For Highways	5
Highway Spending As Percent Of Total	6

Welfare

Percent Of Births To Unwed Mothers	46
AFDC Recipients As Percent Of Population	49
Food Stamp Recipients As Percent Of Population	41
SSI Recipients As Percent Of Population	40
Change In AFDC Recipients	42
Condition Of Children Index	3
Percent Of Families With Single Parent	48
Typical Monthly AFDC Payments	15
Welfare As Percent Of Poverty Level Income	22
Average SSI State Supplements Per Recipient	25
State Income Tax Liability Of Typical Family In Poverty	22
Child Support Collections Per $ Of Administrative Costs	18
Percent Of Children In Foster Care	20
State And Local Welfare Spending Per Capita	19
Welfare Spending As Percent Of Total	27
Administrative Costs Per AFDC Case	20

Debt As Percent Of Revenue	45
Full Faith And Credit Debt	32
Bond Ratings	3
State Solvency Index	26
Pension Plan Assets	4
State Reserves	24
State Budget Process Quality	21
Relative State Spending "Needs"	29

Education

Math Proficiency, 8th Grade	18
AFQT Ranks	36
SAT Scores	n/a
ACT Scores	11
Over-25 Population Without High School Diploma	30
Private School Students	10
Percent Students Finishing High School	34
Pupil-Teacher Ratio	26
Public School Enrollment	37
Library Holdings Per Capita	16
Education Spending As Percent Of Total	29
Spending Per Pupil	15
Average Teacher Salary	19
State Aid Per Pupil	29
State And Local Spending For Higher Education	31
Higher Education Spending As Percent Of Total	28
Public Higher Education Enrollment	37
State Per Pupil Support Of Higher Education	38
Tuition And Fees	11
Average Professor Salary	15
Education Employees	39
R&D Spending	16

Health

Infant Mortality Rates	10
State Health Rankings	19
Population Without Health Insurance	44
Abortions	22

Alcohol Consumption	40
Percent Non-Smokers	33
Percent Obese	20
AIDS Cases	34
Physicians Per 100,000 Population	22
Medicaid Recipients Related To Poverty Population	13
Health/Hospital Spending As Percent Of Total	25
Per Capita Medicaid Spending	11
Medicaid Spending Per Aged Recipient	12
Medicaid Spending Per AFDC Child	15
Medicare Payment Per Hospital-Day	17
Population In HMOs	17

Crime And Law Enforcement

Crime Rate	33
Violent Crime Rate	26
Murder Rate	
Property Crime Rate	35
Motor Vehicle Theft Rate	25
Violent Crime Rate Change	36
Incarceration Rate	16
Juvenile Arrest Rate	26
Proportion Of Sentence Served	39
Law Enforcement Employees	29
Corrections Employees	39
Costs Per Inmate-Day	42
State Corrections Spending	32
Spending For Law Enforcement	27
Law Enforcement Spending As Percent Of Total	20

Transportation

Percent Of Travel On Interstates	15
Interstate Mileage In Poor Condition	37

Deficient Bridges	24
Traffic Deaths Per 100 Million Vehicle-miles	38
Seat Belt Use	27
Vehicle Miles Traveled Per Capita	37
Workers Using Public Transportation	18
Road And Street Miles Under State Control	21
Highway Employees	36
Public Transit Employees	13
State And Local Spending For Highways	36
Highway Spending As Percent Of Total	30

Welfare

Percent Of Births To Unwed Mothers	15
AFDC Recipients As Percent Of Population	8
Food Stamp Recipients As Percent Of Population	15
SSI Recipients As Percent Of Population	23
Change In AFDC Recipients	41
Condition Of Children Index	22
Percent Of Families With Single Parent	28
Typical Monthly AFDC Payments	32
Welfare As Percent Of Poverty Level Income	33
Average SSI State Supplements Per Recipient	43
State Income Tax Liability Of Typical Family In Poverty	19
Child Support Collections Per $ Of Administrative Costs	4
Percent Of Children In Foster Care	21
State And Local Welfare Spending Per Capita	15
Welfare Spending As Percent Of Total	8
Administrative Costs Per AFDC Case	44

Population

Population	28
Percent Population Change	30
Population 2000	28
Median Age	23
Percent Population African-American	23
Percent Population in Poverty	9
Percent Population Female	27
Birth Rates	20
Death Rates	9
Illegal Immigrant Population	22

Economies

Personal Income	29
Per Capita Personal Income	45
Percent of Personal Income from Wages & Salaries	42
Average Annual Pay	41
Cost Of Living	41
Average Annual Pay in Manufacturing	36
Average Annual Pay in Retailing	40
Unemployment Rate	33
Government Employment	27
Manufacturing Employment	33
Fortune 500 Companies	24
Tourism Spending	34
Export-related Jobs	33
Change in Price of Existing Homes	n/a
Net Farm Income	15
Bankruptcy Filings	8
Patents Issued	25
WC Disability Payments	47
UC Average Weekly Benefit	28
Economic Momentum	38
Employment Change	21
Manufacturing Employment Change	13
Home Ownership	18
Gambling Losses	40
Electricity Use Per Residential Customer	17
Revenue Per Kwh	16
New Companies	28

Geography

Total Land Area	19
Federally-Owned Land	35
State Park Visitors	13
State Park Acreage	33
Hunters With Firearms	21
Registered Boats	21
Per Capita State Spending For the Arts	13
Energy Consumption Per Capita	9
Toxic Chemical Release Per Capita	30
Hazardous Waste Sites	37
Polluted Rivers	5
Air Quality	1

Government

Members Of US House	23
Legislators Per Million Population	22
Units Of Government	15
Female Legislators	47
Turnover In Legislatures	36
Democrats in State Legislatures	10
Number Of Statewide Elected Officials	3
State And Local Government Employees	11
State And Local Average Salaries	46
Local Employment	37
Registered Voters	19
Statewide Initiatives	17

Federal

Per Capita Federal Spending	27
Increase In Federal Spending	26
Federal Grants To State And Local Government	34
Per Capita Federal Spending On Procurement	32
Per Capita Federal Spending On Social Security And Medicare	23
Social Security Benefits	36

Federal Spending On

Employee Wages & Salaries	9
Federal Grant Spending Per $ Of State Tax Revenue	36
General Revenue From Federal Government	30
Federal Tax Burden Per Capita	42
Highway Charges Returned To States	41
Terms Of Trade	18
Per Capita Federal Income Tax Liability	46

Taxes

Tax Revenue	39
Per Capita Tax Revenue	44
Tax Effort	30
Tax Capacity	39
Percent Change In Taxes	40
Property Taxes Per Capita	48
Property Tax Revenue As Percent Of Three-Tax Revenue	47
Sales Taxes Per Capita	24
Sales Tax Revenue As Percent Of Three-Tax Revenue	13
Services With Sales Tax	30
Income Taxes Per Capita	32
Income Tax Revenue As Percent Of Three-Tax Revenue	15
Highest Personal Income Tax Rate	23
Motor Fuel Taxes	37
Tobacco Taxes	31
Tax Burden On High Income Family	31
Progressivity Of Taxes	31

Revenues And Finances

State And Local Revenue	29
Non-Tax Revenue	29
State And Local Expenditures	29
Per Capita State And Local General Expenditures	43
Change In General Expenditures	43
State Government General Spending	30

Debt As Percent Of Revenue	30
Full Faith And Credit Debt	49
Bond Ratings	3
State Solvency Index	37
Pension Plan Assets	32
State Reserves	21
State Budget Process Quality	20
Relative State Spending "Needs"	39

Education

Math Proficiency, 8th Grade	18
AFQT Ranks	37
SAT Scores	n/a
ACT Scores	19
Over-25 Population Without High School Diploma	36
Private School Students	41
Percent Students Finishing High School	24
Pupil-Teacher Ratio	13
Public School Enrollment	12
Library Holdings Per Capita	34
Education Spending As Percent Of Total	18
Spending Per Pupil	46
Average Teacher Salary	46
State Aid Per Pupil	18
State And Local Spending For Higher Education	26
Higher Education Spending As Percent Of Total	18
Public Higher Education Enrollment	14
State Per Pupil Support Of Higher Education	23
Tuition And Fees	45
Average Professor Salary	40
Education Employees	10
R&D Spending	46

Health

Infant Mortality Rates	8
State Health Rankings	33
Population Without Health Insurance	1
Abortions	32

Alcohol Consumption	45
Percent Non-Smokers	40
Percent Obese	19
AIDS Cases	38
Physicians Per 100,000 Population	44
Medicaid Recipients Related To Poverty Population	44
Health/Hospital Spending As Percent Of Total	8
Per Capita Medicaid Spending	26
Medicaid Spending Per Aged Recipient	44
Medicaid Spending Per AFDC Child	5
Medicare Payment Per Hospital-Day	40
Population In HMOs	37

Crime And Law Enforcement

Crime Rate	20
Violent Crime Rate	21
Murder Rate	
Property Crime Rate	19
Motor Vehicle Theft Rate	19
Violent Crime Rate Change	5
Incarceration Rate	3
Juvenile Arrest Rate	22
Proportion Of Sentence Served	34
Law Enforcement Employees	20
Corrections Employees	25
Costs Per Inmate-Day	47
State Corrections Spending	44
Spending For Law Enforcement	37
Law Enforcement Spending As Percent Of Total	31

Transportation

Percent Of Travel On Interstates	34
Interstate Mileage In Poor Condition	33

Deficient Bridges	30
Traffic Deaths Per 100 Million Vehicle-miles	17
Seat Belt Use	45
Vehicle Miles Traveled Per Capita	5
Workers Using Public Transportation	46
Road And Street Miles Under State Control	38
Highway Employees	19
Public Transit Employees	41
State And Local Spending For Highways	23
Highway Spending As Percent Of Total	15

Welfare

Percent Of Births To Unwed Mothers	24
AFDC Recipients As Percent Of Population	30
Food Stamp Recipients As Percent Of Population	12
SSI Recipients As Percent Of Population	18
Change In AFDC Recipients	26
Condition Of Children Index	29
Percent Of Families With Single Parent	34
Typical Monthly AFDC Payments	34
Welfare As Percent Of Poverty Level Income	35
Average SSI State Supplements Per Recipient	16
State Income Tax Liability Of Typical Family In Poverty	16
Child Support Collections Per $ Of Administrative Costs	33
Percent Of Children In Foster Care	38
State And Local Welfare Spending Per Capita	32
Welfare Spending As Percent Of Total	26
Administrative Costs Per AFDC Case	10

Population

Population	29
Percent Population Change	11
Population 2000	29
Median Age	4
Percent Population African-American	41
Percent Population in Poverty	27
Percent Population Female	37
Birth Rates	43
Death Rates	26
Illegal Immigrant Population	16

Economies

Personal Income	28
Per Capita Personal Income	26
Percent of Personal Income from Wages & Salaries	29
Average Annual Pay	24
Cost Of Living	22
Average Annual Pay in Manufacturing	21
Average Annual Pay in Retailing	11
Unemployment Rate	36
Government Employment	29
Manufacturing Employment	27
Fortune 500 Companies	20
Tourism Spending	27
Export-related Jobs	24
Change in Price of Existing Homes	3
Net Farm Income	28
Bankruptcy Filings	7
Patents Issued	19
WC Disability Payments	15
UC Average Weekly Benefit	22
Economic Momentum	6
Employment Change	6
Manufacturing Employment Change	8
Home Ownership	40
Gambling Losses	19
Electricity Use Per Residential Customer	6
Revenue Per Kwh	35
New Companies	4

Geography

Total Land Area	10
Federally-Owned Land	7
State Park Visitors	5
State Park Acreage	29
Hunters With Firearms	18
Registered Boats	24
Per Capita State Spending For the Arts	46
Energy Consumption Per Capita	27
Toxic Chemical Release Per Capita	31
Hazardous Waste Sites	33
Polluted Rivers	26
Air Quality	23

Government

Members Of US House	29
Legislators Per Million Population	33
Units Of Government	19
Female Legislators	7
Turnover In Legislatures	11
Democrats in State Legislatures	37
Number Of Statewide Elected Officials	16
State And Local Government Employees	33
State And Local Average Salaries	17
Local Employment	28
Registered Voters	8
Statewide Initiatives	2

Federal

Per Capita Federal Spending	40
Increase In Federal Spending	9
Federal Grants To State And Local Government	24
Per Capita Federal Spending On Procurement	50
Per Capita Federal Spending On Social Security And Medicare	20
Social Security Benefits	13

Federal Spending On

Employee Wages & Salaries	38
Federal Grant Spending Per $ Of State Tax Revenue	13
General Revenue From Federal Government	26
Federal Tax Burden Per Capita	26
Highway Charges Returned To States	29
Terms Of Trade	26
Per Capita Federal Income Tax Liability	28

Taxes

Tax Revenue	12
Per Capita Tax Revenue	21
Tax Effort	20
Tax Capacity	20
Percent Change In Taxes	17
Property Taxes Per Capita	11
Property Tax Revenue As Percent Of Three-Tax Revenue	6
Sales Taxes Per Capita	50
Sales Tax Revenue As Percent Of Three-Tax Revenue	50
Services With Sales Tax	50
Income Taxes Per Capita	6
Income Tax Revenue As Percent Of Three-Tax Revenue	2
Highest Personal Income Tax Rate	5
Motor Fuel Taxes	6
Tobacco Taxes	14
Tax Burden On High Income Family	12
Progressivity Of Taxes	38

Revenues And Finances

State And Local Revenue	26
Non-Tax Revenue	25
State And Local Expenditures	27
Per Capita State And Local General Expenditures	16
Change In General Expenditures	16
State Government General Spending	27

Debt As Percent Of Revenue — 34
Full Faith And Credit Debt — 5
Bond Ratings — 3
State Solvency Index — 4
Pension Plan Assets — 29
State Reserves — 4
State Budget Process Quality — 6
Relative State Spending "Needs" — 18

Education

Math Proficiency, 8th Grade — n/a
AFQT Ranks — 1
SAT Scores — 3
ACT Scores — n/a
Over-25 Population Without
  High School Diploma — 9
Private School Students — 38
Percent Students Finishing
  High School — 31
Pupil-Teacher Ratio — 44
Public School Enrollment — 28
Library Holdings Per Capita — 31
Education Spending As
  Percent Of Total — 30
Spending Per Pupil — 14
Average Teacher Salary — 12
State Aid Per Pupil — 33
State And Local Spending
  For Higher Education — 15
Higher Education Spending
  As Percent Of Total — 24
Public Higher Education
  Enrollment — 16
State Per Pupil Support Of
  Higher Education — 7
Tuition And Fees — 17
Average Professor Salary — 42
Education Employees — 33
R&D Spending — 40

Health

Infant Mortality Rates — 31
State Health Rankings — 22
Population Without Health
  Insurance — 18
Abortions — 13

Alcohol Consumption — 19
Percent Non-Smokers — 13
Percent Obese — 28
AIDS Cases — 22
Physicians Per 100,000
  Population — 17
Medicaid Recipients Related
  To Poverty Population — 34
Health/Hospital Spending
  As Percent Of Total — 28
Per Capita Medicaid
  Spending — 41
Medicaid Spending Per
  Aged Recipient — 31
Medicaid Spending Per
  AFDC Child — 36
Medicare Payment Per
  Hospital-Day — 12
Population In HMOs — 2

Crime And Law Enforcement

Crime Rate — 13
Violent Crime Rate — 27
Murder Rate —
Property Crime Rate — 11
Motor Vehicle Theft Rate — 16
Violent Crime Rate Change — 47
Incarceration Rate — 42
Juvenile Arrest Rate — 20
Proportion Of Sentence
  Served — 24
Law Enforcement
  Employees — 41
Corrections Employees — 22
Costs Per Inmate-Day — 28
State Corrections Spending — 17
Spending For Law
  Enforcement — 22
Law Enforcement Spending
  As Percent Of Total — 26

Transportation

Percent Of Travel On
  Interstates — 16
Interstate Mileage In
  Poor Condition — 44

Deficient Bridges — 22
Traffic Deaths Per
  100 Million Vehicle-miles — 19
Seat Belt Use — 6
Vehicle Miles Traveled
  Per Capita — 25
Workers Using Public
  Transportation — 13
Road And Street Miles
  Under State Control — 39
Highway Employees — 22
Public Transit Employees — 8
State And Local Spending
  For Highways — 31
Highway Spending As
  Percent Of Total — 39

Welfare

Percent Of Births To
  Unwed Mothers — 27
AFDC Recipients As
  Percent Of Population — 36
Food Stamp Recipients As
  Percent Of Population — 26
SSI Recipients As
  Percent Of Population — 36
Change In AFDC Recipients — 22
Condition Of Children Index — 18
Percent Of Families With
  Single Parent — 25
Typical Monthly AFDC
  Payments — 13
Welfare As Percent Of
  Poverty Level Income — 13
Average SSI State Supplements
  Per Recipient — 18
State Income Tax Liability Of
  Typical Family In Poverty — 8
Child Support Collections Per $
  Of Administrative Costs — 8
Percent Of Children In
  Foster Care — 17
State And Local Welfare
  Spending Per Capita — 35
Welfare Spending As
  Percent Of Total — 42
Administrative Costs Per
  AFDC Case — 3

Population

Population	5
Percent Population Change	45
Population 2000	5
Median Age	3
Percent Population African-American	20
Percent Population in Poverty	24
Percent Population Female	3
Birth Rates	44
Death Rates	5
Illegal Immigrant Population	30

Economies

Personal Income	6
Per Capita Personal Income	17
Percent of Personal Income from Wages & Salaries	37
Average Annual Pay	11
Cost Of Living	9
Average Annual Pay in Manufacturing	17
Average Annual Pay in Retailing	23
Unemployment Rate	16
Government Employment	7
Manufacturing Employment	7
Fortune 500 Companies	5
Tourism Spending	8
Export-related Jobs	7
Change in Price of Existing Homes	27
Net Farm Income	21
Bankruptcy Filings	38
Patents Issued	17
WC Disability Payments	11
UC Average Weekly Benefit	8
Economic Momentum	46
Employment Change	46
Manufacturing Employment Change	38
Home Ownership	5
Gambling Losses	12
Electricity Use Per Residential Customer	32
Revenue Per Kwh	26
New Companies	49

Geography

Total Land Area	32
Federally-Owned Land	37
State Park Visitors	7
State Park Acreage	11
Hunters With Firearms	15
Registered Boats	11
Per Capita State Spending For the Arts	22
Energy Consumption Per Capita	35
Toxic Chemical Release Per Capita	36
Hazardous Waste Sites	2
Polluted Rivers	41
Air Quality	41

Government

Members Of US House	5
Legislators Per Million Population	42
Units Of Government	21
Female Legislators	44
Turnover In Legislatures	44
Democrats in State Legislatures	25
Number Of Statewide Elected Officials	35
State And Local Government Employees	50
State And Local Average Salaries	16
Local Employment	11
Registered Voters	39
Statewide Initiatives	n/a

Federal

Per Capita Federal Spending	19
Increase In Federal Spending	17
Federal Grants To State And Local Government	20
Per Capita Federal Spending On Procurement	31
Per Capita Federal Spending On Social Security And Medicare	1
Social Security Benefits	7
Federal Spending On Employee Wages & Salaries	35
Federal Grant Spending Per $ Of State Tax Revenue	30
General Revenue From Federal Government	4
Federal Tax Burden Per Capita	16
Highway Charges Returned To States	24
Terms Of Trade	32
Per Capita Federal Income Tax Liability	20

Taxes

Tax Revenue	25
Per Capita Tax Revenue	17
Tax Effort	24
Tax Capacity	22
Percent Change In Taxes	18
Property Taxes Per Capita	29
Property Tax Revenue As Percent Of Three-Tax Revenue	27
Sales Taxes Per Capita	38
Sales Tax Revenue As Percent Of Three-Tax Revenue	31
Services With Sales Tax	18
Income Taxes Per Capita	13
Income Tax Revenue As Percent Of Three-Tax Revenue	10
Highest Personal Income Tax Rate	41
Motor Fuel Taxes	12
Tobacco Taxes	23
Tax Burden On High Income Family	25
Progressivity Of Taxes	9

Revenues And Finances

State And Local Revenue	4
Non-Tax Revenue	5
State And Local Expenditures	5
Per Capita State And Local General Expenditures	19
Change In General Expenditures	19
State Government General Spending	4

Debt As Percent Of Revenue	20
Full Faith And Credit Debt	16
Bond Ratings	4
State Solvency Index	33
Pension Plan Assets	10
State Reserves	32
State Budget Process Quality	22
Relative State Spending "Needs"	13

Education

Math Proficiency, 8th Grade	14
AFQT Ranks	21
SAT Scores	9
ACT Scores	n/a
Over-25 Population Without High School Diploma	35
Private School Students	2
Percent Students Finishing High School	11
Pupil-Teacher Ratio	28
Public School Enrollment	50
Library Holdings Per Capita	36
Education Spending As Percent Of Total	26
Spending Per Pupil	6
Average Teacher Salary	6
State Aid Per Pupil	7
State And Local Spending For Higher Education	27
Higher Education Spending As Percent Of Total	31
Public Higher Education Enrollment	50
State Per Pupil Support Of Higher Education	39
Tuition And Fees	2
Average Professor Salary	11
Education Employees	49
R&D Spending	12

Health

Infant Mortality Rates	28
State Health Rankings	21
Population Without Health Insurance	41
Abortions	16

Alcohol Consumption	38
Percent Non-Smokers	37
Percent Obese	2
AIDS Cases	17
Physicians Per 100,000 Population	8
Medicaid Recipients Related To Poverty Population	8
Health/Hospital Spending As Percent Of Total	39
Per Capita Medicaid Spending	32
Medicaid Spending Per Aged Recipient	13
Medicaid Spending Per AFDC Child	34
Medicare Payment Per Hospital-Day	11
Population In HMOs	13

Crime And Law Enforcement

Crime Rate	44
Violent Crime Rate	33
Murder Rate	
Property Crime Rate	45
Motor Vehicle Theft Rate	24
Violent Crime Rate Change	33
Incarceration Rate	33
Juvenile Arrest Rate	38
Proportion Of Sentence Served	16
Law Enforcement Employees	34
Corrections Employees	35
Costs Per Inmate-Day	15
State Corrections Spending	25
Spending For Law Enforcement	29
Law Enforcement Spending As Percent Of Total	32

Transportation

Percent Of Travel On Interstates	43
Interstate Mileage In Poor Condition	15

Deficient Bridges	7
Traffic Deaths Per 100 Million Vehicle-miles	30
Seat Belt Use	8
Vehicle Miles Traveled Per Capita	46
Workers Using Public Transportation	7
Road And Street Miles Under State Control	6
Highway Employees	38
Public Transit Employees	6
State And Local Spending For Highways	44
Highway Spending As Percent Of Total	44

Welfare

Percent Of Births To Unwed Mothers	18
AFDC Recipients As Percent Of Population	17
Food Stamp Recipients As Percent Of Population	23
SSI Recipients As Percent Of Population	25
Change In AFDC Recipients	33
Condition Of Children Index	20
Percent Of Families With Single Parent	41
Typical Monthly AFDC Payments	23
Welfare As Percent Of Poverty Level Income	17
Average SSI State Supplements Per Recipient	17
State Income Tax Liability Of Typical Family In Poverty	22
Child Support Collections Per $ Of Administrative Costs	1
Percent Of Children In Foster Care	5
State And Local Welfare Spending Per Capita	6
Welfare Spending As Percent Of Total	5
Administrative Costs Per AFDC Case	35

Population

Population	43
Percent Population Change	50
Population 2000	43
Median Age	10
Percent Population African-American	33
Percent Population in Poverty	37
Percent Population Female	4
Birth Rates	36
Death Rates	11
Illegal Immigrant Population	12

Economies

Personal Income	42
Per Capita Personal Income	19
Percent of Personal Income from Wages & Salaries	38
Average Annual Pay	21
Cost Of Living	7
Average Annual Pay in Manufacturing	33
Average Annual Pay in Retailing	18
Unemployment Rate	3
Government Employment	47
Manufacturing Employment	39
Fortune 500 Companies	31
Tourism Spending	50
Export-related Jobs	37
Change in Price of Existing Homes	n/a
Net Farm Income	48
Bankruptcy Filings	20
Patents Issued	15
WC Disability Payments	19
UC Average Weekly Benefit	5
Economic Momentum	48
Employment Change	48
Manufacturing Employment Change	47
Home Ownership	44
Gambling Losses	34
Electricity Use Per Residential Customer	48
Revenue Per Kwh	48
New Companies	16

Geography

Total Land Area	50
Federally-Owned Land	50
State Park Visitors	40
State Park Acreage	50
Hunters With Firearms	46
Registered Boats	47
Per Capita State Spending For the Arts	24
Energy Consumption Per Capita	42
Toxic Chemical Release Per Capita	38
Hazardous Waste Sites	34
Polluted Rivers	21
Air Quality	43

Government

Members Of US House	38
Legislators Per Million Population	6
Units Of Government	45
Female Legislators	17
Turnover In Legislatures	33
Democrats in State Legislatures	3
Number Of Statewide Elected Officials	35
State And Local Government Employees	45
State And Local Average Salaries	8
Local Employment	44
Registered Voters	26
Statewide Initiatives	n/a

Federal

Per Capita Federal Spending	9
Increase In Federal Spending	20
Federal Grants To State And Local Government	6
Per Capita Federal Spending On Procurement	26
Per Capita Federal Spending On Social Security And Medicare	5
Social Security Benefits	15
Federal Spending On Employee Wages & Salaries	21
Federal Grant Spending Per $ Of State Tax Revenue	11
General Revenue From Federal Government	37
Federal Tax Burden Per Capita	13
Highway Charges Returned To States	4
Terms Of Trade	13
Per Capita Federal Income Tax Liability	21

Taxes

Tax Revenue	19
Per Capita Tax Revenue	15
Tax Effort	4
Tax Capacity	37
Percent Change In Taxes	36
Property Taxes Per Capita	9
Property Tax Revenue As Percent Of Three-Tax Revenue	9
Sales Taxes Per Capita	31
Sales Tax Revenue As Percent Of Three-Tax Revenue	39
Services With Sales Tax	34
Income Taxes Per Capita	21
Income Tax Revenue As Percent Of Three-Tax Revenue	29
Highest Personal Income Tax Rate	2
Motor Fuel Taxes	2
Tobacco Taxes	4
Tax Burden On High Income Family	3
Progressivity Of Taxes	25

Revenues And Finances

State And Local Revenue	42
Non-Tax Revenue	48
State And Local Expenditures	42
Per Capita State And Local General Expenditures	8
Change In General Expenditures	8
State Government General Spending	40

Debt As Percent Of Revenue	3
Full Faith And Credit Debt	9
Bond Ratings	4
State Solvency Index	45
Pension Plan Assets	14
State Reserves	33
State Budget Process Quality	9
Relative State Spending "Needs"	9

Education

Math Proficiency, 8th Grade	23
AFQT Ranks	30
SAT Scores	7
ACT Scores	n/a
Over-25 Population Without High School Diploma	40
Private School Students	11
Percent Students Finishing High School	23
Pupil-Teacher Ratio	4
Public School Enrollment	49
Library Holdings Per Capita	9
Education Spending As Percent Of Total	46
Spending Per Pupil	9
Average Teacher Salary	11
State Aid Per Pupil	31
State And Local Spending For Higher Education	40
Higher Education Spending As Percent Of Total	44
Public Higher Education Enrollment	28
State Per Pupil Support Of Higher Education	15
Tuition And Fees	10
Average Professor Salary	19
Education Employees	47
R&D Spending	6

Health

Infant Mortality Rates	45
State Health Rankings	19
Population Without Health Insurance	48
Abortions	3

Alcohol Consumption	23
Percent Non-Smokers	24
Percent Obese	36
AIDS Cases	9
Physicians Per 100,000 Population	5
Medicaid Recipients Related To Poverty Population	1
Health/Hospital Spending As Percent Of Total	40
Per Capita Medicaid Spending	2
Medicaid Spending Per Aged Recipient	28
Medicaid Spending Per AFDC Child	43
Medicare Payment Per Hospital-Day	43
Population In HMOs	6

Crime And Law Enforcement

Crime Rate	32
Violent Crime Rate	34
Murder Rate	
Property Crime Rate	31
Motor Vehicle Theft Rate	10
Violent Crime Rate Change	43
Incarceration Rate	40
Juvenile Arrest Rate	45
Proportion Of Sentence Served	n/a
Law Enforcement Employees	7
Corrections Employees	20
Costs Per Inmate-Day	5
State Corrections Spending	5
Spending For Law Enforcement	19
Law Enforcement Spending As Percent Of Total	30

Transportation

Percent Of Travel On Interstates	22
Interstate Mileage In Poor Condition	21

Deficient Bridges	4
Traffic Deaths Per 100 Million Vehicle-miles	49
Seat Belt Use	32
Vehicle Miles Traveled Per Capita	47
Workers Using Public Transportation	18
Road And Street Miles Under State Control	10
Highway Employees	42
Public Transit Employees	17
State And Local Spending For Highways	41
Highway Spending As Percent Of Total	48

Welfare

Percent Of Births To Unwed Mothers	21
AFDC Recipients As Percent Of Population	5
Food Stamp Recipients As Percent Of Population	25
SSI Recipients As Percent Of Population	16
Change In AFDC Recipients	10
Condition Of Children Index	16
Percent Of Families With Single Parent	13
Typical Monthly AFDC Payments	8
Welfare As Percent Of Poverty Level Income	5
Average SSI State Supplements Per Recipient	11
State Income Tax Liability Of Typical Family In Poverty	22
Child Support Collections Per $ Of Administrative Costs	13
Percent Of Children In Foster Care	14
State And Local Welfare Spending Per Capita	8
Welfare Spending As Percent Of Total	13
Administrative Costs Per AFDC Case	12

Population

Population	25
Percent Population Change	25
Population 2000	26
Median Age	40
Percent Population African-American	3
Percent Population in Poverty	22
Percent Population Female	13
Birth Rates	15
Death Rates	36
Illegal Immigrant Population	39

Economies

Personal Income	27
Per Capita Personal Income	43
Percent of Personal Income from Wages & Salaries	15
Average Annual Pay	38
Cost Of Living	45
Average Annual Pay in Manufacturing	38
Average Annual Pay in Retailing	36
Unemployment Rate	24
Government Employment	24
Manufacturing Employment	20
Fortune 500 Companies	35
Tourism Spending	23
Export-related Jobs	18
Change in Price of Existing Homes	20
Net Farm Income	31
Bankruptcy Filings	44
Patents Issued	32
WC Disability Payments	30
UC Average Weekly Benefit	39
Economic Momentum	28
Employment Change	35
Manufacturing Employment Change	42
Home Ownership	12
Gambling Losses	20
Electricity Use Per Residential Customer	4
Revenue Per Kwh	10
New Companies	40

Geography

Total Land Area	40
Federally-Owned Land	33
State Park Visitors	26
State Park Acreage	30
Hunters With Firearms	20
Registered Boats	10
Per Capita State Spending For the Arts	14
Energy Consumption Per Capita	19
Toxic Chemical Release Per Capita	10
Hazardous Waste Sites	15
Polluted Rivers	37
Air Quality	1

Government

Members Of US House	23
Legislators Per Million Population	21
Units Of Government	35
Female Legislators	43
Turnover In Legislatures	40
Democrats in State Legislatures	26
Number Of Statewide Elected Officials	3
State And Local Government Employees	15
State And Local Average Salaries	41
Local Employment	41
Registered Voters	33
Statewide Initiatives	n/a

Federal

Per Capita Federal Spending	29
Increase In Federal Spending	31
Federal Grants To State And Local Government	30
Per Capita Federal Spending On Procurement	17
Per Capita Federal Spending On Social Security And Medicare	39
Social Security Benefits	40
Federal Spending On Employee Wages & Salaries	18
Federal Grant Spending Per $ Of State Tax Revenue	19
General Revenue From Federal Government	24
Federal Tax Burden Per Capita	45
Highway Charges Returned To States	50
Terms Of Trade	16
Per Capita Federal Income Tax Liability	45

Taxes

Tax Revenue	42
Per Capita Tax Revenue	45
Tax Effort	35
Tax Capacity	42
Percent Change In Taxes	28
Property Taxes Per Capita	37
Property Tax Revenue As Percent Of Three-Tax Revenue	33
Sales Taxes Per Capita	42
Sales Tax Revenue As Percent Of Three-Tax Revenue	22
Services With Sales Tax	29
Income Taxes Per Capita	29
Income Tax Revenue As Percent Of Three-Tax Revenue	18
Highest Personal Income Tax Rate	15
Motor Fuel Taxes	39
Tobacco Taxes	47
Tax Burden On High Income Family	29
Progressivity Of Taxes	42

Revenues And Finances

State And Local Revenue	28
Non-Tax Revenue	26
State And Local Expenditures	26
Per Capita State And Local General Expenditures	36
Change In General Expenditures	36
State Government General Spending	25

Debt As Percent Of Revenue	22	Alcohol Consumption	25	Deficient Bridges	31
Full Faith And Credit Debt	29	Percent Non-Smokers	44	Traffic Deaths Per	
Bond Ratings	1	Percent Obese	14	100 Million Vehicle-miles	6
State Solvency Index	39	AIDS Cases	12	Seat Belt Use	22
Pension Plan Assets	26	Physicians Per 100,000		Vehicle Miles Traveled	
State Reserves	6	Population	38	Per Capita	16
State Budget Process Quality	11	Medicaid Recipients Related		Workers Using Public	
Relative State Spending "Needs"	36	To Poverty Population	36	Transportation	36

Education

Math Proficiency, 8th Grade	29	Health/Hospital Spending		Road And Street Miles	
AFQT Ranks	47	As Percent Of Total	3	Under State Control	5
SAT Scores	19	Per Capita Medicaid		Highway Employees	35
ACT Scores	n/a	Spending	22	Public Transit Employees	30
Over-25 Population Without		Medicaid Spending Per		State And Local Spending	
High School Diploma	44	Aged Recipient	48	For Highways	50
Private School Students	35	Medicaid Spending Per		Highway Spending As	
Percent Students Finishing		AFDC Child	16	Percent Of Total	45
High School	49	Medicare Payment Per			
Pupil-Teacher Ratio	28	Hospital-Day	28		
Public School Enrollment	20	Population In HMOs	40		
Library Holdings Per Capita	48				
Education Spending As					
Percent Of Total	19				
Spending Per Pupil	38				
Average Teacher Salary	38	**Crime And Law Enforcement**		**Welfare**	
State Aid Per Pupil	32	Crime Rate	12	Percent Of Births To	
State And Local Spending		Violent Crime Rate	5	Unwed Mothers	6
For Higher Education	22	Murder Rate		AFDC Recipients As	
Higher Education Spending		Property Crime Rate	16	Percent Of Population	34
As Percent Of Total	19	Motor Vehicle Theft Rate	29	Food Stamp Recipients As	
Public Higher Education		Violent Crime Rate Change	14	Percent Of Population	20
Enrollment	36	Incarceration Rate	4	SSI Recipients As	
State Per Pupil Support Of		Juvenile Arrest Rate	19	Percent Of Population	10
Higher Education	4	Proportion Of Sentence		Change In AFDC Recipients	23
Tuition And Fees	16	Served	31	Condition Of Children Index	46
Average Professor Salary	31	Law Enforcement		Percent Of Families With	
Education Employees	24	Employees	30	Single Parent	16
R&D Spending	44	Corrections Employees	8	Typical Monthly AFDC	
		Costs Per Inmate-Day	44	Payments	45
		State Corrections Spending	42	Welfare As Percent Of	
		Spending For Law		Poverty Level Income	44
		Enforcement	26	Average SSI State Supplements	
		Law Enforcement Spending		Per Recipient	28
		As Percent Of Total	14	State Income Tax Liability Of	
				Typical Family In Poverty	22
				Child Support Collections Per $	
				Of Administrative Costs	20
				Percent Of Children In	
				Foster Care	34
Health				State And Local Welfare	
Infant Mortality Rates	10	**Transportation**		Spending Per Capita	36
State Health Rankings	46	Percent Of Travel On		Welfare Spending As	
Population Without Health		Interstates	20	Percent Of Total	32
Insurance	14	Interstate Mileage In		Administrative Costs Per	
Abortions	33	Poor Condition	28	AFDC Case	45

Population

Population	45
Percent Population Change	33
Population 2000	45
Median Age	39
Percent Population African-American	46
Percent Population in Poverty	17
Percent Population Female	35
Birth Rates	16
Death Rates	1
Illegal Immigrant Population	50

Economies

Personal Income	47
Per Capita Personal Income	33
Percent of Personal Income from Wages & Salaries	50
Average Annual Pay	50
Cost Of Living	44
Average Annual Pay in Manufacturing	50
Average Annual Pay in Retailing	49
Unemployment Rate	49
Government Employment	45
Manufacturing Employment	43
Fortune 500 Companies	41
Tourism Spending	48
Export-related Jobs	45
Change in Price of Existing Homes	n/a
Net Farm Income	12
Bankruptcy Filings	45
Patents Issued	48
WC Disability Payments	41
UC Average Weekly Benefit	47
Economic Momentum	39
Employment Change	11
Manufacturing Employment Change	2
Home Ownership	31
Gambling Losses	30
Electricity Use Per Residential Customer	26
Revenue Per Kwh	32
New Companies	26

Geography

Total Land Area	16
Federally-Owned Land	17
State Park Visitors	33
State Park Acreage	28
Hunters With Firearms	5
Registered Boats	41
Per Capita State Spending For the Arts	25
Energy Consumption Per Capita	33
Toxic Chemical Release Per Capita	41
Hazardous Waste Sites	47
Polluted Rivers	11
Air Quality	1

Government

Members Of US House	44
Legislators Per Million Population	8
Units Of Government	2
Female Legislators	33
Turnover In Legislatures	17
Democrats in State Legislatures	41
Number Of Statewide Elected Officials	16
State And Local Government Employees	19
State And Local Average Salaries	47
Local Employment	34
Registered Voters	5
Statewide Initiatives	10

Federal

Per Capita Federal Spending	12
Increase In Federal Spending	44
Federal Grants To State And Local Government	12
Per Capita Federal Spending On Procurement	39
Per Capita Federal Spending On Social Security And Medicare	22
Social Security Benefits	44
Federal Spending On Employee Wages & Salaries	13
Federal Grant Spending Per $ Of State Tax Revenue	3
General Revenue From Federal Government	48
Federal Tax Burden Per Capita	35
Highway Charges Returned To States	7
Terms Of Trade	10
Per Capita Federal Income Tax Liability	33

Taxes

Tax Revenue	46
Per Capita Tax Revenue	46
Tax Effort	43
Tax Capacity	41
Percent Change In Taxes	43
Property Taxes Per Capita	28
Property Tax Revenue As Percent Of Three-Tax Revenue	10
Sales Taxes Per Capita	16
Sales Tax Revenue As Percent Of Three-Tax Revenue	10
Services With Sales Tax	5
Income Taxes Per Capita	44
Income Tax Revenue As Percent Of Three-Tax Revenue	44
Highest Personal Income Tax Rate	n/a
Motor Fuel Taxes	30
Tobacco Taxes	31
Tax Burden On High Income Family	45
Progressivity Of Taxes	3

Revenues And Finances

State And Local Revenue	50
Non-Tax Revenue	49
State And Local Expenditures	50
Per Capita State And Local General Expenditures	41
Change In General Expenditures	41
State Government General Spending	50

Debt As Percent Of Revenue	18
Full Faith And Credit Debt	50
Bond Ratings	n/a
State Solvency Index	10
Pension Plan Assets	28
State Reserves	42
State Budget Process Quality	24
Relative State Spending "Needs"	45

Education

Math Proficiency, 8th Grade	n/a
AFQT Ranks	13
SAT Scores	n/a
ACT Scores	11
Over-25 Population Without High School Diploma	24
Private School Students	30
Percent Students Finishing High School	6
Pupil-Teacher Ratio	12
Public School Enrollment	9
Library Holdings Per Capita	7
Education Spending As Percent Of Total	28
Spending Per Pupil	37
Average Teacher Salary	50
State Aid Per Pupil	47
State And Local Spending For Higher Education	44
Higher Education Spending As Percent Of Total	38
Public Higher Education Enrollment	30
State Per Pupil Support Of Higher Education	18
Tuition And Fees	26
Average Professor Salary	49
Education Employees	7
R&D Spending	45

Health

Infant Mortality Rates	1
State Health Rankings	33
Population Without Health Insurance	26
Abortions	48

Alcohol Consumption	28
Percent Non-Smokers	18
Percent Obese	15
AIDS Cases	48
Physicians Per 100,000 Population	45
Medicaid Recipients Related To Poverty Population	38
Health/Hospital Spending As Percent Of Total	43
Per Capita Medicaid Spending	21
Medicaid Spending Per Aged Recipient	18
Medicaid Spending Per AFDC Child	14
Medicare Payment Per Hospital-Day	44
Population In HMOs	43

Crime And Law Enforcement

Crime Rate	47
Violent Crime Rate	44
Murder Rate	
Property Crime Rate	48
Motor Vehicle Theft Rate	50
Violent Crime Rate Change	1
Incarceration Rate	32
Juvenile Arrest Rate	9
Proportion Of Sentence Served	n/a
Law Enforcement Employees	45
Corrections Employees	47
Costs Per Inmate-Day	40
State Corrections Spending	38
Spending For Law Enforcement	45
Law Enforcement Spending As Percent Of Total	43

Transportation

Percent Of Travel On Interstates	24
Interstate Mileage In Poor Condition	5

Deficient Bridges	48
Traffic Deaths Per 100 Million Vehicle-miles	17
Seat Belt Use	47
Vehicle Miles Traveled Per Capita	11
Workers Using Public Transportation	50
Road And Street Miles Under State Control	45
Highway Employees	3
Public Transit Employees	50
State And Local Spending For Highways	6
Highway Spending As Percent Of Total	2

Welfare

Percent Of Births To Unwed Mothers	29
AFDC Recipients As Percent Of Population	46
Food Stamp Recipients As Percent Of Population	36
SSI Recipients As Percent Of Population	28
Change In AFDC Recipients	46
Condition Of Children Index	13
Percent Of Families With Single Parent	40
Typical Monthly AFDC Payments	16
Welfare As Percent Of Poverty Level Income	17
Average SSI State Supplements Per Recipient	35
State Income Tax Liability Of Typical Family In Poverty	n/a
Child Support Collections Per $ Of Administrative Costs	9
Percent Of Children In Foster Care	44
State And Local Welfare Spending Per Capita	41
Welfare Spending As Percent Of Total	34
Administrative Costs Per AFDC Case	24

Population

Population	17
Percent Population Change	14
Population 2000	17
Median Age	16
Percent Population African-American	10
Percent Population in Poverty	16
Percent Population Female	9
Birth Rates	33
Death Rates	25
Illegal Immigrant Population	42

Economies

Personal Income	20
Per Capita Personal Income	36
Percent of Personal Income from Wages & Salaries	10
Average Annual Pay	28
Cost Of Living	35
Average Annual Pay in Manufacturing	37
Average Annual Pay in Retailing	21
Unemployment Rate	25
Government Employment	18
Manufacturing Employment	12
Fortune 500 Companies	21
Tourism Spending	15
Export-related Jobs	16
Change in Price of Existing Homes	14
Net Farm Income	24
Bankruptcy Filings	1
Patents Issued	34
WC Disability Payments	36
UC Average Weekly Benefit	44
Economic Momentum	11
Employment Change	16
Manufacturing Employment Change	44
Home Ownership	21
Gambling Losses	n/a
Electricity Use Per Residential Customer	1
Revenue Per Kwh	50
New Companies	31

Geography

Total Land Area	34
Federally-Owned Land	29
State Park Visitors	8
State Park Acreage	22
Hunters With Firearms	25
Registered Boats	16
Per Capita State Spending For the Arts	18
Energy Consumption Per Capita	18
Toxic Chemical Release Per Capita	5
Hazardous Waste Sites	23
Polluted Rivers	27
Air Quality	24

Government

Members Of US House	15
Legislators Per Million Population	38
Units Of Government	37
Female Legislators	40
Turnover In Legislatures	18
Democrats in State Legislatures	16
Number Of Statewide Elected Officials	45
State And Local Government Employees	37
State And Local Average Salaries	40
Local Employment	18
Registered Voters	27
Statewide Initiatives	n/a

Federal

Per Capita Federal Spending	26
Increase In Federal Spending	11
Federal Grants To State And Local Government	25
Per Capita Federal Spending On Procurement	9
Per Capita Federal Spending On Social Security And Medicare	27
Social Security Benefits	42

Federal Spending On Employee Wages & Salaries	32
Federal Grant Spending Per $ Of State Tax Revenue	9
General Revenue From Federal Government	14
Federal Tax Burden Per Capita	32
Highway Charges Returned To States	48
Terms Of Trade	21
Per Capita Federal Income Tax Liability	29

Taxes

Tax Revenue	50
Per Capita Tax Revenue	48
Tax Effort	44
Tax Capacity	44
Percent Change In Taxes	38
Property Taxes Per Capita	42
Property Tax Revenue As Percent Of Three-Tax Revenue	39
Sales Taxes Per Capita	10
Sales Tax Revenue As Percent Of Three-Tax Revenue	2
Services With Sales Tax	12
Income Taxes Per Capita	43
Income Tax Revenue As Percent Of Three-Tax Revenue	43
Highest Personal Income Tax Rate	n/a
Motor Fuel Taxes	17
Tobacco Taxes	44
Tax Burden On High Income Family	46
Progressivity Of Taxes	1

Revenues And Finances

State And Local Revenue	18
Non-Tax Revenue	19
State And Local Expenditures	19
Per Capita State And Local General Expenditures	47
Change In General Expenditures	47
State Government General Spending	21

Debt As Percent Of Revenue	37	
Full Faith And Credit Debt	27	
Bond Ratings	1	
State Solvency Index	19	
Pension Plan Assets	13	
State Reserves	34	
State Budget Process Quality	14	
Relative State Spending "Needs"	31	

Education

Math Proficiency, 8th Grade	34
AFQT Ranks	39
SAT Scores	n/a
ACT Scores	19
Over-25 Population Without High School Diploma	45
Private School Students	25
Percent Students Finishing High School	39
Pupil-Teacher Ratio	45
Public School Enrollment	32
Library Holdings Per Capita	49
Education Spending As Percent Of Total	41
Spending Per Pupil	43
Average Teacher Salary	35
State Aid Per Pupil	49
State And Local Spending For Higher Education	36
Higher Education Spending As Percent Of Total	22
Public Higher Education Enrollment	38
State Per Pupil Support Of Higher Education	16
Tuition And Fees	41
Average Professor Salary	21
Education Employees	44
R&D Spending	25

Health

Infant Mortality Rates	18
State Health Rankings	42
Population Without Health Insurance	28
Abortions	20

Alcohol Consumption	44
Percent Non-Smokers	43
Percent Obese	15
AIDS Cases	21
Physicians Per 100,000 Population	19
Medicaid Recipients Related To Poverty Population	10
Health/Hospital Spending As Percent Of Total	5
Per Capita Medicaid Spending	17
Medicaid Spending Per Aged Recipient	46
Medicaid Spending Per AFDC Child	27
Medicare Payment Per Hospital-Day	34
Population In HMOs	24

Crime And Law Enforcement

Crime Rate	21
Violent Crime Rate	13
Murder Rate	
Property Crime Rate	24
Motor Vehicle Theft Rate	15
Violent Crime Rate Change	8
Incarceration Rate	27
Juvenile Arrest Rate	18
Proportion Of Sentence Served	36
Law Enforcement Employees	30
Corrections Employees	16
Costs Per Inmate-Day	30
State Corrections Spending	12
Spending For Law Enforcement	31
Law Enforcement Spending As Percent Of Total	19

Transportation

Percent Of Travel On Interstates	11
Interstate Mileage In Poor Condition	34

Deficient Bridges	21
Traffic Deaths Per 100 Million Vehicle-miles	9
Seat Belt Use	30
Vehicle Miles Traveled Per Capita	13
Workers Using Public Transportation	32
Road And Street Miles Under State Control	25
Highway Employees	29
Public Transit Employees	43
State And Local Spending For Highways	33
Highway Spending As Percent Of Total	19

Welfare

Percent Of Births To Unwed Mothers	13
AFDC Recipients As Percent Of Population	11
Food Stamp Recipients As Percent Of Population	6
SSI Recipients As Percent Of Population	7
Change In AFDC Recipients	9
Condition Of Children Index	48
Percent Of Families With Single Parent	3
Typical Monthly AFDC Payments	48
Welfare As Percent Of Poverty Level Income	47
Average SSI State Supplements Per Recipient	46
State Income Tax Liability Of Typical Family In Poverty	n/a
Child Support Collections Per $ Of Administrative Costs	6
Percent Of Children In Foster Care	6
State And Local Welfare Spending Per Capita	23
Welfare Spending As Percent Of Total	11
Administrative Costs Per AFDC Case	46

Population

Population	2
Percent Population Change	8
Population 2000	2
Median Age	48
Percent Population African-American	17
Percent Population in Poverty	4
Percent Population Female	38
Birth Rates	4
Death Rates	44
Illegal Immigrant Population	4

Economies

Personal Income	3
Per Capita Personal Income	32
Percent of Personal Income from Wages & Salaries	18
Average Annual Pay	18
Cost Of Living	42
Average Annual Pay in Manufacturing	18
Average Annual Pay in Retailing	17
Unemployment Rate	11
Government Employment	2
Manufacturing Employment	3
Fortune 500 Companies	4
Tourism Spending	3
Export-related Jobs	2
Change in Price of Existing Homes	24
Net Farm Income	2
Bankruptcy Filings	35
Patents Issued	22
WC Disability Payments	20
UC Average Weekly Benefit	17
Economic Momentum	9
Employment Change	10
Manufacturing Employment Change	20
Home Ownership	43
Gambling Losses	7
Electricity Use Per Residential Customer	10
Revenue Per Kwh	7
New Companies	21

Geography

Total Land Area	2
Federally-Owned Land	19
State Park Visitors	10
State Park Acreage	3
Hunters With Firearms	24
Registered Boats	5
Per Capita State Spending For the Arts	49
Energy Consumption Per Capita	4
Toxic Chemical Release Per Capita	8
Hazardous Waste Sites	14
Polluted Rivers	39
Air Quality	39

Government

Members Of US House	3
Legislators Per Million Population	49
Units Of Government	31
Female Legislators	31
Turnover In Legislatures	38
Democrats in State Legislatures	15
Number Of Statewide Elected Officials	16
State And Local Government Employees	15
State And Local Average Salaries	32
Local Employment	4
Registered Voters	42
Statewide Initiatives	n/a

Federal

Per Capita Federal Spending	38
Increase In Federal Spending	16
Federal Grants To State And Local Government	38
Per Capita Federal Spending On Procurement	20
Per Capita Federal Spending On Social Security And Medicare	44
Social Security Benefits	37
Federal Spending On Employee Wages & Salaries	28
Federal Grant Spending Per $ Of State Tax Revenue	17
General Revenue From Federal Government	3
Federal Tax Burden Per Capita	29
Highway Charges Returned To States	46
Terms Of Trade	34
Per Capita Federal Income Tax Liability	22

Taxes

Tax Revenue	30
Per Capita Tax Revenue	31
Tax Effort	37
Tax Capacity	21
Percent Change In Taxes	7
Property Taxes Per Capita	17
Property Tax Revenue As Percent Of Three-Tax Revenue	11
Sales Taxes Per Capita	8
Sales Tax Revenue As Percent Of Three-Tax Revenue	8
Services With Sales Tax	9
Income Taxes Per Capita	45
Income Tax Revenue As Percent Of Three-Tax Revenue	45
Highest Personal Income Tax Rate	n/a
Motor Fuel Taxes	20
Tobacco Taxes	11
Tax Burden On High Income Family	44
Progressivity Of Taxes	6

Revenues And Finances

State And Local Revenue	3
Non-Tax Revenue	3
State And Local Expenditures	3
Per Capita State And Local General Expenditures	42
Change In General Expenditures	42
State Government General Spending	3

Debt As Percent Of Revenue	13
Full Faith And Credit Debt	18
Bond Ratings	3
State Solvency Index	14
Pension Plan Assets	22
State Reserves	15
State Budget Process Quality	27
Relative State Spending "Needs"	47

Education

Math Proficiency, 8th Grade	25
AFQT Ranks	33
SAT Scores	14
ACT Scores	n/a
Over-25 Population Without High School Diploma	39
Private School Students	44
Percent Students Finishing High School	48
Pupil-Teacher Ratio	16
Public School Enrollment	5
Library Holdings Per Capita	38
Education Spending As Percent Of Total	8
Spending Per Pupil	29
Average Teacher Salary	34
State Aid Per Pupil	28
State And Local Spending For Higher Education	30
Higher Education Spending As Percent Of Total	21
Public Higher Education Enrollment	20
State Per Pupil Support Of Higher Education	26
Tuition And Fees	47
Average Professor Salary	27
Education Employees	5
R&D Spending	21

Health

Infant Mortality Rates	30
State Health Rankings	32
Population Without Health Insurance	4
Abortions	17

Alcohol Consumption	16
Percent Non-Smokers	20
Percent Obese	12
AIDS Cases	11
Physicians Per 100,000 Population	34
Medicaid Recipients Related To Poverty Population	41
Health/Hospital Spending As Percent Of Total	17
Per Capita Medicaid Spending	42
Medicaid Spending Per Aged Recipient	42
Medicaid Spending Per AFDC Child	39
Medicare Payment Per Hospital-Day	9
Population In HMOs	31

Crime And Law Enforcement

Crime Rate	5
Violent Crime Rate	14
Murder Rate	
Property Crime Rate	5
Motor Vehicle Theft Rate	8
Violent Crime Rate Change	31
Incarceration Rate	1
Juvenile Arrest Rate	33
Proportion Of Sentence Served	28
Law Enforcement Employees	19
Corrections Employees	6
Costs Per Inmate-Day	34
State Corrections Spending	41
Spending For Law Enforcement	24
Law Enforcement Spending As Percent Of Total	8

Transportation

Percent Of Travel On Interstates	27
Interstate Mileage In Poor Condition	8

Deficient Bridges	44
Traffic Deaths Per 100 Million Vehicle-miles	22
Seat Belt Use	12
Vehicle Miles Traveled Per Capita	27
Workers Using Public Transportation	24
Road And Street Miles Under State Control	13
Highway Employees	44
Public Transit Employees	15
State And Local Spending For Highways	43
Highway Spending As Percent Of Total	36

Welfare

Percent Of Births To Unwed Mothers	49
AFDC Recipients As Percent Of Population	28
Food Stamp Recipients As Percent Of Population	4
SSI Recipients As Percent Of Population	24
Change In AFDC Recipients	14
Condition Of Children Index	28
Percent Of Families With Single Parent	32
Typical Monthly AFDC Payments	47
Welfare As Percent Of Poverty Level Income	47
Average SSI State Supplements Per Recipient	47
State Income Tax Liability Of Typical Family In Poverty	n/a
Child Support Collections Per $ Of Administrative Costs	48
Percent Of Children In Foster Care	46
State And Local Welfare Spending Per Capita	44
Welfare Spending As Percent Of Total	35
Administrative Costs Per AFDC Case	39

Population

Population	34
Percent Population Change	5
Population 2000	34
Median Age	50
Percent Population African-American	43
Percent Population in Poverty	48
Percent Population Female	43
Birth Rates	1
Death Rates	49
Illegal Immigrant Population	20

Economies

Personal Income	36
Per Capita Personal Income	46
Percent of Personal Income from Wages & Salaries	3
Average Annual Pay	36
Cost Of Living	16
Average Annual Pay in Manufacturing	39`
Average Annual Pay in Retailing	34
Unemployment Rate	45
Government Employment	35
Manufacturing Employment	34
Fortune 500 Companies	36
Tourism Spending	33
Export-related Jobs	35
Change in Price of Existing Homes	1
Net Farm Income	37
Bankruptcy Filings	13
Patents Issued	20
WC Disability Payments	32
UC Average Weekly Benefit	16
Economic Momentum	3
Employment Change	2
Manufacturing Employment Change	1
Home Ownership	19
Gambling Losses	n/a
Electricity Use Per Residential Customer	37
Revenue Per Kwh	14
New Companies	14

Geography

Total Land Area	11
Federally-Owned Land	5
State Park Visitors	31
State Park Acreage	27
Hunters With Firearms	14
Registered Boats	37
Per Capita State Spending For the Arts	10
Energy Consumption Per Capita	28
Toxic Chemical Release Per Capita	3
Hazardous Waste Sites	26
Polluted Rivers	31
Air Quality	30

Government

Members Of US House	34
Legislators Per Million Population	19
Units Of Government	25
Female Legislators	39
Turnover In Legislatures	24
Democrats in State Legislatures	46
Number Of Statewide Elected Officials	42
State And Local Government Employees	35
State And Local Average Salaries	33
Local Employment	46
Registered Voters	38
Statewide Initiatives	17

Federal

Per Capita Federal Spending	48
Increase In Federal Spending	49
Federal Grants To State And Local Government	45
Per Capita Federal Spending On Procurement	23
Per Capita Federal Spending On Social Security And Medicare	49
Social Security Benefits	28
Federal Spending On Employee Wages & Salaries	11
Federal Grant Spending Per $ Of State Tax Revenue	21
General Revenue From Federal Government	36
Federal Tax Burden Per Capita	48
Highway Charges Returned To States	31
Terms Of Trade	20
Per Capita Federal Income Tax Liability	41

Taxes

Tax Revenue	14
Per Capita Tax Revenue	40
Tax Effort	28
Tax Capacity	44
Percent Change In Taxes	30
Property Taxes Per Capita	36
Property Tax Revenue As Percent Of Three-Tax Revenue	36
Sales Taxes Per Capita	27
Sales Tax Revenue As Percent Of Three-Tax Revenue	19
Services With Sales Tax	22
Income Taxes Per Capita	25
Income Tax Revenue As Percent Of Three-Tax Revenue	19
Highest Personal Income Tax Rate	30
Motor Fuel Taxes	24
Tobacco Taxes	26
Tax Burden On High Income Family	20
Progressivity Of Taxes	35

Revenues And Finances

State And Local Revenue	36
Non-Tax Revenue	35
State And Local Expenditures	35
Per Capita State And Local General Expenditures	38
Change In General Expenditures	38
State Government General Spending	38

Debt As Percent Of Revenue	1
Full Faith And Credit Debt	34
Bond Ratings	1
State Solvency Index	13
Pension Plan Assets	34
State Reserves	27
State Budget Process Quality	12
Relative State Spending "Needs"	44

Education

Math Proficiency, 8th Grade	8
AFQT Ranks	25
SAT Scores	n/a
ACT Scores	5
Over-25 Population Without High School Diploma	2
Private School Students	49
Percent Students Finishing High School	12
Pupil-Teacher Ratio	50
Public School Enrollment	1
Library Holdings Per Capita	28
Education Spending As Percent Of Total	1
Spending Per Pupil	50
Average Teacher Salary	42
State Aid Per Pupil	40
State And Local Spending For Higher Education	5
Higher Education Spending As Percent Of Total	1
Public Higher Education Enrollment	9
State Per Pupil Support Of Higher Education	31
Tuition And Fees	31
Average Professor Salary	37
Education Employees	38
R&D Spending	18

Health

Infant Mortality Rates	45
State Health Rankings	3
Population Without Health Insurance	46
Abortions	46

Alcohol Consumption	50
Percent Non-Smokers	1
Percent Obese	41
AIDS Cases	40
Physicians Per 100,000 Population	30
Medicaid Recipients Related To Poverty Population	41
Health/Hospital Spending As Percent Of Total	32
Per Capita Medicaid Spending	49
Medicaid Spending Per Aged Recipient	27
Medicaid Spending Per AFDC Child	25
Medicare Payment Per Hospital-Day	8
Population In HMOs	18

Crime And Law Enforcement

Crime Rate	22
Violent Crime Rate	39
Murder Rate	
Property Crime Rate	15
Motor Vehicle Theft Rate	39
Violent Crime Rate Change	24
Incarceration Rate	46
Juvenile Arrest Rate	29
Proportion Of Sentence Served	21
Law Enforcement Employees	48
Corrections Employees	35
Costs Per Inmate-Day	17
State Corrections Spending	4
Spending For Law Enforcement	35
Law Enforcement Spending As Percent Of Total	29

Transportation

Percent Of Travel On Interstates	1
Interstate Mileage In Poor Condition	41

Deficient Bridges	20
Traffic Deaths Per 100 Million Vehicle-miles	23
Seat Belt Use	41
Vehicle Miles Traveled Per Capita	31
Workers Using Public Transportation	23
Road And Street Miles Under State Control	28
Highway Employees	45
Public Transit Employees	12
State And Local Spending For Highways	39
Highway Spending As Percent Of Total	35

Welfare

Percent Of Births To Unwed Mothers	50
AFDC Recipients As Percent Of Population	46
Food Stamp Recipients As Percent Of Population	47
SSI Recipients As Percent Of Population	49
Change In AFDC Recipients	35
Condition Of Children Index	6
Percent Of Families With Single Parent	50
Typical Monthly AFDC Payments	21
Welfare As Percent Of Poverty Level Income	17
Average SSI State Supplements Per Recipient	39
State Income Tax Liability Of Typical Family In Poverty	21
Child Support Collections Per $ Of Administrative Costs	40
Percent Of Children In Foster Care	49
State And Local Welfare Spending Per Capita	46
Welfare Spending As Percent Of Total	40
Administrative Costs Per AFDC Case	9

Population

Population	49
Percent Population Change	34
Population 2000	49
Median Age	11
Percent Population African-American	48
Percent Population in Poverty	50
Percent Population Female	32
Birth Rates	50
Death Rates	31
Illegal Immigrant Population	37

Economies

Personal Income	49
Per Capita Personal Income	31
Percent of Personal Income from Wages & Salaries	36
Average Annual Pay	33
Cost Of Living	12
Average Annual Pay in Manufacturing	24
Average Annual Pay in Retailing	29
Unemployment Rate	39
Government Employment	50
Manufacturing Employment	44
Fortune 500 Companies	n/a
Tourism Spending	46
Export-related Jobs	42
Change in Price of Existing Homes	n/a
Net Farm Income	43
Bankruptcy Filings	49
Patents Issued	12
WC Disability Payments	6
UC Average Weekly Benefit	31
Economic Momentum	42
Employment Change	39
Manufacturing Employment Change	16
Home Ownership	15
Gambling Losses	45
Electricity Use Per Residential Customer	39
Revenue Per Kwh	46
New Companies	15

Geography

Total Land Area	43
Federally-Owned Land	40
State Park Visitors	50
State Park Acreage	35
Hunters With Firearms	12
Registered Boats	45
Per Capita State Spending For the Arts	26
Energy Consumption Per Capita	41
Toxic Chemical Release Per Capita	49
Hazardous Waste Sites	43
Polluted Rivers	32
Air Quality	1

Government

Members Of US House	44
Legislators Per Million Population	2
Units Of Government	6
Female Legislators	4
Turnover In Legislatures	13
Democrats in State Legislatures	19
Number Of Statewide Elected Officials	16
State And Local Government Employees	23
State And Local Average Salaries	24
Local Employment	45
Registered Voters	14
Statewide Initiatives	n/a

Federal

Per Capita Federal Spending	43
Increase In Federal Spending	30
Federal Grants To State And Local Government	13
Per Capita Federal Spending On Procurement	49
Per Capita Federal Spending On Social Security And Medicare	29
Social Security Benefits	21
Federal Spending On Employee Wages & Salaries	37
Federal Grant Spending Per $ Of State Tax Revenue	8
General Revenue From Federal Government	49
Federal Tax Burden Per Capita	30
Highway Charges Returned To States	10
Terms Of Trade	14
Per Capita Federal Income Tax Liability	34

Taxes

Tax Revenue	7
Per Capita Tax Revenue	14
Tax Effort	20
Tax Capacity	14
Percent Change In Taxes	10
Property Taxes Per Capita	7
Property Tax Revenue As Percent Of Three-Tax Revenue	8
Sales Taxes Per Capita	33
Sales Tax Revenue As Percent Of Three-Tax Revenue	41
Services With Sales Tax	39
Income Taxes Per Capita	20
Income Tax Revenue As Percent Of Three-Tax Revenue	30
Highest Personal Income Tax Rate	4
Motor Fuel Taxes	41
Tobacco Taxes	34
Tax Burden On High Income Family	24
Progressivity Of Taxes	40

Revenues And Finances

State And Local Revenue	49
Non-Tax Revenue	50
State And Local Expenditures	49
Per Capita State And Local General Expenditures	13
Change In General Expenditures	13
State Government General Spending	48

Debt As Percent Of Revenue	1
Full Faith And Credit Debt	34
Bond Ratings	1
State Solvency Index	13
Pension Plan Assets	34
State Reserves	27
State Budget Process Quality	12
Relative State Spending "Needs"	44

Education

Math Proficiency, 8th Grade	8
AFQT Ranks	25
SAT Scores	n/a
ACT Scores	5
Over-25 Population Without High School Diploma	2
Private School Students	49
Percent Students Finishing High School	12
Pupil-Teacher Ratio	50
Public School Enrollment	1
Library Holdings Per Capita	28
Education Spending As Percent Of Total	1
Spending Per Pupil	50
Average Teacher Salary	42
State Aid Per Pupil	40
State And Local Spending For Higher Education	5
Higher Education Spending As Percent Of Total	1
Public Higher Education Enrollment	9
State Per Pupil Support Of Higher Education	31
Tuition And Fees	31
Average Professor Salary	37
Education Employees	38
R&D Spending	18

Health

Infant Mortality Rates	45
State Health Rankings	3
Population Without Health Insurance	46
Abortions	46

Alcohol Consumption	50
Percent Non-Smokers	1
Percent Obese	41
AIDS Cases	40
Physicians Per 100,000 Population	30
Medicaid Recipients Related To Poverty Population	41
Health/Hospital Spending As Percent Of Total	32
Per Capita Medicaid Spending	49
Medicaid Spending Per Aged Recipient	27
Medicaid Spending Per AFDC Child	25
Medicare Payment Per Hospital-Day	8
Population In HMOs	18

Crime And Law Enforcement

Crime Rate	22
Violent Crime Rate	39
Murder Rate	
Property Crime Rate	15
Motor Vehicle Theft Rate	39
Violent Crime Rate Change	24
Incarceration Rate	46
Juvenile Arrest Rate	29
Proportion Of Sentence Served	21
Law Enforcement Employees	48
Corrections Employees	35
Costs Per Inmate-Day	17
State Corrections Spending	4
Spending For Law Enforcement	35
Law Enforcement Spending As Percent Of Total	29

Transportation

Percent Of Travel On Interstates	1
Interstate Mileage In Poor Condition	41

Deficient Bridges	20
Traffic Deaths Per 100 Million Vehicle-miles	23
Seat Belt Use	41
Vehicle Miles Traveled Per Capita	31
Workers Using Public Transportation	23
Road And Street Miles Under State Control	28
Highway Employees	45
Public Transit Employees	12
State And Local Spending For Highways	39
Highway Spending As Percent Of Total	35

Welfare

Percent Of Births To Unwed Mothers	50
AFDC Recipients As Percent Of Population	46
Food Stamp Recipients As Percent Of Population	47
SSI Recipients As Percent Of Population	49
Change In AFDC Recipients	35
Condition Of Children Index	6
Percent Of Families With Single Parent	50
Typical Monthly AFDC Payments	21
Welfare As Percent Of Poverty Level Income	17
Average SSI State Supplements Per Recipient	39
State Income Tax Liability Of Typical Family In Poverty	21
Child Support Collections Per $ Of Administrative Costs	40
Percent Of Children In Foster Care	49
State And Local Welfare Spending Per Capita	46
Welfare Spending As Percent Of Total	40
Administrative Costs Per AFDC Case	9

Population

Population	12
Percent Population Change	17
Population 2000	12
Median Age	37
Percent Population African-American	8
Percent Population in Poverty	35
Percent Population Female	29
Birth Rates	22
Death Rates	42
Illegal Immigrant Population	17

Economies

Personal Income	11
Per Capita Personal Income	13
Percent of Personal Income from Wages & Salaries	17
Average Annual Pay	17
Cost Of Living	24
Average Annual Pay in Manufacturing	29
Average Annual Pay in Retailing	19
Unemployment Rate	38
Government Employment	9
Manufacturing Employment	18
Fortune 500 Companies	13
Tourism Spending	10
Export-related Jobs	21
Change in Price of Existing Homes	28
Net Farm Income	26
Bankruptcy Filings	11
Patents Issued	31
WC Disability Payments	22
UC Average Weekly Benefit	26
Economic Momentum	21
Employment Change	20
Manufacturing Employment Change	34
Home Ownership	30
Gambling Losses	18
Electricity Use Per Residential Customer	8
Revenue Per Kwh	9
New Companies	25

Geography

Total Land Area	37
Federally-Owned Land	23
State Park Visitors	39
State Park Acreage	34
Hunters With Firearms	33
Registered Boats	20
Per Capita State Spending For the Arts	48
Energy Consumption Per Capita	37
Toxic Chemical Release Per Capita	20
Hazardous Waste Sites	16
Polluted Rivers	40
Air Quality	35

Government

Members Of US House	11
Legislators Per Million Population	41
Units Of Government	49
Female Legislators	46
Turnover In Legislatures	49
Democrats in State Legislatures	21
Number Of Statewide Elected Officials	44
State And Local Government Employees	21
State And Local Average Salaries	25
Local Employment	29
Registered Voters	36
Statewide Initiatives	n/a

Federal

Per Capita Federal Spending	3
Increase In Federal Spending	22
Federal Grants To State And Local Government	50
Per Capita Federal Spending On Procurement	2
Per Capita Federal Spending On Social Security And Medicare	43
Social Security Benefits	35
Federal Spending On Employee Wages & Salaries	3
Federal Grant Spending Per $ Of State Tax Revenue	48
General Revenue From Federal Government	21
Federal Tax Burden Per Capita	18
Highway Charges Returned To States	43
Terms Of Trade	50
Per Capita Federal Income Tax Liability	13

Taxes

Tax Revenue	44
Per Capita Tax Revenue	27
Tax Effort	34
Tax Capacity	15
Percent Change In Taxes	23
Property Taxes Per Capita	27
Property Tax Revenue As Percent Of Three-Tax Revenue	23
Sales Taxes Per Capita	40
Sales Tax Revenue As Percent Of Three-Tax Revenue	36
Services With Sales Tax	44
Income Taxes Per Capita	16
Income Tax Revenue As Percent Of Three-Tax Revenue	13
Highest Personal Income Tax Rate	31
Motor Fuel Taxes	36
Tobacco Taxes	50
Tax Burden On High Income Family	34
Progressivity Of Taxes	23

Revenues And Finances

State And Local Revenue	15
Non-Tax Revenue	11
State And Local Expenditures	14
Per Capita State And Local General Expenditures	35
Change In General Expenditures	35
State Government General Spending	15

Debt As Percent Of Revenue	35
Full Faith And Credit Debt	22
Bond Ratings	3
State Solvency Index	42
Pension Plan Assets	49
State Reserves	50
State Budget Process Quality	50
Relative State Spending "Needs"	11

Education

Math Proficiency, 8th Grade	n/a
AFQT Ranks	14
SAT Scores	16
ACT Scores	n/a
Over-25 Population Without High School Diploma	12
Private School Students	28
Percent Students Finishing High School	9
Pupil-Teacher Ratio	2
Public School Enrollment	27
Library Holdings Per Capita	3
Education Spending As Percent Of Total	2
Spending Per Pupil	5
Average Teacher Salary	20
State Aid Per Pupil	34
State And Local Spending For Higher Education	8
Higher Education Spending As Percent Of Total	11
Public Higher Education Enrollment	41
State Per Pupil Support Of Higher Education	48
Tuition And Fees	1
Average Professor Salary	32
Education Employees	8
R&D Spending	27

Health

Infant Mortality Rates	35
State Health Rankings	6
Population Without Health Insurance	33
Abortions	8

Alcohol Consumption	11
Percent Non-Smokers	16
Percent Obese	29
AIDS Cases	44
Physicians Per 100,000 Population	6
Medicaid Recipients Related To Poverty Population	5
Health/Hospital Spending As Percent Of Total	50
Per Capita Medicaid Spending	13
Medicaid Spending Per Aged Recipient	30
Medicaid Spending Per AFDC Child	48
Medicare Payment Per Hospital-Day	42
Population In HMOs	27

Crime And Law Enforcement

Crime Rate	41
Violent Crime Rate	49
Murder Rate	
Property Crime Rate	38
Motor Vehicle Theft Rate	49
Violent Crime Rate Change	49
Incarceration Rate	44
Juvenile Arrest Rate	1
Proportion Of Sentence Served	10
Law Enforcement Employees	43
Corrections Employees	46
Costs Per Inmate-Day	9
State Corrections Spending	9
Spending For Law Enforcement	39
Law Enforcement Spending As Percent Of Total	47

Transportation

Percent Of Travel On Interstates	29
Interstate Mileage In Poor Condition	47

Deficient Bridges	8
Traffic Deaths Per 100 Million Vehicle-miles	20
Seat Belt Use	18
Vehicle Miles Traveled Per Capita	10
Workers Using Public Transportation	43
Road And Street Miles Under State Control	20
Highway Employees	7
Public Transit Employees	29
State And Local Spending For Highways	8
Highway Spending As Percent Of Total	10

Welfare

Percent Of Births To Unwed Mothers	43
AFDC Recipients As Percent Of Population	23
Food Stamp Recipients As Percent Of Population	16
SSI Recipients As Percent Of Population	20
Change In AFDC Recipients	17
Condition Of Children Index	7
Percent Of Families With Single Parent	42
Typical Monthly AFDC Payments	3
Welfare As Percent Of Poverty Level Income	4
Average SSI State Supplements Per Recipient	12
State Income Tax Liability Of Typical Family In Poverty	40
Child Support Collections Per $ Of Administrative Costs	37
Percent Of Children In Foster Care	2
State And Local Welfare Spending Per Capita	13
Welfare Spending As Percent Of Total	18
Administrative Costs Per AFDC Case	28

Population

Population	15
Percent Population Change	13
Population 2000	15
Median Age	24
Percent Population African-American	35
Percent Population in Poverty	29
Percent Population Female	41
Birth Rates	18
Death Rates	40
Illegal Immigrant Population	15

Economies

Personal Income	15
Per Capita Personal Income	12
Percent of Personal Income from Wages & Salaries	27
Average Annual Pay	14
Cost Of Living	14
Average Annual Pay in Manufacturing	10
Average Annual Pay in Retailing	10
Unemployment Rate	10
Government Employment	13
Manufacturing Employment	21
Fortune 500 Companies	17
Tourism Spending	20
Export-related Jobs	10
Change in Price of Existing Homes	17
Net Farm Income	18
Bankruptcy Filings	14
Patents Issued	23
WC Disability Payments	8
UC Average Weekly Benefit	9
Economic Momentum	13
Employment Change	13
Manufacturing Employment Change	41
Home Ownership	41
Gambling Losses	17
Electricity Use Per Residential Customer	5
Revenue Per Kwh	6
New Companies	1

Geography

Total Land Area	20
Federally-Owned Land	12
State Park Visitors	4
State Park Acreage	13
Hunters With Firearms	37
Registered Boats	18
Per Capita State Spending For the Arts	44
Energy Consumption Per Capita	13
Toxic Chemical Release Per Capita	35
Hazardous Waste Sites	7
Polluted Rivers	20
Air Quality	37

Government

Members Of US House	15
Legislators Per Million Population	34
Units Of Government	26
Female Legislators	1
Turnover In Legislatures	7
Democrats in State Legislatures	36
Number Of Statewide Elected Officials	3
State And Local Government Employees	23
State And Local Average Salaries	12
Local Employment	35
Registered Voters	19
Statewide Initiatives	4

Federal

Per Capita Federal Spending	21
Increase In Federal Spending	34
Federal Grants To State And Local Government	32
Per Capita Federal Spending On Procurement	15
Per Capita Federal Spending On Social Security And Medicare	38
Social Security Benefits	9
Federal Spending On Employee Wages & Salaries	10
Federal Grant Spending Per $ Of State Tax Revenue	43
General Revenue From Federal Government	15
Federal Tax Burden Per Capita	11
Highway Charges Returned To States	15
Terms Of Trade	41
Per Capita Federal Income Tax Liability	10

Taxes

Tax Revenue	11
Per Capita Tax Revenue	12
Tax Effort	17
Tax Capacity	12
Percent Change In Taxes	6
Property Taxes Per Capita	22
Property Tax Revenue As Percent Of Three-Tax Revenue	31
Sales Taxes Per Capita	2
Sales Tax Revenue As Percent Of Three-Tax Revenue	3
Services With Sales Tax	3
Income Taxes Per Capita	n/a
Income Tax Revenue As Percent Of Three-Tax Revenue	46
Highest Personal Income Tax Rate	n/a
Motor Fuel Taxes	10
Tobacco Taxes	3
Tax Burden On High Income Family	43
Progressivity Of Taxes	5

Revenues And Finances

State And Local Revenue	13
Non-Tax Revenue	16
State And Local Expenditures	11
Per Capita State And Local General Expenditures	11
Change In General Expenditures	11
State Government General Spending	12

Debt As Percent Of Revenue	26
Full Faith And Credit Debt	24
Bond Ratings	1
State Solvency Index	29
Pension Plan Assets	35
State Reserves	43
State Budget Process Quality	41
Relative State Spending "Needs"	10

Education

Math Proficiency, 8th Grade	18
AFQT Ranks	30
SAT Scores	4
ACT Scores	n/a
Over-25 Population Without High School Diploma	32
Private School Students	31
Percent Students Finishing High School	30
Pupil-Teacher Ratio	19
Public School Enrollment	39
Library Holdings Per Capita	28
Education Spending As Percent Of Total	15
Spending Per Pupil	24
Average Teacher Salary	25
State Aid Per Pupil	50
State And Local Spending For Higher Education	28
Higher Education Spending As Percent Of Total	26
Public Higher Education Enrollment	21
State Per Pupil Support Of Higher Education	24
Tuition And Fees	6
Average Professor Salary	9
Education Employees	19
R&D Spending	4

Health

Infant Mortality Rates	22
State Health Rankings	9
Population Without Health Insurance	24
Abortions	14

Alcohol Consumption	36
Percent Non-Smokers	27
Percent Obese	45
AIDS Cases	19
Physicians Per 100,000 Population	15
Medicaid Recipients Related To Poverty Population	28
Health/Hospital Spending As Percent Of Total	21
Per Capita Medicaid Spending	45
Medicaid Spending Per Aged Recipient	35
Medicaid Spending Per AFDC Child	12
Medicare Payment Per Hospital-Day	31
Population In HMOs	34

Crime And Law Enforcement

Crime Rate	39
Violent Crime Rate	35
Murder Rate	
Property Crime Rate	41
Motor Vehicle Theft Rate	37
Violent Crime Rate Change	22
Incarceration Rate	13
Juvenile Arrest Rate	12
Proportion Of Sentence Served	n/a
Law Enforcement Employees	34
Corrections Employees	14
Costs Per Inmate-Day	31
State Corrections Spending	24
Spending For Law Enforcement	23
Law Enforcement Spending As Percent Of Total	11

Transportation

Percent Of Travel On Interstates	17
Interstate Mileage In Poor Condition	24

Deficient Bridges	26
Traffic Deaths Per 100 Million Vehicle-miles	44
Seat Belt Use	8
Vehicle Miles Traveled Per Capita	18
Workers Using Public Transportation	10
Road And Street Miles Under State Control	3
Highway Employees	26
Public Transit Employees	27
State And Local Spending For Highways	28
Highway Spending As Percent Of Total	23

Welfare

Percent Of Births To Unwed Mothers	25
AFDC Recipients As Percent Of Population	42
Food Stamp Recipients As Percent Of Population	31
SSI Recipients As Percent Of Population	27
Change In AFDC Recipients	19
Condition Of Children Index	15
Percent Of Families With Single Parent	37
Typical Monthly AFDC Payments	38
Welfare As Percent Of Poverty Level Income	28
Average SSI State Supplements Per Recipient	27
State Income Tax Liability Of Typical Family In Poverty	9
Child Support Collections Per $ Of Administrative Costs	11
Percent Of Children In Foster Care	43
State And Local Welfare Spending Per Capita	48
Welfare Spending As Percent Of Total	44
Administrative Costs Per AFDC Case	29

Population

Population	35
Percent Population Change	44
Population 2000	35
Median Age	2
Percent Population African-American	34
Percent Population in Poverty	5
Percent Population Female	8
Birth Rates	49
Death Rates	2
Illegal Immigrant Population	47

Economies

Personal Income	37
Per Capita Personal Income	47
Percent of Personal Income from Wages & Salaries	47
Average Annual Pay	34
Cost Of Living	47
Average Annual Pay in Manufacturing	22
Average Annual Pay in Retailing	45
Unemployment Rate	1
Government Employment	37
Manufacturing Employment	38
Fortune 500 Companies	n/a
Tourism Spending	43
Export-related Jobs	38
Change in Price of Existing Homes	n/a
Net Farm Income	45
Bankruptcy Filings	34
Patents Issued	46
WC Disability Payments	29
UC Average Weekly Benefit	30
Economic Momentum	33
Employment Change	26
Manufacturing Employment Change	12
Home Ownership	1
Gambling Losses	31
Electricity Use Per Residential Customer	20
Revenue Per Kwh	28
New Companies	34

Geography

Total Land Area	41
Federally-Owned Land	28
State Park Visitors	27
State Park Acreage	17
Hunters With Firearms	7
Registered Boats	39
Per Capita State Spending For the Arts	16
Energy Consumption Per Capita	6
Toxic Chemical Release Per Capita	15
Hazardous Waste Sites	44
Polluted Rivers	10
Air Quality	19

Government

Members Of US House	34
Legislators Per Million Population	12
Units Of Government	23
Female Legislators	38
Turnover In Legislatures	14
Democrats in State Legislatures	7
Number Of Statewide Elected Officials	16
State And Local Government Employees	36
State And Local Average Salaries	44
Local Employment	40
Registered Voters	33
Statewide Initiatives	n/a

Federal

Per Capita Federal Spending	15
Increase In Federal Spending	4
Federal Grants To State And Local Government	5
Per Capita Federal Spending On Procurement	44
Per Capita Federal Spending On Social Security And Medicare	3
Social Security Benefits	34

Federal Spending On Employee Wages & Salaries	40
Federal Grant Spending Per $ Of State Tax Revenue	6
General Revenue From Federal Government	33
Federal Tax Burden Per Capita	49
Highway Charges Returned To States	12
Terms Of Trade	1
Per Capita Federal Income Tax Liability	49

Taxes

Tax Revenue	18
Per Capita Tax Revenue	42
Tax Effort	10
Tax Capacity	49
Percent Change In Taxes	47
Property Taxes Per Capita	45
Property Tax Revenue As Percent Of Three-Tax Revenue	43
Sales Taxes Per Capita	28
Sales Tax Revenue As Percent Of Three-Tax Revenue	14
Services With Sales Tax	6
Income Taxes Per Capita	34
Income Tax Revenue As Percent Of Three-Tax Revenue	26
Highest Personal Income Tax Rate	22
Motor Fuel Taxes	4
Tobacco Taxes	40
Tax Burden On High Income Family	22
Progressivity Of Taxes	36

Revenues And Finances

State And Local Revenue	37
Non-Tax Revenue	38
State And Local Expenditures	36
Per Capita State And Local General Expenditures	37
Change In General Expenditures	37
State Government General Spending	37

Debt As Percent Of Revenue	5
Full Faith And Credit Debt	8
Bond Ratings	3
State Solvency Index	36
Pension Plan Assets	18
State Reserves	21
State Budget Process Quality	42
Relative State Spending "Needs"	15

Education

Math Proficiency, 8th Grade	n/a
AFQT Ranks	5
SAT Scores	2
ACT Scores	n/a
Over-25 Population Without High School Diploma	4
Private School Students	33
Percent Students Finishing High School	25
Pupil-Teacher Ratio	48
Public School Enrollment	25
Library Holdings Per Capita	25
Education Spending As Percent Of Total	23
Spending Per Pupil	18
Average Teacher Salary	17
State Aid Per Pupil	4
State And Local Spending For Higher Education	16
Higher Education Spending As Percent Of Total	30
Public Higher Education Enrollment	22
State Per Pupil Support Of Higher Education	30
Tuition And Fees	24
Average Professor Salary	29
Education Employees	46
R&D Spending	17

Health

Infant Mortality Rates	50
State Health Rankings	16
Population Without Health Insurance	12
Abortions	7

Alcohol Consumption	18
Percent Non-Smokers	14
Percent Obese	43
AIDS Cases	20
Physicians Per 100,000 Population	13
Medicaid Recipients Related To Poverty Population	2
Health/Hospital Spending As Percent Of Total	19
Per Capita Medicaid Spending	36
Medicaid Spending Per Aged Recipient	20
Medicaid Spending Per AFDC Child	45
Medicare Payment Per Hospital-Day	14
Population In HMOs	23

Crime And Law Enforcement

Crime Rate	11
Violent Crime Rate	25
Murder Rate	
Property Crime Rate	7
Motor Vehicle Theft Rate	20
Violent Crime Rate Change	37
Incarceration Rate	36
Juvenile Arrest Rate	31
Proportion Of Sentence Served	5
Law Enforcement Employees	42
Corrections Employees	23
Costs Per Inmate-Day	11
State Corrections Spending	7
Spending For Law Enforcement	11
Law Enforcement Spending As Percent Of Total	17

Transportation

Percent Of Travel On Interstates	8
Interstate Mileage In Poor Condition	14

Deficient Bridges	14
Traffic Deaths Per 100 Million Vehicle-miles	43
Seat Belt Use	3
Vehicle Miles Traveled Per Capita	36
Workers Using Public Transportation	9
Road And Street Miles Under State Control	17
Highway Employees	24
Public Transit Employees	4
State And Local Spending For Highways	30
Highway Spending As Percent Of Total	41

Welfare

Percent Of Births To Unwed Mothers	37
AFDC Recipients As Percent Of Population	12
Food Stamp Recipients As Percent Of Population	29
SSI Recipients As Percent Of Population	30
Change In AFDC Recipients	21
Condition Of Children Index	12
Percent Of Families With Single Parent	24
Typical Monthly AFDC Payments	10
Welfare As Percent Of Poverty Level Income	8
Average SSI State Supplements Per Recipient	20
State Income Tax Liability Of Typical Family In Poverty	n/a
Child Support Collections Per $ Of Administrative Costs	35
Percent Of Children In Foster Care	30
State And Local Welfare Spending Per Capita	22
Welfare Spending As Percent Of Total	36
Administrative Costs Per AFDC Case	11

Population

Population	18
Percent Population Change	31
Population 2000	19
Median Age	25
Percent Population African-American	28
Percent Population in Poverty	44
Percent Population Female	30
Birth Rates	42
Death Rates	29
Illegal Immigrant Population	33

Economies

Personal Income	18
Per Capita Personal Income	21
Percent of Personal Income from Wages & Salaries	19
Average Annual Pay	26
Cost Of Living	27
Average Annual Pay in Manufacturing	23
Average Annual Pay in Retailing	42
Unemployment Rate	46
Government Employment	20
Manufacturing Employment	10
Fortune 500 Companies	25
Tourism Spending	25
Export-related Jobs	13
Change in Price of Existing Homes	5
Net Farm Income	25
Bankruptcy Filings	40
Patents Issued	16
WC Disability Payments	16
UC Average Weekly Benefit	15
Economic Momentum	19
Employment Change	17
Manufacturing Employment Change	14
Home Ownership	28
Gambling Losses	26
Electricity Use Per Residential Customer	34
Revenue Per Kwh	13
New Companies	48

Geography

Total Land Area	25
Federally-Owned Land	15
State Park Visitors	19
State Park Acreage	23
Hunters With Firearms	6
Registered Boats	6
Per Capita State Spending For the Arts	32
Energy Consumption Per Capita	38
Toxic Chemical Release Per Capita	27
Hazardous Waste Sites	8
Polluted Rivers	42
Air Quality	40

Government

Members Of US House	15
Legislators Per Million Population	37
Units Of Government	16
Female Legislators	15
Turnover In Legislatures	45
Democrats in State Legislatures	27
Number Of Statewide Elected Officials	16
State And Local Government Employees	32
State And Local Average Salaries	11
Local Employment	9
Registered Voters	4
Statewide Initiatives	n/a

Federal

Per Capita Federal Spending	49
Increase In Federal Spending	40
Federal Grants To State And Local Government	42
Per Capita Federal Spending On Procurement	43
Per Capita Federal Spending On Social Security And Medicare	18
Social Security Benefits	10

Federal Spending On Employee Wages & Salaries	50
Federal Grant Spending Per $ Of State Tax Revenue	41
General Revenue From Federal Government	17
Federal Tax Burden Per Capita	23
Highway Charges Returned To States	33
Terms Of Trade	38
Per Capita Federal Income Tax Liability	23

Taxes

Tax Revenue	6
Per Capita Tax Revenue	13
Tax Effort	3
Tax Capacity	35
Percent Change In Taxes	29
Property Taxes Per Capita	14
Property Tax Revenue As Percent Of Three-Tax Revenue	19
Sales Taxes Per Capita	30
Sales Tax Revenue As Percent Of Three-Tax Revenue	40
Services With Sales Tax	14
Income Taxes Per Capita	8
Income Tax Revenue As Percent Of Three-Tax Revenue	12
Highest Personal Income Tax Rate	18
Motor Fuel Taxes	9
Tobacco Taxes	14
Tax Burden On High Income Family	6
Progressivity Of Taxes	19

Revenues And Finances

State And Local Revenue	14
Non-Tax Revenue	18
State And Local Expenditures	16
Per Capita State And Local General Expenditures	15
Change In General Expenditures	15
State Government General Spending	16

Debt As Percent Of Revenue	17
Full Faith And Credit Debt	45
Bond Ratings	4
State Solvency Index	46
Pension Plan Assets	46
State Reserves	18
State Budget Process Quality	30
Relative State Spending "Needs"	42

Education

Math Proficiency, 8th Grade	34
AFQT Ranks	43
SAT Scores	n/a
ACT Scores	24
Over-25 Population Without High School Diploma	48
Private School Students	46
Percent Students Finishing High School	22
Pupil-Teacher Ratio	8
Public School Enrollment	22
Library Holdings Per Capita	31
Education Spending As Percent Of Total	11
Spending Per Pupil	19
Average Teacher Salary	32
State Aid Per Pupil	6
State And Local Spending For Higher Education	34
Higher Education Spending As Percent Of Total	29
Public Higher Education Enrollment	26
State Per Pupil Support Of Higher Education	21
Tuition And Fees	38
Average Professor Salary	43
Education Employees	13
R&D Spending	26

Health

Infant Mortality Rates	34
State Health Rankings	48
Population Without Health Insurance	8
Abortions	49

Alcohol Consumption	49
Percent Non-Smokers	38
Percent Obese	4
AIDS Cases	43
Physicians Per 100,000 Population	34
Medicaid Recipients Related To Poverty Population	13
Health/Hospital Spending As Percent Of Total	31
Per Capita Medicaid Spending	7
Medicaid Spending Per Aged Recipient	33
Medicaid Spending Per AFDC Child	41
Medicare Payment Per Hospital-Day	46
Population In HMOs	48

Crime And Law Enforcement

Crime Rate	50
Violent Crime Rate	45
Murder Rate	45
Property Crime Rate	50
Motor Vehicle Theft Rate	45
Violent Crime Rate Change	2
Incarceration Rate	48
Juvenile Arrest Rate	3
Proportion Of Sentence Served	11
Law Enforcement Employees	50
Corrections Employees	50
Costs Per Inmate-Day	41
State Corrections Spending	36
Spending For Law Enforcement	50
Law Enforcement Spending As Percent Of Total	50

Transportation

Percent Of Travel On Interstates	13
Interstate Mileage In Poor Condition	10

Deficient Bridges	6
Traffic Deaths Per 100 Million Vehicle-miles	3
Seat Belt Use	32
Vehicle Miles Traveled Per Capita	28
Workers Using Public Transportation	36
Road And Street Miles Under State Control	2
Highway Employees	5
Public Transit Employees	26
State And Local Spending For Highways	21
Highway Spending As Percent Of Total	14

Welfare

Percent Of Births To Unwed Mothers	26
AFDC Recipients As Percent Of Population	8
Food Stamp Recipients As Percent Of Population	2
SSI Recipients As Percent Of Population	6
Change In AFDC Recipients	43
Condition Of Children Index	41
Percent Of Families With Single Parent	35
Typical Monthly AFDC Payments	42
Welfare As Percent Of Poverty Level Income	42
Average SSI State Supplements Per Recipient	47
State Income Tax Liability Of Typical Family In Poverty	11
Child Support Collections Per $ Of Administrative Costs	25
Percent Of Children In Foster Care	19
State And Local Welfare Spending Per Capita	16
Welfare Spending As Percent Of Total	7
Administrative Costs Per AFDC Case	50

Population

Population	50
Percent Population Change	16
Population 2000	50
Median Age	38
Percent Population African-American	42
Percent Population in Poverty	41
Percent Population Female	47
Birth Rates	47
Death Rates	32
Illegal Immigrant Population	45

Economies

Personal Income	50
Per Capita Personal Income	27
Percent of Personal Income from Wages & Salaries	40
Average Annual Pay	43
Cost Of Living	26
Average Annual Pay in Manufacturing	45
Average Annual Pay in Retailing	47
Unemployment Rate	37
Government Employment	48
Manufacturing Employment	50
Fortune 500 Companies	n/a
Tourism Spending	44
Export-related Jobs	50
Change in Price of Existing Homes	n/a
Net Farm Income	42
Bankruptcy Filings	31
Patents Issued	41
WC Disability Payments	31
UC Average Weekly Benefit	24
Economic Momentum	24
Employment Change	37
Manufacturing Employment Change	32
Home Ownership	23
Gambling Losses	47
Electricity Use Per Residential Customer	30
Revenue Per Kwh	17
New Companies	8

Geography

Total Land Area	9
Federally-Owned Land	8
State Park Visitors	44
State Park Acreage	26
Hunters With Firearms	2
Registered Boats	49
Per Capita State Spending For the Arts	29
Energy Consumption Per Capita	2
Toxic Chemical Release Per Capita	6
Hazardous Waste Sites	48
Polluted Rivers	9
Air Quality	1

Government

Members Of US House	44
Legislators Per Million Population	4
Units Of Government	7
Female Legislators	24
Turnover In Legislatures	25
Democrats in State Legislatures	48
Number Of Statewide Elected Officials	16
State And Local Government Employees	1
State And Local Average Salaries	34
Local Employment	24
Registered Voters	17
Statewide Initiatives	n/a

Federal

Per Capita Federal Spending	24
Increase In Federal Spending	35
Federal Grants To State And Local Government	2
Per Capita Federal Spending On Procurement	42
Per Capita Federal Spending On Social Security And Medicare	40
Social Security Benefits	24

Federal Spending On Employee Wages & Salaries	12
Federal Grant Spending Per $ Of State Tax Revenue	1
General Revenue From Federal Government	45
Federal Tax Burden Per Capita	21
Highway Charges Returned To States	9
Terms Of Trade	3
Per Capita Federal Income Tax Liability	17

Taxes

Tax Revenue	4
Per Capita Tax Revenue	11
Tax Effort	46
Tax Capacity	3
Percent Change In Taxes	50
Property Taxes Per Capita	6
Property Tax Revenue As Percent Of Three-Tax Revenue	3
Sales Taxes Per Capita	35
Sales Tax Revenue As Percent Of Three-Tax Revenue	26
Services With Sales Tax	16
Income Taxes Per Capita	n/a
Income Tax Revenue As Percent Of Three-Tax Revenue	46
Highest Personal Income Tax Rate	n/a
Motor Fuel Taxes	47
Tobacco Taxes	45
Tax Burden On High Income Family	49
Progressivity Of Taxes	8

Revenues And Finances

State And Local Revenue	47
Non-Tax Revenue	46
State And Local Expenditures	47
Per Capita State And Local General Expenditures	3
Change In General Expenditures	3
State Government General Spending	49

Debt As Percent Of Revenue	41
Full Faith And Credit Debt	11
Bond Ratings	3
State Solvency Index	16
Pension Plan Assets	5
State Reserves	29
State Budget Process Quality	45
Relative State Spending "Needs"	24

Education

Math Proficiency, 8th Grade	6
AFQT Ranks	10
SAT Scores	n/a
ACT Scores	1
Over-25 Population Without High School Diploma	21
Private School Students	7
Percent Students Finishing High School	10
Pupil-Teacher Ratio	13
Public School Enrollment	34
Library Holdings Per Capita	20
Education Spending As Percent Of Total	14
Spending Per Pupil	8
Average Teacher Salary	16
State Aid Per Pupil	24
State And Local Spending For Higher Education	12
Higher Education Spending As Percent Of Total	20
Public Higher Education Enrollment	10
State Per Pupil Support Of Higher Education	12
Tuition And Fees	25
Average Professor Salary	12
Education Employees	31
R&D Spending	41

Health

Infant Mortality Rates	22
State Health Rankings	13
Population Without Health Insurance	50
Abortions	30

Alcohol Consumption	6
Percent Non-Smokers	26
Percent Obese	13
AIDS Cases	41
Physicians Per 100,000 Population	26
Medicaid Recipients Related To Poverty Population	15
Health/Hospital Spending As Percent Of Total	37
Per Capita Medicaid Spending	19
Medicaid Spending Per Aged Recipient	14
Medicaid Spending Per AFDC Child	46
Medicare Payment Per Hospital-Day	35
Population In HMOs	11

Crime And Law Enforcement

Crime Rate	40
Violent Crime Rate	42
Murder Rate	
Property Crime Rate	39
Motor Vehicle Theft Rate	28
Violent Crime Rate Change	26
Incarceration Rate	39
Juvenile Arrest Rate	30
Proportion Of Sentence Served	29
Law Enforcement Employees	25
Corrections Employees	41
Costs Per Inmate-Day	22
State Corrections Spending	8
Spending For Law Enforcement	17
Law Enforcement Spending As Percent Of Total	21

Transportation

Percent Of Travel On Interstates	49
Interstate Mileage In Poor Condition	20

Deficient Bridges	33
Traffic Deaths Per 100 Million Vehicle-miles	41
Seat Belt Use	22
Vehicle Miles Traveled Per Capita	22
Workers Using Public Transportation	18
Road And Street Miles Under State Control	41
Highway Employees	33
Public Transit Employees	19
State And Local Spending For Highways	20
Highway Spending As Percent Of Total	28

Welfare

Percent Of Births To Unwed Mothers	34
AFDC Recipients As Percent Of Population	27
Food Stamp Recipients As Percent Of Population	49
SSI Recipients As Percent Of Population	22
Change In AFDC Recipients	48
Condition Of Children Index	9
Percent Of Families With Single Parent	30
Typical Monthly AFDC Payments	12
Welfare As Percent Of Poverty Level Income	12
Average SSI State Supplements Per Recipient	5
State Income Tax Liability Of Typical Family In Poverty	38
Child Support Collections Per $ Of Administrative Costs	41
Percent Of Children In Foster Care	7
State And Local Welfare Spending Per Capita	11
Welfare Spending As Percent Of Total	14
Administrative Costs Per AFDC Case	14

Index

395